INTELLECTUALS

AND

SOCIETY

Revised and Enlarged Edition

THOMAS SOWELL

BASIC
BOOKS

A Member of the Perseus Books Group
New York

Copyright © 2011 by Thomas Sowell
Published by Basic Books,
A Member of the Perseus Books Group

All rights reserved. Printed in the United States of America. No part of this book
may be reproduced in any manner whatsoever without written permission except
in the case of brief quotations embodied in critical articles and reviews.
For information, address Basic Books,
387 Park Avenue South, New York, NY 10016-8810.

Books published by Basic Books are available at special discounts for
bulk purchases in the United States by corporations, institutions,
and other organizations. For more information,
please contact the Special Markets Department at the Perseus Books Group,
2300 Chestnut Street, Suite 200, Philadelphia, PA 19103,
or call (800) 810-4145, ext. 5000,
or e-mail special.markets@perseusbooks.com.

A CIP catalog record for this book is available from
the Library of Congress.

LCCN 2011945721
ISBN: 978-0-465-02522-0 (paperback)
ISBN: 978-0-465-03110-8 (e-book)

10 9 8 7 6 5 4 3

CONTENTS

PREFACE

This extensively revised and greatly enlarged edition of *Intellectuals and Society* contains not only four new chapters on intellectuals and race but also additions, revisions and reorganizations of other chapters. The new material includes a critique of John Rawls' conception of justice and a re-examination of what has been called the "trickle-down theory" behind "tax cuts for the rich." Yet the basic themes and structure of this book remain, and are strengthened by the new material and its implications. This will become especially apparent in the much revised final section, summarizing the main themes of the book.

There has probably never been an era in history when intellectuals have played a larger role in society than the era in which we live. When those who generate ideas, the intellectuals proper, are surrounded by a wide penumbra of those who disseminate those ideas— whether as journalists, teachers, staffers to legislators or clerks to judges, and other members of the intelligentsia— their influence on the course of social evolution can be considerable, or even crucial. That influence has of course depended on the surrounding circumstances, including how free intellectuals have been to propagate their own ideas, rather than being instruments of state propaganda, as in totalitarian countries.

There would of course be little point in studying the ideas expressed by prominent writers like Ilya Ehrenburg during the era of the Soviet Union, for these were simply the ideas permitted or advocated by the Soviet dictatorship. In short, the study of the influence of intellectuals is here a study of their influence where they have been freest to exert that influence, namely in modern democratic nations.

For very different reasons, this study of patterns among intellectuals will pay less attention to such an intellectual giant as Milton Friedman as to any number of intellectuals of lesser eminence, simply because Professor Friedman was in many ways very atypical of the intellectuals of his time, both in his scholarly work that won him a Nobel Prize and in his work as a popular commentator on issues of the day. A "balanced" general intellectual history of our times would have to give Professor Friedman a far larger amount of attention than a study which focuses on *general patterns*, to which he was an outstanding exception. Aleksandr Solzhenitsyn was another landmark figure in the intellectual, moral and political history of his age who was likewise too atypical of contemporary intellectuals to be included in a study of the general patterns of the profession.

Because this is a study of *patterns*, it is not confined to contemporary intellectuals but includes patterns that have, in many cases, existed among the intelligentsia for at least two centuries. Because it is a study of *general* patterns, it does not attempt to account for "every sparrow's fall." Nor is it simply a series of critiques of particular intellectuals or particular issues, though one cannot critique a pattern of thinking without examining concrete examples of that thinking.

In this context, the purpose of discussing the Iraq wars or the war in Vietnam, for example, is not to determine the wisdom or unwisdom of Americans becoming involved in those wars, but to understand the role of intellectuals in relation to those wars. Similarly, the purpose of discussing *The Bell Curve* is not to determine the merits or demerits of *The Bell Curve* itself— something I have written about elsewhere[*]— but to show the implications of the intellectuals' contentions regarding that book, neither of whose authors has been sufficiently typical of the patterns found among intellectuals to make *The Bell Curve* itself the main focus.

Many books have been written about intellectuals. Some take in-depth looks at particular prominent figures, Paul Johnson's *Intellectuals* being an especially incisive example. Other books on intellectuals seek general patterns, *Ideology and the Ideologists* by Lewis S. Feuer being a very thoughtful and insightful example of this approach. Richard A. Posner's *Public Intellectuals* is about those intellectuals who directly address the public, while the focus in *Intellectuals and Society* is on intellectuals who influence— sometimes shape— public attitudes and beliefs, whether or not

---

[*] See Thomas Sowell, "Ethnicity and IQ" in *The Bell Curve Wars*, edited by Steven Fraser (New York: Basic Books, 1995), pp. 70–79.

they are widely read by the population at large. As J.A. Schumpeter said, "there are many Keynesians and Marxians who have never read a line of Keynes or Marx."[1] They have gotten their ideas second- or third-hand from the intelligentsia. Many school teachers may not have read anything by John Dewey, and yet their whole approach to education may reflect a vision and an agenda formulated a century ago by Dewey, and permeating schools of education today.

Among the many things said by those who have studied intellectuals, a comment by Professor Mark Lilla of Columbia University in his book *The Reckless Mind* is especially striking:

> Distinguished professors, gifted poets, and influential journalists summoned their talents to convince all who would listen that modern tyrants were liberators and that their unconscionable crimes were noble, when seen in the proper perspective. Whoever takes it upon himself to write an honest intellectual history of twentieth-century Europe will need a strong stomach.
>
> But he will need something more. He will need to overcome his disgust long enough to ponder the roots of this strange and puzzling phenomenon.[2]

While *Intellectuals and Society* is not an intellectual history of twentieth-century Europe— that would be a much larger project for someone much younger— it does attempt to unravel some of the puzzling phenomena in the world of the intellectuals, as that world impacts society at large. Rather than simply generalizing from the writings or behavior of particular intellectuals, this book will analyze both the vision and the incentives and constraints behind the general patterns found among members of the intelligentsia, past and present, as well as what they have said and its impact on the societies in which they said it.

Although we already know much about the biographies or ideologies of particular prominent intellectuals, systematic analyses of the nature and role of intellectuals as a group in society are much less common. This book seeks to develop such an analysis and to explore its implications for the direction in which the intelligentsia are taking our society and Western civilization in general.

Intellectuals and Society

Although this book is about intellectuals, it is not written *for* intellectuals. Its purpose is to achieve an understanding of an important social phenomenon and to share that understanding with those who wish to share it, in whatever walk of life they might be. Those among the intelligentsia who are looking for points to score or things at which to take umbrage will be left to their own devices.* This book is written for those readers who are willing to join with me in a search for some understanding of a distinct segment of the population whose activities can have, and have had, momentous implications for nations and civilizations.

While some studies of intellectual history, and especially studies of ideological differences, seek to explain conflicting social visions by differing "value premises" among those on opposing sides of various issues, *Intellectuals and Society* seeks instead to explain ideological differences by differing underlying assumptions about the facts of life, the nature of human beings and the nature and distribution of knowledge.

Ideological differences based on differing value premises are ultimately differing tastes, on which there is said to be no disputing. But differences based on beliefs about facts, causation, human nature, and the character and distribution of knowledge, are ultimately questions about different perceptions of the real world, leading to hypotheses which can be tested empirically.

Beliefs about facts and causation can change— sometimes suddenly— in the wake of new empirical evidence or a new analysis. The long history of large and sweeping changes in individuals' ideological positions— sometimes rather abruptly, like "road to Damascus" conversions— seems far more consistent with discovering that the facts about the world are very

---

* Despite my reiterated statements that this book is about *general patterns* among intellectuals, some reviewers of the first edition seemed to find its limited coverage of Milton Friedman, among others, either a puzzle or a defect, even though the reasons for such omissions were explained on the first page of the preface, mentioning Milton Friedman by name as one of those whose eminence would not be reflected in their coverage here, because they are atypical of the general patterns being explored. Obviously, general patterns are not the same as universal patterns. One of the benefits of writing for the general public, as distinguished from writing for intellectuals, is that you can usually assume that readers have common sense and are not looking for opportunities to be clever.

different from what had been initially assumed, sometimes as a result of some dramatic event such as the French Revolution or the Nazi-Soviet Pact, and sometimes as a result of a more gradual or more personal unfolding of events inconsistent with expectations based on an existing ideological vision. Such changes apply far beyond intellectuals, and have been captured in such phrases as "radicals in their twenties and conservatives in their forties." But intellectuals have left us concrete records of their changes in ideological orientations and those records are worth exploring.

A remarkable and moving record of such personal changes was a book written long ago, titled *The God That Failed*. It chronicled various intellectuals' breaks with communism, which captured the essence of a process that has applied far more widely, over many centuries, to many visions of the world, both secular and religious, which have been abandoned in the light of experience, and often more rapidly than one is likely to abandon what one fundamentally values. Those who saw Marxism as the way to improve the lot of the poor, for example, may come to see other paths to that goal as more promising, without having changed the goal at all or the value premises behind that goal. For our purposes— trying to understand general patterns of beliefs and tactics among intellectuals— the validity of their assumptions and the consequences of their conclusions are things we can test, in a way that we cannot test opaque value premises. We can also observe the consequences of the prevailing views among intellectuals on the larger society around them, often with dismay.

Thomas Sowell

Hoover Institution
Stanford University

ACKNOWLEDGMENTS

Like other books of mine, this one owes much to the dedicated work of my outstanding research assistants, Na Liu and Elizabeth Costa. Ms. Liu, having worked with me for more than twenty years, has not only ferreted out many facts but contributed many insights to this book, as she has to others. Now she also creates the computer files from which my books can be printed directly. My other assistant in recent years, Ms. Costa, does the copy-editing and fact-checking for me, and seldom does a lapse on my part escape her scrutiny. I have also benefitted from information or comments supplied by Dr. Gerald P. O'Driscoll of the Cato Institute, Professor Lino A. Graglia of the University of Texas at Austin, Dr. Victor Davis Hanson of the Hoover Institution and Professor William R. Allen of the University of California at Los Angeles. Any errors or shortcomings which survive despite their efforts can only be my responsibility.

PART I

INTRODUCTION

Chapter 1

Intellect and Intellectuals

> *Intelligence is quickness to apprehend as distinct from ability, which is capacity to act wisely on the thing apprehended.*
>
> *Alfred North Whitehead*[1]

Intellect is not wisdom. There can be "unwise intellect," as Thomas Carlyle characterized the thinking of Harriet Taylor,[2] the friend and later wife of John Stuart Mill. Sheer brainpower— intellect, the capacity to grasp and manipulate complex concepts and ideas— can be put at the service of concepts and ideas that lead to mistaken conclusions and unwise actions, in light of all the factors involved, including factors left out of some of the ingenious theories constructed by the intellect.

Brilliance— even genius— is no guarantee that consequential factors have not been left out or misconceived. Karl Marx's *Capital* was a classic example of an intellectually masterful elaboration of a fundamental misconception— in this case, the notion that "labor," the physical handling of the materials and instruments of production, is the real source of wealth. Obviously, if this were true, countries with much labor and little technology or entrepreneurship would be more prosperous than countries with the reverse, when in fact it is blatantly obvious that the direct opposite is the case. Similarly with John Rawls' elaborate and ingenious *A Theory of Justice*, in which justice becomes categorically more important than any other social consideration. But, obviously, if any two things have any value at all, one cannot be categorically more valuable than the other. A diamond may be worth far more than a penny, but enough pennies will be worth more than any diamond.

INTELLIGENCE VERSUS INTELLECT

The capacity to grasp and manipulate complex ideas is enough to define intellect but not enough to encompass intelligence, which involves combining intellect with judgment and care in selecting relevant explanatory factors and in establishing empirical tests of any theory that emerges.

Intelligence minus judgment equals intellect.

Wisdom is the rarest quality of all— the ability to combine intellect, knowledge, experience, and judgment in a way to produce a coherent understanding. Wisdom is the fulfillment of the ancient admonition, "With all your getting, get understanding." Wisdom requires self-discipline and an understanding of the realities of the world, including the limitations of one's own experience and of reason itself. The opposite of high intellect is dullness or slowness, but the opposite of wisdom is foolishness, which is far more dangerous.

George Orwell said that some ideas are so foolish that only an intellectual could believe them, for no ordinary man could be such a fool. The record of twentieth century intellectuals was especially appalling in this regard. Scarcely a mass-murdering dictator of the twentieth century was without his intellectual supporters, not simply in his own country, but also in foreign democracies, where people were free to say whatever they wished. Lenin, Stalin, Mao, and Hitler all had their admirers, defenders, and apologists among the intelligentsia in Western democratic nations, despite the fact that these dictators each ended up killing people of their own country on a scale unprecedented even by despotic regimes that preceded them.

Defining Intellectuals

We must be clear about what we mean by intellectuals. Here "intellectuals" refers to an *occupational* category, people whose occupations deal primarily with ideas— writers, academics, and the like.* Most of us do not think of brain surgeons or engineers as intellectuals, despite the demanding mental training that each goes through and despite the intellectual challenges of their

---

* For those few people whose wealth enables them to pursue a career that is not the source of their livelihood, "occupation" need not mean a paying occupation.

occupations. Similarly, virtually no one regards even the most brilliant and successful financial wizard as an intellectual.

At the core of the notion of an intellectual is the dealer in ideas, as such—not the personal application of ideas, as engineers apply complex scientific principles to create physical structures or mechanisms. A policy wonk whose work might be analogized as "social engineering" will seldom personally administer the schemes that he or she creates or advocates. That is left to bureaucrats, politicians, social workers, the police or whoever else might be directly in charge of carrying out the ideas of the policy wonk. Such labels as "applied social science" may be put on the policy wonk's work but that work is essentially the application of general ideas only to produce more specific ideas about social policies, to be turned into action by others.

The policy wonk's work is not personally carrying out those specific ideas, as a physician applies medical science to particular flesh-and-blood human beings or as an engineer stands in hip boots on a construction site where a building or a bridge is being built. The output— the end product— of an intellectual consists of ideas.

Jonas Salk's end product was a vaccine, as Bill Gates' end product was a computer operating system. Despite the brainpower, insights, and talents involved in these and other achievements, such individuals are not intellectuals. *An intellectual's work begins and ends with ideas*, however influential those ideas may be on concrete things— in the hands of others. Adam Smith never ran a business and Karl Marx never administered a Gulag. They were intellectuals. Ideas, as such, are not only the key to the intellectual's function, but are also the criteria of intellectual achievements and the source of the often dangerous seductions of the occupation.

The quintessential intellectuals of the academic world, for example, are those in fields which are more pervaded by ideas, as such. A university's business school, engineering school, medical school, or athletics department is not what usually comes to mind when we think of academic intellectuals. Moreover, the prevailing ideologies and attitudes among academic intellectuals are usually least prevalent in these particular parts of an academic campus. That is, sociology departments have generally been found to be more one-sidedly to the left politically compared to medical schools, psychology departments more to the left than engineering schools, English departments to the left of economics departments, and so on.[3]

The term "pseudo-intellectual" has sometimes been applied to the less intelligent or less knowledgeable members of this profession. But just as a bad cop is still a cop— no matter how much we may regret it— so a shallow, confused, or dishonest intellectual is just as much a member of that occupation as is a paragon of the profession. Once we are clear as to whom we are talking about when we speak of intellectuals— that it is an occupational description rather than a qualitative label or an honorific title— then we can look at the characteristics of such occupations and the incentives and constraints faced by the people in those occupations, in order to see how those characteristics relate to how such people behave. The larger question, of course, is how their behavior affects the society in which they live.

The impact of an intellectual, or of intellectuals in general, does not depend on their being so-called "public intellectuals" who directly address the population at large, as distinct from those intellectuals whose ideas are largely confined to others in their respective specialties or to other intellectuals in general. Books with some of the biggest impacts on the twentieth century were written by Karl Marx and Sigmund Freud in the nineteenth century— and seldom read, much less understood, by the general public. But the conclusions— as distinguished from the intricacies of the analyses— of these writers inspired vast numbers of intellectuals around the world and, through them, the general public. The high repute of these writings added weight and provided confidence to many followers who had not personally mastered these writings or perhaps had not even tried to.

Even intellectuals whose very names have been little known to the general public have had worldwide impacts. Friedrich Hayek, whose writings— notably *The Road to Serfdom*— began an intellectual counter-revolution against the prevailing ideas of his time, a counter-revolution later joined by Milton Friedman, William F. Buckley and others, reaching a political climax with the rise of Margaret Thatcher in Britain and Ronald Reagan in the United States, was little known or read even in most intellectual circles. But Hayek inspired many public intellectuals and political activists around the world, who in turn made his ideas the subject of wider discourse and an influence on the making of government policies. Hayek was a classic example of the kind of intellectual described by Justice Oliver Wendell Holmes as a thinker who, "a hundred years after he is dead and forgotten, men who never heard of him will be moving to the measure of his thought."[4]

The Intelligentsia

Around a more or less solid core of producers of ideas there is a penumbra of those whose role is the use and dissemination of those ideas. These latter individuals would include those teachers, journalists, social activists, political aides, judges' clerks, and others who base their beliefs or actions on the ideas of intellectuals. Journalists in their roles as editorial writers or columnists are both consumers of the ideas of intellectuals and producers of ideas of their own, and so may be considered intellectuals in such roles, since originality is not essential to the definition of an intellectual, so long as the end product is ideas. But journalists in their roles as reporters are supposed to be reporting facts and, in so far as these facts are filtered and slanted in accordance with the prevailing notions among intellectuals, these reporters are part of the penumbra surrounding intellectuals. They are part of the *intelligentsia*, which includes but is not limited to the intellectuals. Finally, there are those whose occupations are not much impacted by the ideas of the intellectuals, but who are nevertheless interested as individuals in remaining *au courant* with those ideas, if only for discussion on social occasions, and who would feel flattered to be considered part of the intelligentsia.

IDEAS AND ACCOUNTABILITY

Because of the enormous impact that intellectuals can have, both when they are well known and when they are unknown, it is critical to try to understand the patterns of their behavior and the incentives and constraints affecting those patterns.

Ideas are of course not the exclusive property of intellectuals. Nor is the complexity, difficulty or qualitative level of ideas the crucial factor in determining whether those who produce these ideas are or are not considered to be intellectuals. Engineers and financiers deal with ideas at least as complex as those of sociologists or professors of English. Yet it is these latter who are more likely to come to mind when intellectuals are discussed. Moreover, it is the latter who most exhibit the attitudes, beliefs, and behavior patterns associated with intellectuals.

Verifiability

The standards by which engineers and financiers are judged are external standards, beyond the realm of ideas and beyond the control of their peers. An engineer whose bridges or buildings collapse is ruined, as is a financier who goes broke. However plausible or admirable their ideas might have seemed initially to their fellow engineers or fellow financiers, the proof of the pudding is ultimately in the eating. Their failure may well be registered in their declining esteem in their respective professions, but that is an effect, not a cause. Conversely, ideas which might have seemed unpromising to their fellow engineers or fellow financiers can come to be accepted among those peers if the empirical success of those ideas becomes manifest and enduring. The same is true of scientists and athletic coaches. But the ultimate test of a deconstructionist's ideas is whether other deconstructionists find those ideas interesting, original, persuasive, elegant, or ingenious. There is no external test.

In short, among people in mentally demanding occupations, the fault line between those most likely to be considered intellectuals and those who are not tends to run between those whose ideas are ultimately subject to internal criteria and those whose ideas are ultimately subject to external criteria. The very terms of admiration or dismissal among intellectuals reflect the non-empirical criteria involved. Ideas that are "complex," "exciting," "innovative," "nuanced," or "progressive" are admired, while other ideas are dismissed as "simplistic," "outmoded" or "reactionary." But no one judged Vince Lombardi's ideas about how to play football by their plausibility *a priori* or by whether they were more complex or less complex than the ideas of other football coaches, or by whether they represented new or old conceptions of how the game should be played. Vince Lombardi was judged by what happened when his ideas were put to the test on the football field.

Similarly, in the very different field of physics, Einstein's theory of relativity did not win acceptance on the basis of its plausibility, elegance, complexity or novelty. Not only were other physicists initially skeptical, Einstein himself urged that his theories not be accepted until they could be verified empirically. The crucial test came when scientists around the world observed an eclipse of the sun and discovered that light behaved as Einstein's theory said it would behave, however implausible that might have seemed beforehand.

The great problem— and the great social danger— with purely internal criteria is that they can easily become sealed off from feedback from the external world of reality and remain circular in their methods of validation. What new idea will seem plausible depends on what one already believes. When the only external validation for the individual is what other individuals believe, everything depends on who those other individuals are. If they are simply people who are like-minded in general, then the consensus of the group about a particular new idea depends on what that group already believes in general— and says nothing about the empirical validity of that idea in the external world.

Ideas sealed off from the outside world in terms of their origin or their validation may nevertheless have great impact on that external world in which millions of human beings live their lives. The ideas of Lenin, Hitler, and Mao had enormous— and often lethal— impact on those millions of people, however little validity those ideas had in themselves or in the eyes of others beyond the circles of like-minded followers and subordinate power-wielders.

The impact of ideas on the real world can hardly be disputed. The converse, however, is not nearly as clear, despite fashionable notions that major changes in ideas are generated by great events.[5] As the late Nobel Prizewinning economist George J. Stigler pointed out, "A war may ravage a continent or destroy a generation without posing new theoretical questions."[6] Wars have all too often done both these things in the course of many centuries, so this hardly presents a new phenomenon for which some new explanation is required.

While one might regard Keynesian economics, for example, as a system of ideas particularly relevant to the events of the era in which it was published— namely, the Great Depression of the 1930s— what is remarkable is how seldom that can be said of other landmark intellectual systems. Were falling objects more common, or more fraught with social impact, when Newton's laws of gravity were developed? Were new species appearing, or old ones disappearing, more often or more consequentially when Darwin's *Origin of Species* was written? What produced Einstein's theory of relativity, other than Einstein's own thinking?

Accountability

Intellectuals, in the restricted sense which largely conforms to general usage, are ultimately unaccountable to the external world. The prevalence and presumed desirability of this are confirmed by such things as academic tenure and expansive concepts of "academic freedom" and academic "self-governance." In the media, expansive notions of freedom of speech and of the press play similar roles. In short, unaccountability to the external world is not simply a happenstance but a principle. John Stuart Mill argued that intellectuals should be free even from social standards— while setting social standards for others.[7] Not only have intellectuals been insulated from material consequences, they have often enjoyed immunity from even a loss of reputation after having been demonstrably wrong. As Eric Hoffer put it:

> One of the surprising privileges of intellectuals is that they are free to be scandalously asinine without harming their reputation. The intellectuals who idolized Stalin while he was purging millions and stifling the least stirring of freedom have not been discredited. They are still holding forth on every topic under the sun and are listened to with deference. Sartre returned in 1939 from Germany, where he studied philosophy, and told the world that there was little to choose between Hitler's Germany and France. Yet Sartre went on to become an intellectual pope revered by the educated in every land.[8]

Sartre was not unique. Environmentalist Paul Ehrlich said in 1968: "The battle to feed all of humanity is over. In the 1970's the world will undergo famines— hundreds of millions of people are going to starve to death in spite of any crash programs embarked upon now."[9] Yet, after that decade—

and later decades— had come and gone, not only had nothing of the sort happened, a growing problem in a growing number of countries was obesity and unsalable agricultural surpluses. But Professor Ehrlich continued to receive not only popular acclaim but also honors and grants from prestigious academic institutions.

Similarly, Ralph Nader first became a major public figure with the 1965 publication of his book *Unsafe at Any Speed*, which depicted American cars in general, and the Corvair in particular, as accident-prone. Yet, despite the fact that empirical studies showed the Corvair to be at least as safe as other cars of its day,[10] Nader not only continued to have credibility but acquired a reputation for idealism and insight that made him something of a secular saint. Innumerable other wrong predictions, about everything from the price of gasoline to the outcome of Cold War policies, have left innumerable other false prophets with just as much honor as if they had been truly prophetic.

In short, constraints which apply to people in most other fields do not apply even approximately equally to intellectuals. It would be surprising if this did not lead to different behavior. Among those differences are the ways they see the world and the way they see themselves in relation to their fellow human beings and the societies in which they live.

Chapter 2

Knowledge and Notions

From an early age, smart people are reminded of their intelligence, separated from their peers in gifted classes, and presented with opportunities unavailable to others. For these and other reasons, intellectuals tend to have an inflated sense of their own wisdom.

Daniel J. Flynn[1]

L ike everyone else, intellectuals have a mixture of knowledge and notions. For some intellectuals in some fields, that knowledge includes knowledge of the systematic procedures available to test notions and determine their validity as knowledge. Since ideas are their life's work, intellectuals might be expected to more thoroughly or more systematically subject notions to such tests. Whether or to what extent they do so in practice is, of course, itself a notion that needs to be tested. There are, after all, other skills in which intellectuals also tend to excel, including verbal skills that can be used to evade the testing of their favorite notions.

In short, the various skills of intellectuals can be used either to foster intellectual standards or to circumvent those standards and promote non-intellectual or even anti-intellectual agendas. In other words, intellectuals— defined as an occupational category— may or may not exemplify the intellectual process. Indeed, it is possible for people *not* defined as intellectuals— engineers, financiers, physicians— to adhere to intellectual procedures more often or more rigorously than some or most intellectuals. The extent to which this is true is another empirical question. What is important here is that the mere word "intellectual," applied to an occupational category, not be allowed to insinuate the presence of intellectual principles or standards which may or may not in fact be present.

However important rigorous intellectual principles may be within particular fields in which some intellectuals specialize, when people operate as "public intellectuals," espousing ideas and policies to a wider population beyond their professional colleagues, they may or may not carry over intellectual rigor into these more general, more policy-oriented, or more ideologically charged discussions.

Bertrand Russell, for example, was both a public intellectual and a leading authority within a rigorous field. But the Bertrand Russell who is relevant here is not the author of landmark treatises on mathematics but the Bertrand Russell who advocated "unilateral disarmament" for Britain in the 1930s while Hitler was re-arming Germany. Russell's advocacy of disarmament extended all the way to "disbanding the army and navy and air force"[2]— again, with Hitler re-arming not far away. The Noam Chomsky who is relevant here is not the linguistics scholar but the Noam Chomsky of similarly extravagant political pronouncements. The Edmund Wilson who is relevant is not the highly regarded literary critic but the Edmund Wilson who urged Americans to vote for the Communists in the 1932 elections. In this he was joined by such other intellectual luminaries of the time as John Dos Passos, Sherwood Anderson, Langston Hughes, Lincoln Steffens and many other well-known writers of that era.[3]

Visiting the United States in 1933, George Bernard Shaw said, "You Americans are so fearful of dictators. Dictatorship is the only way in which government can accomplish anything. See what a mess democracy has led to. Why are you afraid of dictatorship?"[4] Leaving London for a vacation in South Africa in 1935, Shaw declared, "It is nice to go for a holiday and know that Hitler has settled everything so well in Europe."[5] While Hitler's anti-Jewish actions eventually alienated Shaw, the famous playwright remained partial to the Soviet dictatorship. In 1939, after the Nazi-Soviet pact, Shaw said: "Herr Hitler is under the powerful thumb of Stalin, whose interest in peace is overwhelming. And every one except myself is frightened out of his or her wits!"[6] A week later, the Second World War began, with Hitler invading Poland from the west, followed by Stalin invading from the east.

The list of top-ranked intellectuals who made utterly irresponsible statements, and who advocated hopelessly unrealistic and recklessly dangerous things, could be extended almost indefinitely. Many public intellectuals have been justly renowned within their respective fields but the point here is that many *did not stay within their respective fields*. As George J. Stigler said of some of his fellow Nobel Laureates, they "issue stern ultimata to the public on almost a monthly basis, and sometimes on no other basis."[7]

The fatal misstep of such intellectuals is assuming that superior ability within a particular realm can be generalized as superior wisdom or morality over all. Chess grandmasters, musical prodigies and others who are as remarkable within their respective specialties as intellectuals are within theirs, seldom make that mistake. Here it is sufficient to make a sharp distinction between the intellectual occupation and intellectual standards which members of that occupation can and do violate, especially in their roles as public intellectuals, making pronouncements about society and advocating government policies. What was said of John Maynard Keynes by his biographer and fellow economist Roy Harrod could be said of many other intellectuals:

> He held forth on a great range of topics, on some of which he was thoroughly expert, but on others of which he may have derived his views from the few pages of a book at which he had happened to glance. The air of authority was the same in both cases.[8]

What many intellectuals seem not to understand is that even being the world's leading authority on a particular subject, such as admiralty law or Mayan civilization, does not confer even minimal competence on other subjects, such as antitrust law, environmental issues or foreign policy. As British writer Lowes Dickinson said of scientists, "beside being prejudiced, they suppose that the fact that they are men of science gives their prejudices value."[9]

COMPETING CONCEPTS OF KNOWLEDGE

The way the word knowledge is used by many intellectuals often arbitrarily limits what verified information is to be considered knowledge. This arbitrary limitation of the scope of the word was expressed in a parody verse about Benjamin Jowett, master of Balliol College at Oxford University:

> My name is Benjamin Jowett.
>> If it's knowledge, I know it.
> I am the master of this college,
>> What I don't know isn't knowledge.

Someone who is considered to be a "knowledgeable" person usually has a special kind of knowledge— perhaps academic or other kinds of knowledge not widely found in the population at large. Someone who has even more knowledge of more mundane things— plumbing, carpentry, or automobile transmissions, for example— is less likely to be called "knowledgeable" by those intellectuals for whom what they don't know isn't knowledge. Although the special kind of knowledge associated with intellectuals is usually valued more, and those who have such knowledge are usually accorded more prestige, it is by no means certain that the kind of knowledge mastered by intellectuals is necessarily more consequential in its effects in the real world.

The same is true even of expert knowledge. No doubt those in charge of the *Titanic* had far more expertise in the many aspects of seafaring than most ordinary people had, but what was crucial in its consequences was the mundane knowledge of where particular icebergs happened to be located on a particular night. Many major economic decisions are likewise crucially dependent on the kinds of mundane knowledge that intellectuals might disdain to consider to be knowledge in the sense in which they habitually use the word.

Location is just one of those mundane kinds of knowledge, and its importance is by no means confined to the location of icebergs. For example, the mundane knowledge of what is located at Broadway and 23rd Street in

Manhattan, and what the surrounding neighborhood is like, may not be considered relevant to determining whether a given individual should be regarded as a knowledgeable person. But, for a business seeking a place to open a store, that knowledge can be the difference between going bankrupt and making millions of dollars.

Enterprises invest much time and money in determining where to locate their operations, and these locations are by no means random. It is not accidental that filling stations are often located on street corners, and often near other filling stations, just as automobile dealers are often located near other automobile dealers, but stationery stores are seldom located near other stationery stores. People knowledgeable about business have cited, as one of the factors behind the spectacular rise of Starbucks, the Starbucks management's careful attention to choosing the locations of their outlets— and one of the factors cited in Starbucks having to close hundreds of outlets in 2008 has been their straying from that practice.[10] It is a cliché among realtors that the three most important factors in determining the value of a house are "location, location, and location."

Location is just one of many mundane facts with major, and often decisive, consequences. A nurse's mundane knowledge of whether a particular patient is allergic to penicillin can be the difference between life and death. When a plane is coming into an airport for a landing, the control tower's observation that the pilot has forgotten to lower the landing gear is information whose immediate conveyance to the pilot can likewise be crucial, even though such knowledge requires nothing more intellectually challenging than eyesight and common sense. Foreknowledge that the D-Day invasion of Europe would take place at Normandy, rather than at Calais where Hitler expected it, would have led to a wholly different concentration of the Nazis' military forces, costing thousands more lives among the troops hitting the beach, perhaps dooming the whole operation and changing the course of the war.

In short, much of the special kind of knowledge concentrated among intellectuals may not have as weighty consequences as much mundane or intellectually unimpressive knowledge, scattered among the population at large. In the aggregate, mundane knowledge can vastly outweigh the special knowledge of elites, both in its amount and in its consequences. While special knowledge is almost invariably articulated knowledge, other kinds of knowledge need not be articulated to others nor even be consciously articulated to ourselves. Friedrich Hayek included in knowledge "all the human adaptations to environment in which past experience has been incorporated." He added:

> Not all knowledge in this sense is part of our intellect, nor is our intellect the whole of our knowledge. Our habits and skills, our emotional attitudes, our tools, and our institutions— all are in this sense adaptations to past experience which have grown up by selective elimination of less suitable conduct. They are as much an indispensable foundation of successful action as is our conscious knowledge.[11]

Concentration and Dispersion of Knowledge

When both special knowledge and mundane knowledge are encompassed within the concept of knowledge, it is doubtful whether the most knowledgeable person on earth has even one percent of the total knowledge on earth, or even one percent of the consequential knowledge in a given society.

There are many serious implications of this which may, among other things, help explain why so many leading intellectuals have so often backed notions that proved to be disastrous. It is not simply with particular policies at particular times that intellectuals have often advocated mistaken and dangerous decisions. Their whole general approach to policy-making— their ideology— has often reflected a crucial misconception about knowledge and its concentration or dispersion.

Many intellectuals and their followers have been unduly impressed by the fact that highly educated elites like themselves have far more knowledge per capita— in the sense of special knowledge— than does the population at large. From this it is a short step to considering the educated elites to be superior guides to what should and should not be done in a society. They have often overlooked the crucial fact that the population at large may have vastly more *total* knowledge— in the mundane sense— than the elites, even if that knowledge is scattered in individually unimpressive fragments among vast numbers of people.

If no one has even one percent of the knowledge currently available, not counting the vast amounts of knowledge yet to be discovered, the imposition from the top down of the notions in favor among elites, convinced of their own superior knowledge and virtue, is a formula for disaster.

Sometimes it is economic disaster, which central planning, for example, turned out to be in so many countries around the world during the twentieth century that even most governments run by communists and socialists began replacing such top-down economic planning by freer markets by the end of that century. No doubt central planners had far more expertise, and far more statistical data at their command, than the average person making transactions in the market. Yet the vastly greater mundane knowledge brought to bear by millions of ordinary people making their own mutual accommodations among themselves almost invariably produced higher economic growth rates and higher standards of living after central planning was jettisoned, notably in China and India, where rates of poverty declined dramatically as their economies grew at accelerated rates.[*]

Central planning is just one of a more general class of social decision-making processes dependent on the underlying assumption that people with more per capita knowledge (in the special sense) should be guiding their societies. Other forms of this general notion include judicial activism, urban planning, and other institutional expressions of the belief that social decisions cannot be left to be determined by the actions and values of the less knowledgeable population at large. But if no one has even one percent of all the knowledge in a society— in the larger sense in which many different kinds of knowledge are consequential— then it is crucial that the other 99 percent of knowledge, scattered in small and individually unimpressive amounts among the population at large, be allowed the freedom to be used in working out mutual accommodations among the people themselves. These innumerable interactions and mutual

---

[*] This would not have been surprising to John Stuart Mill, who said in the nineteenth century, "even if a government were superior in intelligence and knowledge to any single individual in the nation, it must be inferior to all the individuals of the nation taken together." John Stuart Mill, *Principles of Political Economy*, edited by W.J. Ashley (New York: Longmans, Green and Co., 1909), p. 947.

accommodations are what bring the other 99 percent of knowledge into play— and generate new knowledge in the process of back and forth bids and offers, reflecting changes in supply and demand.

That is why free markets, judicial restraint, and reliance on decisions and traditions growing out of the experiences of the many— rather than the presumptions of an elite few— are so important to those who do *not* share the social vision prevalent among intellectual elites. In short, ideological fault lines divide those who have different conceptions of the meaning of knowledge, and who consequently see knowledge as being concentrated or dispersed. "In general, 'the market' is smarter than the smartest of its individual participants,"[12] is the way the late Robert L. Bartley, editor of the *Wall Street Journal*, expressed his belief that systemic processes can bring into play more knowledge for decision-making purposes, through the interactions and mutual accommodations of many individuals, than any one of those individuals possesses.

Systemic processes are essentially trial-and-error processes, with repeated or continuous— and consequential— feedback from those involved in these processes. By contrast, political and legal processes are processes in which initial decisions are harder to change, whether because of the high cost to political careers of admitting a mistake or— in the law— the legal precedents that are set. Why the transfer of decisions from those with personal experience and a stake in the outcome to those with neither can be expected to lead to better decisions is a question seldom asked, much less answered. Given the greater cost of correcting surrogate decisions, compared to correcting individual decisions, and the greater cost of persisting in mistaken decisions by those making decisions for themselves, compared to the lower cost of making mistaken decisions for others, the economic success of market economies is hardly surprising and neither are the counterproductive and often disastrous results of various forms of social engineering.

People on both sides of the ideological fault line may believe that those with the most knowledge should have the most weight in making decisions that impact society, but they have radically different conceptions of just where in society there is in fact the most knowledge. If knowledge is defined expansively, including much mundane knowledge whose presence or absence is consequential and often crucial, then individuals with Ph.D.s are as grossly ignorant of most consequential things as other individuals are, since no one can be truly knowledgeable, at a level required for consequential decision-making for a whole society, except within a narrow band out of the vast spectrum of human concerns.

The ignorance, prejudices, and groupthink of an educated elite are still ignorance, prejudice, and groupthink— and for those with one percent of the knowledge in a society to be guiding or controlling those with the other 99 percent is as perilous as it is absurd. The difference between special knowledge and mundane knowledge is not simply incidental or semantic. Its social implications are very consequential. For example, it is far easier to concentrate power than to concentrate knowledge. That is why so much social engineering backfires and why so many despots have led their countries into disasters.

Where knowledge is conceived of as Hayek conceived of it, to include knowledge unarticulated even to ourselves, but expressed in our individual habits and social customs, then the transmission of such knowledge from millions of people to be concentrated in surrogate decision-makers becomes very problematic, if not impossible, since many of those operating with such knowledge have not fully articulated such knowledge even to themselves, and so can hardly transmit it to others, even if they might wish to.

Since many, if not most, intellectuals operate under the implicit assumption that knowledge is already concentrated— in people like themselves— they are especially susceptible to the idea that a corresponding concentration of decision-making power in a public-spirited elite can benefit society. That assumption has been the foundation for reform movements like Progressivism in the United States and revolutionary movements in various other countries around the world. Moreover, with sufficient knowledge being considered already concentrated, those with this view often conceive that what needs to be done is to create an accompanying will and power to deal collectively with a wide array of social problems. Emphasis on "will," "commitment," "caring" or "compassion," as crucial ingredients for dealing with social issues implicitly assumes away the question whether those who are presumed to have these qualities also have sufficient knowledge.

Sometimes the sufficiency of knowledge is explicitly asserted and any questions about that sufficiency are then dismissed as reflecting either ignorance or obstruction. John Dewey, for example, spelled it out: "Having the knowledge we may set hopefully at work upon a course of social invention and experimental engineering."[13] But the ignored question is: Who— if anybody— has that kind of knowledge?

Since intellectuals have every incentive to emphasize the importance of the special kind of knowledge that they have, relative to the mundane knowledge that others have, they are often advocates of courses of action which ignore the value, the cost, and the consequences of mundane knowledge. It is common, for example, for the intelligentsia to deplore many methods of sorting and labeling things and people, often saying in the case of people that "each person should be judged as an individual." The cost of the knowledge necessary to do that is almost never considered. Lower cost substitutes for that knowledge of individuals— ranging from credit reports to IQ tests— are used precisely because judging "the whole person" means acquiring and weighing vast amounts of knowledge at vast costs that can include delayed decisions in circumstances where time is crucial. Depending on how expansively "judging the whole person" is defined, the time required can exceed the human lifespan, which would make it impossible for all practical purposes.

Armies sort people into ranks, colleges sort applicants into ranges of SAT scores, and virtually everyone else sorts people by innumerable other criteria. Many, if not most, of these sorting methods are criticized by the intelligentsia, who fail to appreciate the scarcity and high cost of knowledge— and the necessity of making consequential decisions despite that scarcity and high cost, which necessarily includes the costs of mistakes. The risks of making decisions with incomplete knowledge (there being no other kind) are part of the tragedy of the human condition. However, that has not stopped intellectuals from criticizing the inherent risks that turn out badly in everything from pharmaceutical drugs to military operations— nor does it stop them from helping create a general atmosphere of unfulfillable expectations, in which "the thousand natural shocks that flesh is heir to" become a thousand bases for lawsuits.

Without some sense of the tragedy of the human condition, it is all too easy to consider anything that goes wrong as being somebody's fault.

It is common for intellectuals to act as if their special kind of knowledge of generalities can and should substitute for, and override, the mundane specific knowledge of others. This emphasis on the special knowledge of intellectuals often leads to the dismissing of mundane, first-hand knowledge as "prejudices" or "stereotypes," in favor of abstract beliefs common among the intelligentsia, who may have little or no first-hand knowledge of the individuals, organizations or concrete circumstances involved. Moreover, such attitudes are not only disseminated far beyond the ranks of the intelligentsia, they have become the basis of policies, laws, and judicial decisions.

One small but revealing example of the social consequences of this attitude is that many company policies of establishing retirement ages for their employees have been made illegal as "age discrimination" because those policies are said to be based on stereotypes about the elderly, who can be productive beyond the age of "mandatory retirement." In other words, third parties with no stake in the outcome, no direct experience in the particular companies or industries, and no knowledge of the particular individual employees involved, are assumed to have superior understanding of the effects of age than those who do have such experience, such a stake, and such direct knowledge, mundane though that knowledge may be. Moreover, employers have economic incentives to hang on to productive employees, especially since employers must pay costs to recruit their replacements and invest in bringing those replacements up to speed, while surrogate decision-makers pay no cost whatever for being mistaken.

The very phrase "mandatory retirement" shows the verbal virtuosity of the intelligentsia— and what a fatal talent that can be in obscuring, rather than clarifying, rational analysis. There has seldom, if ever, been any such thing as mandatory retirement. Particular employers had set an age beyond which they automatically ceased to employ people. Those people remained free to go work elsewhere and many did. Even within a company with an automatic retirement policy, those particular employees who clearly remained productive and valuable could find the retirement policy waived, either for a particular span of time or indefinitely. But such waivers would be based on specific knowledge of specific individuals, not abstract generalities about how productive older people can be.

Virtually all adverse conclusions about any ethnic minority are likewise dismissed as "prejudices," "stereotypes" and the like by the intelligentsia. For example, a biographer of Theodore Roosevelt said, "During his years as a rancher, Roosevelt had acquired plenty of anti-Indian prejudice, strangely at odds with his enlightened attitude to blacks."[14] Here was a writer, nearly a hundred years removed from the particular Indians that Theodore Roosevelt dealt with personally in the west, declaring *a priori* that Roosevelt's conclusions were mistaken and based on prejudice, even while conceding that racial prejudice was not a general feature of TR's outlook.

It would probably never occur to that writer that it was he who was reaching a conclusion based on prejudgment— prejudice— even if it was a prejudice common among intellectuals, while Theodore Roosevelt's conclusions were based on his own direct personal experience with particular individuals. Many intellectuals seem unwilling to concede that the man on the scene at the time could reach accurate conclusions about the particular individuals he encountered or observed— and that the intellectuals far removed in space and time could be mistaken when reaching conclusions based on their own shared preconceptions.

Another writer, even further removed in space and time, dismissed as prejudice Cicero's advice to his fellow Romans not to buy British slaves because they were so hard to teach.[15] Considering the enormous difference between the primitive, illiterate, tribal world of the Britons of that era and the sophisticated world of the Romans, it is hard to imagine how a Briton taken in bondage to Rome could comprehend the complex circumstances, methods, and expectations of such a radically different society. But the very possibility that Cicero might have known what he was talking about from direct experience received no attention from the writer who dubbed him prejudiced without further ado.

A much more recent example of intellectuals dismissing the first-hand experience of others, in favor of prevailing assumptions among themselves, involved nationally publicized charges of rape filed against three students at Duke University in 2006. These students were members of the men's lacrosse team and, in the wave of condemnation that instantly swept the campus and the media, the only defenders of these students at the outset were members of the women's lacrosse team. These particular women had long associated socially with the accused men and were adamant from the beginning that the three young men in question were not the kind of people to do what they were accused of. Since this case involved race as well as rape, it should also be noted that a black woman on the lacrosse team took the lead in defending these men's character.[16]

In the absence of any evidence on either side of the issue at the outset, there was no reason why unsubstantiated statements for or against the accused should have been uncritically accepted or uncritically rejected. But the statements of members of the women's lacrosse team were not merely dismissed but denounced.

The Duke women lacrosse players were characterized as "stupid, spoiled little girls" in remarks quoted in *The Atlanta Journal- Constitution*, people who "negate common sense" according to a *New York Times* writer, who were "dumb" according to a writer in the *Philadelphia Daily News*, and "ignorant or insensitive" according to a *Philadelphia Inquirer* writer.[17]

In other words, members of the intelligentsia, hundreds of miles away, who had never laid eyes on the men in question, were so convinced of their guilt, on the basis of commonly shared *a priori* notions among the intelligentsia, that they could assail young women who had had direct personal knowledge of the individuals in question, including their attitudes and behavior toward women in general and a black woman in particular. Despite the utter certainty and condescension in the media, devastating facts that later came out— exonerating the accused men and leading to the resignation and disbarment of the district attorney who prosecuted them— showed that it was the women on the Duke lacrosse team who were right and the media wrong. It was a classic example of the presumption of superior knowledge on the part of intellectuals with less knowledge than those whose conclusions they dismissed and denounced. Unfortunately, it was not the only example, nor even a rare example.

Experts

A special occupation which overlaps that of intellectuals, but is not wholly coincident with it, is that of the expert. One may, after all, be an expert on Spanish literature or existentialist philosophy— where one's end product in either case consists of ideas— or one may be an expert on repairing automobile transmissions or extinguishing oil field fires, where the end product is a service rendered. Obviously only the former experts would fit our definition of intellectuals.

Experts of whatever sort are especially clear examples of people whose knowledge is concentrated within a narrow band out of the vast spectrum of human concerns. Moreover, the interactions of innumerable factors in the real world mean that, even within that narrow band, factors from outside that band can sometimes affect outcomes in ways that mean an expert whose expertise does not encompass those other factors can be an amateur when it comes to making consequential decisions, even within what is normally thought of as that expert's field of expertise. For example, in early twentieth century America, experts on forestry predicted a "timber famine" that never materialized because these forestry experts did not know enough economics to understand how prices allocate resources over time, as well as allocating resources among alternative users at a given time.[18]

Similar hysteria about an impending exhaustion of other natural resources, such as oil, has flourished for well over a century, despite repeated predictions that we had only enough oil reserves to last for a dozen or so years and repeated experiences that there were more known oil reserves at the end of the dozen or so years than there were at the beginning.[19]

With experts, as with non-profit organizations or movements with idealistic-sounding names, there is often an implication of disinterested endeavors, uncorrupted by the bias of self-interest. This is one of many perceptions which cannot survive empirical scrutiny— but which is seldom subjected to such scrutiny. Quite aside from the vested interest that experts have in the use of expertise— rather than other economic or other social mechanisms— to shape consequential decisions, there is much empirical evidence of their biases. City planners are a typical example:

Planners often call for visioning sessions in which the public are consulted about their desires for their regions.

In a typical visioning session, members of the public are asked leading questions about their preferences. Would you like to have more or less pollution? Would you like to spend more or less time commuting? Would you like to live in an ugly neighborhood or a pretty one? Planners interpret the answers as support for their preconceived notions, usually some form of smart growth. If you want less pollution, you must want less auto driving. If you want to spend less time getting to work, you must want a denser city so you live closer to work. If you want apple pie, you must oppose urban sprawl that might subdivide the apple orchard.[20]

Quite aside from the tendentiousness of the questions, even an honest attempt to get meaningful input into a decision-making process from answers to questions that neither cost anything to answer nor even include any notion of costs in the questions, would be relevant only to a costless world, while the crucial fact of the world we live in is that all actions or inactions entail costs which have to be taken into account in order to reach a rational decision. "Rational" is used here in its most basic sense— the ability to make a ratio, as in "rational numbers" in mathematics— so that rational decisions are decisions that weigh one thing against another, a trade-off as distinguished from a crusade to achieve some "good thing" without weighing costs.

City planners, like other experts, are also well aware that their own incomes and careers depend on providing ideas that are saleable to those who employ them, including politicians, whose goals and methods become the experts' goals and methods. Even where experts go through the formality of weighing costs against benefits, that can remain only a formality in a process where a goal has been chosen politically. For example, after a planning expert was ordered by a politician who wanted a rail system built to "revise rail ridership estimates upward and costs downward," later cost over-runs and revenue shortfalls became a public scandal. But the politician was able to say: "It's not my fault; I relied on forecasts made by our staff, and they seem to have made a big mistake."[21]

In other words, experts are often called in, not to provide factual information or dispassionate analysis for the purpose of decision-making by responsible officials, but to give political cover for decisions already made and based on other considerations entirely. The shifting of socially consequential decisions from systemic processes, involving millions of people making mutual accommodations— at their own costs and risks— to experts imposing a master plan on all would be problematic even if the experts were free to render their own best judgment. In situations where experts are simply part of the window dressing concealing arbitrary and even corrupt decisions by others, reliance on what "all the experts" say about a given issue is extremely risky. Even where the experts are untrammeled, what "all the experts" are most likely to agree on is the need for using expertise to deal with problems.

Experts have their place and can be extremely valuable in those places, this no doubt being one reason for the old expression, "Experts should be on tap, not on top." For broader social decision-making, however, experts are no substitute for systemic processes which engage innumerable factors on which no given individual can possibly be expert, and engage the 99 percent of consequential knowledge scattered in fragments among the population at large and coordinated systemically during the process of their mutual accommodations to one another's demand and supply.

The simple fact that central planners in the Soviet Union had more than 24 million prices to set[22] shows the absurdity of the task undertaken by central planning. That central planning has failed repeatedly in countries around the world, among both democracies and dictatorships, can hardly be surprising because the central planners could not possibly be experts— or even competent— on all the things under their control. The fact that central planning was abandoned by country after country in the late twentieth century— even in countries with communist or socialist governments— suggests the depth and undeniability of that failure.

Economic central planning is just one aspect of top-down social engineering in general, but bad outcomes in other fields are not always so blatantly obvious, so readily quantifiable, and so undeniable as in the economy, though these other social outcomes may be just as bad or worse.[23] While lawyers and judges are experts on legal principles, and have valuable roles to play within their expertise, both have over the years increasingly moved beyond those roles to using law "as an instrument of social change"—

which is to say, making amateur decisions on complex matters extending far beyond the narrow boundaries of their professional expertise. Moreover, the consensus of like-minded experts on matters beyond their expertise has emboldened many legal experts— like experts in other fields— to imagine that the difference between their elite group perceptions and those of other people is almost axiomatically a difference between knowledgeable people and the uninformed masses.

Among the many examples of this attitude was a 1960s judicial conference where a retired police commissioner attempted to explain to the judges and law professors present how the courts' recent expansions of criminals' legal rights undermined the effectiveness of law enforcement. Among those present were Supreme Court Justice William J. Brennan and Chief Justice Earl Warren, both of whom remained "stony-faced" during the police commissioner's presentation, according to a *New York Times* account, but later "roared with laughter" after a law professor arose to pour ridicule on what the police commissioner had just said.[24] Yet such scornful dismissal was not based on any factual evidence— and evidence subsequently accumulating over the years made painfully clear that law enforcement was in fact breaking down, to an accompanying skyrocketing of crime rates.

Prior to the revolution in judicial interpretations of criminal law in the early 1960s, the murder rate in the United States had been going down for decades, and was by 1961 less than half of what it had been back in 1933.[25] But this long downward trend in murder rates suddenly reversed during the 1960s, and by 1974 the murder rate was double what it was in 1961.[26] Yet here, as elsewhere, the first-hand observations and years of personal day-to-day experience— in this case, by a retired police commissioner— were not merely dismissed but ridiculed by people who relied instead on shared but unsubstantiated assumptions among the elite. Neither this issue nor this episode was unique as an example of those with the vision of the anointed scornfully dismissing alternative views instead of answering them.

THE ROLE OF REASON

There are as many conceptions of reason and its social role as there are conceptions of knowledge and its social role. Both merit scrutiny.

Reason and Justification

The implicit assumption of superior knowledge among intellectual elites underlies one of the demands of intellectuals that goes back at least as far as the eighteenth century— namely, that actions, policies, or institutions "justify themselves before the bar of reason." As William Godwin said in 1793, "we must bring every thing to the standard of reason."[27] The words in which this demand is expressed have changed since the eighteenth century, but the basic premise has not. Many intellectuals today, for example, find it a weighty consideration that they do not understand how corporate executives can be worth such high salaries as they receive— as if there is any inherent reason why third parties should be expected to understand, or why their understanding or acquiescence should be necessary, in order for those who are directly involved in hiring and paying corporate executives to proceed on the basis of their own knowledge and experience, in a matter in which they have a stake and intellectuals do not.[*]

Similarly, many of the intelligentsia express not only surprise but outrage at the number of shots fired by the police in some confrontation with a criminal, even if many of these intellectuals have never fired a gun in their lives, much less faced life-and-death dangers requiring split-second decisions. Seldom, if ever, do the intelligentsia find it necessary to seek out any information on the accuracy of pistols when fired under stress, before venting their feelings and demanding changes. In reality, a study by the New

---

[*] Some try to claim that, as consumers who buy the products of the companies whose executives receive high pay, they are affected in the prices of the products they buy. However, if all the executives of oil companies, for example, agreed to work for no salary at all, that would not be enough to reduce the price of a gallon of gasoline by a dime, since the total profits of the oil companies are a small fraction of the price of a gallon of gasoline— usually much less than the taxes levied by governments at state and national levels. For a fuller discussion of executives' pay, see my *Economic Facts and Fallacies*, second edition, (New York: Basic Books, 2011), pp. 159–164.

York City Police Department found that, even within a range of only six feet, just over half the shots fired by police missed completely. At distances from 16 to 25 yards— less than the distance from first base to second base on a baseball diamond— only 14 percent of the shots hit.[28]

However surprising such facts might be to those who have never fired a pistol, even at a stationary target in the safety and calm of a pistol range, much less in the scramble and stress of life-and-death dangers with moving targets, what is crucial here is that so many of the intelligentsia and those whom they influence have seen no reason to seek such factual information before venting their outrage, in utter ignorance of the facts. Moreover, even a criminal who is hit by a bullet is not necessarily rendered instantly harmless, so there is no reason to stop firing, so long as that criminal continues to be a danger. But such mundane knowledge has been of no interest to those joining elite group expressions of indignation over things beyond their experience or competence.[*]

To demand that things justify themselves before the bar of reason, in a world where no one has even one percent of all consequential knowledge, is to demand that ignorance be convinced and its permission obtained. How can a brain surgeon justify what he does to someone who knows nothing about the brain or about surgery? How can a carpenter justify his choice of nails and woods to people who know nothing about carpentry, especially if the carpenter is being accused of wrongdoing by lawyers or politicians, whose articulation skills may greatly exceed those of the carpenter, while their knowledge of carpentry is far less? The confidence born of their generally superior special knowledge may conceal from these elites themselves the extent of their ignorance and their resulting misconception of the issue at hand. Moreover, arguments against the carpenter by articulate but ignorant elites to a general public that is equally ignorant on this subject— whether the public are on juries or in election booths— may easily prove to be convincing, even if those same arguments would seem absurd to other carpenters.

---

[*] As a personal note, I once taught pistol shooting in the Marine Corps and have not been at all surprised by the number of shots fired by the police.

It is one thing for the population at large to make their own individual transactions and accommodations on matters pertaining to themselves individually, and something quite different for them to make collective decisions for the society at large as voters or jurors. Collective decision-making, whether through democratic processes or through top-down commands, involves people making decisions for other people, rather than for themselves. The same problem of inadequate knowledge afflicts both these processes. To revert for a moment to central planning as a proxy for surrogate decision-making in general, when central planners in the days of the Soviet Union had to set more than 24 million prices it was an impossible task for any manageably sized group of central planners, but far less of a problem in a country with hundreds of millions of people, each making decisions about the relatively few prices relevant to their own economic transactions.

Incentives as well as knowledge are different. There are far more incentives to invest time and attention in decisions with major direct personal consequences to oneself than to invest similar amounts of time and attention to casting one vote among millions in decisions that will affect mostly other people, and whose effect on oneself is unlikely to be changed by how one's own single vote among millions is cast.

The notion that things must justify themselves before the bar of reason opens the floodgates to sweeping condemnations of things not understood by people with credentialed ignorance. Differences in incomes and occupations not understood by intellectual elites, usually without much knowledge of either the mundane specifics or of economics in general, readily become "disparities" and "inequities" without further ado, just as intellectuals who have never fired a gun in their lives do not hesitate to express their outrage at the number of bullets fired by the police in a confrontation with a criminal. In these and other ways, notions trump knowledge— when these are notions prevalent among intellectuals.

This key fallacy— and the bad social consequences to which it can lead— is not limited to intellectual elites. The squelching of individual decision-making by the imposition of collective decisions arrived at by third parties, whether those third parties are elites or masses, usually means essentially allowing ignorance to overrule knowledge. A public opinion poll or a popular vote on an issue involving carpentry would be as irrelevant as the views prevalent in elite circles. The only saving grace is that the masses are much less likely than the elites to think that they should be overruling people whose stake and whose relevant knowledge for the issue at hand are far greater than their own. Moreover, the masses are less likely to have the rhetorical skills to conceal from others, or from themselves, that this is what they are doing.

The intellectuals' exaltation of "reason" often comes at the expense of experience, allowing them to have sweeping confidence about things in which they have little or no knowledge or experience. The idea that what they don't know isn't knowledge may also be a factor in many references to "earlier and simpler times" by people who have made no detailed study of those times, and who are unlikely even to suspect that it is their knowledge of the complexities of those times which is lacking, not the complexities themselves.

Oliver Wendell Holmes pointed out that Roman law contained "a set of technicalities more difficult and less understood than our own."[29] Similar views have been expressed in the twenty-first century by Professor Richard A. Epstein of the University of Chicago, who has also taught Roman law at Oxford: "The private law controversies that generate such animated discussions among lawyers and scholars today were often argued with great ingenuity and imagination hundreds of years ago."[30] In a similar vein, distinguished historian N.J.G. Pounds said, "The evolution of the family and of familial structures, like most other human institutions, shows a progression from the complex towards the simple."[31]

Central planners are not the only elites whose special knowledge has proved less effective in practice than the vastly greater amount of mundane knowledge in the population at large, nor is the economic marketplace the only place where the knowledge imbalance between the elites and the masses can be the opposite of the way this imbalance is perceived by the elites. If, as Oliver Wendell Holmes said, the life of the law has not been logic but experience,[32] then here too it is the millions— and especially the successive generations of millions— who have vastly more knowledge in the form of personal experience than do the relatively small circles of experts in the law. This is not to say that experts have no role to play, whether in the law or in other aspects of life. But the nature of that role is very different when both elite expertise and mass experience must be combined, as in countries where laws are passed by elected representatives of the people and are carried out by judges and other legal experts.

Within a sufficiently circumscribed area of decision-making, experts on that particular circumscribed area can have a vital role to play. The few with legal expertise can make court decisions applying the laws that developed out of the experiences of the many. But that is fundamentally different from creating or changing the law to suit the notions of judges or the notions in vogue among law school professors. Likewise, someone with the special talents and skills to collect information and convey it to the public through the media can be an indispensable part of the functioning of a democratic society, but that is wholly different from journalists taking on the role of filtering and slanting the news to buttress conclusions reflecting notions common within journalistic circles, as will be documented in Chapter 10.

The difference between the carrying out of circumscribed roles and using those roles to exert power or influence to try to shape wider social decisions also applies to those teachers who are classroom indoctrinators or those religious leaders promoting liberation theology, as well as generals who displace civilian government with military coups. What the various non-military ambitious elites are doing is essentially creating smaller and more numerous coups, pre-empting social decisions that others have been authorized to make, in order to acquire power or influence in matters for which they have neither expertise nor, in many cases, even simple competence.

In short, whether one stays within a circumscribed role, based on one's expertise, or ventures beyond that role into areas beyond one's expertise, depends in part on whether one presumes oneself to have more knowledge than those whose decisions are being preempted. How knowledge is seen affects how society is seen, and how one's own role within that society is seen.

"One Day at a Time" Rationalism

Intellectuals' faith in "reason" sometimes takes the form of believing themselves capable of deciding each issue ad hoc as it arises. In principle, reason can be applied to as limited or as expansive a time period as one wishes— a day, a year, a generation, or a century, for example— by analyzing the implications of decisions over whatever span of time may be chosen. One-day-at-a-time rationalism risks restricting its analysis to the immediate implications of each issue as it arises, missing wider implications of a decision that may have merit as regards the issue immediately at hand, considered in isolation, but which can be disastrous in terms of the ignored longer-term repercussions. A classic example was a French intellectual's response to the Czechoslovakian crisis that led to the Munich conference of 1938:

> An eminent French political scientist, Joseph Barthélemy, who taught constitutional law at the University of Paris and was French representative at the League of Nations, asked in *Le Temps* the question French leaders had to answer: "Is it worthwhile setting fire to the world in order to save the Czechoslovak state, a heap of different nationalities? Is it necessary that three million Frenchmen, all the youth of our universities, of our schools, our countryside and our factories would be sacrificed to maintain three million Germans under Czech sovereignty?"[33]

Since it was not France that was threatening to set fire to the world, but Hitler, the larger question was whether someone who was threatening to set fire to the world if he didn't get his way was someone who should be appeased in this one-day-at-a-time approach, without regard to what this appeasement could do to encourage a never-ending series of escalating demands. By contrast, Winston Churchill had pointed out, six years earlier, that "every concession which has been made" to Germany "has been followed immediately by a fresh demand."[34] Churchill clearly rejected one-day-at-a-time rationalism.

By the time that Barthélemy addressed the Czechoslovakian crisis, Hitler had already taken the crucial step toward preparing for war by remilitarizing the Rhineland, in defiance of treaty commitments, had initiated military conscription when there was no military threat against Germany, and had seized Austria by force. As Winston Churchill said at the time, "Europe is confronted with a program of aggression, nicely calculated and timed, unfolding stage by stage." This raised the longer run question posed by Churchill: "How many friends would be alienated, how many potential allies should we see go, one by one, down the grisly gulf, how many times would bluff succeed, until behind bluff ever-gathering forces had accumulated reality?"[35] In short, the handwriting was on the wall for anyone who wanted to read it, and presenting the immediate Czechoslovakian crisis in isolation was one way of not facing the implications of a series of actions over a longer span of time, leading toward a growing threat, as more and more resources came under the control of Nazi Germany, increasing its military potential.

That threat would be even greater with the significant resources of Czechoslovakia under Hitler's control— as France would discover just two years later, when an invading German army battered them into quick submission, using among other things tanks manufactured in Czechoslovakia.

The one-day-at-a-time approach has been applied to numerous issues, foreign and domestic. At the heart of this approach is the implicit notion that intellectuals can define an issue in ways they find convenient— and that what happens in the real world will remain within the confines of their definition. But time is just one of the many things that can move beyond the boundaries of man-made definitions and conceptions. For example, however humane it may seem to have "forgiveness" of loans to Third World countries, at least in a one-day-at-a-time perspective, what happens today affects how people will behave tomorrow. In this case, Third World countries repeatedly borrow money that they repeatedly do not repay, either because of explicit "forgiveness" or because international aid agencies allow them to repeatedly borrow ever larger amounts, using the proceeds of later loans to pay off previous loans, but with no end in sight as far as ever paying off any loan with their own resources. Fiscal irresponsibility has seldom provided a way out of poverty, whether for individuals or for nations.

Hurricanes in Florida and wildfires in southern California are likewise recurrent phenomena over the years but each individual natural catastrophe is treated as an immediate and discrete crisis, bringing not only government rescue efforts but also vast amounts of the taxpayers' money to enable people who live in these places to rebuild in the known path of these dangers.[*] Any administration which might refuse to saddle taxpayers with the huge costs of subsidizing the rebuilding would no doubt be roundly condemned, not only by its political opponents but also by much of the media and the intelligentsia, looking at each particular hurricane or wildfire in a one-day-at-a-time perspective, rather than as part of an on-going sequence with a long history and a predictable future.

---

[*] An economist has estimated that the cost of rebuilding New Orleans was enough to instead give every New Orleans family of four $800,000, which they would be free to use to relocate to some safer place. But the idea of not rebuilding New Orleans has been seen as part of "the apparently heartless reaction of many urban economists to the devastation of New Orleans." Tim Harford, *The Logic of Life* (New York: Random House, 2008), p. 170.

PART II

INTELLECTUALS

AND ECONOMICS

Whether one is a conservative or a radical, a protectionist or a free trader, a cosmopolitan or a nationalist, a churchman or a heathen, it is useful to know the causes and consequences of economic phenomena.

George J. Stigler[1]

Chapter 3

"Income Distribution"

M ost intellectuals outside the field of economics show remarkably little interest in learning even the basic fundamentals of economics. Yet they do not hesitate to make sweeping pronouncements about the economy in general, businesses in particular, and the many issues revolving around what is called "income distribution." Famed novelist John Steinbeck, for example, commented on the many American fortunes which have been donated to philanthropic causes by saying:

> One has only to remember some of the wolfish financiers who spent two thirds of their lives clawing a fortune out of the guts of society and the latter third pushing it back.[1]

Despite the verbal virtuosity involved in creating a vivid vision of profits as having been clawed out of the guts of society, neither Steinbeck nor most other intellectuals have bothered to demonstrate how society has been made poorer by the activities of Carnegie, Ford, or Rockefeller, for example— all three of whom (and many others) made fortunes by reducing the prices of their products below the prices of competing products. Lower prices made these products affordable to more people, simultaneously increasing those people's standard of living and creating fortunes for sellers who greatly expanded the numbers of their customers. In short, this was a process in which wealth was created, not a process by which some could get rich only by making others poorer.

Nevertheless, negative images of market processes have been evoked with such phrases as "robber barons" and "economic royalists"— without answering such obvious questions as "Just who did the robber barons rob when they lowered their prices?" or "How is earning money, often starting from modest circumstances (or even poverty-stricken circumstances in the case of J.C. Penney and F.W. Woolworth) the same as simply inheriting wealth and power like royalty?" The issue here is not the adequacy or inadequacy of intellectuals' answers to such questions because, in most cases, such questions are not even asked, much less answered. The vision, in effect, serves as a substitute for both facts and questions.

This is not to suggest that nobody in business ever did anything wrong. Saints have been no more common in corporate suites than in government offices or on ivy-covered campuses. However, the question here is not one of individual culpability for particular misdeeds. The question raised by critics of business and its defenders alike has been about the merits or demerits of alternative *institutional processes* for serving the economic interests of society at large. Implicit in many criticisms of market processes by intellectuals is the assumption that these are zero-sum processes, in which what is gained by some is lost by others. Seldom is this assumption spelled out but, without it, much of what is spelled out would have no basis.

Perhaps the biggest economic issue, or the one addressed most often, is that of what is called "income distribution," though the phrase itself is misleading, and the conclusions about income reached by most of the intelligentsia are still more misleading.

Variations in income can be viewed empirically, on the one hand, or in terms of moral judgments, on the other. Most of the contemporary intelligentsia do both. But, in order to assess the validity of the conclusions they reach, it is advisable to assess the empirical issues and the moral issues separately, rather than attempt to go back and forth between the two, with any expectation of rational coherence.

EMPIRICAL EVIDENCE

Given the vast amounts of statistical data on income available from the Census Bureau, the Internal Revenue Service and innumerable research institutes and projects, one might imagine that the bare facts about variations in income would be fairly well known by informed people, even though they might have differing opinions as to the desirability of those particular variations. In reality, however, the most fundamental facts are in dispute, and variations in what are claimed to be facts seem to be at least as great as variations in incomes. Both the magnitude of income variations and the trends in these variations over time are seen in radically different terms by those with different visions as regards the current reality, even aside from what different people may regard as desirable for the future.

Perhaps the most fertile source of misunderstandings about incomes has been the widespread practice of confusing statistical categories with flesh-and-blood human beings. Many statements have been made in the media and in academia, claiming that the rich are gaining not only larger incomes but a growing share of all incomes, widening the income gap between people at the top and those at the bottom. Almost invariably these statements are based on confusing what has been happening over time in statistical categories with what has been happening over time with actual flesh-and-blood people.

A *New York Times* editorial, for example, declared that "the gap between rich and poor has widened in America."[2] Similar conclusions appeared in a 2007 *Newsweek* article which referred to this era as "a time when the gap is growing between the rich and the poor— and the superrich and the merely rich,"[3] a theme common in such other well-known media outlets as the *Washington Post* and innumerable television programs. "The rich have seen far greater income gains than have the poor," according to *Washington Post* columnist Eugene Robinson.[4] A writer in the *Los Angeles Times* likewise declared, "the gap between rich and poor is growing."[5] E.J. Dionne of the *Washington Post* described "the wealthy" as "people who have made almost all the income gains in recent years" and added that they are "undertaxed."[6]

Similar statements have been made by academics. According to Professor Peter Corning of Stanford University, in his book *The Fair Society*, "the income gap between the richest and the poorest members of our society has been growing rapidly."[7] Professor Andrew Hacker of Queens College likewise declared in his book *Money*: "While all segments of the population enjoyed an increase in income, the top fifth did twenty-four times better than the bottom fifth. And measured by their shares of the aggregate, not just the bottom fifth but the three above it all ended up losing ground."[8]

Although such discussions have been phrased in terms of *people*, the actual empirical evidence cited has been about what has been happening over time to *statistical categories*— and that turns out to be the direct opposite of what has happened over time to flesh-and-blood human beings, most of whom *move* from one income category to another over time.

In terms of statistical categories, it is indeed true that both the amount of income and the proportion of all income received by those in the top 20 percent bracket have risen over the years, widening the gap between the top and bottom quintiles.[9] But U.S. Treasury Department data, following specific individuals over time from their tax returns to the Internal Revenue Service, show that in terms of *people* the incomes of those particular taxpayers who were in the bottom 20 percent in income in 1996 rose 91 percent by 2005, while the incomes of those particular taxpayers who were in the top 20 percent in 1996 rose by only 10 percent by 2005— and the incomes of those in the top 5 percent and top one percent actually declined.[10]

While it might seem as if both these radically different sets of statistics cannot be true at the same time, what makes them mutually compatible is that flesh-and-blood human beings move from one statistical category to another over time. When those taxpayers who were initially in the lowest income bracket had their incomes nearly double in a decade, that moved many of them up and out of the bottom quintile— and when those in the top one percent had their incomes cut by about one-fourth, that may well have dropped many, if not most, of them out of the top one percent. Internal Revenue Service data can follow particular individuals over time from their tax returns, which have individual Social Security numbers as identification, while data from the Census Bureau and most other sources follow what happens to statistical categories over time, even though it is not the same individuals in the same categories over the years.

Many of the same kinds of data used to claim a widening income gap between "the rich" and "the poor"— names usually given to people with different incomes, rather than different amounts of wealth, as the terms rich and poor might seem to imply— have led many in the media to likewise claim a growing income gap between the "super-rich" and the "merely rich." Under the headline "Richest Are Leaving Even the Rich Far Behind," a front-page *New York Times* article dubbed the "top 0.1 percent of income earners— the top one-thousandth" as the "hyper-rich" and declared that they "have even left behind people making hundreds of thousands of dollars a year."[11] Once again, the confusion is between what is happening to statistical categories over time and what is happening to flesh-and-blood individuals over time, as they move from one statistical category to another.

Despite the rise in the income of the top 0.1 percent of taxpayers as a statistical category, both absolutely and relative to the incomes in other categories, as flesh-and-blood human beings those individuals who were in that category initially had their incomes actually *fall* by a whopping 50 percent between 1996 and 2005.[12] It is hardly surprising when people whose incomes are cut in half drop out of the top 0.1 percent. What happens to the income of the category over time is not the same as what happens to the people who were in that category at any given point in time. But many among the intelligentsia are ready to seize upon any numbers that seem to fit their vision.[13]

It is much the same story with data on the top four hundred income earners in the country. As with other data, data on those who were among the top 400 income earners from 1992 to 2000 were not data on the same 400 people throughout that span of time. During that span, there were thousands of people in the top 400— which is to say, turnover was high. Fewer than one-fourth of all the people in that category during that span of years were in that category more than one year, and fewer than 13 percent were in that same category more than two years.[14]

Behind many of those numbers and the accompanying alarmist rhetoric is a very mundane fact: Most people begin their working careers at the bottom, earning entry-level salaries. Over time, as they acquire more skills and experience, their rising productivity leads to rising pay, putting them in successively higher income brackets. These are not rare, Horatio Alger stories. These are common patterns among millions of people in the United States and in some other countries. A University of Michigan study which followed the same working individuals over time found a pattern very similar to that in the Internal Revenue Service data. More than three-quarters of those working Americans whose incomes were in the bottom 20 percent in 1975 were also in the *top* 40 percent of income earners at some point by 1991. Only 5 percent of those who were initially in the bottom quintile were still there in 1991, while 29 percent of those who were initially at the bottom quintile had risen to the top quintile.[15]

Yet verbal virtuosity has transformed a transient cohort in a given statistical category into an enduring class called "the poor." Just as most Americans in statistical categories identified as "the poor" are not an enduring class there, studies in Britain, Canada, New Zealand and Greece show similar patterns of transience among those in low-income brackets at a given time.[16] Just over half of all Americans earning at or near the minimum wage are from 16 to 24 years of age[17]— and of course these individuals cannot *remain* from 16 to 24 years of age indefinitely, though that age category can of course continue indefinitely, providing many intellectuals with data to fit their preconceptions.

Only by focussing on the income brackets, instead of the actual people moving between those brackets, have the intelligentsia been able to verbally create a "problem" for which a "solution" is necessary. They have created a powerful vision of "classes" with "disparities" and "inequities" in income, caused by "barriers" created by "society." But the routine rise of millions of people out of the lowest quintile over time makes a mockery of the "barriers" assumed by many, if not most, of the intelligentsia.

Far from using their intellectual skills to clarify the distinction between statistical categories and flesh-and-blood human beings, the intelligentsia have instead used their verbal virtuosity to equate the changing numerical relationship between statistical categories over time with a changing relationship between flesh-and-blood human beings ("the rich" and "the poor") over time, even though data that follow individual income-earners over time tell a diametrically opposite story from that of data which follow the statistical categories which people are moving into and out of over time.

The confusion between statistical categories and flesh-and-blood human beings is compounded when there is confusion between income and wealth. People called "rich" or "super-rich" have been given these titles by the media on the basis of income, not wealth, even though being rich means having more wealth. According to the Treasury Department: "Among those with the very highest incomes in 1996— the top 1/100 of 1 percent— only 25 percent remained in this group in 2005."[18] If these were genuinely super-rich people, it is hard to explain why three-quarters of them are no longer in that category a decade later.

A related, but somewhat different, confusion between statistical categories and human beings has led to many claims in the media and in academia that Americans' incomes have stagnated or grown only very slowly over the years. For example, over the entire period from 1967 to 2005, median real household income— that is, money income adjusted for inflation— rose by 31 percent.[19] For selected periods within that long span, real household incomes rose even less, and those selected periods have often been cited by the intelligentsia to claim that income and living standards have "stagnated."[20] Meanwhile, real per capita income rose by 122 percent over that same span, from 1967 to 2005.[21] When a more than doubling of real income per person is called "stagnation," that is one of the many feats of verbal virtuosity.

The reason for the large discrepancy between growth rate trends in household income and growth rate trends in individual income is very straightforward: The number of persons per household has been declining over the years. As early as 1966, the U.S. Bureau of the Census reported that the number of households was increasing faster than the number of people, and concluded: "The main reason for the more rapid rate of household formation is the increased tendency, particularly among unrelated individuals, to maintain their own homes or apartments rather than live with relatives or move into existing households as roomers, lodgers, and so forth."[22] Increasing individual incomes made this possible. As late as 1970, 21 percent of American households contained 5 or more people. But, by 2007, only 10 percent did.[23]

Despite such obvious and mundane facts, household or family income statistics continue to be widely cited in the media and in academia— and per capita income statistics continue to be widely ignored, despite the fact that households are variable in size, while per capita income always refers to the income of one person. However, the statistics that the intelligentsia keep citing are much more consistent with their vision of America than the statistics they keep ignoring.

Just as household statistics understate the rise in the American standard of living over time, they *overstate* the degree of income inequality, since lower income households tend to have fewer people than upper income households. While there are 39 million people in households whose incomes are in the bottom 20 percent, there are 64 million people in households whose incomes are in the top 20 percent.[24] There is nothing mysterious about this either, given the number of low-income mothers living with fatherless children, and low-income lodgers in single room occupancy hotels or rooming houses, for example.

Even if every *person* in the entire country received exactly the same income, there would still be a significant "disparity" between the average incomes received by *households* containing 64 million people compared to the average income received by households containing 39 million people. That disparity would be even greater if only the incomes of working adults were counted, even if those working adults all had identical incomes. There are more adult heads of household working full-time and year-around in even the top *five* percent of households than in the bottom *twenty* percent of households.[25]

Many income statistics are misleading in another sense, when they leave out the income received in kind— such as food stamps and subsidized housing— which often exceeds the value of the cash income received by people in the lower-income brackets. In 2001, for example, transfers in cash or in kind accounted for more than three-quarters of the total economic resources at the disposal of people in the bottom 20 percent.[26] In other words, the standard of living of people in the bottom quintile is about three times what their earned income statistics would indicate. As we shall see, their personal possessions are far more consistent with this fact than with the vision of the intelligentsia.

MORAL CONSIDERATIONS

The difference between statistical categories and actual people affects moral, as well as empirical, issues. However concerned we might be about the economic fate of flesh-and-blood human beings, that is very different from being alarmed or outraged about the fate of statistical categories. Michael Harrington's best-selling book *The Other America*, for example, dramatized income statistics, lamenting "the anguish" of the poor in America, tens of millions "maimed in body and spirit" constituting "the shame of the other America," people "caught in a vicious circle" and suffering a "warping of the will and spirit that is a consequence of being poor."[27] But investing statistical data with moral angst does nothing to establish a connection between a transient cohort in statistical categories and an enduring class conjured up through verbal virtuosity.

There was a time when such rhetoric might have made some sense in the United States, and there are other countries where it may still make sense today. But most of those Americans now living below the official poverty line have possessions once considered part of a middle class standard of living, just a generation or so ago. As of 2001, three-quarters of Americans with incomes below the official poverty level had air-conditioning (which only one-third of all Americans had in 1971), 97 percent had color television (which fewer than half of all Americans had in 1971), 73 percent owned a microwave oven (which fewer than one percent of all Americans had in 1971) and 98 percent of "the poor" had either a videocassette recorder or a DVD player (which no one had in 1971). In addition, 72 percent of "the poor" owned a motor vehicle.[28]

None of this has done much to change the rhetoric of the intelligentsia, however much it may reflect major changes in the standard of living of Americans in the lower income brackets. Professor Peter Corning, for example, has called the American economy "an ever-spreading wasteland of poverty" and said that "close to one-quarter of our population" are "struggling to meet their basic needs."[29] Similarly, Professor Andrew Hacker declared that "a rising proportion of children are growing up in homes without the means even for basic necessities."[30]

Undefined terms like "basic necessities" and arbitrarily defined terms like "poverty" allow such rhetoric to flourish, independently of documented facts about rising living standards in the lower income brackets. While such alarmist rhetoric abounds, specifics are conspicuous by their absence. At one time, poverty meant that people were hungry or couldn't afford adequate clothing to protect themselves against the elements. Today it means whatever those who define the official poverty level want it to mean, so that saying that X percent of the American population live in poverty is to say that they meet some ultimately arbitrary definition, which could be set higher or lower, causing half as many or twice as many to be called "poor." Moreover, the income statistics so often cited tell us very little about the actual standard of living among people who receive the majority of their economic resources *over and above* whatever incomes they may be earning.

In this situation, income statistics for the largely non-working, low-income population tell us more about the notions or agendas in the minds of those who define statistical categories than they tell us about the actual living conditions of flesh-and-blood human beings in the real world.

Misconceptions of how the economy functions have been as common as misstatements of facts. Typical of the mindset of many intellectuals was a book by Professor Andrew Hacker which referred to the trillions of dollars that become "the personal income of Americans" each year, and said: "Just how this money is apportioned will be the subject of this book."[31] But this money is not *apportioned* at all. It becomes income through an entirely different process.

The very phrase "income distribution" is tendentious. It starts the economic story in the middle, with a body of income or wealth existing *somehow*, leaving only the question as to how that income or wealth is to be distributed or "apportioned" as Professor Hacker puts it. In the real world, the situation is quite different. In a market economy, most people receive income as a result of what they produce, supplying other people with some goods or services that those people want, even if that service is only labor. Each recipient of these goods and services pays according to the value which that particular recipient puts on what is received, choosing among alternative suppliers to find the best combination of price and quality— both as judged by the individual who is paying.

This mundane, utilitarian process is quite different from the vision of "income distribution" projected by those among the intelligentsia who invest that vision with moral angst. If there really were some pre-existing body of income or wealth, produced *somehow*— manna from heaven, as it were— then there would of course be a moral question as to how large a share each member of society should receive. But wealth is *produced*. It does not just exist *somehow*. Where millions of individuals are paid according to how much what they produce is valued subjectively by millions of other individuals, it is not at all clear on what basis third parties could say that some goods or services are over-valued or under-valued, that cooking should be valued more or carpentry should be valued less, for example, much less that not working at all is not rewarded enough compared to working.

Nor is there anything mysterious in the fact that at least a thousand times as many people would pay to hear Pavarotti sing as would pay to hear the average person sing.

Where people are paid for what they produce, one person's output can easily be worth a thousand times as much as another person's output to those who are the recipients of that output— if only because thousands more people are interested in receiving some products or services than are interested in receiving other products and services— or even the same product or service from someone else. For example, when Tiger Woods left the golf tournament circuit for several months because of an injury, television audiences for the final round of major tournaments declined by varying amounts, ranging up to 61 percent.[32] That can translate into millions of dollars' worth of advertising revenue, based on the number of television viewers.

The fact that one person's productivity may be a thousand times as valuable as another's does not mean that one person's *merit* is a thousand times as great as another's. Productivity and merit are very different things, though the two things are often confused with one another. Moreover, an individual's productivity is affected by innumerable factors besides the efforts of that individual— being born with a great voice being an obvious example. Being raised in a particular home with a particular set of values and behavior patterns, living in a particular geographic or social environment, merely being born with a normal brain, rather than a brain damaged during the birth process, can make enormous differences in what a given person is capable of producing.

More fundamentally, third parties are in no position to second-guess the felt value of someone's productivity to someone else, and it is hard even to conceive how someone's merit could be judged accurately by another human being who "never walked in his shoes." An individual raised in terrible home conditions or terrible social conditions may be laudable for having become an average, decent citizen with average work skills as a shoe repairer, while someone raised from birth with every advantage that money and social position can confer may be no more laudable for becoming an eminent brain surgeon. But that is wholly different from saying that repairing shoes is just as valuable to others as being able to repair maladies of the brain.

To say that merit may be the same is not to say that productivity is the same. Nor can we logically or morally ignore the discrepancy in the relative urgency of those who want their shoes repaired versus those in need of brain surgery. In other words, it is not a question of simply weighing the interest of one income recipient versus the interest of another income recipient, while ignoring the vastly larger number of other people whose well-being depends on what these individuals produce.

If one prefers an economy in which income is divorced from productivity, then the case for that kind of economy needs to be made explicitly. But that is wholly different from making such a large and fundamental change on the basis of verbal virtuosity in depicting the issue as being simply that of one set of "income distribution" statistics today versus an alternative set of "income distribution" statistics tomorrow.

As for the moral question, whether any given set of human beings can be held responsible for disparities in other people's productivity— and consequent earnings— depends on how much control any given set of human beings has maintained, or can possibly maintain, over the innumerable factors which have led to existing differences in productivity. Since *no* human being has control over the past, and many deeply ingrained cultural differences are a legacy of the past, limitations on what can be done in the present are limitations on what can be regarded as moral failings by society.

Still less can statistical differences between groups be automatically attributed to "barriers" created by society. Barriers exist in the real world, just as cancer exists. But acknowledging that does not mean that all deaths— or even most deaths— can be automatically attributed to cancer or that most economic differences can be automatically attributed to "barriers," however fashionable this latter non sequitur may be in some quarters.

Within the constraints of circumstances, there are things which can be done to make opportunities more widely available, or to help those whose handicaps are too severe to expect them to utilize whatever opportunities are already available. In fact, much has already been done and is still being done in a country like the United States, which leads the world in philanthropy, not only in terms of money but also in terms of individuals donating their time to philanthropic endeavors. But only by assuming that everything that has not been done could have been done, disregarding costs and risks, can individuals or societies be blamed because the real world does not match some vision of an ideal society. Nor can the discrepancy between the real and the vision of the ideal be automatically blamed on the existing reality, as if visionaries cannot possibly be mistaken.

THE POOR AS CONSUMERS

Although most people in the lower income brackets as of a given time do not remain there permanently, some people do. Moreover, particular neighborhoods may remain the homes of poor people for generations, no matter how many people from those neighborhoods move out to a better life as they move up from one income bracket to another. Complete racial or ethnic turnovers in neighborhoods— Harlem having once been a middle-class Jewish community[33]— are just one sign of such economic mobility.

Low-income neighborhoods tend to have their own economic characteristics, regardless of who lives in them— one of the most salient of these characteristics being that prices tend to be higher there than in other neighborhoods. Intellectuals' discussions of the fact that "the poor pay more" are often indignant indictments and condemnations of those who charge higher prices to people who can least afford to pay them. The *causes* of those high prices are implicitly assumed to originate with those who charge them, and in particular to be due to malign dispositions such as "greed," "racism" and the like. Seldom is the possibility even mentioned, much less investigated, that whoever or whatever *conveys* high prices may not be the same as whoever or whatever *causes* those prices to be higher than in other neighborhoods.

Confusing conveyance with causation is at the heart of many intellectuals' discussions of "social problems." In many very different contexts, prices often convey an underlying reality without being the cause of that reality.

Among the underlying realities in many low-income neighborhoods are higher rates of crime, vandalism, and violence, as well as a lack of the economic prerequisites for the economies of scale which enable big chain stores to charge lower prices and still make profits on higher rates of inventory turnover in more affluent neighborhoods. But such mundane considerations do not present intellectuals with either an opportunity to display their special kind of knowledge or an opportunity to display their presumptions of superior virtue by condemning others. If stores in low-income neighborhoods were in fact making higher rates of profit on their investments, it would be hard to explain why national store chains and many other businesses avoid locating in such places, which are often painfully lacking in many businesses that are common in more affluent neighborhoods.

The underlying costs of providing financial services to people in low-income neighborhoods are likewise ignored by much, if not most, of the intelligentsia. Instead, the high rates of interest charged on personal loans to the poor are enough to set off orgies of denunciation and demands for government intervention to put an end to "exploitative" and "unconscionable" interest rates. Here verbal virtuosity is often used by stating interest rates in *annual* percentage terms, when in fact loans made in low-income neighborhoods are often made for a matter of weeks, or even days, to meet some exigency of the moment. The sums of money lent are usually a few hundred dollars, lent for a few weeks, with interest charges of about $15 per $100 lent. That works out to annual interest rates in the hundreds— the kind of statistics that produce sensations in the media and in politics.

The costs behind such charges are seldom, if ever, investigated by the intelligentsia, by so-called "consumer advocates" or by others in the business of creating sensations and denouncing businesses that they know little or nothing about. The economic consequences of government intervention to limit the annual interest rate can be seen in a number of states where such limits have been imposed. After Oregon imposed a limit of 36 percent annual interest, three-quarters of its "payday loan" businesses closed down.[34]

Nor is it hard to see why— if one bothers to look at facts. At a 36 percent limit on the annual interest rate, the $15 in interest charged for every $100 lent would be reduced to less than $1.50 for a loan payable in two weeks— an amount not likely to cover even the cost of processing the loan, much less the risks of making the loan.*

As for the low-income borrower, supposedly the reason for the concern of the moral elites, denying the borrower the $100 needed to meet some exigency must be weighed against the $15 paid for getting the money to meet that exigency. Why that trade-off decision should be forcibly removed by law from the person most knowledgeable about the situation, as well as most affected by it, and transferred to third parties far removed in specific knowledge and general circumstances, is a question that is seldom answered or even asked. With intellectuals who consider themselves knowledgeable, as well as compassionate, it would seldom occur to them to regard themselves as interfering with things of which they are very ignorant— and doing so at costs imposed on people far less fortunate than themselves.

A *New York Times* editorial, for example, denounced the payday loan providers' "triple-digit annual interest rates, milking people's desperation" and "profiteering with the cloak of capitalist virtue." It described a 36 percent interest rate ceiling as something needed to prevent "the egregious exploitation of payday loans."[35] How much good it may have done the *New York Times* to say such things tells us nothing about whether it did any good for the poor to have one of their already limited options taken off the table.

None of this, however, is peculiar to the *New York Times* or to payday loans. Any number of ways in which poor people adjust to their poverty are shocking to people who have more money and more options— as well as more presumptions. The housing that the poor live in, for example, has long offended more affluent third party observers, who have often led political crusades to tear down "substandard" housing, removing the "blight" (and the

---

* One of the problems is that what is called "interest" includes processing costs— and these processing costs tend to be a higher percentage of the total costs for smaller loans. In other words, the processing cost is not likely to vary much between a one hundred dollar loan and a thousand dollar loan. For a ten thousand dollar loan, the same processing cost may be an insignificant fraction of the interest charged.

poor) from their sight. This usually leaves the poor with no better options than before, unless forcing them to pay more for more upscale housing than they wanted— and which they had the option to pay for before— is somehow considered to be better. Reducing people's already limited options can hardly be considered to be making them better off, unless you are convinced of your own superior wisdom and virtue. But, as someone has pointed out, a fool can put on his coat better than a wise man can put it on for him.

Nothing is easier than coming up with housing standards reflecting what upscale third party "reformers" would like to see, at no cost to themselves. Such housing reformers have destroyed whole neighborhoods as "blighted," over the years chasing the poor from one neighborhood to another. In San Francisco, the net effect of such zealotry has been to chase huge numbers of blacks completely out of the city. By the early twenty-first century, the black population of San Francisco was less than half of what it had been in 1970. None of this is peculiar to blacks or to San Francisco, or even to housing reformers or critics of payday loans. These are just some of the ways in which the anointed can feel good about themselves, while leaving havoc in their wake.

Chapter 4

Economic   Systems

The most fundamental fact of economics, without which there would be no economics, is that what everybody wants always adds up to more than there is. If this were not true, then we would be living in a Garden of Eden, where everything is available in unlimited abundance, instead of in an economy with limited resources and unlimited desires. Because of this inherent .scarcity— regardless of whether a particular economic system is one of capitalism, socialism, feudalism, or whatever— an economy not only organizes production and the distribution of the resulting output, it must by its very nature also have ways to *prevent* people from completely satisfying their desires. That is, it must *convey* the inherent scarcity, without which there would be no real point to economics, even though the particular kind of economy does not *cause* that scarcity.

In a market economy, prices convey the inherent scarcity through competing bids for resources and outputs that are inherently inadequate to supply all the bidders with all that they want. This may seem like a small and obvious point, but even such renowned intellectuals as the philosopher John Dewey have grossly misconceived it, blaming the particular economic system that *conveys* scarcity for *causing* the scarcity itself. Dewey saw the existing market economy as one "maintaining artificial scarcity" for the sake of "personal profit."[1] George Bernard Shaw likewise saw "restricting output" as the principle on which capitalism was founded.[2] Bertrand Russell depicted a market economy as one in which "wealthy highwaymen are allowed to levy toll upon the world for the use of indispensable minerals."[3]

According to Dewey, to make "potential abundance an actuality" what was needed was to "modify institutions."[4] But he apparently found it unnecessary to specify any alternative set of economic institutions in the real world which had in fact produced greater abundance than the institutions he blamed for "maintaining artificial scarcity." As in many other cases, the utter absence of factual evidence or even a single step of logic often passes unnoticed among the intelligentsia, when someone is voicing a view common among their peers and consistent with their general vision of the world.

Similarly, a twenty-first century historian said in passing, as something too obvious to require elaboration, that "capitalism created masses of laborers who were poverty stricken."[5] There were certainly many such laborers in the early years of capitalism, but neither this historian nor most other intellectuals have bothered to show that capitalism *created* this poverty. If in fact those laborers were more prosperous before capitalism, then not only would such a fact need to be demonstrated, what would also need to be explained is why laborers gave up this earlier and presumably higher standard of living to go work for capitalists for less. Seldom is either of these tasks undertaken by intellectuals who make such assertions— and seldom do their fellow intellectuals challenge them to do so, when they are saying things that fit the prevailing vision.

Social critic Robert Reich has likewise referred in passing to twentieth-century capitalism as producing, among other social consequences, "urban squalor, measly wages and long hours for factory workers"[6] but without a speck of evidence that any of these things was better before twentieth-century capitalism. Nothing is easier than simply *assuming* that things were better before, and nothing is harder than finding evidence of better housing, higher wages and shorter hours in the nineteenth and earlier centuries, whether in industry or agriculture.

The difference between creating a reality and conveying a reality has been crucial in many contexts. The idea of killing the messenger who brings bad news is one of the oldest and simplest examples. But the fundamental principle is still alive and well today, when charges of racial discrimination are made against banks that turn down a higher proportion of black applicants for mortgage loans than of white applicants.

Even when the actual decision-maker who approves or denies loan applications does so on the basis of paperwork provided by others who interview loan applicants face-to-face, and the actual decision-maker has no idea what race any of the applicants are, the decisions made may nevertheless *convey* differences among racial groups in financial qualifications without being the *cause* of those differences in qualifications, credit history or the outcomes that result from those differences. The fact that black-owned banks also turn down black applicants at a higher rate than white applicants, and that white-owned banks turn down white applicants at a higher rate than Asian American applicants,[7] reinforces the point— but only for those who check out the facts that are seldom mentioned in the media, which is preoccupied with moral melodrama that fits their vision.[*] Among the many differences among black, white and Asian Americans is that the average credit rating among whites is higher than among blacks and the average credit rating of Asian Americans is higher than among whites.[8]

In light of the many differences among these three groups, it is hardly surprising that, while blacks were turned down for mortgage loans at twice the rate for whites in 2000, whites were turned down at nearly twice the rate for Asian Americans.[9] But only the black-white comparison saw the light of day in much of the media. To have included data comparing mortgage loan denial rates between Asian Americans and whites would have reduced a moral melodrama to a mundane example of elementary economics.

CHAOS VERSUS COMPETITION

Among the other unsubstantiated notions about economics common among the intelligentsia is that there would be chaos in the economy without government planning or control. The order created by a deliberately controlled process may be far easier to conceive or understand than an order

---

[*] Attempts to claim that comparing blacks and whites with the same income means eliminating economic differences that might explain different loan denial rates ignore the many other economic variables that differ, such as net worth and credit histories, which vary greatly even among blacks and whites with the same incomes. These issues are explored in greater detail in my *The Housing Boom and Bust*, revised edition (New York: Basic Books, 2010), pp. 101–109.

emerging from an uncontrolled set of innumerable interactions. But that does not mean that the former is necessarily more common, more consequential or more desirable in its consequences.

Neither chaos nor randomness is implicit in uncontrolled circumstances. In a virgin forest, the flora and fauna are not distributed randomly or chaotically. Vegetation growing on a mountainside differs systematically at different heights. Certain trees grow more abundantly at lower elevations and other kinds of trees at higher elevations. Above some altitude no trees at all grow and, at the summit of Everest, no vegetation at all grows. Obviously, none of this is a result of any decisions made by the vegetation, but depends on variations in surrounding circumstances, such as temperature and soil. It is a *systemically* determined outcome with a pattern, not chaos.

Animal life also varies with environmental differences and, while animals like humans (and unlike vegetation) have thought and volition, that thought and volition are not always the decisive factors in the outcomes. That fish live in the water and birds in the air, rather than vice versa, is not strictly a matter of their choices, though each has choices of behavior within their respective environments. Moreover, what kinds of choices of behavior will survive the competition that weeds out some kinds of responses to the environment and lets others continue is likewise not wholly a matter of volition. In short, between individual volition and general outcomes are systemic factors which limit or determine what will survive, creating a pattern, rather than chaos.

None of this is difficult to understand in the natural environment. But the difference between individual, volitional causation and constraining systemic causation is one seldom considered by intellectuals when discussing economies, unless they happen to be economists. Yet that distinction has been commonplace among economists for more than two centuries. Nor has this been simply a matter of opinion or ideology. Systemic analysis was as common in Karl Marx's *Capital* as in Adam Smith's *The Wealth of Nations*, and it existed in the eighteenth century school of French economists called the Physiocrats before either Marx or Smith wrote about economics.

Even the analogy between systemic order in nature and in an economy was suggested by the title of one of the Physiocratic writings of the eighteenth century, *L'Ordre Naturel* by Mercier de la Rivière. It was the Physiocrats who coined the phrase *laissez-faire*, later associated with Adam Smith, based on their conviction that an uncontrolled economy was not one of chaos but of order, emerging from systemic interactions among the people competing with, and accommodating to, one another.

Karl Marx, of course, had a less benign view of the pattern of outcomes of market competition than did the Physiocrats or Adam Smith, but what is crucial here is that he too analyzed the market economy in terms of its systemic interactions, rather than its volitional choices, even when these were the choices of its economic elites, such as capitalists. Marx said that "competition" creates economic results that are "wholly independent of the will of the capitalist."[10] Thus, for example, while a new technology with lower production costs *enables* the capitalist to lower his prices, the spread of that technology to competing capitalists *compels* him to lower his prices, according to Marx.[11]

Likewise in his analysis of downturns in the economy— depressions or economic "crises" in Marxian phraseology— Marx made a sharp distinction between systemic causation versus volitional causation:

> A man who has produced has not the choice whether he will sell or not. He *must* sell. And in crises appears precisely the circumstance that he cannot sell, or only below the price of production, or even that he must sell at a positive loss. What does it avail him or us, therefore, that he has produced in order to sell? What concerns us is precisely to discover what has cut across this good intention of his.[12]

Neither in his theory of economics nor in his theory of history did Marx make end results simply the carrying out of individual volition, even the volition of elites. As his collaborator Friedrich Engels put it, "what each individual wills is obstructed by everyone else, and what emerges is something that no one willed."[13] Economics is about the pattern that emerges. Historian Charles A. Beard could seek to explain the Constitution of the United States by the economic interests of the individuals who wrote it, but that volitional approach was not the approach used by Marx and Engels, despite how often Beard's theory of history has been confused with the Marxian theory of history. Marx dismissed a similar theory in his own day as "facile anecdote-mongering and the attribution of all great events to petty and mean causes."[14]

The question here is not whether most intellectuals agree with systemic analysis, either in economics or elsewhere. Many have never even considered, much less confronted, that kind of analysis. Those who reason in terms of volitional causation see chaos from conflicting individual decisions as the alternative to central control of economic processes. John Dewey, for example, said, "comprehensive plans" are required "if the problem of social organization is to be met."[15] Otherwise, there will be "a continuation of a regime of accident, waste and distress."[16] To Dewey, "dependence upon intelligence" is an alternative to "drift and casual improvisation"[17]— that is, chaos— and those who are "hostile to intentional social planning" were depicted as being in favor of "atomistic individualism."[18]

Here, as in other cases, verbal virtuosity transforms the arguments of people with opposing views into mere emotions. In this case the emotion is *hostility* to social planning. That hostility is presumably due to the leftover notions of a by-gone era that society can depend on "the unplanned coincidence of the consequences of a vast multitude of efforts put forth by isolated individuals without reference to any social end," according to Dewey's characterization of those with whom he disagreed.[19] By the time John Dewey said all this—1935— it was more than a century and a half since the Physiocrats first wrote their books, explaining how competitive markets systemically coordinate economic activities and allocate resources through supply and demand adjustments to price movements.

Whether or not one agrees with the Physiocrats' explanations, or the similar and more sophisticated explanations of later economists, these are the arguments that would have to be answered if such arguments were not so widely evaded by reducing them to emotions or by using other arguments without arguments. Professor Ronald Dworkin of Oxford, for example, simply dismissed arguments for systemic causation in general, whether in the economy or elsewhere, as "the silly faith that ethics as well as economics moves by an invisible hand, so that individual rights and the general good will coalesce, and law based on principle will move the nation to a frictionless utopia where everyone is better off than he was before."[20]

Here again, verbal virtuosity *transforms* an opposing argument, rather than answering it with either logic or evidence. Moreover, as of the time when Professor Dworkin made this claim, there were numerous examples of countries whose economies were primarily market economies and others whose economies clearly were not, so that empirical comparisons were readily available, including comparisons of countries composed of the same peoples— East Germany versus West Germany or North Korea versus South Korea, for example. But verbal virtuosity made both analytical and empirical arguments unnecessary.

Economic competition is what forces innumerable disparate individual decisions to be reconciled with one another, as transactions terms are forced to change in response to changes in supply and demand, which in turn change economic activities. This is not a matter of "faith" (as Dworkin would have it) or of ideology (as Dewey would have it), but of economic literacy. John Dewey could depict businesses as controlling markets but that position is not inherent in being ideologically on the left. Karl Marx was certainly on the left, but the difference was that he had studied economics, as deeply as anyone of his time.

Just as Karl Marx did not attribute what he saw as the detrimental effects of a market economy to the ill will of individual capitalists, so Adam Smith did not attribute what he saw as the beneficial effects of a market economy to the good will of individual capitalists. Smith's depictions of businessmen were at least as negative as those of Marx,[21] even though Smith is rightly regarded as the patron saint of free market economics. According to Smith, the beneficial social effects of the businessman's endeavors are "no part of his intention."[22] Both in Adam Smith's day and today, more than two centuries later, arguments for a free market economy are based on the systemic effects of such economies in allocating scarce resources which have alternative uses through competition in the marketplace. Whether one agrees or disagrees with the conclusions, this is the argument that must be confronted— or evaded.

Contrary to Dewey and many others, systemic arguments are independent of any notions of "atomistic individualism." These are *not* arguments that each individual's well-being adds up to the well-being of society. Such an argument would ignore the systemic interactions which are at the heart of economic analysis, whether by Adam Smith, Karl Marx or other economists. These economic arguments need not be elaborated here, since they are spelled out at length in economics textbooks.[23] What is relevant here is that those intellectuals who see chaos as the alternative to government planning or control have seldom bothered to confront those arguments and have instead misconceived the issue and distorted the arguments of those with different views.

Despite the often expressed dichotomy between chaos and planning, what is called "planning" is the forcible *suppression* of millions of people's plans by a government-imposed plan. What is considered to be chaos are systemic interactions whose nature, logic and consequences are seldom examined by those who simply assume that "planning" by surrogate decision-makers must be better. Herbert Croly, the first editor of the *New Republic* and a major intellectual figure in the Progressive era, characterized Thomas Jefferson's conception of limited government as "the old fatal policy of drift," as contrasted with Alexander Hamilton's policy of "energetic and intelligent assertion of the national good." According to Croly, what was needed was "an energetic and clear-sighted central government."[24] In this conception, progress depends on surrogate decision-makers, rather than on millions of others making their own decisions and exerting their own efforts.

Despite the notion that scarcity is contrived for the sake of profit in a market economy, that scarcity is at the heart of any economy— capitalist, socialist, feudal or whatever. Given that this scarcity is inherent in the system as a whole— *any* economic system— this scarcity must be conveyed to each individual in some way. In other words, it makes no sense for any economy to produce as much as physically possible of any given product, because that would have to be done with scarce resources which could be used to produce other products, whose supply is also inherently limited to less than what people want.

Markets in capitalist economies reconcile these competing demands for the same resources through price movements in both the markets for consumer goods and the market for the resources which go into producing those consumer goods. These prices make it unprofitable for one producer to use a resource beyond the point where that resource has a greater value to some competing producer who is bidding for that same resource, whether for making the same product or a different product.

For the individual manufacturer, the point at which it would no longer be profitable to use more of some factor of production— machinery, labor, land, etc.— is indeed the point which provides the limit of that manufacturer's output, even when it would be physically possible to produce more. But, while profitability and unprofitability *convey* that limit, they are not what *cause* that limit— which is due to the scarcity of resources inherent in any economic system, whether or not it is a profit-based system. Producing more of a given output in disregard of those limits does not make an economy more prosperous. On the contrary, it means producing an excess of one output at the cost of a shortage of another output that could have been produced with the same resources. This was a painfully common situation in the government-run economy of the Soviet Union, where unsold goods often piled up in warehouses while dire shortages had people waiting in long lines for other goods.[25]

Ironically, Marx and Engels had foreseen the economic consequences of fiat prices created by government, rather than by supply and demand, long before the founding of the Soviet Union, even though the Soviets claimed to be following Marxian principles. When publishing a later edition of Marx's 1847 book, *The Poverty of Philosophy*, in which Marx rejected fiat pricing, Engels spelled out the problem in his editor's introduction. He pointed out that it is price fluctuations which have "forcibly brought home to the individual commodity producers what things and what quantity of them society requires or does not require." Without such a mechanism, he demanded to know "what guarantee we have that necessary quantity and not more of each product will be produced, that we shall not go hungry in regard to corn and meat while we are choked in beet sugar and drowned in potato spirit, that we shall not lack trousers to cover our nakedness while trouser buttons flood us in millions."[26]

On this point, the difference between Marx and Engels, on the one hand, and many other intellectuals of the left on the other, was simply that Marx and Engels had studied economics and the others usually had not. John Dewey, for example, demanded that "production for profit be subordinated to production for use."[27] Since nothing can be sold for a profit unless some buyer has a use for it, what Dewey's proposition amounts to is that third-party surrogates would define which use must be subordinated to which other use, instead of having such results be determined systemically by millions of individuals making their own mutual accommodations in market transactions.

As in so many other situations, the most important decision is who makes the decision. The abstract dichotomy between "profit" and "use" conceals the real conflict between millions of people making decisions for themselves and having anointed surrogates taking those decisions out of their hands.

A volitional view of economics enables the intelligentsia, like politicians and others, to dramatize economics, explaining high prices by "greed"[*] and low wages by a lack of "compassion," for example. While this is part of an ideological vision, an ideology of the left is not sufficient by itself to explain this approach. "I paint the capitalist and the landlord in no sense *couleur de rose*," Karl Marx said in the introduction to the first volume of *Capital*. "My stand-point," he added, however, "can less than any other make the individual responsible for relations whose creature he socially remains, however much he may subjectively raise himself above them."[28] In short, prices and wages were not determined volitionally but systemically.

Understanding that was not a question of being on the left or not, but of being economically literate or illiterate. The underlying notion of volitional pricing has, in our own times, led to at least a dozen federal investigations of American oil companies over the years, in response to either gasoline shortages or increases in gasoline prices— with none of these investigations turning up facts to support the sinister explanations abounding in the media and in politics when these investigations were launched. Many people find it hard to believe that negative economic events are not a result of villainy, even though they accept positive economic events— the declining prices of computers that are far better than earlier computers, for example— as being just a result of "progress" that happens *somehow*.

---

* "Greed," as a volitional explanation of economic actions, has the same problem as gravity would have as an explanation of plane crashes. Although gravity certainly pulls crashing planes to the ground, nevertheless when thousands of planes fly millions of miles every day without crashing, using gravity as an explanation of why a particular plane crashed is an explanation that gets us nowhere.

In a market economy, prices convey an underlying reality about supply and demand— and about production costs behind supply, as well as innumerable individual preferences and trade-offs behind demand. By regarding prices as merely arbitrary social constructs, some can imagine that existing prices can be replaced by prices controlled by government, reflecting wiser and nobler notions, such as "affordable housing" or "reasonable" health care costs. A history of price controls going back for centuries, in countries around the world, shows negative and even disastrous consequences from treating prices as mere arbitrary constructs, rather than as symptoms and conveyances of an underlying reality that is not nearly as susceptible of control as the prices are.[*]

As far as many, if not most, intellectuals are concerned, history *would* show that but does not, because they often see no need to consult history or any other validation process beyond the peer consensus of other similarly disposed intellectuals when discussing economic issues.

The crucial distinction between market transactions and collective decision-making is that in the market people are rewarded according to the value of their goods and services to those particular individuals who receive those goods and services, and who have every incentive to seek alternative sources, so as to minimize their costs, just as sellers of goods and services have every incentive to seek the highest bids for what they have to offer. But collective decision-making by third parties allows those third parties to superimpose their preferences on others at no cost to themselves, and to become the arbiters of other people's economic fate without accountability for the consequences.

Nothing better illustrates the difference between a volitional explanation of economic activity and a systemic explanation than the use of "greed" as an explanation of high incomes. Greed may well explain an individual's *desire* for more money, but income is determined by what *other people* pay, whether those other people are employers or consumers. Except for criminals, most people in a market economy receive income as a result of voluntary transactions. How much income someone receives voluntarily depends on

---

[*] See, for example, Chapter 3 of my *Basic Economics*, fourth edition (New York: Basic Books, 2011).

other people's willingness to part with their money in exchange for what the recipient offers, whether that is labor, a commodity or a service. John D. Rockefeller did not become rich simply because he wanted money; he became rich because other people preferred to buy his oil, for example, because it was cheaper. Bill Gates became rich because people around the world preferred to buy his computer operating system rather than other operating systems that were available.

None of this is rocket science, nor is it new. A very old expression captured the fallacy of volitional explanations when it said, "If wishes were horses, beggars would ride." Yet volitional explanations of prices and incomes continue to flourish among the intelligentsia. Professor Peter Corning of Stanford University, for example, attributes high incomes to personality traits found supposedly in one-third of the population because "the 'free market' capitalist system favors the one-third who are the most acquisitive and egocentric and the least concerned about fairness and justice."[29] This description would apply as readily to petty criminals who rob local stores and sometimes shoot their owners to avoid being identified, often for small sums of money that would never support the lifestyle of the rich and famous. The volitional explanation of high incomes lacks even correlation, much less causation.

The tactical advantage of volitional explanations is not only that it allows the intelligentsia to be on the side of the angels against the forces of evil, but also that it avoids having to deal with the *creation* of wealth, an analysis of which could undermine their whole social vision. By focussing on the money that John D. Rockefeller received, rather than the benefits that millions of other people received from Rockefeller— which provided the reason for turning their money over to him in the first place, rather than buying from somebody else— such transactions can be viewed as moral melodramas, rather than mundane transactions for mutual advantage. Contrary to "robber baron" rhetoric, Rockefeller did not reduce the wealth of society but added to it, his own fortune being a share in that additional wealth, as his production efficiencies and innovations reduced the public's cost of oil to a fraction of what it had been before.

ZERO-SUM ECONOMICS

Among the consequences of the economic illiteracy of most intellectuals is the zero-sum vision of the economy mentioned earlier, in which the gains of one individual or one group represent a corresponding loss to another individual or another group. According to noted twentieth-century British scholar Harold Laski, "the interests of capital and labor are irreconcilable in fundamentals— there's a sum to divide and each wants more than the other will give."[30] This assumption is seldom spelled out this plainly, perhaps not even in the minds of most of those whose conclusions require such an implicit zero-sum assumption as a foundation. But the widespread notion, coalescing into a doctrine, that one must "take sides" in making public policy or even in rendering judicial decisions, ignores the fact that economic transactions would not continue to take place unless *both* sides find these transactions preferable to not making such transactions.

Contrary to Laski and many others with similar views, there is no given "sum to divide," as there would be with manna from heaven. It is precisely the cooperation of capital and labor which *creates* a wealth that would not exist otherwise, and that both sides would forfeit if they did not reconcile their conflicting desires at the outset, in order to agree on terms under which they can join together to produce that output. It is literally preposterous (putting in front what comes behind) to begin the analysis with "a sum to divide"— that is, wealth— when that wealth can be created only *after* capital and labor have already reconciled their competing claims and agreed to terms on which they can operate together to produce that wealth.

Each side would of course prefer to have the terms favor themselves more, but both sides must be willing to accept some mutually agreeable terms or no such transaction will take place at all, much less continue. Far from being an "irreconcilable" situation, as Laski claimed, it is a situation reconciled millions of times each day. Otherwise, the economy could not function. Indeed, a whole society could not function without vast numbers of both economic and non-economic decisions to cooperate, despite the fact that no two sets of interests, even among members of the same family, are exactly the same. The habit of many intellectuals to largely ignore the prerequisites, incentives and constraints involved in the production of wealth has many ramifications that can lead to many fallacious conclusions, even if their verbal virtuosity conceals those fallacies from others and from themselves.

Intervention by politicians, judges, or others, in order to impose terms more favorable to one side— minimum wage laws or rent control laws, for example— reduces the overlapping set of mutually agreeable terms and, almost invariably, reduces the number of mutually acceptable transactions, as the party disfavored by the intervention makes fewer transactions subsequently. Countries with generous minimum wage laws, for example, often have higher unemployment rates and longer periods of unemployment than other countries, as employers offer fewer jobs to inexperienced and low-skilled workers, who are typically the least valued and lowest paid— and who are most often priced out of a job by minimum wage laws.

It is not uncommon in European countries with generous minimum wage laws, as well as other worker benefits that employers are mandated to pay for, to have inexperienced younger workers with unemployment rates of 20 percent or more.[31] Employers are made slightly worse off by having to rearrange their businesses and perhaps pay for more machinery to replace the low-skilled workers whom it is no longer economic to hire. But those low-skilled, usually younger, workers may be made much worse off by not being able to get jobs as readily, losing both the wages they could earn otherwise and sustaining the perhaps greater loss of not acquiring the work experience that would lead to better jobs and higher pay.

In short, "taking sides" often ends up making both sides worse off, even if in different ways and to different degrees. But the very idea of taking sides is based on treating economic transactions as if they were zero-sum events. This zero-sum vision of the world is also consistent with the disinterest of many intellectuals in what promotes or impedes the *creation* of wealth, on which the standard of living of a whole society depends, even though the creation of more wealth has lifted "the poor" in the United States today to economic levels not reached by most of the American population in past eras or in many other countries even today.

Just as minimum wage laws tend to reduce employment transactions with those whose pay is most affected, so rent control laws have been followed by housing shortages in Cairo, Melbourne, Hanoi, Paris, New York and numerous other places around the world. Here again, attempts to make transactions terms better for one party usually lead the other party to make fewer transactions. Builders especially react to rent control laws by building fewer apartment buildings and, in some places, building none at all for years on end.

Landlords may continue to rent existing apartments but often they cut back on ancillary services such as painting, repairs, heat and hot water— all of which cost money and all of which are less necessary to maintain at previous levels to attract and keep tenants, once there is a housing shortage. The net result is that apartment buildings that receive less maintenance deteriorate faster and wear out, without adequate numbers of replacements being built. In Cairo, for example, this process led to families having to double up in quarters designed for only one family. The ultimate irony is that such laws can also lead to *higher* rents on average— New York and San Francisco being classic examples— when luxury housing is exempted from rent control, causing resources to be diverted to building precisely that kind of housing.

The net result is that tenants, landlords, and builders can all end up worse off than before, though in different ways and to different degrees. Landlords seldom end up living in crowded quarters or on the street, and builders can simply devote more of their time and resources to building other structures such as warehouses, shopping malls and office buildings, as well as luxury housing, all of which are usually not subject to rent control laws. But, again, the crucial point is that both sides can end up worse off as a result of laws and policies based on "taking sides," as if economic transactions were zero-sum processes.

One of the few writers who has explicitly proclaimed the zero-sum vision of the economy— Professor Lester C. Thurow of M.I.T., author of *The Zero-Sum Society*— has also stated that the United States has been "consistently the industrial economy with the worst record" on unemployment. He spelled it out:

> Lack of jobs has been endemic in peacetime during the past fifty years of American history. Review the evidence: a depression from 1929 to 1940, a war from 1941 to 1945, a recession in 1949, a war from 1950 to 1953, recessions in 1954, 1957–58, and 1960–61, a war from 1965 to 1973, a

recession in 1969–70, a severe recession in 1974–75, and another recession probable in 1980. This is hardly an enviable economic performance.[32]

Several things are remarkable about Professor Thurow's statement. He reaches sweeping conclusions about the record of the United States *vis-à-vis* the record of other industrial nations, based solely on a recitation of events within the United States— *a one-nation international comparison* when it comes to facts, rather than rhetoric. Studies which in fact compare the unemployment rate in the United States versus Western European nations, for example, almost invariably show Western European nations with *higher* unemployment rates, and longer periods of unemployment, than the United States.[33] Moreover, the wars that Professor Thurow throws in, in what is supposed to be a discussion of unemployment, might leave the impression that wars contribute to unemployment, when in fact unemployment virtually disappeared in the United States during World War II and has been lower than usual during the other wars mentioned.[34]

Professor Thurow's prediction about a recession in 1980 turned out to be true, though that was hardly a daring prediction in the wake of the "stagflation" of the late 1970s. What turned out to be false was the idea that large-scale government intervention was required to head off more unemployment— that, in Thurow's words, the government needed to "restructure the economy so that it will, in fact, provide jobs for everyone."[35] What actually happened was that the Reagan administration took office in 1981 and did the exact opposite of what Lester Thurow advocated— and, after the recession passed, there were twenty years of economic growth, low unemployment and low inflation.[36]

Professor Thurow was not, and is not, some fringe kook. According to the material on the cover of the 2001 reprint of his 1980 book *The Zero-Sum Society*, "Lester Thurow has been professor of management and economics at MIT for more than thirty years." He is also the "author of several books, including three *New York Times* best sellers, he has served on the editorial board of the *New York Times*, as a contributing editor of *Newsweek*, and as a member of *Time* magazine's Board of Economics." He could not be more mainstream— or more wrong. But what he said apparently found resonance among the elite intelligentsia, who made him an influence on major media outlets.

Similar prescriptions for active government intervention in the economy have abounded among intellectuals, past and present. John Dewey, for example, used such attractive phrases as "socially organized intelligence in the conduct of public affairs,"[37] and "organized social reconstruction"[38] as euphemisms for the plain fact that third-party surrogate decision-makers seek to have their preferences imposed on millions of other people through the power of government. Although government is often called "society" by those who advocate this approach, what is called "social" planning are in fact *government orders* over-riding the plans and mutual accommodations of millions of people subject to those orders.

Despite whatever vision may be conjured up by euphemisms, government is not some abstract embodiment of public opinion or Rousseau's "general will." Government consists of politicians, bureaucrats, and judges— all of whom have their own incentives and constraints, and none of whom can be presumed to be any less interested in the promotion of their own interests or notions than are people who buy and sell in the marketplace. Neither sainthood nor infallibility is common in either venue. The fundamental difference between decision-makers in the market and decision-makers in government is that the former are subject to continuous and consequential feedback which can force them to adjust to what others prefer and are willing to pay for, while those who make decisions in the political arena face no such inescapable feedback to force them to adjust to the reality of other people's desires and preferences.

A business with red ink on the bottom line knows that this cannot continue indefinitely, and that they have no choice but to change whatever they are doing that produces red ink, for which there is little tolerance even in the short run, and which will be fatal to the whole enterprise in the long run. In short, financial losses are not merely informational feedback but *consequential* feedback which cannot be ignored, dismissed or spun rhetorically through verbal virtuosity.

In the political arena, however, only the most immediate and most attention-getting disasters— so obvious and unmistakable to the voting public that there is no problem of "connecting the dots"— are comparably consequential for political decision-makers. But laws and policies whose consequences take time to unfold are by no means as consequential for those who created those laws and policies, especially if the consequences emerge after the next election. Moreover, there are few things in politics as unmistakable in its implications as red ink on the bottom line is in business. In politics, no matter how disastrous a policy may turn out to be, if the causes of the disaster are not understood by the voting public, those officials responsible for the disaster may escape any accountability, and of course they have every incentive to deny having made mistakes, since admitting mistakes can jeopardize a whole career.

Why the transfer of economic decisions from the individuals and organizations directly involved— often depicted collectively and impersonally as "the market"— to third parties who pay no price for being wrong should be expected to produce better results for society at large is a question seldom asked, much less answered. Partly this is because of rhetorical packaging by those with verbal virtuosity. To say, as John Dewey did, that there must be "social control of economic forces"[39] sounds good in a vague sort of way, until that is translated into specifics as the holders of political power forbidding voluntary transactions among the citizenry.

Chapter 5

Government and the Economy

Governments can intervene in a market economy in a number of ways, and intellectuals tend, by and large, to favor such interventions. Two of the most common forms of intervention have been in particular businesses and intervention in the economy as a whole, especially during recessions or depressions.

BUSINESS

The organizations, large and small, which produce and distribute most of the goods and services that make up a modern standard of living— businesses— have long been targets of the intelligentsia. Accusations against businesses have been as specific as charging excessively high prices and as nebulous as failing to live up to their social responsibilities.

Management

Intellectuals who have never run any business have often been remarkably confident that they know when businesses have been run wrongly or when their owners or managers are overpaid. John Dewey, for example, declared, "Industrial entrepreneurs have reaped out of all proportion to what they sowed."[1] Evidence? None. This is one of many assertions that can pass unchallenged among the intelligentsia, its familiarity and its consonance with the prevailing vision being substitutes for evidence or analysis. The ease of running a business has been a common belief going back at least as far as Edward Bellamy's *Looking Backward* in the nineteenth century.[2] Lenin said that running a business involved "extraordinarily simple operations" which "any literate person can perform," so that those in charge of such enterprises need not be paid more than any ordinary worker.[3] Just three years after taking power, however, and with his post-capitalist economy facing what Lenin himself later called "ruin, starvation and devastation,"[4] he reversed himself and declared to the 1920 Communist Party Congress: "Opinions on corporate management are all too frequently imbued with a spirit of sheer ignorance, an antiexpert spirit."[5] Lenin reversed himself in deeds as well as in words, creating his New Economic Policy which allowed more leeway for markets to function, and the Soviet economy began to recover.

In short, the first time that the theory of how easy it is to run a business was put to a test, it failed that test disastrously. As the twentieth century unfolded, that theory would fail repeatedly in other countries around the world, to the point where even most communist and socialist governments began to free up markets by the end of the twentieth century, usually leading to higher economic growth rates, as in China and India.

When judging those who run businesses, the criteria applied, either implicitly or explicitly, by many intellectuals are often remote from any relevance to the operation of an economic enterprise. Theodore Roosevelt, for example, said: "It tires me to talk to rich men. You expect a man of millions, the head of a great industry, to be a man worth hearing; but as a rule they don't know anything outside their own businesses."[6]

That certainly could not be said of Theodore Roosevelt himself. In addition to his political experience at municipal, state, national, and international levels, TR was not only a well-educated and widely read man but also a scholar in his own right, having published books on a wide range of subjects, including a naval history of the war of 1812 that was required reading at naval academies on both sides of the Atlantic for decades. The author of fifteen books,[7] Theodore Roosevelt was for many years an intellectual in our sense, as someone who earned his living from his writings, especially during the years when his pay as a municipal or state official was inadequate to support his family, and during the years when his business ventures on the western frontier were losing money.

"Few, if any Americans could match the breadth of his intellect," according to a biographer of Theodore Roosevelt.[8] Certainly few, if any, business leaders were at all comparable to TR in intellectual scope or depth. *Nor was there any reason why they should be.* In many fields, it is often the specialist— sometimes the monomaniac— who is most likely to produce the peak achievements. No one expected Babe Ruth or Bobby Fischer to be a Renaissance Man, and anyone who might have would have been very badly disappointed. The judging of people in non-intellectual fields by intellectual criteria will almost inevitably find them unworthy of the rewards they receive— which would be a legitimate conclusion only if non-intellectual endeavors were automatically less worthy than intellectual endeavors. Few would argue explicitly for this premise but, as John Maynard Keynes pointed out, conclusions often continue on without the premises on which they were based.[9]

Another common misconception among the intelligentsia is that individual business entrepreneurs should— or could— be "socially responsible" by taking into account the wider consequences of the entrepreneur's business decisions. This idea goes back at least as far as Woodrow Wilson, another intellectual in our sense, because of his academic career before entering politics:

> We are not afraid of those who pursue legitimate pursuits, provided they link those pursuits in at every turn with the interest of the community as a whole; and no man can conduct a legitimate business if he conducts it in the interest of a single class.[10]

In other words, it is not considered sufficient if a manufacturer of plumbing fixtures produces high-quality faucets, pipes and bathtubs, and sells them at affordable prices, if this entrepreneur does not also take on the role of philosopher-king and try to decide how this business affects "the interest of the community," however that nebulous notion might be conceived. It is a staggering requirement which few, if any, people in business, academia, politics, or other fields of endeavor could meet. John Dewey likewise lamented that workers, like their employers, had "no social outlook upon the consequences and meaning of what they are doing."[11]

Intellectuals may choose to imagine what are the wider social consequences of their own actions, inside or outside their fields of professional competence, but there is little or no consequential feedback when they are wrong, no matter how wrong or for how long. That both business owners and workers usually avoid taking on such a cosmic task suggests that they may have a more realistic assessment of human limitations.

Although businesses produce most of the things that make up the standard of living in a modern society, there is remarkably little interest among the intelligentsia in a causal analysis of the things that promote or inhibit the production of output, on which everyone's economic well-being ultimately depends. Instead, business issues are often approached as moral melodramas, starring the anointed intelligentsia on the side of the angels against the forces of evil. As Theodore Roosevelt put it, in accepting the Progressive Party's nomination for President of the United States in 1912, "We stand at Armageddon, and we battle for the Lord." Business men were a special target: "Whenever in any business the prosperity of the business man is obtained by lowering the wages of his workmen and charging an excessive price to the consumers, we wish to interfere and stop such practices."[12]

In other words, third party observers, usually without any business experience or (like TR) with no successful business experience, can somehow determine what prices are "excessive" and what wages are too low— and make their uninformed beliefs determine the law of the land. This emboldened ignorance led Theodore Roosevelt, and innumerable others after him, to attack businesses that were *lowering* prices, as a result of production efficiencies, rather than by paying workers less than other businesses. But such mundane facts have seldom been allowed to spoil a heady vision of moral melodramas.

Business "Power" or "Control"

One of the many signs of verbal virtuosity among intellectuals is the repackaging of words to mean things that are not only different from, but sometimes the direct opposite of, their original meanings or the meaning that most other people attach to those words. "Freedom" and "power" are among the most common of these repackaged words. The basic concept of freedom as not being subjected to other people's restrictions, and of power as the ability to restrict other people's options, have both been stood on their heads in some of the repackaging of these words by intellectuals discussing economic issues. Thus business enterprises which *expand* the public's options, either quantitatively (through lower prices) or qualitatively (through better products) are often spoken of as "controlling" the market, whenever this results in a high percentage of consumers choosing to purchase their particular products rather than the competing products of other enterprises.

In other words, when consumers decide that particular brands of products are either cheaper or better than competing brands of those products, third parties take it upon themselves to depict those who produced these particular brands as having exercised "power" or "control." If, at a given time, three-quarters of the consumers prefer to buy the Acme brand of widgets to any other brand, then Acme Inc. will be said to "control" three-quarters of the market, even though consumers control 100 percent of the market, since they can switch to another brand of widgets tomorrow if someone else comes up with a better widget, or stop buying widgets altogether if a new product comes along that makes widgets obsolete.

Any number of companies that have been said to "control" a majority of their market have not only lost that market share but have gone bankrupt within a few years of their supposed dominance of the market. Smith Corona, for example, sold over half the typewriters and word processors in the United States in 1989 but, just six years later, it filed for bankruptcy, as the spread of personal computers displaced both typewriters and word processors. Yet the verbal packaging of sales statistics *ex post* as market "control" *ex ante* has been common, not only in the writings of the intelligentsia but even in courts of law in anti-trust cases. Even at its peak, Smith Corona controlled nothing. Every consumer was free to buy any other brand of typewriter or word processor, or refrain from buying any.

The verbal packaging of consumer choice as business "control" has become so widespread that few people seem to feel a need to do anything so basic as thinking about the meaning of the words they are using, which transform an *ex post* statistic into an *ex ante* condition. By saying that businesses have "power" because they have "control" of their markets, this verbal virtuosity opens the way to saying that government needs to exercise its "countervailing power" (John Kenneth Galbraith's phrase) in order to protect the public. Despite the verbal parallels, government power is in fact power, since individuals do not have a free choice as to whether or not to obey government laws and regulations, while consumers are free to ignore the products marketed by even the biggest and supposedly most "powerful" corporations in the world. There are people who have never set foot in a Wal-Mart store and there is nothing that Wal-Mart can do about it, despite being the world's largest retailer.

One of John Kenneth Galbraith's earliest and most influential books, *American Capitalism: The Concept of Countervailing Power*, declared that "power on one side of a market creates both the need for, and the prospect of reward to, the exercise of countervailing power from the other side."[13] Thus, according to Professor Galbraith, the rise of big corporations gave them an oppressive power over their employees, which led to the creation of labor unions in self-defense.[14] As a matter of historical fact, however, it was not in large, mass-production industries that American labor unions began but in industries with numerous smaller businesses, such as construction, trucking and coal mining— all of which were unionized years before the steel or automobile industries.

But, whatever the genesis of union power, the crucial countervailing power for Galbraith was that of the government, both in support of private countervailing power with such legislation as the National Labor Relations Act of 1935 and legislation to help coal producers and others supposedly oppressed by the "power" of big business.[15] Such government "countervailing power performs a valuable— indeed an indispensable— regulatory function in the modern economy,"[16] according to Galbraith. But this formulation depends crucially on redefining "power" to include its opposite— the expansion of consumer options by businesses, in order to increase sales.

John Kenneth Galbraith was perhaps the most prominent, and certainly one of the most verbally gifted, of the advocates of a theory of volitional pricing. According to Professor Galbraith, the output of a given industry tends to become more concentrated over time in the hands of a few producers, who acquire decisive advantages that make it difficult for a new company without the same amount of experience to enter the industry and compete effectively against the leading incumbents. Therefore, according to Galbraith, "sellers have gained authority over prices," which are "tacitly administered by a few large firms."[17] In reality, one of the most common reasons for buyers buying disproportionately from a particular seller is that this seller has a lower price. After Galbraith has redefined power as a concentration of sales and of resulting profits and size, he is able to depict that "power" of the seller as a reason why that seller can now set prices different from— and implicitly higher than— those of a competitive market.

In this formulation, "the size of the corporation which the individual heads is again a rough index of the power the individual exercises."[18] However plausible all this might seem, Galbraith did not venture very far in the direction of empirical verification. The *insinuation* of Galbraith's— and many others'— discussions of the "power" of big business is that the growth of ever larger businesses means the growth of their power to raise prices. This insinuation— as distinguished from either a demonstrated fact or even a testable hypothesis— was a staple among the intelligentsia long before Galbraith's time, and provided the impetus for the Sherman Anti-Trust Act of 1890, among other attempts to contain the "power" of big business.

In reality, the era leading up to the Sherman Act was not an era of rising prices imposed by monopolies, even though it was an era of growing sizes of businesses in many industries, often through consolidation of smaller businesses into giant corporations. Far from leading to higher prices, however, this was an era of *falling* prices charged by these larger businesses, whose size created economies of scale, which meant lower production costs that enabled them to profit from *lower* prices, thereby expanding their sales. Crude oil, which sold for $12 to $16 a barrel in 1860, sold for less than one dollar a barrel in every year from 1879 to 1900. Railroad freight costs fell by 1887 to 54 percent of what they had been in 1873. The price of steel rails fell from $68 in 1880 to $32 in 1890. The prices of sugar, lead, and zinc all fell during this period.[19]

Henry Ford pioneered in mass production methods, and had some of the highest paid workers of his day— decades before the industry was unionized—

and the lowest priced cars, notably the legendary Model T, which made the automobile no longer a luxury confined to the wealthy. But none of these plain facts prevailed against the vision of the Progressive era intelligentsia, who in this case included President Theodore Roosevelt. His administration launched anti-trust prosecutions against some of the biggest price-cutters, including Standard Oil and the Great Northern Railroad. Theodore Roosevelt sought the power, in his words, to "control and regulate all big combinations."[20] He declared that "of all forms of tyranny the least attractive and the most vulgar is the tyranny of mere wealth, the tyranny of a plutocracy."[21]

No doubt it was true, as TR said, that Standard Oil created "enormous fortunes" for its owners "at the expense of business rivals,"[22] but it is questionable whether consumers who paid lower prices for oil felt that they were victims of a tyranny. One of the popular muckraking books of the Progressive era was *The History of the Standard Oil Company* by Ida Tarbell, which said among other things that Rockefeller "should have been satisfied"[23] with what he had achieved financially by 1870, implying greed in his continued efforts to increase the size and profitability of Standard Oil.

A study done a century later, however, pointed out: "One might never know from reading *The History of Standard Oil* that oil prices were actually falling."[24] That fact had been filtered out of the story, as it has been filtered out of other stories of that time and of later times. The presumably key question whether Rockefeller's pursuit of a larger fortune actually made the consuming public worse off was seldom even addressed. How consumers would have been better off if a man who introduced extraordinary efficiencies into the production and distribution of oil had ended his career earlier, leaving both the cost of producing oil and the resulting prices higher, is a question not raised, much less answered.

One of the common complaints against Standard Oil was that it was able to get railroads to charge them less for shipping their oil than was charged to competing businesses shipping oil. Such an inequality was of course anathema to those who thought in terms of abstract people in an abstract world— ignoring what there was specifically about Standard Oil that was different, which was the very reason why John D. Rockefeller amassed a fortune in an industry in which many others went bankrupt. For example, oil shipped in Standard Oil's tank cars was easier to transport than oil shipped in barrels by other companies.[25] Since the railroads had lower costs of handling Rockefeller's oil, shipped in tank cars, than handling other producers' oil shipped in barrels, Rockefeller paid less for shipping his oil.

There was nothing mysterious, much less sinister, about this. Yet Theodore Roosevelt— who knew little or no economics and had lost a large portion of his inheritance in his one business venture— said that discount shipping rates were discriminatory and should be forbidden "in every shape and form."[26] Senator John Sherman, author of the Sherman Anti-Trust Act, also introduced legislation to ban differential shipping rates, apparently at the prompting of a refinery that shipped its oil in barrels.[27] Today, oil is still *measured* in barrels but it is *shipped* in tanker cars on railroads, in tanker trucks on land and in ocean-going oil tankers, as the whole industry now follows methods pioneered by John D. Rockefeller.

Businesses which charge lower prices often lead to losses by competing businesses that charge higher prices. But, obvious as this might seem, it has not stopped outcries over the years from the intelligentsia, legislation from politicians and adverse court decisions from judges, aimed not only at Standard Oil in the early twentieth century but also later at other businesses that reduced prices in other industries, ranging from the A&P grocery chain in the past to Wal-Mart today.

In short, the verbal transformation of lower prices and larger sales into an exercise of "power" by business that has to be counteracted by more government power has more than purely intellectual implications. It has led to many laws, policies and court decisions that punish lower prices in the name of protecting consumers.

As a result of the spread of globalization, even if a particular company is the only producer of a given product in a given country, that monopoly means little if foreign producers of the same product compete in supplying that product to the consumers. Eastman Kodak has long been the only major American producer of film but camera stores across the United States also sell film produced in Japan (Fuji) and sometimes in England (Ilford), and in other countries, quite aside from the sweeping competition from digital cameras, produced primarily overseas. In short, Kodak's ability to jack up film prices without suffering lost sales is hemmed in by substitutes. The fact that Eastman Kodak is a huge enterprise does not change any of that, except in the visions and rhetoric of the intelligentsia.

The straining of words to depict particular businesses as exercising "power" in situations where consumers simply buy more of their products, has been used to justify depriving people who run businesses of the rights exercised by other people. As we shall see in Chapter 13, this attitude can even extend to putting the burden of proof on businesses to rebut accusations in certain anti-trust cases and civil rights cases. A somewhat similar mindset was expressed in a question asked in *The Economist* magazine: "Why should companies be allowed to dodge taxes and sack workers by shifting operations overseas?"[28] In free countries, no one else's right to relocate for their own benefit is treated as something requiring some special justification. Indeed, workers who relocate to other countries in violation of the recipient country's immigration laws are often defended by those who consider it wrong for businesses to relocate legally.

RECESSIONS AND DEPRESSIONS

Nothing established the idea that government intervention in the economy is essential like the Great Depression of the 1930s. The raw facts tell the story of that historic tragedy: National output fell by one-third between 1929 and 1933, thousands of banks failed, unemployment peaked at 25 percent, and the entire corporate sector as a whole lost money, two years in a row, at the depth of the Great Depression.

Prior to that time, no president had attempted to have the federal government intervene to bring a depression to an end. Many at the time saw in the Great Depression the failure of free market capitalism as an economic system, and a reason for seeking a radically different kind of economy— for some Communism, for some Fascism and for some the New Deal policies of Franklin D. Roosevelt's administration. Whatever the particular alternative favored by particular individuals, what was widely believed then and later was that the stock market crash of 1929 was not only a failure of the free market but the cause of the massive unemployment that persisted for years during the 1930s.

Given the two most striking events of that era— the huge stock market crash and a widespread government intervention in the economy— it is not immediately obvious which of these was more responsible for the dire economic conditions that followed. But remarkably little effort has been made by most of the intelligentsia to try to distinguish the effects of one of these events from the effects of the other. It has been largely a foregone conclusion that the market was the cause and that government intervention was the saving grace. Yet it is hard to maintain that conclusion after following the specific sequence of events.

Both at the time and since then, many or most of the intelligentsia have assumed that there had to be government intervention in a depression where mass unemployment reached as high as 25 percent at its worst. But unemployment never reached 25 percent until *after* massive government intervention. Unemployment never reached double digits during any of the 12 months that followed the stock market crash of 1929. When the first major federal government intervention was made in June 1930, the unemployment rate was 6.3 percent— down from a peak of 9 percent two months after the stock market crash of October 1929.[29] It was only after this intervention— the Smoot-Hawley tariffs of 1930— that the downward movement in unemployment reversed and rose within six months to double digits.

In the wake of this government intervention under President Herbert Hoover, followed by new and more sweeping interventions under President Franklin D. Roosevelt, unemployment remained in double digits for the entire remainder of the decade. In short, the brief (one-month) 9 percent unemployment rate in the wake of the stock market crash of 1929 was dwarfed by later unemployment rates that soared after government interventions under both Hoover and FDR. The unemployment rate never fell below 20 percent for any month over a period of 35 consecutive months, from the Hoover administration into the Roosevelt administration. Moreover, even after the unemployment rate eventually fell below 20 percent, it rose again to 20 percent in the spring of 1939,[30] nearly a decade after the stock market crash that has been widely blamed for the mass unemployment of the 1930s.

Presidents Hoover and FDR were not the only sources of federal intervention. One of the few things on which people across the ideological spectrum agreed upon in later years was that the Federal Reserve System mishandled its job during the Great Depression. Looking back at that period, Milton Friedman called the people who ran the Federal Reserve "inept" and John Kenneth Galbraith said that Federal Reserve officials showed "startling incompetence."[31] For example, as the country's money supply declined by one-third in the wake of massive bank failures, the Federal Reserve raised the interest rate, creating further deflationary pressures.

Congress also passed laws more than doubling the tax rates on the upper income brackets under Hoover and raised them still higher under FDR. President Hoover urged business leaders not to reduce workers' wage rates during the depression, even though the greatly reduced money supply made the previous wage-rates unpayable with full employment. Both Hoover and his successor, FDR, sought to keep prices from falling, whether the price of labor, farm produce, or industrial output, assuming that this would keep purchasing power from falling. However, purchasing power depends not only on what prices are charged but on how many transactions will actually be made at those prices. With a reduced money supply, neither the previous amount of employment of labor nor the previous sales of farm or industrial products could continue at the old prices.*

Neither Hoover nor FDR seemed to understand this nor to have thought this far. However, columnist Walter Lippmann pointed out the obvious in 1934 when he said, "in a depression men cannot sell their goods or their service at pre-depression prices. If they insist on pre-depression prices for goods, they do not sell them. If they insist on pre-depression wages, they become unemployed."[32] Though neither the sellers nor the unemployed workers were demanding prices or wages that were unsustainable under depression conditions, with a greatly reduced money supply, the federal

---

* In his memoirs, Herbert Hoover pointed out that there were many times as many firms cutting wage rates in 1921 as under his administration a decade later— and counted that among his "accomplishments." He did not explore the implications of the fact that the economy rebounded far faster from the earlier recession. Herbert Hoover, *The Memoirs of Herbert Hoover: The Great Depression 1929–1941* (New York: The Macmillan Company, 1952), p. 46.

government was doing just that by mandating prices and wages that made both goods and labor unsaleable, through the National Industrial Recovery Act, the Agricultural Adjustment Act, the Fair Labor Standards Act and other legislation and policies.

There is little empirical evidence to suggest that the many government interventions during the 1930s helped the economy and much evidence to suggest that they made matters worse.[*] A 2004 study by economists in a leading scholarly journal concluded that government policies prolonged the Great Depression by several years.[33]

There is of course no way to re-run the stock market crash of 1929 and have the federal government let the market adjust on its own, in order to see how that experiment would turn out. The closest thing to such an experiment was the 1987 stock market crash, when stock prices fell further in one day than on any day in 1929. The Reagan administration did nothing, despite outrage in the media at the government's failure to act.

"What will it take to wake up the White House?" the *New York Times* asked, declaring that "the President abdicates leadership and courts disaster."[34] *Washington Post* columnist Mary McGrory said that Reagan "has been singularly indifferent" to the country's "current pain and confusion."[35] The *Financial Times* of London said that President Reagan "appears to lack the capacity to handle adversity" and "nobody seems to be in charge."[36] A former official of the Carter administration criticized President Reagan's "silence and inaction" following the 1987 stock market crash and compared him unfavorably to President Franklin D. Roosevelt, whose "personal style and bold commands would be a tonic" in the current crisis.[37]

The irony in this comparison was that FDR presided over an economy with seven consecutive years of double-digit unemployment, while Reagan's policy of letting the market recover on its own, far from leading to another Great Depression, led instead to one of the country's longest periods of sustained economic growth, low unemployment and low inflation, lasting twenty years.[38]

---

[*] For details, see *FDR's Folly* by Jim Powell (New York: Crown Forum, 2003), which also mentions some of Hoover's folly.

Like many other facts at variance with the prevailing vision, this one received remarkably little attention at the time or since. While it might be possible to debate the wisdom or effectiveness of various government responses or non-responses to economic crises, there has been very little awareness of anything to debate by intellectuals outside the economics profession. Histories of the Great Depression by leading historians such as Arthur M. Schlesinger, Jr. and Henry Steele Commager made FDR the hero who came to the rescue, though Schlesinger himself admitted that he— Schlesinger— "was not much interested in economics,"[39] despite his willingness to make historic assessments of how FDR's policies affected the economy. However, Professor Schlesinger was by no means unusual among intellectuals for reaching sweeping conclusions about economic issues without feeling any need to understand economics.

PART III

INTELLECTUALS AND

SOCIAL VISIONS

At the core of every moral code there is a picture of human nature, a map of the universe, and a version of history. To human nature (of the sort conceived), in a universe (of the kind imagined), after a history (so understood), the rules of the code apply.

Walter Lippmann[1]

Chapter 6

A Conflict of Visions

Intellectuals do not simply have a series of isolated opinions on a variety of subjects. Behind those opinions is usually some coherent over-arching conception of the world, a social vision. Intellectuals are like other people in having visions— some intuitive sense of how the world works, what causes what. The vision around which most contemporary intellectuals tend to coalesce has features that distinguish it from other visions prevalent in other segments of contemporary society or among elites or masses in earlier times.

While visions differ, a vision of some kind or other underlies attempts to explain either physical or social phenomena, whether by intellectuals or by others. Some visions are more sweeping and dramatic than others, as well as differing in the particular assumptions on which they are based, but all kinds of thinking, whether formal or informal, must start somewhere with a hunch, a suspicion, or an intuition of some sort— in short, with a vision of causal connections. Systematically working out the implications of that vision can produce a theory, which in turn can be refined into specific hypotheses that can be tested against empirical evidence. But "the preconceived idea— supposedly 'unscientific'— must nearly always be there," as British historian Paul Johnson put it.[1] Economist J.A. Schumpeter defined a vision as a "preanalytic cognitive act."[2]

What then is the prevailing vision of the intelligentsia, including both the solid core of intellectuals and the surrounding penumbra of those who follow their lead? And what alternative vision opposes them?

OPPOSING SOCIAL VISIONS

At the heart of the social vision prevalent among contemporary intellectuals is the belief that there are "problems" created by existing institutions and that "solutions" to these problems can be excogitated by intellectuals. This vision is both a vision of society and a vision of the role of intellectuals within society. In short, intellectuals have seen themselves not simply as an elite— in the passive sense in which large landowners, rentiers, or holders of various sinecures might qualify as elites— but as an *anointed* elite, people with a mission to lead others in one way or another toward better lives.

John Stuart Mill, who epitomized the intellectual in many ways, expressed this view explicitly, when he said that the "present wretched education" and "wretched social arrangements" were "the only real hindrance" to attaining general happiness among human beings.[3] Moreover, Mill saw the intelligentsia— "the most cultivated intellects in the country," the "thinking minds," "the best and wisest"— as guides to a better world in their role of "those who have been in advance of society in thought and feeling."[4] This has been the role of the intelligentsia, as seen by the intelligentsia, both before and after Mill's time— that of intellectual leaders whose broader knowledge and deeper insights can liberate people from the needless restrictions of society.

Jean-Jacques Rousseau's famous declaration— "Man was born free, and he is everywhere in chains"[5]— summarizes the heart of the vision of the anointed, that social contrivances are the root cause of human unhappiness. This vision seeks to explain the fact that the world we see around us differs so greatly from the world that we would like to see. In this vision, oppression, poverty, injustice and war are all products of existing institutions— problems whose solutions require changing those institutions, which in turn requires changing the ideas behind those institutions. In short, the ills of society have been seen as ultimately an intellectual and moral problem, for which intellectuals are especially equipped to provide answers, by virtue of their greater knowledge and insight, as well as their not having vested economic interests to bias them in favor of the existing order and still the voice of conscience.

this author's BIAS
is annoying.

Large, unmerited differences in the economic and social prospects of people born into different social circumstances have long been a central theme of intellectuals with the vision of the anointed. Contrasts between the grinding poverty of some and the luxurious extravagance of others, compounded by similar unmerited contrasts in social status, are among the problems that have long dominated the agenda of those with the vision of the anointed.

More general sources of unhappiness among people across the social spectrum— the psychic problems created by moral stigma, as well as the horrors of war, for example— are also things for which intellectual solutions are sought.

This vision of society, in which there are many "problems" to be "solved" by applying the ideas of morally anointed intellectual elites is by no means the only vision, however much that vision may be prevalent among today's intellectuals. A conflicting vision has co-existed for centuries—a vision in which the inherent flaws of human beings are the fundamental problem, and social contrivances are simply imperfect means of trying to cope with those flaws— the imperfections of these contrivances being themselves products of the inherent shortcomings of human beings. A classical scholar has contrasted modern visions of the anointed with "the darker picture" painted by Thucydides of "a human race that escaped chaos and barbarism by preserving with difficulty a thin layer of civilization," based on "moderation and prudence" growing out of experience.[6] This is a tragic vision of the human condition that is very different from the vision of the anointed.

"Solutions," are not expected by those who see many of the frustrations, ills, and anomalies of life— the tragedy of the human condition— as being due to constraints inherent in human beings, singly and collectively, and in the constraints of the physical world in which they live. In contrast to the vision of today's anointed, where existing society is discussed largely in terms of its inadequacies and the improvements which the anointed have to offer, the tragic vision regards civilization itself as something that requires great and constant efforts merely to be preserved— with these efforts to be based on actual experience, not on "exciting" new theories.

In the tragic vision, barbarism is always waiting in the wings and civilization is simply "a thin crust over a volcano." This vision has few solutions to offer and many painful trade-offs to ponder. Commenting on Felix Frankfurter's references to the success of various reforms, Oliver Wendell Holmes wanted to know what the costs— the trade-offs— were. Otherwise, while lifting up society in one respect, "how the devil can I tell whether I am not pulling it down more in some other place," he asked.[7] This constrained vision is thus a tragic vision— not in the sense of believing that life must always be sad and gloomy, for much happiness and fulfillment are possible within a constrained world, but tragic in inherent limitations that cannot be overcome merely by changing institutions or by compassion, commitment, or other virtues which those with the vision of the anointed advocate or attribute to themselves.

In the tragic vision, social contrivances seek to restrict behavior that leads to unhappiness, even though these restrictions themselves cause a certain amount of unhappiness. As Professor Richard A. Epstein of the University of Chicago put it: "The study of human institutions is always a search for the most tolerable imperfections."[8] The tragic vision is a vision of trade-offs, rather than solutions, and a vision of wisdom distilled from the experiences of the many, rather than the brilliance of a few.

Because there are inherent limitations on the human brain and on the human lifespan, those with the tragic vision have tended to be advocates of specialization, exemplified by Adam Smith's praise of the division of labor in *The Wealth of Nations*.[9] But those with the opposite vision tend to lament so much specialization, seeking for example to transcend the specialization of academic disciplines with "interdisciplinary" courses and programs— and more generally projecting a vision of the future in which individuals will each have wide-ranging skills and interests, much like those of an idealized Renaissance Man.[10] Those with this vision of the anointed need not *deny* human limitations. They simply do not build those limitations into the foundations of their vision, as those with the tragic vision do.

The conflict between these two visions goes back for centuries.[11] Those with the tragic vision and those with the vision of the anointed do not simply happen to differ on a range of policy issues. They *necessarily* differ, because they are talking about very different worlds which exist inside their minds. Moreover, they are talking about different creatures who inhabit that world, even though both call these creatures human beings, for the nature of those human beings is also fundamentally different as seen in the two visions.[12]

In the tragic vision, there are especially severe limits on how much any given individual can know and truly understand, which is why this vision puts such emphasis not only on specialization but also on systemic social processes whose economic and social transactions draw upon the varied knowledge and experience of millions, past and present. In the vision of the anointed, however, far more knowledge and intelligence are available to some people than to others, and the differences between them and the masses are far greater than in the tragic vision.[13]

These opposing visions differ not only in what they believe exists and in what they think is possible, but also in what they think needs explaining. To those with the vision of the anointed, it is such evils as poverty, crime, war, and injustice which require explanation. To those with the tragic vision, however, it is prosperity, law, peace, and such justice as we have achieved, which require not only explanation but constant efforts, trade-offs, and sacrifices, just to maintain them at their existing levels, much less promote their enhancement over time. While those with the vision of the anointed seek the causes of war,[14] for example, those with the tragic vision say such things as "No peace keeps itself,"[15] that peace "is an unstable equilibrium, which can be preserved only by acknowledged supremacy or equal power,"[16] that a nation "despicable by its weakness, forfeits even the privilege of being neutral,"[17] and that "nations in general will make war whenever they have a prospect of getting anything by it."[18]

A tragic vision is a sort of zero-based vision of the world and of human beings, taking none of the benefits of civilization for granted. It does not assume that we can begin with what we already have and simply tack on improvements, without being concerned at every step with whether these innovations jeopardize the very processes and principles on which our existing level of well-being rests. It does not assume that the chafing restrictions *conveyed* to us by social contrivances— from prices to stigmas— are *caused* by those contrivances. Above all, it does not assume that untried theories stand on the same footing as institutions and practices whose very

[handwritten margin note: realist vs. Liberal]

existence demonstrate their ability to survive in the world of reality, however much that reality falls short of what can be imagined as a better world.

The two visions differ fundamentally, not only in how they see the world but also in how those who believe in these visions see themselves. If you happen to believe in free markets, judicial restraint, traditional values and other features of the tragic vision, then you are just someone who believes in free markets, judicial restraint and traditional values. There is no personal exaltation inherent in those beliefs. But to be for "social justice" and "saving the environment," or to be "anti-war" is more than just a set of hypotheses about empirical facts. This vision puts you on a higher moral plane as someone concerned and compassionate, someone who is for peace in the world, a defender of the downtrodden, and someone who wants to preserve the beauty of nature and save the planet from being polluted by others less caring.

In short, one vision makes you somebody special and the other vision does not. These visions are not symmetrical. Their asymmetry, as we shall see in later chapters, affects not only how their respective advocates see themselves but how they see those who disagree with them.

THE LEFT-RIGHT DICHOTOMY

One of the fertile sources of confusion in discussions of ideological issues is the dichotomy between the political left and the political right. Perhaps the most fundamental difference between the left and the right is that only the former has even a rough definition. What is called "the right" are simply the various and disparate opponents of the left. These opponents of the left may share no particular principle, much less a common agenda, and they can range from free-market libertarians to advocates of monarchy, theocracy, military dictatorship or innumerable other principles, systems and agendas.

To people who take words literally, to speak of "the left" is to assume implicitly that there is some other coherent group which constitutes "the right." Perhaps it would be less confusing if what we call "the left" would be designated by some other term, perhaps just as X. But the designation as being on the left has at least some historical basis in the views of those deputies who sat on the left side of the president's chair in France's Estates General in the eighteenth century. A rough summary of the vision of the political left today is that of collective decision-making through government, directed toward— or at least rationalized by— the goal of reducing economic and social inequalities. There may be moderate or extreme versions of the left vision or agenda but, among those designated as "the right," the difference between free market libertarians and military juntas is not simply one of degree in pursuing a common vision, because there is no common vision among these and other disparate groups opposed to the left— which is to say, there is no such definable thing as "the right," though there are various segments of that omnibus category, such as free market advocates, which can be defined.

The heterogeneity of what is called "the right" is not the only problem with the left-right dichotomy. The usual image of the political spectrum among the intelligentsia extends from the Communists on the extreme left to less extreme left-wing radicals, more moderate liberals, centrists, conservatives, hard right-wingers, and ultimately Fascists. But, like so much that is believed by the intelligentsia, it is a conclusion without an argument, unless endless repetition can be regarded as an argument. When we turn from such images to specifics, there is remarkably little difference between Communists and Fascists, except for rhetoric, and there is far more in common between Fascists and even the moderate left than between either of them and traditional conservatives in the American sense. A closer look makes this clear.

Communism is socialism with an international focus and totalitarian methods. Benito Mussolini, the founder of Fascism, defined Fascism as *national* socialism in a state that was totalitarian, a term that he also coined. The same idea was echoed in Germany, in the name of the National Socialist German Workers' Party, Hitler's party, now almost always abbreviated as Nazis, thereby burying its socialist component.

Viewed in retrospect, the most prominent feature of the Nazis— racism in general and anti-Jewish racism in particular— was not inherent in the Fascist vision, but was an obsession of Hitler's party, not shared by the Fascist government of Mussolini in Italy or that of Franco in Spain. At one time, Jews were in fact over-represented among Fascist leaders in Italy. Only after Mussolini became Hitler's junior partner in the Axis alliance of the late 1930s were Jews purged from Italy's Fascist party. And only after Mussolini's Fascist government in Rome was overthrown in 1943, and was replaced in northern Italy by a rump puppet government that the Nazis set up, were Jews in that part of Italy rounded up and sent off to concentration camps.[19] In short, official and explicit government racist ideology and practice distinguished the Nazis from other Fascist movements.

What distinguished Fascist movements in general from Communist movements was that Communists were officially committed to government ownership of the means of production, while Fascists permitted private ownership of the means of production, so long as government directed the private owners' decisions and limited what profit rates they could receive. Both were totalitarian dictatorships but Communists were officially internationalist while Fascists were officially nationalist. However, Stalin's proclaimed policy of "socialism in one country" was not very different from the Fascists' proclaimed policy of national socialism.

When it came to practice, there was even less difference, since the Communist International served the *national* interests of the Soviet Union, despite whatever internationalist rhetoric it used. The way Communists in other countries, including the United States, reversed their opposition to Western nations' military defense efforts in World War II, within 24 hours after the Soviet Union was invaded by Hitler's armies, was only the most dramatic of many examples that could be cited.

As regards Fascists' supposed restriction of their interests to those within their own respective countries, that was belied by both Hitler's and Mussolini's invasions of other countries and by Nazi international networks, operating among Germans living in other countries ranging from the United States to Brazil to Australia[20]— all focused on Germany's national interest, as distinguished from seeking ideological purity or the interests of Germans living in these other countries. Thus the grievances of the Sudeten Germans in Czechoslovakia were pressed during the Munich crisis of 1938 as part of Germany's national expansion, while Germans living in Italy were told to squelch their grievances, since Mussolini was Hitler's ally.[21]

While the Soviet Union proclaimed its internationalism as it set up various officially autonomous nations within its borders, the people who wielded the real power in those nations— often under the official title of "Second Secretary" of the Communist Party in these ostensibly autonomous nations— were usually Russians,[22] just as in the days when the czars ruled what was more candidly called the Russian Empire.

In short, the notion that Communists and Fascists were at opposite poles ideologically was not true, even in theory, much less in practice. As for similarities and differences between these two totalitarian movements and liberalism, on the one hand, or conservatism on the other, there was far more similarity between these totalitarians' agendas and those of the democratic left than with the agendas of most conservatives. For example, among the items on the agendas of the Fascists in Italy and/or the Nazis in Germany were (1) government control of wages and hours of work, (2) higher taxes on the wealthy, (3) government-set limits on profits, (4) government care for the elderly, (5) a decreased emphasis on the role of religion and the family in personal or social decisions and (6) government taking on the role of changing the nature of people, usually beginning in early childhood.[23] This last and most audacious project has been part of the ideology of the left— both democratic and totalitarian— since at least the eighteenth century, when Rousseau and Godwin advocated it, and it has been advocated by innumerable intellectuals since then,[24] as well as being put into practice in various countries, under names ranging from "re-education" to "values clarification."[25]

These are of course things opposed by most people who are called "conservatives" in the United States, and they are things much more congenial to the general approach of people who are called "liberals" in the American political context. It should be noted also that neither "liberal" nor "conservative," as those terms are used in the American context, has much relationship to their original meanings. Milton Friedman, one of the leading American "conservative" intellectuals of his time, advocated radical changes in the country's school system, in the role of the Federal Reserve System, and in the economy in general. One of his books was titled *The Tyranny of the Status Quo*. He, like Friedrich Hayek, called himself a "liberal" in the original sense of the word, but that sense has been irretrievably lost in general discussions in the United States, though people with similar views are still called liberals in some other countries.

Despite all this, even scholarly studies of intellectuals have referred to Hayek as a defender of the "status quo," and as one of those whose "defense of the existing state of affairs" has "furnished justifications for the powers that be."[26] Whatever the merits or demerits of Hayek's ideas, those ideas were far more distant from the status quo than were the ideas of those who criticized him. In general, people such as Hayek, who are referred to in the American context as "conservatives," have a set of ideas which differ not only in degree, but in kind, from the ideas of many others who are said to be on the right politically. Perhaps if liberals were simply called X and conservatives were called Y there would be less confusion.

Conservatism, in its original sense, has no specific ideological content at all, since everything depends on what one is trying to conserve. In the last days of the Soviet Union, for example, those who were trying to preserve the existing Communist regime were rightly referred to as "conservatives," though what they were trying to conserve had nothing in common with what was advocated by Milton Friedman, Friedrich Hayek or William F. Buckley in the United States, much less Cardinal Joseph Ratzinger, a leading conservative in the Vatican who subsequently became Pope. Specific individuals with the "conservative" label have specific ideological positions, but there is no commonality of specifics among "conservatives" in different venues.

If we attempt to define the political left by its proclaimed goals, it is clear that very similar goals have been proclaimed by people whom the left repudiates and anathematizes, such as Fascists in general and Nazis in particular. Instead of defining these (and other) groups by their proclaimed goals, we can define them by the specific institutional mechanisms and policies they use or advocate for achieving their goals. More specifically, they can be defined by the institutional mechanisms they seek to establish for making decisions with impacts on society at large. In order to keep the discussion manageable, the vast sweep of possible decision-making mechanisms can be dichotomized into those in which individuals make decisions individually for themselves and those in which decisions are made collectively by surrogates for society at large.

In market economies, for example, consumers and producers make their own decisions individually and the social consequences are determined by the effect of those individual decisions on the way resources are allocated in the economy as a whole, in response to the movements of prices and incomes— which in turn respond to supply and demand.

While this vision of the economy is often considered to be "conservative" (in the original sense of the word), in the long view of the history of ideas it has been revolutionary. From ancient times to the present, and in highly disparate societies around the world, there have been the most varied systems of thought— both secular and religious— seeking to determine how best the wise and virtuous can influence or direct the masses, in order to create or maintain a happier, more viable or more worthy society. In this context, it was a revolutionary departure when, in eighteenth-century France, the Physiocrats arose to proclaim that, for the economy at least, the best that the reigning authorities could do would be to leave it alone— *laissez-faire* being the term they coined. To those with this vision, whether in France or elsewhere, for the authorities to impose economic policies would be to give "a most unnecessary attention," in Adam Smith's words,[27] to a spontaneous system of interactions that would go better without government intervention— not perfectly, just better.

Variations of this vision of spontaneous order can also be found in other areas, ranging from language to the law. No elites sat down and planned the languages of the world or of any given society. These languages evolved from the systemic interactions of millions of human beings over the generations, in the most varied societies around the world. Linguistic scholars study and codify the rules of language— but after the fact. Young children learn words and usage, intuiting the rules of that usage before they are taught these things explicitly in schools. While it was possible for elites to create languages such as Esperanto, these artificial languages have never caught on in a way that would displace historically evolved languages.

In law, a similar vision was expressed in Justice Oliver Wendell Holmes' statement that "The life of the law has not been logic: it has been experience."[28] In short, whether in the economy, language, or the law, this vision sees social viability and progress as being due to systemic evolution rather than elite prescription.

Reliance on systemic processes, whether in the economy, the law, or other areas, is based on the constrained vision— the tragic vision— of the severe limitations on any given individual's knowledge and insight, however knowledgeable or brilliant that individual might be, compared to other individuals. Systemic processes which tap vastly more knowledge and experience from vastly more people, often including traditions evolved from the experiences of successive generations, are deemed more reliable than the intellect of the intellectuals.

By contrast, the vision of the left is one of surrogate decision-making by those presumed to have not only superior knowledge but sufficient knowledge, whether these surrogates are political leaders, experts, judges or others. This is the vision that is common to varying degrees on the political left, whether radical or moderate, and common also to totalitarians, whether Communist or Fascist. A commonality of purpose in society is central to collective decision-making, whether expressed in town-meeting democracy or totalitarian dictatorship or other variations in between. One of the differences between the commonality of purposes in democratic systems of government and in totalitarian systems of government is in the range of decisions infused with that commonality of purpose and in the range of decisions reserved for individual decision-making outside the purview of government.

The free market, for example, is a huge exemption from government power. In such a market, there is no commonality of purpose, except among such individuals and organizations as may choose voluntarily to coalesce into groups ranging from bowling leagues to multinational corporations. But even these aggregations typically pursue the interests of their own respective constituents and compete against the interests of other aggregations. Those who advocate this mode of social decision-making do so because they believe that the systemic results of such competition are usually better than a society-wide commonality of purpose imposed by surrogate decision-makers superintending the whole process in the name of "the national interest" or of "social justice."

The totalitarian version of collective surrogate decision-making by government was summarized by Mussolini, who defined "totalitarianism" in the motto: "Everything in the State, nothing outside the State, nothing against the State."[29] Moreover, the state ultimately meant the political leader of the state, the dictator. Mussolini was known as *Il Duce*— the leader— before Hitler acquired the same title in German as the *Führer*.

Democratic versions of collective surrogate decision-making by government choose leaders by votes and tend to leave more areas outside the purview of government. However, the left seldom has any explicit principle by which the boundaries between government and individual decision-making can be determined, so that the natural tendency over time is for the scope of government decision-making to expand, as more and more decisions are taken successively from private hands, since government officials constantly have incentives to expand their powers while the voters' attention is not constantly focussed on maintaining limits on those powers.

Preferences for collective, surrogate decision-making from the top down are not all that the democratic left has shared with the original Italian Fascists and with the National Socialists (Nazis) of Germany. In addition to political intervention in economic markets, the democratic left has shared with the Fascists and the Nazis the underlying assumption of a vast gap in understanding between ordinary people and elites like themselves. Although both the totalitarian left— that is, the Fascists, Communists and Nazis— and the democratic left have widely used in a positive sense such terms as "the people," "the workers" or "the masses," these are the ostensible beneficiaries of their policies, but *not* autonomous decision-makers. Although much rhetoric on both the democratic left and the totalitarian left has long papered over the distinction between ordinary people as beneficiaries and as decision-makers, it has long been clear in practice that decision-making has been seen as something reserved for the anointed in these visions.

Rousseau, for all his emphasis on "the general will," left the interpretation of that will to elites. He likened the masses of the people to "a stupid, pusillanimous invalid."[30] Godwin and Condorcet, also on the eighteenth century left, expressed similar contempt for the masses.[31] Karl Marx said, "The working class is revolutionary or it is nothing"[32]— in other words, millions of human beings mattered only if they carried out his vision. Fabian socialist George Bernard Shaw included the working class among the "detestable" people who "have no right to live." He added: "I should despair if I did not know that they will all die presently, and that there is no need on earth why they should be replaced by people like themselves."[33] As a young man serving in the U.S. Army during the First World War, Edmund Wilson wrote to a friend: "I should be insincere to make it appear that the deaths of this 'poor white trash' of the South and the rest made me feel half so bitter as the mere conscription or enlistment of any of my friends."[34]

The totalitarian left has been similarly clear that decision-making power should be confined to a political elite— the "vanguard of the proletariat," the leader of a "master race," or whatever the particular phrase that might become the motto of the particular totalitarian system. In Mussolini's words, "The mass will simply follow and submit."[35]

The similarity in underlying assumptions between the various totalitarian movements and the democratic left was openly recognized by leaders of the left themselves in democratic countries during the 1920s, when Mussolini was widely lionized by intellectuals in the Western democracies, and even Hitler had his admirers among prominent intellectuals on the left. It was only as the 1930s unfolded that Mussolini's invasion of Ethiopia and Hitler's violent anti-Semitism at home and military aggression abroad made these totalitarian systems international pariahs that they were repudiated by the left— and were thereafter depicted as being on "the right."*

During the 1920s, however, radical writer Lincoln Steffens wrote positively about Mussolini's Fascism as he had more famously written positively about Soviet Communism.[36] As late as 1932, famed novelist and Fabian socialist H.G. Wells urged students at Oxford to be "liberal fascists" and "enlightened Nazis."[37] Historian Charles Beard was among Mussolini's apologists in the Western democracies, as was the *New Republic* magazine.[38] The poet Wallace Stevens even justified Mussolini's invasion of Ethiopia.[39]

---

*The Nazis street battles with the Communists in 1920s Germany were internecine warfare among groups competing for the allegiance of the same constituency, much as the Communists killed socialists during the Spanish civil war, and as Stalin purged Trotskyites in the Soviet Union.

W.E.B. Du Bois was so intrigued by the Nazi movement in the 1920s that he put swastikas on the cover of an issue of a magazine he edited, despite protests from Jews.[40] Even though Du Bois was conflicted by the Nazis' anti-Semitism, he said in the 1930s that creation of the Nazi dictatorship had been "absolutely necessary to get the state in order" in Germany, and in a speech in Harlem in 1937 he declared that "there is today, in some respects, more democracy in Germany than there has been in years past."[41] More revealing, Du Bois saw the Nazis as part of the political left. In 1936, he said, "Germany today is, next to Russia, the greatest exemplar of Marxian socialism in the world."[42]

The heterogeneity of those later lumped together as the right has allowed those on the left to dump into that grab-bag category many who espouse some version of the vision of the left, but whose other characteristics make them an embarrassment to be repudiated. Thus the popular 1930s American radio personality Father Coughlin— who was, among other things, an anti-Semite— has been verbally banished to "the right," even though he advocated so many of the policies that became part of the New Deal that many Congressional Democrats at one time publicly praised him and some progressives urged President Franklin D. Roosevelt to make him a Cabinet member.[43]

During this early period, it was common on the left, as well as elsewhere, to compare as kindred experiments Fascism in Italy, Communism in the Soviet Union and the New Deal in the United States.[44] Such comparisons were later as completely rejected as the inclusion of Father Coughlin as a figure of the left was. These arbitrary changes in classifications not only allowed the left to distance themselves from embarrassing individuals and groups, whose underlying assumptions and conclusions bore many similarities to their own, these classification changes also allowed the left to verbally transfer these embarrassments to their ideological opponents. Moreover, such changes in nomenclature greatly reduced the likelihood that observers would see the negative potential of the ideas and agendas being put forth by the left in its bid for influence or power.

The kinds of concentrations of government power sought by the left may be proclaimed to be in the service of various sorts of lofty goals, but such concentrations of power also offer opportunities for all sorts of abuses, ranging up to and including mass murder, as Hitler, Stalin, Mao, and Pol Pot demonstrated. These leaders did *not* have a tragic vision of man, such as that underlying what is called "conservative" thought in America today. It was precisely these dictators' presumptions of their own vastly greater knowledge and wisdom than that of ordinary people which led to such staggering tragedies for others.

YOUTH AND AGE

Given the very different conceptions of knowledge by those with the tragic vision and those with the vision of the anointed, it is virtually inevitable that they would have different conceptions of the role and competence of the young. Where knowledge is conceived of as more or less the kinds of things taught in schools and universities, and intelligence is conceived of as sheer brainpower in manipulating concepts and articulating conclusions, there is no inherent reason why the young would not be at least as accomplished in such things as the old, since brain development is said to reach its peak in early adulthood. Moreover, the young, having been more recently educated, have the advantage of the most updated and newly discovered knowledge. As the Marquis de Condorcet said in the eighteenth century: "A young man now leaving school possesses more real knowledge than the greatest geniuses— not of antiquity, but even of the seventeenth century— could have acquired by long study."[45]

This is yet another example of how one conceives of knowledge affects how one conceives of other things, including in this case the relative advantages of youth and age. Views such as those of Condorcet contrast with the views of those with the tragic vision, where consequential knowledge is often mundane knowledge, accumulated by experience, and wisdom is also primarily distilled from experience. Therefore, almost by definition, the younger generation is not usually in as good a position to make wise decisions— for themselves, much less for society— as those who have much more experience to draw upon.

Accordingly, those with the vision of the anointed have for centuries put great hopes in the young, while those with the tragic vision have relied far more on those with mature experience.

The 1960s notion that "we should learn from our young people" had antecedents going back to the eighteenth century. Such subsidiary social phenomena as lowering the voting age, and reducing the deference to the older generation in general and to parents in particular, are likewise very consistent with, if not inescapable corollaries from, the over-all conception of knowledge and intelligence prevalent among those with the vision of the anointed. Where social problems are seen as being consequences of existing institutions and prejudices, the young are often seen as less wedded to the status quo, and thus as hopes for the future.

Back in the eighteenth century, William Godwin articulated this argument when he said, "The next generation will not have so many prejudices to subdue."[46] Children, according to Godwin, "are a sort of raw material put into our hands."[47] Their minds "are like a sheet of white paper."[48] At the same time, they are oppressed by their parents and must go through "twenty years of bondage" before they receive "the scanty portion of liberty, which the government of my country happens to concede to its adult subjects!"[49] Clearly the young have been seen as candidates for "liberation," both of themselves and of society, in this view— a view still very much alive among intellectuals, more than two centuries later. Advocates of "children's rights" are advocating rights that children themselves obviously will not be exercising, so this amounts to another way for third party surrogates to intervene in families, without having to pay any price when they are wrong.

All these conclusions change completely, however, if knowledge and wisdom are conceived as they are conceived by those with the tragic vision. Adam Smith, for example, said, "The wisest and most experienced are generally the least credulous." In short, the old are generally not as susceptible to heady notions, according to Smith: "It is acquired wisdom and experience only that teach incredulity, and they very seldom teach it enough."[50] The zeal and enthusiasm of the young, much praised by many of those with the vision of the anointed, have long been seen very differently by those with the tragic vision. Burke, for example, said: "It is no excuse for presumptuous ignorance that it is directed by insolent passion."[51] Some have even referred to a perennial invasion of civilization by barbarians, namely the new-born, whom families and social institutions must civilize, because they enter the world no different from babies born in the days of the caveman.

People with opposing visions of the world do not simply happen to reach different conclusions about the young and the old. On these and innumerable other issues, the conclusions reached by each are entailed as corollaries of their underlying assumptions about knowledge and wisdom. The education of the young has long been a battleground between adherents of the two visions of the nature of human beings and the nature of knowledge and wisdom. William Godwin's notion that the young "are a sort of raw material put into our hands" remains, after two centuries, a powerful temptation to classroom indoctrination in schools and colleges. In the early twentieth century, Woodrow Wilson wrote of his years as an academic administrator when he felt "I should like to make the young gentlemen of the rising generation as unlike their fathers as possible."[52]

This indoctrination can start as early as elementary school, where students are encouraged or required to write about controversial issues, sometimes in letters to public officials. More fundamentally, the indoctrination process habituates them to taking sides on weighty and complex issues after hearing just one side of those issues. Moreover, they are habituated to venting their emotions instead of analyzing conflicting evidence and dissecting conflicting arguments. In short, they are led to prepackaged conclusions, instead of being equipped with the intellectual tools to reach their own conclusions, including conclusions different from those of their teachers. In many colleges and universities, whole academic departments are devoted to particular prepackaged conclusions— whether on race, the environment or other subjects, under such names as black, women's or environmental "studies." Few, if any, of these "studies" include conflicting visions and conflicting evidence, as educational rather than ideological criteria might require.

Critics of ideological indoctrination in schools and colleges often attack the particular ideological conclusions, but that is beside the point educationally. Even if we were to assume, for the sake of argument, that all the conclusions reached by all the various "studies" are both logically and factually valid, that still does not get to the heart of the educational issue. Even if students were to leave these "studies" with 100 percent correct conclusions about issues *A*, *B* and *C*, that would in no way equip them intellectually with the tools needed to confront very different issues *X*, *Y* and *Z* that are likely to arise over the course of their future years. For that they would need knowledge and experience in how to analyze and weigh conflicting viewpoints. As John Stuart Mill said:

> He who knows only his own side of the case, knows little of that. . . Nor is it enough that he should hear the arguments of adversaries from his own teachers, presented as they state them, and accompanied by what they offer as refutations. That is not the way to do justice to the arguments, or bring them into real contact with his own mind. He must be able to hear them from persons who actually believe them; who defend them in earnest, and do their very utmost for them. He must know them in their most plausible and persuasive form. . .[53]

One of the remarkable self-indulgences of contemporary educators in the public schools has been the introduction into classrooms of programs which systematically undermine moral principles that have come down over the centuries, and which children have been taught by their parents. These programs have usually been developed by intellectuals outside the field of education, extensively marketed by both commercial firms and non-profit organizations, and are often eagerly embraced by educators who have been taught in schools of education that their role is to be that of agents of social "change," not simply transmitters of a heritage of knowledge. These programs have a remarkable variety of names and ostensible goals, one of the earliest names being "values clarification," though other names have proliferated after parents and others discovered what "values clarification" really meant in practice and raised objections.

The phrase "values clarification" is very misleading. When parents tell their children not to steal or lie, or engage in violence, there is no ambiguity as to what they mean. Ambiguity is *introduced* by programs which confront students with carefully crafted moral dilemmas, such as a situation where a ship is sinking and there are more people than the lifeboats can hold, so that decisions have to be made as to who is to be left to drown, perhaps beaten off when they try to climb out of the water onto a lifeboat that is already so full that it will capsize if another person climbs in. Because received moral principles do not always apply, the implication is that each individual should develop his or her own situational ethics to replace traditional morality— not only where traditional moral principles fail but in the vast range of more ordinary situations where there are no such dilemmas as those in contrived examples.

If such exercises seem remote from the purposes of a public school education, they are not remote from the philosophy introduced into education by John Dewey a century ago and promoted by schools of education to the present day. Nor were they remote from the thinking by Woodrow Wilson. Like so much in the vision of the anointed, this view of education exalts those who believe in it, and so it is not simply a set of testable hypotheses about social events. Also like other aspects of that vision, there is no price to be paid by its promoters for being wrong, however large a price ends up being paid by individual students or by society at large.

"Values clarification" has been just one of a wide range of high-sounding names for classroom programs to re-shape the attitudes and consciousness of the younger generation. Other names have included "affective education," "decision-making," "Quest," "sex education" and many other imaginative titles. Such titles are often simply flags of convenience, under which schools set sail on an "exciting" voyage in an uncharted sea of social experimentation in the re-shaping of young people's beliefs and attitudes. The ever-changing names for these programs reflect the need for concealment or misdirection, since few parents want to be told that schools are out to undo what the parents have taught their children or to mold those children to be what third parties want them to be.

Enigmatic writing is another way of concealing what is being done. Many people— including many who have respected and agreed with his conclusions— have commented on the difficulty of trying to understand the writings of philosopher John Dewey who, in addition to his other roles, was the leading educational theorist of the twentieth century. William James, a contemporary and fellow leader in the development of the philosophy of pragmatism, called Dewey's writing style "damnable." In a later era, Richard Hofstadter said of Dewey, "He wrote a prose of terrible vagueness and plasticity."[54] Yet anyone who reads Dewey's 1935 book *Liberalism and Social Action* will find its writing clear as a bell, whatever its merits or demerits otherwise. Nor can the subject matter of technical philosophy be the sole reason for the difficulties of trying to pin down what Dewey was saying in most of his earlier writings. Even books by Dewey with such a familiar and non-technical subject matter as *The Child and the Curriculum* have a vagueness that sometimes makes trying to grasp his meanings seem like trying to grab a handful of fog.

What Hofstadter regarded as a defect of Dewey's writings on education— that a "variety of schools of educational thought have been able to read their own meanings into his writings"[55]— has been a source of the enduring influence of those writings. Moreover, it was a protective obscurity, since Dewey espoused ideas that could have set off more than one hornet's nest of opposition if expressed in plain words in the early twentieth century. By 1935, when *Liberalism and Social Action* was published, the kinds of social and political notions expressed in that book were very much in keeping with the spirit of the 1930s and required no camouflage.

Writing in the early twentieth century, however, Dewey's notion that education should be a means to "eliminate obvious social evils" through its "development of children and youth but also of the future society of which they will be the constituents"[56] was a fundamental change in the role of schools. The notion that the school should be run as a microcosm of society— "a miniature community, an embryonic society"[57]— and as a place for conditioning students to want a very different kind of society, unlike the current society, was not something likely to find approval or perhaps even toleration. In the early twentieth century especially, parents were not sending their children to school to become guinea pigs in someone else's social experiments to use education as a means of subverting existing values in order to create a new society based on new values, those of a self-anointed elite, more or less behind the backs of parents, voters and taxpayers.

Chapter 7

Abstract People in an Abstract World

One of the bases for many of the intellectuals' sweeping pronouncements about whole societies is conceiving of people in the abstract, without the innumerable specific, systematic and consequential *differences* in characteristics found among flesh-and-blood human beings as they exist in the real world. For example, the intellectuals' consuming preoccupation with various inequalities in outcomes is understandable if the individuals or groups that differ in their outcomes do not differ in the many things which produce those outcomes— as they would not with abstract people.

Abstract people are very convenient for intellectuals' discussions or research. Abstract people can be aggregated into statistical categories such as households, families, and income brackets, without the slightest concern for whether those statistical categories contain similar people, or even the same numbers of people, or people who differ substantially in age, much less in such finer distinctions as whether or not they are working or whether they are the same people in the same categories over time. The gross contrast between the impression created by income data from the Census Bureau and income data from the Internal Revenue Service, as noted in Chapter 3, is due essentially to the Census' data being about unspecified people in abstract brackets over time, and the IRS data being compiled from identifiable flesh-and-blood individuals as they move massively from one bracket to another over time.

Thinking of people in the abstract, and dismissing observed differences between them as mere "perceptions," or "stereotypes" provides the intelligentsia with innumerable occasions for waxing morally indignant at the concrete differences in economic and other outcomes among different individuals and groups as they exist in the real world.

Reluctance to associate with any group, whether at work or in neighborhood or other settings, is almost automatically attributed by the intelligentsia to ignorance, prejudice or malice— in utter disregard of not only the first-hand experience of those who are reluctant, but also of objective data on vast differences in rates of crime, alcoholism, and substandard school performances between groups, even though such differences have been common in countries around the world for centuries.

Cholera, or example, was unknown in America until large numbers of Irish immigrants arrived in the nineteenth century, and cholera outbreaks in New York and Philadelphia went largely through Irish neighborhoods.[1] People who did not want to live near Irish immigrants, as a result of diseases, violence and other social pathology rampant in the Irish communities of that era, cannot be automatically dismissed as blinded by prejudice or deceived by stereotypes.* Strenuous efforts, especially by the Catholic Church, to change the behavior patterns within Irish American communities,[2] suggest that it was not all a matter of other people's "perceptions" or "stereotypes." Moreover, these efforts within Irish American communities ultimately paid off, as barriers against the Irish, epitomized by employers' signs that said "No Irish Need Apply," faded away over the generations.

Such barriers were not simply a matter of mistaken or malign ideas in other people's heads, nor were the Irish simply abstract people in an abstract world, however much that vision may flatter intellectuals' desires to be on the side of the angels against the forces of evil. There is no need to go to the opposite extreme and claim that *all* negative views of all groups are based on valid reasons. The point here is that this is an empirical question to be investigated in terms of the particular facts of the particular group at a

---

* "The Germans in St. Louis were principally concentrated in the northern and southern sections of the city. The Irish also had their own special area, and it was never safe to venture from one section into the other... Rioting occurred also when Irish rowdies interfered with German picnics, frequently for no apparent reason except to add excitement to an otherwise dull Sunday." Carl Wittke, *The Irish in America* (New York: Russell & Russell, 1970), p. 183.

particular time and place— a process circumvented by reasoning as if discussing abstract people in an abstract world.

In the real world, people do not behave randomly. Studies have shown the correlation between the IQs of husbands and their wives to be similar to— and sometimes greater than— the correlation between the IQs of brothers and sisters,[3] even though there is no genetic or biological reason for spouses to be similar in IQ. Only the fact that people behave differently toward people whom they perceive as similar to themselves seems likely to explain IQ correlations between people who get married, even though they do not give IQ tests to one another before deciding to wed.

Considering an opposite approach may make the difference between reasoning in the abstract and reasoning in the concrete stand out more sharply. When a scholarly study of economic development in Latin America concluded, "Costa Rica is different from Nicaragua *because Costa Ricans are different from Nicaraguans*,"[4] its conclusion— whatever its merits or demerits— was one almost unthinkable within the confines of the vision of the anointed, even as a hypothesis to be tested. The opposite approach— treating Costa Ricans and Nicaraguans as if they were abstract people in an abstract world, whose differences in outcomes could only be a result of external circumstances, has been far more common among the intelligentsia.

DISPARITIES AND THEIR CAUSES

The grand social dogma of our time, that statistical disparities in outcomes between groups are presumptive evidence of differential treatment by others— a presumption that employers, lenders and others accused of discriminatory behavior must rebut to the satisfaction of commissions or courts, or else face penalties that can amount to millions of dollars— is sheer presumption. *No evidence whatsoever* is required to be presented to commissions or courts to substantiate that presumption. Moreover, such evidence as history offers goes completely counter to that presumption.

In the nineteenth century, Scottish highlanders were not as prosperous as Scottish lowlanders, whether in Scotland itself or as immigrants living in

Australia or the United States.[5] In the twentieth century, Gaelic-speaking children in the Hebrides Islands off Scotland did not score as high on IQ tests as the English-speaking children there.[6] Rates of alcoholism among Irish-Americans have at one time been some multiple of the rates of alcoholism among Italian Americans or Jewish Americans.[7] In the days of the Soviet Union, the consumption of cognac in Estonia was more than seven times what it was in Uzbekistan.[8] In Malaysia during the 1960s, students from the Chinese minority earned more than 400 degrees in engineering, while students from the Malay majority earned just four engineering degrees during that same decade.[9]

To those who think in terms of abstract people in an abstract world, it may be surprising, or even shocking, to discover large intergroup disparities in incomes, I.Q.s and numerous other social variables. Although such disparities are common in many very different societies around the world, intellectuals in each society tend to regard these disparities in their own country as strange, if not sinister. In some countries, particular minorities have been accused of "taking over" whole industries, when in fact those industries did not exist until those minorities created them.[10]

Sometimes minorities are on the short end of disparities (as in the United States, Britain and France), and sometimes it is a majority that lags behind (as in Malaysia, Indonesia or the Ottoman Empire). Sometimes the disparities are blamed on discrimination, sometimes on genes, but in any event the disparities are treated as oddities that need explaining, *no matter how common such supposed oddities are in countries around the world* or in how many centuries they have been common. Because intellectuals' assumptions about these disparities are so deeply ingrained, so widely disseminated, and have such powerful ramifications on so many issues, it is worth taking a closer and longer look beyond abstract people in an abstract world to the hard facts about real people in the real world, now and in the past.

Where minorities have outperformed politically dominant majorities, it is especially difficult to make the case that discrimination is the cause.

A study of the Ottoman Empire, for example, found that "of the 40 private bankers listed in Istanbul in 1912 not one bore a Muslim name." Nor was even one of the 34 stockbrokers in Istanbul a Turk. Of the capital assets of 284 industrial firms employing five or more workers, 50 percent were owned by Greeks and another 20 percent by Armenians.[11] In the seventeenth century Ottoman Empire, the palace medical staff consisted of 41 Jews and 21 Muslims.[12]

The racial or ethnic minorities who have owned or directed more than half of whole industries in particular nations have included the Chinese in Malaysia,[13] the Lebanese in West Africa,[14] Greeks in the Ottoman Empire,[15] Britons in Argentina,[16] Belgians in Russia,[17] Jews in Poland,[18] and Spaniards in Chile[19]— among many others. As of 1921, members of the Tamil minority in Ceylon outnumbered members of the Sinhalese majority in that country's medical profession.[20]

Groups have differed greatly in innumerable endeavors in countries around the world. In 1908, Germans were the sole producers of the following products in Brazil's state of São Paulo: metal furniture, trunks, stoves, paper, hats, neckties, leather, soap, glass, matches, beer, confections, and carriages.[21] People of Japanese ancestry who settled in that same state produced more than two-thirds of the potatoes and more than 90 percent of the tomatoes.[22] Exporters from the Lebanese minority in the African nation of Sierra Leone accounted for 85 percent of the exports of ginger in 1954 and 93 percent in 1955.[23] In 1949, Lebanese truckers in Sierra Leone outnumbered African truckers and European truckers combined.[24] In 1921, more than three-fifths of all the commerce in Poland was conducted by Jews, who were only 11 percent of the population.[25] In 1948, members of the Indian minority owned roughly nine-tenths of all the cotton gins in Uganda.[26] In colonial Ceylon, the textile, retailing, wholesaling, and import businesses were all largely in the hands of people of Indian ancestry, rather than in the hands of the Sinhalese majority.[27]

As early as 1887, more than twice as many Italians as Argentines had bank accounts in the *Banco de la Provincia de Buenos Aires*,[28] even though most nineteenth-century Italian immigrants arrived in Argentina destitute and began working in the lowest, hardest, and most "menial" jobs. In the United States, knowledge of the frugality of Italian immigrants, and their reliability in repaying debts, even when they had low incomes, caused a bank to be set up to attract this clientele in San Francisco, under the name "Bank of Italy." It became so successful that it spread out to the larger society, and eventually became the largest bank in the world under its new name, "Bank of America."[29] The frugality of Italians was not simply a "perception" or a "stereotype," as A.P. Giannini well knew when he set up this bank.

At one period of history or another, when it was not one specific racial or ethnic minority dominating an industry or occupation, it has often been foreigners in general, leaving the majority population of a country outnumbered, or even non-existent, in whole sectors of their own economy. Even after the middle of the twentieth century, most of the industrial enterprises in Chile were controlled by either immigrants or the children of immigrants.[30] At various times and places, foreign minorities have predominated in particular industries or occupations over the majority populations of Peru,[31] Switzerland,[32] Malaysia,[33] Argentina,[34] Russia,[35] much of the Balkans,[36] the Middle East,[37] and Southeast Asia.[38] Indeed, it has been a worldwide phenomenon, found even in some economically advanced countries, as well as being common in less advanced countries.

Such examples could be extended almost indefinitely,* and so could the reasons for the disparities. But a more fundamental question must be faced: Was there ever any realistic chance that the various races would have had the same skills, experience and general capabilities, even if they had the same genetic potential and faced no discrimination?

Different races, after all, developed in different parts of the world, in very different geographic settings, which presented very different opportunities

---

* For example, a study of military forces in countries around the world found that "militaries fall far short of mirroring, even roughly, the multi-ethnic societies" from which they come. Cynthia H. Enloe, *Police, Military and Ethnicity: Foundations of State Power* (New Brunswick: Transaction Books, 1980), p. 143. Another massive scholarly study of ethnic groups in countries around the world concluded that, when discussing "proportional representation" of ethnic groups, "few, if any, societies have ever approximated this description." Donald L. Horowitz, *Ethnic Groups in Conflict* (Berkeley: University of California Press, 1985), p. 677. Yet another such international study of ethnic groups referred to "the universality of ethnic inequality" and pointed out that these inequalities are multi-dimensional: "All multi-ethnic societies exhibit a tendency for ethnic groups to engage in different occupations, have different levels (and, often, types) of education, receive different incomes, and occupy a different place in the social hierarchy." Myron Weiner, "The Pursuit of Ethnic Equality Through Preferential Policies: A Comparative Public Policy Perspective," *From Independence to Statehood*, edited by Robert B. Goldmann and A. Jeyaratnam Wilson (London: Frances Pinter, 1984), p. 64.

and restrictions on their economic and cultural evolution over a period of centuries.

There is no way, for example, that the patterns of economic and social life which originated and evolved in Europe could have originated among the indigenous peoples of the Western Hemisphere, where the horses that were central to everything from farming to transportation to warfare in Europe simply did not exist anywhere in the Western Hemisphere when the European invaders arrived and began transplanting horses across the Atlantic to the New World. Take horses out of the history of Europe and a very different kind of economy and society would have had to evolve, in order to be viable. Not only horses were lacking in the Western Hemisphere, neither were there oxen, which were common in both Europe and Asia. There were, in short, no such heavy-duty beasts of burden in the Western Hemisphere as existed on the vast Eurasian land mass, where most of the human race has lived throughout recorded history. The way of life in these different regions of the world had no basis on which to be the same— which is to say, there was no way for the skills and experiences of the races in these regions to be the same.

The wheel has often been regarded as fundamental to economic and social advances but, for most of the history of the human race, the value of wheeled vehicles depended to a great extent on the presence of draft animals to pull those vehicles— and there were no wheeled vehicles in any of the economies of the Western Hemisphere when the Europeans arrived. The Mayans had invented wheels, but they were used on children's toys,[39] so the issue was not the intellectual capacity to invent the wheel but the circumstances that make wheels more valuable or less valuable. Clearly, the way of life among the indigenous peoples of the Western Hemisphere could not have been the same as that on the Eurasian land mass, when there were neither wheeled vehicles nor draft animals in the Western Hemisphere when the Europeans and their animals arrived.

Geographic differences between Europe and sub-Saharan Africa are even more numerous and more drastic than those between Europe and the Western Hemisphere.[40] In addition to severe geographic limitations on the production of wealth, due to deficiencies of soil and unreliable rainfall patterns,[41] sub-Saharan Africa has had severe geographic restrictions on communications among its fragmented peoples, and of these peoples with the peoples of the outside world, due to a dearth of navigable waterways within sub-Saharan Africa, as well as a dearth of natural harbors, the difficulties of maintaining draft animals because of the disease-carrying tsetse fly, and the vast barrier of the Sahara desert, which is several times the size of any other desert in the world, and as large as the 48 contiguous states of the United States. With an expanse of sand that size standing between them and the outside world to the north, and with three oceans on the other sides of them, the peoples of sub-Saharan Africa have long been among the most insulated from the rest of the human race.

Isolated peoples have for centuries lagged behind others, whether the isolation has been caused by mountains, deserts, or islands far from the nearest mainland. Eminent French historian Fernand Braudel pointed out, "mountain life persistently lagged behind the plain."[42] The inhabitants of the Canary Islands were people of a Caucasian race who were living at a stone-age level when they were discovered by the Spaniards in the fifteenth century.[43] On the other side of the world, the similarly isolated Australian aborigines similarly lagged far behind the progress of the outside world.[44] Sub-Saharan Africans have been part of a worldwide pattern of isolated peoples lagging behind others in technology, organization and in other ways.

In addition to having many geographic barriers limiting their access to the peoples and cultures of other lands, sub-Saharan Africans also faced internal geographic barriers limiting their access to each other. The resulting internal cultural fragmentation is indicated by the fact that, while Africans are only about ten percent of the world's population, they have one-third of the world's languages.[45]

Eventually, the severe isolation of many sub-Saharan Africans was ended in the modern era, as that of other severely isolated peoples was ended, but that was after millennia in which these isolated peoples had developed whole ways of life very different from the ways of life that developed among those peoples of Europe and Asia who had far greater access to a far wider cultural universe. Moreover, cultures— whole ways of life— do not simply evaporate when conditions change, whether among Africans or others.

Long-standing and deep-seated cultural differences can become cultural barriers, even after the geographical barriers that created cultural isolation have been overcome with the growth of modern transportation and communication. As distinguished cultural historian Oscar Handlin put it: "men are not blank tablets upon which the environment inscribes a culture which can readily be erased to make way for a new inscription."[46] As another noted historian put it: "We do not live in the past, but the past in us."[47]

Even the geographic differences between Eastern Europe and Western Europe[48] have left the peoples of Eastern Europe with a lower standard of living than that of Western Europeans for centuries, including in our own times a larger economic disparity between the people in these two regions of Europe than the per capita income disparity between blacks and whites in the United States.[49] As Professor Angelo Codevilla of Boston University put it, "a European child will have a very different life depending on whether that baby was born east or west of a line that starts at the Baltics and stretches southward along Poland's eastern border, down Slovakia's western border and along the eastern border of Hungary, then continues down through the middle of Bosnia to the Adriatic Sea."[50] Both geography and history have for centuries presented very different opportunities to people born east and west of that line.[51]

In addition to the inherent geographic advantages that Western Europe has had over Eastern Europe— for example, more navigable waterways leading to the open seas, with Western European rivers and harbors not being frozen over as often or as long in winter as rivers and harbors in Eastern Europe, due to the warming effect of the Gulf Stream on Western Europe— another major historic advantage growing out of geography is that Western Europe was more readily accessible to invasion by Roman conquerors. Despite the ruthless slaughters in those conquests and the subsequent brutal oppressions by the Roman overlords, among the lasting advantages which the Roman conquests brought to Western Europe were Roman letters, so that Western European languages had written versions, centuries before the languages of Eastern Europe did. To the enormous advantages of literacy, as such, Western Europeans had the further advantage of a far greater accumulation of written knowledge in their languages, even after the languages of Eastern Europe began to develop written versions, but still had not yet caught up with the centuries-long accumulations of knowledge written in Western European languages.

Literacy was not the only thing that moved from west to east in Europe. So did coins, printing presses, castles, crossbows, paved streets, and vaccinations, among other economic and social advances. But all of this took time, sometimes centuries. Moreover, people from Western Europe— Germans, Jews and others— were often a majority of the population in Eastern European cities in earlier centuries, while Slavs remained a huge majority in the surrounding countrysides. For example, before 1312 the official records of the city of Cracow were kept in German— and the transition, at that point, was to Latin. Only decades later did Poles become a majority of the population in Cracow.[52] The towns of medieval East Central Europe were often cultural enclaves of foreigners— again, mostly Germans, but with many Jews as well and, in the Balkans, Greeks and Armenians, joined in later centuries by Turks.[53]

In short, there has been for centuries, not only a disparity between the opportunities and advances in the two halves of Europe, but great disparities within Eastern Europe itself between the indigenous peoples of the region and the transplanted Western Europeans living in Eastern Europe, the Baltic and the Balkans. Neither genes nor discrimination are necessary to explain this situation, though some intellectuals and politicians have chosen to claim that the differences have been due to race and others have chosen to blame social injustices. Many other racial and other groups in many other parts of the world have likewise ended up with large disparities in opportunities and achievements, for reasons that range across a wide spectrum and cannot be reduced to genes or injustices.

There is no need to replace genetic determinism with geographic determinism. While there are other factors which operate against the presumed equality of developed capabilities among people with equal potential, the point here is that geography alone is enough to prevent equality of developed capabilities, even if all races have identical potentialities and there is no discrimination. Nor is it necessary to determine the relative weights of geographic, demographic, cultural and other factors, when the more fundamental point is that each of these factors makes equal outcomes among races, classes or other subdivisions of the human species less likely.

Historical happenstances— the fact that certain decisive battles could easily have gone the other way and changed the future of whole nations and races— are among those other factors. Had the battle of Tours in 732 or the siege of Vienna in 1529 gone the other way, this could be a very different world today. But these other factors besides geography tend to remove equal developed capabilities even further from the realm of reality. Moreover, since the geography of the planet is not something "socially constructed," the misfortunes of lagging groups are not automatically a *social* injustice, even if they are injustices from some cosmic perspective, in the sense that many peoples have suffered serious deprivations through no fault of their own. Putting the onus on society by calling these deprivations a violation of "social justice" may be a verbal sop to those who are lagging, but it points them away from the paths by which other lagging groups have advanced themselves in the past.

Cultural attitudes, which in some societies create a rigid division between "women's work" and "men's work," or which make manual labor repugnant to people with education, or caste-ridden societies which drastically limit the sources from which particular talents can be drawn for accomplishing particular tasks, all affect the economic potential of a given society. A society which throws away the talents and potentialities of half its population by making many economic roles and endeavors off-limits to women can hardly be expected to match the economic performances of societies which do not restrict their own prospects like this. In a society with rigid class or caste divisions, the highly varied talents and potentialities which arise among individuals may not arise solely, or even predominantly, among those individuals who happen to be born within the rigid class or caste stratifications in which their talents and potentialities are appropriate, or in which they can reach fruition.

This is yet another reason why societies, races and civilizations are extremely unlikely to have identical achievements, even in the complete absence of genetic deficiencies or social injustices.

Examples of differences in particular capabilities and achievements, among groups, nations or civilizations around the world that are *not* due to discrimination could be multiplied almost without limit.[54] But what is crucial is that *no* examples of an even or statistically random distribution of groups in any country have been necessary to establish the prevailing dogma, the vision to which American employers, lenders and others must conform, at the risk of facing the heavy penalties of the law.

The views of those who reason as if discussing abstract people in an abstract world were exemplified in the dissenting opinion of Justice Ruth Bader Ginsburg in the 2011 U.S. Supreme Court case of *Wal-Mart v. Dukes*. Justice Ginsburg objected to Wal-Mart's "system of delegated discretion" in which individual managers in its stores across the country assess the job performances of the individuals working under them, and determine pay and promotions accordingly. This can lead to "discriminatory outcomes," she said, due to "arbitrary and subjective criteria."[55]

While discrimination can certainly affect outcomes, it does not follow that outcomes tell you whether or not there is discrimination. To believe the latter would be to say that those whose managerial decisions *convey* differences among groups are the *cause* of those differences among groups— that the groups themselves cannot possibly behave or perform differently. Moreover, to say that judgments made by those directly observing the behavior or performances of individuals are "subjective" is to imply that "objective" standards prescribed by distant third parties who have never laid eyes on the individuals involved would be more accurate.

That would be true if the individual workers' performances could be assessed from afar as if they were abstract people in an abstract world, rather than having all the differences that have been common for centuries among individuals and groups. Alternatively, it would be true if those making managerial decisions were so vastly inferior to distant third parties, either intellectually or morally, that surrogate decision-makers' unsubstantiated assumptions could be relied upon to produce more accurate assessments.

What does all this boil down to?

1. Grossly uneven distributions of racial, ethnic and other groups in numerous fields of endeavor have been common in countries around the world and for centuries of recorded history.

2. The even, proportional or statistically random distribution of these groups, which has been taken as a norm, deviations from which have been regarded as evidence of either genetic differences in ability (in the early 20th century) or as evidence of maltreatment by others (in the late 20th century) has seldom, if ever, been demonstrated empirically, or even been asked to be demonstrated.

3. The current widespread use of an even, proportional or statistically random distribution of groups in particular fields of endeavor, or at particular income levels, as a benchmark from which to measure maltreatment by others, is taken as axiomatic, not because of empirical support for this conclusion but because that benchmark is a foundation for other social beliefs and political agendas.

INTERTEMPORAL ABSTRACTIONS

Abstract people have an immortality which flesh-and-blood people have yet to achieve. Thus, a historian writing about the newly-created state of Czechoslovakia after the First World War, said that its policies regarding the ethnic groups within it were designed "to correct social injustice" and to "put right the historic wrongs of the seventeenth century"[56]— despite the fact that actual flesh-and-blood people from the seventeenth century had died long before, putting the redressing of their wrongs beyond the reach of human power.

Much the same kind of reasoning has continued to be ideologically powerful among the intelligentsia in twenty-first century America, who speak of "whites" and "blacks" as intertemporal abstractions with centuries-old issues to be redressed, rather than as flesh-and-blood individuals who take their sins and their sufferings with them to the grave. There is surely no more profound difference between human beings than the difference between the dead and the living. Yet even that difference is glided over verbally when speaking of races as intertemporal abstractions, of whom the current living generation is just the latest embodiment.

Unlike real people, abstract people can be sent "back" to places where they have never been. Thus millions of descendants of German families who had lived for centuries in parts of Eastern Europe and the Balkans were sent "back" to Germany after the Second World War, as the majority populations of these regions reacted bitterly to having been mistreated during Nazi occupation by imposing a massive ethnic cleansing of Germans from their midst after the war. Many of these flesh-and-blood individuals of German ancestry had never laid eyes on Germany, to which they were being sent "back." Only as intertemporal abstractions had they come from Germany.

It was much the same story with so-called Indian Tamils in Sri Lanka who, in the 1960s, were sent "back" to India, from which their ancestors had emigrated in the nineteenth century. Similarly, when people of Indian and Pakistani heritage were expelled from Uganda in the 1970s, most of them had been born in Uganda and more of them resettled in Britain than in India or Pakistan. Perhaps the most persistent efforts to repatriate intertemporal abstractions were nineteenth-century American proposals to free the slaves and then send them "back to Africa"— a continent which in most cases neither they nor their grandparents had ever seen.

Intertemporal abstractions are especially useful to those intellectuals who tend to conceive of social issues in terms which allow the intelligentsia to be on the side of the angels against the forces of evil. When intellectuals are unable to find enough contemporary grievances to suit their vision or agenda, they can mine the past for harm inflicted by some on others. By conceiving of those involved in the past as members of intertemporal abstractions, the intelligentsia can polarize contemporary descendants of those involved in past acts. The kind of society to which that leads is one in which a newborn baby enters the world supplied with prepackaged grievances against other babies born the same day.

It is hard to imagine anything more conducive to unending internal strife and a weakening of the bonds that hold a society together. The tragic history of territorial irredentism offers little reason for optimism about moral irredentism.

EQUALITY

Abstract people are implicitly either equal or at least randomly variable among individuals, which would amount to being equal as groups, where the groups are large enough for these random variations to preclude substantial *systematic* differences between groups containing millions of people. But actual flesh-and-blood people are remote from any such condition or ideal.

Inequalities of income, power, prestige, and other things have long preoccupied intellectuals, both as things to explain and things to correct. The time and attention devoted to these inequalities might suggest that equality is so common or so automatic that its absence is what requires an explanation.

Various causes of this apparently inexplicable inequality of outcomes have been suggested— racism, sexism, or class bias, for example. But seldom is it considered necessary to demonstrate the automatic equality which makes an explanation of its absence necessary. Anyone who suggests that individuals— or, worse yet, groups— are unequal in behavior or performance risks being written off intellectually and denounced morally as biased or bigoted toward those considered less than equal in some respects. Yet the empirical case for equality of consequential characteristics ranges from meager to non-existent.

Once the focus shifts from abstract potential to empirical capabilities, the notion of equality is not merely unproven but unlikely to the point of being absurd. How could people living in the Himalayas develop the seafaring skills of people living in ports around the Mediterranean? How could the Bedouins of the Sahara know as much about fishing as the Polynesians of the Pacific— or the Polynesians know as much about camels as the Bedouins? How could Eskimos be as proficient at growing tropical crops as the people of Hawaii or the Caribbean?

Such considerations are far more crucial for mundane knowledge than for academic knowledge. Ph.D.s in mathematics can have the same knowledge in Delhi as in Paris. However, in the world of mundane but consequential knowledge, how could an industrial revolution have originated in places which lack the key natural resources— iron ore and coal— and are too geographically inaccessible for those resources to be transported to them without prohibitive costs? The industrial revolution could hardly have begun in the Balkans or Hawaii, regardless of what people were living there— *and neither could the people in those places have developed the same industrial skills, habits and ways of life* at the same time as people in other places where the industrial revolution in fact began.

Differences among racial, national or other groups range from the momentous to the mundane, whether in the United States or in other countries around the world and down through the centuries.

Empirically observable skills have always been grossly unequal— which is to say, real people have never been even close to the equality of abstract people, when it comes to developed capabilities, as distinguished from abstract potential. Among the many different groups in countries around the world, very few have ever matched the major role played by the Jains from India in the cutting of diamonds for the world market, whether the Jains lived in India or in Amsterdam. People of German ancestry have been similarly prominent in the brewing of beer, whether in Germany or in the United States, where the best-selling brands of beer were created by people of German ancestry, as was true of China's famous Tsingtao beer. In nineteenth century Argentina, German beer drove English beer from the local market, while Germans also established breweries in Australia and Brazil, as they had brewed beer in the days of the Roman Empire.

Jews have been similarly prominent, if not predominant, in the apparel industry, whether in medieval Spain, the Ottoman Empire, Eastern Europe, Argentina or the United States. Yet intellectuals' emphasis on external circumstances over internal cultures led an academic historian to say that Jewish immigrants to the United States were fortunate that they arrived in this country just when the garment industry was about to take off.[57] The same coincidence seems to have occurred in a number of other countries, just as the arrival of large numbers of overseas Chinese in various countries in Southeast Asia galvanized particular sectors of the economies there, and the arrival of the Huguenots galvanized the watch-making industry in seventeenth-century England.

Innumerable other examples could be cited, involving other groups in countries around the world. But none of that has made a dent in the intelligentsia's indignant responses when discovering statistical disparities in outcomes among groups. The burden of proof to the contrary is put on others, rather than on those whose presumptions are based on nothing more than reasoning as if they were discussing abstract people in an abstract world, and applying statistical techniques that would be appropriate to such homogeneous human beings or people who are in effect essentially random events, on which much statistical analysis is based.

Whatever the abstract potential of individuals and groups, the distinction between abstract potential and developed capabilities is not trivial, even though that distinction is often lost sight of, or is finessed, by intellectuals who speak in generalities about "equality." Abstract potential carries very little weight anywhere in the real world, when people are making decisions for themselves. Performance is what counts. What we want to know is what real people can actually do, not what abstract potential there is in abstract people.

The exceptional facility of intellectuals with abstractions, including the application of statistical probabilities to these abstractions, does not eliminate the difference between those abstractions and real people in the real world. Nor does it guarantee that what is true of those abstractions is necessarily true of reality, much less that intellectuals' sophisticated visions about these abstractions should over-ride other people's very different direct experiences in the real world. Intellectuals may indeed dismiss the "perceptions" of others and label them as "stereotypes" or "myths," but that is not the same as proving them wrong empirically, even if a remarkable number of intellectuals act as if it does.

Behind the widespread practice of regarding group differences in demographic "representation" in various occupations, institutions, or income levels as evidence of social barriers or discrimination, there is the implicit notion that the groups themselves cannot be different, or that any differences are the fault of "society," which must correct its own mistakes or sins.

Since there is no one named "society," what such intellectuals usually turn to for redress is the government. Implicit in all this is the assumption that there is something wrong about individuals and groups being different in their empirical capabilities, since their abstract potentials have been presumed to be the same.

In addition to intergroup differences in particular occupational skills, there are large and consequential differences in median age. Some groups differ by a decade in median age and others differ by two decades or more.[58] Large differences among groups in median age occur both within nations and between nations. Just among Asian Americans, the median age ranges from 43 years old for Japanese Americans to 24 years old for Americans of Cambodian ancestry.[59] Among nations, the median age in Germany and Japan is over forty while the median age in Afghanistan and Yemen is under twenty.[60] How a group of people, whether races or nations, whose median ages are decades apart could have the same knowledge, skills and experience— or have the same outcomes that depend on such knowledge, skills and experience— is a question that need not be faced by those who proceed as if they are discussing abstract people in an abstract world. None of these empirical facts disturbs the vision of abstract equality or curbs the outrage of the intelligentsia at discovering the real world consequences of these differences, which are just some of the many differences among races, nations and other subdivisions of the human species.

When *some* of the many consequential differences among groups are taken into account and that still does not reduce their differences in outcomes to zero, the unexplained residual is more or less automatically attributed to discrimination. For example, when black and white Americans in the same income brackets were turned down for mortgage loans at different rates, that was enough for editorials in *USA Today* and in the *St. Louis Post-Dispatch*, among others, to conclude that this was due to racial discrimination, and for a front-page news story in the *New York Times* to imply as much.[61] But that ignores other economic variables affecting the acceptance or rejection of mortgage loan applications, such as credit scores, which are different on average between blacks and whites.

What most media accounts have also left out is that Asian Americans had higher average credit scores than those of whites, which in turn were higher than those of blacks. In 2000, when blacks were turned down for conventional mortgage loans at double the rate for whites, the whites were in turn denied conventional mortgage loans at nearly double the rate for Asian Americans.[62] But including Asian Americans in these comparisons would have undermined the racial discrimination theory. So would inclusion of the fact that banks owned by blacks also turned down black applicants— at a rate higher than the rejection rates of black applicants by white-owned banks.[63] All of these real world differences were avoided by reasoning as if discussing abstract people whose differences in outcomes could only be due to mistaken or malign decisions made by others.

Where concrete information is lacking or unstudied, equality tends to be the default assumption of the intelligentsia when comparing groups, no matter how many, or how large, are the inequalities that have already been found in factors that have been studied. Whether in a racial or other context, where some— sometimes just one— of these factors have been held constant and the differences in outcomes do not completely disappear, that is often taken as proof that bias or discrimination explains the remaining differences in outcomes.

The fundamental flaw in such reasoning can be illustrated in a non-controversial area such as baseball. There were two players on the 1927 New York Yankees with identical batting averages of .356, one of whom has remained famous to this day, while the other is almost completely forgotten. Their equality in one dimension in no way implied equality in other dimensions. In this case, one .356 hitter hit 6 home runs that year (Earle Combs) and the other hit 60 (Babe Ruth).

Similarly, when Lewis Terman's famous decades-long study of unusually high-IQ children assessed their achievements in adulthood, many had very high achievements but, as a later writer observed, "almost *none* of the genius children from the lowest social and economic class ended up making a name for themselves." Almost a third of these high-IQ children "from the other side of the tracks" had "a parent who had dropped out of school before the eighth grade."[64] They were like the other children in the sense of having IQs of 140 or above, but not in terms of the cultural background factors involved in high achievements.

The same principle applies in innumerable contexts, not only in American society but in other countries around the world. University students in India who came from families with similar incomes were found to come from families with very different levels of literacy when comparing students who were Dalits (formerly called "untouchables") with students who were caste Hindus— illiteracy being higher in the families of the Dalits.[65] Equality of income did not imply equality of other consequential characteristics. In other countries, people with the "same" education— measured quantitatively— have had very different *qualities* of education, whether measured by their own performances as students, by their choices of specialization or by the quality rankings of the institutions in which they were educated.[66] Only abstract people in an abstract world are the same.

In a world where consequential characteristics are multi-dimensional, equality in one dimension says nothing about whether other dimensions are equal or unequal between particular groups. Yet a vast literature on socioeconomic "disparities" and "gaps"— transformed verbally into "inequities," if not deliberate discrimination— proceeds as if the causes behind these effects must be external, especially if these differences in outcomes do not disappear completely when holding constant some given dimension or dimensions of the factors involved, such as income among black and white mortgage loan applicants.

Equality is one of the most widespread and long-lived ideals, especially among modern intellectuals.[*] Its variety of very different, and even mutually contradictory, meanings may be part of the reason for its longevity, since many people with very different substantive ideas can espouse and believe in equality as a vague generality. Moreover, the same individual can shift from one concept of equality to another as the convenience of the argument might require.

---

[*] This sometimes extends to avoidance of titles that distinguish either varying achievements or the varying personal relationships among individuals. Calling a stranger named William Smith "Bill"— instead of Mr. Smith, Dr. Smith, Colonel Smith or whatever his title might be— is just one of these increasingly common practices which verbally banish differences. This can extend to children calling adults, including their teachers or even parents, by their first names. But a mother is not just another woman named Mary or Elizabeth. Her relationship to the child is one unlike any other that the child is likely to encounter in a lifetime. Moreover, a given individual will have many different names, denoting widely varying relationships with others. William Smith, for example, may be Uncle Bill to his siblings' children, "Billy" as a small child, "honey" to his wife, "coach" to a Little League team and so on. These are often relationships that people on both ends of a relationship may need to keep in mind, in order to remind themselves that they are not just abstract people in an abstract world but people with limited roles or particular responsibilities *vis-à-vis* particular others.

Like many emotionally powerful concepts, equality is seldom defined with any precision. Equality might mean that everyone should be regarded as equally important, that their interests should be regarded as being of equal concern to others. Thus a baby's interests are as important as an adult's, even though the baby lacks the capabilities of an adult. Alternatively, equality might mean that everyone should be treated equally— that they should all be judged by the same criteria and rewarded or punished by the same standards. Another meaning of equality might be that the people themselves are equal in either their potential or their developed capabilities. Yet another meaning of equality might be that people are entitled to equal prospects of success or reward, even if that requires those with lesser potentialities or capabilities to receive compensatory advantages, as Condorcet advocated in the eighteenth century[67] and as John Rawls advocated in the twentieth century.[68]

The point here is that all these very different notions are encompassed by the undefined word "equality." Abstract people may have equality in all these senses simultaneously, but that is very different from saying that the same is true of flesh-and-blood human beings in the real world.

Similar principles are involved when discussing differences between the sexes, as well as differences among races or other subdivisions of the human species. The fact that the widest income differences between the sexes are between men with children and women with children[69] is hardly surprising, when recognizing the mundane fact that how those children are produced and raised differs radically between mothers and fathers, however much fathers and mothers can be made verbally equivalent as parents when discussing people in the abstract.

Empirical data suggest that being a mother increases the importance of a particular job's working conditions relative to the importance of its pay— especially when some higher paid occupations require very long hours of work, including unpredictable demands to work nights and weekends, or to fly off to other cities or countries on short notice for indefinite amounts of time, as high-powered lawyers or executives may have to do. But to be a father with a family to support can have the opposite effect of being a mother, making higher pay more important to fathers than to single men, childless husbands or to women— all of whom have lower incomes than fathers— even if that means taking jobs whose working conditions are not particularly desirable or even as safe as most jobs. More than 90 percent of job-related deaths occur among men, for example.[70] Given their respective incentives and constraints, the fact that parenthood has opposite effects on the incomes of women and men is by no means mysterious.

With sexes, as with races, taking more causal factors into account tends to substantially reduce statistical differences in incomes, sometimes to the vanishing point, where a very large number of relevant factors can be both identified and quantified— which is by no means always possible as a practical matter. But, where an unexplained residual difference in outcomes remains after taking various factors into account, christening that unexplained residual "discrimination" presupposes that either all the relevant dimensions have been identified and reliably quantified by observers or that the remaining unidentified relevant factors are equal, despite how unequal the identified relevant factors may have been.

In the case of income differences between women and men, where the very same factor— parenthood— can have opposite effects on income, holding parenthood constant as a factor does not mean comparing women and men who are comparable. Where women and men are truly comparable— for example, when they are older than the usual child-bearing years and both have worked continuously and full-time in the same occupations— various studies have found the women making the same incomes as the men, or more than the men.[71] Diana Furchtgott-Roth, a Senior Fellow at the Hudson Institute, has pointed out that empirical studies using fewer explanatory variables concluded that there was sex discrimination more often than studies that used a larger number of explanatory variables.[72]

In general, income differences between women and men are more often found where they do different jobs, or have the same jobs but with different working conditions, work different numbers of hours annually, have differences in continuous years of employment, or have other such work-related differences, rather than where they do the same job, under the same conditions and with the same qualifications and experience.[73] But mundane reasons for income differences between the sexes have no such attraction for much of the intelligentsia as external reasons, such as employer discrimination, which allow the intelligentsia to be on the side of the angels against the forces of evil.

With both the sexes and the races, empirical evidence may not only be mishandled but even deemed unnecessary, as exemplified in the phrase "glass ceiling" as an explanation for the under-representation of women in higher levels of employment. Defined as an "invisible but impenetrable barrier between women and the executive suite,"[74] the term "glass ceiling" implies that even in the absence of any tangible empirical evidence of that barrier— since it is "invisible"— we are to accept its existence, much as people in a well-known fable were to accept the emperor's new clothes.[*] In other words, the whole question of the existence or effect of the posited barrier is taken out of the realm of empirical evidence. Such verbal virtuosity simply preempts the question as to whether there is an internal reason or an external obstruction that explains the differential advancement of women to higher management positions.

Where that question is *not* finessed aside by sheer assertion, however, the evidence against the external barrier theory is considerable. For example, Diana Furchtgott-Roth has pointed out that the "top corporate jobs require one to be in the pipeline for at least 25 years" and that "less than 5 percent of the qualified candidates for these jobs were women."[75] A Canadian study found similar differences between male and female executives there.[76] In the United States, a report by the Government Accountability Office found that female managers were younger than male managers, had less education and were more often part-time workers.[77] Numerous other specific differences in both the qualifications and the preferences of women have been found in other studies.[78]

---

[*] Similar reasoning— or lack of reasoning— is common in discussions of discriminatory barriers as the reason for the underrepresentation of particular racial or ethnic groups. The absence of evidence is taken to mean that discrimination has simply become "more subtle, less overt, and harder to detect." Thomas J. Espenshade and Alexandria Walton Radford, *No Longer Separate, Not Yet Equal: Race and Class in Elite College Admission and Campus Life* (Princeton: Princeton University Press, 2009), p. 1.

The point here is not that the intelligentsia were mistaken or ill-informed on particular issues. The more fundamental point is that, by proceeding as if discussing abstract people in an abstract world, intellectuals evade the responsibility and the arduous work of learning the real facts about real people in the real world— facts which often explain the discrepancies between what intellectuals see and what they would prefer to see.

Many of what are called social problems are differences between the theories of intellectuals and the realities of the world— differences which many intellectuals interpret to mean that it is the real world that is wrong and needs changing. Apparently their theories, and the vision behind them, cannot be wrong.

Chapter 8

Arguments Without Arguments

We fight for and against not men and things as they are, but for and against the caricatures we make of them.

J.A. Schumpeter[1]

Intellectuals with opposing visions are usually well equipped, in terms of mental ability, to argue their respective beliefs and thereby enlighten others while debating each other. What is remarkable, however, is how many substitutes for doing that have been found. While the conflicts between the tragic vision and the vision of the anointed can lead to innumerable arguments on a wide range of issues, these conflicts can also lead to presentations of views that take the outward form of an argument without the inner substance of facts or analysis— in other words, arguments without arguments.

Although such tactical evasions are in principle available to intellectuals in any part of the ideological spectrum, only when these evasions are deployed in defense of the prevailing vision are they likely to be uncritically accepted by the intelligentsia, or even by the lay public, which has heard the prevailing vision so much through the media, the educational system and in political discussions that familiarity gives that vision an acceptance which competing visions cannot expect to achieve with a similar lack of substantive arguments.

Although the talents and education of intellectuals would seem to enable them to be proficient at engaging in logically structured arguments, using empirical evidence to analyze contending ideas, many of their political or ideological views are promoted by verbal virtuosity in *evading* both structured arguments and empirical evidence. Among their many arguments without arguments are claims that opposing views are "simplistic." In addition, there are their own arbitrary assertions of "rights" and their caricaturing of adversaries as unworthy and as believing in things they never expressed a belief in, including in some cases things that are the direct opposite of their expressed beliefs. There is also what is perhaps the most widespread of the many arguments without arguments— "social justice."

"SIMPLISTIC" ARGUMENTS

Many among the intelligentsia dismiss opponents' arguments as "simplistic"— not as a conclusion from counter-evidence or counter-arguments, but in *lieu* of counter-evidence or counter-arguments. It is a very effective debating tactic. With one word, it preempts the intellectual high ground without offering anything substantive. Using that word insinuates, rather than demonstrates, that a more complex explanation is more logically consistent or more empirically valid. But the fact that one argument may be simpler than another says nothing about which argument reaches conclusions that turn out to be validated by empirical evidence more often. Certainly the explanation of many physical phenomena— the sun setting over the horizon, for example— by the argument that the earth is round is simpler than the more complex explanations of the same phenomena by members of the Flat Earth Society. Evasions of the obvious can become very complex.

Before an explanation can be *too* simple, it must first be wrong. But often the fact that some explanation seems too simple becomes a *substitute* for showing that it is wrong. For example, when Professor Orley Ashenfelter, an economist at Princeton University, began to predict the prices of particular vintages of wine, based solely on weather statistics during the grapes' growing season, without bothering to taste the wines or to consult experts who had tasted the wines, his method was dismissed as simplistic by wine connoisseurs, one of whom referred to the "self-evident silliness"[2] of this method. Nevertheless, Professor Ashenfelter's price predictions have turned out to be substantiated more often than those of wine experts.[3]

Only after a given method has turned out to be wrong is it legitimate to call it "simplistic." Otherwise, its use of smaller amounts of information to produce validated conclusions is greater efficiency. But the term "simplistic" has become a widely used argument without an argument, a way of dismissing opposing views without confronting them with either evidence or analysis.

Virtually any answer to virtually any question can be made to seem simplistic by *expanding* the question to unanswerable dimensions and then deriding the now inadequate answer. For example, in the 1840s, an Austrian doctor collected statistics showing a substantial difference in mortality rates among women in maternity clinics in Vienna when they were examined by doctors who had washed their hands before examining them and doctors who had not. He sought to get all doctors to wash their hands before examining patients. But his suggestion was rejected, essentially as being simplistic, using a kind of argument that is still with us today. He was challenged to explain *why* washing one's hands would affect maternal mortality— and, since this was before the germ theory of diseases was developed and accepted, he could not do so.[4]

In short, the question was expanded to the point where it could not be answered (at the current state of knowledge), thereby making any answer seem "simplistic." However, the real issue was *not* whether the statistically minded doctor could explain the larger question but whether his evidence on the more modest and mundane question was valid— and could therefore save lives, based on empirical facts alone. The danger of committing the *post hoc* fallacy could have been easily avoided by continuing to collect data on whether more washing of hands by more doctors reduced current maternal mortality rates.

Today, those who reject stronger police action and more severe punishment as ways of dealing with crime, and who prefer social programs and rehabilitation efforts instead, often stigmatize the traditional "law and order" approach as "simplistic" by *expanding* the question to that of finding the "root causes" of crime, a question that police action and punishment cannot answer. Neither may alternative theories provide an answer that is convincing to those who require something more than an answer whose only basis is consonance with the prevailing vision. But the substitution of a much larger and more sweeping question for the more pragmatic and empirical question of which alternative approach to crime control has a better track record accomplishes the tactical purpose of derailing an alternative to the prevailing vision by making the alternative seem simplistic.

Ironically, many of those who emphasize the complexities of real-world problems and issues nevertheless often also regard people with opposing views of those problems and issues as either intellectually or morally unworthy. In other words, despite an emphasis on the complexities involved, these problems or issues are *not* regarded as being so complex that a different person could weigh the various probabilities or values differently and legitimately arrive at a different conclusion.

A variation on the theme of opponents' "simplistic" arguments is to say that whatever they advocate is "no panacea"— as indeed nothing is a panacea or else, by definition, all the problems of the world would already have been solved. When the collapse of the Communist bloc in Eastern Europe left Czechoslovakia celebrating its freedom, *New York Times* columnist Tom Wicker cautioned that freedom is "not a panacea; and that Communism has failed does not make the Western alternative perfect, or even satisfying for millions of those who live under it."[5]

Another variation on this theme includes the assertion that there was never a "golden age," often said in answer to people who never claimed that there was, but who happened to think that some past practice produced better results than some present practice. Instead of offering evidence that the present practice produces better results, panaceas and golden ages are dismissed. Sometimes the same notion is expressed by saying that we cannot or should not "turn back the clock." But unless one accepts as dogma that all things subsequent to some arbitrary date are automatically better than all things prior to that date, this is another evasion of specifics, another argument without an argument.

UNWORTHY OPPONENTS

Because the vision of the anointed is a vision of themselves as well as a vision of the world, when they are defending that vision they are not simply defending a set of hypotheses about external events, they are in a sense defending their souls— and the zeal and even ruthlessness with which they may defend their vision are not surprising under these circumstances. But for people with opposite views, who may for example believe that most things work out better if left to such systemic processes as free markets, families, and traditional values, these are just a set of hypotheses about external events, rather than badges of moral superiority, so there is no such huge personal ego stake in whether or not those hypotheses are confirmed by empirical evidence. Obviously, everyone would prefer to be proved right rather than proved wrong, but the point here is that there are no such comparable ego stakes involved among believers in the tragic vision.

This asymmetry between the two visions may help explain a striking pattern that goes back at least two centuries— the greater tendency of those with the vision of the anointed to see those they disagree with as enemies who are morally lacking. While there are individual variations in this, as with most things, there are nevertheless general patterns, which many have noticed, both in our times and in earlier centuries. For example, a contemporary account has noted:

> Disagree with someone on the right and he is likely to think you obtuse, wrong, foolish, a dope. Disagree with someone on the left and he is more likely to think you selfish, a sell-out, insensitive, possibly evil.[6]

Supporters of both visions, by definition, believe that those with the opposing vision are mistaken. But that is not enough for those with the vision of the anointed. It has long been taken for granted by those with the vision of the anointed that their opponents are lacking in compassion. Moreover, there was no felt need to test that belief empirically.

As far back as the eighteenth century, the difference between supporters of the two visions in this regard was apparent in a controversy between Thomas Malthus and William Godwin. Malthus said of his opponents, "I cannot doubt the talents of such men as Godwin and Condorcet. I am unwilling to doubt their candour."[7] But when Godwin referred to Malthus, he called Malthus "malignant," questioned "the humanity of the man," and said "I profess myself at a loss to conceive of what earth the man was made."[8]

Edmund Burke was a landmark figure among those with the tragic vision but, despite his all-out attacks on the *ideas* and *deeds* of the French Revolution, Burke nevertheless said of those with the opposing vision that they "may do the worst of things, without being the worst of men."[9] Similarly in eighteenth-century America, the first essay in *The Federalist*— a publication permeated with the tragic vision— declared: "So numerous indeed and so powerful are the causes which serve to give a false bias to the judgment, that we, upon many occasions, see wise and good men on the wrong as well as on the right side of questions of the first magnitude to society"— and added, "we are not always sure that those who advocate the truth are influenced by purer principles than their antagonists."[10]

It would be hard, if not impossible, to find similar statements about ideological adversaries from those with the vision of the anointed, either in the eighteenth century or today. Yet such a view of opponents— as mistaken, or even dangerously mistaken, but not necessarily evil personally— has continued to be common among those with the tragic vision.

When Friedrich Hayek in 1944 published *The Road to Serfdom*, his landmark challenge to the prevailing social vision among the intelligentsia, setting off an intellectual and political counter-revolution later joined by Milton Friedman, William F. Buckley and others intellectually and by Margaret Thatcher and Ronald Reagan politically, he characterized his adversaries as "single-minded idealists" and "authors whose sincerity and disinterestedness are above suspicion."[11] Clearly, however, sincerity was not considered sufficient to prevent opponents from being considered to be not only mistaken but dangerously mistaken, as illustrated by Hayek's belief that they were putting society on "the road to serfdom."

In the tenth anniversary edition of Charles Murray's devastating critique of social welfare policies— *Losing Ground*— he said that before writing that book "I had been working for years with people who ran social programs at street level, and knew the overwhelming majority of them to be good people trying hard to help."[12] Again, it would be difficult, if not impossible, to find similar statements about people with opposing views among those with the vision of the anointed, who so often see themselves as being on the side of the angels against the forces of evil.

Similarly, Winston Churchill never questioned the good intentions of those like Prime Minister Neville Chamberlain who had ignored his warnings about the dangers from Nazi Germany throughout the 1930s, and whose policies ended up getting Britain into the largest and most bloody war in history. Writing in his six-volume *History of the Second World War*, Churchill characterized what had happened as a "sad tale of wrong judgments formed by well-meaning and capable people."[13] At the time of Chamberlain's death in 1940, Churchill rose in the House of Commons to say:

> The only guide to a man is his conscience; the only shield to his memory is the rectitude and sincerity of his actions. It is very imprudent to walk through life without this shield, because we are so often mocked by the failure of our hopes and the upsetting of our calculations; but with this shield, however the fates may play, we march always in the ranks of honour. . . . Neville Chamberlain acted with perfect sincerity. . .[14]

Even in the midst of a political campaign in 1945, when Churchill warned of authoritarian rule if the opposing Labor Party won, he added that this was not because they wanted to reduce people's freedom but because "they do not see where their theories are leading them."[15] Similar concessions to the sincerity and good intentions of opponents can be found in Milton Friedman and other exponents of the constrained or tragic vision. But such a view of ideological opponents has been much rarer among those with the vision of the anointed, where the presumed moral and/or intellectual failings of opponents have been more or less a staple of discourse from the eighteenth century to the present.[16] When British journalist Edmund Morel ran for Parliament in 1922 against Winston Churchill, Morel said that he looked upon Churchill "as such a personal force for evil that I would take up the fight against him with a whole heart."[17]

While sincerity and humane feelings are often denied to ideological opponents by those with the vision of the anointed, whether or not opposition to particular policies, such as minimum wage laws or rent control laws, for example, is in fact due to a lack of compassion for the poor is irrelevant to the question whether the arguments for or against such policies have either empirical or analytical validity. Even if it could be proved to a certainty that opponents of these and other "progressive" policies were veritable Scrooges, or even venal, that would still be no answer to the arguments they make. Yet claims that opponents are racist, sexist, homophobic or "just don't get it" are often advanced by the intelligentsia today in lieu of specific refutations of their specific arguments.

"What often distinguishes liberals from others," according to best-selling author Andrew Hacker, is that they are "ready to share some of what they have with others less fortunate than themselves."[18] This is not a view peculiar to Professor Hacker. It reflects an opinion that was widespread among those with the vision of the anointed before he was born. But here, as elsewhere, the power of a vision is shown not by the evidence offered in favor of it, but precisely by the lack of any sense of need for evidence— in this case, evidence of the lesser humanitarianism among conservatives opposed to "progressive" policies.

An empirical study by Professor Arthur C. Brooks of Syracuse University, to test the extent to which liberals and conservatives in America donated money, blood, and time to philanthropic endeavors, found that conservatives donated on average both a larger amount of money and a higher percentage of their incomes (which were slightly lower than liberals' incomes) to philanthropic causes, that they donated more hours of their time as volunteers, and that they donated far more blood.[19] It might come as a surprise to many among the intelligentsia that Ronald Reagan donated a higher percentage of his income to philanthropic causes than did either Ted Kennedy or Franklin D. Roosevelt,[20] though that is in fact consistent with a much larger empirical pattern, however inconsistent it is with the prevailing vision.

This, of course, in no way proves that conservatives' arguments on social or political issues are more valid. What it does show is how far wrong people can go when they believe what is convenient for their vision and see no need to test such convenient assumptions against any empirical evidence. The fact that the assumption that conservatives were less concerned about other people's well-being prevailed so strongly and so unquestioningly for so long— literally for centuries— before even being tested, reinforces the point.

Similarly, when those with the vision of the anointed advocate disarmament and international agreements among potential adversary nations as the way to preserve peace, and are opposed by those with the tragic vision who advocate military deterrence and military alliances as the way to preserve peace, these are seldom seen as simply different hypotheses about prospects and risks in the external world. Those with the vision of the anointed have far more often, and for a very long time, seen such differences as signs of internal defects in those who disagree with them. Those who rely on stronger military forces, rather than disarmament or international agreements, to deter war have often been depicted by intellectuals as being in *favor* of war. Bertrand Russell, for example, said:

> If you address an audience of unselected men on the prevention of war, you are sure to come up against the middle-aged man who says, with a sneer: "Wars will never stop; it would be contrary to human nature". It is quite obvious that the man who says this delights in war, and would hate a world from which it had been eliminated.[21]

Nor was Bertrand Russell the only internationally known philosopher to make this kind of argument, as he did in 1936, against those who wanted Britain to rearm in the face of Hitler's massive buildup of military forces that would be unleashed just three years later to begin the Second World War. Earlier, back in the 1920s, when many intellectuals were in favor of international agreements renouncing war, such as the Kellogg-Briand Pact of 1928, those who opposed this approach were depicted by John Dewey as people "who believe in the war system."[22]

British writer J.B. Priestley likewise explained the failure of the pacifism common among his fellow intellectuals in the 1930s to catch on with the general public by saying that the public *favored war* out of "boredom," a boredom leading to "the widespread desire for some grand piece of excitement, for fiery speeches and flag-waving, for special editions, troop trains, casualty lists."[23] While acknowledging "the enormous sales" of the anti-war novel *All Quiet on the Western Front*, Priestley said of the people who read it, "The very horrors fascinated them," that the book was "too good a show as a tragic spectacle."[24]

In short, no matter what the empirical facts might be, they would simply be interpreted to fit Priestley's vision. The desires arbitrarily attributed to the public made it unnecessary for Priestley to confront opposing arguments or to confront the possibility that there were gaps or flaws in the arguments advanced by pacifists like himself, which left the public unconvinced that the pacifists' approaches— disarmament and treaties— were likely to reduce the dangers of war.

There has been a long history of a similar approach to issues of war and peace by intellectuals, going back at least as far as Godwin and Condorcet in the eighteenth century, and often depicting those who disagreed with them as people who favored war for some malign or irrational reason.[25] Moreover, that practice is as common today as in the past. In 2010, the *Chronicle of Higher Education* ran two feature articles on the theme, "America's Love Affair With War." One of these articles was titled "Why Conservatives Love War," going all the way back to Edmund Burke, while the other article referred to a "great American proclivity to war."[26] It so happens that Edmund Burke opposed the war that Britain fought to keep the American colonies from becoming independent, as did Adam Smith, who opposed having overseas colonies in the first place. Neither were pacifists, however, and both recognized that some wars had to be fought, which is hardly a "love affair with war."

The contrast between how those with the tragic vision and those with the vision of the anointed see opponents has been too widespread and too long-lasting to be attributed simply to differences in particular personalities, even if there are individual variations on both sides. The visions themselves involve very different personal ego stakes. To believe in the vision of the anointed is to be oneself one of the anointed. To believe in the tragic vision offers no such exaltation. Discordant evidence can embarrass believers in either vision but evidence or arguments against their vision presents, in addition, a threat against the ego for those with the vision of the anointed, who accordingly often treat opposing arguments as dismissively as they treat individuals with opposing views.

UNWORTHY ARGUMENTS

Not only are *people* who oppose the vision of the anointed deemed to be unworthy, *arguments* inconsistent with that vision are likewise often deemed

to be unworthy of serious engagement, and are accordingly treated as
something to be discredited, rather than answered. This process has produced
many examples of Schumpeter's observation about fighting not against people
and ideas as they are but against caricatures of those people and those ideas.
Among other things, this has produced two of the most fashionable political
catch phrases of our time, "tax cuts for the rich" and the "trickle-down theory."
An examination of these particular phrases may shed light on how other such
phrases are generated and keep getting repeated, without benefit of either
evidence or analysis— in short, as arguments without arguments.

At various times and places, particular individuals have argued that
existing tax *rates* are so high that the government could collect more tax
revenues if it lowered those tax rates, because the changed incentives would
lead to more economic activity, resulting in more tax revenues out of rising
incomes, even though the tax rate was lowered. This is clearly a testable
hypothesis that people might argue for or against, on either empirical or
analytical grounds. But that is seldom what happens.

Even when the particular tax cut proposal is to cut tax rates in all income
brackets, including reducing tax rates by a higher percentage in the lower
income brackets than in the upper income brackets, such proposals have
nevertheless often been characterized by their opponents as "tax cuts for the
rich" because the total amount of money saved by someone in the upper
income brackets is often larger than the total amount of money saved by
someone in the lower brackets. Moreover, the reasons for proposing such tax
cuts are verbally transformed from those of the advocates— namely,
changing economic behavior in ways that generate more output, income and
resulting higher tax revenues— to a very different theory attributed to the
advocates by the opponents, namely "the trickle-down theory."

No such theory has been found in even the most voluminous and learned
histories of economic theories, including J.A. Schumpeter's monumental
1,260-page *History of Economic Analysis*. Yet this non-existent theory has
become the object of denunciations from the pages of the *New York Times*
and the *Washington Post* to the political arena. It has been attacked by
Professor Paul Krugman of Princeton and Professor Peter Corning of
Stanford, among others, and similar attacks have been repeated as far away

as India.[27] It is a classic example of arguing against a caricature instead of confronting the argument actually made.

While arguments for cuts in high tax rates have often been made by free-market economists or by conservatives in the American sense, such arguments have also sometimes been made by people who were neither, including John Maynard Keynes[28] and President John F. Kennedy, who in fact got tax rates cut during his administration.[29] But the claim that these are "tax cuts for the rich," based on a "trickle-down theory" also has a long pedigree.

President Franklin D. Roosevelt's speech writer Samuel Rosenman referred to "the philosophy that had prevailed in Washington since 1921, that the object of government was to provide prosperity for those who lived and worked at the top of the economic pyramid, in the belief that prosperity would trickle down to the bottom of the heap and benefit all."[30] The same theme was repeated in the election campaign of 2008, when presidential candidate Barack Obama attacked what he called "the economic philosophy" which "says we should give more and more to those with the most and hope that prosperity trickles down to everyone else."[31]

When Samuel Rosenman referred to what had been happening "since 1921," he was referring to the series of tax rate reductions advocated by Secretary of the Treasury Andrew Mellon, and enacted into law by Congress during the decade of the 1920s. But the actual arguments advocated by Secretary Mellon had nothing to do with a "trickle-down theory." Mellon pointed out that, under the high income tax rates at the end of the Woodrow Wilson administration in 1921, vast sums of money had been put into tax shelters such as tax-exempt municipal bonds, instead of being invested in the private economy, where this money would create more output, incomes and jobs.[32] It was an argument that would be made at various times over the years by others— and repeatedly evaded by attacks on a "trickle-down" theory found only in the rhetoric of opponents.[33]

What actually followed the cuts in tax rates in the 1920s were rising output, rising employment to produce that output, rising incomes as a result and rising tax *revenues* for the government because of the rising incomes, even though the tax *rates* had been lowered. Another consequence was that people in higher income brackets not only paid a larger total amount of taxes than before, but a higher percentage of all taxes, after what have been called "tax cuts for the rich." There were somewhat similar results in later years after high tax rates were cut during the John F. Kennedy, Ronald Reagan and George W. Bush administrations.[34] After the 1920s tax cuts, it was not simply that investors' incomes rose but that this was now *taxable* income, since the lower tax rates made it profitable to get higher returns by investing outside of tax shelters.

The facts are unmistakably plain, for those who bother to check the facts. In 1921, when the tax rate on people making over $100,000 a year was 73 percent, the federal government collected a little over $700 million in income taxes, of which 30 percent was paid by those making over $100,000. By 1929, after a series of tax rate reductions had cut the tax rate to 24 percent on those making over $100,000, the federal government collected more than a billion dollars in income taxes, of which 65 percent was collected from those making over $100,000.[35]

There is nothing mysterious about this. Under the sharply rising tax rates during the Woodrow Wilson administration, fewer and fewer people reported high taxable incomes, whether by putting their money into tax-exempt securities or by any of the other ways of rearranging their financial affairs to minimize their tax liability. Under Woodrow Wilson's escalating income tax rates, to pay for the high costs of the First World War, the number of people reporting taxable incomes of more than $300,000— a huge sum in the money of that era— declined from well over a thousand in 1916 to fewer than three hundred in 1921. The total amount of taxable income earned by people making over $300,000 declined by more than four-fifths during those years.[36] Since these were years of generally rising incomes, as Mellon pointed out, there was no reason to believe that the wealthy were suddenly suffering drastic reductions in their own incomes,[37] but considerable reason to believe that they were receiving tax-exempt incomes that did not have to be reported under existing laws at that time.

By the Treasury Department's estimate, the money invested in tax-exempt securities had nearly tripled in a decade.[38] The total value of these securities was almost three times the size of the federal government's annual budget and more than half as large as the national debt.[39] Andrew Mellon pointed out that "the man of large income has tended more and more to invest his capital in such a way that the tax collector cannot reach it."[40] The value of tax-exempt securities, he said, "will be greatest in the case of the wealthiest taxpayer" and will be "relatively worthless" to a small investor, so that the cost of such tax losses by the government must fall on those other taxpayers "who do not or cannot take refuge in tax-exempt securities."[41] Mellon called it an "almost grotesque" result to have "higher taxes on all the rest in order to make up the resulting deficiency in the revenues."[42]

Secretary Mellon repeatedly sought to get Congress to end tax-exemptions for municipal bonds and other securities,[43] pointing out the inefficiencies in the economy that such securities created.[44] He also found it "repugnant" in a democracy that there should be "a class in the community which cannot be reached for tax purposes." Secretary Mellon said: "It is incredible that a system of taxation which permits a man with an income of $1,000,000 a year to pay not one cent to the support of his Government should remain unaltered."[45]

Congress, however, refused to put an end to tax-exempt securities.[*] They continued what Mellon called the "gesture of taxing the rich," while in fact high tax rates on paper were "producing less and less revenue each year and at the same time discouraging industry and threatening the country's future prosperity."[46] Unable to get Congress to end what he called "the evil of tax-exempt securities,"[47] Secretary Mellon sought to reduce the incentives for investors to divert their money from productive investments in the economy to putting it into safe havens in these tax shelters:

> Just as labor cannot be forced to work against its will, so it can be taken for granted that capital will not work unless the return is worth while. It will continue to retire into the shelter of tax-exempt bonds, which offer both security and immunity from the tax collector.[48]

---

[*] However economically inconsistent it was to have very high tax rates on high incomes, while providing a large loophole through which the wealthy could avoid paying those taxes, it was politically beneficial to elected officials, who could attract votes with class-warfare rhetoric and at the same time attract donations from the wealthy by providing an easy escape from actually paying these taxes— and sometimes any taxes at all.

In other words, high tax rates *that many people avoid paying* do not necessarily bring in as much revenue to the government as lower tax rates that more people are in fact paying, when these lower tax rates make it safe to invest their money where they can get a higher rate of return in the economy than they get from tax-exempt securities. The facts are plain: There were 206 people who reported annual taxable incomes of one million dollars or more in 1916. But, as the tax rates rose, that number fell to just 21 people by 1921. Then, after a series of tax rate cuts during the 1920s, the number of individuals reporting taxable incomes of a million dollars or more rose again to 207 by 1925.[49] Under these conditions, it should not be surprising that the government collected more tax revenue after tax rates were cut. Nor is it surprising that, with increased economic activity following the shift of vast sums of money from tax shelters into the productive economy, the annual unemployment rate from 1925 through 1928 ranged from a high of 4.2 percent to a low of 1.8 percent.[50]

The point here is not simply that the weight of evidence is on one side of the argument rather than the other but, more fundamentally, that *there was no serious engagement with the arguments actually advanced* but instead an evasion of those arguments by depicting them as simply a way of transferring tax burdens from the rich to other taxpayers. What Senators Robert La Follette and Burton K. Wheeler said in their political campaign literature during the 1924 election campaign— that "the Mellon tax plan" was "a device to relieve multimillionaires at the expense of other tax payers," and "a master effort of the special privilege mind," to "tax the poor and relieve the rich"[51]— would become perennial features of both intellectual and political discourse to the present day.

Even in the twenty-first century, the same arguments used by opponents of tax cuts in the 1920s were repeated in the book *Winner-Take-All Politics*, whose authors refer to "the 'trickle-down' scenario that advocates of helping the have-it-alls with tax cuts and other goodies constantly trot out."[52] No one who actually trotted out any such scenario was cited, much less quoted.

Repeatedly, over the years, the arguments of the proponents and opponents of tax rate reductions have been arguments about two fundamentally different things— namely (1) the distribution of *existing* incomes and existing tax liabilities versus (2) incentives to *increase* incomes by reducing tax rates, so as to get individuals and institutions to take their money out of tax shelters and invest it in the productive economy. Proponents and opponents of tax rate reductions not only had different arguments, they were arguments about very different things, and the two arguments largely went past each other untouched. Empirical evidence on what happened to the economy in the wake of those tax cuts in four different administrations over a span of more than eighty years has also been largely ignored by those opposed to what they call "tax cuts for the rich."

Confusion between reducing tax *rates* on individuals and reducing tax *revenues* received by the government has run through much of these discussions over these many years. Famed historian Arthur M. Schlesinger, Jr., for example, said that although Andrew Mellon advocated balancing the budget and paying off the national debt, he "inconsistently" sought a "reduction of tax rates."[53] In reality, the national debt was reduced, as more revenue came into the government under the lowered tax rates. The national debt was just under $24 billion in 1921 and it was reduced to under $18 billion in 1928.[54] Nor was Professor Schlesinger the only highly regarded historian to perpetuate economic confusion between tax rates and tax revenues.

Today, widely used textbooks by various well-known historians have continued to grossly misstate what was advocated in the 1920s and what the actual consequences were. According to the textbook *These United States* by Pulitzer Prize winner Professor Irwin Unger of New York University, Secretary of the Treasury Andrew Mellon, "a rich Pittsburgh industrialist," persuaded Congress to "reduce income tax rates at the upper levels while leaving those at the bottom untouched." Thus "Mellon won further victories for his drive to shift more of the tax burden from high-income earners to the middle and wage-earning classes."[55] But hard data show that, in fact, both the amount and the proportion of taxes paid by those whose net income was no higher than $25,000 went *down* between 1921 and 1929, while both the amount and the proportion of taxes paid by those whose net incomes were between $50,000 and $100,000 went up— and the amount and proportion of taxes paid by those whose net incomes were over $100,000 went up even more sharply.[56]

Another widely used textbook, co-authored by a number of distinguished historians, two of whom won Pulitzer Prizes, said of Andrew Mellon: "It was better, he argued, to place the burden of taxes on lower-income groups" and that a "share of the tax-free profits of the rich, Mellon reassured the country, would ultimately trickle down to the middle- and lower-income groups in the form of salaries and wages."[57] What Mellon actually said was that tax policy "must lessen, so far as possible, the burden of taxation on those least able to bear it."[58] He therefore proposed sharper percentage cuts in tax rates at the lower income levels[59]— and that was done. Mellon also proposed eliminating federal taxes on movie tickets, because such taxes were paid by "the great bulk of the people whose main source of recreation is attending the movies in the neighborhood of their homes."[60] In short, Mellon advocated the direct opposite of the policies attributed to him.

The very idea that profits "trickle down" to workers depicts the economic sequence of events in the opposite order from that in the real world. Workers must first be hired and commitments made to pay them, *before* there is any output produced to sell for a profit, and independently of whether that output subsequently sells for a profit or at a loss. With investments, whether they lead to a profit or a loss can often be determined only years later, and workers have to be paid in the meantime, rather than waiting for profits to "trickle down" to them. The real effect of tax rate reductions is to make the *future prospects* of profit look more favorable, leading to more *current* investments that generate more current economic activity and more jobs.

Those who attribute a trickle-down theory to others are attributing their own misconceptions to others, as well as distorting both the arguments used and the hard facts about what actually happened after the recommended policies were put into effect.

Another widely used history textbook, a best-seller titled *The American Nation* by Professor John Garraty of Columbia University, said that Secretary Mellon "opposed lower tax rates for taxpayers earning less than $66,000."[61] Still another best-selling textbook, *The American Pageant* with multiple authors, declared: "Mellon's spare-the-rich policies thus shifted much of the tax burden from the wealthy to the middle-income groups."[62]

There is no need to presume that the scholars who wrote these history textbooks were deliberately lying, in order to protect a vision. They may simply have relied on a peer consensus so widely held and so often repeated as to be seen as "well-known facts" requiring no serious re-examination. The results show how unreliable peer consensus can be, even when it is a peer consensus of highly intellectual people,* if those people share a very similar vision of the world and treat its conclusions as axioms rather than as hypotheses that need to be checked against facts. These history textbooks may also reflect the economic illiteracy of many leading scholars outside the field of economics, who nevertheless insist on proclaiming their conclusions on economic issues.

When widely recognized scholars have been so cavalier, it is hardly surprising that the media have followed suit. For example, *New York Times* columnist Tom Wicker called the Reagan administration's tax cuts "the old Republican 'trickle-down' faith."[63] *Washington Post* columnist David S. Broder called these tax cuts "feeding the greed of the rich" while "adding to the pain of the poor"— part of what he called the "moral meanness of the Reagan administration."[64] Under the headline, "Resurrection of Coolidge," another *Washington Post* columnist, Haynes Johnson, characterized the Reagan tax rate cuts as part of the "help-the-rich-first, and let-the-rest-trickle-down philosophies."[65]

John Kenneth Galbraith characterized the "trickle-down effect" as parallel to "the horse-and-sparrow metaphor, holding that if the horse is fed enough oats, some will pass through to the road for the sparrows."[66] Similar characterizations of a "trickle-down" theory were common in op-ed columns

---

* Such reliance on peer consensus has not been confined to historians or to our times. Even such a landmark intellectual figure as John Stuart Mill attacked the critics of the economic proposition known as Say's Law, without citing a single actual statement of those critics on that subject, while mischaracterizing their arguments, in his huge and hugely successful book, *Principles of Political Economy*. The peer consensus that John Stuart Mill relied on included the views of his father, James Mill, a defender of Say's Law and a contributor to the development of that law. See Thomas Sowell, *On Classical Economics* (New Haven: Yale University Press, 2006), pp. 135–136. As J.A. Schumpeter put it, in his *History of Economic Analysis*, "Mill, however modest on his own behalf, was not at all modest on behalf of his time." (J.A. Schumpeter, *History of Economic Analysis* [New York: Oxford University Press, 1954]), p. 530). In other words, John Stuart Mill relied on peer consensus among the leading economists of his time, instead of personally re-examining the writings of those economists who dissented from Say's Law.

by Leonard Silk, Alan Brinkley and other well-known writers of the time, as well as in *New York Times* editorials.[67]

When President George W. Bush proposed his tax rate cuts in 2001, citing the Kennedy administration and Reagan administration precedents,[68] denunciations of "trickle-down" economics came from, among others, Arthur M. Schlesinger, Jr., Paul Krugman, and Jonathan Chait. *Washington Post* columnist David S. Broder denounced "the financial bonanza that awaits the wealthiest Americans in the Bush plan."[69]

Implicit in the approach of both academic and media critics of what they call "tax cuts for the rich" and a "trickle-down theory" is a zero-sum conception of the economy, where the benefits of some come at the expense of others. That those with such a zero-sum conception of the economy often show little or no interest in the factors affecting the creation of wealth— as distinguished from their preoccupation with its distribution— is consistent with their vision, however inconsistent it is with the views of others who are focussed on the growth of the economy, as emphasized by both Presidents John F. Kennedy and Ronald Reagan, for example.

What is also inconsistent is attributing one's own assumptions to those who are arguing on the basis of entirely different assumptions. Challenging those other assumptions, or the conclusions which derive from them, on either analytical or empirical grounds would be legitimate, but simply attributing to them arguments that they never made is not.

In the 1960s, President Kennedy, like Andrew Mellon decades earlier, pointed out that "efforts to avoid tax liabilities" make "certain types of less productive activity more profitable than other more valuable undertakings" and "this inhibits our growth and efficiency." Therefore the "purpose of cutting taxes" is "to achieve the more prosperous, expanding economy."[70] *"Total output and economic growth"* were italicized words in the text of John F. Kennedy's address to Congress in January 1963, urging cuts in tax rates.[71] Much the same theme was repeated yet again in President Ronald Reagan's February 1981 address to a joint session of Congress, pointing out that "this is not merely a shift of wealth between different sets of taxpayers." Instead, basing himself on a "solid body of economic experts," he expected that "real production in goods and services will grow."[72]

Even when empirical evidence substantiates the arguments made for cuts in tax rates, such facts are not treated as evidence relevant to testing a disputed hypothesis, but as isolated curiosities. Thus, when tax revenues rose in the wake of the tax rate cuts made during the George W. Bush administration, the *New York Times* reported: "An unexpectedly steep rise in tax revenues from corporations and the wealthy is driving down the projected budget deficit this year."[73] Expectations, of course, are in the eye of the beholder. However surprising the increases in tax revenues may have been to the *New York Times*, they are exactly what proponents of reducing high tax rates have been expecting, not only from these particular tax rate cuts, but from similar reductions in high tax rates at various times going back more than three-quarters of a century.

THE RHETORIC OF "RIGHTS"

Much advocacy by intellectuals involve assertions of "rights," for which no basis is asked or given. Neither constitutional provisions, legislative enactments, contractual obligations, nor international treaties are cited as bases for these "rights." Thus there are said to be "rights" to "a living wage," "decent housing," "affordable health care," and numerous other benefits, material and psychic. That such things may be desirable is not the issue. The real issue is why such things are regarded as obligations— the logical corollary of rights— upon other people who have agreed to no such obligation to provide these things. If someone has a right, someone else has an obligation. But the proposed right to a "living wage," for example, is not based on any obligation agreed to by an employer. On the contrary, this "right" is cited as a reason why government should force the employer to pay what third parties would like to see paid.

"Rights," as the term is used ideologically, imply no mutual agreement of any kind, whether among individuals, enterprises or nations. Captured terrorists, for example, have been deemed by some to have a right to the same treatment prescribed for prisoners of war by the Geneva Convention, even though terrorists have neither agreed to the terms of the Geneva

Convention nor are among those whom the signers of that convention designated as covered by the convention. Again, "rights," as the term is used ideologically, are ultimately assertions of arbitrary authority by third parties to prescribe things that others have never agreed to.

The same principle is expressed when terms like "social responsibility" or "social contract" are used to describe what third parties want done, regardless of whether any others have agreed to do it. Thus business is said to have a "social responsibility" to provide various benefits to various individuals or to society at large, regardless of whether or not those businesses have chosen to assume such a responsibility. Nor are these responsibilities necessarily based on laws that have been enacted. On the contrary, the asserted "responsibilities" are the basis for advocating the passing of such laws, even though the responsibilities have no basis themselves, other than the fact that third parties want them imposed.

The same principle can be seen in assertions of figurative "promises," as in the title of *The Promise of American Life* by Herbert Croly, the Progressive-era first editor of the *New Republic* magazine. These "promises" are found nowhere except in the desires of Herbert Croly and like-minded Progressives, including some a hundred years later.[74] Similarly with "contracts" that no one has signed or even seen. Thus Social Security has been described as a "contract between the generations" when, obviously, generations yet unborn could not have agreed to any such contract.

Legal obligations can of course be imposed on unborn generations, whether through Social Security or the national debt, but the argument is not about what is physically possible but what has any logical or empirical foundation. To say that it has a moral foundation, without providing any specifics, is only to say that some people feel that way. But there would be no issue in the first place unless other people felt differently. Nor are the asserted "rights," "social responsibilities," or fictitious "contracts" or "promises" necessarily based on claims of demonstrable majorities favoring such things. On the contrary, they are asserted as reasons why the majority or political leaders or the courts *ought* to impose what third parties want imposed. They are arguments without arguments.

Sometimes the term "social justice" is used to provide the semblance of a basis for these arbitrary assertions. But "justification," even as the term is used in carpentry or printing, means aligning one thing with another. But what are these assertions to be aligned with, other than the feelings, visions or groupthink that happen to prevail currently among the intelligentsia? The groupthink of the intelligentsia is still groupthink and their prejudices are still prejudices.

Justice Oliver Wendell Holmes said, "the word 'right' is one of the most deceptive of pitfalls" and "a constant solicitation to fallacy."[75] But while Justice Holmes rejected abstract rights, he regarded those rights actually "established in a given society" to have a different basis.[76] Holmes was particularly troubled about the notion that judges should be enforcing abstract rights for which there was no concrete basis:

> There is a tendency to think of judges as if they were independent mouthpieces of the infinite, and not simply directors of a force that comes from the source that gives them their authority. I think our court has fallen into the error at times and it is that that I have aimed at when I have said that the Common Law is not a brooding omnipresence in the sky and that the U.S. is not subject to some mystic overlaw that it is bound to obey.[77]

Holmes' original statement that the common law "is not a brooding omnipresence in the sky" was made in the 1917 U.S. Supreme Court case of *Southern Pacific Co. v. Jensen*, where he explained that law is "the articulate voice of some sovereign or quasi-sovereign that can be identified."[78] Assertions of abstract "rights" by intellectuals in effect verbally transform themselves into self-authorized sovereigns.

"SOCIAL JUSTICE"

Among the many arguments without arguments, none is more pervasive or more powerful than that of what is called "social justice." Yet it is a term with no real definition, even though it is a term that has been in use for more than a century. All justice is inherently social, since someone alone on a desert island cannot be either just or unjust. What seems to be implied by adding the word "social" to the concept of justice is that justice is to be established among groups, rather than just among individuals. But this collectivizing of justice does little to make the concept of social justice any clearer. However, the term does at least signal a dissatisfaction with conventional notions of formal justice, such as applying the same rules to all. Anatole France made this dissatisfaction plain when he said: "The law, in its majestic equality, forbids the rich as well as the poor to sleep under bridges, to beg in the streets, and to steal bread."[79]

In short, the equality of formal justice is an equality of processes, not an equality of impact or consequences. This criticism has long been made by those with the vision of the anointed. But those with the tragic vision see formal justice as the best we are likely to achieve or should attempt to achieve. In Burke's words, "all men have equal rights; but not to equal things."[80] Alexander Hamilton likewise considered "all men" to be "entitled to a parity of privileges,"[81] though he expected that economic inequality "would exist as long as liberty existed."[82]

By contrast, intellectuals with the unconstrained vision have long been offended, not only by unequal end results but also— and perhaps more fundamentally— by the fact that different end results often seem to have been virtually foreordained from birth. In short, they consider it to be not simply a misfortune, but an injustice, to be born into circumstances that make one's chances in life far less promising than the circumstances into which others are born. Peter Sacks, for example, said:

> Colleges, once seen as beacons of egalitarian hope, are becoming bastions of wealth and privilege that perpetuate inequality. The chance of a low-income child obtaining a bachelor's degree has not budged in three decades: Just 6 percent of students from the lowest-income families earned a bachelor's degree by age 24 in 1970, and in 2002 still only 6 percent did. Lower still is that child's chance of attending one of America's top universities.[83]

Similar conceptions of socioeconomic mobility and similar ways of measuring it have been used by many others, focusing on statistical probabilities of outcomes— "life chances"— for individuals born into differing circumstances. Since it is not just individuals, but whole groups, whose life chances differ, this is one of the concerns addressed by those seeking "social justice." Yet statistical differences in achievements tell us nothing about the *reasons* for those differences, even though Professor Sacks chooses to attribute these disparities to external institutions, such as colleges, rather than to internal differences in values, discipline, ability or innumerable other factors that affect outcomes. The setting into which one happens to be born can affect some or all of these factors, including how far one's innate potential is turned into developed capabilities. In assessing life chances, two very different questions are often confused with one another:

1. Is **life** fair?

2. Is **society** fair?

The first question is much easier to answer. Life has seldom, if ever, been fair or even close to fair. The family or culture into which one is born can affect the direction one's life takes, as can the happenstance of the individuals encountered in the journey through life, who may influence one's outlook and aspirations, for good or ill. These are just some of the factors affecting one's life chances— and affecting them very differently from the life chances of others born into different circumstances and encountering very different influences in their formative years.

The second question is whether the rules and practices of a given society are fair or unfair. To answer that question requires, at a minimum, recognizing that factors internal to individuals and groups cannot be disregarded, and all differences in their life chances arbitrarily attributed to particular external institutions or to society as a whole. Nor can it be assumed that any society has either the omniscience or the omnipotence to eliminate differences in life chances among individuals or groups. Moreover, the extent to which these differences in life chances can be mitigated by such things as widespread access to education or the alleviation of grinding poverty is a question, rather than a foregone conclusion.

The unfairness or injustice that remains after society has done its best cannot be called a *social* injustice, though it is an injustice in some cosmic sense— extending beyond society's rules and practices— because it goes back to happenstances into which people are born. What many are seeking, in the name of "social justice," could more accurately be called *cosmic justice*— and the failure to find it in any society might caution against what is to be risked or sacrificed in the quest for cosmic justice.

John Rawls' *A Theory of Justice* is a landmark for those who espouse social justice, even though Rawls, like others who have used the term, provided no clear-cut definition. Instead, he delineated his view of the importance of justice in general:

> Justice is the first virtue of social institutions, as truth is of systems of thought. A theory however elegant and economical must be rejected or revised if it is untrue; likewise laws and institutions no matter how efficient and well-arranged must be reformed or abolished if they are unjust. Each person possesses an inviolability founded on justice that even the welfare of society as a whole cannot override. For this reason justice . . . does not allow that the sacrifices imposed on a few are outweighed by the larger sum of advantages enjoyed by many. . . . The only thing that permits us to acquiesce in an erroneous theory is the lack of a better one; analogously, an injustice is tolerable only when it is necessary to avoid an even greater injustice. Being first virtues of human activities, truth and justice are uncompromising.[84]

Like many others who argue in terms of life chances, Rawls assumes in passing that these differences in life chances are externally "imposed"— presumably by society— rather than being internally produced differences, due to individual or group behavior patterns that are less successful in educational institutions and in the economy, for example. The correlation between family income and subsequent individual educational achievement tells us nothing about the nature, or even the direction, of causation. Low income might lead to low educational achievements, or both might be results of a set of attitudes, behavior or capabilities among the less successful individuals or groups.

Similarly, Professor Peter Corning's observation that "the children of affluent parents have a far better than average chance of doing well economically, whereas the offspring of the poor generally do much worse than average,"[85] tells us nothing about whether the reasons are external or internal. Statisticians have often warned against confusing correlation with causation, a warning all too often ignored.

While Rawls systematized much of the moral dimension of the prevailing social vision among contemporary intellectuals, he was also in a long tradition that goes back at least as far as William Godwin, whose 1793 treatise, *An Enquiry Concerning Political Justice*, was a study of *social* justice— the term "political" in the context of the times referring to society as a whole, in the same way as the term "political economy" was used in that era to refer to the economics of society as a whole, the polity, as distinguished from the economics of an individual, a household or other organization within the society or polity.

The *categorical* primacy of justice claimed by Rawls has been part of the thinking of such contemporaries of his as Ronald Dworkin and Laurence Tribe, who have referred to legal rights as "trumps" that over-ride mere interests or other considerations that may have to be sacrificed in order to vindicate those rights.[86] The "superior claims of justice" have been part of the unconstrained vision at least as far back as William Godwin.[87] Defining some considerations as categorically preemptive over other considerations— whether in the manner of Rawls, Dworkin or Tribe— is one of the most sweeping of the arguments without arguments, unless simply elaborating the desirability of the thing that is made preemptive is considered an argument, in a world where there are innumerable desirable things, most of which can be achieved more fully only by sacrificing other desirable things.

One could just as easily, and just as arbitrarily, have chosen health, wealth, happiness or something else as categorically preemptive over everything else. But Rawls' arbitrary choice of a preemptive concern fits the concerns of contemporary intellectuals, and so his choice has passed muster with them and allowed his *A Theory of Justice* to become a landmark.

Virtually every aspect of Rawls' vision, however, is incompatible with the tragic vision. While Adam Smith, writing as a professor of moral philosophy in his *Theory of Moral Sentiments*, nearly two decades before he became famous as an economist with *The Wealth of Nations*, also made justice a prime virtue, his specifics made his claim nearly the opposite of Rawls'. Smith said: "Society may subsist, though not in the most comfortable state, without beneficence; but the prevalence of injustice must utterly destroy it."[88] The crucial difference between Smith and Rawls, however, is that in

Smith justice was *instrumentally* important, in order to preserve society, and need only be "tolerably observed" to fulfill that purpose.[89] Edmund Burke likewise spoke of "justice without which human society cannot subsist,"[90] but justice was not *categorically* preemptive over other considerations. "Nothing is good," Burke said in another context, "but in proportion, and with Reference"[91]— in short, as a trade-off.

Although justice has been seen as very important, both by those with the tragic vision and those with the vision of the anointed, the rejection of the concept of "*social* justice" has been as complete among today's believers in the tragic vision as its acceptance has been among believers in the vision of the anointed. Hayek, for example, called social justice a concept that "does not belong to the category of error but to that of nonsense."[92] Others in the tradition of the tragic vision do not even bother to mention it. Professor Richard A. Posner of the University of Chicago Law School, for example, wrote a whole treatise on justice without even mentioning social justice.[93] Both the central role of social justice in the vision of the anointed and its utter banishment from the tragic vision make sense within the very different assumptions of these two visions.

Those with the vision of the anointed proceed on the assumption that surrogate decision-makers can directly prescribe and create socially desirable *results*, while those with the tragic vision regard that as beyond any human being's capabilities, which can at best create social *processes* that will enable vast numbers of other people to make their own mutual accommodations among themselves, reflecting their own individual desires, direct knowledge of their individual circumstances, and individual senses of what is best, whether these mutual accommodations are done through the economic marketplace or in various other political or social processes. When Rawls repeatedly called upon society to "arrange"[94] social results for individuals or groups, that sidestepped the question which is central to those with the tragic vision— the specific nature of the processes by which social decisions are to be made and the incentives, constraints and dangers of those processes.

Instead, like many others with the vision of the anointed, Rawls employed the euphemistic and question-begging term "society" to refer to what only government would have the power to do, thereby side-stepping the crucial and painful question of the consequences of concentrating the vast new powers required for seeking social justice in the hands of political leaders, even though the history of the twentieth century provided all too many ghastly examples of what such concentrations of power can lead to.

With Rawls, as with others, the sweep of what is called "social justice" is far more than social, and can even be *anti-social* in its consequences. Even if one could somehow create equal results for social groups, that would still not satisfy Rawls' criterion of fairness to individuals. While Rawls was concerned with the general question of what he called "the distribution of income and wealth," in this and other things he advocated "a conception of justice that nullifies the accidents of natural endowment and the contingencies of social circumstance."[95] In other words, his concerns included individuals' life chances, not just aggregate results for groups.

"No one deserves his place in the distribution of native endowments, any more than one deserves one's initial starting place in society,"[96] Rawls said. Therefore his conception of justice requires that people "should have the same prospects of success regardless of their initial place in the social system."[97] According to Rawls, "The unequal inheritance of wealth is no more inherently unjust than the unequal inheritance of intelligence."[98] In short, this conception of justice seeks to correct the happenstances of fate, the gods or the cosmos, and could more fittingly be called *cosmic justice* instead of social justice, since these happenstances include things *not* caused by the institutions or policies of any society— and are by no means necessarily correctable by social institutions or social policies.

Seeking to make life chances equal is very different from simply prescribing equal treatment by the law or other social institutions, since people born with very different natural endowments— whether of brains, physique, voice, or beauty— or with different social endowments according to the different knowledge and values imparted by the families in which they were raised, may be unlikely to have even approximately equal outcomes.

To ask whether life chances are equal or fair is to ask a very *different* question from asking whether a particular institution or a particular society treats individuals equally or fairly, though these two very different questions are often confused with one another.

To take a small and simple example, various mental tests or scholastic tests have been criticized as unfair because different groups perform very differently on such tests. But one reply to critics summarized the issue succinctly: "The tests are not unfair. *Life* is unfair and the tests measure the results." Here, as in economic and other contexts, there is a fundamental distinction between *conveying* a difference that already exists and *causing* a difference to exist.

Abandoning these tests would not make life any fairer. Those who lag in mental development or academic skills, for whatever reason, would still lag. If tests were no longer conveying these deficiencies beforehand, then performances on the job or in educational institutions would reveal the deficiencies later. It is doing no favor to those who lag to postpone the revelation of those lags. On the contrary, the earlier the lags are discovered, the greater the chances of their being overcome. Nor is verbal virtuosity in defining these lags out of existence, as with multiculturalist doctrines, any favor, for the same reason.

Life chances have seldom, if ever, been even approximately equal in any society. Yet many with the vision of social justice attribute unequal or unfair outcomes to the defects of "our society," and imagine that they are able not only to conceive, but to create, a different society that will achieve what innumerable other societies of the past and present have not even come close to achieving. Equal treatment may be rightly seen as falling far short of the cosmic justice being sought but, nevertheless, even the merely "formal" justice disdained by those seeking cosmic justice remains a rare achievement in the annals of human societies. Moreover, formal justice— equality before the law and "a government of laws, not of men"— has taken centuries of struggle to achieve, even approximately, and has cost many lives in the process.

Even in an open society where one can literally go from rags to riches, how many people are even oriented toward doing that, much less equipped with the attitudes and self-discipline that are as essential as ability, is often dependent on the family and community in which they were raised, or on a chance encounter with someone who helped set them on the path to personal achievement— or to ruin. There are things societies can do to mitigate the inherent unfairness of life. But there are also limits to what society can do. No society can change the past— and, as a noted historian once said, "We do not live in the past, but the past in us."

To suggest that "society" can simply "arrange" better outcomes *somehow*, without specifying the processes, the costs or the risks, is to ignore the tragic history of the twentieth century, written in the blood of millions, killed in peacetime by their own governments that were given extraordinary powers in the name of lofty goals.

In focussing on results rather than systemic processes, Rawls' conception makes the nature of those processes either less important than justice or expendable. For example, a "competitive price system gives no consideration to needs and therefore it cannot be the sole device of distribution,"[99] according to Rawls. But determining what constitutes "needs" implies third-party surrogates with concentrations of power sufficient to make their conception prevail over the conceptions or priorities of millions of others, and presumes a corresponding concentration of knowledge and wisdom, which may or may not exist or even be possible.

The same process question arises when Rawls proposes the principle of "equal life prospects in all sectors of society for those similarly endowed and motivated."[100] But what third parties can possibly know when individuals or groups are similarly endowed, much less similarly motivated as well? The cost to society of such a concentration of power, on the dubious assumption of a similar concentration of knowledge and in the name of social justice, has too often turned out to be a gamble with catastrophic consequences— hardly a gamble to be repeated on the strength of soothing words about what results "society" can *somehow* "arrange."

When John Rawls said, "Each person possesses an inviolability founded on justice that even the welfare of society as a whole cannot override,"[101] he was making the individuals' right to justice preemptive over the well-being of others. Thus what has been called social justice could be more accurately called *anti-social* justice, in so far as it is to be imposed for the benefit of some in disregard of the costs to society as a whole.

This categorical priority of cosmic justice to selected individuals or groups, in disregard of the consequences for others, is a violation of the rights of others by those with the vision of the anointed, and is in complete contradiction to the tragic vision. Justice Oliver Wendell Holmes exemplified this opposite, tragic vision when he made social well-being preemptive over that of individuals, as when he said, "the public welfare may call upon the best citizens for their lives."[102] Consistent with this, he said:

> If we want conscripts, we march them up to the front with bayonets in their rear to die for a cause in which perhaps they do not believe. The enemy we treat not even as a means but as an obstacle to be abolished, if so it may be.[103]

"I feel no pangs of conscience over either step," he added.[104] In *The Common Law* Holmes said, "No society has ever admitted that it could not sacrifice individual welfare to its own existence."[105] Thus "justice to the individual is rightly outweighed by the larger interests on the other side of the scales."[106] Accordingly, he wrote elsewhere, "I have no scruples about a draft or the death penalty."[107] The woman known as "typhoid Mary" was quarantined— incarcerated— for years, through no fault of her own, because she was a carrier of a lethal disease for which medical science had no cure at the time, even though she herself was unaffected by the disease which she spread to others, initially without even realizing it.

In the tragic vision, it is society which makes the individual's life possible— not just his prosperity or happiness, but even his physical survival. A new-born baby can be kept alive only by enormous efforts and resources supplied by others, whom the baby is in no position to compensate— and those efforts and resources are forthcoming as a result of the norms of society. So too are years of further investments of time, efforts and resources by others, until the recipient of those efforts has grown up to the point of being self-supporting, which can be decades later for those who go through college and then on to postgraduate training.

Thus, in the tragic vision, the rights of individuals cannot take precedence over the preservation of society, for the individual would not even survive physically without society, and the very concept of the rights of individuals comes from society. Where society breaks down and anarchy reigns, it can quickly become painfully clear how little the rights of individuals matter without a functioning society to enforce them.

Oliver Wendell Holmes' view that the preservation of society takes precedence over the rights of individuals was shared by others with the tragic vision. Something similar was implied in Edmund Burke's statement about the inapplicability of the usual legal processes when the state itself is threatened, as in times of war or insurrection. "Laws are commanded to hold their tongues amongst arms," he said, when an issue is "an extraordinary question of state, and wholly out of the law."[108] Something similar was also implied in Justice Robert Jackson's statement that the "doctrinaire logic" of the Supreme Court could "convert the constitutional Bill of Rights into a suicide pact."[109]

In short, justice cannot be *categorically* more important than other considerations within the framework of the tragic vision, however central social justice may be in the vision of the anointed. Indeed, the term "social" hardly seems to cover the vast scope of what Rawls and others propose, which goes beyond correcting inequalities caused by the decisions or practices of society.

These philosophic issues have ramifications far beyond the confines of academic seminars and scholarly journals. They have been echoed in declarations by a head of the National Association for the Advancement of Colored People that "each group must advocate and insist upon its piece of the pie"[110] and by a President of the United States who said in 1965:

> You do not take a person who, for years, has been hobbled by chains and liberate him, bring him up to the starting line of a race and then say, "you are free to compete with all the others," and still justly believe that you have been completely fair.[111]

It would be hard to find a more eloquent expression of Rawls' conception of social justice. But the same question that applies to Lyndon Johnson's statement— Just who is "you" in this case?— applies more generally to John Rawls' statements: Just who concretely is responsible, either causally or morally, for the failure of life to be fair? One can say "society" but there is no one named "society." Moreover, much that happens in a given society is beyond the control of any institution in that society, including cultures that originated in other times and places, individual happenstances ranging from birth defects to being born to loving, wise and dedicated parents, as well as choices made by millions of individuals within that society. What living, breathing, flesh-and-blood human being today is either causally or morally responsible for the past— or has either the superhuman knowledge or wisdom to be trusted with the power to preempt millions of other peoples' decisions for the indefinite future?

Saying that "society" should *somehow* "arrange" things better evades, rather than answers, such questions. But to recognize the limitations on what any society is capable of doing is not to claim that what exists represents justice from a cosmic perspective.

Both John Rawls and Adam Smith before him— operating from within opposite visions— posited an abstract being from whose perspective principles of justice could be derived. Rawls conceived of a disembodied being in the "original position" of contemplating the desirability of different kinds of society into which to be born, without knowing into what position one would be born in that society. The just society, according to Rawls, is the kind of society into which one would wish to be born, if not biased by knowledge of one's own personal starting position in that society.

Adam Smith's abstract being, from whose perspective justice was to be determined, was what he called an "impartial spectator," whose role was very much like that of the abstract being in Rawls' "original position." Smith never imagined that there was in fact such an impartial spectator, any more than Rawls would claim that there was someone in his "original position" of contemplating what kind of society to be born into. The point in both cases was to imagine how the world would look from the perspective of such a being and to derive principles of justice from that perspective.

The difference between the approach in Rawls' *A Theory of Justice* and in Adam Smith's *Theory of Moral Sentiments* was that Rawls sought to have a society directly "arrange" outcomes according to principles of justice that were categorically preemptive over other considerations, while Adam Smith sought only to have principles of justice "tolerably observed" in order to have a viable society. Smith had a very constrained vision of what results anyone could directly "arrange":

> The man of system. . . seems to imagine that he can arrange the different members of a great society with as much ease as the hand arranges the different pieces upon a chess-board; he does not consider that the pieces upon the chess-board have no other principle of motion besides that which the hand impresses upon them; but that, in the great chess-board of human society, every single piece has a principle of motion of its own, altogether different from that which the legislature might choose to impress upon it.[112]

The difference between Smith and Rawls was not a difference in "value premises," but a difference in what they thought possible, and at what cost. Smith contrasted the doctrinaire "man of system" with the man of "humanity and benevolence," whose approach he preferred. "When he cannot establish the right," Smith said, "he will not disdain to ameliorate the wrong," and will "endeavour to establish the best that the people can bear." The fundamental difference between Smith and Rawls was not a difference in "value premises" as to what is right and wrong, but a difference in beliefs about what the constraints of life imply, and the costs of trying to proceed in disregard of those constraints as to what one can "arrange."

Chapter 9

Patterns of the Anointed

The behavior of those who follow the vision of the anointed has long included certain patterns. They tend to see themselves as advocates of change and their opponents as defenders of the status quo. Their behavior often reflects attitudes rather than principles. They often see issues in terms of crusades and their vision as something to protect, virtually at all costs, even if that means keeping it sealed inside a bubble where discordant facts cannot get in to threaten it.

"CHANGE" VERSUS THE STATUS QUO

The intelligentsia often divide people into those who are for "change" and those who are for the status quo. John Dewey's *Liberalism and Social Action*, for example, begins with these words:

> Liberalism has long been accustomed to onslaughts proceeding from those who oppose social change. It has long been treated as an enemy by those who wish to maintain the *status quo*.[1]

As already noted in Chapter 6, even such landmark "conservative" figures as Milton Friedman and Friedrich Hayek advocated policies radically different from those in existing institutions or societies. No book was more completely based on the constrained or tragic vision of human nature than *The Federalist*— and yet its authors had not only rebelled against British colonial rule, but had created a new form of government, radically at variance with the autocracies that prevailed around the world at the time. To call such people defenders of the status quo is to completely divorce words from realities.

Similarly among their contemporaries in eighteenth century England, where Edmund Burke and Adam Smith were towering figures among those with the tragic vision. Both Burke and Smith advocated such drastic changes as freeing the American colonies instead of fighting to retain them, as the British government did, and both also opposed slavery at a time when few others did in the Western world, and virtually no one did outside of Western civilization. Burke even worked out a plan for preparing slaves for freedom and providing them with property to begin their lives as free people.[2] Adam Smith not only opposed slavery but also dismissed with contempt the theory that black slaves in America were racially inferior to the whites who enslaved them.[3]

Calling those with the tragic vision defenders of the status quo is a triumph of verbal virtuosity over plain and demonstrable facts. That such a lazy way of evading critics' arguments should have prevailed unchallenged from the eighteenth century to the present, among those who consider themselves "thinking people," is a sobering sign of the power of a vision and rhetoric to shut down thought.

More generally, it is doubtful whether there are many— if any— individuals in a free society who are completely satisfied with all the policies and institutions of their society. In short, virtually everybody is in favor of some changes. Any accurate and rational discussion of differences among them would address which particular changes are favored by which people, based on what reasons, followed by analysis and evidence for or against those particular reasons for those particular changes. But all of this is by-passed by those who simply proclaim themselves to be in favor of "change" and label those who disagree with them as defenders of the status quo. It is yet another of the many arguments without arguments.

People who call themselves "progressives" assert not merely that they are for changes but that these are beneficial changes— that is, progress. But other people who advocate other very different changes likewise proclaim those to be changes for the better. In other words, *everybody* is a "progressive" by their own lights. That some people should imagine that they are peculiarly in favor of progress is not only another example of self-flattery but also an example of an evasion of the work of trying to show, with evidence and analysis, where and why their particular proposed changes would produce better end results than other people's proposed changes. Instead, proponents of other changes have been dismissed by many, including John Dewey, as "apologists for the *status quo*."[4]

Despite such dismissals in lieu of arguments, anyone with a knowledge of the history of eighteenth-century Britain must know that Adam Smith's *The Wealth of Nations* was hardly a defense of the status quo, and in fact went completely counter to the vested interests of the political, economic, and social elites of his time. It would be hard even to imagine why Adam Smith, or anyone else, would spend a whole decade writing a 900-page book to say how contented he was with the way things were. The same could be said of the voluminous writings of Milton Friedman, Friedrich Hayek, William F. Buckley, and many other writers labeled "conservative."

The very concept of change used by the intelligentsia of the left— which is to say, most of the intelligentsia— is arbitrarily restrictive and tendentious. It means in practice the particular kinds of changes, through the particular kinds of social mechanisms that they envision. Other changes— no matter how large or how consequential for the lives of millions of people— tend to be ignored if they occur through other mechanisms and in ways not contemplated by the intelligentsia. At the very least, such unprescribed developments outside the scope of the vision of the anointed are denied the honorific title of "change."

The 1920s, for example, were a decade of huge changes in the lives of the people of the United States: the change from a predominantly rural to a predominantly urban society, the spread of electricity, automobiles, and radios to vastly more millions of Americans, the beginning of commercial air travel, the revolutionizing of retail selling, with resulting lower prices, by the rapid spread of nationwide chain stores that made more products more affordable to more people. Yet when intellectuals refer to eras of "change," they almost never mention the 1920s— because these sweeping changes in the way millions of Americans lived their lives were not the particular kinds of changes envisioned by the intelligentsia, through the particular kinds of social mechanisms envisioned by the intelligentsia. In the eyes of much of the intelligentsia, the 1920s (when that decade is thought of at all) are seen as a period of a stagnant status quo, presided over by conservative administrations opposed to "change."

ATTITUDES VERSUS PRINCIPLES

Ideally, the work of intellectuals is based on certain principles— of logic, of evidence, and perhaps of moral values or social concerns. However, given the incentives and constraints of the profession, intellectuals' work need not be. There is ample room for attitudes, rather than principles, to guide the work of intellectuals, especially when these are attitudes prevalent among their peers and insulated from consequential feedback from the outside world.

While logic and evidence are ideal criteria for the work of intellectuals, there are many ways in which much of what is said and done by intellectuals has less to do with principles than with attitudes. For example, intellectuals who are receptive to claims of mitigation on the part of murderers who profess to have been battered wives, or others who are said to have had traumatic childhoods of one sort or another, or the less fortunate in general, are seldom receptive to claims that policemen who had a split second to make a life-and-death shooting decision, at the risk of their own lives, should be cut some slack.

Some intellectuals who have been opposed to the principle of racism have nevertheless remained either silent or apologetic when black community leaders have made racist attacks on Asian storekeepers in black ghettos, or on whites in general or Jews in particular. The beating up of Asian American school children by their black classmates— for years[5]— likewise elicits little interest, much less outrage, from the intelligentsia. Some intellectuals have even redefined racism in a way to make blacks ineligible for the label[*]— another exercise in verbal virtuosity.

---

[*] On grounds that only those with power can be racists— a proviso never part of the definition before and one which would imply that Nazis were not racists during the 1920s, before they took power.

Many among the intelligentsia have denounced "greed" among corporate executives whose incomes are a fraction of the incomes of professional athletes or entertainers who are seldom, if ever, accused of greed.

The intelligentsia have led outraged outcries against oil companies' profits when gasoline prices have risen, though the amount of profits in the price of a gallon of gasoline is much less than the amount of taxes. But the concept of "greed" is almost never applied to government, whether in the amount of taxes it collects or even when working class homes, often representing the labors and sacrifices of a lifetime, are confiscated wholesale for "redevelopment" of an area in ways that will bring in more taxes to the local jurisdiction (at the expense of other jurisdictions), thereby enabling local politicians to do more spending to enhance their chances of being reelected. It is not uncommon among the intelligentsia to consider it "selfish" if you object to others taxing away what you have earned, but it is not considered selfish for politicians to want to tax away any amount of the earnings, not only of contemporaries, but also of generations yet unborn, to whom the national debt will be passed on.

Such responses and non-responses by intellectuals not only represent attitudes rather than principles, often they represent attitudes that over-ride principles. Nor are such biases confined to reactions to particular groups of human beings. They apply even to concepts, such as risk, for example.

Intellectuals who are highly critical of any risks associated with particular pharmaceutical drugs, and consider it the government's duty to ban some of these drugs because of risks of death, see no need for the government to ban sky-diving or white-water rafting, even if the latter represent higher risks of death for the sake of recreation than the risks from medicines that can stave off pain or disability, or which may save more lives than they cost. Similarly, when a boxer dies from a beating in the ring, that is almost certain to set off demands in the media or among the intelligentsia that boxing be banned, but no such demands are likely to follow deaths from skiing accidents, even if these are far more common than deaths from boxing. Again, it is not the principle but the attitude.

While attitudes can vary from individual to individual, the attitudes of intellectuals are often group attitudes. Moreover, these attitudes change collectively over time, becoming transient moods of a given era and badges of identity in those eras, rather than permanent attitudes, much less permanent principles. Thus in the Progressive era of the early twentieth century, racial and ethnic minorities were viewed in largely negative terms, and Progressive support of the eugenics movement was not unrelated to the presumed desirability of preventing these minorities from propagating "too many" of their own kind. This mood had largely passed by the 1930s, and in later times racial and ethnic minorities became objects of special solicitude. After the 1960s, this solicitude became virtually an obsession, however inconsistent it was with earlier and opposite obsessions about the same people among intellectuals considered "progressive" in the early twentieth century.

During the earlier era, when farmers and workers were the special focus of solicitude, no one paid much attention to how what was done for the benefit of these groups might adversely affect minorities or others. Likewise, in a later era, little attention was paid by "progressive" intellectuals to how affirmative action for minorities or women might adversely affect others. There is no principle that accounts for such collective mood swings. There are simply mascots du jour, much like adolescent fads that are compulsive badges of identity for a time and afterwards considered passé— but seldom treated as subject to logic or evidence during either the period of their obsession or the period of their dismissal. Back in the 1920s, when the Sacco-Vanzetti case was an international *cause célèbre* because of the presumed injustice of their trial, Justice Oliver Wendell Holmes wrote in a letter to Harold Laski about the arbitrary focus of that time:

> I cannot but ask myself why this so much greater interest in red than black. A thousand-fold worse cases of negroes come up from time to time, but the world does not worry over them. It is not a mere simple abstract love of justice that has moved people so much.[6]

A SEALED BUBBLE

The dangers of living in a sealed bubble of ideas should be obvious. But history offers examples for those who need them. China's centuries-long intellectual and technological superiority to Europe not only ended, but reversed, after the fateful, fifteenth-century decision of China's rulers to discontinue international explorations and deliberately become an inward-looking society, disdainful of peoples elsewhere, who were dismissed as "barbarians." At that time, China's capacity for exploration was one of many areas in which its progress greatly exceeded that of Europe:

> These flotillas far surpassed in grandeur the small Portuguese fleets that came later. The ships were probably the largest vessels the world had seen. . . .The biggest were about 400 feet long, 160 wide (compare the 85 feet of Columbus's *Santa Maria*), had nine staggered masts and twelve square sails of red silk.[7]

Decades before Columbus, a Chinese admiral led a voyage of exploration that took far more ships a far longer distance, from China to the east coast of Africa, with stops in between. China also had huge drydocks on the Yangtze River, technologically preceding Europe by centuries.[8] But at the height of its preeminence, China's rulers decreed that such explorations would cease, and even made it a capital offense for anyone to build ships above a certain size, so as to insulate the country and its people from foreign ideas.[9]

A century later, Japan's rulers imposed a similar policy of sealing its people off from foreign influence. Thus Japan sealed itself off from the scientific and technological advances being made in the Western world and, in the middle of the nineteenth century, found itself helpless when Commodore Matthew Perry forced his way into Japanese waters and forced Japan to open itself up to the outside world. The later rise of Japan to the forefront of technology demonstrated not only the capacity of its people but, implicitly, also what a waste of that capacity had been imposed by sealing them off from the rest of the world for more than two centuries.

Similar things have happened in other countries from similar policies that sealed their people off from the ideas of others, even when they did not go to the extremes of China or Japan. Portugal had been one of the leading nations in maritime explorations, but it lost its lead in navigational proficiency when the Inquisition made astronomy a dangerous field in which to teach the condemned advances of Copernicus and Galileo. As a narrow and persecuting orthodoxy stifled intellectual curiosity, "the Portuguese lost competence even in those areas they had once dominated."[10]

In the first half of the twentieth century, Germany was a world leader in nuclear physics, and Hitler had a program to produce an atomic bomb before the United States did. Indeed, fear of Nazi Germany's getting such a weapon spurred the creation and acceleration of the Manhattan Project. But Hitler's intolerance toward Jews led Jewish scientists to flee not only Germany but other countries in Europe living in the shadow of Nazi domination or conquest— and Jewish scientists from Europe and America played key roles in making the United States the first nuclear power.

Whatever the country, the century or the subject, sealing ideas in a bubble protects those with the power to seal the bubble, but often at a huge cost to those who are sealed inside the bubble with them. In contemporary America, no one has the power to seal the whole population off from ideas that clash with the prevailing vision. But the institutions most under the control of intellectuals— the leading colleges and universities— are not only among the most one-sided ideologically, but also the most restrictive in what students can say without running afoul of vague speech codes and punishments that can range from "re-education" on up to expulsion. While this is a sealing off of a limited segment of the population for a limited number of years, the students who have been sealed off are a segment of society that can be expected to have a disproportionate influence in later years, and the years in which the ideas that influence these students are crucial formative years.

CRUSADES OF THE ANOINTED

To understand intellectuals' role in society, we must look beyond their rhetoric, or that of their critics, to the reality of their revealed preferences.

How can we tell what anyone's goals and priorities are? One way might be to pay attention to what they say. But of course outward words do not always accurately reflect inward thoughts. Moreover, even the thoughts which people articulate to themselves need not reflect their actual behavior pattern. Goals, preferences and priorities articulated either inwardly or outwardly need not be consistent with the choices actually made when confronted with the options presented by the real world. A man may claim or believe that keeping the lawn mowed is more important than watching television but, if he is found spending hours in front of the TV screen, day in and day out for weeks on end, while weeds and tall grass take over the lawn, then the preferences revealed by his behavior are a more accurate indicator of that individual's priorities than either his expressed words or even whatever beliefs he may have about himself.

What preferences are revealed by the actual behavior of intellectuals— especially in their social crusades— and how do such revealed preferences compare with their rhetoric? The professed beliefs of intellectuals center about their concern for others— especially for the poor, for minorities, for "social justice" and for protecting endangered species and saving the environment, for example. Their rhetoric is too familiar and too pervasive to require elaboration here. The real question, however, is: What are their revealed preferences?

The phrase "unintended consequences" has become a cliché precisely because so many policies and programs intended, for example, to better the situation of the less fortunate have in fact made their situation worse, that it is no longer possible to regard good intentions as automatic harbingers of good results. Anyone whose primary concern is in improving the lot of the less fortunate would therefore, by this time, after decades of experience with negative "unintended consequences," see a need not only to invest time and efforts to turn good intentions into policies and programs, but also to invest time and efforts afterwards into trying to ferret out answers as to what the actual consequences of those policies and programs have been.

Moreover, anyone whose primary concern was improving the lot of the less fortunate would also be alert and receptive to other factors from *beyond* the vision of the intellectuals, when those other factors have been found empirically to have helped advance the well-being of the less fortunate, even if in ways not contemplated by the intelligentsia and even if in ways counter to the beliefs or visions of the intelligentsia.

In short, one of the ways to test whether expressed concerns for the well-being of the less fortunate represent primarily a concern for that well-being or a use of the less fortunate as a means to condemn society, or to seek either political or moral authority over society— to be on the side of the angels against the forces of evil— would be to see the revealed preferences of intellectuals in terms of how much time and energy they invest in promoting their vision, as compared to how much time and energy they invest in scrutinizing (1) the actual consequences of things done in the name of that vision and (2) benefits to the less fortunate created outside that vision and even counter to that vision.

Crusaders for a "living wage" or to end "sweatshop labor" in the Third World, for example, may invest great amounts of time and energy promoting those goals but virtually none in scrutinizing the many studies done in countries around the world to discover the actual consequences of minimum wage laws in general or of "living wage" laws in particular. These consequences have included such things as higher levels of unemployment and longer periods of unemployment, especially for the least skilled and least experienced segments of the population. Whether one agrees with or disputes these studies, the crucial question here is *whether one bothers to read them at all.*

If the real purpose of social crusades is to make the less fortunate better off, then the actual consequences of such policies as wage control become central and require investigation, in order to avoid "unintended consequences" which have already become widely recognized in the context of many other policies. But if the real purpose of social crusades is to proclaim oneself to be on the side of the angels, then such investigations have a low priority, if any priority at all, since the goal of being on the side of the angels is accomplished when the policies have been advocated and then instituted, after which social crusaders can move on to other issues. The revealed preference of many, if not most, of the intelligentsia has been to be on the side of the angels.

The same conclusion is hard to avoid when looking at the response of intellectuals to improvements in the condition of the poor that follow policies or circumstances which offer no opportunities to be on the side of the angels against the forces of evil. For example, under new economic policies beginning in the 1990s, tens of millions of people in India have risen above that country's official poverty level. In China, under similar policies begun earlier, a million people a month have risen out of poverty.[11] Surely anyone concerned with the fate of the less fortunate would want to know how this desirable development came about for such vast numbers of very poor people— and therefore how similar improvements might be produced elsewhere in the world. But these and other dramatic increases in living standards, based ultimately on the production of more wealth, arouse little or no interest among most intellectuals.

However important for the poor, these developments offer no opportunities for the intelligentsia to be on the side of the angels against the forces of evil— and that is what their revealed preferences show repeatedly to be their real priority. Questions about what policies or conditions increase or decrease the rate of growth of output seldom arouse the interest of most intellectuals, even though such changes have done more to reduce poverty— in both rich and poor countries— than changes in the distribution of income have done. French writer Raymond Aron has suggested that achieving the ostensible goals of the left without using the methods favored by the left actually provokes resentments:

> In fact the European Left has a grudge against the United States mainly because the latter has succeeded by means which were not laid down in the revolutionary code. Prosperity, power, the tendency towards uniformity of economic conditions— these results have been achieved by private initiative, by competition rather than State intervention, in other words by capitalism, which every well-brought-up intellectual has been taught to despise.[12]

Similarly, despite decades of laments in the United States about the poor quality of education in most black schools, studies of particular schools where black students meet or exceed national norms[13] arouse little or no interest among most intellectuals, even those who are active in discussions of racial issues. As with people rising out of poverty in Third World countries, lack of interest in academically successful black schools by people who are otherwise vocal and vehement on racial issues suggests a revealed preference for the condemnation of unsuccessful schools and of the society that maintains such schools. Investigating successful black schools could offer hope of finding a possible source of knowledge and insights into how to improve education for a group often lagging far behind in educational achievement and in the incomes and occupations that depend on education. But it would not offer an opportunity for the anointed to be on the side of the angels against the forces of evil.

That many, if not most, of these successful black schools do not follow educational notions in vogue among the intelligentsia may be part of the reason for the lack of interest in such schools, just as the lack of interest in how India and China managed to raise the living standards of many millions of poor people may be in part because it was done by moving away from the kinds of economic policies long favored by the left.

It has often been said that intellectuals on the left are "soft on criminals" but, even here, the question is whether those people accused of crime or convicted and in prison are the real objects of intellectuals' concern or are incidental props in a larger picture— and expendable like others who are used as props. For example, one of the horrific experiences of many men in prison is being gang-raped by other male prisoners. Yet any attempt to reduce the incidence of such lasting traumatic experiences by building more prisons, so that each prisoner could be housed alone in a single cell, is bitterly opposed by the same people who are vehement in defense of prisoners' "rights." Those rights matter as a means of condemning "society" but so does opposition to the building of more prisons. When the actual well-being of prisoners conflicts with the symbolic issue of preventing more prisons from being built, prisoners become just another sacrifice on the altar to a vision.

In many ways, on a whole range of issues, the revealed preference of intellectuals is to gain moral authority— or, vicariously, political power— or both, over the rest of society. The desires or interests of the ostensible beneficiaries of that authority or power— whether the poor, minorities, or criminals in prison— are seldom allowed to outweigh the more fundamental issue of gaining and maintaining the moral hegemony of the anointed.

One of the sources of the credibility and influence of intellectuals with the vision of the anointed is that they are often seen as people promoting the interests of the less fortunate, rather than people promoting their own financial self-interest. But financial self-interests are by no means the only self-interests, nor necessarily the most dangerous self-interests. As T.S. Eliot put it:

Half of the harm that is done in this world is due to people who want to feel important. They don't mean to do harm— but the harm does not interest them. Or they do not see it, or they justify it because they are absorbed in the endless struggle to think well of themselves.[14]

Few things illustrate the heedlessness of social crusades so plainly or so painfully as the consequences of the worldwide environmentalist crusade to ban the insecticide DDT, on grounds of its adverse effects on some birds' eggs— leading to the melodramatic title of Rachel Carson's best-selling book, *Silent Spring*, silent presumably because of the extinction of song birds.

But, whatever the harm that DDT might do to the reproduction rates of some birds, it had a very dramatic effect in reducing the incidence of lethal malaria among human beings, by killing the mosquitoes which transmit that disease. For example, before the use of DDT on a mass scale was first introduced into Ceylon (now Sri Lanka) in 1946, there was an average of more than 40,000 cases of malaria annually in Ceylon in the years from 1937 through 1945. But, after the introduction of DDT, the number of cases of malaria there was cut by more than three-quarters by 1949, was under a thousand by 1955, and was in single digits by 1960.

There were similarly steep reductions in the incidence of malaria in other tropical and sub-tropical countries, saving vast numbers of lives around the world.[15] Conversely, after the political success of the anti-DDT crusade by environmentalists, the banning of this insecticide was followed by a resurgence of malaria, taking millions of lives, even in countries where the disease had been all but eradicated. Rachel Carson may have been responsible for more deaths of human beings than anyone without an army. Yet she remains a revered figure among environmental crusaders.

The point here is not that one particular crusade had catastrophic effects but that the crusading spirit of those with the vision of the anointed makes effects on others less important than the self-exaltation of the crusaders. The idea that crusaders "don't mean to do harm— but the harm does not interest them," when they are "absorbed in the endless struggle to think well of themselves" applies far beyond any particular social crusade.

This preoccupation with self-exaltation was perhaps epitomized in the greeting of a Yale law school dean to incoming students as "Citizens of the republic of conscience," saying, "We are not just a law school of professional excellence; we are an intellectual community of high moral purpose."[16] In other words, the students were not simply entering an institution designed to teach them legal principles, they were joining those who were on the side of the angels.

PART IV

OPTIONAL REALITY

A screen has been fashioned through which our contemporary age reads its filtered information.

Jean-François Revel[1]

Chapter 10

Filtering Reality

The preservation of the vision of the anointed has led many among the intelligentsia to vigorous and even desperate expedients, including the filtering out of facts, the redefinition of words and— for some intellectuals— challenging the very idea of truth itself. Many among the intelligentsia create their own reality— whether deliberately or not— by filtering out information contrary to their conception of how the world is or ought to be.

Some have gone further. J.A. Schumpeter said that the first thing a man will do for his ideals is lie.[1] It is not necessary to lie, however, in order to deceive, when filtering will accomplish the same purpose. This can take the form of reporting selective and atypical samples, suppressing some facts altogether, or filtering out the inconvenient meanings or connotations of words.

SELECTIVE SAMPLES

Filtering the sample of information available to the public can take many forms. For example, Bennett Cerf, the founder of Random House publishers, at one time during the Second World War suggested that books critical of the Soviet Union be withdrawn from circulation.[2]

When the American economy was recovering from a recession in 1983 and unemployment was down in 45 out of the 50 states, ABC News simply chose to feature a report on one of the five states where that was not so or, as they put it, "where unemployment is most severe"[3]— as if these states were just more severe examples of a more general condition, when in fact they were very atypical of existing trends in unemployment.

Filtering can also take the form of incessantly reporting data showing blacks or other non-white groups as being worse off than whites in income, rejection of mortgage loan applications or lay-offs during economic downturns— and *not* reporting that whites are in all these same respects worse off than another non-white group, Asian Americans.[4] Even when data are available for all these groups, Asian Americans tend to be filtered out in "news" stories that are de facto editorials, whose clear thrust is that white racism is the reason for the lower incomes or lower occupational status, or other misfortunes, of non-white groups.

Including Asian Americans in these comparisons would not only introduce a discordant note, it would raise the possibility that these various groups differ in their own behavior or performances— contrary to implicit assumptions— and that such differences are reflected in the outcomes being studied. In short, the performance of Asian Americans, whether in the economy or in educational institutions, has implications going far beyond Asian Americans themselves, for it is a threat to a whole vision of American society in which many have a large stake— ideologically and sometimes politically and economically.[*]

Homelessness is another area where much of the media filters what kind of reality gets through to their audience. During his time at CBS News, Bernard Goldberg noticed the difference between what he saw on the street and what was being broadcast on television:

> In the 1980s, I started noticing that the homeless people we showed on the news didn't look very much like the homeless people I was tripping over on the sidewalk.
> The ones on the sidewalk, by and large, were winos or drug addicts or schizophrenics. They mumbled crazy things or gave you the evil eye when they put paper coffee cups in your face and "asked" for money. . . .
> But the ones we liked to show on television were different. They looked as if they came from your neighborhood and mine. They looked like us. And the message from TV news was that they didn't just *look* like us— they *were* like us! On NBC, Tom Brokaw said that the homeless are "people you know."[5]

---

[*] One of the small but revealing signs of the high stakes that many have in the prevailing vision is the adverse reaction of many among the intelligentsia to Asian Americans being called a "model minority." Considering all the things that various minorities have been called at various times and places, the fierceness of the reaction against this particular label suggests far more at stake than the felicity of a phrase.

If the homeless tend to be sanitized in television news, businessmen tend to be demonized in movies and television dramas, as another study found:

> Only 37 percent of the fictional entrepreneurs played positive roles, and the proportion of "bad guy businessmen" was almost double that of all other occupations. What's more, they were *really* nasty, committing 40 percent of the murders and 44 percent of the vice crimes. . . Only 8 percent of prime-time criminals were black. . .[6]

In real life, as well as in fiction, what was presented to television audiences was highly atypical of what existed in the real world:

> ■During the period studied, 6 percent of the people with AIDS shown on the evening news were gay men. But in real life 58 percent were gay men.
> ■On TV, 16 percent were blacks and Hispanics. But in real life 46 percent were black or Hispanic.
> ■On TV, 2 percent of the AIDS sufferers were IV drug users. In real life 23 percent were.[7]

This creation of a picture reflecting the vision of the anointed, rather than the realities of the world, extends to textbooks used in schools. Publishers such as McGraw-Hill, for example, have percentage guidelines as to how many of the people shown in photographs in their textbooks have to be black, white, Hispanic and disabled. Moreover, the way these individuals are portrayed must also reflect the vision of the anointed. According to the *Wall Street Journal*, "one major publisher vetoed a photo of a barefoot child in an African village, on the grounds that the lack of footwear reinforced the stereotype of poverty on that continent."[8] In short, the painfully blatant reality of desperate poverty in much of Africa is waved aside as a "stereotype" because it does not fit the vision to be portrayed, even if it does fit the facts.

SUPPRESSING FACTS

One of the historic examples of suppressing facts was the reporting and non-reporting of the Soviet Union's government-created famine in the Ukraine and the North Caucasus that killed millions of people in the 1930s. *New York Times*

Moscow correspondent Walter Duranty wrote, "There is no famine or actual starvation, nor is there likely to be."[9] He received a Pulitzer Prize, the Pulitzer panel commending him for his reports, "marked by scholarship, profundity, impartiality, sound judgment and exceptional clarity."[10]

Meanwhile, British writer Malcolm Muggeridge reported from the Ukraine that peasants there were in fact starving: "I mean starving in its absolute sense; not undernourished as, for instance, most Oriental peasants. . . and some unemployed workers in Europe, but having had for weeks next to nothing to eat."[11] Muggeridge wrote in a subsequent article that the man-made famine was "one of the most monstrous crimes in history, so terrible that people in the future will scarcely be able to believe it ever happened."[12] Decades later, a scholarly study by Robert Conquest, *The Harvest of Sorrow*, estimated that six million people had died in that famine over a period of three years.[13] Still later, when the official archives were finally opened in the last days of the Soviet Union under Mikhail Gorbachev, new estimates of the deaths from the man-made famine were made by various scholars who had studied material from those archives. Most of their estimates equalled or exceeded Dr. Conquest's earlier estimates.[14]

At the time of the famine, however, this was one of the most successful filtering operations imaginable. What Muggeridge said was dismissed as "a hysterical tirade" by Beatrice Webb, co-author with her husband Sidney Webb of an internationally known study of the Soviet Union.[15] Muggeridge was vilified and was unable to get work as a writer, after his dispatches from the Soviet Union, and was so financially strapped that he, his wife and two small children had to move in with friends. There is no need to believe that there was any conspiracy among editors or journalists to silence and ostracize Malcolm Muggeridge. Nor is a conspiracy necessary for successfully filtering out things that do not fit the prevailing vision— either then or now.

Except for Muggeridge and a very few other people, a famine deliberately used to break the back of resistance to Stalin— killing a comparable or larger number of people as those who died in the Nazi Holocaust— would have been filtered completely out of history, instead of being merely ignored, as it usually is today. This was not a matter of honest mistakes by Duranty and others. What Duranty said privately to some other journalists and to diplomats at the time was radically different from what he said in his dispatches to the *New York Times*. For example, in 1933 a British diplomat reported to London: "Mr. Duranty thinks it quite possible that as many as 10 million people may have died directly or indirectly from lack of food in the Soviet Union during the past year."[16]

Statistical data can also be filtered, whether by omitting data that go counter to the desired conclusion (such as data on Asian Americans) or by restricting the release of data to only those researchers whose position on the issue at hand is in accord with that of those who control the data. For example, a statistically based study by former college presidents William Bowen and Derek Bok was widely hailed for its conclusions supporting affirmative action in college admissions.[17] But when Harvard Professor Stephan Thernstrom, whose views on affirmative action did not coincide with theirs, sought to get the raw data on which the study's conclusions were based, he was refused.[18] Similarly, when UCLA professor of law Richard Sander sought to test competing theories about the effect of affirmative action in law schools by getting data on bar examination pass rates by race in California, supporters of affirmative action threatened to sue if the state bar released such data— and the state bar then refused to release the data.[19]

In these and other cases, statistics are filtered at the source, even when these are taxpayer-financed statistics, collected for the ostensible purpose of providing facts on which informed policy choices can be made, but in practice treated as if their purpose is to protect the prevailing vision.

Rummaging through numbers can turn up statistical data consistent with a given vision and rummaging through other numbers— or perhaps even the same numbers viewed or selected differently— can produce data consistent with the opposite vision. But only when numbers are in accord with a prevailing vision are they likely to be accepted uncritically, without considering other statistics that tell a very different story. For example, much of what is said about the effect of gun control on crime rates in general, or on the murder rate in particular, is based on what kinds of statistics are repeated endlessly and what kinds of data seldom, if ever, reach the general public.

It has, for example, been repeated endlessly in the media and in academia that Britain and various other countries with stronger gun control laws than those in the United States have murder rates that are only a fraction of the murder rate in the United States— the clear implication being that it is the gun control which accounts for the difference in murder rates. Having reached this conclusion, most of the intelligentsia have seen no reason to proceed further. But a serious attempt to test the hypothesis of an inverse relationship between restricted gun ownership and the murder rate would make other comparisons and other breakdowns of statistical data necessary. For example:

1. Since we know that murder rates are lower in some countries with stronger gun control laws than in the United States, are there other countries with stronger gun control laws than the United States that have *higher* murder rates?
2. Are there countries with widespread gun ownership which have lower murder rates than some other countries with lower gun ownership rates?
3. Did the murder rate differential between the United States and Britain originate with the onset of gun control laws?

Those who were content to stop when they found the kinds of statistics they were looking for were unlikely to ask such questions. The answers to these three questions, incidentally, are yes; yes; and no.

Russia and Brazil have tougher gun control laws than the United States and much higher murder rates.[20] Gun ownership rates in Mexico are a fraction of what they are in the United States, but Mexico's murder rate is more than double that in the United States. Handguns are banned in Luxembourg but not in Belgium, France or Germany; yet the murder rate in Luxembourg is several times the murder rate in Belgium, France or Germany.[21]

As for Britain's lower murder rate than that in the United States, history undermines the notion that gun control laws explain the difference. New York City has had a murder rate some multiple of the murder rate in London for more than two centuries— and for most of those two centuries *neither* place had serious restrictions on acquiring firearms.[22] At the beginning of the twentieth century, anyone in England "could buy any type of gun, no questions asked."[23] Murders committed without guns have also been several times as high in New York as in London.[24]

Within England, eras of increasing ownership of guns have not been eras of increasing murder rates, nor have eras of reduced gun ownership been eras of reduced murder rates. A scholarly history of guns in England concluded: "Firearms first entered general circulation and then became commonplace during the sixteenth and seventeenth centuries. This was the same time that homicides and other violent crimes decreased dramatically."[25] This decline continued in the eighteenth century, when "firearms had largely replaced traditional weapons."[26] In the nineteenth century, "violent crime reached a record low."[27] This was the situation in the early 1890s:

> In the course of three years, according to hospital reports, there were only 59 fatalities from handguns in a population of nearly 30 million people. Of these, 19 were accidents, 35 were suicides, and only 3 were homicides— an average of one a year.[28]

By contrast, in later years, especially after the Second World War, Britain began severely tightening up its gun control laws. As it did so, the murder rate *rose*. By 1963, the murder rate was nearly double what it had been at the beginning of the twentieth century.[29] Nevertheless, the fact that the murder rate in England is lower than that in the United States continues to be cited as proof that gun control laws reduce the murder rate.

Considering how many intellectuals have not only supported existing gun control laws, but have actively promoted more and stronger gun control laws, it can hardly be supposed that all these highly educated and very brainy people were incapable of performing very straightforward tests of the hypothesis of an inverse correlation between gun control and murder rates. Nor need we suppose that they knew better and were deliberately lying. What seems more likely is that, once they found statistics to support their preconception, they had no incentive to go any further.

Just as it is hard to find any consistent correlation between gun ownership and violent crime rates internationally, it is hard to find any such correlation from historical statistics within the United States. As one study noted:

The United States experienced an extraordinary increase in violent crime in the 1960s and 1970s and a remarkable drop in violent crime in the 1990s. The number of firearms, especially handguns, in private hands increased by several million every year during this period. The relentless growth in the privately held stock of firearms cannot explain both the crime wave of the first period and the crime drop of the second period.[30]

Few of these facts detrimental to gun control advocates' case reach the general public, though there is no organized conspiracy to block the truth. Individual ad hoc filtering of what gets through the media to the public can readily add up to as complete a distortion of reality as if there were a conscious coordination by a heavy-handed censorship or propaganda agency— if those individual journalists and editors who do the filtering share the same general vision of what is and what ought to be. What seems plausible to those who share that vision can become the criterion of both believability and newsworthiness. Plausibility, however, is the most treacherous of all criteria, for what will seem plausible in a particular case depends on what one already believes in general.

It is not necessary for either individuals or a cabal to work out a plan of deliberate deception for filtering of information to produce a distorted picture that resembles the vision of the anointed rather than the reality of the world. All that is necessary is that those in a position to filter— whether as reporters, editors, teachers, scholars, or movie-makers— decide that there are certain aspects of reality that the masses would "misunderstand" and which a sense of social responsibility requires those in a position to filter to leave out. This applies far beyond issues of gun control.

Data showing the poverty rate among black married couples in America to have been in single digits for every year since 1994 are unlikely to get much, if any, attention in most of the media. Still less is it likely to lead to any consideration of the implications of such data for the view that the high poverty rate among blacks reflects the larger society's racism, even though married blacks are of the same race as unmarried mothers living in the ghetto on welfare, and would therefore be just as subject to racism, if that was the main reason for poverty. Still less are such data likely to be examined as to their implications for the notion that marriage is just one "lifestyle" choice among many, with no weightier implications for individual or social consequences.

No factual information that could reflect negatively on homosexuals is likely to find its way through either media or academic filters, but anything that shows gays as victims can get massive coverage. A search by journalist William McGowan found more than 3,000 media stories about a gay man in Wyoming who was beaten unconscious by thugs and left to die, but fewer than 50 media stories about a teenage boy who was captured and repeatedly raped for hours by two homosexual men, who likewise left him to die. McGowan's search indicated that the second story was not mentioned at all in the *New York Times* or the *Los Angeles Times*, nor was it broadcast on CBS, NBC, ABC or CNN.[31]

Despite an abundance of statistical data being published on virtually every conceivable comparison among groups, no data on the average lifespan of homosexuals compared to the national average, the cost of AIDS to the taxpayers compared to the cost of other diseases, much less a comparison of the incidence of child molestation among heterosexual and homosexual men, is likely to find its way through the filters of the intelligentsia to reach the public, even though there is a well-known national organization openly promoting homosexual relations between men and boys. Conceivably, data on such matters might lay to rest some concerns about homosexuality expressed in some quarters,[32] but few among the intelligentsia seem prepared to risk what the data might show if not filtered out. In this, as in many other cases, it is too much for some to gamble the fate of a vision on a roll of the dice, which is what empirical verification amounts to for those dedicated to a vision.

This is especially true for reporters who are themselves homosexual—and there are enough such reporters to have a National Lesbian and Gay Journalists Association. One homosexual reporter, who has worked for the *Detroit News* and the *New York Times*, knew about the role of public bathhouses frequented by gay men in spreading AIDS, but decided not to write about it because "I was hesitant to do a story that would give comfort to our enemies."[33] Nor is this attitude peculiar to homosexual reporters. Journalists hired under a "diversity" rationale as representatives of blacks, Hispanics or women have the same conflict between reporting news and filtering news for the benefit of the group they were hired to represent.

A black reporter for the *Washington Post*, for example, wrote in her memoirs that she saw her role as being "a spokeswoman for the race" and she excoriated a fellow black reporter on the *Washington Post* for writing about corruption in the local D.C. government, where black officials predominate.[34] "The National Association of Hispanic Journalists has long cautioned journalists against using the word 'illegal' in copy and headlines" about people who crossed the border into the United States without authorization, according to the *Washington Times*. "The practice is 'dehumanizing' and 'stereotypes undocumented people who are in the United States as having committed a crime,' said Joseph Torres, the group's president."[35]

In short, the first loyalty of many journalists is not to their readers or television audiences who seek information from them, but to protecting the image and interests of the groups they represent under a "diversity" hiring rationale. Such journalists are also under peer pressure to filter the news, rather than report the facts straight.

Conversely, information or allegations reflecting negatively on individuals or groups seen less sympathetically by the intelligentsia pass rapidly into the public domain with little scrutiny and much publicity. Two of the biggest proven hoaxes of our time have involved allegations of white men gang-raping a black woman— first the Tawana Brawley hoax of 1987 and later the false rape charges against three Duke University students in 2006. In both cases, editorial indignation rang out across the land, without a speck of evidence to substantiate either of these charges. Moreover, the denunciations were not limited to the particular men accused, but were often extended to society at large, of whom these men were deemed to be symptoms or "the tip of the iceberg." In both cases, the charges fit a pre-existing vision, and that apparently made mundane facts unnecessary.

Another widely publicized hoax— one to which the President of the United States added his sub-hoax— was a 1996 story appearing in *USA Today* under the headline, "Arson at Black Churches Echoes Bigotry of the Past." There was, according to *USA Today*, "an epidemic of church burning," targeting black churches. Like the gang-rape hoaxes, this story spread rapidly through the media. The *Chicago Tribune* referred to "an epidemic of criminal and cowardly arson"[36] leaving black churches in ruins.

As with the gang-rape hoaxes, comments on the church fire stories went beyond those who were supposed to have set these fires to blame forces at work in society at large. Jesse Jackson was quoted in the *New York Times* as calling these arsons part of a "cultural conspiracy" against blacks, which "reflected the heightened racial tensions in the south that have been exacerbated by the assault on affirmative action and the populist oratory of Republican politicians like Pat Buchanan." *Time* magazine writer Jack White likewise blamed "the coded phrases" of Republican leaders for "encouraging the arsonists." Columnist Barbara Reynolds of *USA Today* said that the fires were "an attempt to murder the spirit of black America." *New York Times* columnist Bob Herbert said, "The fuel for these fires can be traced to a carefully crafted environment of bigotry and hatred that was developed over the last quarter century."[37]

As with the gang-rape hoaxes, the charges publicized were taken as reflecting on the whole society, not just those supposedly involved in what was widely presumed to be arson, rather than fires that break out for a variety of other reasons. *Washington Post* columnist Dorothy Gilliam said that society in effect was "giving these arsonists permission to commit these horrible crimes."[38] The climax of these comments came when President Bill Clinton, in his weekly radio address, said that these church burnings recalled similar burnings of black churches in Arkansas when he was a boy. There were more than 2,000 media stories done on the subject after the President's address.

This story began to unravel when factual research showed that (1) *no* black churches were burned in Arkansas while Bill Clinton was growing up, (2) there had been no increase in fires at black churches, but an actual decrease over the previous 15 years, (3) the incidence of fires at white churches was similar to the incidence of fires at black churches, and (4) where there was arson, one-third of the suspects were black. However, retractions of the original story— where there were retractions at all— typically were given far less prominence than the original banner headlines and heated editorial comments.[39]

Other stories that reflect adversely on America can spread rapidly through the media, with little evidence and less skepticism, whether these are racial stories or not. For example, Dan Rather began the CBS News broadcast of March 26, 1991 by proclaiming "A startling number of American children in danger of starving." He added: "One out of eight American children under the age of twelve is going hungry tonight. That is the finding of a new two-year study."[40] Despite the portentous word "study," this was all based on five questions asked by a radical advocacy group which classified as "hungry" children whose parents answered "yes" to five out of eight questions. Two of these questions did not even deal with children but asked about the eating habits of adults. One of the questions about children was: "Do you ever rely on a limited number of foods to feed your children because you are running out of money to buy food for a meal?"[41] In other words, did you ever fill them up with hot dogs when you would have preferred to have given them more of a variety of foods?

It is a long way from "ever" to "every night" and a still longer way from a limited variety of foods to hunger, much less starvation. But verbal virtuosity papered over such distinctions. Nor was Dan Rather unique. "Hunger in America" became a theme of news and commentary elsewhere in the media. *Newsweek*, the Associated Press, and the *Boston Globe* were among those who repeated the one-in-eight statistic from this "study."[42] Meanwhile, when actual flesh-and-blood people were examined by the Centers for Disease Control and the U.S. Department of Agriculture, no evidence of malnutrition among Americans with poverty-level incomes was found, nor any significant difference in their intake of vitamins and minerals from that among people in higher income brackets. The only real difference, in this regard, among people in different income brackets, was that being overweight was much more prevalent among the poor than among the affluent.[43] But, as in other contexts, when a story fits the vision, people in the media do not always find it necessary to check whether it also fits the facts.

FICTITIOUS PEOPLE

Filtering and slanting can create not only fictitious facts but also fictitious people. This is obvious in the case of totalitarian dictatorships, where mass-murdering tyrants are depicted in official propaganda as kindly, wise and all-caring leaders of their people, while all those who might oppose the dictator at home or abroad are depicted as the lowest sorts of villains. But something very similar can happen in free, democratic nations without any official propaganda agency, but with an intelligentsia bent on seeing the world in a particular way.

Perhaps the most striking example in twentieth-century America of a fictitious persona being created for a public figure, without any conscious coordination among the intelligentsia, was that of Herbert Hoover. Hoover's misfortune was to be President of the United States when the stock market crash of 1929 was followed by the beginning of the Great Depression of the 1930s. Had he never become president, Herbert Hoover could have gone down in history as one of the greatest humanitarians of the century. It was not simply the amount of money he donated to philanthropic causes before he became president, but the way he risked his own personal fortune to rescue starving people in Europe during the First World War, that made him unique.

Because the blockades, destruction and disruptions of the war had left millions of people across Europe suffering from hunger, or even starving, Hoover formed a philanthropic organization to get food to them on a massive scale. However, realizing that if he operated in the usual way, by first raising money from donations and then buying the food, people would be dying while he was raising money, Hoover bought the food first, putting his own personal fortune at risk if he could not raise the money to pay for it all. Eventually, enough donations came in to cover the cost of the food, but there was no guarantee that this would happen when he began.

Hoover also served as head of the Food Administration in Woodrow Wilson's administration during the war, where he apparently sufficiently impressed supporters of another member of that administration— a rising young man named Franklin D. Roosevelt— that these FDR supporters sought to interest Hoover in becoming the Democrats' nominee for president in 1920, with FDR as his vice-presidential running mate.[44] However, only the latter came to pass, with Roosevelt being the running mate for Democratic presidential candidate James M. Cox, who lost in 1920, while Hoover went on to serve as Secretary of Commerce under Republican Presidents Warren Harding and Calvin Coolidge.

So much for the real Herbert Hoover. What whole generations have heard and read about is the fictitious Herbert Hoover— a cold, heartless man who let millions of Americans suffer needlessly during the Great Depression of the 1930s because of his supposedly doctrinaire belief that the government should leave the economy alone. In short, the image of Hoover depicted by the intelligentsia was that of a do-nothing president.[45] According to this view— widely disseminated in both the popular media and in academia, as well as repeated at election time for decades— it was only the replacement of Hoover by FDR that got the federal government involved in trying to counter the effects of the Great Depression.

The falsity of this picture was exposed back during the Great Depression itself by leading columnist Walter Lippmann, and that falsity was confirmed in later years by former members of Roosevelt's own administration, who acknowledged that much— if not most— of the New Deal was simply a further extension of initiatives already taken by President Hoover.[46] Lippmann, writing in 1935, said:

> The policy initiated by President Hoover in the autumn of 1929 was something utterly unprecedented in American history. The national government undertook to make the whole economic order operate prosperously. . . the Roosevelt measures are a continuous evolution of the Hoover measures.[47]

Herbert Hoover was quite aware— and proud— of the fact that he was the first President of the United States to make getting the country out of a depression a federal responsibility. "No President before had ever believed there was a government responsibility in such cases," he said in his memoirs.[48] Nor was such interventionism a new departure for Hoover who, earlier as Secretary of Commerce, had urged a mandated reduction in the hours of labor and advocated a Constitutional amendment to forbid child labor, among other interventionist initiatives.[49] As President, Hoover responded to a growing federal deficit during the depression by proposing, and later signing into law, a large increase in tax rates— from the existing rate of between 20 and 30 percent for people in the top income brackets to new rates of more than 60 percent in those brackets.[50]

None of this, of course, means that either Hoover's or FDR's interventions were helpful on net balance, nor is that the point, which is that a completely fictitious Herbert Hoover was created, not only in politics but in the writings of the intelligentsia. For example, the fictitious Hoover cared only for the rich— whose taxes the real Hoover more than doubled, taking more than half their income. The fictitious Hoover was unconcerned about ordinary working people, but the real Hoover was praised by the head of the American Federation of Labor for his efforts to keep industry from cutting workers' wages during the depression.[51]

The intelligentsia of the times created the fictitious Hoover, and the intelligentsia of later times perpetuated that image. In 1932, Oswald Garrison Villard, editor of *The Nation*, said that President Hoover "failed for lack of sympathy."[52] A *New Republic* editorial said of Hoover: "He has been the living embodiment of the thesis that it is the function of the government not to govern."[53] Noted literary critic Edmund Wilson said that Hoover "made no effort to deal with the breakdown"[54] and called him "inhuman."[55] Joint columnists Robert S. Allen and Drew Pearson denounced Hoover's "do-nothingness."[56] As far away as England, Harold Laski said, "Mr. Hoover has done nothing to cope with the problem."[57]

In politics as well, the fictitious Hoover had the same image— and that image lived on. In 1936, when Herbert Hoover was no longer a candidate, FDR's Secretary of the Interior, Harold Ickes, nevertheless attacked Hoover for having been a "do-nothing" president[58]— a trend that continued for many elections in later years, as Democrats repeatedly pictured a vote for Republican presidential candidates as a vote to return to the days of Herbert Hoover. It was twenty years after Hoover left the White House before there was another Republican president.

As late as the 1980s, President Ronald Reagan was characterized by the Democrats' Speaker of the House Tip O'Neill as "Hoover with a smile" and, when Reagan's Secretary of the Treasury defended the administration's economic policies in a statement to Congress, Democratic Senator Ernest Hollings said, "That's Hoover talk, man!"[59]— even though Reagan's tax cut policy was the direct opposite of Hoover's tax increases. As late as the twenty-first century, the 2008 financial crisis provoked a *New York Times* columnist to express fear that the 50 state governors would become "50 Herbert Hoovers."[60] In short, Hoover's image was still politically useful as a bogeyman, decades after his presidency and even after his death.

One of the signs of the great sense of decency of Harry Truman was that, a month after he became president in 1945, he sent a handwritten letter to Herbert Hoover, inviting him to the White House for the first time since Hoover left it in 1933, to seek his advice on food aid to Europe after the disruptions of the Second World War.[61] Hoover was both surprised by the letter from President Truman and moved to tears when he met with Truman in the White House.[62] Later, Truman's appointment of Hoover to head a commission to investigate the efficiency of government agencies enabled this much-hated man to regain some public respect in his later years and shake off some of the opprobrium that went with the intelligentsia's creation of a fictitious Herbert Hoover.

Fictitious positive images can of course also be created, not only by propaganda agencies in totalitarian countries but also by the intelligentsia in democratic countries. No politician in the second half of the twentieth century was regarded by intellectuals as more of an intellectual than Adlai Stevenson, the suave and debonair former governor of Illinois, who twice ran for President of the United States against Dwight Eisenhower in the 1950s. The *New York Times* called him "the best kind of intellectual."[63] Russell Jacoby's study, *The Last Intellectuals* depicted "Eisenhower's resounding defeat of Adlai Stevenson" as showing "the endemic anti-intellectualism of American society."[64] Yet Stevenson "could go quite happily for months or years without picking up a book,"[65] according to noted historian Michael Beschloss, among others who reported Stevenson's disinterest in books.

Meanwhile, no one thought of Harry Truman as an intellectual, though he was a voracious reader, whose fare included heavyweight books like the works of Thucydides and Shakespeare, and who was "a president who enjoyed Cicero in the original Latin"[66]— someone who was able to correct Chief Justice Fred M. Vinson when Vinson quoted in Latin.[67] However, Adlai Stevenson had the rhetoric and the airs of an intellectual, and Harry Truman did not.[*]

---

[*] Neither was of course an intellectual in the sense defined here but the point is that intellectuals saw Stevenson as one of their own, but not Truman, who was far more involved in matters of the mind.

Many among the intelligentsia regarded the unpretentious and plain-spoken Truman as little more than a country bumpkin. These included not only those who were politically or ideologically opposed to him, but also fellow liberals and Democrats. For example, a front-page banner headline on the *New Republic* of April 5, 1948 said: "TRUMAN SHOULD QUIT." In the accompanying editorial, Michael Straight said, "we call upon Truman to quit," adding "To recognize his incapacity is not to deny his good intentions."[68] In a long, unsigned article the next month, the *New Republic* said, "the presidency demands the very finest in leadership that our nation possesses" but "today in the White House there sits a little man." It added:

> Harry Truman has none of the qualities demanded by the presidency. The tasks are utterly beyond his narrow intelligence and limited capacity, as everyone who has worked with him knows.[69]

There were clearly some White House aides who took the same condescending attitude toward Truman. Columnist Drew Pearson reported:

> Certain White House speech-writers were so sure of Truman's defeat they were ashamed to let anybody know they had a hand in his speeches. Of Truman's last speech tour they said: "We are just rehashing old stuff and dishing it out to keep poor old Truman slap-happy."

Pearson noted that most of these speech-writers "had tried to ditch Truman at the Philadelphia Convention."[70] However, despite the *New Republic*'s claim that "everyone who has worked with him" saw President Truman as someone of limited intellect, that was certainly not true of then Assistant Secretary of State Dean Acheson, who later became Secretary of State, though there were many, inside and outside the White House, who under-estimated the scope and depth of President Truman's knowledge and understanding. At a White House conference in 1946, for example, General Dwight D. Eisenhower raised a question as to whether the president understood the grave implications of American foreign policy as regards the Dardanelles. Dean Acheson, who was present at that meeting, later described how President Truman "reached in a drawer, took out a large and clearly much-studied map of the area" and proceeded to give an extended account of the history of that area of the world in what Acheson described as "a masterful performance"— after which Truman turned to Eisenhower to ask whether the general was satisfied that the president understood the implications of American foreign policy in that area.[71]

A contemporary public figure who has had a fictitious personality created for him by the media is Supreme Court Justice Clarence Thomas. The fictitious Clarence Thomas has been described as a loner, permanently embittered by his controversial Senate confirmation hearings, "a virtual recluse in private life."[72] A reporter for the *Wall Street Journal* called him "Washington's most famous recluse."[73] Justice Thomas was depicted in a *New Yorker* article as someone who can really talk only to his wife and "the couple's life appears to be one of shared, brooding isolation."[74] Because Justice Thomas and Justice Antonin Scalia have voted together so often in Supreme Court cases, he has been variously described as "a clone" of Scalia by syndicated columnist Carl Rowan[75] and a "puppet" of Scalia by a lawyer from the American Civil Liberties Union.[76] Similar statements about Justice Thomas' role on the Supreme Court have been common in the media.

Those who have bothered to check out the facts, however, have discovered a flesh-and-blood Clarence Thomas the exact opposite of the fictitious Clarence Thomas portrayed in the media. Reporters for the *Washington Post*— hardly a supporter of Justice Thomas— interviewed colleagues and former clerks of his, as well as consulting notes made by the late Justice Harry Blackmun at private judicial conferences among the justices, and came up with a radically different picture of the man:

> Thomas is perhaps the court's most accessible justice— except to journalists. . . He is known to spot a group of schoolchildren visiting the court and invite the students to his chambers. Students from his alma mater, family members of former clerks, people he encounters on his drives across the country in his 40-foot Prevost motor coach— all are welcome. . .
>
> Thomas seems to have an unquenchable thirst for conversation. . . . A planned 15-minute drop-by invariably turns into an hour, then two, sometimes three, maybe even four, according to interviews with at least a dozen people who have visited with Thomas in his chambers. . . . Washington lawyer Tom Goldstein, whose firm devotes itself primarily

to Supreme Court litigation, has met all the justices and has declared Thomas "the most real person" of them all.[77]

Far from being a recluse permanently scarred by his Senate confirmation hearings, Justice Thomas frequently goes back to the Senate at mealtimes, according to the *Washington Post*:

> Thomas is hardly a stranger in the Senate. He can be spotted in the Dirksen Senate Office Building cafeteria, eating the hot buffet lunch with his clerks. He is chummy with the women who cook and waitress. He has breakfasted among senators in their private dining room, just a whisper away from some of the lawmakers who virulently opposed his nomination. Who would have imagined that the U.S. Senate, the stage for Thomas's "high-tech lynching," as he angrily charged during his 1991 confirmation hearings, is where he enjoys meals?[78]

Others who have actually studied Justice Thomas and interviewed those who have worked with him or encountered him socially have likewise been struck by the difference between the public image and the man himself:

> He made a point of introducing himself to every employee at the Court, from cafeteria cooks to the nighttime janitors. He played hoops with the marshals and security guards. He stopped to chat with people in the hallways. Clerks say Thomas had an uncanny ability to recall details of an employee's personal life. He knew their children's names and where they went to school. He seemed to see people who would otherwise go unnoticed. Stephen Smith, a former clerk, recalls an instance when Thomas, on a tour of the maritime courts in 1993 or 1994, was talking to a group of judges. "There was this old woman standing there in one of those blue janitor's uniforms and a bucket, a black woman," Smith recalled. "And she was looking at him, wouldn't dare go up and talk to this important guy. He left the judges there, excused himself, and went over to talk to her. He put out his hand to shake her hand, and she threw her arms around him and gave him a big bear hug."
>
> Among his eight colleagues, Thomas was similarly outgoing and gregarious. Justice Ginsburg said Thomas sometimes dropped by her chambers with a bag of Vidalia onions from Georgia, knowing that her husband was a devoted chef. "A most congenial colleague," said Ginsburg of Thomas. . .
>
> Thomas took an especially keen interest in his clerks and often developed an almost paternal relationship with them. . . When he noticed the treads on Walker's car were thin, he showed her how to measure them for wear and tear. "The next Monday," Walker recalled, "he came in and said, 'I saw some great tires at Price Club, they're a good

deal. You should really get them.' And I'm sitting there thinking, here's a Supreme Court justice who's worried about whether my tires are safe." Many of Thomas's clerks have similar stories to tell.[79]

Another study chronicled Clarence Thomas' life away from Washington:

Behind the wheel of his forty-foot RV, Clarence Thomas couldn't be happier. The '92 Prevost motor coach has a bedroom in the back, plush gray leather chairs, a kitchen, satellite television, and a computerized navigational system. "It's a condo on wheels," he has said— a condo from which he observes the nation and, when he chooses, engages with fellow citizens. He is drawn mostly to small towns and RV campgrounds, national parks, and historic landmarks. Thomas has told friends he has never had a bad experience traveling by motor coach. Away from the urban centers, he often encounters people who don't recognize him or don't care that he's a Supreme Court justice. He loves to pull into a Wal-Mart parking lot in jeans and deck shoes, a cap pulled over his head. Plopped outside the vehicle in a lawn chair, he can sit for hours, chatting up strangers about car waxes and exterior polishes, sipping lemonade.[80]

Justice Thomas also gives talks to "audiences of thousands at major universities," according to the *Washington Times*.[81] But, since he has seldom been seen at fashionable social gatherings of Washington's political and media elites, that makes him a "recluse" as far as the intelligentsia are concerned.

What of Clarence Thomas' work as a Supreme Court justice? The fact that his votes and those of Justice Scalia often coincide says nothing about who persuaded whom, but the media have automatically assumed that it was Scalia who led and Justice Thomas who followed. To know the facts would require knowing what happens at the private conferences among the nine justices, where even their own clerks are not present. Despite sweeping assumptions that reigned for years in the media, a radically different picture emerged when notes taken by the late Justice Harry Blackmun at these conferences became available among his posthumous papers. Author Jan Crawford Greenburg, who consulted Blackmun's notes when writing a book about the Supreme Court (*Supreme Conflict*), found an entirely different pattern from that of the prevailing media vision. Moreover, that pattern emerged early, during Clarence Thomas' first year on the Supreme Court.

In only the third case in which he participated, Justice Thomas initially agreed with the rest of his colleagues and the case looked like it was headed for a 9-to-nothing decision. But Thomas thought about it overnight and decided to dissent from the views of his eight senior colleagues:

> As it turned out, Thomas was not alone for long. After he sent his dissent to the other justices, Rehnquist and Scalia sent notes to the justices that they too were changing their votes and would join his opinion. Kennedy declined to join Thomas's dissent, but he also changed his vote and wrote his own dissent. . .[82]

This was something that happened several times that first year alone. Some of Justice Blackmun's notes indicated his surprise at the independence of this new member of the court.

Political figures are not the only ones given fictitious personas in the media, creating impressions that are the opposite of the facts. Famous 1930s German boxer and former heavyweight champion Max Schmeling was widely depicted in the American media as a Nazi. He was called "the Nazi fighter" in the *Chicago Tribune*,[83] and "the Nazi nailer" in the *Los Angeles Times*.[84] He was described in the *Washington Post* as "a close personal friend of Hitler."[85] Famed syndicated columnist Westbrook Pegler called him "Der Fuehrer's boy."[86] Nazi propaganda minister Joseph Goebbels was described in the *New York Times* as "a good friend of Schmeling."[87] As late as 1991, the *American Heritage* magazine described him as "vehemently pro-Hitler,"[88] though by this time facts to the contrary had come out and were widely available.

First of all, in the context of the times, Schmeling's agreeing to a match with a black boxer— then rising contender Joe Louis— was criticized in Nazi Germany.[89] Even in the United States, none of the leading black heavyweight boxing contenders of the 1920s had been given a title bout. Although Schmeling was no longer champion and this was not a title fight, it was a match that was especially distasteful to the authorities in Germany because of the Nazis' racial ideology. Only after Schmeling created a sensation with his upset knockout of Louis in their first fight was he then lionized by Nazi leaders. As the *New York Times* reported at the time:

> Max Schmeling, who was ignored and in disgrace for signing to fight a Negro when he left for his winning bout with Joe Louis, returned today a national hero.[90]

Schmeling was then invited to dine with Hitler— and turning down the Nazi dictator was not something to be done lightly. Schmeling accepted the invitation and was reported to have also dined with Joseph Goebbels, in addition to being showered with praises. However, as the *New York Times* also reported at the time:

> Max smiled, bowed and made all the proper responses to the official honors paid him. He did not appear to be carried away with enthusiasm, however. Perhaps he recalled the very cold send-off he received when it seemed likely that the German would be defeated by the American Negro.[91]

Neither in word nor in deed did Schmeling promote the Nazi racial ideology. As sports writer Shirley Povich reported in 1936, before Max Schmeling's first fight with Joe Louis, "With a fine disregard for Nazi policy, Schmeling is training at a Jewish country club" in upstate New York.[92] Schmeling's manager was Jewish and Schmeling retained him as manager despite being pressured by the Nazis to break with him. On his arrival back in the United States, Max Schmeling was photographed warmly embracing both his manager and the fight promoter, Mike Jacobs— both Jews.[93]

As for his behavior toward Joe Louis, after scoring his upset knockout in their first fight, Schmeling went over and helped Louis back to his feet. Before the second fight, which was ballyhooed as a battle between dictatorship and democracy and a test of Nazi racial doctrines, Schmeling's first act, upon entering the ring, was to go straight over to Louis' corner and shake his hand, even though boxers almost invariably go to their own corner first. He went as far as a man living under a dictatorship could safely go in symbolically distancing himself from the Nazi racial ideology.

During *Kristallnacht* in 1938, the night of Nazi-orchestrated mob violence against Jews in Nazi Germany, Schmeling hid two Jewish teenagers— sons of an old friend of his— in his hotel suite. One of those youngsters— Henri Lewin— grew up to become a hotel owner in the United States. In 1989, at a dinner in Las Vegas at which Max Schmeling was present, Lewin publicly told the story of Schmeling's rescue of him and his brother, with tears in his eyes.[94] Schmeling wept as well, but said that he did not like to be "glorified." However, Lewin added, "If they had caught him hiding us, they would have shot him. Let me tell you: If I had been Max Schmeling in Germany in 1938, I wouldn't have done it."[95] How many of those who called Schmeling a Nazi would have done it is another question.

Not only individuals, but whole nations, can be given fictitious characteristics in furtherance of a prevailing vision. Intellectuals' admiration for the presumed virtues of foreign nations has often served as a means of rebuke to their own country. This pattern goes back at least as far as Jean-Jacques Rousseau in the eighteenth century, whose depiction of "the noble savage" served as a rebuke to European civilization.

While it is legitimate to compare some nations to other nations, or perhaps to some ideal vision of what nations should be like, too often Western intellectuals in general, or American intellectuals in particular, make comparisons with a fictitious image of other nations— at one time, especially during the 1930s, with the image of the Soviet Union as conceived by the intelligentsia of the times, with the help of pro-Soviet writers like Walter Duranty or Sidney and Beatrice Webb. Famed literary critic Edmund Wilson, for example, called the Soviet Union the "moral top of the world"[96] at a time when there were mass starvation and slave labor camps under Stalin. When too many facts about the Soviet Union eventually became too well known and too chilling for the fictitious image to hold up, the search for other foreign nations to admire as a rebuke to their own shifted for a while to Communist China or to various Third World nations such as India or some of the newly independent nations in sub-Saharan Africa.

India has perhaps survived in this role longer than others, partly as "the world's largest democracy" and partly because its democratic socialism under Nehru and his successors was so similar to what Western intellectuals favored. The fictitious India was depicted as not being materialistic, intolerant, or violent like the United States. It was as if India was a country of Mahatma Gandhis, when in fact Gandhi was assassinated precisely because of his attempts to dampen the violent intolerance rampant among India's population. The hundreds of thousands of Hindus and Muslims killed in riots between the two groups that followed India's independence in 1947, as the subcontinent was divided into India and Pakistan, somehow faded away into the mists of time. Even lethal violence between Hindus and

Muslims in India today, in the twenty-first century— hundreds killed in riots in just one state in 2002, for example[97]— has done little to change the image of the fictitious India. Nor has the treatment of untouchables.

The Indian government outlawed untouchability in 1949 and the term "untouchable" was replaced in polite conversation by "Harijan"— "children of God," as Mahatma Gandhi called them— then by "Dalits" (the downtrodden) and, in official government reports, "scheduled castes." But many of the old oppressive discriminations continued, especially in the countrysides. Years after racial lynchings had become a thing of the past in the United States, the Indian publication *The Hindu* in 2001 reported that attacks "and even massacres of men, women and children belonging to the lowest rungs of the social order" were still "a regular feature in most parts of the country."[98]

Such practices are not universal across India today. An official report in 2001 found that just three states in India produced nearly two-thirds of all the thousands of atrocities committed against untouchables annually, while there were several states with none at all.[99] But, where atrocities against untouchables continue, they are indeed atrocities. A June 2003 article in *National Geographic* magazine, complete with photographs of untouchable men mutilated by acid because they dared to fish in a pond used by higher caste Indians, detailed a chilling picture of the continuing oppressions and violence against untouchables.[100]

Nor are untouchables the only victims of caste intolerance in India. There are still "honor killings" of young women or couples who marry, or seek to marry, outside their castes. In 2010, the killing of a Brahmin woman who sought to marry a man from a caste that is not ranked as high as Brahmins sparked protests in India but it was not unique. The *New York Times* reported: "New cases of killings or harassment appear in the Indian news media almost every week." A United Nations survey found 76 percent of Indian respondents saying that marriage outside one's caste is unacceptable.[101]

During the era of slavery, India was estimated to have more slaves than the entire Western Hemisphere.[102] Nor has the buying and selling of human beings died out even today. In the June 2, 2011 *New York Times*, columnist Nicholas D. Kristof wrote from India of prostitution traffickers there who "offer families hundreds of dollars for a pretty girl," some not yet teenagers.

Nor are these isolated events: "This country almost certainly has the largest number of human-trafficking victims in the world today."[103]

The point here is not to make a general assessment of India, which would have to include its positive as well as negative features, but to show how, just as fictitious people have been created by the intelligentsia, a whole fictitious country can be created, totally different from the real country it is said to be. Indeed, many such fictitious countries have been created over many generations by intellectuals disdaining their own countries.[104]

Paul Hollander's book *Political Pilgrims*— a study of intellectuals whose visits to Communist countries like the Soviet Union, China and Cuba produced glowing accounts of those totalitarian societies— attributes part of the reason to an asymmetry of information. The "unavailability of unflattering visual information about the most repressive police states" visited by intellectuals contrasts with the "vivid images of the worst aspects of their societies."[105] False interpretations of facts are to some extent inevitable, given the limitations of information and the limitations of human beings. But the creation of fictitious people and fictitious nations goes beyond that, especially when the intelligentsia who are in the business of gathering and disseminating information reach sweeping conclusions in the absence of information or in defiance of information that is available.

Facts about India, including its treatment of untouchables, honor killings, and atrocities against both Muslims and Christians are freely reported in India's own media,* and there are even official Indian government reports on the atrocities committed against untouchables. The same is not true of

---

* In 1994, for example, the *Far Eastern Economic Review* reported on mass riots in Bombay (Mumbai), including quotes from *The Times of India*: "These statistics convey little of the real horror of hordes 'stopping vehicles and setting passengers ablaze'; of 'men brought bleeding to hospital who were knifed afresh'; of the autorickshaw driver who 'decoyed a Muslim couple into a fatal ambush'; of 'neighbours leading long-time friends to gory deaths'; of women driven mad having 'seen their children thrown into fires, husbands hacked, daughters molested, sons dragged away,' and of the 150,000 people hounded out of the city." ("Devils and Enemies," *Far Eastern Economic Review*, July 7, 1994), p. 53. In 2001, Christians were the targets, as reported in the March 11, 2001 issue of the Indian publication *The Hindu*: "Bibles were burnt, priests and nuns assaulted, churches damaged and chapels set afire. Graham Staines charred to death with his children. Father Christudas paraded naked and humiliated on the streets of Dumka and a nun in Bihar forced to drink human refuse."

secretive, totalitarian governments, of course. But, even as regards totalitarian states, much information can become available to intellectuals in the outside world, and the crucial factor can be their willingness to believe it. As British writer Anthony Daniels put it:

> One of the abiding myths of the twentieth century is that many Western intellectuals sympathized with the Soviet Union because they were unaware of the true nature of the regime established by the Bolsheviks. According to this mythology, a lack of information allowed or encouraged them to fix their minds on the regime's declared ideals, and to ignore its terrible realities. Their sympathy, therefore, was a manifestation of generosity of spirit; they were guilty (if of anything at all) only of an error of judgment.
> Nothing could be further from the truth. . . My own small collection of books published in Britain, France and the United States in the 1920s and 1930s contains many volumes that, by themselves, prove beyond reasonable doubt that every class of atrocity, if not every atrocity itself, was made known in the West as or soon after it occurred.[106]

The crucial factor does not seem to be what information is available but the predispositions— the vision— with which intellectuals approach the available information, whether information about nations or information about individuals. Certainly there have been no serious barriers to information about American public figures who have been either exalted or denigrated by intellectuals.

Often fictitious individuals and nations have characteristics that are not merely different from, but the direct opposite of, those of the flesh-and-blood people to whom they are supposed to correspond. With the various fictitious personas which have been created for public figures and foreign countries by the intelligentsia, the only consistency has been a consonance with the intelligentsia's vision of the world and of themselves in that world, leading them to exalt or denigrate according to whose views coincide with or differ from their own— exaltation and denigration often taking the place of facts and analysis about individuals and the issues with which they are involved.

VERBAL CLEANSING

The numerous filters at work in both the media and in academia are not random. They reflect a common vision and filter out innumerable things that could threaten that vision. The verbal virtuosity of the intellectuals filters words as well as facts, through what might be called verbal cleansing, much like ethnic cleansing. Words which have acquired particular connotations over the years from the experiences of millions of people in successive generations now have those connotations systematically stripped away by a relatively small number of contemporary intellectuals, who simply substitute different words for the same things until the new words replace the old in the media. Thus "bums" has been replaced by "the homeless," "swamps" by "wetlands," and "prostitutes" by "sex workers," for example.

All the things that generations of people have learned from experience about bums, swamps, and prostitutes are in effect erased by the substitution of new words, cleansed of those connotations. Swamps, for example, are often unsightly, slimy, and smelly places, where mosquitoes breed and spread diseases. Sometimes swamps are also places where dangerous creatures like snakes or alligators lurk. But "wetlands" are spoken of in hushed and reverential tones, as one might speak of shrines.

Newly coined words for old things appear in many contexts, often erasing what experience has taught us about those things. Thus "light rail" has become the fashionable term used by mass transit advocates for things that are very much like what were once called trolleys or street cars, and which were once common in hundreds of American cities. Trolleys were replaced by buses in almost all those cities— for a reason. But now the inconveniences and inefficiencies of trolleys vanish into thin air when they are presented as that new-sounding thing called "light rail," whose prospective wonders can be described in glowing terms by city planners and other advocates, secure against experience rearing its ugly head through memories or histories of the decline and fall of the trolley car.

Another significant development in the art of verbal cleansing has been changing the names used to describe people who espouse government intervention in the economy and society, as most intellectuals tend to do. In the United States, such people changed their own designation more than once during the course of the twentieth century. At the beginning of that century, such people called themselves "Progressives." However, by the 1920s, experience had led American voters to repudiate Progressivism and to elect national governments with a very different philosophy throughout that entire decade. When the Great Depression of the 1930s again brought to power people with the government intervention philosophy— many of whom had served in the Progressive Woodrow Wilson administration— they now changed their name to "liberals," escaping the connotations of their earlier incarnation, much as people escape their financial debts through bankruptcy.

The long reign of "liberalism" in the United States— which lasted, with few interruptions, from President Franklin D. Roosevelt's New Deal in the 1930s through President Lyndon B. Johnson's Great Society of the 1960s— ultimately ended with liberalism being so discredited that later Presidential and other political candidates with long records of liberalism rejected that label or rejected labeling altogether as somehow misleading or unworthy. By the end of the twentieth century, many liberals began calling themselves "progressives," thus escaping the connotations which liberalism had acquired over the years, but which connotations no longer applied to the word "progressive," which was from an era too far in the past for most people to associate any experience with that word.

On October 26, 1988, a long list of leading intellectuals— including John Kenneth Galbraith, Arthur Schlesinger, Jr., Daniel Bell, and Robert Merton, among others— signed an advertisement in the *New York Times*, protesting what they called President Ronald Reagan's "vilifying one of our oldest and noblest traditions" by making "'liberal' and 'liberalism' terms of opprobrium."[107] Reverting to the original meaning of liberalism as "the freedom of individuals to attain their fullest development," the advertisement did not even recognize— much less defend— what liberalism had come to mean in practice, widespread government interventions in the economy and social engineering.

Whatever the merits or demerits of those interventions, these were the actual policies advocated and carried out by contemporary liberals, regardless of what the original dictionary definition of the word "liberal" might have meant in times past. But the impassioned advertisement did not even consider the possibility that the actual track record of liberals when in power might have had more to do with the term becoming one of opprobrium than the criticisms made by those with a different philosophy. Moreover, it was presented as something odd and unworthy that conservatives like Ronald Reagan would criticize liberals, as liberals so often criticized conservatives like President Reagan.

Just as people who criticize liberalism on the basis of the actual behavior of liberals are accused of being against liberalism in its dictionary definition, so people who criticize the actual behavior of intellectuals are often accused of being "anti-intellectual" in the sense of being against intellectual pursuits themselves. Richard Hofstadter's well-known book *Anti-Intellectualism in American Life* equated the two things, both in its title and in its text, where he referred to "the national disrespect for mind" and "the qualities in our society that make intellect unpopular."[108] *New York Times* columnist Nicholas D. Kristof was one of many who wrote of "the anti-intellectualism that has long been a strain in American life."[109] Even distinguished scholar Jacques Barzun said: "Intellect is despised,"[110] though he himself has been critical of intellectuals, without being someone who despised intellect. Nor did he find it necessary to try to show that scientists or engineers were despised by most Americans or even by those who were highly critical of the track record of intellectuals in the sense of people whose work begins and ends with ideas.

OBJECTIVITY VERSUS IMPARTIALITY

Verbal virtuosity has enabled many intellectuals to escape responsibility for filtering reality to create a virtual reality more closely resembling their vision. Some among the intelligentsia inflate to insoluble levels the problem of choosing between filtering and non-filtering, and then dismiss critics as expecting the impossible— namely, perfect objectivity or complete impartiality. "None of us are objective," according to the *New York Times*' public editor.[111]

Of course no one is objective or impartial. Scientific *methods* can be objective but individual scientists are not— and need not be. For that matter, mathematicians are not objective, but that does not mean that quadratic equations or the Pythagorean Theorem are just matters of opinion. Indeed, the whole point of developing and agreeing to objective scientific *methods* is to seek reliable information not dependent upon the subjective beliefs or predilections of particular individual scientists or on any hope that most scientists would be personally objective. If scientists themselves were objective, there would be little need to spend time and effort to work out and agree upon objective scientific methods.

Even the most rigorous scientist is not objective as a person or impartial in scientific pursuits. Scientists studying the growth of cancer cells in human beings are clearly not impartial as between the life of those cancers and the lives of human beings. Cancers are not studied just to acquire academic information but precisely in order to learn how best to destroy existing cancers and, if possible, prevent new cancers from coming into existence, in order to reduce human suffering and prolong human life. There could hardly be any activity more partial. What makes this activity scientific is that it uses methods devised to get at the truth, not to support one belief or another. On the contrary, scientific methods which have evolved to put competing beliefs to the test of facts, implicitly recognize how ill-advised it would be to rely on *personal* objectivity or impartiality among scientists.

Although J.A. Schumpeter said, "The first thing a man will do for his ideals is lie," he also said that what makes a field scientific are "rules of procedure" which can "crush out ideologically conditioned error" from an analysis.[112] Such rules of procedure are an implicit recognition of the unreliability of personal objectivity or impartiality.

A scientist who filtered out facts contrary to some preferred theory of cancer would be regarded as a disgrace and discredited, while an engineer who filtered out certain facts in building a bridge could be prosecuted for criminal negligence if that bridge collapsed as a result, with people on it. But those intellectuals whose work has been analogized as "social engineering" face no such liability— in most cases, no liability at all— if their filtering out of known facts leads to social disasters.

That so many intellectuals could use the unattainability of personal objectivity and impartiality as a reason to justify their own filtering of facts— and make their argument seem plausible— shows again that they have much intellect and much verbal virtuosity, even if they do not always have much wisdom. Ultimately, the issue is not, as so often misstated, a question of being "fair" to those on "both sides" of an issue. What is far more important is being *honest* with the reader, who after all has usually not paid to learn about the psyche or ideology of the writer, but to acquire some information about the real world.

When the *New York Times* listed three best-selling political books, written respectively by Mike Huckabee, Dick Morris and Frank I. Luntz— all Fox News Channel commentators— among books on personal advice, listing these political books among books on such subjects as how to lose weight,[113] instead of on the more prominent "hardcover non-fiction" list, this was not simply a question of being "unfair" to these particular authors but, more fundamentally, a misleading of the paper's general readers and of bookstores across the country, who use the list of the best-selling, hardcover non-fiction books to determine what books to order and feature in their displays.

Intellectuals who take it upon themselves to filter facts, in the interest of their own vision, are denying to others the right they claim for themselves, to look at the world as it is and reach their own conclusions. Having an opinion, or expressing an opinion, is radically different from blocking information from reaching others who could form their own opinions.

Chapter 11

Subjective Truth

Truth— empirical facts or compelling logic— is an enemy of dogmas, and one dealt with as an enemy by small but growing numbers of modern intellectuals, demonstrating again the divergence between intellectual standards and the self-serving interests of intellectuals. It is not simply particular truths that are attacked or evaded but in many cases the very concept of truth itself.

The discrediting of truth as a decisive criterion has been attempted systematically by some with deconstruction, or ad hoc by others with assertions of what is "my truth" versus "your truth"— as if truth could be made private property, when its whole significance is in interpersonal communication. For example, when Robert Reich was challenged on the factual accuracy of his published accounts of various meetings that had been videotaped by others, showing situations radically different from what he had described in his book, his reply was: "I claim no higher truth than my own perceptions."[1] If truth is subjective, then its entire purpose becomes meaningless. However, that may seem to some to be a small price to pay in order to preserve a vision on which many intellectuals' sense of themselves, and of their role in society, depends.

The seeming sophistication of the notion that all reality is "socially constructed" has a superficial plausibility but it ignores the various validation processes which test those constructions. Much of what is said to be socially "constructed" has been in fact socially *evolved* over the generations and socially *validated* by experience. Much of what many among the intelligentsia propose to replace it with is in fact *constructed*— that is, created deliberately at a given time and place— and with no validation beyond the consensus of like-minded peers. If facts, logic, and scientific procedures are all just arbitrary "socially constructed" notions, then all that is left is consensus— more specifically peer consensus, the kind of consensus that matters to adolescents or to many among the intelligentsia.

In a very limited sense, reality is indeed constructed by human beings. Even the world that we see around us is ultimately constructed inside our brains from two very small patches of light falling on our retinas. Like images seen in the back of a view camera, the image of the world in the back of our eyes is upside down. Our brain turns it right side up and reconciles the differences between the image in one eye with the image in the other eye by perceiving the world as three-dimensional.

Bats do not perceive the world in the same way humans do because they rely on signals sent out like sonar and bounced back. Some creatures in the sea perceive through electrical fields that their bodies generate and receive. While the worlds perceived by different creatures through different mechanisms obviously differ from one another, these perceptions are not just free-floating notions, but are subjected to validation processes on which matters as serious as life and death depend.

The specific image of a lion that you see in a cage may be a construct inside your brain, but entering that cage will quickly and catastrophically demonstrate that there is a reality beyond the control of your brain. Bats do not fly into brick walls during their nocturnal flights because the very different reality constructed within their brains is likewise subject to validation by experience in a world that exists outside their brains. Indeed, bats do not fly into plate glass windows, as birds sometimes do when relying on sight— indicating both differences in perception systems and the existence of a reality independent of those perception systems.

Even the more abstract visions of the world can often be subject to empirical validation. Einstein's vision of physics, which was quite different from that of his predecessors, was shown at Hiroshima to be not just Einstein's vision of physics— not just *his* truth versus somebody else's truth, but an inescapable reality for everyone present at that tragic place at that catastrophic time. Validation processes are the crucial ignored factor which allows many intellectuals to regard all sorts of phenomena— whether social, economic or scientific— as mere subjective notions, implicitly allowing them to substitute their own preferred subjective notions as to what is, as well as what ought to be.

One of the ways of making reality seem optional is to refuse to be judgmental about various preferences, behaviors and lifestyles. "Who am I to say?" or "Who are we to say?" sound like self-denying expressions of generosity toward other people's choices. In practice, they can be denials of consequences— a sort of tactical agnosticism to finesse unwelcome facts.

To say that marriage, for example, is just one of a spectrum of lifestyles that individuals may choose is not only to state an empirical fact but to evade the question of the *consequences* that follow from these various lifestyle choices, not only to the individuals who choose them but for others, including a whole society. Marriage and other living arrangements, after all, can produce children— people who did *not* have a choice of what kind of living arrangement to be born into and raised within. Empirical consequences of raising children in different lifestyles include not only higher rates of poverty in single-parent homes and costs to taxpayers who end up having to support many children raised in such homes, but also other third parties who become victims of higher crime rates by people who were raised in single-parent homes. When poverty rates among black married couples have been in single digits, every year since 1994,[2] this suggests that some lifestyle choices are not only *different* from others but produce *better* consequences.

Many other aspects of culture have weighty consequences. To automatically and non-judgmentally celebrate cultural "diversity" is to refuse to confront consequences that can affect not only the lives of individuals but the fate of society as a whole. However clever tactical agnosticism may be as an exercise in verbal virtuosity, would anyone say that Nazism was just Hitler's "lifestyle"? Or would the consequences be too overwhelming to be finessed aside with a few phrases? Non-judgmentalism is one of the most dangerous of all the arguments without arguments, for no *reason* is given for being non-judgmental,[*] unless endless repetition or peer consensus are considered to be reasons.

---

[*] To justify non-judgmentalism would be to violate the premise of non-judgmentalism itself, for it would say that it is not just *different* to be non-judgmental, but *better*.

Somewhat related to the undermining of the idea of objective truth has been the undermining of standards in various fields, including music, art and literature. "There are no hard distinctions between what is real and what is unreal, nor between what is true and what false," according to playwright Harold Pinter.[3] Nor is this idea confined to playwrights. Distinguished British historian Paul Johnson has pointed out, for example, that a novelist has achieved "aesthetic dominance when those who cannot understand what he is doing or why he is doing it are inclined to apologize for their own lack of comprehension rather than blame his failure to convey his meaning."[4]

The same enviably self-serving result has likewise been achieved by painters, sculptors, poets and musical composers, among others, many of whom draw financial support from taxpayers whom they have no need to please, nor even to make their work comprehensible to them. In some cases, the "artistic" products of these subsidized artists are clearly intended to mock, shock or insult the public, and may even be questionable as art. But, as Will Rogers said long ago, "When you ain't nothing else, you can claim to be an artist— and nobody can prove you ain't."[5] Jacques Barzun has aptly called artists "the most persistent denouncers of Western civilization,"[6] which is perfectly understandable when there is no price to pay for such self-indulgences.

THE LOCALIZATION OF EVIL

Many among the intelligentsia see themselves as agents of "change," a term often used loosely, almost generically, as if things are so bad that "change" can be presupposed to be a change for the better. The history of changes that turned out to be for the worse, even in countries that were pretty bad to begin with— czarist Russia or Cuba under Batista, for example— receives remarkably little attention. But for an agenda of comprehensive and beneficial social change even to seem plausible, it must implicitly assume a localization of evil in some class, institution or officials, since sins and shortcomings universally present in human beings would leave little reason to hope for something dramatically better in a rearranged society, so that even a revolution could be much like rearranging the deck chairs on the *Titanic*.

Incremental reforms, evolving out of trial-and-error experience, may over the course of time amount to a profound change in society, but this is wholly different from the kind of sweepingly imposed prepackaged changes to smite the wicked and exalt the anointed, in keeping with the invidious and dramatic vision of the intellectuals. That vision requires villains, whether individuals or groups or a whole society permeated by wrong ideas that can be corrected by those with right ideas. Nor will it do if these villains are in some distant place, oblivious to the exhortations or condemnations of the intelligentsia. Home-grown villainy is much more accessible and a more attackable target, with more probability of being overthrown by the home audience for the vision of the intelligentsia.

In short, what must be attacked is "our society," to be subjected to the particular "change" favored by the intellectual elite. Society's sins, past and present, must be the focus. For example, imperialism has been seen by much of the intelligentsia, as an evil of "our society." But it is impossible to read much of the history of the world, ancient or modern, without encountering the bloody trail of conquerors and the sufferings they inflicted on the conquered. Like slavery, imperialism encompassed every branch of the human race, both as conquerors and conquered. It was an evil that was never localized in fact, however much some conquered peoples have been portrayed as noble victims by intellectuals— even on the eve of those victims assuming the role of victimizers when they got the chance, as many did after Woodrow Wilson's right of "self-determination" of peoples led to oppressed minorities in the dismembered Habsburg and Ottoman Empires acquiring their own nations, in which one of the first orders of business was the oppression of other minorities now living under their thumb.

Yet the story of conquest today is wholly disproportionately told as the story of brutal Europeans conquering innocent native peoples, the latter often depicted as "living in harmony with nature" or some other version of what Jean-François Revel has aptly called "the lyricism of Third World mythology."[7] This localization of evil is made to seem plausible by the fact that Europeans have in recent centuries had more wealth, more technology and more firepower with which to do what everyone else had done for thousands of years. But Europeans have not always been in the vanguard of technology or wealthier than other peoples— and during the centuries that preceded the rise of Europe on the world stage, millions of Europeans were subjugated by conquerors invading from Asia, the Middle East, and North Africa.

In medieval times, the empire of the Golden Horde of Genghis Khan extended across Asia to deep inside Eastern Europe, controlling without directly occupying what is today Russia, and ruling through Russian leaders chosen by Mongol overlords.

Slavs in general were part of a chain reaction set in motion by various invaders from Central Asia who drove portions of the Slavic populations before them out of the Ukrainian steppes into the Balkans and into what is today East Central Europe, where Slavs in turn forced Germanic and other populations farther west and farther south.

The conquests of the Ottoman Empire in medieval times brought many Slavs under the dominion of the Turks. Ottoman rule in the Balkans lasted five centuries. Among the things it imposed on the conquered European population was a turning over of a certain percentage of their boys, who were taken away as slaves, converted to Islam and trained for military roles in the corps of the Janissaries or in various civil positions. This practice did not die out until the latter part of the seventeenth century, by which time approximately 200,000 boys had been taken from their families in this way.[8] Like other non-Muslim conquered peoples in the Ottoman Empire, the Slavs were explicitly assigned a lower position in the laws and policies of the empire.

It took centuries of fighting before Spain finally expelled the last of its North African conquerors— in the very same year in which it sent Christopher Columbus on the voyage that would open a whole new hemisphere to conquest by Spaniards and other Europeans. Both slavery and brutal conquest were already common in the Western Hemisphere, long before Columbus' ships appeared on the horizon. Indeed, the emergence of the idea that conquest *per se* was wrong—as slavery *per se* was wrong— regardless of who did it to whom, was a slowly evolving notion, as a corollary to a sense of universalism pioneered by Western civilization. Yet today this history, too, is often stood on its head in depictions of peculiar Western evil, inheritable guilt and— not incidentally— liability for reparations.

THE INVIDIOUS AND THE DRAMATIC

The invidious and the dramatic play an especially large role in the careers of intellectuals— and almost inevitably so. Although thinking is the core activity of intellectuals, thinking is something that everyone does. The only rationale or justification for there being a special class of intellectuals is that they do it better— *from an intellectual standpoint*, in terms of the originality, complexity and internal consistency of their ideas, together with a large knowledge base of a certain kind of knowledge, and the consonance of these ideas with accepted premises among intellectuals— but not necessarily from the standpoint of empirical consequences to others.

The Invidious

In an era of widespread access to higher education for those who pass through successive screenings, being in the top five or ten percent by various criteria is often crucial to getting into elite academic institutions, from which careers as intellectuals are most readily launched with the greatest promise of success. A preoccupation with the invidious is thus not simply an individual idiosyncrasy but part of a group experience that goes with the territory of becoming an intellectual and having passed through successive intellectual filters on the road to that occupation. Even those individual intellectuals who have had a more modest educational background imbibe the heady atmosphere of the leading intellectuals, and are able to believe that intellectuals as such are a very special and precious group.

A sense of superiority is not an incidental happenstance, for superiority has been essential to getting intellectuals where they are. They are in fact often very superior within the narrow band of human concerns with which they deal. But so too are not only chess grandmasters and musical prodigies but also computer software engineers, professional athletes and people in many mundane occupations whose complexities can only be appreciated by those who have had to master them. The fatal misstep of many among the intelligentsia is in generalizing from their mastery of a certain kind of knowledge to a general wisdom in the affairs of the world— which is to say, in the affairs of other people, whose knowledge of their own affairs is far greater than what any given intellectual can hope to have. It has been said that a fool can put on his coat better than a wise man can put it on for him.

Many intellectuals are so preoccupied with the notion that their own special knowledge exceeds the *average* special knowledge of millions of other people that they overlook the often far more consequential fact that their mundane knowledge is not even one-tenth of the *total* mundane knowledge of those millions. However, to many among the intelligentsia, transferring decisions from the masses to people like themselves is transferring decisions from where there is less knowledge to where there is more knowledge. That is the fatal fallacy behind much that is said and done by intellectuals, including the repeated failures of central planning and other forms of social engineering which concentrate power in the hands of people with less total knowledge but more presumptions, based on their greater average knowledge of a special kind.

As already noted, there were 24 million prices to be set by central planners in the Soviet Union[9]— an impossible task if those prices were to bear any rational relationship to one another as means of reflecting the relative scarcities or costs of goods and services or the relative desires of consumers of those 24 million goods and services, compared to one another, and allocating the resources for their production accordingly. But while this was an overwhelming task for any central planning commission, it has been a very manageable task in market economies for millions of individual consumers and producers, each keeping track of only those relatively few prices relevant to their own personal decision-making, with the coordination of the allocation of resources and the distribution of products and services in the economy as a whole being done through price competition in the market for inputs and outputs.

In short, the millions know far more than any central planning commission can possibly know, even if the central planners all have advanced degrees and most other people do not. Credentialed ignorance is still ignorance. Ironically, the big problem for supposedly knowledgeable intellectuals is that they do not have nearly enough knowledge to do what they set out to do. Nobody does. But intellectuals have every incentive to claim to be able to do more than anyone can do, and their education and that of their like-minded peers are enough to make these claims seem plausible. Yet, with the ever-narrower specialization of academic intellectuals, it becomes ever more unlikely that even the most outstanding scholars in a given specialty can comprehend all the factors that go into a practical problem in the real world, since many or perhaps most of those factors almost inevitably fall beyond the scope of a given specialty.

The moral dimensions of the invidious seem also to have a widespread attraction among the intelligentsia. Opportunities to be morally one-up on others— sometimes including their whole society— have been eagerly seized, whether in opposing stern punishment of criminals or insisting on applying the Geneva Convention to captured terrorists who neither subscribe to the Geneva Convention nor are covered by it. Moral double standards— denouncing the United States for actions that are passed over with little or no comment when other nations do the same things or worse— are defended on grounds that we should have higher moral standards. Thus an incidental comment that can be construed as "racist" can provoke more outrage in the American media than the beheading of innocent people by terrorists and the dissemination of the videotapes of these beheadings to eager audiences in the Middle East.

Seldom is there much concern expressed by the intelligentsia about the cumulative effect of such biased filtering of information and comments on the public at large or on students who receive a steady diet of such filtered information from the elementary schools to the universities. What is called "multiculturalism" is seldom a warts-and-all picture of societies around the world. Far more common is an emphasis on warts when it comes to discussing the history and current condition of the United States or of Western civilization, and a downplaying or ignoring of warts when discussing India or other non-Western societies.

Since every society is challenged from within and without, distortions that denigrate a society have consequences, including a reluctance to defend one's own society against even unreasonable demands or deadly threats. As will become clear in Chapter 14, this can include a reluctance to respond even to military dangers, sometimes giving potential enemies such as Hitler every benefit of the doubt until it is too late.

The very discussion of both domestic and international issues often reflects the invidious preoccupations of the intelligentsia. These issues are often discussed as competitions in verbal virtuosity, as attempts to show who has the quicker or better talking points, rather than as a search for which conclusion is closer to the truth.

The focus on personal, invidious importance provides incentives for many intellectuals to see social issues in ways that enhance their own sense of superior wisdom and virtue— ways that permit them to be on the side of the angels against the forces of evil, whether discussing payday loans, income differences, high prices in low-income neighborhoods, or the failure of the statistical "representation" of women or minorities to match the preconceptions of the intelligentsia. Given the inability of any particular individual to master more than a small fraction of the consequential endeavors in the real world, the ignorance of the intelligentsia provides a fertile spawning ground for uninformed attacks on social institutions in any society. However superior that society may be to other societies, it is virtually guaranteed to be inferior to what can be imagined in the unconstrained, abstract world existing inside the head of intellectuals.

In short, the invidious is not simply a happenstance or an individual idiosyncrasy. It is an essential factor in the careers of intellectuals, and often a major component in their sense of themselves.

The Dramatic

What of the dramatic? The vision of the anointed lends itself to dramatic, categorical decisions— a proliferation of "rights," for example— rather than to incremental trade-offs. Whatever the benefits and losses to the general public from each of these decision-making approaches in particular instances, the benefits to the anointed come from making categorical decisions which ringingly and dramatically affirm their loftier vision, while trade-offs reduce issues to undramatic quibbling over more or less— with all of this being done on a plane of moral equality with their adversaries, at that, this itself being a violation of the vision of the anointed.

This bias toward categorical decisions has fateful consequences to the larger society. It almost doesn't matter what policy you believe in, if you believe in it categorically, because almost any policy can be pushed to the point where it becomes counterproductive. The institutions through which decisions are made can be crucial, when some institutions tend to be categorical and others incremental. Political, and especially legal, institutions tend toward categorical decisions while families and markets tend toward incremental trade-offs because of an unwillingness to sacrifice completely either love or wealth, for example. It is completely consistent with the vision of the anointed that they wish to have so many decisions made categorically as "rights."

There are other reasons for a tendency toward the dramatic. It is worth noting again that those who are intellectuals in our sense are not dealing primarily with mathematics, science, medicine or engineering, but with things like language, literature, history, or psychology. While the most routine saving of a human life by a doctor using common medical methods has a socially recognized importance, the mere recording of hum-drum events does not make history or journalism interesting, much less important in the eyes of society or a path to distinction, acclaim or influence for the individual intellectual conveying such information. It is exceptional individuals or momentous events that make history worth reading. In journalism, the adage "dog bites man is not news," but the reverse is, conveys the same point. In literature or psychology as well, it is the exceptional subject or the exceptional theory that gives importance to the practitioner or to the field itself.

By contrast, a doctor who never does a thing outside the normal practice of medical science is nevertheless accorded recognition and respect for contributing to the health, and saving the lives, of fellow human beings. There need be no claim of originality or superiority to other doctors in order to receive both the material and moral rewards of the profession. However, in most of the fields in which the intelligentsia work, no such automatic importance is accorded. Only the new, the exceptional, or the dramatic, puts the practitioner or the field on the map, as far as public recognition is concerned. Indeed, even within these fields, complete mastery of the subject matter may mean little for a career in the academic world, without some personal contribution to the development of the field. Hence the imperative among academics to "publish or perish."

Both the invidious process which gives birth to intellectuals from exceptional individuals and the incentives to continue to demonstrate one's exceptional nature contribute to a pattern summarized in Eric Hoffer's observation that "the intellectual cannot operate at room temperature."[10] The mundane cannot sustain them, as the mundane sustains people in fields where the mundane involves something widely recognized as vital in itself, such as health or economic production. Given the process which selects and rewards intellectuals, and the incentives they continue to face, it is understandable that their attention is drawn toward exceptional things that demonstrate their own specialness and away from things that may be vital to others, but are too mundane to serve the interests of intellectuals.

As noted in Chapter 3, most of the intelligentsia show little or no interest in what facilitates or impedes economic production, even though it is ultimately increased production which has relieved the mass poverty that intellectuals have been preoccupied with lamenting for centuries. Much of what is called poverty in the industrialized nations today would have been considered prosperity by most people in times past or in some contemporary Third World nations. But contemporary intellectuals who show little interest in such things are enormously interested in the relative shares of existing wealth that go to various segments of society, and in the ways and means of redistributing existing wealth— even though, historically, the growth of the economic pie, as it were, has done far more to reduce poverty than changing the relative sizes of the slices going to different segments of the population.

Even whole societies created for the express purpose of changing the relative size of the slices— Communist countries, for example— have done much less to reduce poverty than countries whose policies have facilitated the creation of a larger pie. It is difficult, if not impossible, to explain the widespread lack of interest in the creation of wealth by intellectuals who are forever discussing and bemoaning poverty, when ultimately increased wealth is the only thing that has cured mass poverty, without understanding that mundane solutions to even vital problems are not promoted by the incentives, constraints, and habits of intellectuals.

To much of the intelligentsia, the solution to great problems like poverty involves great *intellectual* input, such as their own. H.G. Wells, for example, said that "escape from economic frustration to universal abundance and social justice" requires "a mighty intellectual effort."[11] Similarly, creating a lasting peace "is a huge, heavy, complex, distressful piece of mental engineering."[12] The coincidence of real world challenge and intellectual challenge, which Wells and others have tended to treat as almost axiomatic, depends on the initial assumptions of one's social vision. Those with opposite assumptions reach opposite conclusions, such as that by George J. Stigler already noted in Chapter 1: "A war may ravage a continent or destroy a generation without posing new theoretical questions."[13] In short, even the gravest catastrophes are not necessarily *intellectual* challenges.

After China's communist government decided in the late twentieth century to make their economy increasingly capitalistic, the dramatically increased economic growth rate led to an estimated one million Chinese per month rising out of poverty.[14] Surely anyone genuinely interested in reducing poverty would be not only pleased but inquisitive as to how such a huge benefit could be achieved. Yet virtually none of the intellectuals who have been preoccupied with poverty for years has shown any real interest in the actual reduction of poverty through market mechanisms in China, India or anywhere else. It did not happen in either the way they predicted or the way they preferred— so it was disregarded, as if it had not happened at all.

Again, it is attitudes rather than principles that are manifested— attitudes towards the kinds of policies and institutions based on the prevailing views of intellectuals versus the kinds of policies and institutions which have produced demonstrable results without reflecting, or even considering, the views of intellectuals.

Journalists and others who write for a popular audience face additional incentives, and few constraints, to explain the world in terms which both their audience and often themselves find emotionally satisfying. Many issues are misconstrued, not because they are too complex for most people to understand, but because a mundane explanation is far less emotionally satisfying than an explanation which produces villains to hate and heroes to exalt. Indeed, the emotionally satisfying explanation may often be more complex than a mundane explanation that is more consonant with verifiable facts. This is especially true of conspiracy theories.

Perhaps the classic example of a widespread preference for emotionally satisfying explanations has been the reaction of the American media, politicians and much of the public to the changing prices— and, in the 1970s, shortages— of gasoline. None of these events has required a level of economic sophistication going beyond that in any standard introductory economics textbook. Indeed, it has not been necessary to rise even to that level of sophistication in order to understand how supply and demand operate for a standard product like oil, traded on a massive scale in a vast world market, in which even companies called "Big Oil" in the United States have little or no control of the price. Nor does it require any breakthroughs on the frontiers to knowledge to understand how price controls on oil in the 1970s led to shortages of gasoline— when price controls have led to shortages of innumerable products in countries around the world, whether in modern societies or in the Roman Empire or ancient Babylon.[*]

None of these mundane explanations, however, has proved to be as popular or as prevalent in the media or in politics as the "greed" of oil companies. Over the years, numerous American oil company executives have been hauled before Congressional committees to be denounced on nationwide television for gasoline prices, gasoline shortages or whatever the issue of the moment might be. Politicians' loudly proclaimed determination to "get to the bottom of this" have launched numerous federal investigations of oil companies over the years, accompanied by banner headlines on newspapers and similar dramatic statements on television. The later anticlimactic conclusions of these investigations typically appear in small items buried deep inside newspapers or in a similarly inconspicuous way on television news programs— or do not appear at all. With the emotional catharsis now over, the mundane conclusions— that no evidence of collusion or market control has been found— may no longer be considered to be news.

---

[*] See, for example, Robert L. Schuettinger and Eamonn F. Butler, *Forty Centuries of Wage and Price Controls: How Not to Fight Inflation* (Washington: Heritage Foundation, 1979) or my own *Basic Economics*, fourth edition (New York: Basic Books, 2011), Chapter 3.

Although intellectuals exist in the first place because they supposedly think better or more knowledgeably than other people, in reality their mental superiority is a superiority within a particular narrow band out of the vast spectrum of human capabilities. Intellectuals are often extraordinary within their own specialties— but so too are chess grandmasters, musical prodigies and many others. The difference is that these other exceptional people seldom imagine that their extraordinary talents in a particular endeavor entitle them to judge, pontificate to, or direct a whole society.

Many people over the years have accused intellectuals of not having common sense. But it may be expecting too much to expect most intellectuals to have common sense, when their whole role in life is based on their being uncommon— that is, saying things that are different from what everyone else is saying. Yet there is only so much genuine originality in anyone. Beyond some point, being uncommon can mean indulging in pointless eccentricities or clever attempts to mock or shock. Politically, it can mean seeking dramatic ideological "solutions" instead of prudent trade-offs. Not only Communist movements, but also Fascist and Nazi movements, have had a special appeal to intellectuals, as noted by historian Paul Johnson:

> The association of intellectuals with violence occurs too often to be dismissed as an aberration. Often it takes the form of admiring those 'men of action' who practise violence. Mussolini had an astonishing number of intellectual followers, by no means all of them Italian. In his ascent to power, Hitler consistently was most successful on the campus, his electoral appeal to students regularly outstripping his performance among the population as a whole. He always performed well among teachers and university professors. Many intellectuals were drawn into the higher echelons of the Nazi Party and participated in the more gruesome excesses of the SS. Thus the four *Einsatzgruppen* or mobile killing battalions which were the spearhead of Hitler's 'final solution' in Eastern Europe contained an unusually high proportion of university graduates among the officers. Otto Ohlendorf, who commanded 'D' Battalion, for instance, had degrees from three universities and a doctorate in jurisprudence. Stalin, too, had legions of intellectual admirers in his time, as did such post-war men of violence as Castro, Nasser and Mao Tse-tung.[15]

It was much the same story later in the infamous killing fields of Cambodia:

> The hideous crimes committed in Cambodia from April 1975 onwards, which involved the deaths of between a fifth and a third of the population, were organized by a group of Francophone middle-class intellectuals known as the Angka Leu ('the Higher Organization'). Of its eight leaders, five were teachers, one a university professor, one a civil servant and one an economist.[16]

Eric Hoffer's claim that intellectuals "cannot operate at room temperature"[17] has had many other confirming examples.

However dramatic or attractive a particular vision may be, ultimately everyone must live in the world of reality. To the extent that reality has been filtered to fit a vision, this filtered information is a misleading guide to making decisions in an unforgiving reality, to which we must all adjust, because it is not going to adjust to us.

PART V

INTELLECTUALS

AND THE LAW

Although science is capable of linear advancement, the same is not true of law, where the same insights and mistakes tend to recur again and again.

Richard A. Epstein[1]

Chapter 12

Changing the Law

The law is one of the many arenas in which the ideological conflict of visions is fought out. Just as a free market economy puts severe limits on the role to be played by the vision of the intellectuals, so too does strict adherence to the rule of law, especially Constitutional law. To those whose vision casts a knowledgeable elite in the role of surrogate decision-makers for society at large, the law must have very different characteristics from what it has in the vision of those who see the vast majority of consequential knowledge scattered among millions of people, with no given individual having more than a minute fraction of that knowledge.

If the law depends on the knowledge, wisdom and virtue of surrogate decision-makers, then it is easy to imagine that it is up to those decision-makers to shape laws that are "fair," "compassionate," or guided by a sense of "social justice." But, since these are all undefined words, malleable in the hands of those with verbal virtuosity, such a concept of law is wholly incompatible with the kind of law desired by those who wish the law to provide a dependable framework of rules, within which independent decisions can be made by millions of people working out their mutual accommodations among themselves.

There can be no dependable framework of law where judges are free to impose as law their own individual notions of what is fair, compassionate or in accord with social justice. Whatever the merits or demerits of particular judges' conceptions of these terms, they cannot be known in advance to others, nor uniform from one judge to another, so that they are not law in the full sense of rules known in advance to those subject to those rules. The Constitution of the United States explicitly forbids *ex post facto* laws,[1] so that citizens cannot be punished or held liable for actions which were not illegal when those actions took place. But judges making decisions on the basis of their own conceptions of fairness, compassion or social justice are, in effect, creating laws after the fact, which those subject to such laws could not have known in advance.

Here, as in so many other situations, the fatal step is in going beyond one's expertise. While judges have specialized knowledge and skills in determining where the law sets the boundaries of citizens' discretion, that is wholly different from having judges become second-guessers as to how citizens exercise whatever discretion belongs to them within those boundaries. Individuals may, for example, choose to take on the responsibilities of marriage or to live together without taking on those responsibilities. But judges who have awarded "palimony" to one of the partners after a breakup have, in effect, retroactively forced the responsibilities of marriage on people who had agreed to avoid those responsibilities when they decided to live together without availing themselves of this well-known institution.

The consequences can spread far beyond the particular cases or the particular issues in those cases. The wider penumbra of uncertainty around *all* laws, when judges indulge their own notions, encourages increased litigation by those who have no real case under the law as written, but who may be able to extort concessions from those they sue, who may not be willing to risk some judge's imaginative interpretation of the law.

METHODS OF CHANGE

Laws must of course change as conditions change in society but there is a fundamental difference between laws that change by the electorate deciding to vote for officials who will pass new legislation that will then become laws announced in advance— versus laws changed individually by judges who inform those standing before them in court how the judge's new interpretation applies to them.

Justice Oliver Wendell Holmes' famous statement, "The life of the law has not been logic: it has been experience,"[2] was more than a judgment about history. It was part of his judicial philosophy. In one of his U.S. Supreme Court opinions, he said:

> Tradition and the habits of the community count for more than logic . . . The plaintiff must wait until there is a change of practice or at least an established consensus of civilized opinion before it can expect this court to overthrow the rules that the lawmakers and the court of his own State uphold.[3]

While relying more on the evolved experience of generations, embodied in law, as against the reasonings of intellectuals, Holmes did not deny that some "great intellects" had made contributions to the development of the law, "the greatest of which," he added, "is trifling when compared with the mighty whole."[4] But if the systemic evolution of the law as conceived by Holmes has not been so much a matter of intellect as of wisdom— a wisdom distilled from the experiences of whole generations, rather than from the brilliance or presumptions of an intellectual elite— then intellectuals who seek more than a "trifling" role have little choice but to try to create a very different kind of law, one more suited to their own particular endowments and aspirations.

That has in fact been the thrust of those with the vision of the anointed for more than two centuries. In the eighteenth century, the Marquis de Condorcet took a view of the law opposite to that later taken by Holmes, and more consonant with that of the twentieth century intelligentsia:

> Laws are better formulated and appear less often to be the vague product of circumstance and caprice; they are made by learned men if not yet by philosophers.[5]

By the second half of the twentieth century, the view of law as something to be deliberately shaped according to the spirit of the times, as interpreted by intellectual elites, became more common in the leading law schools and among judges. Professor Ronald Dworkin of Oxford University epitomized this approach when he dismissed the systemic evolution of the law as a "silly faith,"[6] based on "the chaotic and unprincipled development of history,"[7]— systemic processes being equated with chaos, as they have been among those who promoted central economic planning rather than the systemic interactions of markets. In both cases, the preference has been for an elite to impose its vision, overriding if necessary the views of the masses of their fellow citizens, for Dworkin also said, "a more equal society is a better society even if its citizens prefer inequality."[8]

In short, this vision has sought to impose social and economic equality through a political inequality that would allow an elite to override what the population at large wants. Despite Professor Dworkin's claim, it hardly seems likely that most people really prefer inequality. What they may prefer is the freedom that systemic processes permit, rather than elite dictation, even if those systemic processes entail a certain amount of economic inequality.

Law— in the full sense of rules known in advance and applied as written— is a major restriction on surrogate decision-making, especially when it is Constitutional law, not readily changed by a simple majority of the moment. Those with the vision of the anointed must either chafe under such restrictions or else use their talents, including verbal virtuosity, to loosen the restrictions of law on government officials— which is to say, they must make law become less than law, and more in the nature of ad hoc decision-making by empowered elites. That has, in fact, long been the general direction taken by intellectuals who favor surrogate decision-making in general and in particular by government officials seeking greater scope for the exercise of their power.

The Constitution and the Courts

Individual intellectuals and individual judges can take any of a number of approaches to interpreting the Constitution. However, there are certain patterns and vogues that can be traced to particular periods of history. The Progressive era, at the beginning of the twentieth century, saw the beginning of a pattern that would become dominant— first among the intellectuals and then in the courts— later in that century. These Progressive era ideas were promoted not only by such legal scholars as Roscoe Pound and Louis Brandeis but also by the only two Presidents of the United States who had for some years been intellectuals in our sense of people earning their livings from intellectual work— Theodore Roosevelt and Woodrow Wilson.

Theodore Roosevelt referred in his memoirs to his policies as President, including "my insistence upon the theory that the executive power was limited only by specific restrictions and prohibitions appearing in the Constitution or imposed by the Congress under its Constitutional powers."[9] This blithely ignored the Tenth Amendment, under which the federal government could exercise only those powers specifically granted to it by the Constitution, with all other powers belonging either to the states or to the people themselves.

Theodore Roosevelt stood the Tenth Amendment on its head, as if all powers not specifically forbidden to the President were his to use. Nor were his words mere theorizing. When Roosevelt authorized troops to seize a coal mine during a strike, he told the general in charge, "I bid you pay no heed to any other authority, no heed to a writ from a judge, or anything else excepting my commands." Nor was he willing to listen to a Congressional official from his own party, who raised questions about the Constitutionality of the President's actions:

> Exasperated, Roosevelt grabbed Watson by the shoulder and shouted, "The Constitution was made for the people and not the people for the Constitution."[10]

With this, Theodore Roosevelt verbally transformed himself into "the people" and transformed the Constitution into an optional or advisory document, defeating the whole purpose of having a Constitution as a check on the powers of government officials. Nor was this an isolated slip of the tongue. The keynote speech of the Progressive Party, on which TR ran in 1912 spelled it out:

> The Progressive party believes that the constitution is a living thing, growing with the people's growth, strengthening with the people's strength, aiding the people in their struggle for life, liberty and the pursuit of happiness, permitting the people to meet all their needs as conditions change.[11]

Theodore Roosevelt pledged to make "the people themselves" the "ultimate makers of their own constitution."[12] Since the millions of people themselves obviously cannot remake the Constitution, this leaves the President again in the role of "the people"— which means that constitutional limits on Presidential power are only whatever the President chooses to acknowledge.

Woodrow Wilson, the other President who was an intellectual in the sense defined here, was less dramatic but just as impatient with the restrictions of the Constitution. He introduced a theme that would long outlive his presidency when he wrote, while still a scholar at Princeton, of "the simple days of 1787" when the Constitution was adopted and of how "each generation of statesmen looks to the Supreme Court to supply the interpretation which will serve the needs of the day."[13] "The courts are the people's forum," he asserted, choosing a different branch of government as a surrogate for the people and, like Theodore Roosevelt, transforming the Constitution into an advisory document, with the courts' role being to determine "the adequacy of the Constitution in respect of the needs and interests of the nation" and to be the nation's "conscience" in matters of law— in short, expecting the courts to be surrogate policy makers, rather than simply legal specialists applying laws created by others. That unelected federal judges with lifetime appointments should be depicted as "the people's forum" was yet another example of verbal virtuosity in transforming an institution specifically insulated from popular opinions into a supposed expression of those opinions.

If courts "interpreted the Constitution in its strict letter, as some proposed," Wilson said, it would turn that document into "a strait-jacket."[14] Wilson used yet another argument that would be repeated by many others, on into the next century— namely, the role of "change" in general and technological change in particular: "When the Constitution was framed there were no railways, there was no telegraph, there was no telephone,"[15] he said. Like others who would repeat this kind of argument for generations to come— citing television, computers, and other new technological marvels[*]— Wilson made no attempt whatever to show how these or other changes specifically required courts to reach new and different interpretations of the Constitution. One could go through a long list of controversial landmark Supreme Court decisions, from *Marbury v. Madison* to *Roe v. Wade*, finding few— if any— where technological change made any difference.

Abortion,[16] prayer in school,[17] the arrest of criminals,[18] the segregation of the races,[19] capital punishment,[20] the displaying of religious symbols on

---

[*] For example, Stephen Breyer, *Making Our Democracy Work: A Judge's View* (New York: Alfred A. Knopf, 2010), p. 78.

government-owned property,[21] and the differential weighting of votes,[22] were all things wholly familiar to those who wrote the Constitution. Melodramatic apostrophes to "change" may be triumphs of verbal virtuosity but they seldom have any relevance to the issues at hand.

Generic "change" is one of the most uncontroverted facts of life among people across the entire ideological spectrum. Nor is there any question whether laws, including sometimes the Constitution, may require changing. Indeed, the Constitution itself recognized a need for such changes and established a process for creating new Amendments. The salient question that is resolutely ignored in all the rhetoric about "change" is the central question of decision-making in general: *Who* is to decide?

There are, after all, legislative bodies and an executive branch of government, not to mention a whole galaxy of private institutions available to respond to changes, as can millions of individuals and families. Merely repeating the mantra of "change" offers no reason why *judges* specifically are the ones to make the changes. It is another of the many arguments without arguments, unless repetition is considered an argument.

Sometimes the "difficulty" of changing laws, and especially the difficulty of amending the Constitution, is invoked as a reason why judges should become the shortcut to change. For example, Herbert Croly, first editor of the *New Republic*, said in his Progressive era classic, *The Promise of American Life*, "every popular government should in the end, and after a necessarily prolonged deliberation, possess the power of taking any action, which, in the opinion of a decisive majority of the people, is demanded by the public welfare." He added, "Such is not the case with the government organized under the Federal Constitution."[23] He deplored what he called "the practical immutability of the Constitution."[24]

Many others have advanced the thesis that the Constitution is difficult to amend, including in later times Supreme Court Justice Stephen Breyer.[25] But difficulty is not determined by frequency. If the people do not want a particular thing done, even if the intelligentsia consider it desirable or even imperative, that is not a difficulty. That is democracy. If the Constitution is not amended very often, that in itself is no evidence of a serious difficulty in amending the Constitution. There is no inherent difficulty in getting up in the morning and putting on one red shoe and one green shoe. It doesn't happen very often because people *don't want it to happen*. When the people wanted it to happen, the Constitution was amended four times in eight years, from 1913 through 1920.

As far back as 1908, Roscoe Pound, later to become dean of the Harvard Law School, referred to the desirability of "a living constitution by judicial interpretation."[26] He called for "an awakening of juristic activity," for "the sociological jurist," and declared that law "must be judged by the results it achieves."[27] What he called "mechanical jurisprudence" was condemned for "its failure to respond to vital needs of present-day life." When law "becomes a body of rules," that "is the condition against which sociologists now protest, and protest rightly,"[28] he said. Although Pound depicted a "gulf between legal thought and popular thought" as a reason to bring the former into line with the latter, in order to have a system of law which "conforms to the moral sense of the community," this apparently populist notion became merely a rhetorical backdrop in the end, as he called for law "in the hands of a progressive and enlightened caste whose conceptions are in advance of the public and whose leadership is bringing popular thought to a higher level."[29]

In short, Roscoe Pound advocated that an anointed elite change the nature of law to conform to what they defined as the "vital needs of present-day life,"[30] despite being at variance with ("in advance of") the public, with whose "moral sense" the law was supposedly being made to conform. Law, according to Pound, should also reflect what he repeatedly called— without definition— "social justice."[31] With Pound, as with Woodrow Wilson, what the public at large wanted faded into the background, except when used as an opaque mandate for "change." Pound lamented that "we still harp upon the sacredness of property before the law" and approvingly cited the "progress of law away from the older individualism" which "is not confined to property rights."[32]

Thus, in 1907 and 1908, Roscoe Pound set forth principles of judicial activism— going beyond interpreting the law to making social policy— that would be dominant a hundred years later. He even anticipated the later practice of referring to foreign law as justifications for judicial decisions about American law[33]— a process removing judicial decisions even further from the legislation it was supposedly interpreting, from the control of citizens subject to those decisions, and from the Constitution of the United States.

In a similar vein, Louis Brandeis spoke of "revolutionary changes" in society to which courts had been "largely deaf and blind," including a need for state governments to be able to "correct the evils of technological unemployment and excess productive capacity."[34] What would qualify judges to go beyond their legal competence, in order to shape economic and social policies, was unspecified. In an article titled "The Living Law," Brandeis asserted that there had been, "a shifting of our longing from legal justice to social justice."[35] Just whose longing this was, Brandeis did not make clear, though his praise of Roscoe Pound and other legal theorists and like-minded judges might suggest that this was the longing of intellectual elites for a broader influence on policy-making via the courts. Brandeis, like Pound, cited foreign legal theories and practices as a reason why American judges should go in that direction. He also cited "social science" as having "raised the doubt whether theft was not perhaps as much the fault of the community as of the individual."[36]

Like Pound, Brandeis argued that courts "continued to ignore newly arisen social needs" and "complacently" applied such old-fashioned notions as "the sacredness of private property."[37] Like many others then and later, Brandeis treated property rights as just special privileges for a fortunate few, rather than as a limitation on the power of politicians. The culmination of the Progressives' conception of property rights came in 2005, when the Supreme Court in *Kelo v. New London* decreed that politicians could seize private property— typically the homes and businesses of working class and middle class people— and turn it over to other private parties, typically developers who would build things for more upscale people, who would pay more in taxes into coffers controlled by politicians.

Again, like Pound, Brandeis noted some recent trends toward "a better appreciation by the courts of existing social needs."[38] Why judges were qualified to be arbiters of what constituted "social needs" was not explained— which is to say, the more general question of elites going beyond the boundaries of their professional competence was not addressed. Brandeis also invoked "social justice,"[39] without definition, as Pound had

done before him and as innumerable others would do after him. He also
justified the kind of law he wanted as one which, as he illustrated with an
example from Montenegro, "expressed the will of the people"[40]— though, in
the American system of government, the will of the people is expressed
through elected officials, rather than through unelected judges. This is so
obvious that it is hard to see why the will of the people is invoked at all,
except as rhetorical window dressing for judicial coups.

Most courts of the Progressive era rejected the kinds of arguments made
by Roscoe Pound and Louis Brandeis. The most famous of these rejections
came in the 1905 case of *Lochner v. New York*, which upheld the
Constitution's ban on government's changing the terms of private contracts.
But the passage of time brought more and more Progressive era legal
doctrines into courts, including the Supreme Court to which Brandeis was
appointed, and these courts overturned not only *Lochner* but other
Constitutional precedents. Roscoe Pound's becoming dean of the leading
law school in the country, at Harvard, likewise marked a turning point in the
evolution of American legal thinking.

In later years, Professor Archibald Cox of the Harvard Law School
acknowledged the "unprecedented judicial undertaking" of policy-making,
with judges telling "the government what to do and how to do it."[41] However,
he sought to justify this expanded role of courts by saying that the legislative
and executive branches of government failed to solve some problems:

> The courts simply are not ideal instruments for these purposes.
> But the true question is not whether the court is an ideal forum.
> Because a plaintiff comes to court to say that the nonjudicial system has
> broken down and that no one else will fix it, the true shortrun question
> is whether the court will do the job so badly that it is better to let the
> breakdown continue rather than suffer judicial intervention in desperate
> last resort. The longrun question for the creators and shapers of
> institutions is whether some other ombudsman or forum of last resort,
> equipped with expertise and tools that no court commands, can be
> created to deal with such disasters.
> In my view, the judges are not so incompetent nor are the courts so ill-
> suited that a judicial remedy would be worse than inaction.[42]

The crucial question here, as in so many other decision-making processes
is not *what* to decide but *who* is to decide. In this case, who is to decide if
some situation has "broken down" and that "inaction" would produce

"disasters"? If neither the legislative nor the executive branch of government sees the situation that way, why is some third party to supersede their decisions, whether that third party is an existing court or a future "ombudsman" with the power to override both Houses of Congress and the President of the United States, when they have violated no explicit provision of the Constitution, but have simply differed from elite opinion as to what does or does not need to be done?

This is not a matter of differences over particular policy issues. It is a more fundamental question about the nature of the American government and American society— whether the people have a right to choose elected officials to make the decisions and pass the laws they live under or whether third party elites are to say, as Professor (and later Justice) Ruth Bader Ginsburg said, "Boldly dynamic interpretation, departing radically from the original understanding, is required."[43]

As with so many other issues, intellectuals have tended to dismiss, rather than answer, the objections of those with opposing views. John Dewey, for example, referred to "verbal and sentimental worship of the Constitution,"[44] once again reducing contrary views to mere emotions, requiring no substantive counter-argument.* Herbert Croly, in his Progressive-era classic, *The Promise of American Life*, likewise caricatured the position of those with opposing views as "the tradition that a patriotic American citizen must not in his political thinking go beyond the formulas consecrated in the sacred American writings." He said, "They adhere to the stupefying rule that the good Fathers of the Republic relieved their children from the necessity of vigorous, independent, or consistent thinking in political matters,— that it is the duty of their loyal children to repeat the sacred words and then await a miraculous consummation of individual and social prosperity."[45]

Here, as elsewhere in later years, the issue was presented— or caricatured— as whether thought and action should be frozen into that of

---

* In a similar vein, economic conclusions have been attributed by a later writer to "the common antagonism of most leading members of the Chicago school to the scientific management of society through government planning and implementation." Robert H. Nelson, *The New Holy Wars: Economic Religion vs. Environmental Religion in Contemporary America* (University Park, PA: Pennsylvania State University Press, 2010), p. 283.

the eighteenth century, rather than *who should decide* what changes should be made in laws, including the Constitution itself. The writers of the Constitution themselves obviously did not expect to freeze laws as they existed then, or there would have been no point in their creating a legislative branch of government and a process for amending the Constitution itself.

While there are many controversies over particular aspects of the law, the most fundamental controversy has long been over who should control the law and who should change the law. American intellectuals, since at least the middle of the twentieth century, have overwhelmingly favored expansion of the role of judges, beyond that of applying laws created by others, to themselves remaking the law to "fit the times"— which is to say, making the law fit the prevailing vision of the times, the vision of the anointed intellectuals.

Where the Constitution of the United States is a barrier to this expanded role of judges, then judges have been urged to "interpret" the Constitution as a set of values to be applied as judges choose, or updated as they think appropriate, rather than as a set of specific instructions to be followed. That is what "judicial activism" means, though verbal virtuosity has managed to confuse that meaning with other meanings.

Judicial Activism

Those who advocate a greatly expanded latitude for judges to "interpret" laws to suit the presumed necessities or spirit of the times, rather than being bound by what the words meant when the laws were enacted, seem implicitly to assume that activist judges will bend the law in the direction preferred by such advocates— in effect, promote the vision of the anointed. But judicial activism is a blank check for going in any direction on any issue, depending on the predilections of particular judges.

While Chief Justice Earl Warren used expansive interpretations of the law to outlaw racial segregation in public schools in 1954, almost exactly a century earlier Chief Justice Roger Taney had used expansive interpretations of the law to say in the *Dred Scott* case that a black man "had no rights which the white man was bound to respect."[46] It was the dissenters in that case who insisted on following the laws as written and the legal precedents, showing that free blacks had exercised legally recognized rights in parts of the country even before the Constitution was adopted, as well as thereafter.[47]

Intellectuals of the Progressive era and later may well have correctly read the tendencies of their times for judicial activism to move the law in the direction of these intellectuals' goals and values. But that is neither inherent nor inevitable. If the principle of free-wheeling judicial law-making becomes established and accepted across the ideological spectrum, then swings of the ideological pendulum over time can unleash a judicial war of each against all, in which the fundamental concept of law itself is undermined, along with the willingness of the people to be bound by the arbitrary dictates of judges. In the meantime, the sophistry of "results"-oriented judges can make a mockery of the very concept of law, including the Constitution of the United States.

A classic case of judicial sophistry for the sake of desired social "results" was the 1942 case of *Wickard v. Filburn*, which established a precedent and a rationale that extended far beyond the issues in that particular case. Under the Agricultural Adjustment Act of 1938, the federal government had the power to control the production and distribution of many agricultural products. That power was said to be derived from the authority of Congress to regulate interstate commerce, as provided by the Constitution. Yet the law was applied to a farmer in Ohio who grew what the Supreme Court itself characterized as "a small acreage of winter wheat"[48] for his own consumption and that of his farm animals. This farmer planted about 12 acres more than the Department of Agriculture permitted but he challenged the federal government's authority to tell him what to grow on his own farm, when that produce did not enter interstate commerce or even intrastate commerce.

The Supreme Court ruled that the federal authority extended to "production not intended in any part for commerce but wholly for consumption on the farm."[49] The reasoning of the High Court was:

> One of the primary purposes of the Act in question was to increase the market price of wheat, and to that end to limit the volume thereof that could affect the market. It can hardly be denied that a factor of such volume and variability as home-consumed wheat would have a substantial influence on price and market conditions. This may arise because being in marketable condition such wheat overhangs the market and, if induced by rising prices, tends to flow into the market and check

> price increases. But if we assume that it is never marketed, it supplies a
> need of the man who grew it which would otherwise be reflected by
> purchases in the open market. Home-grown wheat in this sense
> competes with wheat in commerce.[50]

Thus wheat which did not enter any commerce at all was ruled to be subject to federal control under the interstate commerce clause of the Constitution. But the fact that the Constitution gives the federal government certain specified powers does not mean that it also grants the government the right to achieve its particular goals in using those powers "by all means necessary," in disregard of individuals' rights. Under such expansive stretching of the law as that in *Wickard v. Filburn*, virtually anything could be called "interstate commerce," since virtually everything has some effect— however small or remote— on virtually everything else. In the wake of this Supreme Court decision "interstate commerce" in fact became a magic phrase justifying virtually any expansion of federal power over the years, contrary to the Tenth Amendment's limitation on federal authority.

In 1995, there was consternation in some quarters when the Supreme Court voted 5 to 4 in *U.S. v. Lopez* that carrying a gun near a school was not "interstate commerce," so that Congress had no authority to ban it, though all the states had that authority and most in fact did ban it. What made the vote close and the result surprising was that it rejected the long-standing practice of courts stretching the phrase "interstate commerce" to cover— and rubber stamp— virtually anything that Congress chose to regulate, ban or impose. The argument that carrying a gun near a school was covered by the interstate commerce clause of the Constitution was later summarized by Justice Stephen Breyer in his book *Making Our Democracy Work: A Judge's View*:

> Possession of guns in schools means violence, and violence means poor
> education. Poor education means an unproductive, noncompetitive
> workforce. And that kind of workforce negatively affects not just one
> state but all states. School violence, of which guns are a part, arguably
> presents a national problem warranting a national solution.[51]

Such reasoning, so reminiscent of that in *Wickard v. Filburn*— which Justice Breyer also rationalized[52]— would make almost anything, in almost any aspect of life, "interstate commerce" and thus nullify the Constitution's limits on the powers of Congress and of the federal government in general.

Some judicial activists not only make rulings that stretch the law but even go directly counter to it. A classic example of this was the 1979 case of *United Steelworkers of America v. Weber*. Section 703(a) of the Civil Rights Act of 1964 made it illegal for an employer "to discriminate against any individual with respect to his compensation, terms, conditions, or privileges of employment, because of such individual's race" or various other characteristics. Section 703(d) more specifically forbade such discrimination in "any program established to provide apprenticeship or other training." Nevertheless, a white employee, Brian F. Weber, was denied admission to a training program where places were awarded on the basis of seniority, even though black employees with less seniority were admitted, because racially separate seniority lists were used and racial quotas were established.

That this was counter to the plain meaning of the Act was not explicitly denied in the U.S. Supreme Court opinion written by Justice William J. Brennan. But Justice Brennan rejected "a literal interpretation" of the Civil Rights Act, preferring instead to seek the "spirit" of the Act in Congress' "primary concern" for "the plight of the Negro in our economy."[53] Because that presumed purpose was not to protect whites from racial discrimination, the Act was deemed not to protect Brian F. Weber, who lost the case. The emergence of this decision, despite the clear language of the Act to the contrary, was likened to the great escapes of Houdini in the dissenting opinion of Justice William H. Rehnquist.[54] As for the supposed "spirit" of the Civil Rights Act of 1964, its Congressional sponsors repeatedly and emphatically denied during Congressional debate that it required, or would even permit, preferences for blacks or discrimination against whites.[55]

In all three of these examples— *Dred Scott, Wickard v. Filburn* and *Weber*— the decisions reflected the "results" preferred rather than the written law on which those results were supposedly based. They are classic concrete examples of judicial activism. Unfortunately, the meaning of the phrase has been obfuscated in recent years and so requires some closer scrutiny.

"Judicial activism" is an idiomatic expression whose meaning cannot be determined by the separate meanings of its words, any more than the meaning of the exclamation "Hot dog!" can be determined by referring to a separate definition of "hot" and "dog." Nevertheless, in recent times, some have attempted to redefine judicial activism by how *active* a judge has been in declaring laws or government actions unconstitutional. However, the Constitution itself is a limitation on the powers of Congress, as well as on the powers of the other branches of government. Judges have been considered duty-bound to invalidate legislation that goes counter to the Constitution, ever since the landmark case of *Marbury v. Madison* in 1803, so how often they perform that duty is not solely in their hands, but depends also on how often others do things that exceed the powers granted them by the Constitution.

The real issue regarding judicial activism is over whether the *basis* of a judge's decisions is the law created by others, including the Constitution, or whether judges base their decisions on their own particular conception of "the needs of the times" or of "social justice" or of other considerations beyond the written law or the legal precedents.

There is another idiomatic expression used for the practice of a judge who confines his role to following the written law— "judicial restraint" or following the "original intent" of laws. Here again, the meaning of these terms cannot be understood simply from the separate meaning of each word. Judicial restraint means making judicial rulings based on laws created by others, rather than being based on the judge's own assessment of what would be best for either the parties in the case at hand or for society at large.

Justice Oliver Wendell Holmes exemplified this legal philosophy when he said that his role as a judge "is to see that the game is played according to the rules whether I like them or not."[56] He also said: "The criterion of constitutionality is not whether we believe the law to be for the public good."[57] But, since the judge who believes in judicial restraint makes the existing law— and especially the Constitution, which is explicitly "the supreme law of the land"[58]— the paramount consideration in deciding cases, that often means that such a judge must be *active* in striking down new laws which violate the restrictions of the Constitution.

In short, activity is *not* what distinguishes the judicial activist from the practitioner of judicial restraint, since these are just idiomatic expressions for different philosophies of carrying out a judge's function. Judges who base their decisions on the kinds of social, economic, or other considerations of the sort urged by Roscoe Pound, Louis Brandeis, or others in later times, are judicial activists in the sense that has stirred controversy, whether they declare many laws unconstitutional or few laws unconstitutional.

Although Justice William O. Douglas was a classic judicial activist in the sense of paying only the most token attention to the Constitution in making rulings based on his own policy preferences— the most famous example being basing his ruling in *Griswold v. Connecticut* on "emanations" from the "penumbras" of the Constitution— he nevertheless deferred to legislators who passed liberal social legislation, using language dear to the heart of advocates of judicial restraint, saying that the court should not be a "super-legislature" but leave social policy to Congress and state legislators.[59] But when the existing law represented social policy that he disapproved, Justice Douglas did not hesitate to intervene and declare it unconstitutional— as he did in *Griswold v. Connecticut*— even if he had nothing more on which to base his ruling than "emanations" that he somehow discerned coming from the "penumbras" of the Constitution,[60] which not even the greatest legal minds, on or off the court, had ever discerned before.

The high tide of judicial activism was the Warren Court of the 1950s and 1960s, when Chief Justice Earl Warren and a like-minded majority on the Supreme Court decided to remake social policy in both civil and criminal areas, almost invariably to the applause of the intelligentsia in the media and in academia. However, as justices with a more judicially restrained view of their role later went on the court, beginning with the Warren Burger Court in 1969, many among the intelligentsia sought to turn the previous complaints about judicial activism against the new judges, by measuring how *active* these judges were in declaring laws unconstitutional or in amending the precedents established by judicial activists such as those of the Warren Court era.

Liberal journalist Michael Kinsley accused Antonin Scalia of judicial activism when Scalia wrote an opinion as a Circuit Court of Appeals judge which, in Kinsley's words, over-ruled "a major piece of legislation passed by large majorities in both houses of Congress and signed with a flourish by a popular president"[61]— as if these were things that make a law Constitutional. Linda Greenhouse of the *New York Times* likewise called the decision that carrying a gun near a school was not interstate commerce an exercise of "raw power" by the Supreme Court because in *U.S. v. Lopez* it "invalidated a law that two houses of Congress and the President of the United States approved"[62]— as if other laws over-ruled by the Supreme Court as unconstitutional, ever since *Marbury v. Madison* in 1803, were not also laws duly passed in the same way.

Under the title, "Dissing Congress," a *Michigan Law Review* article said that "the Court in *Lopez* had taken an important step in developing its new version of judicial activism, under which Congress was accorded less respect for its handiwork."[63] Senator Herb Kohl likewise denounced the *Lopez* decision as "a piece of judicial activism that ignores children's safety for the sake of legal nit-picking." However, the *Washington Post* took a more measured view in its editorial on the case:

> One would never guess from the senator's comment, for example, that most states already prohibit the carrying of weapons in schools. In fact, Alfonso Lopez, the San Antonio teenager whose conviction was reversed in this case, was initially arrested on state charges that were dropped only when the federal government took over the prosecution. Clearly, the invalidation of this statute does not leave the nation's children vulnerable at their desks. And it may cause federal legislators to think twice about rushing into every problem area without even considering "nit-picking" questions of federalism.[64]

Senator Kohl was by no means the only law-maker to argue in "results"-oriented terms, rather than in terms of Constitutional limitations on federal power. Senator Arlen Specter said, "I think that crime is a national problem" and "Guns and drugs are the principal instrumentalities of crime." But liberal law professor Laurence Tribe saw beyond "results"-oriented criteria in this case, as reported in the *Chicago Sun-Times*:

> "Congress has pushed the outer edge of the envelope rather carelessly," said Harvard Law School professor Laurence H. Tribe, who noted that lawmakers did not present findings of a link between interstate commerce and the dangers of guns on school grounds. He said the ruling revealed that "this court takes structural limits (to Congress' power) more seriously than people had thought. . . which liberals and pragmatists find dismaying."[65]

The new definition of judicial activism included not only failing to defer to Congress but also the overturning of judicial precedents. In Linda Greenhouse's words, the *Lopez* case "was the first time in 60 years that the Court had invalidated a Federal law on the ground that Congress had exceeded its constitutional authority to regulate interstate commerce."[66] But judges take an oath to uphold the Constitution, not an oath to uphold precedents. Otherwise, *Dred Scott* and *Plessy v. Ferguson* could have been set in concrete forever.

The *Lopez* case was by no means the only one that caused many among the intelligentsia to denounce the later Supreme Court for "judicial activism" on the basis of its having declared some law or policy unconstitutional. Professor Cass Sunstein of the University of Chicago lamented in 2001: "We are now in the midst of a remarkable period of right-wing judicial activism." This has produced, among other things, he said, an "undemocratic judiciary"[67]— when in fact an appellate court with the power to overrule laws passed by elected officials is inherently undemocratic, so that Professor Sunstein's complaint would apply to the Constitution of the United States itself, rather than to those who carry out their function under that Constitution, as they took an oath to do.

Sunstein complained again in 2003 that "the Rehnquist Court has struck down at least 26 acts of Congress since 1995," and is thereby "guilty of *illegitimate activism*" for— among other things— having "struck down a number of affirmative action programs" as well as striking down "federal legislation as beyond congressional power under the Commerce Clause." According to Professor Sunstein, the Supreme Court has "forbidden Congress from legislating on the basis of its own views" of what the Fourteenth Amendment means.[68] But if Congress can determine the extent of its own powers under the Fourteenth Amendment, or under any other provision of the Constitution, then the Constitution becomes meaningless as a limit on Congressional power or on government power in general. The fundamental idea of checks and balances among the three branches of government would vanish into thin air.

In a similar vein, an article in the *New Republic* titled "Hyperactive: How the Right Learned to Love Judicial Activism" claimed that conservative judges "have turned themselves into the mirror image of the judicial activists whom they have spent their careers attacking."[69] Using this new redefinition of judicial activism, a *New York Times* writer charged Chief Justice John Roberts with sometimes supporting "judicial action, even if it meant trampling on Congress and the states."[70] A later *New York Times* editorial declared "a willingness to strike down Congressional laws" to be "the most common objective criteria"[71] of judicial activism. This redefinition sidesteps the whole crucial question whether the laws over-ruled were in fact consistent or inconsistent with the Constitution of the United States. But this key issue is repeatedly left out of claims that the Supreme Court is "activist" when it fails to uphold legislation or particular precedents.

No provision of the Constitution is more plainly stated than the First Amendment, which begins, "Congress shall make no law" and includes among the forbidden legislation laws "abridging the freedom of speech." Yet there was consternation in the media, in politics and in academia when the Supreme Court in 2010 declared unconstitutional sections of the McCain-Feingold law, which forbade unions or corporations from running television advertisements opposing or endorsing political candidates.

The President of the United States called the decision "devastating" and Professor Ronald Dworkin denounced the decision for having "overruled established precedents and declared dozens of national and state statutes unconstitutional." Both lamented the presumed *results* of the decision, President Obama saying that it "will open the floodgates for special interests." Professor Dworkin said the decision "will further weaken the quality and fairness of our politics."[72] Professor Alan Blinder of Princeton called the decision "outrageous" because "it will strengthen the hands of industry lobbyists"[73]— another results-oriented criterion, substituting for legal principles the question of whose ox is gored.

Dworkin questioned the motives of the five justices in the majority— their "instinctive favoritism of corporate interests" and their "partisan zeal" for Republicans."[74] He said:

> They have changed the American electoral system to make the election
> of Republican candidates more likely, for example by guaranteeing

corporations a constitutional right to spend as much as they wish denouncing candidates they dislike.[75]

Since everyone else is free to denounce candidates they dislike, why people who run corporations should be denied the same right was not explained by Dworkin. He nowhere addressed the fundamental constitutional question, whether stopping particular segments of the population from running political ads was "abridging the freedom of speech," something for which "Congress shall make no law."[76] He dismissed "a shallow, simplistic understanding of the First Amendment, one that actually undermines one of the most basic purposes of free speech, which is to protect democracy."[77] In other words, the plain, explicit and unmistakable statement of the Constitution— that "Congress shall make no law"— is to be superseded by an inferred purpose and/or presumed results. Moreover, justices who prefer to read the law as it was written are to be considered judicial activists, standing the definition of judicial activism on its head, as well as standing the Constitution on its head.

The new definition of judicial activism lends itself to a purely numerical basis for deciding who is and who is not a judicial activist— Professor Sunstein, for example, basing his charges on how many "federal laws per year" the Supreme Court has declared unconstitutional.[78] That notion has spread from the intelligentsia into politics.

Thus Senator Patrick Leahy used this new definition of judicial activism when he asserted, "The two most activist judges we have right now are Justice Thomas and Justice Scalia, who have struck down and thus written laws of their own in place of congressional laws more than anybody else on the current Supreme Court."[79] Since these are the two justices most identified with judicial restraint, it was a verbal coup to turn the tables and label them conservative activists. Such verbal virtuosity, blurring the line between judicial activism and judicial restraint, not only defuses criticism of liberal activist judges but enables points to be scored by invoking moral equivalence against judicially restrained judges who can also be called "activist" by simply redefining the term.

Genuine judicial activism, like many other social phenomena, may be more readily understood by examining the incentives and constraints facing those involved. One constraint on judges' actions that has clearly weakened over the years is the disapproval of peers, whether in the judiciary or among legal scholars in the law schools. Judicial activism for litigants or causes currently favored by the prevailing vision of the intellectuals can expect acceptance, at a minimum, and in many cases celebration or lionizing of activist judges. In short, incentives favor judicial activism.

Judges, like intellectuals, usually become famous among the general public only when they step out beyond the bounds of their professional competence to become philosopher-kings deciding social, economic or political issues. Not even Chief Justice Earl Warren's admirers tried to portray him as a great legal scholar.[80] Both he and Chief Justice Roger Taney a century earlier became famous for making sweeping pronouncements about society on a sociological, rather than a legal, basis for their landmark rulings. With pronouncements going beyond the range of their expertise or competence being virtually a prerequisite for popular prominence, it is hardly surprising that so many judges, like so many intellectuals, have said so many things that make no sense.

Judicial Restraint and "Original Intent"

"Judicial restraint" has sometimes been summed up in another idiomatic expression— namely, following the "original intent" of the law. Many among the intelligentsia have seized upon the word "intent" to claim that it is difficult or impossible to discern exactly what those who wrote the Constitution, or legislation for that matter, actually intended, especially after the passing of many years. Thus Professor Jack Rakove of Stanford University said: "Establishing the intention behind any action is a tricky business" and "The task grows geometrically more complex when we try to ascribe intent to groups of people— especially men who were acting two centuries ago, who left us incomplete records of their motives and concerns, and who reached their decisions through a process that fused principled debate with hard-driven bargains."[81]

The key word in all of this— and the key fallacy in this common line of reasoning— is the word "behind." Practitioners of judicial restraint are seeking to understand and apply the written law as it stands— as instructions for both judges and the citizenry— *not* discover the motivations, beliefs, hopes or fears that might have been behind the writing of the law. Judicial restraint means undertaking an inherently less complicated task. Even the simplest law, such as a 65 miles an hour speed limit, can be expanded into a complex question of unanswerable dimensions if looked at in terms of the attitudes, values, etc., *behind* the intentions of those who created that law, rather than being looked at as an explicit instruction, readily understood.

Looking at laws in terms of the subjective intentions of those who wrote them is not only a more complicated approach, it is an approach that seeks or claims to discern the value judgments or the "spirit" behind the laws— which gives judges far greater latitude for interpretation, and thus far more opportunities to adjust the laws to meet "the needs of the time," "social justice," or whatever other synonym for the individual predilections of particular judges. Critics of judicial restraint project such difficulties onto others who are not looking behind laws, but undertaking a far more straightforward task of reading laws as explicit instructions, rather than as general statements of values.

As Justice Antonin Scalia put it, "despite frequent statements to the contrary, we do not really look for subjective legislative intent." What he is seeking is "the original meaning of the text," adding: "Often— indeed, I dare say usually— that is easy to discern and simple to apply."[82] Nor is Justice Scalia unique in this. From William Blackstone in eighteenth century England to Oliver Wendell Holmes and Robert Bork in twentieth century America, those seeking to stick to the original meaning of laws have made it very clear that they were *not* talking about events taking place within the inner recesses of the minds of those who write laws.

For one thing, the votes which provide the political, legal and moral authority of laws are votes on what was publicly set before those who voted. In other words, *nobody voted on what was in the back of somebody else's mind.* Moreover, nobody knows how to obey or disobey what is in the back of somebody else's mind.

It was the publicly known meaning of the words of the laws, "to be understood in their usual and most known signification" as of the time they were used, according to Blackstone,[83] that determines how a judge should interpret them. For Holmes as well, legal interpretation of what the law-maker said did not mean trying to "get into his mind."[84] Holmes said: "We do not inquire what the legislature meant; we ask only what the statute means."[85] In a letter to British jurist Sir Frederick Pollock, Holmes said "we don't care a damn for the meaning of the writer."[86] The judge's job, according to Holmes, is to "read English intelligently— and a consideration of consequences comes into play, if at all, only when the meaning of the words used is open to reasonable doubt."[87] Judge Robert H. Bork has likewise argued that judges should render decisions "according to the historical Constitution."[88]

What is different about the *original* meaning of a law, as compared to other meanings that might later be read into its words? It is a meaning *already known* by those subject to that law— and ultimately laws are written for the citizenry, not for judges. To subject citizens to the penalties of the law for things that the law never meant before is, in effect, to create *ex post facto* laws, in defiance of the Constitutional ban on such laws[89] and the fundamental principles of a self-governing nation, whose laws are passed by elected officials. When it comes to interpreting laws, each appellate court cannot act as if it is a new Constitutional Convention, which is what Justice Stephen Breyer's advice amounts to when he says that the Court should "consider the basic values that underlie a constitutional provision and their contemporary significance."[90]

Oliver Wendell Holmes saw it differently: "Men should know the rules by which the game will be played. Doubt as to the value of some of those rules is no sufficient reason why they should not be followed by the courts."[91] What "the needs of the times," "values," "modern social science," and foreign laws all have in common is that they expand the arbitrary power of judges beyond the written laws passed by elected representatives of the people and beyond that of the Constitution of the United States.

Despite many plain statements by advocates and practitioners of judicial restraint over a long span of years, much verbal virtuosity has been deployed by others to expand the task of judicial interpretation to unachievable dimensions by turning the question into one of discerning subjective values, motives, beliefs, hopes and fears *behind* the creation of the law, or which "underlie" the law, in Justice Breyer's words. Professor Rakove, for example, said that at the time of the Constitutional Convention in 1787, James Madison "approached the Convention in the grip of a great intellectual passion,"[92] that he had "fear" of certain policies regarding property and religion,[93] and that he "privately described" Constitutional amendments in a particular way.[94] But nobody voted on Madison's private thoughts and fears.

Professor Ronald Dworkin has likewise argued at considerable length against original intent on grounds that the "mental events" in the minds of legislators or writers of the Constitution are difficult or impossible to discern,[95] that "it seems even plainer that we have no fixed concept of a group intention," nor any way of deciding "which aspects of individual mental states are relevant to a group intention."[96] Similarly, Justice William J. Brennan spoke of the "sparse or ambiguous evidence of the original intention" of the framers of the Constitution.[97] Long-time *New York Times* writer Anthony Lewis likewise declared, "it is seldom possible to know with assurance what the delegates to the Constitutional Convention of 1787, or the hundreds at the state ratifying conventions, thought about the particular issues that arise today."[98]

These laments about the difficulty of mind-reading ignore the plainly stated and repeated declarations over the past two centuries that believers in judicial restraint are *not* trying to read minds.

Such attempts to change the question from the plain *meaning* of a law, as a set of instructions to citizens and judges alike, to an esoteric quest for discovering what was *behind* the creation of the law are often used by those who espouse judicial interpretations which go beyond what the law explicitly says— and sometimes even directly counter to the written law, as Justice William J. Brennan did in the *Weber* case. Professor Ronald Dworkin defended the *Weber* decision on grounds that "the question of how Title VII should be interpreted cannot be answered simply by staring at the words Congress used."[99] The verbal virtuosity of referring to simply "staring" at words— apparently as the only alternative to adventurous reinterpretations— contrasts sharply with Holmes' statement about simply reading English intelligently.

To Dworkin, the significance of the *Weber* decision was that it was "another step in the Court's efforts to develop a new conception of what equality requires in the search for racial justice."[100] Why judges are to preempt such decisions and rule on the basis of their own new conceptions of social issues, under the guise of interpreting the existing law, while going directly counter to what the law actually says, was a question not raised, much less answered.

Saying that it is hard or impossible to discern what was meant by a law has often been a prelude to making decisions that ignore even the plainest meanings— as in the *Weber* case— in order to impose notions currently in vogue in elite circles as the law of the land. Dworkin and others have openly advocated as much, which makes their tactical agnosticism about "intent" a red herring. For those who do not intend to follow the original meaning of laws, the ease or difficulty of discovering that meaning is irrelevant, except as a distracting talking point.

The Constitution was a very plainly written document, and when it used phrases like "an establishment of religion," for example, it referred to something well known to people who had already lived under an established church, the Church of England. The prohibition against an establishment of religion had nothing to do with a "wall of separation" between church and state, which appears nowhere in the Constitution, but was a phrase from Thomas Jefferson. There was nothing esoteric about the phrase "an establishment of religion." For more than a hundred years after the Constitution was written, it never meant that it was illegal to display religious symbols on government property, however much some people in later times might wish that this was what it meant, and however much some modern judges might be willing to accommodate that wish.

Similarly with phrases like "due process" or "freedom of speech," which had a long history in British law before those same phrases were placed in the Constitution of the United States by people who had only recently ceased to be British subjects. They were not coining new phrases for new or esoteric concepts whose meanings judges would have to divine *de novo*.

Judicial restraint involves not only upholding Constitutional provisions and the provisions of legislation that are within the authority of Congress or the states, it also involves a reluctance to over-rule prior court decisions. Without such a reluctance, laws could become so changeable with the changing personnel of courts that citizens would find it difficult to plan economic or other endeavors that take time to come to fruition, for it would be impossible to predict what the turnover of judges and their changing of laws would be in the meantime.

Needless to say, this reluctance to overturn prior court decisions cannot be absolute, but must be a matter of cautious judgment. If some legal scholar today should publish an article or book showing convincingly that *Marbury v. Madison* was wrongly decided in 1803, no court today would be likely to over-rule that decision, on which two centuries of legal precedents have been built and under which all sorts of endeavors and commitments have been undertaken during those centuries, relying on the legal system that evolved in the wake of *Marbury v. Madison.*

Yet, ironically, many of the same intellectuals who heartily supported the Warren Court's overturning of long-standing precedents during the 1950s and 1960s also bitterly condemned later and more conservative courts which cut back on some of the new precedents established by liberal justices, especially in decisions during the Warren Court era. Thus, under the headline "The High Court Loses Restraint," a *New York Times* editorial reacted to the *Lopez* decision by saying: "In deciding that Congress lacks the power to outlaw gun possession within 1,000 feet of a school, the Supreme Court has taken an unfortunate historical turn and needlessly questioned previously settled law."[101] Citing Justice Stephen Breyer, the *Times* emphasized "the value of judicial restraint," defined by them as "deferring to Congress when Congress showed a rational basis for finding an interstate commercial impact in its law." But to *defer* to those whose powers the Constitution specifically limited would be to make a mockery of those limitations. If Congress itself is to decide how far its powers extend, what purpose can there be in Constitutional limitations on the power of Congress or of the federal government?

Inconsistent as such reactions from the intelligentsia have been, when viewed as commentary on jurisprudence, these reactions are perfectly consistent when viewed as part of a "results"-oriented role for courts, since the intelligentsia clearly preferred the social results of the Warren Court's decisions to the social results of many decisions of later courts. But court decisions based on the social results preferred by judges, rather than on the law as written, have a number of adverse effects on law as a fundamental framework within which members of society can plan their own actions. The most obvious effect is that no one can predict what social results judges will turn out to prefer in the future, leaving even the most clearly written laws surrounded by a fog of uncertainty that invites increased litigation.

The opposite of the results-oriented judge is the judge who will rule in favor of litigants whose beliefs or behavior the judge may not view with approval, or may even despise, if the law is on that side in that case. Justice Oliver Wendell Holmes, for example, voted in favor of Benjamin Gitlow in the 1925 case of *Gitlow v. New York*— and then said afterwards, in a letter to Harold Laski, that he had just voted for "the right of an ass to drool about proletarian dictatorship."[102] Likewise, Holmes dissented in *Abrams v. United States* in favor of appellants whose views he characterized in his judicial opinion itself as "a creed that I believe to be the creed of ignorance and immaturity."[103] As he told Laski, "I loathed most of the things in favor of which I decided."[104] Conversely, he could rule against litigants he personally viewed favorably. In another letter to Laski, Holmes said that he had to "write a decision against a very thorough and really well expressed argument by two colored men— one bery black— that even in intonations was better than, I should say, the majority of white discourses that we hear."[105] Holmes was not taking sides or seeking particular "results," but applying the law.

Chapter 13

Law and "Results"

Fundamental rights of individuals guaranteed by the Constitution of the United States, and by legal traditions that go back even farther than the Constitution, can be lost as a result of judicial rulings based on seeking particular social results in accordance with judges' social visions. In so far as the nebulous phrase "social justice" might have any discernible meaning, it seems to be that merely *formal* justice is not enough, but must be either supplemented or superseded by a kind of justice based on desirable social results. In any event, the rule of law— "a government of laws and not of men"— is the antithesis of results-oriented "social justice," for the results are to be chosen according to the preferences of particular individuals empowered to pick and choose desirable outcomes, rather than applying rules known in advance to all and binding on both citizens and judges.

Perhaps the ultimate in results-oriented law was that dispensed by "Representatives on Mission" in revolutionary France during the 1790s. Representatives on Mission were particular members of the ruling Convention, chosen to go about the country righting wrongs, empowered to act "above all existing laws and authorities":

> They could make arrests, create revolutionary courts, conduct trials, erect guillotines. They could nullify, extend or curtail the force of any law. They could issue decrees and proclamations on any subject. They could fix prices, requisition goods, confiscate property, collect taxes. They could purge any existing government body, or, if they chose, dissolve government bodies altogether, replacing them with committees of their own nomination.[1]

This was the ultimate in results-oriented law. While no one is advocating creating Representatives on Mission today, this is the general direction in which many are urging courts to move, by emphasizing "results" over rules. Particular judges have in fact appointed people— aptly called "masters"— to prescribe and oversee the policies and operations of prisons, schools or other governmental institutions, and judges have even ordered state legislators to raise taxes.[2]

Going by results seems especially questionable in a court of law, which inherently lacks institutional mechanisms for monitoring what are in fact the results of judicial decisions, as their repercussions spread in all directions throughout society— as distinguished from how judges might have imagined what the results of their decision would be. Some results have in fact been the direct opposite of what "results"-based judicial decisions sought to do.

BURDENS OF PROOF

Perhaps nothing is more fundamental to the American legal tradition than the requirement that the burden of proof be on the prosecution in criminal cases and on the plaintiff in civil cases. Yet the zeal for "results" has led to putting the burden of proof on the accused to prove their innocence in certain arbitrarily chosen classes of cases. This principle, or lack of principle, appeared in anti-trust law before being applied in civil rights cases.

The Robinson-Patman Act, for example, made price discrimination illegal, except under certain conditions. But once a *prima facie* case was made that different prices had been charged to different customers, the accused business then had to prove that the exceptions— such as cost differences in serving those particular customers, sufficient to justify the price differences— applied. Since the apparently simple word "cost" conceals complexities that can keep accountants, economists and lawyers on both sides tied up in endless disputes, it may not be possible for either the accuser or the accused to prove anything conclusively. This means that the accused either loses those cases or else settles them out of court on whatever terms can be negotiated, given the virtual impossibility of proving one's innocence in many cases.

The more fundamental problem, however, is that the burden of proof has been put on the accused, contrary to centuries-old legal traditions applied in most other kinds of cases.

The same results-oriented legal principle of putting the burden of proof on the accused reappeared later in court cases involving civil rights laws and policies. Here again, all it takes is a *prima facie* case— that is, an accusation not meeting even the civil law standard of a preponderance of evidence— based simply on statistical "under-representation" of minorities or women in an enterprise's workforce, to put the burden of proof on the employer to show that discrimination is not the reason. No burden of proof whatever is put on those who presuppose an even or random distribution of achievements or rewards between racial or other groups in the absence of discrimination, despite vast amounts of evidence from both history and contemporary life of wholly disproportionate achievements among individuals, groups and nations.[3]

An employer who has hired, paid and promoted individuals without regard to race or sex can nevertheless find it either impossible or prohibitively expensive to disprove the accusation of discrimination. For example, the Equal Employment Opportunity Commission brought a sex discrimination case against the Sears department store chain in 1973, based solely on statistics, without being able to produce even one woman, either currently or previously employed in any of Sears' hundreds of stores across the country, to claim that she had personally been discriminated against. Yet this case dragged on through the courts for 15 years, and cost Sears $20 million to litigate, before the Seventh Circuit Court of Appeals eventually ruled in Sears' favor.

Since very few employers have that kind of money to spend on litigation, or can afford the negative publicity of such a damning charge hanging over them for so many years, most settle such cases out of court on whatever terms they can get— and these numerous settlements are then cited in the media and elsewhere as proof of how much discrimination there is. Again, all of this goes back to the practice of putting the burden of proof on the accused. Had the burden of proof been put on the E.E.O.C., the case might never have gotten as far as a trial in the first place, since the E.E.O.C. did not have even one woman who claimed that she had been discriminated against. All it had were statistics that did not fit the prevailing preconception that all groups would tend to be proportionally represented in the absence of discrimination.

A similar case, one that went all the way up to the Supreme Court, again taking 15 years from the time of the original trial, produced a decision in favor of the accused employer that was subsequently overturned when Congress passed a new law restoring the burden of proof to the accused. In this case, the Wards Cove Packing Company, based in Washington state and Oregon, ran a fish canning operation up in Alaska. Since it recruited its management where the firm's main offices were located and recruited its canning workforce where the fish were caught, this led to a predominantly white management, based in Washington and Oregon, and a predominantly non-white workforce in Alaska. This statistical fact became the basis for charges of discrimination. The Ninth Circuit Court of Appeals upheld the charge of discrimination but the Supreme Court over-ruled that decision and remanded the case for reconsideration. This set off a storm of criticism in the media and among academics.

New York Times Supreme Court reporter Linda Greenhouse said that the ruling in *Wards Cove v. Atonio* "shifted the burden of proof on a central question from employers to employees charging job discrimination"[4]— expressing what happened in terms of social groups and social results, rather than in terms of legal principles and legal categories (plaintiffs and respondents), where the burden has for centuries been put on plaintiffs to back up their accusations. According to Linda Greenhouse, the *Wards Cove* decision "relieved employers of some of the burden of justifying practices that are shown to have a discriminatory impact."[5]

What Ms. Greenhouse chose to call "a discriminatory impact" were employee demographics not matching population demographics— which is to say, real world facts not matching the vision of the anointed. As in other contexts, the vision was taken as axiomatically true, so that statistical deviations from an even or random distribution of members of different groups in a business' workforce could be taken as evidence of employer bias, a presumption which it was then the employer's responsibility to refute or else be judged guilty of violating federal law.

New York Times columnist Tom Wicker likewise accused the Supreme Court, in its "radical Ward's Cove decision" of "overturning established law" by having "assigned the burden of proof to an *employee* who charged an employer with discriminatory hiring and employment practices." Previously, according to Wicker, the Supreme Court, "in keeping with overall legal custom, had placed the burden on the party best able to show that the procedures at issue were fair and necessary— obviously, the *employer.*" Again, legal precedents were taken as preemptive, even though the particular precedent in this case— *Griggs v. Duke Power*— was not nearly as long-lived as *Plessy v. Ferguson* was when it was overturned by *Brown v. Board of Education.*

Nothing in Wicker's discussion gave the readers any inkling that putting the burden of proof on the accused was a rare exception to legal traditions going back for centuries, an exception for certain classes of cases where social "results" were the primary concern and where the particular defendants— businesses— were out of favor among the intelligentsia, whether in anti-trust cases under the Robinson-Patman Act or in civil rights cases.

When Congress developed legislation to overturn the *Wards Cove* decision and President George H.W. Bush threatened a veto, Tom Wicker said, "he threatens to make it easier for employers to discriminate and harder for employees (often members of minority groups) to get relief in court."[6]

The *New York Times* editorials made similar arguments. The *Wards Cove* decision, it said, "placed new, heavy burdens on civil rights plaintiffs."[7] Again, there was no inkling given to the readers that what the *New York Times* called the "heavy burdens on civil rights plaintiffs" were the same burdens that most other plaintiffs in most non-civil-rights cases had been carrying for centuries, on the basis of the legal principle that the accused are not required to prove their innocence.

An op-ed column in the *Washington Post* likewise used a "results" criterion, complaining that the *Wards Cove* decision was one "making it far harder for plaintiffs to win such cases."[8] An editorial in the *Boston Globe* likewise complained that the *Wards Cove* decision was one "making it virtually impossible for employees to win discrimination suits."[9] Another *Boston Globe* editorial complained that the burden of proof "now shifts to the plaintiff"[10]— as if this were an unusual place for the burden of proof to be.

The response from academics was no less strident, no less filtered in its presentation of facts, and no less focused on "results." Professor Ronald Dworkin of Oxford wrote of the "brutal disparity" between the races in the *Wards Cove* case, which he called "structural discrimination," and of the "impossible burden" put on plaintiffs.[11] Professor Paul Gewirtz of Yale

University said, "the Supreme Court has dealt body blows to two of the most important mechanisms for integrating the American work force."[12] Clearly, his focus was on social results— "integrating the American work force"— not law. Professor Reginald Alleyne of the UCLA law school was no less "results"-oriented and attributed the *Wards Cove* decision to judges who "simply dislike civil-rights legislation."[13] Professor Howard Eglit of the Chicago-Kent College of Law characterized the decision in the *Wards Cove* case as a "disingenuous revisionist treatment of the burden of proof."[14]

Another law professor, Alan Freeman of the State University of New York at Buffalo, likewise used the unworthy opponent notion, dubbing the justices who rendered the *Wards Cove* decision "reactionary apologists for the existing order" who deserved "contempt."[15] Law Professor Candace S. Kovacic-Fleischer of American University called for Congress to "restore the normal allocation of burdens of proof; that is, if plaintiff proves an employment practice or practices caused a disparate-impact, the burden then should shift to the employer to prove a business necessity for the practice."[16] But this allocation of burdens of proof was "normal" only in civil rights cases and in some anti-trust cases, contrary to centuries of normal practice elsewhere in Anglo-American law.

This burden of proof on employers was not mandated by the Civil Rights Act of 1964. On the contrary, in the Congressional debates preceding passage of that Act, Senator Hubert Humphrey and other leaders of the fight to pass this legislation explicitly repudiated the idea that statistical disparities would be enough to force an employer to try to prove that he was not discriminating.[17] Senator Joseph Clark, another advocate for the Civil Rights Act of 1964, said that the Equal Employment Opportunity Commission established by that Act "must prove by a preponderance that the discharge or other personnel action was because of race"[18]— a preponderance of evidence, as in other civil cases, not a *prima facie* case, with the burden of proof then shifting to the employer, as later became the standard, as a result of judicial rulings.

It was the Supreme Court's *Griggs v. Duke Power* decision in 1971 which shifted the burden of proof to the employer when there were hiring criteria which had a "disparate impact" on minority workers— in that case, a mental test or a high school diploma. The *Griggs* decision— less than 20 years old at the time of the *Wards Cove* decision— was the "established" law from which Tom Wicker saw the *Wards Cove* decision as a "radical" departure. The concept of "disparate impact" is in effect a judicial codification of the confusion between saying that a given institution *conveys* a difference that already exists and saying that that institution causes that difference. But this distinction was made during the Congressional debates leading up to passage of the original Civil Rights Act of 1964, where supporters of that Act said that under its subsection 706(g), an employer was held liable only for his own "intentional" discrimination,[19] not for societal patterns reflected in his work force.

Apparently those journalists, academics and others who expressed outrage at the *Wards Cove* decision somehow just *know* that employer discrimination is the reason for statistical disparities, so apparently it is only a matter of making it easier for courts to reach that same conclusion. What this amounts to is that those members of society who are viewed unfavorably by the anointed are not to have the same rights as the general population, much less the privileges of those whom the anointed view favorably. The idea that law is about making it harder or easier for some preselected segment of society to win lawsuits against some other preselected segment of society runs through many, if not most, of the criticisms of the *Wards Cove* decision by intellectuals. In short, they wanted "results"— and Congress gave it to them with the Civil Rights Restoration Act of 1991, which put the burden of proof back on the employer, unlike the original Civil Rights Act of 1964.

PROPERTY RIGHTS

Nowhere have the actual results of "results"-oriented judicial rulings been more radically different from what was contemplated than in the case of property rights, which have long been a battleground between those with opposing social visions. As ideas of a "living Constitution," to be applied to current conditions as judges see fit, became dominant in the second half of the twentieth century, property rights have been reduced to second-class status, at best. As distinguished urban economist Edwin S. Mills put it, "the courts have virtually abolished the Fifth Amendment as it applies to urban real estate."[20]

Property rights are seen in radically different terms by those with the tragic vision and those with the vision of the anointed. Those with the tragic vision of human flaws and failings see property rights as necessary limitations on the power of government officials to seize the belongings of the populace, whether for their own use or for dispersal as largesse to various constituencies whose political or financial support the politicians seek. Such actions by power holders were common in ancient despotisms and not unknown in modern democracies. Those who founded the United States of America, and wrote the Constitution, saw property rights as essential for safeguarding all other rights. The right to free speech, for example, would be meaningless if criticisms of the authorities could lead to whatever you owned being seized in retaliation.

Economists have seen property rights as essential to (1) keeping economic decision-making in the hands of private individuals— that is, out of the hands of politicians, and (2) maintaining incentives for private individuals to invest time, talents and resources, in the expectation of being able to reap and retain the rewards of their efforts. However, those with the vision of the anointed, in which surrogate decision-makers are better equipped than others to make wise decisions, see property rights as obstacles to the achievement of various desirable social goals through government action. Property rights simply protect those individuals fortunate enough to own substantial property from the greater interests of society at large, according to those with this vision. Professor Laurence Tribe of the Harvard Law School, for example, said that property rights represent simply an individual benefit to "entrenched wealth."[21]

In other words, property rights are seen in terms of their individual results, rather than in terms of the social processes facilitated by a property rights system of economic decision-making. By contrast, free speech rights are almost never seen in such narrow terms, as special interest benefits for that very small proportion of the population who are professional writers, media journalists or political activists. Instead, free speech rights are seen as rights essential to the functioning of the whole system of representative government, though property rights are seldom seen by intellectuals as similarly essential to the functioning of a market economy. Instead, property rights are readily disdained as special protections of the economically privileged, as they are by Professor Tribe and as they were before him by Roscoe Pound, Louis Brandeis, and many others.

Those who take this dismissive view of property rights not only promote their own vision but often also filter out the opposite vision of property rights, or distort it as just a defense of existing "entrenched wealth,"[22] so that much of the public does not even learn what the issue is, making the question of how to resolve the issue moot. Once property rights are reduced by verbal virtuosity to simply a special benefit for a privileged few, these rights are then seen as less important than benefits to the larger society. It follows from this that property rights must often give way in clashes with other rights, when the issue is posed as opposing courts' exalting "property rights over human rights" or posed as property rights versus "the public interest."[*]

Such arguments, however, make sense only within the framework of the vision of the anointed. Otherwise, there is no clash between property rights and human rights because (1) property itself has no rights and (2) only human beings have rights. Any clash is between different sets of human beings. Property rights are legal barriers to politicians, judges or bureaucrats arbitrarily seizing the assets of some human beings to transfer those assets to other human beings.

Those who see surrogate decision-makers with both the right and the duty to make "income distribution" more equal or more just see property rights as a barrier that should not stand in the way of that over-riding goal. As the ideas of Progressive era intellectuals became dominant in the law schools and in the courts during the second half of the twentieth century, property rights have been eroded by judicial decisions, and the ability of government officials to over-ride the rights of property owners has been justified on grounds of a greater public interest, supposedly for the benefit of the less fortunate. However, here as elsewhere, because certain notions fit the vision there has

---

[*] Such phrases go back at least as far as Theodore Roosevelt. See, for example, Theodore Roosevelt, *The Rough Riders: An Autobiography* (New York: The Library of America, 2004), pp. 720–721.

been remarkably little attention paid to whether they also fit the facts. In other words, the notion that an erosion of property rights benefits those with limited incomes, and who lack any substantial property, is taken as axiomatic, rather than as a hypothesis to be tested empirically.

The implicit assumption that the weakening of property rights would benefit the less fortunate, at the expense of the more fortunate, has turned out to be in innumerable cases the very opposite of what has in fact happened. Given a freer hand in confiscating property, government officials at all levels have for decades promoted massive demolitions of working class and low-income neighborhoods in "urban renewal" or "redevelopment" programs that replaced these neighborhoods with more upscale housing, shopping malls and other attractions for the more affluent members of society.

The larger amounts of taxes that such "redeveloped" areas would pay locally provided obvious incentives for local political leaders to benefit themselves at the expense of the displaced population. These displaced populations have been predominantly low-income and minority groups, primarily blacks.[23]

The ultimate consummation of the legal trends toward reducing property rights as restrictions on government action came with the 2005 case of *Kelo v. New London*, in which the Constitution's provision that private property could be taken for "public use" was expanded to mean that such property could be taken for a "public *purpose*." While a public use would include such things as the government's building a reservoir, a bridge, a highway or some other such facility, "public purpose" could mean almost anything— and in the *Kelo* case it meant confiscating people's homes to turn the property over to developers who would build various upscale facilities.

It should also be noted that the things built on the land taken through eminent domain from homeowners and businesses in low-income neighborhoods are seldom things that would not or could not be built somewhere else. Rather, these are things that local political leaders seek to attract to their own particular taxing jurisdiction, rather than let them be built somewhere else, in someone else's taxing jurisdiction. In other words, these things for which hundreds, or even thousands, of people's homes and businesses are sacrificed, and their lives disrupted, are not net additions to the national wealth, however much they may add to tax revenues in a particular place, instead of in some other place.

An even more direct benefit to the affluent and the wealthy, at the expense of people of low or moderate incomes, has resulted from the ever greater scope allowed government officials to over-ride property rights in the name of "open space," "smart growth" and other forms of arbitrary building restrictions, politically packaged under a variety of rhetorically attractive labels. Banning the building of homes or other structures in or around upscale communities greatly reduces the ability of less affluent people to move into such communities, both because of the reduction in the physical supply of land for housing and because of skyrocketing housing prices resulting from vastly increased land prices when the supply of buildable land has been artificially restricted by law.

The doubling, tripling, or more, of housing prices in the wake of building restrictions— such as happened in various parts of the United States, beginning in the 1970s[24]— does not adversely affect those already living in upscale communities (except for renters) but in fact benefits homeowners by raising the value of their own homes in an artificially restricted market.

In addition, the arbitrary powers of planning commissions, zoning boards and environmental agencies to restrict or forbid the use of private property in ways they choose to disapprove gives them leverage to extract concessions from those who seek to build anything under their jurisdiction. These concessions may be extracted either illegally in the form of direct personal bribes or legally through forcing the property owner to contribute part of the property to the local jurisdiction. In the town of San Mateo, California, for example, approval of a housing development was made contingent on the builders turning over to local authorities "a 12-acre plot on which the city will build a public park," contributing $350,000 toward "public art," and selling about 15 percent of the homes below their market value.[25]

Chief Justice John Marshall said that the power to tax is the power to destroy. The power of arbitrary regulation is the power to extort— just as is the power to put the burden of proof on the accused. Among the justifications offered by contemporary judges for politicians' extraction of concessions from builders— in this case, selling a certain percentage of the housing they build at prices below the usual market price— is that this is done in exchange for "benefits" to the builders. One of these "benefits" is being eligible for "expedited processing."[26] In other words, by the power of delay, local authorities can extract concessions. By this reasoning, blackmailers confer a "benefit" by not revealing damaging information, and kidnappers confer a "benefit" by returning their hostage after the ransom is paid.

In the case of housing, the "concessions" extorted from builders are ultimately paid for by people who buy or rent the homes or apartments that they build. The erosion of property rights permitted by courts affect even people who own no property but who have to pay more to rent, or who are unable to afford to either rent or buy in communities where housing prices have been artificially inflated by land use restrictions to levels unaffordable to any but the affluent or wealthy, thus establishing a *cordon sanitaire* around upscale communities, keeping out people of moderate or low incomes. Whatever the "results" being sought by those who urged a weakening of property rights, these are the results actually achieved.

Even low- or moderate-income people already living within communities that over-ride property rights with arbitrary building restrictions can be forced out as rent rises steeply. In San Francisco, for example, the black population has been cut in half since 1970, and in some other coastal California counties it has not been uncommon for the black population to decline by 10,000 or more just between the 1990 and 2000 censuses,[27] even when the total population of these counties was growing.

One of the many problems of "results"-oriented judicial decisions is that actual results cannot be confined to the particular results that judges had in mind and that other results are seldom predictable. Given legal precedents, these "results"-oriented decisions are seldom reversible, no matter how far the actual results differ from what was expected.

CRIME

The vision of crime common among intellectuals goes back at least two centuries but it gained the ascendancy in practice only during the second half of the twentieth century. Louis Brandeis' claim— that modern "social science" had raised the issue whether the surrounding community was not as much responsible for theft as the thief himself— ignored the fact that blaming crime on society was a common notion among those with the vision of the anointed, as far back as the eighteenth century— which is to say, before modern "social science,"[28] though these earlier speculations antedated the practice of wrapping themselves in the mantle of science.

The vision of the anointed has long de-emphasized punishment and emphasized prevention by getting at the social "root causes" of crime beforehand and by "rehabilitation" of criminals afterwards. Subsidiary themes in this vision include mitigation of personal responsibility on the part of criminals as a result of unhappy childhoods, stressful adulthoods or other factors assumed to be beyond the control of the individual. Conflicting theories of crime can be debated endlessly, and no doubt will be, as will many other questions expanded to unanswerable dimensions. What is relevant here, however, is what the evidence of actual results has been from the ascendancy and pervasive prevalence of the intellectuals' vision of crime— and what the intellectuals' reactions have been to that evidence.

In the United States, where murder rates had been going down for decades, and were in 1961 less than half of what they had been in 1933, the legal reforms of the 1960s— applying the ideas of intellectuals and widely applauded by the intelligentsia— were followed almost immediately by a sharp reversal of this long downward trend, with the murder rate doubling by 1974.[29] In Britain, the ascendancy of the same vision of crime was followed by similarly sudden reversals of previous downward trends in crime rates. As one study noted:

> Scholars of criminology have traced a long decline in interpersonal violence since the late Middle Ages until an abrupt and puzzling reversal occurred in the middle of the twentieth century. . . And a statistical comparison of crime in England and Wales with crime in America, based on 1995 figures, discovered that for three categories of violent crime— assaults, burglary, and robbery— the English are now at far greater risk than Americans.[30]

The abruptness of the reversal of a long downward trend in crime rates, on both sides of the Atlantic, greatly reduces the likelihood that the results were due to the kinds of complex social changes which take years to gradually unfold. But, within a relatively short span of time, legislation, court decisions, and government policy changes in both Britain and the United States greatly reduced the likelihood that a criminal would be convicted and punished for a given crime, reduced the severity of the punishment for those who were punished, and simultaneously reduced the ability of law-abiding citizens to defend themselves when confronted with a criminal or to be armed to deter criminal attacks.[31] In Britain, the anti-gun ideology is so strong that even the use of toy guns in self-defense is forbidden:

> Merely threatening to defend oneself can also prove illegal, as an elderly lady discovered. She succeeded in frightening off a gang of thugs by firing a blank from a toy gun, only to be arrested for the crime of putting someone in fear with an imitation firearm. Use of a toy gun for self-defence during a housebreak is also unacceptable, as a householder found who had detained with an imitation gun two men who were burgling his home. He called the police, but when they arrived they arrested him for a firearms offence.[32]

British intellectuals have long been zealous advocates of gun control. A 1965 article in the *New Statesman* declared that firearms in private hands "serve no conceivable civilised purpose," that "the possession or use of pistols or revolvers by civilians" was something that "cannot be justified for any purpose whatsoever."[33] A 1970 article in the same publication urged laws banning "all firearms"— whether concealed or not— "from the entire civilian population."[34]

Like so many ideas in vogue among the intelligentsia, the zeal for gun control laws has defied years of mounting evidence of the futility and counterproductive consequences of such laws. For example, a scholarly study in 2001 found that "the use of handguns in crime rose by 40 per cent in the two years after such weapons were banned in the UK."[35] An earlier study found: "In homicide involving organized crime and drugs no legally-owned firearms were used at all, but forty-three illegal ones were."[36] Other studies likewise indicated that, in England as in the United States, laws against owning guns had no discernible effect on people who make their livings by breaking laws:

In 1954 there were only twelve cases of robbery in London in which a firearm was used, and on closer inspection eight of these were only "supposed firearms." But armed robberies in London rose from 4 in 1954, when there were no controls on shotguns and double the number of licensed pistol owners, to 1,400 in 1981 and to 1,600 in 1991. In 1998, a year after a ban on virtually all handguns, gun crime was up another 10 percent.[37]

As gun control laws were made ever tighter in Britain toward the end of the twentieth century, murder rates rose by 34 percent, while murder rates in Canada and the United States were falling by 34 percent and 39 percent, respectively. Murder rates in France and Italy were also falling, by 25 percent and 59 percent, respectively.[38] Britain, with its strong anti-gun ideology among the intellectual and political elites, was an exception to international trends. Meanwhile, Americans' purchases of guns increased during this same period, gun sales surging "to a peak in 1993 of nearly 8 million small arms, of which 4 million were handguns."[39] Far from leading to more murders, this was a period of declining murder rates in the United States. Altogether, there were an estimated 200 million guns in the United States, and rates of violent crime have been lowest in those places where there have been the highest incidence of gun ownership. The same has been true of Switzerland.[40]

Yet none of this has caused second thoughts about gun control among either the American or British intelligentsia. In Britain, both ideology and government policy have taken a negative view of other measures of self-defense as well. Opposition to individual self-defense by law-abiding citizens extends even beyond guns or imitation guns. A middle-aged man attacked by two thugs in a London subway car "unsheathed a sword blade in his walking stick and slashed at one of them"— and was arrested along with his assailants, for carrying an offensive weapon.[41] Even putting up barbed wire around a garden and its shed that had been broken into several times was forbidden by local authorities, fearful of being sued if a thief injured himself while trying to break in.[42] That such a lawsuit would be taken seriously is another sign of the prevailing notions among British officials, operating in a climate of opinion created by the British intelligentsia.

The "root causes" theory of crime has likewise remained impervious to evidence on both sides of the Atlantic. In both the United States and

England, crime rates soared during years when the supposed "root causes of crime"— poverty and barriers to opportunity— were visibly lessening. As if to make a complete mockery of the "root causes" theory, the ghetto riots that swept across American cities in the 1960s were less common in Southern cities, where racial discrimination was still most visible, and the most lethal riot of that era occurred in Detroit, where the poverty rate among blacks was only half that of blacks nationwide, while the homeownership rate among blacks was higher than among blacks in any other city, and the black unemployment rate in Detroit was 3.4 percent, which was lower than the unemployment rate among *whites* nationwide.[43]

Urban riots were most numerous during the administration of President Lyndon Johnson, which was marked by landmark civil rights legislation and a massive expansion of social programs called "the war on poverty." Conversely, such riots became virtually non-existent during the eight years of the Reagan administration, which de-emphasized such things.

It would be hard to think of a social theory more consistently and unmistakably belied by the facts. But none of this has made a dent on those who have espoused the "root causes" theory of crime or the general social vision behind it. The United States was not the only country in which the supposed "root causes" of crime showed no correlation with the actual crime rate. Britain was another:

> Against prodigious odds violent crime plummeted during the nineteenth century. From midcentury up to the First World War reported assaults fell by 71 percent, woundings by 20 percent, and homicides by 42 percent. . . The age was cursed with every ill modern society pegs as a cause of crime— wrenching poverty alongside growing prosperity, teeming slums, rapid population growth and dislocation, urbanization, the breakdown of the working family, problematic policing, and, of course, wide ownership of firearms.[44]

Even the most blatant facts can be sidestepped by saying that the causes of crime are too "complex" to be covered by a "simplistic" explanation. This verbal tactic simply expands the question to unanswerable dimensions, as a prelude to dismissing any explanation not consonant with the prevailing vision as "simplistic" because it cannot fully answer the expanded question. But no one has to master the complexities of Newton's law of gravity to know that stepping off the roof of a skyscraper will have consequences. Similarly, no one has to unravel the complexities of the innumerable known and unknown reasons why people commit crimes to know that putting criminals behind bars has a better track record of reducing the crime rate than any of the complex theories or lofty policies favored by the intelligentsia.[45]

Expanding the question to unanswerable dimensions, and then deriding any unwelcome answer as "simplistic," is just one of the ways that intellectuals' rhetorical skills have been deployed against facts. As another example, to demand a return to "law and order" was long stigmatized as a sign of covert racism, since the crime rate among blacks was higher than among whites.

As noted in Chapter 2, a retired New York police commissioner who tried to tell a gathering of judges of the dangerous potential of some of their rulings was literally laughed at by the judges and lawyers present.[46] In short, theory trumped experience, as the vision has so often trumped facts, and the benighted were treated as not even worth taking seriously by the anointed.

Similar attitudes have accompanied the same vision in Britain, where much of the media, academia and the intelligentsia in general, as well as university-trained public officials, treat the public's complaints about rising crime rates, and demands for some serious sanctions against criminals, as mere signs of the public's lesser understanding of the deeper issues involved. On both sides of the Atlantic, the elites put their emphasis on the problems experienced by the people who commit crimes, and on how various social programs to solve those problems will be the real solution to the crime problem in society. In the United States, even such things as "prompt collection" of garbage has been depicted by *New York Times* columnist Tom Wicker as part of the "social justice" needed to stem crime.[47]

No amount of hard evidence has been able to burst through the sealed bubble of this elite vision in Britain. On the contrary, data that contradict that vision have been suppressed, filtered out or spun rhetorically by British officials— so much so that the British magazine *The Economist* reported "widespread distrust of official figures"[48]— while the British media have tried to make the public feel guilty for the imprisonment of those relatively few criminals who are in fact imprisoned.[49] Typical of the disdain for public complaints has been the response, or non-response, to the experiences of people living in neighborhoods in which institutions for released criminals have been placed:

> They spoke of a living nightmare brought about by the non-stop crime, intimidation, vandalism and harassment inflicted on them by their criminal residents. All spoke of their total failure to get local politicians, MPs, criminal justice officials, police, or indeed anyone to take any notice of their desperate situation.[50]

For many of those with the vision of the anointed, a wide difference between the beliefs and concerns of the population at large and the beliefs and concerns of themselves and like-minded peers is not a reason for reconsideration, but a source of pride in being one of the anointed with a higher vision. Peer consensus inside the sealed bubble of their vision can be enough to prevent the intrusion of facts from outside.

Meanwhile, in the United States, after many years of rising crime rates had built up sufficient public outrage to force a change in policy, rates of imprisonment rose— and crime rates began falling for the first time in years. Those with the vision of the anointed lamented the rising prison population in the country and, when they acknowledged the declining crime rate at all, confessed themselves baffled by it, as if it were a strange coincidence that crime was declining as more criminals were taken off the streets. In 1997, for example, *New York Times* writer Fox Butterfield wrote under the headline, "Crime Keeps on Falling, but Prisons Keep on Filling"— as if there were something puzzling about this:

> It has become a comforting story: for five straight years, crime has been falling, led by a drop in murder.
>
> So why is the number of inmates in prisons and jails around the nation still going up? . . . Already, California and Florida spend more to incarcerate people than to educate their college-age populations.[51]

The irrelevant comparison of prison costs versus college costs became a staple of critics of imprisonment. A *New York Times* editorial in 2008 was still repeating this argument in its laments about a growing prison population:

> After three decades of explosive growth, the nation's prison population has reached some grim milestones: More than 1 in 100 American adults are behind bars. One in nine black men, ages 20 to 34, are serving time, as are 1 in 36 adult Hispanic men.
>
> Nationwide, the prison population hovers at almost 1.6 million, which surpasses all other countries for which there are reliable figures. The 50 states last year spent about $44 billion in tax dollars on corrections, up from nearly $11 billion in 1987. Vermont, Connecticut, Delaware, Michigan and Oregon devote as much money or more to corrections as they do to higher education.[52]

This was by no means the first time that rising rates of imprisonment were denounced in the *New York Times*. Years earlier, in 1991, *New York Times* columnist Tom Wicker said that "crimes of violence have not decreased at all" in the wake of rising levels of imprisonment— a claim that later statistics disproved— and urged shorter sentences, as well as "improved educational and vocational services and drug treatment" in prisons, and deplored "panicky public fears and punitive public attitudes."[53] Here, as with many other issues, the differing views of others were verbally reduced to mere emotions ("panicky"), rather than arguments that had to be analyzed and answered with facts.

Within prisons themselves, the changed public attitudes toward prisoners in the United States were reflected in tougher measures against inmates who caused trouble:

> Assaults at Folsom dropped 70 percent in four years, from 6.9 for every 100 inmates in 1985 to 1.9 in 1989. Despite a steep rise in the nation's prison population in the 1980's and despite occasional frightening outbreaks of violence like the one at Rikers Island in New York this summer, stories like Folsom's are being repeated all over the country. Prison officials, emboldened by a public mood that brooks no patience for criminals, say they have taken greater control of their institutions.[54]

Hard evidence about the effectiveness of asserting law enforcement authority, both in prison and outside, made no discernible difference to those with the vision of the anointed, either in the United States or in Britain. Yet an inverse correlation between imprisonment rates and crime rates could also be found in Australia and New Zealand, where a trend back toward more imprisonment was likewise accompanied by a decline in crime rates.[55]

The British intelligentsia have been no more impressed with facts than their American counterparts. The British media and academia abound with people opposed to imprisonment.[56] *The Economist* magazine, for example, referred to "America's addiction to incarceration"[57]— the reduction of opposing views to mere emotions being a pattern among the intelligentsia on both sides of the Atlantic. A probation officer's account of the difference between vision and reality, derived from his listening to his car radio while driving to work at a prison, was revealing. On the radio, a government minister was being questioned by an interviewer:

> A well-known presenter introduced his question to a minister with the statement, 'We all know that we send too many people to prison in this country...' This introductory remark was made with great assurance and confidence; it conveyed the belief that this statement was something 'everyone knew' and was beyond question. Yet as I listened, I knew I was driving to a prison which, despite its huge catchment area (it served magistrates' courts districts from several parts of the country) was only half-full. What is more this institution took the seventeen to twenty-year-old offender age group, known to be highly prolific offenders. If any prison was going to be full, it should have been ours. Yet for some years it had only ever been half-full at the most, and was often far less occupied than that. At the very time that the *Today* programme was confidently misleading the public over the numbers of offenders being given custodial sentences, the Home Office were drawing up plans to close our prison and many more besides.[58]

In Britain, as in the United States, it is often taken as axiomatic that "prisons are ineffective," as *The Economist* magazine put it. The reason: "They may keep offenders off the streets, but they fail to discourage them from offending. Two-thirds of ex-prisoners are re-arrested within three years of being released."[59] By this kind of reasoning, food is ineffective as a response to hunger because it is only a matter of time after eating before you get hungry again— a kind of recidivism, if you will. Like many other things, incarceration only works when it is done. The fact that criminals commit crimes when they are no longer incarcerated says nothing about whether incarceration is effective in reducing crime. The empirical question of the effect on the crime rate of keeping more criminals off the streets was not even considered in this sweeping dismissal of prisons as "ineffective."

The ideology of "alternatives to incarceration" is not only a shibboleth among the British intelligentsia, but is also backed up by the self-interest of government officials in reducing expenditures on prisons. Although statements about how much it costs to keep a prisoner behind bars, as compared to the cost of keeping a student at some expensive college, have become staples in arguments against incarceration, the relevant comparison would be between the cost of keeping someone in prison versus the costs of letting a career criminal loose in society. In Britain, the total cost of the prison system per year was found to be £1.9 billion, while the financial cost alone of the crimes committed per year by criminals was estimated at £60 billion.[60]

In the United States, the cost of incarcerating a criminal has been estimated as being at least $10,000 a year *less* than the cost of turning him loose in society.[61] Despite all empirical evidence, however, the *New York Times* in 2008 continued to speak of imprisonment as "a terrible waste of money and lives," lamented that "incarceration rates have continued to rise while crime rates have fallen" and repeated the old argument that some states "devote as much money or more to corrections as they do to higher education."[62]

In Britain, the anti-incarceration ideology is so strong that only 7 percent of convicted criminals end up behind bars.[63] In December 2008, London's *Daily Telegraph*, in its on-line publication *Telegraph.co.uk*, reported: "Thousands of criminals spared prison go on to offend again." It said: "More than 21,000 offenders serving non-custodial sentences committed further crimes last year, casting doubt over Labour's pledge to make the punishments a tough alternative to jail."[64] The transformation of Britain wrought by the triumph of the vision of the anointed may be summarized by noting that Britain, which had long had one of the lowest crime rates in the world, had by the end of the twentieth century seen its crime rate in most categories rise several-fold and eventually surpass that of the United States.[65]

As a young man visiting Britain shortly after the Second World War, Lee Kuan Yew was so impressed with the orderly and law-abiding people of London that he returned to his native Singapore determined to transform it from the poverty-stricken and crime-ridden place that it was at the time. Later, as a leader of the city-state of Singapore for many years, Lee Kuan Yew instituted policies that resulted in Singapore's rise to unprecedented levels of prosperity, with an equally dramatic fall in crime. By the beginning of the twenty-first century, the crime rate per 100,000 people in Singapore was 693 and in Britain was over 10,000.[66] Singapore had, in effect, gone back in time to policies and methods now disdained by the intelligentsia as "outmoded" and "simplistic."

In light of the fact that a wholly disproportionate amount of crime is committed by a relatively small segment of the population, it is hardly surprising that putting a small fraction of the total population behind bars has led to substantial reductions in the crime rate. However, that is not sufficient for those who take a cosmic view of justice and lament that some people, through no fault of their own, are born into circumstances far more likely to result in criminal behavior than the circumstances into which others are born.

While those with this vision tend to regard those circumstances as economic or social, the same injustice— as viewed from the same cosmic perspective— is involved when people are born into *cultural* circumstances that are more likely to lead them into crime. Yet, far from taking on the daunting task of trying to change cultures or subcultures, many of the intelligentsia are adherents of the multicultural ideology, according to which cultures are all on a plane of equality, so that trying to change some cultures would be an unwarranted intrusion, cultural imperialism as it were.

Like so many other nice-sounding notions, the multicultural ideology does not distinguish between an arbitrary definition and a verifiable proposition. That is, it does not distinguish between how one chooses to use words within one's own mind and the empirical validity of those words outside in the real world. Yet consequences, for both individuals and society, follow from mundane facts in the real world, not from definitions inside people's heads. Empirically, the question whether or not cultures are equal becomes: *Equal in what demonstrable way?* That question is seldom, if ever, asked, much less answered, by most of the intelligentsia.

In addition to claims that crime can be reduced by getting at its supposed "root causes," many among the intelligentsia also advocate "rehabilitation" of criminals, "anger management" and other therapeutic approaches to reducing crime— not simply as a supplement to traditional imprisonment but also as a substitute. Like other "alternatives to incarceration," these are not treated as hypotheses to be tested but as axioms to be defended. No matter how high the rate of recidivism among those who have been through "rehabilitation" programs or how much violence continues to be committed by those who have been in "anger management" programs, these notions are never considered to be refuted. Between the suppression of evidence by officials[67] and its evasion through the verbal virtuosity of the intelligentsia, these theories can seldom be defeated by mere facts.

By the same token, none of the traditional methods of crime control that have been supplanted by newer and more fashionable methods can be resurrected on the basis of factual evidence. The very mention of "Victorian" ideas about society in general, or crime control in particular, is virtually guaranteed to evoke a sneer from the intelligentsia.* The fact that the Victorian era was one of a decades-long decline in alcoholism, crime and social pathology in general, both in Britain and in the United States[68]— in contrast to more modern ideas with the opposite results in both countries— carries virtually no weight among the intelligentsia, and such facts remain largely unknown among those in the general public who depend on either the media or academia for information.

The fact that ordinary, common sense measures against crime are effective remains a matter of surprise among many of the intelligentsia. After decades of controversy over ways of reducing crime, in 2009 such news rated a headline in the *San Francisco Chronicle*: "Homicides Plummet as Police Flood Tough Areas." The account began: "San Francisco's homicide total for the first half of 2009 hit a nine-year low— falling more than 50 percent from last year— a drop that police officials attribute to flooding high-crime areas with officers and focusing on the handful of people who commit most of the crimes."[69]

A few intellectuals— James Q. Wilson being the most prominent— have bucked the tide when it comes to crime, but most of their work consists of showing what is wrong with the work of the far more numerous intellectuals

---

* "Victorian" was called in the *New York Review of Books* "a byword for quaint, antiquated, repressed, or repressive attitudes toward modern manners, mores, and morals." Martin Filler, "The Most Happy Couple," *New York Review of Books*, August 19, 2010, p. 67.

whose theories of crime and prescriptions for crime control have been pervasive and have, in practice, led only to rising crime rates. The net cost of intellectuals to society as regards crime would include not only the vast sums of money lost by the general public— greatly exceeding the cost of keeping criminals behind bars— but also the impact of policies based on intellectuals' theories on the lives of ordinary law-abiding citizens, demoralized by fear, brutalized by violence, or cut short by criminals or rioters. If it were possible to quantify the cost of turning the theories of the intellectuals into the law of the land, the total cost would undoubtedly be enormous, just as regards crime.

PART VI

INTELLECTUALS AND WAR

It is too true, however disgraceful it may be to human nature, that nations in general will make war whenever they have a prospect of getting anything by it.

-John Jay, *The Federalist*, Number 4.

Chapter 14

The World Wars

Bad ages to live through are good ages to learn from.

Eugen Weber[1]

Like virtually everyone else, intellectuals generally prefer peace to war. However, as already noted in Chapter 6, there are some very fundamental differences in ideas on how to prevent wars. Just as the vision of crime prevention among intellectuals goes back at least as far as the eighteenth century, so too does their vision of war and peace. In contrast to the tragic vision, which sees military strength as the key to deterrence, the vision of the intellectuals has long been one that relies on international negotiations and/or disarmament agreements to avoid wars.

Regardless of intellectuals' vision of war in general, there are no wars in general. The real question is: How have intellectuals reacted to particular wars, or particular threats of war, at particular times? Since our focus is on intellectuals from an era when their influence has had a major impact on public opinion and government policies, that confines the question largely to intellectuals in Western nations in recent times. Within this era, intellectuals have sometimes been strong supporters of particular wars and sometimes strong opponents of other wars. There are elements of their vision consistent with either position.

Sometimes the position of intellectuals for or against a particular war seems to have been a matter of whether the time was one of a long period of peace or one in which the horrors of war had been a recent and indelible memory. The period leading up to the First World War, for example, was one in which the United States had not experienced a major war, involving a large part of its population, for more than a generation. In Europe, it had been nearly a century since the Napoleonic wars ravaged the continent. In Germany during the mid 1890s— two decades since the Franco-Prussian war— many intellectuals, including university professors, supported the Kaiser's government in its plans to build a big and expensive navy,[2] as part of a more aggressive international stance in general, even though Germany was a land power with few overseas interests to protect.

In such a time, it was easy for many intellectuals and others to think of war in the abstract, and to find in its excitement and sense of social cohesion and national purpose positive virtues, while its devastating human costs receded into the background of their thoughts. Even those mindful of the carnage and devastation of war could speak, as William James did, of a need for "the moral equivalent of war" to mobilize people behind a common purpose and common aspirations. It was part of a long-standing assumption among many intellectuals of a *dirigiste* orientation that it is the role of third parties to bring meaning into the lives of the masses.

As already noted, the vision of the anointed is a vision of intellectual and moral elites being surrogate decision-makers, imposing an over-arching common purpose to supersede the disparate and conflicting individual purposes and individual decisions of the population at large. War creates a setting in which this vision can flourish. It also creates many other things, so that the net effect is very much influenced by the conditions of the times. In the twentieth century, the First World War presented both an opportunity for the vision of the anointed to flourish— and later, after the fact, a devastating reminder of the horrors of war which had been ignored or under-estimated.

The postwar backlash against those horrors then set in motion a radically different view of war, leading to widespread pacifism among intellectuals. But, even though many intellectuals radically changed their view of war within a relatively few years, what they did *not* change was their conviction that they as the anointed were to continue to act as guides to the masses and to take the lead in promoting government policies in line with their new anti-war vision. These various periods in the history of intellectuals' pro-war and anti-war visions need to be examined individually.

THE FIRST WORLD WAR

The First World War was a shock to many people in many ways. Nearly a century without a major war on the European continent had lulled some into a comfortable feeling that European civilization had somehow left war behind, as a thing of the past. Many on the far left believed that international working class solidarity would prevent the workers of different countries from killing each other on the battlefields, supposedly for the benefit of their exploiters. In countries on both sides, generations that had no experience with war marched off to war with great public fanfare, exhilaration, and a sense of assurance that it would all be over— victoriously— in a relatively short time.[3]

Few had any idea of how modern technology would make this the most lethal and ghastly war the world had yet seen, for both soldiers and civilians alike, how many of the survivors across the continent of Europe would end up hungry or starving amid the ruins and rubble of war, or how many centuries-old empires would be shattered into oblivion by the war, much less what a monstrous new phenomenon— totalitarianism— would be spawned in the chaotic aftermath of that war. Intellectuals were among the many whose illusions would be brutally smashed by the catastrophes of the First World War.

The Pre-War Era

At the beginning of the twentieth century, the only war that most Americans had experienced was the Spanish-American war, in which the overwhelming power of the United States had quickly driven Spain from its colonies in Cuba, Puerto Rico, and the Philippines. Looking back at the Spanish-American war, Woodrow Wilson approved of the annexation of Puerto Rico by President William McKinley, saying of those annexed, "they are children and we are men in these deep matters of government and justice." Wilson disdained what he called "the anti-imperialist weepings and wailings" of critics of these actions.[4] As for Theodore Roosevelt, even before becoming President, he was not only a supporter of the Spanish-American war, but a major participant. It was in fact his own military exploits in that war, as a leader of the men called "rough riders," that first made him a national figure.

This was an era when imperialism was seen as an international mission of America to spread democracy, and as such was supported by many Progressive-era intellectuals.[5] The Progressive-era classic, *The Promise of American Life* by *New Republic* editor Herbert Croly, argued that most Asians and Africans had little chance of developing modern democratic nations without the superintendence of Western democracies. He said: "The majority of Asiatic and African communities can only get a fair start politically by some such preliminary process of tutelage; and the assumption by a European nation of such a responsibility is a desirable phase of national discipline and a frequent source of genuine national advance."[6] More generally, "A war waged for an excellent purpose contributes more to human amelioration than a merely artificial peace," according to Croly.[7]

However much intellectuals have traditionally been opposed to imperialism for the benefit of economic interests, military interests, territorial expansion or the self-aggrandizement of reigning political leaders, interventions in other countries in the absence of these factors and for ideological reasons have by no means been so universally condemned by the intelligentsia. Indeed, the complete absence of any national interest in a particular intervention has often been treated by intellectuals as exempting that intervention from the moral condemnation applied to other cases of imperialism.

Seen in this light, substantial support from intellectuals of the Progressive era for American military interventions in poor countries, from which no serious material benefit could be expected, was quite understandable at a time when those interventions posed virtually no danger to the United States, and when a long preceding era of peace allowed the brutal realities of war to recede into the background in people's minds. In such special circumstances, imperialism was simply an extension across national boundaries of the notion that the special wisdom and virtue of the anointed should be guiding other people's lives.

Famed editor William Allen White said, "Only Anglo-Saxons can govern themselves," and declared, "It is the Anglo-Saxon's manifest destiny to go forth as a world conqueror." Crusading Progressive journalist Jacob Riis, who knew Theodore Roosevelt from the days when TR was a police commissioner in New York City, said, "Cuba is free and she thanks President Roosevelt for her freedom." He also said, "I am not a jingo; but when some things happen I just have to get up and cheer. The way our modern American diplomacy goes about things is one of them."[8] Willard D. Straight, who financed the founding of the *New Republic* magazine and Herbert Croly, its first editor, both supported the imperial adventurism of Theodore Roosevelt.

Croly declared that "the forcible pacification of one or more such centers of disorder" in the Western Hemisphere was a task for the United States, which "has already made an effective beginning in this great work, both by the pacification of Cuba and by the attempt to introduce a little order into the affairs of the turbulent Central American republics."[9] Croly saw no contradiction between the principles behind Progressive domestic reforms and Progressives' support for foreign adventurism:

> That war and its resulting policy of extra-territorial expansion, so far from hindering the process of domestic amelioration, availed, from the sheer force of the national aspirations it aroused, to give a tremendous impulse to the work of national reform. . . and it indirectly helped to place in the Presidential chair the man who, as I have said, represented both the national idea and the spirit of reform.[10]

John Dewey likewise saw war as constraining "the individualistic tradition" which he opposed, and establishing "the supremacy of public need over private possessions."[11]

As for Woodrow Wilson, not only was he a believer in the rightness of McKinley's intervention in Spain's colonies, as President he ordered a number of military interventions of his own in Latin America[12] before he made his biggest and most fateful intervention, in the First World War raging in Europe.

America at War

The ostensible cause of the entry of the United States into the stalemated carnage in Europe during the First World War was German submarines sinking passenger ships which had American passengers on board. But these were ships entering a war zone in which both the British and the Germans were maintaining naval blockades, the former with surface ships and the latter with submarines— and each with the intention of denying the other both war materiel and food.[13] Moreover, the most famous of these sinkings by German submarines, that of the *Lusitania*, was of a British passenger ship that was, years later, revealed to have been secretly carrying military supplies.

By the very nature of submarine warfare, these undersea craft could not give the warnings and pauses to let crews and passengers disembark before sinking passenger ships. This was especially so when many civilian ships entering war zones were armed and when the advent of radio meant that any ship that had been warned could immediately summon warships to the scene to sink the submarine. The sudden, surprise attacks of submarines— the only way they could operate without endangering themselves— added to the shock at the loss of innocent lives. But it was the insistence by Woodrow Wilson on a right of Americans to sail safely into blockaded ports during wartime which created the setting for these tragedies. He had on his side international conventions created before the submarine became a major factor in naval warfare. Eventually, he made Germany's submarine warfare against ships sailing to enemy ports the centerpiece of his appeal to Congress in 1917 to declare war on Germany.

Whether that was Wilson's real reason for wanting war or instead a convenient occasion for launching an international ideological crusade is not clear, especially in view of the war message itself and subsequent statements and actions by President Wilson. Woodrow Wilson could not resist inserting into his war message to Congress criticisms of the autocratic nature of the German government and a reference to "heartening things that have been happening within the last few weeks in Russia,"[14] with the overthrow of the czar's autocratic government there. This was in keeping with his more famous characterization of the First World War as a war in which "The world must be made safe for democracy"[15] and his later postwar efforts to remake nations and empires in the image of his vision of what they should be like— which was a continuation on a larger scale of his interventionist policies in Latin America.

Before the war was over, Wilson was publicly demanding "the destruction of every arbitrary power anywhere that can separately, secretly and of its single choice disturb the peace of the world." This was not just idle rhetoric. Wilson sent a note to Germany demanding that Kaiser Wilhelm abdicate.[16]

Like many other intellectuals, Wilson depicted actions taken without material motives to be somehow on a higher moral plane than actions taken to advance the economic interests of individuals or the territorial interests of nations[17]— as if sacrificing countless lives to enable the anointed to play a historic role on the world stage in furthering their vision was not at least as selfish and calloused as seeking material ends would be. In a later time, Adolf Hitler would say, "I have to attain immortality, even if the whole German nation perishes in the process."[18] Woodrow Wilson was too moralistic to say such a thing but, given the power of human rationalization, the net difference in this respect may not have been great.

Sinking the blood and treasure of a nation for ideological aggrandizement was equated with idealism by many intellectuals of the time, as well as in later times. Moreover, like many other issues addressed by intellectuals, Woodrow Wilson's policies and actions have not been judged nearly as often by their actual empirical consequences as by how well their goals fit the vision of the anointed. Among the Progressives and others on the left who rallied to President Wilson's war efforts were *New Republic* editor Herbert Croly, John Dewey, Clarence Darrow, Upton Sinclair, Walter Lippmann, John Spargo and George Creel, a former muckraker who spearheaded the wartime propaganda efforts of the Wilson administration. Dewey, for example, declared: "I have been a thorough and complete sympathizer with the part played by this country in this war, and I have wished to see the resources of this country used for its successful prosecution."[19]

Since Wilson had been, for much of his adult life, a quintessential academic intellectual, it is hardly surprising that his words as President repeatedly found resonance among many other intellectuals and evoked lavish praise from them. For example, one of Woodrow Wilson's speeches about the right of self-determination of peoples in 1916 elicited these responses:

> The president of Williams College, for instance, compared it to the Gettysburg Address. Walter Lippmann, using the Monroe Doctrine as his point of reference, wrote: "In historic significance it is easily the most important diplomatic event that our generation has known." Hamilton

Holt proclaimed that the address "cannot fail to rank in political importance with the Declaration of Independence." In an editorial entitled "Mr. Wilson's Great Utterance," the *New Republic* suggested that the President might have engineered "a decisive turning point in the history of the modern world."[20]

Not only has history failed to rank President Wilson's remarks with the historic pronouncements with which they were compared, at the time his own Secretary of State, Robert Lansing, was deeply troubled by the concept of the self-determination of peoples. He wrote in his diary:

These phrases will certainly come home to roost and cause much vexation. The President is a phrase-maker par excellence. He admires trite sayings and revels in formulating them. But when he comes to their practical application he is so vague that their worth may well be doubted. He apparently never thought out in advance where they would lead or how they would be interpreted by others. In fact he does not seem to care so that his words sound well. The gift of clever phrasing may be a curse unless the phrases are put to the test of sound, practical application before being uttered.[21]

Ten days later, Secretary Lansing returned to this subject in his diary:

The phrase is simply loaded with dynamite. It will raise hopes which can never be realized. It will, I fear, cost thousands of lives. In the end it is bound to be discredited, to be called the dream of an idealist who failed to realize the danger until too late to check those who attempt to put the principle into force. What a calamity that the phrase was ever uttered! What misery it will cause! Think of the feelings of the author when he counts the dead who died because he coined a phrase![22]

It should be noted that Lansing did not simply reach a different conclusion from that of Wilson's admirers. He applied an entirely different criterion—concrete results, rather than resonance with a vision. The military, economic and social viability of the nations created by fiat after the First World War was not a question that the victors had sufficient time to address, much less answer. As in so many other contexts in which "the people" are invoked, the people themselves actually had little to say about the decisions involved. The so-called self-determination of peoples was in fact the determination of peoples' fate by foreigners, arrogating the role of surrogate decision-makers, while having neither the degree of knowledge nor the accountability for consequences that might have made their decisions even plausible.[*]

Although the concept of the self-determination of peoples has been identified with Woodrow Wilson, the idea of a sweeping redrawing of national boundaries was already in the air. H.G. Wells, as early as 1914, had written of a need for "a re-mapped and pacified Europe"[23] after the war and said: "We are fighting now for a new map of Europe."[24] In other words, his was the vision of the anointed shaping other people's lives, including the lives of whole foreign nations, the vision later expressed and carried out by Woodrow Wilson.

Writing in 1915, Walter Lippmann, who would four years later become a member of President Wilson's delegation in Paris, saw the gross lack of knowledge of the peoples who were being proposed to be dealt with as if they were chess pieces being arranged to carry out some grand design:

> We are feeding on maps, talking of populations as if they were abstract lumps, and turning our minds to a scale unheard of in history. . . When you consider what a mystery the East Side of New York is to the West Side, the business of arranging the world to the satisfaction of the people in it may be seen in something like its true proportions.[25]

The very idea of having each "people" have their own homeland ignored both history and demography, not to mention economics and military security. Locations of peoples and of national boundaries had already changed repeatedly and drastically throughout history. Much of the land in the world, and most of the land in the dismembered Habsburg and Ottoman Empires, belonged to different sovereignties at different periods of history. The number of cities in those empires with multiple names from different languages over the centuries should have been a tip-off, quite aside from the mosques converted to churches and the churches converted to mosques.

The idea of rescuing oppressed minorities ignored the prospect— since become a reality— that oppressed minorities who became rulers of their

---

[*] A member of the British delegation to the Paris conference that shaped the postwar world wrote to his wife describing the leaders of the victorious allies— Wilson, Britain's Prime Minister David Lloyd George and France's Premier Georges Clemenceau— as "three ignorant and irresponsible men cutting Asia Minor to bits as if they were dividing a cake." Daniel Patrick Moynihan, *Pandaemonium*, (Oxford: Oxford University Press, 1993), p. 102.

own nations would immediately begin oppressing other minorities under their control. The solution sought by Wilson and applauded by other intellectuals was as illusory as it was dangerous. Small and vulnerable states created by the dismemberment of the Habsburg Empire were later picked off, one by one, by Hitler in the 1930s— an operation that would have been much more difficult and hazardous if he had to confront a united Habsburg Empire instead. The harm done extended beyond the small states themselves; a larger state like France was more vulnerable after Hitler took control of the military and other resources of Czechoslovakia and Austria. Today, NATO is in effect an attempt to consolidate individually vulnerable states, now that the empires of which some had been part are gone.

As for Wilson's other famous sweeping phrase, "The world must be made safe for democracy,"[26] the actual concrete results of his policies led in the directly opposite direction— to brutal totalitarian regimes replacing the autocratic governments in Russia, Italy, and Germany. Despite the "heartening" news of the fall of the czarist government in Russia, to which Wilson referred in his speech asking Congress to declare war on Germany, the Kerensky regime that followed was then undermined by the Wilson administration itself, which made the granting of desperately needed loans to Russia contingent on Russia's continuing to fight a losing, disastrous, and bitterly unpopular war, leading within a year to the Bolshevik revolution, inaugurating one of the bloodiest totalitarian regimes of the twentieth century.

In short, the end of autocracy, which Wilson and the intelligentsia in general so much welcomed, was followed not by the democratic governments which were expected to replace them, but by regimes much worse than those they replaced. The czars, for example, did not execute as many political prisoners in 92 years as the Soviets executed in a single year.[27] As in other contexts, intellectuals tended to act as if incessant criticisms and all-out opposition to the shortcomings of existing governments will lead to "change," implicitly assumed to be a change for the better, no matter how often it has led to changes for the worse. Wilson was thus a quintessential intellectual in this as well. In later years, other autocratic governments denounced by later intellectuals— whether in China, Iran or Cuba— were followed by totalitarian regimes more brutal and repressive internally and more dangerous on the world stage.

The effects of Woodrow Wilson's administration on democracy within the United States were likewise negative, despite the rhetoric of making the world safe for democracy. Wartime restrictions on civilian liberties were much more widespread during America's relatively brief involvement in the First World War— all of it fought overseas— than during the much longer involvement of the United States in the Second World War, where the war was brought much closer to home, with Japanese attacks on Pearl Harbor and the Aleutian Islands, and German submarine attacks on American ships off the east coast. Some of the landmark Supreme Court decisions on freedom of speech grew out of the Wilson administration's attempts to silence criticisms of its conduct of the war.

During the relatively brief period of American military involvement in the First World War— little more than a year and a half— a remarkably large set of pervasive federal controls over the internal life of the United States were put into operation, confirming the Progressive intellectuals' view of war as a golden opportunity for replacing traditional American individual economic and social decision-making processes with collectivist control and indoctrination. Quickly created boards, commissions, and committees were directed by the War Industries Board, which governed much of the economy, creating rationing and fixing prices. Meanwhile, the Committee on Public Information, aptly described as "the West's first modern ministry for propaganda," was created and run by Progressive George Creel, who took it as his mission to turn public opinion into "one white-hot mass" of support for the war, in the name of "100 percent Americanism, with anyone who "refuses to back the President in this crisis" being branded "worse than a traitor."[28]

While the public was being propagandized on a mass scale— by tens of millions of pamphlets and with "war studies" created in high schools and colleges, for example— a Sedition Act was passed which forbade "uttering, printing, writing, or publishing any disloyal, profane, scurrilous, or abusive language about the United States government or the military." Even the pro-war *New Republic* was warned that it could be banned from the mails if it continued to publish advertisements by the National Civil Liberties Bureau.[29] All of this was promoted by the Progressives— not inconsistently, but very consistently with their *dirigiste* vision, the vision of the anointed taking control of the masses in the name of collective goals to supersede the individual decisions that Progressives saw as chaotic.

The ultimate irony was that all this economic, political and social repression was justified as part of the war in which "The world must be made safe for democracy"— a goal which itself was far removed from the ostensible cause of American military involvement, German submarine warfare.

Just as the international repercussions of American involvement in the First World War did not end when the war ended, so the repercussions of the domestic policies of the Wilson administration did not end when the war ended. The widespread government control of the economy demonstrated, to John Dewey for example, "the practicable possibilities of governmental regulation of private business" and that "public control was shown to be almost ridiculously easy."[30] As elsewhere, government orders were verbally transformed into the more politically acceptable euphemism "public control," and the ease of imposing such orders was equated with success at achieving their proclaimed goals. Moreover, the Wilson administration did not last long enough after wartime controls were instituted to determine their long-run effects in peacetime.

As for the public, as distinguished from those who invoked its name in euphemisms, the public repudiated Wilson's Progressivism at the polls and elected conservative administrations throughout the ensuing decade of the 1920s. But the heady experience of government intervention and control of the economy in wartime shaped the thinking of individuals who would later be supporters or participants in the New Deal administration of the 1930s, headed by Wilson's Assistant Secretary of the Navy, Franklin D. Roosevelt.

THE SECOND WORLD WAR

Intellectuals Between the World Wars

While the First World War reinforced the *dirigiste* tendencies of both the intelligentsia and of many in the political arena, it devastated the notions of those intellectuals who saw war as a beneficial social tonic domestically or as a good means to spread Progressive policies internationally. Despite those intellectuals who had rallied to the military interventionist policies of Woodrow Wilson in Latin America and in Europe, the unprecedented horrors and devastations of the First World War turned virtually the whole intellectual community of the Western world in the opposite direction, toward pacifism. Indeed, pacifism became a widespread attitude among much of the population at large and therefore a potent political force in democratic nations.

No matter how drastically intellectuals had been forced to change their minds in the wake of the First World War, they remained as convinced as ever that their views on the subject of war and peace were vastly superior to the views of the general public. Circumstances were part of the reason for the spread of pacifism, especially the grim and heart-rending experiences of the First World War. But part was due to how people reacted to circumstances, especially the intelligentsia, most severely the intelligentsia in France, which suffered most among the Western democracies. The most fundamental of these circumstances were the stark facts of that war itself:

> About 1,400,000 French lost their lives; well over 1,000,000 had been gassed, disfigured, mangled, amputated, left permanent invalids. Wheelchairs, crutches, empty sleeves dangling loosely or tucked into pockets became common sights. More than that had suffered some sort of wound: Half of the 6,500,000 who survived the war had sustained injuries. Most visible, 1,100,000, were those who had been evidently diminished and were described as *mutilés*, a term the dictionary translates as "maimed" or "mangled," and English usage prefers to clothe in an euphemism: "disabled."[31]

With most of the war on the western front fought on its own territory, France suffered tremendous casualties in the First World War. More than one-fourth of all Frenchmen between the ages of 18 and 27 were killed in the First World War.[32] Moreover, neither the financial nor the human costs of the First World War ended when the war itself ended. Although the numbers of males and females in France's population were roughly equal before the war, the massive wartime casualties among young Frenchmen meant that in the 1930s the number of women between the ages of twenty and forty exceeded the number of men of those ages by more than a million— meaning that more than a million women in the prime of life could not fulfill traditional expectations of becoming wives and mothers. During the 1930s, there were not enough babies born in France to replace the people who died during that decade.[33]

The sense of faith in the French government was also devastated, as people who had patriotically invested in bonds to help finance the First World War saw the value of those bonds drastically reduced by inflation, cheating some citizens out of their life's savings. No country was more fertile soil for pacifism and demoralization, and no one created more of both than France's intelligentsia.

Anti-war novels and the memoirs of military veterans found a vast market in France. A translation of the anti-war classic *All Quiet on the Western Front* sold 72,000 copies in ten days and nearly 450,000 copies by Christmas, *L'Humanité* serialized it and *Vie intellectuelle* praised it. In 1938, the year of the Munich appeasement of Hitler, *Echo de la Nièvre* said, "anything rather than war."[34] Novelist Jean Giono, long critical of his own French government, likewise urged acceptance of Hitler's terms at Munich.[35]

Very similar trends were apparent in Britain in the years between the two World Wars where, for example, *All Quiet on the Western Front* sold 300,000 copies in six months[36]:

> In the late 1920s and early 1930s, the pacifist mood was being fuelled by the flow of memoirs and novels exploring the horrors of the Great War— Richard Aldington's *Death of a Hero* and Siegfried Sassoon's *Memoirs of a Fox-hunting Man* were published in 1928, and Robert Graves' *Goodbye to All That*, Ernest Hemingway's *Farewell to Arms* and Erich Maria Remarque's *All Quiet on the Western Front* appeared in 1929. Lewis Milestone's film of Remarque's book had a powerful impact.[37]

In addition to many anti-war novels about the First World War, eighty or more novels about the horrors of future wars were published in Britain between the First and Second World Wars.[38]

One of the remarkable developments of the 1920s was an international movement among intellectuals, promoting the idea that nations should get together and publicly renounce war. As prominent British intellectual Harold Laski put it: "The experience of what world-conflict has involved seems to have convinced the best of this generation that the effective outlawry of war is the only reasonable alternative to suicide."[39] In the United States, John Dewey spoke of those who were skeptical of this movement for the international renunciation of war that he supported, which led to the Kellogg-Briand Pact of 1928, as people with "the stupidity of habit-bound minds." He saw arguments against the renunciation of war as coming "from those who believe in the war system."[40] With Laski, Dewey and others, the issue was not simply a matter of one hypothesis about war and peace versus another but was a question of the anointed versus the benighted— the latter being dismissed with contempt, rather than having their arguments answered.

Being a pacifist in the 1920s and 1930s was a badge of honor, and pacifist phrases facilitated admission to the circles of the self-congratulatory elites. At a 1935 rally of the British Labor Party, economist Roy Harrod heard a candidate proclaim that Britain ought to disarm "as an example to the others"— a very common argument at that time. His response and the answer it provoked captured the spirit of the times:

> 'You think our example will cause Hitler and Mussolini to disarm?' I asked.
> 'Oh, Roy', she said, 'have you lost all your idealism?'[41]

Others likewise presented pacifism in personal, rather than policy, terms. Author J.M. Murry, for example, said: "What matters is that men and women should bear their witness."[42] However, pacifist Margery South objected to pacifism becoming a "precious" doctrine "which has as its objective the regeneration of the individual rather than the prevention of war."[43] Here, as in other cases, the vision of the anointed was a vision about themselves, not just about the ostensible issue at hand. Like Margery South, John Maynard Keynes also objected to having national policies be based on the "urge to save *one's own soul*."[44]

Given the high personal psychic stakes for pacifists, it is not surprising that those with a contrary opinion on issues of war and peace— as on other issues— were lashed out at, as personal enemies or as people threatening their soul, and were demonized rather than answered. As noted in Chapter 8, Bertrand Russell claimed that the man who opposed pacifism was someone who "delights in war, and would hate a world from which it had been eliminated."[45]

In a very similar vein, H.G. Wells spoke of a substantial portion of "human beings who definitely like war, know they like war, want it and seek it."[46]

Kingsley Martin, long-time editor of the influential *New Statesman*, likewise characterized Winston Churchill in 1931 as someone whose mind "is confined in a militaristic mould," as a psychological explanation of Churchill's advocacy of "keeping the French Army and the British Navy at full strength."[47] More generally, Kingsley Martin treated those with views different from his own regarding war and peace as having psychological defects, rather than having arguments that required being answered with other arguments:

> To have a foreign enemy in the offing enables us to hate with a good conscience. . . It is only in time of war that we get a complete moral holiday, when all the things which we have learned at our mother's knee, all the moral inhibitions imposed by education and society, can be whole-heartedly thrown aside, when it becomes justifiable to hit below the belt, when it is one's duty to lie, and killing is no longer murder.[48]

In short, the unworthiness of opponents was taken as axiomatic, making substantive arguments against their arguments unnecessary. Kingsley Martin was not alone. Churchill's colleagues in Parliament were equally dismissive.[49]

Such views were not peculiar to British and American intellectuals. The French intelligentsia played a major role in the promotion of pacifism between the two World Wars. Even before the Treaty of Versailles was signed, internationally renowned French writer Romain Rolland— recipient of France's Grand Prix de Littérature, later elected to the Russian Academy of Sciences and offered the Goethe Prize by Germany, as well as recipient of the Nobel Prize for Literature— issued a manifesto calling on intellectuals in all countries to oppose militarism and nationalism, in order to promote peace.[50]

In 1926, prominent intellectuals from a number of countries signed an internationally publicized petition calling for "some definite step toward complete disarmament and the demilitarizing of the mind of civilized nations." Among those who signed were H.G. Wells and Bertrand Russell in England and Romain Rolland and Georges Duhamel in France. The petition called for a ban on military conscription, in part "to rid the world of the spirit of militarism."[51]

Behind such arguments was the crucial assumption that both physical and moral disarmament were necessary to sustain peace. Neither in this petition nor in other statements expressing similar views was there much, if any, expressed concern that both kinds of disarmament would leave the disarmed nations at the mercy of those nations which did not disarm in either sense, thus making a new war look more attractive to the latter because it would look more winnable. Hitler, for example, banned the anti-war classic *All Quiet on the Western Front*, as he wanted neither moral nor physical disarmament in Germany, but carefully followed both phenomena in Western democracies, as he plotted his moves against them.

Pacifists of this era seemed not to think of other nations as prospective enemies but of *war itself* as the enemy, with weapons of war and those who manufactured these weapons— "merchants of death" being the fashionable phrase of the times and the title of a best-selling 1934 book[52]— also being enemies. The "merchants of death wax fat and bloated," declared John Dewey in 1935.[53] Romain Rolland called them "profiteers of massacre."[54] H.G. Wells said, "war equipment has followed blindly upon industrial advance until it has become a monstrous and immediate danger to the community."[55] Harold Laski spoke of the "wickedness of armaments."[56] Aldous Huxley referred to a battleship as a "repulsive" insect, a "huge bug," which "squatted there on the water, all its poisonous armory enlarged into instruments of destruction, every bristle a gun, every pore a torpedo tube," and added: "Men had created this enormous working model of a loathsome insect for the express purpose of destroying other men."[57]

Pacifists did not see military forces as deterrents to other nations' military forces but as malign influences in and of themselves. J.B. Priestley, for example, said "we should distrust any increase in armaments," one reason being that "heavy competitive arming produces fear." Moreover, "Once a nation is heavily armed, it has to keep playing at war, and from playing at war to the actual waging of war is a very short step."[58] Famed author E.M. Forster (*A Passage to India*) said that he was "shocked" to realize that his stock in Imperial Chemicals was stock in a company that *potentially* could produce war weapons, even though currently (1934) it was "not an armament firm"— and he promptly sold all his shares of that stock. A year later, he said, "One of my reasons for voting Labour last week was that I hoped it would arm us inadequately: would, in more decorous language, keep us out of the armament race when disaster seems assured."[59]

Such views— seeing weapons rather than other nations as the danger— were not simply intellectual fashions but created political bases for national policies and international agreements, beginning with the Washington Naval Agreements of 1921–1922 among the leading naval powers of the world to limit the number and size of warships, agreements hailed by John Dewey among others,[60] and the Kellogg-Briand Pact of 1928, renouncing war. "Away with rifles, machine guns, and cannon!" said France's Foreign Minister, Aristide Briand,[61] co-author of the Kellogg-Briand Pact. In a letter to the *New Republic* in 1932, Romain Rolland urged, "Unite, all of you, against the common enemy. Down with war!"[62] Later, Georges Duhamel, looking back on the interwar pacifists in France, including himself, summarized their approach, which avoided seeing other nations as potential enemies:

> For more than twelve years Frenchmen of my kind, and there were many of them, spared no pains to forget what they knew about Germany. Doubtless it was imprudent, but it sprang from a sincere desire on our part for harmony and collaboration. We were willing to forget. And what were we willing to forget? Some very horrible things.[63]

The view of war itself, rather than other nations, as the enemy began shortly after the end of the First World War, as did the idea that patriotism must be superseded by internationalism, in the interests of peace. Addressing school teachers in 1919, Anatole France urged that they use the schools to promote pacifism and internationalism. "In developing the child, you will determine the future," he said. "The teacher must make the child love peace and its works; he must teach him to detest war; he will banish from education all that which excites hate for the stranger, even hatred of the enemy of yesterday," he added. Anatole France declared, "we must be citizens of the world or see all civilization perish."[64] Such ideas became dominant in French schools during the next two decades.

A key role in the spread of pacifism in France was played by the schools— more specifically, by the French teachers' unions, which began organized campaigns in the 1920s, objecting to postwar textbooks favorably depicting the French soldiers who had defended their country against German invaders in the First World War. Such textbooks were called "bellicose"— a verbal tactic still common among those with the vision of the anointed, of reducing views different from their own to mere emotions, as if in this case only pugnaciousness could account for resisting invaders or for praising those who had put their lives on the line to do so. The leading teachers' union, the *Syndicat national des instituteurs* (SN) launched a campaign against those textbooks "of bellicose inspiration" which it characterized as "a danger for the organization of peace." Since nationalism was said to be one of the causes of war, internationalism or "impartiality" among nations was considered to be a required feature of textbooks.[65]

This was not thought of as being against patriotism but, at the very least, it lessened the sense of obligation to those who had died to protect the nation, with its implicit obligation on members of generations that followed to do the same, if and when that became necessary again.

Leaders of the drive to rewrite history textbooks called their goal "moral disarmament" to match the military disarmament which many regarded as another key to peace. Lists of textbooks targeted for removal from the schools were made by Georges Lapierre, one of the SN leaders. By 1929, he was able to boast of all the "bellicose" books the SN campaign had gotten taken out of the schools, rewritten, or replaced. Faced with the threat of losing a share of the large textbook market, French publishers caved in to union demands that books about the First World War be revised to reflect "impartiality" among nations and to promote pacifism.

The once epic story of French soldiers' heroic defense at Verdun, despite their massive casualties, was now transformed into a story of horrible suffering by *all* soldiers at Verdun, presented in the much sought after spirit of impartiality: "Imagine the life of these combatants— French, allies, or enemies."[66] In short, men who had once been honored as patriotic heroes for having sacrificed their lives in a desperate struggle to hold off the invaders of their country were now verbally reduced to *victims*, and put on the same plane as other victims among the invaders. Ceremonies dedicating monuments to commemorate soldiers who had died in battle were sometimes turned into occasions for speeches promoting the pacifist ideology.[67]

Among those who tried to warn against "moral disarmament" was Marshal Philippe Pétain, the victor of the battle of Verdun, who in 1934 said that French teachers were out to "raise our sons in ignorance of or in contempt of the fatherland."[68] Years later, during the Second World War, one of the alerts issued to French soldiers said, "Remember the Marne and Verdun!"[69] But this was said to a generation that had been taught to see the Marne and Verdun not as historic sites of patriotic heroism by French soldiers but as places where soldiers on all sides had been victims alike.

France's behavior in the Second World War was in extraordinary contrast with its behavior in the First World War. France fought off the German invaders for four long years during the First World War, despite suffering horrendous casualties— more wartime deaths than a larger country like the United States has ever suffered in any war or in all its wars put together. Yet, during the Second World War, France surrendered after just six weeks of fighting in 1940. In the bitter moment of defeat, the head of the teachers' union was told: "You are partially responsible for the defeat."[70] Charles de Gaulle, François Mauriac, and many other Frenchmen blamed a lack of national will, or general moral decay, for the sudden and humiliating collapse of France in 1940.[71]

Although France's sudden collapse caught much of the world by surprise, Winston Churchill had said, as far back as 1932: "France, though armed to the teeth, is pacifist to the core."[72] Hitler was not surprised by France's sudden collapse, and had in fact predicted it.[73] When he pressed his generals to draw up plans for the invasion of France immediately after the swift German victory in Poland in the autumn of 1939, the generals' analyses of the various military and logistical factors involved led them to doubt that such a project could be undertaken, with any realistic hope of success, before 1941 or perhaps even 1942. But the most delay that Hitler would grant them was until the spring of 1940, which in fact was when the German invasion of France began. Hitler's reasons were wholly different from the objective factors which German generals had analyzed. It was based on his analysis of the French themselves.

Hitler said that France was no longer the same country as the France that had fought doggedly through four years of the First World War, that the contemporary French were lacking in the personal strengths necessary for victory, and would falter and surrender.[74] That is in fact largely what happened. The objective factors, such as the number and quality of military equipment available to France and its British allies versus those available to the German invaders led military leaders in both France and Germany to conclude at the outset that France had the greater prospects of victory.[75] But Hitler had long made a study of public opinion, as well as official opinion, in France and Britain.[76] The words and deeds of both politicians and pacifists in those countries went into Hitler's calculations.

The invasion of France took place when it did only because Hitler insisted upon it, dismissing the contrary advice of his own top generals. Decades later, scholarly studies in both France and Germany reached the same conclusion as that of French and German military leaders in 1940, that the objective military factors favored a French victory[77]— and certainly nothing like the swift and total collapse that occurred. How much of that collapse can be attributed to the large role of chance and misjudgments inherent in war, and how much to a fundamental inner erosion of morale, patriotism and resolution among the French themselves, is a question unlikely to be answered definitively.

What is clear, however is that the irresolution which marked French political responses to the German threat in the years leading up to the Second World War carried over into the war itself, beginning with the long months of the "phony war" from September 1939 to May 1940, during which France had overwhelming military superiority on Germany's western front, while German military forces were concentrated in the east, fighting Poland— and yet France did nothing. The German general responsible for defending the vulnerable western front said, "Every day of calm in the West is for me a gift from God."[78] In the earliest days of the war, when German military forces were most heavily concentrated on the eastern front, one of the generals under his command had informed him that, if the French attacked, he did not have enough resources to stop them for even one day.[79] Even a civilian like American foreign correspondent William L. Shirer was amazed as he observed the French inaction during the "phony war" and their irresolution and ineptness when the Germans attacked in 1940.[80]

While France was the most dramatic example of "moral disarmament" during the interwar years, it was by no means the only country in which such views prevailed among the intelligentsia. British pacifists likewise often depicted wars as being a result of national emotions or attitudes, rather than calculations of self-interest by aggressive rulers. In a 1931 editorial in the *New Statesman and Nation*, Kingsley Martin said that "modern war is the product of ignorance and idealism, not of far-sighted wickedness." Therefore what was needed to prevent a future war was "bringing up a new generation to recognise that martial patriotism is an out-of-date virtue" because taking part in a future war would be "something that is individually shameful as well as socially suicidal."[81] Bertrand Russell defined patriotism as "a willingness to kill and be killed for trivial reasons."[82]

In 1932, British author Beverley Nichols publicly declared himself in favor of peace at any price, and later wrote *Cry Havoc!*, one of the most prominent pacifist books of the decade.[83] In 1933, students at Oxford University publicly pledged themselves *not* to fight in defense of their country, and what became known as "the Oxford pledge" spread rapidly to other British universities, as well as being echoed in Britain by such intellectuals as Cyril Joad and A.A. Milne, famous author of *Winnie the Pooh*, and in France by André Gide, who spoke of "the courageous students of Oxford."[84] Joad said that "the best way to ensure peace is to refuse in any circumstances to make war." He urged "an intensive campaign to induce the maximum number of young people to announce their refusal to fight in any war between nations."[85]

Joad was one of those who wrote graphically of the horrors and agonies of war, though Winston Churchill warned that Britain "cannot avoid war by dilating upon its horrors."[86] In Britain, as in France, patriotism was considered suspect as a cause of war. H.G. Wells, for example, declared himself against "the teaching of patriotic histories that sustain and carry on the poisonous war-making tradition of the past" and wanted British citizenship replaced by "world citizenship."[87] He regarded patriotism as a useless relic to be replaced by "the idea of cosmopolitan duty."[88] J.B. Priestley likewise saw patriotism as "a mighty force, chiefly used for evil."[89] A letter to *The Times* of London in 1936, signed by such prominent intellectuals as Aldous Huxley, Rebecca West, and Leonard Woolf, called for "the spread of the cosmopolitan spirit" and called for "writers in all countries" to "help all peoples to feel their underlying kinship."[90]

Meanwhile, Hitler was following such developments in Britain and France,[91] as he made his own plans and assessed the prospects of military victory.

Almost as remarkable as the lengths to which the pacifists of the 1930s went was the verbal virtuosity with which they downplayed the dangers of the pacifism they were advocating while Hitler was rearming on a massive scale in Germany and promoting the very patriotism among Germans that was being eroded by the intelligentsia in the democracies. Bertrand Russell used an argument that went as far back as 1793, when William Godwin claimed that a country which presented no military threat or provocation to other nations would not be attacked.[92] If Britain would reduce its armed forces, as Bertrand Russell advocated, "we should threaten no one, and no one would have any motive to make war on us." Russell explained further:

> When disarmament is suggested, it is natural to imagine that foreign conquest would inevitably follow, and would be accompanied by all the horrors that characterize warlike invasions. This is a mistake, as the example of Denmark shows. Probably, if we had neither armaments nor Empire, foreign States would let us alone. If they did not, we should have to yield without fighting, and we should therefore not arouse their ferocity.[93]

According to Russell, if you declare "that you are prepared to be defenceless and trust to luck, the other people, having no longer any reason to fear you, will cease to hate you, and will lose all incentive to attack you." The reason for this conclusion was Lord Russell's claim: "In most civilized men, resistance is necessary to arouse ferocity."[94] From this it followed that fear of an impending war should lead to "unilateral disarmament."[95] Such reasoning was not peculiar to Bertrand Russell nor unique to Britain. In France, a book by the head of the French socialist party— and later premier— Léon Blum said:

> If a nation thus undertook to disarm, it would not in reality incur any risk, because the moral prestige which it would acquire would render it invulnerable to attack and the force of its example would induce all other States to follow.[96]

Another element in the pacifist case of the 1930s, in both France and Britain, was that even a victory in war would make no real difference. According to Bertrand Russell, "victory will be no less disastrous to the world than defeat would have been." Because of the need for tight wartime control of a panicked population, the result "will be the substitution of an English Hitler for the German one."[97] Kingsley Martin likewise saw a new war as one "from which no one can emerge victorious,"[98] that "war would totally end civilisation."[99] In France, novelist Jean Giono asked what was the worst that could happen if the Germans invaded France. The French would become Germans, he said. "I prefer being a living German to being a dead Frenchman."[100] Literary figure Simone Weil argued along similar lines, asking "why is the possibility of German hegemony worse than French hegemony?"[101]

Just a little over two years after this abstract question about abstract people, the Nazi conquest of France made the consequences of Hitler's hegemony much more painfully specific. In the aftermath of France's defeat, Simone Weil fled to England to escape the dangers of genocidal Nazi rule in France because, though a practicing Christian, her ancestors were Jewish and that was enough to get other Jews in France sent to Nazi death camps. After the German invasion of France, even Bertrand Russell changed his mind and declared that fighting back was a lesser evil than submitting to the Nazis.[102] In France, Georges Lapierre, who had spearheaded the drive against "bellicose" textbooks in French schools became, in the wake of France's defeat, part of the underground resistance to Nazi rule, but was captured and sent to the Dachau concentration camp, where he died.[103] Weil and Lapierre learned from experience, but too late to spare themselves or their country the consequences of the things they had advocated. Meanwhile, Jean Giono collaborated with the Nazi conquerors.

Widespread pacifist sentiments among the intelligentsia in Britain during the interwar period were echoed in the political arena by leaders of the British Labor Party:

> In June 1933, at the East Fulham by-election, the Labour candidate received a message from the Labour Party leader, George Lansbury: 'I would close every recruiting station, disband the Army and disarm the Air Force. I would abolish the whole dreadful equipment of war and say

to the world "do your worst".' Clement Attlee, who was to succeed him
as leader, told the Commons, 21 December 1933: 'We are unalterably
opposed to anything in the nature of rearmament.' Labour consistently
voted, spoke and campaigned against rearmament right up to the
outbreak of war.[104]

Two years later, Attlee said, "Our policy is not of seeking security through
rearmament but through disarmament."[105] As late as 1937, Harold Laski
said, "Are we really to support this reactionary Government. . . in rearming
for purposes it refuses specifically to declare?"[106] The Labor Party's
opposition to military preparedness did not change until the working class
component of the Labor Party, represented by its unions, eventually
overcame its intellectual component, represented by Laski and others with a
doctrinaire opposition to military defense.[107]

A 1938 editorial in the *New Statesman and Nation* deplored the labor
unions' "supporting rearmament" without getting some quid pro quo in the
form of influence over the government's international policies or forcing the
government "to limit effectively the profits of the arms industry."[108] In
short, to intellectual supporters of the Labor Party, rearmament was still an
ideological issue a year before the Second World War began, rather than a
matter of national survival.

Similar anti-military and anti-armament views were common among the
American intelligentsia. John Dewey, Upton Sinclair, and Jane Addams
were among the American signers of a 1930 manifesto against military
training for youths.[109] In 1934, Oswald Garrison Villard urged a "decrease
by one-third of the United States army and the mustering out of 50 per cent
of our reserve officers as evidence of our good faith."[110] Nor were such
sentiments among intellectuals without influence upon holders of political
power. When the Roosevelt administration cut the Army's budget, Army
Chief of Staff General Douglas MacArthur had an angry confrontation
with the President, offered his resignation, and was still so upset as he left
the White House that he vomited on the steps.[111]

In such an atmosphere between the two World Wars, international
disarmament conferences and agreements in which nations renounced war
became very popular in the Western democracies. But, as with domestic
gun-control laws, the real question is whether arms-limitation treaties

actually limit the arms of anyone except those who respect the law, whether international or domestic. Both Japan and Germany violated armaments limitations agreements that they had signed, producing among other things larger battleships than these treaties allowed and larger than anything in either the British or American navies.

Violations of arms control treaties are not a happenstance. Such agreements are inherently one-sided. Leaders of democratic nations are under more pressure to sign such agreements than are leaders of dictatorships that can control, suppress or ignore public opinion. In democratic nations, neither academic nor media intellectuals are usually as concerned with scrutinizing the specifics of disarmament agreements as they are with celebrating the symbolism of the signing of such agreements and the "easing of international tensions" that they bring, as if emotional catharsis will deflect governments bent on military aggression. Thus intellectuals like John Dewey had cheered on the Washington Naval Agreements of 1921–1922,[112] and *The Times* of London praised the Anglo-German Naval Agreement of 1935 as "the outstanding fact in Anglo-German relations," as an "emphatic renunciation of hostile purpose towards this country" by Germany, and a "clear-sighted decision of HERR HITLER himself."[113]

Conversely, those with this vision roundly condemn leaders of their own country who refuse to compromise in order to reach such agreements. In addition to terms that explicitly tend to favor those nations whose intelligentsia are not free to criticize their governments, subsequent violations of these agreements by aggressor nations are more likely to be tolerated by leaders of democratic nations, who have no incentive to be quick to announce to their own citizens that they have been "had" in signing agreements that were widely publicized and widely celebrated when they were signed.

The intelligentsia do not need to convert political leaders to their own pacifist views in order to affect government policy. Leaders of democratic nations must always face the prospect of elections, and the atmosphere in which those elections are held is a fact of life to politicians seeking to keep their careers alive and their party in power. Thus, although clandestine German rearmament in violation of treaties began even before Hitler came to power in 1933, this was "secret" only in the sense that the German government did not acknowledge it and the general public in Western democratic countries were not made aware of it. But it was not secret from democratic leaders who received intelligence reports.

Stanley Baldwin, who was Britain's Deputy Prime Minister in 1933, was well aware of what was going on— but was also well aware of the political repercussions if he publicly announced German rearmament. In response to a speech in the House of Commons in 1936 by Winston Churchill, then a back-bencher, charging that the British government had engaged in "one-sided disarmament" and that the British army "lacks almost every weapon which is required for the latest form of modern war,"[114] now Prime Minister, Stanley Baldwin replied in terms of what the political realities were at the time of the 1933 elections:

> Supposing I had gone to the country and said that Germany was rearming, and that we must rearm, does anybody think that this pacific democracy would have rallied to that cry at that moment? *I cannot think of anything that would have made the loss of the election from my point of view more certain.*[115]

Even a dozen years later, writing his monumental postwar, six-volume history, *The Second World War*, Churchill remained repelled by Baldwin's answer:

> This was indeed appalling frankness. It carried naked truth about his motives into indecency. That a Prime Minister should avow that he had not done his duty in regard to national safety because he was afraid of losing the election was an incident without parallel in our parliamentary history. Mr. Baldwin was, of course, not moved by any ignoble wish to remain in office. He was in fact in 1936 earnestly desirous of retiring. His policy was dictated by the fear that if the Socialists came into power, even less would be done than his Government intended. All their declarations and votes against defence measures are upon record.[116]

Here, as in many other situations, the intelligentsia's effect on the course of events did not depend upon their convincing the holders of power. All they had to do was convince enough of the public so that the holders of power became fearful of losing that power if they went against the prevailing vision— pacifism, in this case. If Stanley Baldwin's Conservative Party had lost power, he would have lost it to those who would turn the pacifist vision into a reality potentially disastrous to the country. Britain, after all, narrowly escaped being invaded and conquered in 1940, and only because of a belated development of its interceptor fighter planes that shot down German bombers during the aerial blitz that was intended to prepare the way for the invasion force being mobilized across the English Channel. Had the pacifists in the Labor Party come to power in 1933, it is by no means clear that this narrow margin of survival would have been in place.

There was a similar reluctance among leaders in France to alert the public to danger, or perhaps even to acknowledge the dangers to themselves. Although French Foreign Minister Aristide Briand was well aware of the dramatically rising political support for the Nazis in the 1930 German elections, and what that portended in terms of a military threat to France, like Baldwin he was not prepared to alarm the public:

> Briand was untroubled: Hitler will not go far, he assured the press while doing his best to keep news of German militarism reviving from the French public. Parades and demonstrations of the German Right were "completely suppressed in newsreels shown in French movie houses," reported the American military attaché.[117]

Even before Hitler came to power, French intelligence agents had already penetrated Germany's clandestine military buildup.[118] But neither the press nor the politicians wanted to tell the French public things that they did not want to hear, after all the traumas that they had been through during the First World War. Even after a further escalation of the vote for the Nazis in the 1932 elections brought Hitler into the German government, evasion or denial of the dangers to France continued:

> In the new German elections the Nazis became the largest party in the Reichstag, but the French press was not impressed. President Hindenburg had brought in General von Schleicher to hold the fort against the house painter-demagogue. Newspapers from Left to Right celebrated "the piteous end of Hitlerism" (*L'Œuvre*, January 1, 1933) and "the decadence of Hitler's movement" (*Paris-Soir*, January 1, 1933). The German Boulanger had missed the boat, exulted *L'Echo de Paris* (Nov. 7, 1932), forgetting how law-abiding the populist nineteenth-century general had been. The Socialist *Populaire* and the royalist *Action française* agreed: Hitler was henceforth excluded from power. But Schleicher resigned as

January 1933 ended, and the demagogue found himself in power after all. A pacifist dedicated his latest book, *Peace on Earth*, to Adolf Hitler.[119]

As in other times and in other contexts, it is worth noting in passing the know-it-all tone of condescension in the press, which is a corollary of self-exaltation among the intelligentsia.

However understandable the French desire to avoid a repetition of the horrors they had experienced in the First World War, their intellectuals' resolute denials of the dangers building up across the Rhine reached high levels of unreality. One of the early signs of this unreality was the celebration of the Kellogg-Briand pact of 1928, outlawing war. Named for an American Secretary of State and the French Foreign Minister, this pact received virtually unanimous approval in the French press.[120] Nothing is easier than to get peaceful people to renounce violence, even when they provide no concrete ways to prevent violence from others.

The French did not want to hear anything bad about Germany. Even Hitler's *Mein Kampf*, which spelled out his hostile intentions toward France, did not get through to the intelligentsia or to the public because a French court stopped its full translation, so that only expurgated versions were available to the few who were interested.[121] By the late 1930s, as refugees from Germany fled to France, bearing stories of the horrors of the Nazi regime, their stories were not only widely rejected but, because many of these refugees were Jewish, this provoked increased anti-Semitism, based on the notion that Jews were trying to provoke a war between France and Germany. Anti-Semitism was not confined to the masses, but was common among French intellectuals as well.[122]

In Britain, as in France, there was strong resistance among the intelligentsia to recognizing the nature of the Nazi regime within Germany or the external threat that it posed to Western democracies. The influential *Manchester Guardian* said that, despite the Nazis' radical ideas, they would act like "ordinary politicians" when they took office. Britain's largest circulation newspaper at the time, the *Daily Herald*, dismissed Hitler as a "clown" and opined that he would share the fate of his immediate predecessors as Chancellor of Germany, whose terms had lasted only a matter of weeks. The *Daily Telegraph* likewise said that Hitler was "done for" and would be gone before the end of 1932.[123] Harold Laski likewise declared in 1932 that "the Hitlerite movement has passed its apogee," that Hitler was "a cheap conspirator rather than an inspired revolutionary, the creature of circumstances rather than the maker of destiny."[124]

The most influential British newspaper, *The Times* of London, considered Hitler a "moderate," at least compared to other members of his party.[125] After Hitler and the Nazis achieved supreme power in Germany in 1933, *The Times* was especially resistant to letting news of the Nazis' domestic oppressions or international threat reach the public. Dispatches from *The Times'* own foreign correspondents in Germany were often filtered, rewritten, and sometimes rejected outright when they reported the raw reality of what was happening under Hitler. Complaints from these correspondents were unavailing, and some resigned in protest against the newspaper's filtering of their dispatches critical of the Nazi regime and reassigning them to places away from crucial events in Germany, while *The Times'* editorials supported Prime Minister Neville Chamberlain's appeasement policies toward Germany. *Times* editor Geoffrey Dawson wrote candidly to his Geneva correspondent:

> I do my utmost, night after night, to keep out of the paper anything that might hurt their [German] susceptibilities. . . . I have always been convinced that the peace of the world depends more than anything else upon our getting into reasonable relations with Germany.[126]

Here, as in other contexts, the harm done by the intelligentsia seems especially great when they step out beyond the bounds of their competence (in this case, gathering and reporting news) to seek a wider and greater role in shaping events (in this case, by filtering news to fit their vision).

Responses to International Crises

The ideas pervasive among the intelligentsia between the two World Wars would be no more than a footnote to the history of the times if these ideas did not have repercussions on the society at large, and indeed on the history of the world. But the influence of the ideas spread by the intelligentsia became apparent in the series of international crises that led up to the Second World War. The first of these crises involved the Rhineland in 1936.

After the shock of the First World War, the Treaty of Versailles sought to render Germany's huge military potential less dangerous through various restrictions, including limitations on the size of German military forces, a ban on military conscription in Germany and forbidding the German government from stationing troops in the Rhineland, the region of Germany where its industrial capacity was concentrated. This last provision meant that any future German attacks on other nations risked having its own undefended industrial sector seized by the French.

These otherwise objectionable limitations on national sovereignty were clearly based on *not* seeing Germany as an abstract nation in an abstract world, but as the most dangerous threat to the nations around it, both from the military prowess it had demonstrated in the First World War— inflicting casualties on its enemies at a much higher rate than its own casualty rate— and from its industrial predominance in Europe and its central location on the continent, from which it could strike in any direction.

With the passage of time, however, the British intelligentsia by the 1930s were discussing these restrictions on Germany as if Germany were an abstract nation in an abstract world. The fact that Germany was being treated *unequally* under the Versailles Treaty was seen by much of the British intelligentsia as a reason why it would be wrong to forbid the German government from doing things that other governments did. As Winston Churchill noted, in his aptly titled book *The Gathering Storm*, when "in 1932 the German delegation to the Disarmament Conference categorically demanded the removal of all restrictions upon their right to rearm, they found much support in the British press." He added:

> *The Times* spoke of "the timely redress of inequality," and *The New Statesman* of "the unqualified recognition of the principle of the equality of states." This meant that the seventy million Germans ought to be allowed to rearm and prepare for war without the victors in the late fearful struggle being entitled to make any objection. Equality of status between victors and vanquished; equality between a France of thirty-nine millions and a Germany of nearly double that number![127]

In short, the mundane specifics— on which matters of life and death depended— were subordinated by the intelligentsia to abstract principles about abstract nations. Germany was to be treated just as if it were Portugal or Denmark, even though the restrictions imposed by the Treaty of Versailles were due precisely to the fact that Germany had *not* behaved like Portugal or Denmark, and had a military capacity vastly greater than that of Portugal or Denmark.

With the rise to power of Adolf Hitler in 1933, unrestricted German rearmament went from being a demand to becoming a reality— in stages, beginning cautiously and then continuing more boldly as the Western democracies did nothing to enforce the restricting provisions of the Treaty of Versailles. Because of the initially small size of the German military under those restrictions, these violations began at a time when France alone had overwhelming military superiority over Germany and could have intervened unilaterally to stop the buildup of the Nazi military machine— a fact of which Hitler was vividly aware, and German military leaders even more fearfully so.[128]

The crucial step, without which the Nazis' wars of aggression would be impossible, was the stationing of German troops in the country's industrial region, the Rhineland. Only after its own industry was secured could Germany attack other nations. Hitler clearly understood both how essential the stationing of German troops in the Rhineland was— and how risky it was, given the relative sizes of the French and German armies at the time:

> "The forty-eight hours after the march into the Rhineland," Paul Schmidt, his interpreter, heard him later say, "were the most nerve-racking in my life. If the French had then marched into the Rhineland, we would have had to withdraw with our tails between our legs, for the military resources at our disposal would have been wholly inadequate for even a moderate resistance."[129]

The stakes were the highest— military conquests abroad or the collapse of the Nazi regime within Germany. "A retreat on our part," Hitler later admitted, "would have spelled collapse."[130] Hitler bet everything on irresolution by the French. He won his bet and tens of millions of people later lost their lives as a result. Yet this action in the Rhineland, like others before it, continued to be viewed among the British intelligentsia as an abstract question about abstract nations. A phrase repeated again and again in the British press after Hitler sent troops into the Rhineland was that "After all, they are only going into their own back-garden."[131] A very similar view was taken in the French press.[132] Despite French military superiority, the lack of political will paralyzed them from using that military superiority to prevent Hitler from remilitarizing the Rhineland:

> Nowhere in France was there the slightest indication that the public wanted or would even tolerate military action on account of German remilitarization of the Rhineland. The satirical weekly *Le Canard enchainé* expressed a common view when it said: "The Germans have invaded— Germany!" Communist leaders, supposedly in the forefront of opposition to Nazism, called stridently for preventing "the scourge of war from falling anew on us." They urged that the whole nation unite "against those who want to lead us to massacre." Socialist spokesmen termed "inadmissible any response that risked war," saying that even reinforcing the Maginot Line would be "provocative." The right-wing dailies *Le Matin* and *Le Jour* declared that conflict with Germany would benefit only communist Russia.[133]

Nor were such views confined to France. When the French Foreign Minister, Pierre-Étienne Flandin, met with British Prime Minister Stanley Baldwin, to ask only for British *political* support for action that France might take in response to German remilitarization of the Rhineland— France already having the *military* means to respond unilaterally— according to Flandin, Baldwin's response was: "You may be right, but if there is *even one chance in a hundred* that war would follow from your police operation, I have not the right to commit England."[134] This kind of thinking was commonplace at the time, as if there were no dangers from *inaction* to be weighed in the balance. In retrospect, we now know that Western democracies' inaction in response to Hitler's repeated provocations were crucial to his decisions to move toward war, confident that Western leaders were too timid to respond in time, or perhaps even at all.

This was especially clear in other international crises leading up to the Second World War. The West's half-hearted and ineffective response to Mussolini's invasion of Ethiopia in 1935, in defiance of the League of

Nations, was one of the inactions which led Hitler to doubt their will. Their inaction in response to the German remilitarization of the Rhineland in 1936, and to both Germany's and Italy's interventions into the Spanish civil war that same year, followed by the Western democracies' inaction in response to Germany's annexation of Austria in 1938, all contributed to his contempt for Western leaders and his confidence that they would do nothing more than talk.

The crisis that most solidified that confidence on Hitler's part was the crisis over his demand to annex Czechoslovakia's Sudetenland, adjacent to Germany and populated mostly by people of German ancestry. At the Munich conference in 1938, France, Britain, and Italy concurred in Hitler's annexation of the Sudetenland, abandoning Czechoslovakia to its fate, despite France's mutual defense treaty with Czechoslovakia.

The power of the intelligentsia is demonstrated not only by their ability to create a general climate of opinion that strikes fear into those who oppose their agenda but also by their ability to create a climate of opinion which richly rewards those political leaders whose decisions are consonant with the vision of the intelligentsia. There has probably never been a leader of a democratic nation more widely or more enthusiastically acclaimed, by the public, in the press, and by members of opposition parties as well as his own, as British Prime Minister Neville Chamberlain was when he returned from the Munich conference of 1938, waving an agreement with Hitler which he characterized as producing "peace for our time."[135] Less than a year later, the biggest and most bloody war in all of human history began.

Seeing each of Hitler's successive demands as a separate issue (the perspective of one-day-at-a-time rationalism), the French press saw the 1938 demand for German annexation of Czechoslovakia's Sudetenland as a question of "Should the French get themselves killed for Beneš, the Free Mason?" as *Je Suis Partout* put it and, in 1939, as Hitler demanded German annexation of Poland's lone port of Danzig (Gdansk), the question was posed as "Do We Have to Die for Danzig?" as a headline in *L'Œuvre* put it.[136] The phrase "Why die for Danzig?" was considered a hallmark of sophistication among the intelligentsia at the time, but was instead a sign of their dangerous talent for verbal virtuosity, which can pose questions in ways that make the desired answer almost inevitable, whatever the substantive merits or demerits of the issue.

Contrary to one-day-at-a-time rationalism, the real question was not whether it was worth dying over the Rhineland, over Czechoslovakia, over Austrian annexation, or over the city of Danzig. The question was whether one recognized in the unfolding pattern of Hitler's actions a lethal threat. By 1939 the French public seemed to have reached a more realistic understanding of what Hitler was doing than some of the country's intelligentsia. A poll in France in 1939 showed 76 percent of the public willing to use force in defense of Danzig.[137] A history of this period noted that French premier Édouard Daladier "complained that he could not appear in an open place or in a bistro without seeing people stand up and cry, 'Lead! We will follow you!'"[138]

Still, this was very late in the day, just months before the outbreak of the Second World War. The pervasive pacifism of that era and its political consequences had left France backed into a corner, where it now faced the prospect of war after having lost potential allies whom it had thrown to the wolves, in the hope of being spared Hitler's wrath themselves. As noted in Chapter 2, among the military equipment used by the Germans when they invaded France in 1940 were tanks manufactured in Czechoslovakia.

Serious questions have been raised as to whether the particular kinds of military equipment that Hitler accumulated, as of 1939, indicated an imminent attack against Britain and France, on the one hand, or attacks eastward, on the other.[139] But, if the latter, whether the British and the French governments chose the best time to fight is a question of military strategy. What is relevant to the role of intellectuals is the atmosphere in which these governments based their previous actions, leading up to this crisis.

The Outbreak of War

The aggressor Axis nations in the Second World War— Germany, Italy and Japan— did not have the resources, and were well aware that they did not have the resources, to match the combined resources of the democratic nations, including Britain, France, and the United States, in an arms race.

Achieving the goals of the Axis powers depended on (1) the Western democracies not mobilizing their resources in time to stave off devastating defeats, which in fact the Axis inflicted time and again during the first three years of the Second World War, and (2) not having the fortitude to continue fighting in the face of an unbroken string of bloody losses and retreats, both in Europe and in Asia, until such time as their greater resources could eventually be mobilized to begin counter-attacks.

That strategy came dangerously close to success. It was November 1942— three years after Britain had entered the Second World War— before British Prime Minister Winston Churchill could say, after the battle of El Alamein in North Africa, "we have a new experience. We have victory."[140] There had been nothing but a steady stream of defeats and retreats for the British up to that point, both in Europe and in Asia, and few expected Britain itself to survive in 1940,[141] after France fell to defeat in just six weeks of fighting and the *Luftwaffe* launched its massive bombings of London and other British cities.[142] Americans also had their first military victory in 1942, with incredible good luck overcoming lopsided Japanese naval superiority at the battle of Midway.[143]

Intellectuals played a major role in bringing both Britain and the United States to such a desperate situation with a steady drumbeat of pacifist, anti-national-defense efforts between the two World Wars. In October 1938, a month after Munich and less than a year before the beginning of the Second World War, the influential British journal *New Statesman and Nation* described rearmament as "only an inefficient and wasteful form of subsidy to industries which can find no better employment for their capital" and declared that "we shall not regain self-respect by trebling the numbers of our aeroplanes."[144] Even in February 1939, just months before the outbreak of the Second World War, the *New Statesman and Nation* referred to "the international Bedlam rearmament race" and questioned the money being made by "makers of aircraft and munitions" who were described as "friends" of the "Tory Government."[145] We now know that those aircraft and munitions provided the narrow margin by which Britain survived Hitler's aerial onslaught a year later, despite a widespread view in 1940 that Britain would not survive. History also suggests that years of "arms race" and "merchants of death" rhetoric contributed to making that margin of survival so narrow and precarious.

Intellectuals played a major role in creating the atmosphere of both military weakness and political irresolution within democratic nations, which made a war against those nations look winnable to the leaders of the Axis dictatorships. In addition to thus helping bring on the most devastating war in human history, intellectuals so impeded the buildup and modernizing of military forces in democratic nations in the years leading up to that war— demonizing military equipment suppliers as "merchants of death," being a classic example— that this ensured that American and British armed forces would often be outgunned in battle,[*] until belated and desperate efforts, both in war industries and on the battlefields, narrowly avoided total defeat and later turned the tide that led ultimately to victory.

The wartime costs of prewar self-indulgences in pacifist moral preening and anti-military crusades by the intelligentsia were staggering in both blood and treasure. Had Hitler and his allies won the Second World War, the enduring costs for the whole human race would have been incalculable.

Neglect of history has allowed us today to forget how narrowly the Western democracies as a whole escaped the ultimate catastrophe of a victory by Hitler and his allies. More important, it has allowed us to forget what brought the Western democracies to such a perilous point in the first place— and the potential for the same notions and attitudes, promoted by today's intelligentsia as by the intelligentsia between the two World Wars, to bring us to the same perilous tipping point again, with no assurance that either the luck or the fortitude that saved us the first time will do so again.

---

[*] As one example of what this meant, obsolete American torpedo bombers at the battle of Midway had a top speed of barely 100 miles an hour, and the much faster Japanese Zero fighter planes shot most of them out of the sky. Of the 82 Americans who flew into the battle of Midway on these planes, only 13 returned alive. Victor Davis Hanson, *Carnage and Culture: Landmark Battles in the Rise of Western Power* (New York: Doubleday, 2001), pp. 342–351.

Chapter 15

The Cold War and Beyond

The timid civilized world has found nothing with which
to oppose the onslaught of a sudden revival of barefaced
barbarity, other than concessions and smiles.

Aleksandr Solzhenitsyn[1]

Many wars have been fought in many parts of the world since the
Second World War but none thus far has been comparable in
magnitude or in the range of its consequences. Like the First World War,
the Second World War brought sweeping changes in the attitudes of
Western intellectuals— but very different changes. As we have seen, many
intellectuals who had rallied behind the Allied cause in the First World War,
especially as that cause was articulated by Woodrow Wilson, turned to
radical pacifism in the aftermath of that brutal and disillusioning carnage.
By contrast, in the period immediately following the end of the Second
World War, the tragic lessons of that war and of the years that had led up to
it were too indelibly etched into people's consciousness for many to return
to the naive and doctrinaire pacifism that had once been so common among
intellectuals in the Western democracies.

The shocking differences between the behavior of democratic nations and
totalitarian nations had been too recently, too graphically and too painfully
demonstrated during the war for "moral equivalence" to be a widely saleable
commodity, even among the intelligentsia. That would come later, as the mass
atrocities of Nazi Germany and imperial Japan faded into the mists of memory
and the similar mass atrocities of the Soviet Union remained largely concealed
or ignored. But in the immediate aftermath of the Second World War, evil and

danger were not things that could be ignored, viewed with an air of sophisticated detachment or verbally shrouded in euphemisms. *Time* magazine, for example, said in May 1945, at the end of the war in Europe:

> This war was a revolution against the moral basis of civilization. It was conceived by the Nazis in conscious contempt for the life, dignity and freedom of individual man and deliberately prosecuted by means of slavery, starvation and the mass destruction of noncombatants' lives. It was a revolution against the human soul.[2]

The difference between the hand-wringing and navel-gazing of the 1930s and the atmosphere in the immediate postwar era was epitomized in the way the decision was made by President Harry Truman to proceed with developing the hydrogen bomb, a weapon vastly more destructive than the atomic bombs that had devastated Hiroshima and Nagasaki. This was President Truman's consultation with his advisers:

> Lilienthal spoke of his fears of an arms race. Acheson countered by pointing out the growing public and political pressures on Truman. Lilienthal again spoke of his own "grave reservations." Truman cut him short. He did not, the President said, believe that an H bomb would ever be used, but because of the way the Russians were behaving, he had no other course. The meeting lasted only seven minutes. "Can the Russians do it?" Truman asked. All three men nodded yes. "In that case," Truman said, "we have no choice. We'll go ahead."[3]

The decade of the 1950s was still too close to the Second World War for the prewar notions, attitudes and blindspots of the intellectuals to make a strong comeback, or for the benefits of a free and decent society to be taken for granted and its human flaws to become a reason for sweeping rejections of its norms and institutions. That would begin in the 1960s, especially among people too young to have known what the Second World War was all about or what had led up to that catastrophe.

The difference between the immediate postwar period and the later period showed up in many ways. When visiting cemeteries and war memorials in Western Europe, decades later, distinguished American military historian Victor Davis Hanson noticed a difference between the messages at American cemeteries and the messages at European war memorials:

> The inscriptions at American graveyards admonish the visitor to remember sacrifice, courage, and freedom; they assume somebody bad once started a war to hurt the weak, only to fail when somebody better stopped them. In contrast, the "folly" of war— to paraphrase Barbara Tuchman— is what one gleans at most World War II museums in Europe. The displays, tapes, and guides suggest that a sudden madness once descended equally on normal-thinking Europeans and Americans at places like Nijmegen and Remagen. "Stupidity," a European visitor at Arnhem lectured me, best explains why thousands of young men killed each other for no good reason over "meaningless" bridges.[4]

Since the American commemorative sites were undoubtedly created first and the European war memorials later, after European economies had recovered from wartime devastations, the differences may reflect differences in time, rather than only differences between Americans and Europeans. In the later era, people living in safety purchased with other people's lives could loftily dismiss bridges as "meaningless," when in warfare the control of bridges can be a matter of life and death for armies and for the fate of whole nations.

A striking example of the wide mood swings to which some intellectuals have been subject was Bertrand Russell's postwar argument that Western nations should present the Soviet Union with an ultimatum to submit to a new world government, with its own armed forces, and— if the ultimatum was rejected, launch a preemptive war against the Soviet Union, while the United States had a nuclear bomb and the Soviets did not yet have one.[5] As reported in *The Observer* of London on November 21, 1948:

> "Either we must have a war against Russia before she has the atom bomb or we will have to lie down and let them govern us.". . . An atomic war would be one of extraordinary horror, but it would be "the war to end wars.". . . Fearing the horror of a future war was no way to prevent it. "Anything is better than submission."[6]

There could hardly be a greater contrast with Bertrand Russell's prewar advocacy of pacifism and unilateral disarmament— or with his subsequent return to that position. A decade later, Lord Russell said "I am for controlled nuclear disarmament." But, if it proved to be impossible to get the Soviet Union to agree to that, he was for "unilateral nuclear disarmament." He added:

> It is a bitter choice. . . Unilateral disarmament is likely to mean, for a while, Communist domination of this world of ours. . . But if the

alternatives are the eventual extinction of mankind and a temporary Communist conquest, I prefer the latter.[7]

After his return to his earlier pacifist and unilateral disarmament position, Bertrand Russell condemned those in the West who supported nuclear deterrence policies as people who "belong to the murderers' club." In this later period, Bertrand Russell described British Prime Minister Harold Macmillan and American President John F. Kennedy as "the wickedest people that ever lived in the history of man" and as "fifty times as wicked as Hitler" because Russell depicted their promotion of nuclear deterrence as "organizing the massacre of the whole of mankind."[8]

Whether as an advocate of preventive war or as a radical pacifist before and afterwards, Bertrand Russell sought sweeping and dramatic "solutions." While his particular solutions were unusual in both cases, what was far more common among intellectuals was to think of the world in terms of dramatic solutions of some sort, and to have their complete reversals of positions as to what specifically those solutions might be— as among intellectuals in general during and then after the First World War— leave them nevertheless confident that their superior wisdom and virtue should guide the masses and influence national policies. Clearly, at least one of their mutually incompatible positions had to be wrong, suggesting the old but apt phrase, "often wrong but never in doubt."

REPLAYING THE 1930s

The 1960s and the Vietnam war brought a more general return to the intellectual and ideological climate that had reigned during the 1920s and 1930s. Indeed, many of the very words and phrases of that earlier time reappeared in the 1960s, often put forth as if they were fresh new insights, instead of old notions already discredited by the course of history. For example, disarmament advocates once again called themselves "the peace movement" and called military deterrence an "arms race." Once again, the argument was made that "war solves nothing." Those who manufactured military equipment, who had been called "merchants of death" in the 1930s were now called "the military-industrial complex" and were once again regarded as a threat to peace, rather than suppliers of the means of deterring aggressor nations. The Oxford Pledge by young Englishmen of the 1930s, to refuse to fight for their country in war, was echoed during the 1960s by young Americans of military draft age who said, "Hell no, I won't go."

Graphic depictions of the horrors of war were once again seen as ways to promote peace, and a one-day-at-a-time rationalism was again considered to be the way to deal with issues that had the potential to escalate into war.[*] Replacing the rhetoric of moral outrage with a more non-judgmental pragmatism and trying to see the other side's point of view were also part of this resurrected vision from the era between the two World Wars. Few who espoused these and other ideas from the 1930s recognized their antecedents, much less the disasters to which those antecedents had led. Most of the notions among the pacifist intelligentsia of the 1960s and later had appeared in British Prime Minister Neville Chamberlain's speeches back in the 1930s that were published as a collection in his book *In Search of Peace*, which appeared just months before the outbreak of the Second World War that these notions help bring on.[**]

More important, as too often happens, words became preemptive— disarmament being axiomatically equated with peace, for example. To

---

[*] When the Western allies refused to give in to Soviet threats to block access to West Berlin in 1961, famed British playwright and critic Kenneth Tynan posed the question as whether it was worth it to risk nuclear annihilation as what his article titled "The Price of Berlin." It was the "Why die for Danzig?" argument of 1939 resurrected and enhanced with depictions of the horrors of nuclear war and a trivializing of the freedoms enjoyed in the West. See Kenneth Tynan, "The Price of Berlin," *Time and Tide*, August 3, 1961, p. 1263.

[**] Neville Chamberlain, *In Search of Peace* (New York: G.P. Putnam's Sons, 1939). These 1930s notions that reappeared in the 1960s and beyond include opposition to a "senseless competition in rearmament" (p. 45), the futility of war (140, 288), assertions that the peoples of all countries are "human beings like ourselves" (252) and desirous of peace (v, 192, 210), morally equating both sides in international conflicts (19, 27), the importance of seeing adversaries' viewpoint (53, 174), assertions that various kinds of psychological problems— enmities, fears, suspicions and misunderstandings— created a danger of war (5, 14, 50, 52, 53, 74, 97, 105, 106, 112, 133, 210, 212, 252), so that a relaxation of international tensions is crucial (158, 185), and for this "personal contact" between heads of state are vital (34, 40, 120, 187, 209, 210, 216, 230, 242, 251–252, 271). What Chamberlain called "personal contacts" between heads of state would be renamed "summit meetings" in the later period but the reasoning and the conclusions were the same.

disarmament advocates of his day, Churchill had said, "When you have peace, you will have disarmament"[9]— not the other way around— but there was seldom even an attempt to test this hypothesis against that of those who automatically transformed disarmament advocates into "the peace movement."

The Vietnam War

Among the many implications of the war in Vietnam was that it once again illuminated the role of the intelligentsia in influencing the policies of a society and the course of history. That role was not the role that Machiavelli once sought, the role of directly influencing the thinking, beliefs or goals of those who wield power. In modern democratic nations, the intelligentsia can have influence— sometimes decisive influence— by creating a general climate of opinion in which it becomes politically impossible for the wielders of power to do what they believe needs to be done.

As already noted in Chapter 14, Stanley Baldwin— by his own later admission— dared not tell the British public that Germany was rearming in 1933 for fear of losing that year's election, because saying that Germany was rearming implied that Britain needed to rearm, and the dominant climate of opinion at the time would have rejected that conclusion and whoever was the messenger bringing that bad news. Baldwin dared not tell what he knew,* not simply to save his own political position, but because he knew that any attempt on his part to sound the alarm about impending dangers from Germany could bring to power the opposition Labor Party, which was totally opposed to military preparedness and would make the nation even more vulnerable than it was.

In short, the climate of opinion of the times made it politically difficult for Britain to rearm adequately, as either a deterrent to war or as a means of defending itself in the event of war, even though its highest officials were fully aware of the dangers of what was at that time clandestine German

---

* Baldwin's veiled public references to things he could say if his lips were not sealed brought him the popular nickname of "Old Sealed Lips" and caused famed British editorial cartoonist David Low to draw caricatures of Baldwin with tape over his mouth. David Low, *Years of Wrath: A Cartoon History 1932–1945* (London: Victor Gollancz, 1949), p. 37.

rearmament, at least in the sense that the general public was not aware of it. Thus the influence of the intelligentsia was decisive, even though they failed completely to convince the country's highest officials that what they said was correct.

Although the Vietnam war involved very different issues and different facts, its outcome reflected the same influence of the intelligentsia on public opinion. Whatever the merits or demerits of the decision of the United States to become a major participant in the war to prevent South Vietnam from being conquered by North Vietnam's Communist government, the stark fact is that more than 50,000 Americans died winning military victories in Vietnam that ended in political defeat because the climate of opinion created by the intelligentsia in the United States made it politically impossible not only to continue the involvement of American troops in the fighting there, but impossible even to continue to supply the resources needed by the South Vietnam government to defend itself after American troops were withdrawn. With one side receiving aid from outside and the other side not, the outcome was inevitable— the conquest of South Vietnam by North Vietnam.

The decisive turning point in the Vietnam war came with a massive 1968 uprising of Communist guerrillas in South Vietnam during a Vietnamese holiday called "Tet"— an uprising which became known as "the Tet offensive," launched during what was supposed to be a holiday truce. After many optimistic statements by American political and military leaders about how well the war was going, it came as a shock to the American public that the Communists were able to launch such a massive effort in the heart of South Vietnam.[10] Moreover, many in the media depicted what happened as a defeat for the United States, when in fact the Communist guerilla movement was decimated in the fighting and was never the same again.[11]

Communist leaders themselves, after taking over South Vietnam, openly admitted in later years that they had lost militarily in their war with American troops in Vietnam, including during their Tet offensive, but pointed out that they had won politically in America. During the war itself, American prisoner of war James Stockdale was told by his North Vietnamese captor, "Our country has no capability to defeat you on the battlefield," but that they expected to "win this war on the streets of New York."[12]

Legendary Communist military leader General Vo Nguyen Giap, who had defeated the French in the decisive battle of Dien Bien Phu in 1954, and who later commanded North Vietnamese forces against the Americans, said candidly in later years, "We were not strong enough to drive out a half-million American troops, but that wasn't our aim." His goal was political: "Our intention was to break the will of the American Government to continue the war. Westmoreland was wrong to expect that his superior firepower would grind us down. If we had focused on the balance of forces, we would have been defeated in two hours." As it was, the North Vietnamese lost "at least a million" troops killed, mostly by American troops, according to one of General Giap's aides— a death toll almost 20 times that of the Americans.[13] Looking back, years later, General Giap's aide called the Communist losses during the Tet offensive "devastating."[14]

A still later interview with a man who had served as a colonel on the staff of the North Vietnamese army, and who had received the surrender of South Vietnam in 1975, told a very similar story. A 1995 interview with Colonel Bui Tin produced these questions and answers:

Q: Was the American antiwar movement important to Hanoi's victory?

A: It was essential to our strategy. Support for the war from our rear was completely secure while the American rear was vulnerable. Every day our leadership would listen to world news over the radio at 9 a.m. to follow the growth of the American antiwar movement. Visits to Hanoi by people like Jane Fonda and former Attorney General Ramsey Clark and ministers gave us confidence that we should hold on in the face of battlefield reverses. We were elated when Jane Fonda, wearing a red Vietnamese dress, said at a press conference that she was ashamed of American actions in the war and that she would struggle along with us.

Q: Did the Politburo pay attention to these visits?

A: Keenly.

Q: Why?

A: Those people represented the conscience of America. The conscience of America was part of its war-making capability, and we were turning that power in our favor. America lost because of its democracy; through dissent and protest it lost the ability to mobilize a will to win.[15]

As regards the pivotal Tet offensive of 1968, the interviewer's question as to the purpose of that operation was answered plainly: "Tet was designed to influence American public opinion." As for the results of the Tet offensive: "Our losses were staggering and a complete surprise. Giap later told me that Tet had been a military defeat, though we had gained the planned political advantages when Johnson agreed to negotiate and did not run for re-election." Militarily, however, "Our forces in the South were nearly wiped out by all the fighting in 1968."[16]

This paradoxical combination of overwhelming American military victories in Vietnam and devastating political defeat in Washington was crucially dependent on the climate of opinion in the United States, a climate to which the intelligentsia made a major contribution.

One of the themes of contemporary critics of the Vietnam War, both before and after the Tet offensive, was that the war was unwinnable because it was essentially a "civil war" conducted by Communist guerrillas within South Vietnam, though aided and abetted by the Communist government of North Vietnam, rather than a war between these two nations. Well-known historian and contemporary commentator Arthur Schlesinger, Jr. opined that these guerrillas could "keep fighting underground for another 20 years."[17] The Tet offensive seemed to be in keeping with this view, especially when those widespread attacks were depicted as a "heavy blow" and a "setback" for American and South Vietnamese military forces and a "success" for the Communists in the *New York Times*,[18] among other places. Nationally syndicated columnist Drew Pearson said that the United States had taken a "shellacking."[19] A month later, Lyndon Johnson announced that he would not seek re-election and that he was seeking negotiations with North Vietnam.

As we now know, North Vietnamese Communist leaders in Hanoi had virtually the same military evaluation of the Tet offensive as American leaders in Washington— namely, that it was an overwhelming defeat for the Communist guerrillas. The Communists' political success consisted precisely in the fact that media outlets like the *New York Times* declared their military offensive successful. The *Wall Street Journal* likewise rejected the Johnson administration's contention that the Tet offensive was a "last gasp" of the Communist Vietcong guerilla movement in South Vietnam.[20]

By this time, the Johnson administration's credibility had been squandered by its own previous words and actions,[21] so that what we now know to be the inaccurate military assessment by the media carried more weight in shaping public opinion than the accurate assessments made by national leaders in both Hanoi and Washington.

The key assumption of anti-war critics was that, in the words of distinguished columnist Walter Lippmann, "The Americans cannot exterminate the Viet Cong" guerrillas in South Vietnam— a view shared by historian Arthur Schlesinger, Jr. and by others.[22] Yet the Tet offensive virtually accomplished that supposedly impossible task, costing the Vietcong guerrillas such a loss of manpower and of areas they had previously controlled, as well as their ability to get new recruits, that what was called a civil war became afterwards more clearly a war between the armies of nations.[23] To Lippmann, writing in 1965, three years before the Tet offensive, what was happening in South Vietnam was a civil war in which "the rebels are winning."[24] Yet Lippmann later considered himself vindicated by the Tet offensive: "The Vietnamese war is, I have always believed, unwinnable."[25] *Washington Post* columnist Joseph Kraft was one of many others who echoed the theme that the Vietnam war was "unwinnable."[26] In a democracy, if enough people believe that a war is unwinnable, that can make it unwinnable.

Like many others, Walter Lippmann's solution from the beginning had been a "negotiated settlement." He paid as little attention to the actual viability of such a settlement as many other intellectuals have paid over the years to the viability of various international disarmament treaties and other agreements with totalitarian dictatorships. Nor was Lippmann alone. Economist John Kenneth Galbraith was among many others who urged that course.[27] In the end, Lyndon Johnson's successor, President Richard Nixon, in fact made a negotiated settlement with North Vietnam— and that settlement proved to be simply a face-saving surrender on the instalment plan to the North Vietnamese, who took over South Vietnam, and made clear to the world what had happened by renaming Saigon, the South Vietnamese capital, Ho Chi Minh City, in honor of the late ruler of North Vietnam.

In the aftermath of the Communist political victory in Vietnam, those in the Western democracies who had opposed American involvement in the

Vietnam war on humanitarian grounds, because of the large casualties among civilians and soldiers alike, were now confronted by the fact that the end of the war did not put an end to the casualties. Military historian Victor Davis Hanson observed:

> A communist victory brought more death and even greater dislocation to the Vietnamese than did decades of war— more often slowly by starvation, incarceration, and flight, rather than by outright mass murder... Exact numbers are in dispute, but most scholars accept that well over 1 million left by boat; and hundreds of thousands of others crossed by land into neighboring Thailand and even China...Those who died in leaky boats or in storms numbered between 50,000 and 100,000...[28]

The Vietnam war also saw the revival in America of a pattern seen in France between the two World Wars— the downgrading of soldiers in battle from the role of patriotic heroes, no matter what acts of bravery and self-sacrifice they engaged in. During the Vietnam war, this tendency was carried even further. Collateral damage to Vietnamese civilians during American military operations, or even allegations of individual misconduct by American troops, led to sweeping moral condemnations of the U.S. military as a whole, often without any examination of the question whether such collateral damage was unusual in warfare or unusually extensive, or whether atrocities were authorized or condoned by authorities.[29] The most widely publicized atrocity against civilians— the "My Lai massacre" by an American military unit against a South Vietnamese village that was suspected of harboring Communist guerrillas— was stopped by other American troops when they arrived on the scene, and the officer in charge was court-martialed for things that the Communist guerrillas did routinely and on a vastly larger scale.[30]

The image, filtered through the media, of those who served in the military during the Vietnam war, like the image of French soldiers who had served in the First World War, often became that of victims. "'Hero stories' were off the menu" in Vietnam, as the head of the *Washington Post*'s bureau in Vietnam later recalled the coverage of the war in the American media.[31] A common image of Vietnam veterans was that they were disproportionately the poor, the uneducated, the minorities— and that the trauma of combat drove them to widespread drug usage in Vietnam and to acts of violence upon returning home with "post-traumatic stress syndrome." Widely hailed motion pictures depicting that era dramatized such images.[32] Hard statistical data, however, contradicted such depictions[33] and some of the Vietnam "combat veterans" featured on television specials by Dan Rather and others later turned out to have never been in combat or never to have been in Vietnam.[34] But what they said fit the vision and that was often enough to get them on television and cited in newspapers and books.

Some among the American media and intelligentsia outdid the interwar French by depicting American combat veterans as villains. The only Pulitzer Prize awarded for coverage of the Tet offensive went to a reporter who wrote about the My Lai massacre without ever setting foot in Vietnam.[35] This tangential tragedy thus overshadowed innumerable battles across South Vietnam in which American troops won overwhelming victories. That much of this fighting against urban guerrillas in civilian clothes took place in residential neighborhoods made the task more difficult for American troops but presented the media with numerous opportunities to criticize those troops:

> Homes surrounding the track were stuffed with hundreds of snipers. It took a week of house-to-house fighting for American army troops and ARVN [South Vietnamese] forces to locate and expel the Vietcong, who rarely surrendered and had to be killed almost to the last man. Yet on television Americans were being blamed for blasting apart residences, as if no one noticed that urban snipers were shooting marines in the middle of a holiday truce.[36]

This battle in Saigon was not the only one reported in this one-sided way. The city of Hué, near the border with North Vietnam, was captured by a large force of Vietcong guerrillas and North Vietnamese troops, after which they massacred thousands of civilians, who were buried in mass graves. The American counter-attack that retook the city was heavily criticized in the media for its destruction of ancient historic structures, such criticisms often being made by journalists who had little or nothing to say about the mass atrocities committed by the Communists there.[37] As a later study put it:

> Probably no war was ever waged with such a one-sided hostile reportage. No North Vietnamese newspaper or cameras covered the Hué massacre during the Tet offensive, which apart from its having been tenfold the

magnitude of My Lai, was executed as part of a deliberate policy to obliterate South Vietnamese civilian leaders and their families; American reporters evinced only a peripheral interest in North Vietnamese cruelties.[38]

Long after the Vietnam war was over, CNN broadcast a story in 1998 suggesting an officially sanctioned American atrocity back in 1970. As the *Wall Street Journal* reported: "A former Green Beret sued Cable News Network and Time magazine for defamation over the now-retracted CNN broadcast, recounted in Time, that accused the U.S. military of using nerve gas to kill American defectors during the Vietnam War."[39] A co-author of that story, Peter Arnett, was also the sole source for a more famous but unsubstantiated remark supposedly made by an American military officer in Vietnam that "It became necessary to destroy the town to save it."[40] As military historian Victor Davis Hanson reported: "Yet there was little evidence— other than from Arnett himself— that any American officer said anything of the sort."[41]

The negative images of American troops filtered through the media were so pervasive and so powerful that Vietnam war veterans returning home were often openly disdained or insulted.

The Cold War

The Cold War between the United States and the Soviet Union began well before Americans' entry into the Vietnam war and continued well after it. If the Western democracies' recognition of the Soviet threat can be dated to a particular event, that event would be Winston Churchill's 1946 speech in Fulton, Missouri, when he pointed out how the Soviets' wartime commitment to providing free elections and independent governments in Eastern Europe had been violated, as part of a process of Soviet expansion and dictatorial rule:

> From Stettin in the Baltic to Trieste in the Adriatic, an iron curtain has descended across the Continent. Behind that line lie all the capitals of the ancient states of Central and Eastern Europe. Warsaw, Berlin, Prague, Vienna, Budapest, Belgrade, Bucharest and Sofia, all these famous cities and the populations around them lie in what I must call the Soviet sphere, and all are subject in one form or another, not only to

Soviet influence but to a very high and, in many cases, increasing measure of control from Moscow.[42]

Among the many efforts to prevent that iron curtain from extending farther west were the Marshall Plan, to aid the rebuilding of Western Europe from the devastations of war, and the North Atlantic Treaty Organization (NATO) to present a united military front of European nations, including American troops in these nations and an American nuclear umbrella over them, with the threat of retaliation by all against a military attack on any one of the NATO member nations. None of this was done without large and continuing controversies within the Western democracies, in which the intelligentsia played major roles.

Churchill's "iron curtain" speech, for example, evoked much adverse reaction among the intelligentsia within both the United States and Britain. Nobel Prize-winning author Pearl Buck, for example, called the Churchill speech a "catastrophe."[43] A *Chicago Tribune* editorial opined that "Mr. Churchill loses a good deal of stature by this speech."[44] Columnist Marquis Childs lamented "the strong anti-Russia bias which ran through the body of the speech."[45] The *Boston Globe*, the *Washington Star* and various other American newspapers also reacted negatively to Churchill's speech, as did leading columnist Walter Lippmann, though the *New York Times* and the *Los Angeles Times* praised it.[46] In Britain, reactions ranged from that of the *Evening News*, which praised Churchill's warning, to George Bernard Shaw, who called the speech "nothing short of a declaration of war on Russia." There were similar conflicting reactions to the "iron curtain" speech in Paris.[47]

In the decades that followed, attempts to bolster Western Europe's military defenses against the Soviet bloc were similarly controversial among the intelligentsia, some of whom asked whether it was "better to be red than dead." These included famed British playwright and critic Kenneth Tynan, who not only answered that question in the affirmative but added, "I would rather live on my knees than die on my knees."[48] Western Europe, however, was just one theater of the Cold War, and military defense was just one of the areas of conflict between the Soviet Union and the United States, which extended into economic, political, social and ideological competition.

Although this was a non-military Cold War in the sense that American and Soviet troops did not fight battles directly against each other, there were many parts of the world in which military battles took place between troops backed respectively by the Soviets and the Americans. Vietnam was just one of those battlefronts. Moreover, even though the war between the United States and the Soviet Union was "cold" in the sense of lacking direct military conflict between these two countries, over it all hung the threat of the ultimate catastrophe of nuclear war.

During the Cold War, and especially after the escalating involvement of the United States in the Vietnam war, many among the intelligentsia began repeating the old notion that war "solves nothing," an echo from the 1930s, where the futility of war was proclaimed, among many others, by Neville Chamberlain, who said that war "wins nothing, cures nothing, ends nothing"[49]— and who was in turn echoing what many among the intelligentsia were saying in his day. But, like so much that has been said by the intelligentsia on so many subjects, the notion that "war solves nothing" had less to do with any empirical evidence than with its consonance with the vision of the anointed, which in turn has had much to do with the exaltation of the anointed.

Had the battle of Tours in 732 or the siege of Vienna in 1529 gone the other way, this could be a very different world today. Had the desperate fighting at Stalingrad and on the beaches at Normandy gone the other way during the Second World War, life might not be worth living for millions of human beings today. Had the British successfully crushed the rebellion of the American colonies in the eighteenth century, slavery in America would have ended a generation earlier than it did. Had the South won the Civil War, slavery would have continued longer than it did.

There have of course been futile wars in which all the nations on both sides ended up far worse off than before— the First World War being a classic example. But no one would make the blanket statement that medical science "solves nothing" because many people die despite treatment and some die because of wrong treatment or even from the remote risks of vaccinations. In short, mundane specifics are more salient in evaluating any particular war than are the sweeping, abstract and dramatic pronouncements so often indulged in by the intelligentsia.

The futility of an "arms race" was another staple of the 1930s that made a comeback in the 1960s, even though it was one-sided disarmament— moral as well as military— in the democratic nations after the First World War which made another war look winnable to the Axis powers, and thus led to the Second World War. The notion that an "arms race" would lead to war, which had been a staple of intellectuals during the interwar era, and which was also echoed in the political arena, notably by Neville Chamberlain,* was a notion that made a comeback during the second half of the twentieth century. Whatever the plausibility of this notion, what is crucial is that few intellectuals saw any reason to go beyond plausibility to seek hard evidence on this crucial assumption as an empirically verifiable proposition, but instead treated it as an unquestionable axiom.

Right after the Second World War had demonstrated tragically the dangers of disarmament and of half-hearted rearmament, the idea of the futility of an arms race receded. But when President John F. Kennedy invoked this lesson of the Second World War by saying in his inaugural address in 1961, "We dare not tempt them with weakness,"[50] despite his youth he was speaking for a passing generation and for ideas that would soon be replaced by opposite ideas, espoused ironically in later years by his own youngest brother in the United States Senate. The idea of military strength as a foundation of peace by deterring potential enemies faded rapidly from the 1960s on, at least among intellectuals. Instead, during the long years of the Cold War between the Soviet Union and the United

---

* "I must confess that the spectacle of this vast expenditure upon means of destruction instead of construction has inspired me with a feeling of revolt against the folly of mankind. The cost is stupendous, and the thought of the sacrifice that it must entail upon us, and upon those who come after us, drives the Government always to search for a way out, to seek to find some means of breaking through this senseless competition in rearmament which continually cancels out the efforts that each nation makes to secure an advantage over the others." Neville Chamberlain, *In Search of Peace* (New York: G.P. Putnam's Sons, 1939), p. 45. The fallacy in this is that not all nations were seeking to get an advantage by rearming. Some were rearming in order to prevent other nations from getting an advantage that would lead those other nations to attack them. Verbal equivalence once more concealed profound differences in the real world. Moreover, "mankind" is not a decision-making unit. Each nation is a decision-making unit and there is no "folly" in any nation's refusal to be disarmed when other nations are armed.

States, arms limitation agreements were advocated by much, if not most, of the Western intelligentsia.

Treaties proclaiming peaceful intentions among nations, especially those limiting military weapons, were once more praised by the intelligentsia for "relaxing tensions" among nations. But international tensions had been relaxed by such agreements many times before, during the period between the two World Wars, by such things as the Washington Naval Agreements of 1921–1922, the Locarno Pact of 1925, the Kellogg-Briand Pact of 1928, the Anglo-German Naval Agreement of 1935 and the grand relaxation of all— the Munich agreement of 1938, in which Britain and France gave away an ally that they would desperately need in the war that began just one year later.

All this history vanished from memory, as if it had never happened, as the Western intelligentsia of the Cold War era repeated Neville Chamberlain's oft-reiterated emphasis on "personal contact"[51] between leaders of opposing nations by celebrating "summit meeting" after "summit meeting" between American and Soviet leaders, christening the afterglow of these meetings as "the spirit of Geneva," "the spirit of Camp David," and of other sites of similar meetings and pacts. It was as if the causes of war were hostile emotions that could be defused by a better understanding between peoples, or misunderstandings between governments that could be cleared up by meetings of opposing heads of state. But the desire of A to ruin or destroy B is not an "issue" that can be resolved amicably around a conference table.

Empirical questions about the mundane specifics of international agreements, such as the verifiability of their terms or whether their restrictions on the West were matched by comparable restrictions on the Soviets, seldom received much attention by the intelligentsia, who were too busy promoting euphoria over the fact that international agreements had been signed, to the accompaniment of lofty rhetoric.

The general asymmetry of international agreements between democratic and autocratic governments goes back well before the Cold War. Not only do the intelligentsia of democratic countries help create a climate of opinion eager for such agreements and uncritical of their specifics, that same public opinion forces democratic governments to live up to the terms of such agreements, while there is no comparable pressure on autocratic governments.

Thus, as noted in Chapter 14, British and American governments restricted the size of their battleships to what was specified in the Washington Naval Agreements of 1921–1922, and the British also did the same as regards the Anglo-German Naval Agreement of 1935— with the net result during the Second World War being that both Japan and Germany had battleships larger than any in the British or American navy, because the totalitarian German and Japanese governments were free to violate those agreements.

Similarly, during the Vietnam war, a cease-fire negotiated in Paris had to be observed by South Vietnam because the South Vietnamese were dependent on American military supplies, and the United States was under the pressure of public opinion to see that the cease-fire was observed. Meanwhile, Communist North Vietnam was free to ignore the agreement that its representative had signed to such international fanfare, which culminated in a Nobel Prize for peace to both North Vietnamese representative Le Duc Tho and American Secretary of State Henry Kissinger.

With North Vietnam free to continue the fighting and South Vietnam inhibited from taking comparable countermeasures, the net result was that North Vietnam conquered South Vietnam.

Once again, the intellectuals' effect on the course of events did not depend their convincing or influencing the holders of power. President Nixon had no regard for intellectuals. It was by helping shape the climate of public opinion that the intelligentsia influenced Nixon's foreign policy decision, at the cost of abandoning South Vietnam to its fate.

Among the many notions of the 1920s and 1930s that returned in the 1960s was the irrelevant claim that the peoples of all countries desire peace— as if what the German people desired mattered to Hitler[52] or what the Soviet peoples wanted mattered to Stalin. As a corollary to this notion, the old idea of more "people to people" contacts for the sake of peace, as urged by John Dewey back in the 1920s,[53] returned as if it were a new idea during the Cold War. It was as if war was a result of some insufficiency of empathy among peoples, or some mass psychological malaise that could be treated therapeutically.

John Dewey said in 1922: "If we succeed in really understanding each other, some way of cooperation for common ends can be found."[54] In the next decade, a similar sentiment was expressed by British Prime Minister Neville Chamberlain[55] and, decades after that, the same idea was revived and became the *leitmotif* of media and academic discourse during the decades of the Cold War. The idea that mutual understanding was the key to peace— and its corollary, that seeing the other side's point of view was crucial— were key to the 1930s diplomacy of Prime Minister Chamberlain.[56] But, like so much in the prevailing vision, it was taken as axiomatic, not as a hypothesis subject to empirical verification from history or from more contemporary events.

The election of Ronald Reagan as President of the United States in 1980 brought policies and practices directly the opposite of those favored by intellectuals. Instead of emphasizing, as Neville Chamberlain had, the importance of understanding an adversary nation's point of view,[57] President Reagan emphasized the importance of making sure that adversary nations understood the American point of view, as when he called the Soviet Union "an evil empire"— to the consternation of the intelligentsia.[58] In his first meeting with Soviet premier Mikhail Gorbachev in Geneva in 1985, Reagan was quite blunt: "We won't stand by and let you maintain weapon superiority over us. We can agree to reduce arms, or we can continue the arms race, which I think you know you can't win."[59]

During a visit to West Berlin in 1987, Reagan was told that the Communists in East Berlin had long-range listening devices. This was his response, as recounted in his autobiography:

> "Watch what you say," one German official said. Well, when I heard that, I went out to a landing that was even closer to the building and began sounding off about what I thought of a government that penned in its people like farm animals.
> I can't remember exactly what I said, but I may have used a little profanity in expressing my opinion of Communism, hoping I would be heard.[60]

Later that day, he went to the infamous Berlin Wall, where he made a public statement that stunned the intelligentsia as much as his "evil empire" remark: "Mr. Gorbachev, tear down this wall!"[61] This was a double insult because, officially at least, it was the sovereign East German government that was responsible for the Berlin Wall. By publicly going over their heads directly to Soviet premier Gorbachev, he was in effect calling the East German regime a puppet government.

Another area in which Ronald Reagan marked a break with past practices of Western leaders was in refusing to make international agreements, when he did not consider the terms right, even if that meant that he came away from a summit meeting empty-handed and would be blamed by the media for not reaching an agreement. At a 1986 summit meeting in Iceland with Soviet leader Mikhail Gorbachev, there were many tentative agreements on arms reductions but, when time came to finalize an accord, Gorbachev said, "This all depends, of course, on you giving up SDI," the Strategic Defense Initiative, the missile defense program called "star wars" by its opponents. Later, recalling this sticking point at the eleventh hour in his autobiography, Reagan said:

> I was getting angrier and angrier.
> I realized he had brought me to Iceland with one purpose: to kill the Strategic Defense Initiative. He must have known from the beginning he was going to bring it up at the last minute.
> "The meeting is over," I said. "Let's go, George, we're leaving."[62]

With that, President Reagan and Secretary of State George Shultz walked out, even though the Soviets had indicated that they were prepared to stay for another day.* There would be later summits, but this summit let the Soviets know that Reagan, unlike previous Western leaders, did not feel a need to come away with an agreement at virtually any cost.

The fact that the Reagan approach, which many among the intelligentsia saw as likely to lead to nuclear war, led instead to the end of the Cold War, while the Chamberlain approach that was supposed to lead to peace led instead to the biggest war in history, has made no dent on the vision of the anointed.

---

* "Gorbachev was stunned. The Soviets had already made it known they were willing to spend another day in Reykjavik. Gorbachev had more to say. As Reagan put his coat on, Gorbachev said to him, 'Can't we do something about this?' Reagan had had enough. 'It's too late,' he said." Lou Cannon, *President Reagan: The Role of a Lifetime* (New York: Public Affairs, 2000), p. 690.

The Cold War Intelligentsia

Verbal virtuosity was as much in evidence among the intelligentsia in the 1960s and afterwards as it was in the world of the 1920s and 1930s. Disarmament advocates called themselves "peace" movements in both eras, preempting the crucial question whether one-sided disarmament was more likely to lead to peace or to war, and whether "relaxing international tensions" was more likely to reduce the drive to war among all nations or to leave the intended victims less mindful of the dangers from aggressors. As in other contexts, the fatal talent of verbal virtuosity often served as a substitute for scrutinizing empirical evidence or engaging in analysis. It was not that the intelligentsia did these things badly. Their clever verbal formulations often made it unnecessary for them to do these things at all.

During the 1980s, when President Reagan met a Soviet nuclear missile buildup in Eastern Europe with an American nuclear missile buildup in Western Europe, this revived the "arms race" arguments of the 1920s and 1930s, polarizing public opinion in Western nations, including the United States.

Washington Post columnist William Raspberry deplored "a protracted, expensive and dangerous nuclear arms race."[63] *New York Times* columnist Anthony Lewis said "it is not a rational response" to Soviet power "to intensify an arms race."[64] Fellow *New York Times* columnist Tom Wicker referred to "an arms race that has grown out of all reason."[65] "Better, surely, to concentrate on the effort to bring the arms race under control, thus keeping civilized life as we know it at least physically intact," said author and former diplomat George F. Kennan.[66] Nobel Peace Prize winner Alva Myrdal said, "I was never able to stop the search for the why's and how's of something so senseless as the arms race."[67] John Kenneth Galbraith referred to "the arms race and its near-certainty of death," and proposed instead to "freeze the competition" and "establish a minimum of confidence between the two countries."[68]

Such views were echoed in the political arena. As already noted, President John F. Kennedy's youngest brother, Senator Edward M. Kennedy of Massachusetts, became a leading political figure making the same argument against an "arms race" as that of many, if not most, of the intelligentsia.

In 1982, Senator Kennedy was among those who objected to President Reagan's military buildup as "a dangerous new spiral in nuclear weapons competition" and called for "reversing the nuclear arms race."[69] In 1983, Senator Kennedy said, "We will seek to freeze the arms race which someday could make a cold wasteland of all the earth."[70] Later that same year, he said "We must stop the arms race before it stops us."[71] Senator Kennedy also joined other Senators in a statement in a letter to the *New York Times* declaring: "Experts and citizens across the country are embracing the freeze as the best way to end the nuclear arms race before it is too late."[72] In other words, once the Soviets' nuclear missile buildup in Eastern Europe gave them military superiority in Europe, we should freeze that superiority instead of restoring the balance. Attacking President Reagan's policies in the Senate, Kennedy called on his fellow Senators to "stop the nuclear arms race before it stops the human race."[73]

Though Senator Kennedy was a leading voice for a nuclear freeze, he was joined by many other prominent political figures and by many in the media who echoed their message. Senator Joseph Biden was one of the sponsors of a bill to freeze American military spending in 1984— which, given the rate of inflation, would mean a reduction of military spending in real terms— and, though the bill was defeated, one-third of the Senate voted for it.[74]

Those who resurrected the "arms race" argument against military deterrence that had been so pervasive in the era between the two World Wars proceeded on the implicit assumption of sufficient resources on all sides to permit indefinite escalation of mutually offsetting military buildups. That assumption was demonstrated to be false when President Reagan's military buildup in the 1980s proved to be more than the Soviet Union's economy could match— as Reagan knew.* The fact that the actual

---

* "At the start of 1986, we were getting more and more evidence that the Soviet economy was in dire shape. It made me believe that, if nothing else, the Soviet economic tailspin would force Mikhail Gorbachev to come around on an arms reduction agreement we both could live with. If we didn't deviate from our policies, I was convinced it would happen." Ronald Reagan, *An American Life* (New York: Simon and Schuster, 1990), p. 660. Arthur M. Schlesinger, Jr., despite his expressed lack of interest in economics, as noted in Chapter 5, declared that those who considered the Soviet Union to be in economic trouble were "kidding themselves." Peter Robinson, "Who Was That Reagan Man?" *Washington Times*, November 12, 1997, p. A19.

consequence of Reagan's policy was the direct opposite of what the "arms race" argument had predicted— that is, the consequence was the end of the Cold War, rather than the beginning of a nuclear war— has had as little effect on the prevailing vision as other facts which directly contradict other premises of that vision.

That more conciliatory policies had failed for decades to end the nuclear threat under which the world had lived during the Cold War decades was likewise ignored. Most of the intelligentsia simply lavished praise on Soviet premier Mikhail Gorbachev for no longer following the policies of his predecessors.[75] The alternative was to admit that there might be something to be said for the Reagan emphasis on military strength and for his rejection of the "arms race" rhetoric which had been so central to the thinking of the intelligentsia for so long.

Some have contested the issue as to whether the end of the Cold War should be credited more to Reagan or to Gorbachev but for many, if not most, of the intelligentsia there was no issue to contest, since it was unthinkable that one of their fundamental assumptions could be wrong. Yet, after the end of the Cold War and the dissolution of the Soviet Union, former Soviet high officials said that Reagan's policies were a crucial factor. According to the *Washington Post*: "Speaking at a Princeton University conference on the end of the Cold War, the officials said former Soviet president Mikhail Gorbachev was convinced any attempt to match Reagan's Strategic Defense Initiative, which was launched in 1983 to build a space-based defense against missiles, would do irreparable harm to the Soviet economy."[76] Yet CNN commentator Wolf Blitzer dismissed the claim that Reagan won the Cold War with the all-purpose put-down, "simplistic."[77]

Calling military deterrence an "arms race" was just one of the many notions of the 1920s and 1930s that were resurrected during the Cold War era. Just as the French teachers' unions turned France's schools into indoctrination centers for pacifism in the 1920s and 1930s, with emphasis on the horrors of war, so in the United States during the Cold War American classrooms became places for indoctrination in the horrors of war. Dramatizations of the nuclear bombing of Japanese cities were one example:

In grisly detail these generally well-off upper middle class kids were obliged to observe Japanese women and children being incinerated by the fire storm set in motion by the dropping of nuclear bombs. The youngsters sat riveted in their seats. Sobbing could be heard. By the conclusion the general mood of the class was well expressed by an emotional young lady who asked, "Why did we do it?" The teacher responded by saying, "We did it once; we can do it again. Whether these weapons of destruction are used depends on you." So began a unit on nuclear weapons.[78]

Reducing children to tears in the classroom, as part of the indoctrination process, had likewise been part of the *modus operandi* in France between the two World Wars:

At a boys' school in Amiens, for example, teachers asked children whose fathers had been killed in combat to speak to the class. "More than one tear was shed," the headmaster reported. Similarly, a teacher from a girls' advanced primary school in Amiens noted that at her school, one student in six had lost a father between 1914 and 1918: "The roll call of the dead was carried out with the most moving reverence," the teacher reported, "and both teachers and students were united by their emotions." Yet another teacher, this time from a girl's school in Pont de Metz, reported that the solemn silence she called for upon the roll call of the dead "was broken by the sobs of many children whose fathers were killed in the war."[79]

It should be noted that here, as in other contexts, the fatal misstep of teachers was in operating beyond their competence— teachers having no professional qualifications for understanding the dangers of manipulating children's emotions, nor any special qualifications for understanding international political complications or what factors make wars less likely or more likely, much less what factors are likely to lead to collapse and defeat, as in France in 1940.

As in interwar France, the leading teachers' union— in America, the National Education Association— was a spearhead of pacifism and a fountainhead of ideas of the left in general. At its annual meetings, the NEA passed innumerable resolutions on subjects ranging far beyond education to issues involving migrant workers, voting laws, gun control, abortion, statehood for the District of Columbia, and many others, including issues of war and peace. Its resolutions, speeches and awards over the years have promoted the same combination of pacifism and internationalism that marked the efforts of the French teachers' unions between the two World Wars.

These resolutions have urged "disarmament agreements that reduce the possibility of war,"[80] urged "that the United States make every effort to strengthen the United Nations to make it a more effective instrument for world peace,"[81] called for "a halt to the arms race,"[82] and declared that "specific materials need to be developed for use in school classrooms in order to attain goals that focus on the establishment of peace and the understanding of nuclear proliferation."[83] The idea so much in vogue in the 1920s and 1930s, that war itself was the enemy, not other nations, reappeared in an NEA resolution that declared nuclear war "the common enemy of all nations and peoples."[84] Trophies were awarded at the NEA's meetings for schools that created programs to promote pacifism and internationalism, in the name of "peace."

In 1982, for example, the National Education Association at its annual meeting awarded a peace trophy to its affiliate in the city of St. Albans, Vermont, because its teachers had organized all sorts of pacifist activities, including having their students send letters to Senators on hunger and peace.[85] Three years later, the West Virginia Education Association was awarded a prize for developing an "educational" project on nuclear issues that had children contacting the White House and the Kremlin.[86] The people-to-people theme of the years between the two World Wars, when the French teachers' union established joint activities with German teachers,[87] was repeated by having school children making and sending symbolic gifts to Japan. The NEA meeting also adopted a resolution calling for "an immediate universal nuclear weapons freeze."[88] In 1982, the Representative Assembly of the National Education Association called for a "freeze" on the development, testing or deployment of nuclear weapons.[89] That same year, NEA president Willard H. McGuire addressed a special session on disarmament held at United Nations headquarters in New York, and declared:

> If wars in the past left almost unimaginable death and destruction in their wake, a future war between the major world Powers could well mean the end of civilization on this planet. So it becomes imperative that we teachers, through our member organizations, work to prevent the

precious instrument of education from ever again becoming the tool of irrational leaders who would pervert the world's youth into believing that there is nobility in militarism, that there can be peace only through deterrence, or that there is safety only if we live frightened lives behind nuclear shields for protection.

We must educate the world's children to believe that real peace is possible, a peace free of nuclear threats and counter-threats, a peace where human life is something more than a list of numbers on some benighted general's chart. Such a peace can only be possible through world disarmament. The world's teachers must work toward this goal.[90]

What qualified him to sweepingly dismiss officials who had far more access to information, and far more experience in foreign affairs, as "irrational" and generals as "benighted," was a question never addressed. Nor was the question of his mandate for turning classrooms into indoctrination centers. But Willard H. McGuire was not unique. Two years later, a new NEA president, Mary Hatwood Futrell, excoriated the Reagan administration for having "escalated the arms race, and increased the risk of world incineration."[91]

In 1990, NEA president Keith Geiger called for putting "human needs above the arms race"[92] and, after Iraq invaded Kuwait, he urged President George H.W. Bush to "continue to pursue peaceful means to end the Iraqi occupation of Kuwait," so as to "avoid war while maintaining inviolable principles in the Persian Gulf."[93] There were no suggestions as to how this remarkable feat might be achieved, much less any discussion of the track record of attempts to undo military conquests through diplomacy or boycotts.

There has also been a repeat of media leaders taking a sympathetic view of nations opposed to their own. Columnist Robert Novak, for example, revealed a discussion he had with Cable News Network (CNN) founder Ted Turner who, as indicated by Novak's account, also repeated the 1920s and 1930s pattern of equating believers in military deterrence with advocates of war:

> As we walked across Lafayette Square on the way to my office, Turner said: "I can't understand, Novak, why you're in favor of all-out nuclear war." He then launched a defense of the Kremlin's arms control policies and lauded the people's paradise in Cuba. I tried to argue back, but it was tough getting a word in edgewise with Ted Turner. When we reached my thirteenth-floor office, I introduced him to a young woman in the Evans & Novak outer office whose main job was handling the phone calls.

Turner looked her in the eye and asked: "How do you feel working for a man who is in favor of a nuclear holocaust?"

The woman looked at Ted as though he were mad, and to a certain extent he was.[94]

THE IRAQ WARS

Two wars against Iraq, beginning respectively in 1991 and in 2003, were fought under the specter of the Vietnam War, with predictions of another "quagmire" in both cases, though the 1991 war in fact successfully drove Iraq out of Kuwait in short order, with minimal American casualties and devastating losses inflicted on Iraqi armed forces. Tom Wicker of the *New York Times*, for example, in 1990 foresaw "a bloody and ill-conceived war against Iraq," one with "devastating casualties for United States forces."[95] Anthony Lewis of the *New York Times* speculated that there might be "20,000 American casualties."[96] A *Washington Post* writer reported a mathematical model developed at the Brookings Institution that produced an "optimistic" estimate of more than a thousand American deaths in the 1991 Iraq war and a "pessimistic" estimate of more than four thousand deaths.[97] In reality, 148 Americans were killed in combat during the first Iraq war.[98]

The second Iraq war, beginning in 2003, was more like most wars, with unforeseen setbacks and unpredictable side effects, quite aside from debatable issues about the wisdom of the invasion or the nature of its goals. Despite the swift military defeat of the Iraqi armed forces, peace was not restored because of a reign of terror directed in part against American troops, but primarily against Iraqi civilians, by both domestic and foreign terrorists, determined to prevent a very different kind of government from being established in the Middle East under American auspices.

As in the case of the Vietnam war, much of the media and the intelligentsia in general declared what was happening in Iraq to be a "civil war" and "unwinnable," and many urged the immediate withdrawal of American troops. When instead there was in 2007 an increase in the number of American troops— called a "surge"— in order to suppress the rampant terrorism, this surge was widely condemned in advance as futile by the intelligentsia, in the media and in Congress.

In January 2007, *New York Times* columnist Maureen Dowd dismissed the idea as President Bush's "nonsensical urge to Surge."[99] *New York Times* columnist Paul Krugman said: "The only real question about the planned 'surge' in Iraq— which is better described as a Vietnam-style escalation— is whether its proponents are cynical or delusional."[100] In February 2007, the *Washington Post* said: "Mr. Bush's surge is unlikely to produce a breakthrough toward peace; in fact the violence may continue to worsen."[101] The *St. Louis Post-Dispatch* said "it's too little, too late."[102] An op-ed column in the *Philadelphia Tribune* called the war "unwinnable."[103] The *New Republic* asked rhetorically: "So who in Washington actually believes this surge will work?" Answering their own question, they said only "one man"— Vice President Dick Cheney. But, they added, "Sooner or later, even for Dick Cheney, reality must intrude."[104] Even the tone of utter certainty and condescension echoed that of the 1920s and 1930s intelligentsia.

Among those in politics who condemned the surge in advance was a future President of the United States, Senator Barack Obama, who said in January 2007 that the impending surge was "a mistake that I and others will actively oppose in the days to come." He called the projected surge a "reckless escalation," and introduced legislation to begin removal of American troops from Iraq no later than May 1, 2007, "with the goal of removing all United States combat forces from Iraq by March 31, 2008."[105] Senator Obama said: "Escalation has already been tried and it has already failed, because no amount of American forces can solve the political differences that lie at the heart of somebody else's civil war."[106] Another 20,000 American troops "will not in any imaginable way be able to accomplish any new progress."[107]

Senator Obama was not alone. Senator Edward Kennedy proposed requiring Congressional approval before there could be a surge.[108] Senate Majority Leader Harry Reid and Speaker of the House Nancy Pelosi sent a letter to President Bush, cautioning against the surge strategy: "Surging forces is a strategy that you have already tried and that has already failed," they said, and called the upcoming surge "a serious mistake."[109] Senator

Hillary Clinton was also among those in Congress opposing the surge, and former Senator John Edwards called for an immediate withdrawal of American troops.[110]

A later (2009) Brookings Institution study of fatalities in 2007 among Iraqi civilians— the main target of terrorist attacks— showed such fatalities to have been an estimated 3,500 per month when predictions of failure for the surge were made in January 2007. In the wake of the surge, however, these fatalities fell to 750 per month by the end of the year. Fatalities among American troops in Iraq were 83 per month in January 2007, rose to a peak of 126 per month as military operations against terrorist strongholds increased, but fell to 23 per month by the end of the year, in the wake of the surge.[111]

At the time, however, there was fierce resistance among the intelligentsia to news that the surge was working. In June 2007, the *Los Angeles Times* said that there was "no evidence that the surge is succeeding."[112] In September 2007, under the title "Snow Job in the Desert," *New York Times* columnist Paul Krugman lamented the Bush administration's "remarkable success creating the perception that the 'surge' is succeeding, even though there's not a shred of verifiable evidence to suggest that it is."[113] *New York Times* columnist Frank Rich declared "The 'decrease in violence' fable" to be "insidious."[114]

Clearly, some people were determined to see this as another "unwinnable" war, another Vietnam. By 2009, however, even the *New York Times* was reporting— though not under banner headlines— that there had been large declines in fatalities among American troops in Iraq, Iraqi security forces and Iraqi civilians, to a fraction of what their fatalities had been two years earlier, before the surge. There had also been an increase in the number of Iraqi security forces and in the country's electricity output.[115]

While the surge was going on in 2007, however, it was something exceptional when two Brookings Institution scholars, identifying themselves as people who had previously criticized "the Bush administration's miserable handling of Iraq" nevertheless said after a visit to that country that "we were surprised by the gains we saw and the potential to produce not necessarily 'victory' but a sustainable stability that both we and the Iraqis could live with."[116] Other on-the-scene reports in 2007 likewise revealed substantial success against the terrorists in Iraq and a corresponding return to normalcy in Iraqi society, including a return of Iraqi expatriates who had fled the terrorism, and resident Iraqis who now frequented public places where they had been fearful of going before.

Those who were committed to the view that the war was "unwinnable," and a surge futile, remained unchanged despite the growing evidence that the surge was working. In September 2007, *New York Times* columnist Paul Krugman said: "To understand what's really happening in Iraq, follow the oil money, which already knows that the surge has failed."[117]

Insistence that the surge was a failure only escalated as signs of its success began to appear. As the September 2007 date for General David Petraeus' report to Congress on the surge which he commanded neared, there were growing outcries in the media and in politics that the general would only try to verbally spin the failure of the surge into success. Senator Dick Durbin, for example, said that "By carefully manipulating the statistics, the Bush-Petraeus report will try to persuade us that violence in Iraq is decreasing and thus the surge is working."[118] "We need to stop the surge and start to get our troops out," said Senator Joseph Biden in August 2007.[119]

These preemptive efforts at discrediting what Petraeus was about to report were climaxed by a full-page advertisement in the *New York Times*, on the day of his report, with a bold headline: "General Petraeus or General Betray Us?" sponsored by the political activist organization MoveOn.org.[120] The subtitle was "Cooking the Books for the White House." The *New York Times* charged MoveOn.org less than half the usual rate for a full-page ad and waived its policy against ads making personal attacks in advertisements.[121]

In short, General Petraeus was accused of lying before he said anything— and in the face of growing evidence from a number of other sources that in fact the surge had substantially reduced violence in Iraq. The hostile atmosphere in which General Petraeus and U.S. ambassador Ryan Crocker testified before Congress was indicated by an account in *USA Today*:

> Following a day-long marathon Monday before two key House committees, they faced some of the Senate's most celebrated talkers— including five presidential candidates— in back-to-back hearings.
> In 10 hours of testimony, the two men got two bathroom breaks and less than 30 minutes for lunch.[122]

During these hearings, Senator Barbara Boxer said to General Petraeus: "I ask you to take off your rosy glasses."[123] Hillary Clinton said that the general's report required "the willing suspension of disbelief."[124] Congressman Rahm Emanuel said that General Petraeus' report could win "the Nobel Prize for creative statistics or the Pulitzer for fiction."[125] Congressman Robert Wexler declared that "among unbiased, non-partisan experts, the consensus is stark: The surge has failed." He compared General Petraeus' testimony to the discredited testimony of General William Westmoreland during the Vietnam war.[126] The same comparison was made by Frank Rich of the *New York Times*, who asserted that there were "some eerie symmetries between General Petraeus's sales pitch" and "Gen. William Westmoreland's similar mission for L.B.J."[127] This was just one of the signs that the ghost of the Vietnam war still loomed over later wars. Even the tactics of opponents of the Vietnam war reappeared in many places. According to *USA Today*: "The testimony was punctuated by anti-war hecklers who rose one by one to shout slogans such as, "Generals lie, children die."[128]

Eventually, claims that the surge had failed as predicted faded away amid increasingly undeniable evidence that it had succeeded. But, far from causing a re-evaluation of the prevailing vision that had been so strident and so discredited by events, the success of the surge simply led to shrinking coverage of news from Iraq in much of the media. Unlike Vietnam, this time the military defeat of the enemy was prevented from being turned into a political surrender, though only at the eleventh hour, when the cries for immediate withdrawal were loudest.

These political developments reflected a prevailing vision of war growing out of the intelligentsia's perception of the Vietnam war which, among other things, left a legacy of catchwords such as the insistently repeated "unwinnable" and "quagmire." As in so many other areas, mundane facts to the contrary had little impact on the prevailing vision. Even when politicians said what they did for their own political purposes, those purposes could be served only because there were many others who sincerely believed the prevailing vision and would support those who espoused those beliefs. Once again, as in other times and places, the influence of the intelligentsia did not depend upon their convincing the holders of power, but only on their creating a climate of opinion providing incentives and constraints affecting what the holders of power could say and do.

Another throwback to the Vietnam war era was the highly publicized "combat veteran" who proclaimed his opposition to the war— and who later turned out not to have been a combat veteran at all. As the *New York Times* reported, after the truth about one of these "combat veterans" came out belatedly:

> The thick-muscled man with close-cropped hair who called himself Rick Duncan seemed right out of central casting as a prop for a Democratic candidate running against Bush administration policies last fall.
>
> A former Marine Corps captain who suffered brain trauma from a roadside bomb in Iraq and was at the Pentagon during the Sept. 11 attacks. An advocate for veterans rights who opposed the war. An Annapolis graduate who was proudly gay. With his gold-plated credentials, he commanded the respect and attention of not just politicians, but also police chiefs, reporters and veterans advocates for the better part of two years.
>
> Yet, except for his first name, virtually none of his story was true.[129]

That this man's easily checked lies passed muster in the media for two years suggests once again the receptivity of the intelligentsia to things that fit their vision, however unsubstantiated those things might be otherwise.

During the second Iraq war, the American intelligentsia repeated the patterns of the intelligentsia in France between the two World Wars— namely, the verbal reduction of combat soldiers from the status of patriotic heroes to that of pitiable victims. Even stories about the financial problems of reservists called away from their jobs to go on active duty in Iraq, or stories about the simple fact of sad goodbyes to friends or family members in the military being sent overseas, made the front pages of the *New York Times*,[130] while stories about the heroism of American troops in combat either went unreported or appeared on inside pages. Stories of extraordinary bravery of Americans under fire that won Congressional Medals of Honor— including men throwing themselves on enemy hand grenades, sacrificing their own lives to save the lives of those around them— were reported on pages 13 and 14, respectively, and one in the second section of the *New York Times.*[131] The *Washington Post* and the *Los Angeles Times* similarly buried these stories of extraordinary heroism on the inside pages and much of television news followed suit, either downplaying or completely ignoring such stories.

Negative stories, on the other hand, found instant prominence in the media, even when unsubstantiated. For example, much outrage was expressed in the media during the early days of the Iraq war when a claim was made that looters had pillaged precious artifacts from an Iraqi museum, which American soldiers had failed to protect.[132] That men fighting, with their lives on the line, were supposed to divert their attention to protecting museums was a remarkable enough premise. But the charge itself turned out to be false.[133] The artifacts in question had been secreted by the museum staff, in order to protect them from looters and from the dangers of war. Yet the media had not waited to substantiate the charges against the American military before bursting into print with these charges and bursting with indignation over them.

The American military's positive achievements in general, whether in battle or in restoring civil order or carrying out humanitarian activities, received little attention in the media. While the Iraq war began to disappear from the front pages of the *New York Times* as terrorist attacks declined in the wake of the surge, and coverage shrank similarly in other media, American casualties continued to be highlighted, even when those casualties were in single digits, and the cumulative casualties were constantly featured, even though these casualties were by no means high compared to other wars. In fact, all the Americans killed in the two Iraq wars put together were fewer than those killed taking the one island of Iwo Jima during the Second World War or one day of fighting at Antietam during the Civil War.[134]

Unless one believes that wars can be fought with no casualties, there was nothing unusual about the casualty rate in the first or second Iraq war, except for its being lower than in most wars. But casualties fit the constant theme of soldiers as victims, and verbal virtuosity has enabled this victimization message to be characterized as "supporting the troops" or even "honoring the troops." When the *New York Times* published photographs of dying and dead American soldiers in Iraq, executive editor Bill Keller declared that "death and carnage are part of the story, and to launder them out of our account of the war would be a disservice."[135] Such verbal virtuosity creates a straw man of "laundering out" the fact of deaths in war— which no one has ever doubted— and equates publishing photos of individual soldiers in the throes of death with just telling the story, while burying stories of soldiers' heroism deep inside the paper.

The same depiction of soldiers as victims dominated news stories of veterans returning home from combat. Problems of returning veterans, such as alcoholism or homelessness, were featured in the media, with no attempt to compare the incidence of such problems to the incidence of the same problems among the civilian population.[136] In other words, if all returning veterans were not completely immune to the problems that civilians experienced, that was presented as if it were a special problem brought on by military service. A front page article in the *New York Times* of January 13, 2008, for example, featured killings in the United States by veterans returning from the wars in Iraq and Afghanistan. "In many of those cases," it said, "combat trauma and the stress of deployment" were among the factors which "appear to have set the stage for a tragedy that was part destruction, part self-destruction."[137]

This particular attempt to picture veterans as victims failed to compare the homicide rate of returning veterans with the homicide rate among civilians of the same ages. Had they done so, it was pointed out in the *New York Post*, they would have found that the homicide rate among returning veterans was *one-fifth* that among civilians of the same ages.[138] Undaunted, the *New York Times* returned to the same theme in a front-page story a year later, in 2009— again going into gory details in individual cases, with no mention of the rate of homicides among military veterans compared to civilians of the same ages.[139]

Another promotion of the image of victimhood among military veterans was a story about suicide rates in the military having reached "the highest since the Army began keeping records," as the *New York Times* put it,[140] in a story echoed throughout the media. Yet, once again, there was no comparison with suicide rates among people of the same demographic characteristics in the civilian population— which was *higher* than among people in the military, as the Associated Press reported,[141] but which few media outlets mentioned. Once again, much of the media filtered out facts that went against their vision, leaving their readers with a wholly distorted picture. Like *The Times* of London in the 1930s, the *New York Times* in a later era took the lead in filtering and slanting news to fit its vision.

PATRIOTISM AND NATIONAL HONOR

No matter how much journalists, politicians or others undermine a war effort, anyone calling such actions unpatriotic is automatically met with the indignant response, "How dare you question my patriotism?" Just why patriotism is something that it is unreasonable or unworthy to question is something for which no argument is advanced, unless endless repetition is considered to be an argument.

This is not to say that anyone with whom one disagrees about a war or any other issue can be automatically called "unpatriotic." That is not a charge to be either automatically accepted or automatically rejected. Even actions detrimental to a country's self-defense are not automatically unpatriotic in intention. It is not necessary to assume that the intelligentsia of the 1930s, for example, deliberately set out to do such things as making their own countries vulnerable to military attack.

As noted in Chapter 14, Georges Lapierre— the leader of the French teachers' union's campaigns to promote pacifism in France's textbooks during the 1920s and 1930s, downplaying national pride and national defense— nevertheless, after the fall of France in 1940, joined the French underground resistance movement against the Nazi conquerors, and as a result ended up being captured and sent to his death in Dachau.[142] He was clearly not an unpatriotic man. But, whatever his intentions during the interwar years, the more important question for the country as a whole is the ultimate effect of his efforts on a whole generation. Many other prewar pacifist teachers also ended up fighting in the French resistance movement after the vision they had promoted for so long had led to opposite results from what they were seeking.

They had, in Burke's words from an earlier time, helped bring about the worst results "without being the worst of men."[143] In their own minds, the teachers "wove together patriotism and pacifism," according to an account of that era[144] but, regardless of what went on inside these educators' minds, the net result out in the real world was the same as if they had deliberately undermined the patriotism of a whole generation of their students, for whom they made internationalism as well as pacifism prime virtues, despite whatever passing mention there might be of love of country as a subordinate aspect of a love of humanity in general.

A much larger question than the patriotism or lack of patriotism of particular individuals or institutions is the question of how consequential patriotism itself is, and the related question of how consequential a sense of national honor is.

Patriotism has long been viewed by many intellectuals as a psychological phenomenon with no substantive basis. Back in the eighteenth century, William Godwin referred to patriotism as "high-sounding nonsense"[145] and "the unmeaning rant of romance."[146]

As noted in Chapter 14, such views were still common in the twentieth century during the period between the two World Wars, among such prominent European intellectuals as Bertrand Russell, H.G. Wells, Romain Rolland, Kingsley Martin, Aldous Huxley, and J.B. Priestley, among others. In America, John Dewey decried patriotism as something that "degenerates into a hateful conviction of intrinsic superiority" and national honor as "a touchy and testy Honor" based on "emotion and fantasy."[147] But how consequential patriotism and national honor are cannot be determined *a priori* by how much either of them does or does not conform to the vision of the anointed.

As with many other things, how consequential they are can be discovered by what happens in their absence. When Hitler launched an invasion of France in 1940, against the advice of his top generals, it was because he was convinced that contemporary France was lacking in these supposedly irrelevant qualities[148]— and the sudden collapse of the French, despite their military advantages, suggests that these qualities are indeed consequential. What is called "national honor" is a long-run perspective on national decisions and their consequences, the opposite of the one-day-at-a-time rationalism by which France had declined to fight over the militarization of the Rhineland in 1936, or to live up to the French mutual defense treaty with Czechoslovakia in 1938, or to seriously engage the Germans militarily during the long months of the "phony war" following the formal declaration of war in 1939, despite France's large military superiority on the western front while Hitler's troops were concentrated in the east, conquering Poland.

A willingness to fight can be a deterrence to attack and, conversely, an unwillingness to meet a challenge or provocation can make a nation a target for an all-out assault. "National honor" is simply an idiomatic expression for this long-run perspective on national interest, as distinguished from a one-day-at-a-time perspective, which may serve the short-run interests of politicians, by sparing them from making the hard decisions which distinguish a politician from a statesman. But many intellectuals have tried to reduce a sense of national honor, like patriotism, to a psychological quirk. However, even British Prime Minister Neville Chamberlain, the man most indelibly identified with the policy of appeasement of Hitler, belatedly seemed to acknowledge that national honor was consequential, just months before the Second World War began:

> I had the opportunity yesterday of exchanging a few words with M. Blum, the French Socialist leader and former Prime Minister, and he said to me that in his view, and in the view of all the Socialist friends with whom he had talked, there was only one danger of war in Europe, and that was a very real one: it was that the impression should get about that Great Britain and France were not in earnest and that they could not be relied upon to carry out their promises. If that were so, no greater, no more deadly mistake could be made— and it would be a frightful thing if Europe were to be plunged into war on account of a misunderstanding.[149]

In short, Europe and the world were on the brink of a catastrophic war because neither friend nor foe believed that Britain and France had national honor. That is, there was no sense of a firm resolve by the British or the French, on which friendly nations could stake their own survival by allying themselves with Britain or France, at the cost of incurring the wrath of Nazi Germany. Likewise, there was no sense among belligerent nations that they need fear anything more serious than temporizing words from Britain and France. What was lacking in Chamberlain's statement, on the eve of war, was any acknowledgment that it was his own policies, and similar policies in France, substituting talk for action, which had created this deadly misconception that all they would ever do was talk. Hitler was in fact quite surprised when his invasion of Poland led to declarations of war by Britain and France.[150]

If the Second World War grew out of a "misunderstanding," British and French sacrifice of national honor one year earlier, at Munich, fostered that misunderstanding and their belated refusal to sacrifice national honor a second time meant war.

The ultimate and bitter irony was that it was Neville Chamberlain's fate to make the declaration of war against Germany in 1939 which turned a regional invasion of Poland into the Second World War— the most catastrophic war in history— a war which he had striven to avoid at virtually all costs, brushing aside two years earlier "the old stand-upon-your-dignity methods"[151] that had once been part of the concept of national honor. Instead, Chamberlain operated on the basis of one-day-at-a-time rationalism in which, as he said in 1938, "we can remove the danger spots one by one," by "our willingness to face realities which we cannot change."[152] But, just one year later, Chamberlain abandoned that one-day-at-a-time-rationalism when he declared, "we are not prepared to sit by and see the independence of one country after another successively destroyed"[153]— even though he now had fewer potential allies left, after having abandoned Austria and Czechoslovakia to Nazi conquest, and was now in a weaker position from which to try to change the reality of Hitler's and Stalin's joint conquest of Poland.

The ultimate issue was never Austria, Czechoslovakia, or Poland, as such. The issue was whether Hitler was to be allowed to upset the whole balance of power in Europe, on which peace depended, to the fatal disadvantage of Britain and France, simply by doing so in installments, with Britain and France posing the issue in each case in terms of one-day-at-a-time rationalism, while Hitler posed the issue explicitly in terms of "the national honour of a great people"[154]— in other words, a long run interest that he was willing to fight for. Chamberlain's belated abandonment of the one-day-at-a-time approach was evident in his August 1939 reversal of what he had said in September 1938. On the eve of the fateful Munich conference in 1938, Prime Minister Chamberlain said in a broadcast to the nation:

> How horrible, fantastic, incredible it is that we should be digging
> trenches and trying on gas masks here because of a quarrel in a far-away
> country between people of whom we know nothing.[155]

But, in August 1939, in the dark shadow of the impending war, Chamberlain said, "we shall not be fighting for the political future of a far away city in a foreign land."[156] He now understood that it was not a question of "Why die for Danzig?"

Many knowledgeable people, then and in later years, criticized Prime Minister Chamberlain's new actions— publicly guaranteeing Poland's independence— as reckless under the circumstances,[157] but it may well be that events and emotions swept the Prime Minister and Britain into a war for which the British were not yet militarily prepared, but which they entered in reaction to the blasting of their earlier illusions at the time of the Munich agreement. Serious questions have been raised as to whether the particular kinds of military equipment that Hitler had accumulated, as of 1939, indicated an imminent attack against Britain and France, on the one hand, or attacks eastward, on the other. But, if the latter, whether the British and the French governments chose the best time to fight is a question of military strategy. What is relevant to the role of intellectuals is the atmosphere in which these governments based their previous actions that led up to this crisis.

As for Chamberlain's earlier dismissal of "the old stand-upon-your-dignity methods" in 1937, John Maynard Keynes saw the flaw in that:

> Our strength is great, but our statesmen have lost the capacity to appear
> formidable. It is in that loss that our greatest danger lies. Our power to
> win a war may depend on increased armaments. But our power to avoid
> a war depends not less on our recovering that capacity to appear
> formidable, which is a quality of will and demeanour.[158]

In other words, being militarily formidable may be enough to fight off an aggressor, but showing yourself a formidable leader beforehand may be enough to make it unnecessary to fight a war in the first place. Chamberlain seems not to have understood this and ended up having to fight what became the biggest war in all of history. Ronald Reagan clearly understood the importance of having the "will and demeanour" to appear formidable—

as he did in Iceland and elsewhere— and was able to put an end to the long, fear-ridden Cold War without firing a shot at the Soviets.

Keynes said of Neville Chamberlain, during the apparent triumph of his policy of appeasement: "He is not escaping the risks of war. He is only making sure that, when it comes, we shall have no friends and no common cause."[159] Just two years later, these words became painfully prophetic, when Britain stood alone facing the wrath of Nazi Germany, as Hitler's *Luftwaffe* began bombing London and other places in the south of England, while a German invasion force was being assembled across the Channel on the coast of conquered France. The misconceptions on which Chamberlain had operated for years did not originate with him. They were part of the atmosphere of the times, an atmosphere to which intellectuals made a major contribution.

Despite a tendency in some intellectual circles to see the nation as just a subordinate part of the world at large— some acting, or even describing themselves, as citizens of the world— patriotism is, in one sense, little more than a recognition of the basic fact that one's own material well-being, personal freedom, and sheer physical survival depend on the particular institutions, traditions and policies of the particular nation in which one lives. There is no comparable world government and, without the concrete institutions of government, there is nothing to be a citizen of or to provide enforceable rights, however lofty or poetic it may sound to be a citizen of the world. When one's fate is clearly recognized as dependent on the surrounding national framework— the institutions, traditions and norms of one's country— then the preservation of that framework cannot be a matter of indifference while each individual pursues purely individual interests.

Patriotism is a recognition of a shared fate and the shared responsibilities that come with it. National honor is a recognition that one-day-at-a-time rationalism is a delusion that enables politicians to escape the responsibilities of statesmanship.

Conditions may become so repugnant in one country that it makes sense to move to another country. But there is no such thing as moving to "the world." One may of course live in a country parasitically, accepting all the benefits for which others have sacrificed— both in the past and in the present— while rejecting any notion of being obliged to do the same. But once that attitude becomes general, the country becomes defenseless against forces of either internal disintegration or external aggression. In short, patriotism and national honor cannot be reduced to simply psychological quirks, to which intellectuals can consider themselves superior, without risking dire consequences, of which France in 1940 was a classic example. It was considered chic in some circles in France of the 1930s to say, "Rather Hitler than Blum."[160] But that was before they experienced living under Hitler or realizing that their fellow countrymen were dying after dehumanization in Hitler's concentration camps.

Disdain for patriotism and national honor was just one of the fashionable attitudes among the intellectuals of the 1920s and 1930s to reappear with renewed force in Western democracies in the 1960s and afterwards. How far history will repeat itself, on this and other issues, is a question for the future to answer. Indeed, it is *the* question for the future of the Western world.

PART VII

INTELLECTUALS
AND RACE

The gods mercifully gave mankind this little moment of peace between the religious fanaticisms of the past and the fanaticisms of class and race that were speedily to arise and dominate time to come.

G.M. Trevelyan[1]

Chapter 16

Disparities and Their Causes

For centuries, there have been beliefs that some races are superior to others. Various developments in the second half of the nineteenth century, and in the early twentieth century, turned such general beliefs into organized ideologies with the aura of "science," often creating the very dogmatism among intellectuals that science is meant to counter. By the end of the twentieth century, opposite ideologies about race would prevail among intellectuals, sometimes also invoking the name of science, with no more justification and with the same dismissive attitude toward those who dared to disagree with the currently prevailing vision.

The term "race," as it was used in the late nineteenth and early twentieth centuries, was not confined to broad divisions of the human species, such as black, white and yellow races. Differences among Slavs, Jews and Anglo-Saxons were often referred to as "racial" differences as well. Madison Grant's influential 1916 best-seller, *The Passing of the Great Race*, was one of those writings which divided Europeans into Nordic, Alpine and Mediterranean "races," among others.[1] However, rather than become bogged down in semantic issues, we can refer to racial and ethnic groups loosely under the rubric of race, in part because more precise definitions could easily lose touch with social realities, in a world of growing racial intermixtures over the generations. These biological intermixtures have accelerated in our own times, even as the stridency of separate racial identity rhetoric has increased. These include people bitterly complaining about how half their ancestors mistreated the other half, as a current grievance of their own, whether among the Maoris of New Zealand or among various American racial or ethnic groups.

With race, as with war, twentieth century intellectuals were concentrated on one end of the spectrum in the early years and then on the opposite end of the spectrum in later years. The vision of the anointed— that is, the preference for surrogate decision-making, inspired by intellectual elites, over systemically evolved mutual accommodations among the people at large— need not require a commitment to a particular view of a particular issue such as race, even though whatever view happened to prevail among the anointed at a given time was often deemed to be almost axiomatically superior to conflicting views held by others— these other views often being treated as unworthy of serious intellectual engagement. In the early twentieth century, Madison Grant referred to those who disagreed with his genetic determinism as sentimentalists[2] and, in the late twentieth century, those who disagreed with the prevailing racial orthodoxy of that era were often dismissed as racists.

Intellectuals on opposite ends of the spectrum in different eras have been similar in another way: Both have tended to ignore the long-standing warning from statisticians that correlation is not causation. Whether they believed that differences among races were caused by genes or caused by society's treatment of those races, they tended to overlook the possibility that what *conveys* differences may not be the same as what *causes* those differences. One race may be more successful than another at a particular endeavor, or a whole range of endeavors, for reasons that are neither genetic nor a result of the way the society in which they live treats them. As noted in Chapter 7, there are many historic, geographic and demographic reasons for groups to differ from one another in their skills, experiences, cultures and values— whether these are different social, national or racial groups.

GENETIC DETERMINISM

The mid-nineteenth century sensation created by Charles Darwin's theory of evolution had ramifications far beyond the field of biology. The idea of "survival of the fittest" among competing species was extended by others into competition among human beings, whether among different classes or different races. The research of Darwin's cousin Francis Galton (1822–1911) culminated in a book titled **Hereditary Genius**, which established that high achievers were concentrated in particular families. Correlation was treated as causation, with genetics being proclaimed to be the reason for the achievement differential.

Similar reasoning was applied to races. As a later scholar said of Galton: "He believed that in his own day the Anglo-Saxons far outranked the Negroes of Africa, who in turn outranked the Australian aborigines, who outranked nobody." Again, correlation was treated as causation, leading to eugenics— a term Galton coined— to promote the differential survival of races. He said, "there exists a sentiment, for the most part quite unreasonable, against the gradual extinction of an inferior race."[3]

Whatever the validity of Galton's assessments of the relative achievements of different races in his own time, profound changes in the relative achievements of different races over the centuries undermine the theory of genetic determinism. China was, for centuries, technologically, economically, and in other ways more advanced than any country in Europe. The later reversals of the relative positions of the Chinese and Europeans in the modern era, without any demonstrable changes in their genes, undermines Galton's genetic arguments, as other major reversals of the positions of other racial groups or subgroups would undermine the later genetic determinism of other intellectuals.

This is not to say that there were no great differences in achievements among different races, either within societies or between societies, as of a given time, nor that all such differences reversed over time, though many did. But once the automatic link between genetics and achievement is broken, it ceases to be a weighty presumption, even in the case of groups that have never been leaders in achievement. Whatever non-genetic factors have been able to produce profound differences in other situations cannot be ruled out *a priori* for any group, and therefore it remains a question to be examined empirically in each particular case— that is, if science is to be something more than an incantation invoked to buttress an ideology and silence its critics.

Much empirical evidence of large and consequential differences among racial or ethnic groups, as well as social classes, accumulated in the late nineteenth and early twentieth centuries. Studies of the histories of families, as well as the spread of mental testing, and sociological studies of differences in crime rates and educational achievements among children from different backgrounds, even when attending the same schools, added weight to the case made by those promoting genetic determinism. Contrary to later verbal fashions, these were not simply "perceptions" or "stereotypes." These were painstakingly established facts, despite the serious problems with the inferences drawn from those facts— such as Madison Grant's sweeping pronouncement, "race is everything."[4]

THE PROGRESSIVE ERA

The Progressive era in early twentieth century America was perhaps the high-water mark of "scientific" theories of racial differences. The increasing immigration from Europe, and especially the shift in its origins from Northern and Western Europe to Eastern and Southern Europe, raised questions about the racial quality of the new people flooding into the country. The beginning of the mass migrations of American blacks from the South to the Northern cities, and their concentration in ghettos there, raised similar questions during the same era. Empirical data on group differences in crime rates, disease rates, mental test scores, and school performances fed all these concerns.

Two huge compilations of empirical data in early twentieth century America stand out particularly. One was the huge, multi-volume report of the federal immigration commission headed by Senator William P. Dillingham and published in 1911. This report showed, among other things, that with children who attended elementary school three-quarters of the school days or more, 30 percent of native-born white children had been denied promotion to the next grade, compared to 61 percent of native-born black children and 67 percent of the children of immigrant Polish Jews.[5] The other huge source of data about differences among racial or ethnic groups during this period was the mental testing of more than 100,000 soldiers by the U.S. Army during the First World War.[6] The proportions of soldiers with different ancestries who exceeded the American national norms on mental tests were as follows:[7]

English	67 percent
German	49 percent
Irish	26 percent
Russian	19 percent
Italian	14 percent
Polish	12 percent

Men from Italy, Poland and Russia scored consistently at or near the bottom among immigrants from Europe on various mental tests, with American blacks scoring at the bottom among soldiers as a whole, though scoring only marginally lower than these Southern and Eastern European immigrants on these tests.[8] Among the civilian population, the same groups scored at or near the bottom in mental test scores, though in a slightly different order. Black children attending schools in Youngstown, Ohio, scored marginally higher on I.Q. tests than the children of Polish, Greek and other immigrants there.[9] In Massachusetts, a larger proportion of black school children scored over 120 on the I.Q. tests than did their schoolmates who were children of Polish, Italian or Portuguese immigrants.[10] During this era, Northern blacks had somewhat higher I.Q.s than Southern blacks.[11]

Another curious fact, which received much less attention at the time, was that the Army tests in the First World War showed white soldiers from Georgia, Arkansas, Kentucky, and Mississippi scoring lower on mental tests than black soldiers from Ohio, Illinois, New York, and Pennsylvania.[12] However, the black population as a whole was overwhelmingly concentrated in the South at that time, which may explain why the Army tests showed blacks scoring below the immigrants that they scored above in civilian tests conducted where they both went to the same schools in the North.

Again, none of this was simply a matter of "perceptions," "stereotypes," or "prejudices." Differences among racial, ethnic and regional groups were very real, sometimes very large and very consequential. What was at issue were the *reasons* for those differences. Moreover, the reasons for such differences that were acceptable to intellectuals changed radically over the generations, much as their support for the First World War and their later pacifism marked drastic changes on that subject.

During the early twentieth century, demonstrable differences among groups were largely attributed to heredity and, during the late twentieth century, these differences were largely— if not solely— attributed to environment, including an environment of discrimination. Nevertheless, the same *general* vision of society prevailed among those who called themselves Progressives at the beginning of the twentieth century and those who called themselves liberals later in that century, however disparate their views on race were between these two eras. Theirs was the vision of the anointed as surrogate decision-makers in both periods, along with such corollaries as an expanded role for government and an expanded role for judges to re-interpret the Constitution, so as to loosen its restrictions on the powers of government.

Progressive-era intellectuals took a largely negative view of the new immigrants from Southern and Eastern Europe, as well as of American blacks in general. Because such a high proportion of the immigrants from Poland and Russia were Jews during this era, Carl Brigham— a leading authority on mental tests, and creator of the College Board's Scholastic Aptitude Test— asserted that the Army test results tended to "disprove the popular belief that the Jew is highly intelligent."[13] H.H. Goddard, who had administered mental tests to immigrant children on Ellis Island, declared: "These people cannot deal with abstractions."[14] Another giant of the mental-testing profession, L.M. Terman, author of the Stanford-Binet I.Q. test and creator of a decades-long study of people with I.Q.s of 140 and above, likewise concluded from his study of racial minorities in the Southwest that children from such groups "cannot master abstractions."[15] It was widely accepted as more or less a matter of course during this era that blacks were incapable of mental performances comparable to whites, and the Army mental test results were taken as confirmation.

The Progressive era was also the heyday of eugenics, the attempt to prevent excessive breeding of the "wrong" kind of people— including, though not limited to, particular races. Eugenicists feared that people of lower mental capacity would reproduce on a larger scale than others, and thus over time bring about a decline in the average I.Q. in the nation.[16] The *New Republic* lamented "the multiplication of the unfit, the production of a horde of unwanted souls."[17]

In Britain, as in the United States, leaders and supporters of the eugenics movement included people on the left, such as John Maynard Keynes, who helped create the Cambridge Eugenics Society, as well as H.G. Wells, George Bernard Shaw, Harold Laski, Sidney Webb and Julian Huxley. Sidney Webb said, "as a nation we are breeding largely from our inferior stocks."[18] But eugenics was by no means exclusively a movement on the left, nor one without opponents on the left. Supporters of eugenics also included conservatives, among them both Neville Chamberlain and Winston Churchill.[19]

In America, among those to whom pioneer birth-control advocate Margaret Sanger took her message was the Ku Klux Klan. Madison Grant's book *The Passing of the Great Race*, expressing fears of a loss of hegemony by whites in general and Nordics in particular, was a landmark book of its era. It was not only a best seller in the United States, it was translated into French, Norwegian and— most fatefully— German. Hitler called it his "Bible."[20]

Despite its international influence, *The Passing of the Great Race* offered extremely little evidence for its sweeping conclusions. The great bulk of the book was a historical account of Alpine, Mediterranean and Nordic peoples in Europe and of the Aryan languages. Yet most of Madison Grant's sweeping conclusions and the policies he recommended were about America— about the "inferior races among our immigrants,"[21] about the need for eugenics[22] and for "laws against miscegenation."[23] He asserted that "Negroes have demonstrated throughout recorded time that they are a stationary species and that they do not possess the potentiality of progress or initiative from within."[24] Yet, as Grant himself said, "the three main European races are the subject of this book,"[25] which contained virtually no factual information about blacks, but only opaque pronouncements. Even Grant's rankings of European groups are essentially pronouncements, with little or no empirical evidence or analysis, despite an abundance of miscellaneous and often arcane information.

What *The Passing of the Great Race* did have was a great display of erudition, or apparent erudition, using numerous technical terms unfamiliar to most people— "brachycephalic skulls,"[26] "Armenoids,"[27] "Paleolithic man,"[28] the "Massagetæ,"[29] "Zendavesta,"[30] the "Aryan Tokharian language,"[31] and the "Miocene" and "Pliocene" eras,[32] as well as such statements as "The Upper Paleolithic embraces all the postglacial stages down to the Neolithic and includes the subdivisions of the Aurignacian, Solutrean, Magdalenian and Azilian."[33] But this all served as an impressive backdrop for unrelated conclusions.

Among Madison Grant's conclusions were that "race lies at the base of all the manifestation of modern society."[34] He also deplored "a sentimental belief in the sanctity of human life," when that is used "to prevent both the elimination of defective infants and the sterilization of such adults as are themselves of no value to the community."[35] He feared "the resurgence of the lower races at the expense of the Nordics"[36] and the "prevailing lack of true race consciousness" among the latter.[37] He saw the immigrants arriving in America as the "sweepings" of the "jails and asylums" of Europe.[38] More generally, he said:

> There exists to-day a widespread and fatuous belief in the power of environment, as well as of education and opportunity to alter heredity, which arises from the dogma of the brotherhood of man, derived in its turn from the loose thinkers of the French Revolution and their American mimics.[39]

> The man of the old stock is being crowded out of many country districts by these foreigners just as he is to-day being literally driven off the streets of New York City by the swarms of Polish Jews.[40]

> We Americans must realize that the altruistic ideals which have controlled our social development during the past century and the maudlin sentimentalism that has made America "an asylum for the oppressed," are sweeping the nation toward a racial abyss.[41]

That *The Passing of the Great Race* was taken seriously says much about the times. But Madison Grant was by no means a fringe crank or an ignorant redneck. He was born into a wealthy family in New York City and was educated at Yale and the Columbia University law school. He was a member of numerous exclusive social clubs. Politically, he was a Progressive and an activist on issues important to Progressives, such as conservation, endangered species, municipal reform and the creation of national parks, as well as being a driving force behind the creation of the world's largest zoo in the Bronx.[42] *The Passing of the Great Race* was recommended not only in a popular publication like *The Saturday Evening Post* but was also reviewed in *Science*, published by the American Association for the Advancement of Science.[43] The maps for a later book of his were prepared with the help of the American Geographical Society.[44]

Madison Grant's thesis elaborated themes introduced by others before him, such as Progressive sociologist Edward A. Ross, who coined the term "race suicide" to describe the demographic replacement of the existing American stock over time by immigrants with higher birthrates from Southern and Eastern Europe, those whom prominent economist Francis A. Walker had even earlier described as "beaten men from beaten races."[45]

Professor Ross declared that "no one can doubt that races differ in intellectual ability"[46] and lamented an "unanticipated result" of widespread access to medical advances— namely "the brightening of the survival prospect of the ignorant, the stupid, the careless and the very poor in comparison with those of the intelligent, the bright, the responsible and the thrifty."[47] Ross' concerns were raised not only about people from different classes but also about the new and massive numbers of immigrants:

> Observe immigrants not as they come travel-wan up the gang-plank, nor as they issue toil-begrimed from pit's mouth or mill gate, but in their gatherings, washed, combed, and in their Sunday best. You are struck by the fact that from ten to twenty per cent. are hirsute, low-browed, big-faced persons of obviously low mentality. Not that they suggest evil. They simply look out of place in black clothes and stiff collar, since clearly they belong in skins, in wattled huts at the close of the Great Ice Age. These oxlike men are descendants of those *who always stayed behind*. . . To the practised eye, the physiognomy of certain groups unmistakably proclaims inferiority of type.[48]

According to Professor Ross, "the new immigrants are inferior in looks to the old immigrants,"[49] apparently because the new immigrants were from Eastern and Southern Europe, unlike earlier immigrants from Northern and Western Europe. As Ross put it:

> The fusing of American with German and Scandinavian immigrants was only a reblending of kindred stocks, for Angles, Jutes, Danes, and Normans were wrought of yore into the fiber of the English breed. But the human varieties being collected in this country by the naked action of economic forces are too dissimilar to blend without producing a good many faces of a "chaotic constitution."[50]

Nor were the differences between the old immigrants and the new limited to intellect or physical appearance, according to Ross: "That the Mediterranean peoples are morally below the races of northern Europe is as certain as any social fact."[51] Moreover, these differences were said to be due to people from Northern Europe surpassing people from Southern Europe "in innate ethical endowment."[52] Ross declared, "I see no reason why races may not differ as much in moral and intellectual traits as obviously they do in bodily traits."[53] Black Americans were mentioned in passing as "several millions of an inferior race."[54] To Ross, the survival of a superior race and culture depended on awareness of, and pride in, that superiority:

> The superiority of a race cannot be preserved without *pride of blood* and an uncompromising attitude toward the lower races. . . Since the higher culture should be kept pure as well as the higher blood, that race is stronger which, down to the cultivator or the artisan, has *a strong sense of its superiority*.[55]

Francis A. Walker was a leading economist of the second half of the nineteenth century. He was not a Progressive, by any means, but his views on immigrants from Southern and Eastern Europe were views that later became dominant in the Progressive era of the early twentieth century. He proposed strict restrictions on immigration, not only quantitatively, but qualitatively. He proposed to measure quality by requiring each immigrant to post a $100 bond upon entering the country— a sum vastly more than most Jewish, Italian or other immigrants from Eastern Europe or Southern Europe had with them at that time. He said that the restrictions he proposed "would not prevent tens of thousands of thrifty Swedes, Norwegians, Germans, and men of other nationalities coming hither at their own charges, since great numbers of these people now bring more than that amount of money with them."[56] Such a requirement, he said, would "raise the average quality, socially and industrially, of the immigrants actually entering the country."[57]

Walker saw a need to protect "the American standard of living, and the quality of American citizenship from degradation through the tumultuous access of vast throngs of ignorant and brutalized peasantry from the countries of eastern and southern Europe."[58] He pointed out that, in earlier times, immigrants "came almost exclusively from western or northern Europe" and "immigrants from southern Italy, Hungary, Austria, and Russia together made up hardly more than one per cent of our immigration." Now those proportions had changed completely, bringing "vast masses of peasantry, degraded below our utmost conceptions." He said: "They are beaten men from beaten races; representing the worst failures in the struggle for existence."[59]

Without restrictions on immigration, Professor Walker declared that "every foul and stagnant pool of population in Europe," from places where "no breath of intellectual life has stirred for ages," would be "decanted upon our shores."[60] Nor were the people of Eastern and Southern Europe the only ones dismissed as hopeless by Walker. The indigenous American Indians Walker dismissed as "savages," who were "without forethought and without self-control, singularly susceptible to evil influences, with strong animal appetites and no intellectual tastes or aspirations to hold those appetites in check."[61]

Another prominent contemporary economist, Richard T. Ely, one of the founders of the American Economic Association, was similarly dismissive of blacks, saying that they "are for the most part grown-up children, and should be treated as such."[62] Professor Ely was also concerned about classes that he considered inferior: "We must give to the most hopeless classes left behind in our social progress custodial care with the highest possible development and with segregation of sexes and confinement to prevent reproduction."[63]

Richard T. Ely was not only a Progressive during the Progressive era, he espoused the kinds of ideas that defined the Progressive era, years before that era began. He rejected free market economics[64] and saw government power as something to be applied "to the amelioration of the conditions under which people live or work." Far from seeing government intervention as a reduction of freedom, he redefined freedom, so that the "regulation by the power of the state of these industrial and other social relations existing among men is a condition of freedom." While state action might "lessen the amount of theoretical liberty" it would "increase control over nature in the individual, and promote the growth of practical liberty."[65]

Like other Progressives, Richard T. Ely advocated the cause of conservation, of labor unions, and favored the "coercive philanthropy" of the state.[66] He said, "I believe that such natural resources as forests and mineral wealth should belong to the people" and also believed that "highways or railroads as well as telegraph and parcels post" should also be owned by "the community." He also favored "public ownership" of municipal utilities[67] and declared that "labor unions should be legally encouraged in their efforts for shorter hours and higher wages" and that "inheritance and income taxes should be generally extended."[68] In short, in the course of his long lifetime Professor Ely was a Progressive before, during and after the Progressive era.

While leading traditional economists of that era, such as Alfred Marshall in England and John Bates Clark in the United States, condemned minimum wage laws for creating unemployment, economists of a Progressive orientation advocated such laws as a way of preventing "low-wage races" such as Chinese immigrants from lowering the standard of living of American workers. Professor John R. Commons, for example, said "The competition has no respect for the superior races," so that " the race with lowest necessities displaces others." Professor Arthur Holcombe of Harvard, and a president of the American Political Science Association, referred approvingly of Australia's minimum wage law as a means to "protect the white Australian's standard of living from the invidious competition of the colored races, particularly of the Chinese."[69]

Eugenics, however, was not confined to trying to reduce the reproduction of particular races. Many of its advocates targeted also people of the sort whom Harvard economist Frank Taussig called "those saturated with alcohol or tainted with hereditary disease," as well as "the irretrievable criminals and tramps." If it was not feasible to "chloroform them once and for all," Professor Taussig said, then "at least they can be segregated, shut up in refuges and asylums, and prevented from propagating their kind."[70] In Sweden in later years, Nobel Prizewinning economist Gunnar Myrdal supported programs which sterilized 60,000 people from 1941 through 1975.[71]

Many academics, including some of great distinction, were supporters of eugenics during the Progressive era. Professor Irving Fischer of Yale, the leading American monetary economist of his day, was one of the founders of the American Eugenics Society. Professor Fischer advocated the prevention of the "breeding of the worst" by "isolation in public institutions and in some cases by surgical operation."[72] Professor Henry Rogers Seager of Columbia University, who would become sufficiently recognized to be selected as president of the American Economic Association, likewise said that "we must courageously cut off lines of heredity that have been proved to be undesirable," even if that requires "isolation or sterilization."[73] Stanford University's president David Starr Jordan declared that a nation's "blood" was what "determines its history."[74] Eugenics outlasted the Progressive era. As late as 1928, there were 376 college courses devoted to eugenics.[75]

Those who promoted genetic determinism and eugenics were neither uneducated nor fringe cranks. Quite the contrary. Edward A. Ross, Francis A. Walker and Richard T. Ely all had Ph.D.s from leading universities and were professors at leading universities. Edward A. Ross was the author of 28 books, whose sales were estimated at approximately half a million copies, and he was regarded as one of the founders of the profession of sociology in the United States.[76] He held a Ph.D. in economics from Johns Hopkins University and, at various times, served as Secretary of the American Economic Association as well as President of the American Sociological Association, and head of the American Civil Liberties Union. Among the places where his articles appeared were the *Annals of the American Academy of Political and Social Science*.

Ross was in the mainstream of Progressive intellectuals at the highest levels. He was a man of the left who had supported Eugene V. Debs in the 1894 Pullman strike and had advocated public ownership and regulation of public utilities. Active as a public intellectual in print and on the lecture circuit, Professor Ross referred to "us liberals" as people who speak up "for public interests against powerful selfish private interests," and denounced those who disagreed with his views as unworthy "kept" spokesmen for special interests, a "mercenary corps" as contrasted with "us champions of the social welfare."[77]

Roscoe Pound credited Ross with setting him "in the path the world is moving in."[78] Ross praised the muckrakers of his day and was also said to have been influential with Progressive Presidents Theodore Roosevelt and Woodrow Wilson.[79] The introduction to one of Ross' books included a letter of fulsome praise from TR.[80] The voters' repudiation of the Progressives in the years after the Woodrow Wilson presidency Ross referred to as the "Great Ice Age (1919–31)."[81] In self-righteousness, as well as in ideology, he was a Progressive, a man of the left.

Francis A. Walker was similarly prominent in the economics profession of his day. He was the first president of the American Economic Association— and the Francis A. Walker medal, created in 1947, was the highest award given by the American Economic Association until 1977, when it was discontinued as a result of the creation of a Nobel Prize in economics. Professor Walker was also General Walker in the Union army during the Civil War. He was, at various times, also president of the American Statistical Association and the Massachusetts Institute of Technology. He was also in charge of the ninth and tenth censuses of the United States, a Commissioner of Indian Affairs, and was elected a fellow of the American Academy of Arts and Sciences.

After Walker's death in 1897, commemorative articles appeared in the scholarly journal of the American Statistical Association, in the *Quarterly Journal of Economics*, the first scholarly journal of the economics profession in the United States, published at Harvard, as well as in the *Journal of Political Economy*, published at the University of Chicago, and an obituary also appeared in the *Economic Journal*, England's premier scholarly journal of the economics profession.

Richard T. Ely received his Ph.D. *summa cum laude* from the University of Heidelberg and was the author of many books, one of which sold more than a million copies.[82] Among the prominent people who were his students were the already mentioned Edward A. Ross and Woodrow Wilson, both of whom studied under him at Johns Hopkins University.[83] He was also considered "a major contributing force in making the University of Wisconsin a vital institution wielding a profound influence upon the political economy of the State and the nation."[84] Ely has been called "the father of institutional economics,"[85] the field in which one of his students, John R. Commons, made his name at the University of Wisconsin. Richard T. Ely's death in 1943 was marked by tributes on both sides of the Atlantic, including an obituary in Britain's *Economic Journal*.[86] On into the twenty-first century, one of the honors awarded annually by the American Economic Association to a distinguished economist has been an invitation to give the association's Richard T. Ely Lecture.

In short, Edward A. Ross, Francis A. Walker and Richard T. Ely were not only "in the mainstream"— to use a term that has become common in our times— they were among the elite of the mainstream. But that was no more indication of the validity of what they said then than it is among today's elite of the mainstream.

While Madison Grant was not an academic scholar, he moved among prominent members of the intelligentsia. His closest friends included George Bird Grinnell, editor of the elite sportsman's magazine *Forest and Stream*, and Henry Fairfield Osborn, a world-renowned paleontologist who coined the term "tyrannosaurus rex." Osborn said, in the wake of mass mental testing: "We have learned once and for all that the negro is not like us."[87] In short, Madison Grant, Edward A. Ross, Francis A. Walker and Richard T. Ely were part of the intellectual currents of the times, in an era when leading intellectuals saw mental test results as confirming innate racial differences, when immigration was severely restricted for racial reasons, and when the Ku Klux Klan was revived and spread beyond the South, becoming an especially strong political force in the Midwest. As even a critical biographer of Madison Grant said:

> Grant was not an evil man. He did not wake up in the morning and think to himself: "Hmm, I wonder what vile deeds I can commit today." To the contrary, he was by all accounts a sweet, considerate, erudite, and infinitely charming figure.[88]

Madison Grant also moved in socially elite and politically Progressive circles. Theodore Roosevelt welcomed Grant's entry into an exclusive social club that TR had founded.[89] Later, Grant became friends for a time with Franklin D. Roosevelt, addressing him in letters as "My dear Frank," while FDR reciprocated by addressing him as "My dear Madison."[90] The two men met while serving on a commission as civic-minded citizens, and the fact that both suffered crippling illnesses during the 1920s created a personal bond. But Madison Grant's ideas moved far beyond such genteel circles in America. They were avidly seized upon in Nazi Germany, though Grant's death in 1937 spared him from learning of the ultimate consequences of such ideas, which culminated in the Holocaust.

George Horace Lorimer, long-time editor of the *Saturday Evening Post*, was another major supporter of the Progressive movement in the early twentieth century and his magazine, with a readership of four to five million readers per week,[91] carried weight politically and socially. He supported both Theodore Roosevelt and Progressive Senator Albert Beveridge.[92] In proposing immigration restrictions, Lorimer— like many others of that era— invoked "science" as opposed to "the Pollyanna school."[93] In an editorial in the *Saturday Evening Post*, Lorimer warned against "our racial degeneration" as a result of immigration, which he said could end with Americans having to "forfeit our high estate and join the lowly ranks of the mongrel races."[94]

In the early 1920s, Lorimer assigned novelist and future Pulitzer Prize winner Kenneth L. Roberts to write a series of articles on immigration for the *Saturday Evening Post*. In one of these articles Roberts referred to "the better-class Northern and Western Europeans" who "are particularly fine types of immigrants," as contrasted with "the queer, alien, mongrelized people of Southeastern Europe."[95] These articles were later republished as a book titled *Why Europe Leaves Home*. In this book, Roberts said, among other things, "the Jews of Poland are human parasites,"[96] that people from the Austro-Hungarian Empire were "inconceivably backward."[97] He added:

> The American nation was founded and developed by the Nordic race, but if a few more million members of the Alpine, Mediterranean and Semitic races are poured among us, the result must inevitably be a hybrid race of people as worthless and futile as the good-for-nothing mongrels of Central America and Southeastern Europe.[98]

Like many others of that era, Roberts invoked the notion of a "scientific" approach to immigration law,[99] while contrasting "the desirable immigrants from Northwestern Europe" with the "undesirables" who "came from Southern and Eastern European countries."[100]

Progressive muckraking journalist George Creel, a former member of Woodrow Wilson's administration, wrote articles on immigration in 1921 and 1922 in *Collier's* magazine, another leading mass circulation publication of that era. In these articles he made the familiar contrast between the peoples of Northern and Western Europe with the people of Eastern and Southern Europe, using the familiar nomenclature of that time, which called the former Nordics and the latter Alpine and Mediterranean peoples:

> The men and women who first came to America were Nordic— clean-blooded, strong-limbed people from England, Ireland, Scotland, Scandinavia, Belgium, Holland, Germany, and France. The millions that followed them, for a full two centuries, were also Nordic, holding the same customs, ideas, and ideals, fitting into the life they found as skin fits the hand.
>
> Not until 1880 was there any vital change in the character of immigration, and then commenced the tidal waves of two new stocks— the Alpine from central Europe, Slavs for the most part, and the Mediterranean, the small swarthy peoples from southern Italy, Greece, Spain, and northern Africa.[101]

These latter immigrants, Creel described as the "failures, unfits, and misfits of the Old World."[102] Creel said, "those coming from eastern Europe were morally, physically, and mentally the worst in the history of immigration."[103]

While H.L. Mencken was another prominent intellectual during the Progressive era, he was by no means a Progressive. Yet his view of blacks was very much like that of other intellectuals of the times. Writing in 1908, he wrote of "the hopelessly futile and fatuous effort to improve the negroes of the Southern United States by education." He added:

> It is apparent, on brief reflection, that the negro, no matter how much he is educated, must remain, as a race, in a condition of subservience; that he must remain the inferior of the stronger and more intelligent white man so long as he retains racial differentiation. Therefore, the effort to educate him has awakened in his mind ambitions and aspirations which, in the very nature of things, must go unrealized, and so, while gaining nothing whatever materially, he has lost all his old contentment, peace of mind and happiness. Indeed, it is a commonplace of observation in the United States that the educated and refined negro is invariably a hopeless, melancholy, embittered and despairing man.[104]

Similar views of blacks were expressed in other early writings by H.L. Mencken, though blacks were not the only group viewed negatively in those writings:

> The negro loafer is not a victim of restricted opportunity and oppression. There are schools for him, and there is work for him, and he disdains both. That his forty-odd years of freedom have given him too little opportunity to show his mettle is a mere theory of the chair. As a matter of fact, the negro, in the mass, seems to be going backward. The most complimentary thing that can be said of an individual of the race today is that he is as industrious and honest a man as his grandfather, who was a slave. There are exceptional negroes of intelligence and ability, I am well aware, just as there are miraculous Russian Jews who do not live in filth; but the great bulk of the race is made up of inefficients.[105]

However, by 1926, H.L. Mencken had changed his position somewhat. In a review of a book of essays by leading black intellectuals, edited by Alain Locke, himself a leading black intellectual of the times, Mencken wrote:

> This book, it seems to me, is a phenomenon of immense significance. What it represents is the American Negro's final emancipation from his inferiority complex, his bold decision to go it alone. That inferiority complex, until very recently, conditioned all of his thinking, even (and perhaps especially) when he was bellowing most vociferously for his God-given rights.
> . . .
> As I have said, go read the book. And, having read it, ask yourself the simple question: could you imagine a posse of *white* Southerners doing anything so dignified, so dispassionate, so striking? . . . As one who knows the South better than most, and has had contact with most of its intellectuals, real and Confederate, I must say frankly that I can imagine no such thing. Here, indeed, the Negro challenges the white Southerner on a common ground, and beats him hands down.[106]

Yet Mencken was by no means sanguine about the prospects of the black population as a whole:

> The vast majority of the people of their race are but two or three inches removed from gorillas: it will be a sheer impossibility, for a long, long while, to interest them in anything above pork-chops and bootleg gin.[107]

Like many other intellectuals of the early twentieth century, H.L. Mencken in 1937 favored eugenics measures— in this case, voluntary sterilization of males, encouraged by rewards to be supplied by private philanthropy. As in the past, he included white Southerners among those considered undesirable. He suggested that the answers to many social problems would be "to sterilize large numbers of American freemen, both white and black, to the end that they could no longer beget their kind." For this "the readiest way to induce them to submit would be to indemnify them in cash." The alternative, he said, would be "supporting an ever-increasing herd of morons for all eternity."[108]

Not all eugenicists were racial determinists, as Mencken's inclusion of white Southerners in his eugenics agenda in 1937 indicated. In England, H.G. Wells rejected the singling out of particular races for extinction, though he recommended that undesirable people of whatever race be targeted.[109] Writing in 1916, Wells said:

> Now I am a writer rather prejudiced against the idea of nationality; my habit of thought is cosmopolitan; I hate and despise a shrewish suspicion of foreigners and foreign ways; a man who can look me in the face, laugh with me, speak truth and deal fairly, is my brother, though his skin is as black as ink or as yellow as an evening primrose.[110]

American novelist and radical Jack London, however, declared, "the Anglo-Saxon is a race of mastery" and is "best fitted for survival." He said, "the inferior races must undergo destruction, or some humane form of economic slavery, is inevitable."[111] While Jack London was a man of the left during the Progressive era, he was not a Progressive. He boldly declared himself a socialist.

Woodrow Wilson, one of two American presidents who was also an intellectual in our sense of one who for years earned his living from the production of ideas (the other being Theodore Roosevelt), praised the movie *The Birth of A Nation*, which glorified the Ku Klux Klan, and had a private showing of it in the White House, to which prominent political figures were invited.[112] It was during the Progressive administration of Woodrow Wilson that the Bureau of the Census and the Bureau of Printing and Engraving began to segregate black and white employees. The Post Office Department not only began to segregate its black and white employees in Washington during the Wilson administration, but also began to fire and downgrade black postal employees in the South, as did the Department of the Treasury. President Wilson expressed his approval of these actions.[113]

The academic world was by no means exempt from the racial and social beliefs of the times. In early twentieth century America, during an era when most applicants to even highly prestigious colleges were admitted, there were both formal and informal restrictions on the admissions of Jews, Harvard being one of the few institutions to openly admit imposing quota limits, though a 1909 article characterized anti-Semitism as "more dominant at Princeton" (under Woodrow Wilson) than at any of the other institutions surveyed. In 1910, students at Williams College demonstrated against the admission of Jews. In 1922, Yale's dean of admission said: "The opinion is general in the Faculty that the proportion of those in college whose racial elements are such as not to permit of assimilation has been exceeded and that the most noticeable representatives among those regarded as undesirable are the Jewish boys."[114]

Such views on race or ethnicity were not inevitably entailed by the principles of Progressivism, though they were not precluded by those principles either. During the Progressive era itself, Theodore Roosevelt had a very different view of the *potential* of blacks than did many other Progressives. In response to a British historian who expressed a fear that the black and yellow races would rise in the world to the point of challenging the white race, Theodore Roosevelt said: "By that time the descendant of the negro may be as intellectual as the Athenian."[115] Moreover, he also believed in equal opportunity for other minorities.[116]

Nevertheless, Roosevelt's low estimate of the *contemporary* level of knowledge and understanding among black Americans[117] might place him under at least a suspicion of racism by those today who project contemporary standards back into the past, or who perhaps think of the black population of the past as if they were simply today's black population living in an earlier time, rather than a population which in that era included millions of people who had not yet acquired even the ability to read and write.

One of the ironies of Madison Grant's theories was that he was a descendant of Scots who emigrated after the failed uprisings against the English in 1745. In earlier centuries, Scotland had been one of the most backward nations on the fringes of European civilization, even though

Grant classified the Scots as Nordics, who were supposedly superior intellectually. Later, Scots had a spectacular rise to the forefront of European and world civilization, in too brief a time— as history is measured— for there to have been any major change in the genetic make-up of Scotland's population. In short, the history of his own ancestral homeland provided some of the strongest evidence against Grant's theories of genetic determinism. So do other major reversals in technological and other leadership among nations, races and civilizations, such as the reversal of the positions of China and Europe already noted. There are many peoples and nations that have experienced their "golden age," only to later fall behind, or even be conquered by, their erstwhile inferiors.

The wider the sweep of history that is surveyed, the more dramatic reversals of the relative positions of nations and races there are. A tenth-century Muslim scholar noted that Europeans grow more pale the farther north you go and also that the "farther they are to the north the more stupid, gross, and brutish they are."[118] However offensive this correlation between skin color and intellectual development may seem today, there is no reason in history to challenge it as an empirical generalization, as of that particular time. Mediterranean Europe was more advanced than northern Europe for centuries, beginning in ancient times, when the Greeks and Romans laid many of the foundations of Western civilization, at a time when the peoples of Britain and Scandinavia lived in illiterate and far less advanced societies.

Like the tenth-century Muslim scholar, Madison Grant saw a correlation between skin color and intelligence, but he explicitly attributed that correlation to genetics. Among other things, he explained the over-representation of mulattoes among the black elite of his day by their Caucasian genes, and Edward Byron Reuter made an empirical sociological study of the same phenomenon, reaching the same conclusion.[119] In a later period, intellectuals would explain the same phenomenon by the bias of whites in favor of people who looked more like themselves.

Regardless of what either theory says, the facts show that the actual skills and behavior of blacks and mulattoes had historically been demonstrably different, especially in nineteenth and early twentieth century America. These were not mere "perceptions" or "stereotypes," as so many inconvenient observations have been labeled. A study of nineteenth century Philadelphia, for example, found crime rates higher among the black population than among the mulatto population.[120] It is not necessary to believe that crime rates are genetically determined, but it is also not necessary to believe that it was all just a matter of perceptions by whites.[121]

During the era of slavery, mulattoes were often treated differently from blacks, especially when the mulattoes were the offspring of the slave owner. This difference in treatment existed not only in the United States but throughout the Western Hemisphere. Mulattoes were a much higher proportion of the population of "free persons of color" than they were of the populations of slaves throughout the Western Hemisphere, and women were far more often freed than were men.[122] These initial differences, based on personal favoritism, led to long-term differences based on earlier opportunities to begin acquiring human capital as free people, generations before the Emancipation Proclamation.

In short, "free persons of color" had a generations-long head start in acculturation, urbanization and general experience as free people. The rate of literacy reached by the "free persons of color" in 1850 would not be reached by the black population as a whole until 70 years later.[123] Neither within groups nor between groups can differences be discussed in the abstract, in a world where the concrete is what determines people's fates. Among Americans of African descent, as within and between other groups, *people are not random events* to which statistical probability theories can be blithely applied— and correlation is not causation.

Against the background of head starts by those freed from slavery generations ahead of others, it is not so surprising that, in the middle of the twentieth century, most of the Negro professionals in Washington, D.C. were by all indications descendants of the antebellum "free persons of color"[124]— a group that was never more than 14 percent of the American Negro population.[125] Because many of these professionals— such as doctors, lawyers and teachers— worked primarily or exclusively within the black community in mid-twentieth-century Washington, favoritism by *contemporary* whites had little or nothing to do with their success, even though the human capital which produced that success developed ultimately from the favoritism shown their ancestors a century or more earlier.

Neither genetics nor contemporary environment is necessary to explain differences in human capital between blacks and mulattoes— differences that were much more pronounced in earlier years than today, after the black population as a whole has had more time and opportunities as free people to acquire more human capital. Similarly, neither genetics nor contemporary environment is necessary to explain differences in skills, behavior, attitudes and values among other racial groups or sub-groups in many other countries around the world, since many of these groups differed greatly in their history, in their geographic settings and in other ways.

Madison Grant asserted that "the intelligence and ability of a colored person are in pretty direct proportion to the amount of white blood he has, and that most of the positions of leadership, influence, and prominence in the Negro race are held not by real Negroes but by Mulattoes, many of whom have very little Negro blood. This is so true that to find a black Negro in a conspicuous position is a matter of comment."[126] But, like so much else that was said by him and by others of like mind, it verbally eternalized a contemporary pattern by attributing that pattern to genetics, just as many Progressive-era intellectuals disdained the peoples of Southern Europe, who had by all indices once been far more advanced in ancient times than the Nordics who were said to be genetically superior. The Greeks and Romans had the Parthenon and the Coliseum, not to mention literature and giants of philosophy, at a time when there was not a single building in Britain, a country inhabited at that time by illiterate tribes.

RESPONSES TO DISPARITIES

We have already seen some of the many disparities in achievements among racial or ethnic groups in Chapter 7. Such examples could be extended almost indefinitely.[127] Although economic and social inequalities among racial and ethnic groups have attracted much attention from intellectuals, seldom today has this attention been directed primarily toward how the less economically successful and less socially prestigious groups might improve themselves by availing themselves of the culture of others around them, so as to become more productive and compete more effectively with other groups in the economy. When David Hume urged his fellow eighteenth-century Scots to master the English language,[128] as they did, both he and they were following a pattern very different from the pattern of most minority intellectuals and their respective groups in other countries around the world. The spectacular rise of the Scots in the eighteenth and nineteenth centuries— eventually surpassing the English in engineering and medicine,[129] for example— was also an exception, rather than the rule.

A much more common pattern has been one in which the intelligentsia have demanded an equality of economic outcomes and of social recognition, irrespective of the skills, behavior or performance of the group to which they belong or on whose behalf they spoke. In some countries today, any claim that intergroup differences in outcomes are results of intergroup differences in skills, behavior or performance are dismissed by the intelligentsia as false "perceptions," "prejudices," or "stereotypes," or else are condemned as "blaming the victim." Seldom are any of these assertions backed up by empirical evidence or logical analysis that would make them anything more than arbitrary assertions that happen to be in vogue among contemporary intellectual elites.

In direct contrast with the Scots, who mastered the language of the English— and the broader range of knowledge, skills and culture to which that language gave them access— other groups in a position to rise by acquiring the knowledge and skills available in another language or culture have resented having to advance in that way.

In the days of the Russian Empire, for example, most of the merchants, artisans, and industrialists in the Baltic port city of Riga were German,[130] even though Germans were less than one-fourth of that city's population.[131] Education at Dorpat University in Riga was conducted in German, as was most of the educational activity in the city.[132] Not only in Riga, but in Latvia as a whole, the upper classes were mostly German and the lower classes mostly Latvian. However, those Latvians who wanted to rise could become part of the elite German culture and intermarry into the German community. But a newly emerging Latvian educated class, many educated at Dorpat

University, resented having to become culturally German in order to rise, and initiated the politics of ethnic identity instead.[133] They saw Latvians as a people "consigned by long oppression to lowly stations in life."[134]

A very similar process occurred in the Habsburg Empire, where the Germans in Bohemia were an educated elite and where Czechs there who wanted to rise into that elite could do so by acquiring the German language and culture. But a new Czech intelligentsia, lincluding university students and school teachers, promoted Czech cultural nationalism.[135] Czech nationalists, for example, insisted that street signs in Prague, which had been in both Czech and German, henceforth be exclusively in Czech.[136] Symbolism— including intolerance toward other people's symbols— has often marked the efforts of an ethnic intelligentsia. The rising indigenous intelligentsia— whether in Latvia, Bohemia or elsewhere— tended to treat the cultural advantages of Germans as a *social* injustice, against which they mobilized other members of their ethnic group to oppose Germans and German culture.

Whether in the Baltic or in Bohemia, the Germans tended to be more cosmopolitan, and initially resisted efforts by the newly arising indigenous intelligentsia to fragment society along ethnic lines. But the persistent and increasing promotion of ethnic identity by the newly rising ethnic intelligentsia eventually led the Germans to abandon their cosmopolitanism and defend themselves as Germans.[137] The net result in both countries was ethnic polarization, often under the banner of some variation of "social justice," requiring the lagging group to be put on a par through some process other than their own acquisition of the same knowledge and skills as others.

Similar polarization has been produced in other countries with the rise of a newly educated intelligentsia— usually educated in "soft" fields, rather than in the sciences or in other subjects that would produce marketable skills with which to compete with members of other ethnic groups who already had such skills and experience. One historical study referred to the "well-educated but underemployed" Czech young men who promoted ethnic identity in the nineteenth century[138]— a description that would apply to many ethnic identity promoters in other parts of Europe and Asia, as well as in the United States, then and now. The "educated unemployed" became a common expression in the twentieth century,[139] whether in Europe, Asia or elsewhere— and such people became common sources of ethnic polarization.

Newly educated classes have been especially likely to specialize in softer subjects and to be prominent among those fostering hostility toward more advanced groups, while promoting ethnic "identity" movements, whether such movements have been mobilized against other ethnic groups, the existing authorities, or other targets. In various periods of history, the intelligentsia in general and newly educated people in particular have inflamed group against group, promoting discriminatory policies and/or physical violence in such disparate countries as India,[140] Hungary,[141] Nigeria,[142] Kazakhstan,[143] Romania,[144] Sri Lanka,[145] Canada,[146] and Czechoslovakia.[147]

Whether at the level of minority activists in a given society or at the level of leaders of national revolts against external imperial powers, promoters of nationalism have been disproportionately intellectuals— and intellectuals from a limited range of fields. "Few nationalist militants were engineers or economists, or professional administrators," as a study of nationalism said of the generation of African leaders during the transition from colonial status to that of independent nations in the twentieth century. For example, Kwame Nkrumah was a British-educated lawyer, Jomo Kenyatta an anthropologist, and Léopold Senghor a poet.[148] Much the same pattern could be found in other parts of the world as well. Leaders of the Basque separatist movement in Spain and of the Quebec separatist movement in Canada were also soft-subject intellectuals.[149]

In the less developed eastern regions of Europe, the rising intellectual class during the years between the two World Wars likewise tended to concentrate in the softer subjects, rather than in science or technology, and to seek careers in politics and government bureaucracies, rather than in industry or commerce. As a scholarly history of that era put it, institutions of higher education in East Central Europe turned out a "surplus academic proletariat" which could not be absorbed into "economically or socially functional employment" because they were trained primarily in law or the humanities.[150] Romanian institutions of higher education were described as "numerically swollen, academically rather lax, and politically overheated," serving as "veritable incubators of surplus bureaucrats, politicians, and demagogues."[151]

Much the same pattern would be apparent decades later in Sri Lanka, which was all too typical of Asian Third World countries in having "a backlog of unemployed graduates" who had specialized in the humanities and the social sciences.[152] Ethnic leaders who would later promote the breakup of Yugoslavia, and the atrocities that followed in the last decade of the twentieth century, included professors in the humanities and the social sciences, as well as a novelist and a psychiatrist.[153] The mass slaughters in Kampuchea under the Khmer Rouge were likewise led principally by intellectuals, including teachers and academics.[154]

Historian A.J.P. Taylor has said that the first stage of nationalism "is led by university professors" and that "the second stage comes when the pupils of the professors get out into the world."[155] Whatever the actual sequence, the intelligentsia in many countries around the world have played a central role in promoting intergroup and international animosities and atrocities— and in trying to artificially preserve, revive, or fabricate past glories.

Conversely, the historic examples of dramatic self-improvement in nineteenth-century Japan and eighteenth-century Scotland— countries that set out to change themselves, rather than to blame others— concentrated on building tangible skills, such as in engineering and medicine in the case of Scotland, and science and technology in the case of Japan.[*] By contrast, in the twentieth century a whole generation of future Third World leaders who went to study in the West seldom concentrated on studying the science, technology or entrepreneurship that produced Western prosperity, but instead concentrated on the social theories and ideologies in vogue among Western intellectuals in academia and elsewhere. The countries they led after independence often paid a high price in economic stagnation or even retrogression, as well as in internal polarization that turned group against group.

Language politics has been one aspect of more general polarization that has poisoned relations between more prosperous and less prosperous groups in India, Malaysia, and Sri Lanka, among other places where the lagging

---

[*] In addition to sending their young people abroad to study Western technology and science, the Japanese brought so many Scottish engineers to their own country that there was a Presbyterian church established in Japan.

majority tried to insulate themselves from competition with more successful minorities by making their own language a prerequisite for education and/or employment.[156] In Asia, as in Europe, Africa and the Western Hemisphere, the intelligentsia have been prominent among those pushing ethnic identity ideology and intergroup polarization.

Under such influences, Sri Lanka went from being a country whose record for harmonious relations between majority and minority were held up to the world as a model by many observers, in the mid-twentieth century, to a country whose later ethnic polarization produced decades of mob violence and then outright civil war, in which unspeakable atrocities were committed, on into the early twenty-first century.[157]

The polarization between Czechs and Germans in nineteenth century Bohemia took longer to reach the level of historic tragedy but nevertheless it did. A key turning point came when the new nation of Czechoslovakia was created in the twentieth century, from the breakup of the Habsburg Empire after the First World War, with the former kingdom of Bohemia now being Czechoslovakia's most economically and culturally advanced region— in part because of the Germans living in a section of that region called the Sudetenland. As one indicator of the wide cultural differences among the various peoples of this small country was that the illiteracy rate in Bohemia was only 2 percent in 1921, while half the people in the province of Ruthenia were illiterate.[158] Much of Czechoslovakia's industry was located in Bohemia and a substantial proportion of it was in the hands of the Sudeten Germans.

Now armed with the power of government of their own country, Czech leaders set about "correcting" both historic and contemporary "injustices" — namely the fact that the Germans were more economically and otherwise advanced than the Czechs and other groups in the country. The government instituted preferential hiring of Czechs in the civil service and transferred capital from German and German-Jewish banks to Czech banks, as well as breaking up large German-owned estates into smaller farms, for the benefit of the Czech peasantry.[159] Violent German protests led to Czech soldiers shooting and killing more than fifty Germans,[160] setting the stage for a continuing bitter escalation of the polarization between Czechs and Germans, leading to larger tragedies in the decades that followed.

Nazi Germany annexed the Sudetenland in 1938 and then took over the rest of Czechoslovakia in 1939. With the country now under Nazi rule, the roles of Czechs and Germans were reversed, with brutal suppression of the Czechs that lasted until the defeat of Germany in 1945 allowed the Czechs to take control of the country once again. In the bitter backlash that followed, there was both official discrimination against Germans in Czechoslovakia and widespread unofficial and often lethal violence against Germans, more than three million of whom were expelled from the country, leaving behind a German population less than one-tenth of what it had once been.[161]

The Germans' skills and experience were of course expelled with them, and these were not easily replaced. Half a century later, there were still deserted towns and farmhouses in the Sudeten region, from which the Germans had been expelled[162]— mute testimony to the inconvenient fact that differences between Czechs and Germans were not simply matters of perceptions or injustices, unless one chooses to characterize historical circumstantial differences as injustices. All this was part of the price paid for seeking cosmic justice for intertemporal abstractions, in a world where maintaining peace and civility among flesh-and-blood contemporaries is often a major challenge by itself.

Whether in Europe, Asia, Africa or the Western Hemisphere, a common pattern among intellectuals has been to seek, or demand, equality of results without equality of causes— or on sheer presumptions of equality of causes. Nor have such demands been limited to intellectuals within the lagging groups, whether minorities or majorities. Outside intellectuals, including intellectuals in other countries, have often discussed statistical differences in incomes and other outcomes as "disparities," and "inequities" that need to be "corrected," as if they were discussing abstract people in an abstract world.

The corrections being urged are seldom corrections within the lagging groups, such as Hume urged upon his fellow Scots in the eighteenth century. Today, the prevailing tenets of multiculturalism declare all cultures equal, sealing members of lagging groups within a bubble of their current habits and practices, much as believers in multiculturalism have sealed themselves within a bubble of peer-consensus dogma.

There are certain possibilities that many among the intelligentsia cannot even acknowledge as possibilities, much less try to test empirically, which would be risking a whole vision of the world— and of themselves— on a roll of the dice. Chief among these is the possibility that the most fundamental disparity among people is in their disparities in wealth-generating capabilities, of which the disparities in income and wealth are results, rather than causes. Other disparities, whether in crime, violence and alcohol intake or other social pathology, may also have internal roots. But these possibilities as well are not allowed inside the sealed bubble of the prevailing vision.

One of the consequences of this vision is that blatant economic and other differences among groups, for which explanations due to factors internal to the lagging group are not allowed inside the sealed bubble of the multicultural vision, must be explained by external causes. If group *A* has higher incomes or higher other achievements than group *B*, then the vision of cosmic justice transforms *A*'s good fortune into *B*'s grievance— and not a grievance against fate, the gods, geography or the cosmos, but specifically a grievance against *A*. This formula has been applied around the world, whether turning Czechs against Germans, Malays against Chinese, Ugandans against Indians, Sinhalese against Tamils or innumerable other groups against those more successful than themselves.

The contribution of the intelligentsia to this process has often been to verbally conjure up a vision in which *A* has acquired wealth by taking it from *B*— the latter being referred to as "exploited," "dispossessed," or in some other verbal formulation that explains the economic disparity by a transfer of wealth from *B* to *A*. It does not matter if there is no speck of evidence that *B* was economically better off before *A* arrived on the scene. Nor does it matter how much evidence there may be that *B* became demonstrably worse off after *A* departed the scene, whether it was the Ugandan economy collapsing after the expulsions of Indians and Pakistanis in the 1970s, the desolation in the Sudeten region of Czechoslovakia after the Germans were expelled in 1945, or the continuing urban desolation of many black ghettoes across the United States, decades after the riots of the 1960s drove out many of the white-owned businesses that were supposedly exploiting ghetto residents.

Not only is empirical evidence that *A* made *B* poorer seldom considered necessary, considerable evidence that *A*'s presence kept *B* from being even poorer is often ignored. In Third World countries whose poverty has often been attributed to "exploitation" by Western nations, it is not uncommon for those indigenous people most in contact with Westerners in port cities and other places to be visibly less poor than indigenous people out in the hinterlands remote from Western contacts or influence.[163]

To think of some people as simply being higher achievers than others, for whatever reason, is a threat to today's prevailing vision, for it implicitly places the onus on the lagging group to achieve more— and, perhaps more important, deprives the intelligentsia of their role of fighting on the side of the angels against the forces of evil. The very concept of achievement fades into the background, or disappears completely, in some of the verbal formulations of the intelligentsia, where those who turn out to be more successful *ex post* are depicted as having been "privileged" *ex ante*.

How far this vision can depart from reality was shown by a report titled ***Ethno-Racial Inequality in the City of Toronto***, which said, "the Japanese are among the most privileged groups in the city"[164] because they were more successful economically than either the other minorities there or the white majority. What makes this conclusion grotesque is a documented history of anti-Japanese discrimination in Canada,[165] where people of Japanese ancestry were interned during the Second World War longer than Japanese Americans were.

Similarly, members of the Chinese minority in Malaysia have been characterized as having "privilege" and the Malay majority as being "deprived," despite a history of official preferential treatment of Malays, going all the way back to British colonial days, when the government provided free education to Malays but the Chinese had to get their own.[166] There is no question that the Chinese greatly *outperformed* the Malays, both in education and in the economy— an inconvenient fact evaded by the rhetoric of privilege and deprivation.

Efforts of the intelligentsia to downplay or discredit achievement by verbally transforming it into "privilege" are by no means confined to the case of the Japanese minority in Canada or the Chinese minority in Malaysia. In many countries around the world, the abandoning or discrediting of the concept of achievement leads to blaming higher achieving groups for the fact that other groups are lower achievers, putting the anointed in the familiar role of being on the side of the angels— and putting many societies on the road to racial or ethnic polarization, and sometimes on the road to ruin. In many places around the world, groups who co-existed peacefully for generations have turned violently against one another when both circumstances and verbally and politically skilled "leaders" appeared at the same time, creating a "perfect storm" of polarization. Intellectuals often help create a climate of opinion in which such perfect storms can occur.

The ego stakes of intellectuals discussing racial issues have led not only to formulating these issues in ways that promote moral melodramas, starring themselves on the side of the angels, but also promoting the depiction of those designated as victims as being people who are especially worthy— the noble oppressed. Thus, much sympathy was generated for the many minority groups in the Habsburg and Ottoman Empires that were dismantled in the wake of Woodrow Wilson's doctrine of the "self-determination" of peoples. But the newly created or newly reconstituted nations carved out of these dismantled empires quickly became places marked by the newly empowered minorities oppressing other minorities in the nations now ruled by the erstwhile minorities of the Habsburg or Ottoman Empires. However, these new oppressions seldom attracted much attention from intellectuals who had championed the cause of the Habsburg or Ottoman minorities who were now the new oppressors.

Something similar has happened in the United States, where intellectuals who protested racism against blacks have seldom criticized anti-Semitism or anti-Asian words and deeds among black Americans. The beating up of Asian American school children by black classmates in New York and Philadelphia, for example, has been going on for years,[167] and yet has attracted little attention, much less criticism, from the intelligentsia. Contrary to visions conjured up by some of the intelligentsia, suffering oppression does not make people noble, nor necessarily even tolerant. Moreover, the behavior of the intelligentsia often reflects a pattern in which principles are less important than fashions— and Asian Americans are not in vogue.

There have also been random outbursts of violence of young blacks against whites in various cities across the United States, but these attacks are either not reported in much of the media or else the racial basis for these attacks on strangers is ignored or downplayed, even when the attackers accompany their attacks with anti-white invective.[168]

Chapter 17

Race and Intelligence

T here are few, if any, issues more explosive than the question of whether there are innate differences in intelligence among the various races. Here it is especially important to be clear as to what is meant, and not meant, by "intelligence" in this context. What is not meant are wisdom, skills or even developed mental capabilities in general. Virtually everyone recognizes that these things depend to some extent on circumstances, including upbringing in general and education in particular. Those on both sides of the question of race and intelligence are arguing about something much more fundamental— the innate potential for thinking, what was defined in Chapter 1 as "intellect," the ability to grasp and manipulate complex concepts, without regard to whatever judgment may or may not have been acquired from experience or upbringing.

This has sometimes been called *native* intelligence— the mental capacity with which one was born— but it could more aptly be called the mental *potential* at the time of conception, since the development of the brain can be affected by what happens in the womb between conception and birth. These things can happen differently according to the behavior of the mother, including diet, smoking and intake of alcohol and narcotics, not to mention damage that can occur to the brain during its passage through the birth canal. Genetic mental potential would therefore mean the potential at the moment of conception, rather than at birth, since "native intelligence" has already been affected by environment.

Similarly, if one is comparing the innate potential of races, rather than individuals, then that innate potential as it existed at the dawn of the human species may be different from what it is today, since all races have been subjected to various environmental conditions that can affect what kinds of individuals are more likely or less likely to survive and leave offspring to carry on their family line and the race. Large disparities in the geographic, historic, economic and social conditions in which different races developed for centuries open the possibility that different kinds of individuals have had different probabilities of surviving and flourishing in these different environmental conditions. No one knows if this is true— and this is just one of the many things that no one knows about race and intelligence.

The ferocity of the assertions on both sides of this issue seems to reflect the ideological importance of the dispute— that is, how it affects the visions and the agendas of intellectuals. During the Progressive era, assertions of innate racial differences in intelligence were the basis for proposing sweeping interventions to keep certain races from entering the country and to suppress the reproduction of particular races already living within the country. During the later twentieth century, assertions of innate equality of the races became the basis for proposing sweeping interventions whenever there were substantial statistical differences among the races in incomes, occupational advances and other social outcomes, since such disparities have been regarded as presumptive evidence of discrimination, given the presumed innate equality of the races themselves.

Innate intellectual ability, however, is just one of the many factors that can cause different groups to have different outcomes, whether these are groups that differ by race, sex, religion, nationality or the many other subdivisions of the human species. In short, innate equality of intellectual potential in races, even if it could be proven, would not prove that their differences in outcomes could only be a result of their being treated differently by others— given the many geographic, historic, demographic and other influences affecting the development of individuals and races.

HEREDITY AND ENVIRONMENT

In principle, all the factors affecting intelligence can be dichotomized into those due to heredity and all the remaining influences, which can be put into the category of environment. However, life does not always cooperate with our analytical categories. If environment can affect which hereditary traits are more likely to survive, then these two categories are no longer hermetically sealed off from one another.

If, for example, we take some characteristic that is widely agreed to be affected primarily by genetics— height, for example— it has been argued that the average height of Frenchmen has been lowered by massive casualties in war, as a result of the decimations of French soldiers during the Napoleonic wars or during the First World War, or both, since the biggest and strongest men have been more likely to have been taken into the military forces and sent into battle. Thus two races with initially identical genetic potential for height can end up with different heights, and different genetic potentials for height in future generations, if one race has been subjected more often to conditions more likely to kill off tall people at an early age, before they reproduce sufficiently to replace their numbers and maintain their share of their race's gene pool.

Similarly, some have sought to explain the over-representation of Jews among people with high intellectual achievements by differential survival rates within the Jewish population. It would be hard to think of any other group subjected to such pervasive and relentless persecution, for thousands of years, as the Jews. Such persecutions, punctuated from time to time by mass lethal violence, obviously reduced Jews' survival prospects. According to this hypothesis, if people of only average or below average intelligence were less likely to survive millennia of such persecutions, then— regardless of Jews' initial genetic intellectual potential— a disproportionate share of those who survived physically, and especially of those who could survive *as Jews*, without converting to another religion to escape persecution, were likely to be among the more ingenious.

Whether or not this hypothesis can be validated by empirical research, like the hypothesis about the heights of Frenchmen it demonstrates that heredity theories and environmental theories of group differences are not hermetically sealed off from one another, since environment can influence the survival rate of hereditary characteristics.

Heredity and environment can also interact in many other ways. For example, it is known that children who are the first born have on average higher IQs than their later born siblings.[1] Whatever the reasons for this, if families in group *A* have an average of two children and families in group *B* have an average of six children, then the average IQ in group *A* is likely to be higher than in group *B*— even if the innate genetic potential of the two groups is the same— because half the people in group *A* are first-borns, while only one-sixth of those in group *B* are.

In some cultures, marriage between first cousins is acceptable, or even common, while in other cultures it is taboo. These differences existed long before science discovered the negative consequences of in-breeding— and in some cultures such patterns have continued long after these scientific discoveries. Races, classes or other social groups with very different incest taboos can therefore start out with identical genetic potential and yet end up with different capabilities. The point here is simply that there are too many variables involved for dogmatic pronouncements to be made on either side of the issue of innate equality or innate inequality of the races.

Since there has been no method yet devised to measure the innate potential of individuals at the moment of conception, much less the innate potential of races at the dawn of the human species, the prospect of a definitive answer to the question of the relationship of race and innate mental ability seems remote, if possible at all.

Put differently, the utter certainty of many who have answered this question in one way or in the opposite way seems premature at best, when all that we have at this point, when it comes to race and intelligence, is a small island of knowledge in a vast sea of the unknown. However, neither certainty nor precision have been necessary for making practical decisions on many other questions, so there needs to be some assessment of the magnitude of what is in dispute and then some assessment of how the evidence bears on that practical question.

THE MAGNITUDES IN QUESTION

The genetic determinists of the late nineteenth and early twentieth centuries asserted not merely that there were differences in the average mental capacity of different races, but also that these differences were of a magnitude sufficient to make it urgent to at least reduce the reproduction of some races, as people like Margaret Sanger and Madison Grant suggested, or even to promote "the gradual extinction of an inferior race"[2] as Sir Francis Galton advocated. The mental test scores of that era, which seemed to support not merely a difference in intellectual capacity between races but a difference of a sufficient magnitude to make drastic actions advisable, have since then been shown to be far from having the permanence that was once assumed.

Both the magnitude and the permanence of racial differences on mental tests have been undermined by later empirical research, quite aside from questions about the validity of such tests. As regards magnitude, Professor Arthur R. Jensen of the University of California at Berkeley, whose research published in 1969 reopened the question of racial differences in mental capacity and set off a storm of controversy,[3] provided an insight that is especially salient, since he has been prominent, if not pre-eminent, among contemporaries on the side of hereditary theories of intelligence:

> When I worked in a psychological clinic, I had to give individual intelligence tests to a variety of children, a good many of whom came from an impoverished background. Usually I felt these children were really brighter than their IQ would indicate. They often appeared inhibited in their responsiveness in the testing situation on their first visit to my office, and when this was the case I usually had them come in on two to four different days for half-hour sessions with me in a "play therapy" room, in which we did nothing more than get better acquainted by playing ball, using finger paints, drawing on the blackboard, making things out of clay, and so forth. As soon as the child seemed to be completely at home in this setting, I would retest him on a parallel form of the Stanford-Binet. A boost in IQ of 8 to 10 points or so was the rule; it rarely failed, but neither was the gain very often much above this.[4]

Since "8 to 10 points" is more than half the average I.Q. difference of 15 points between black and white Americans, the disappearance of that much I.Q. differential from a simple change of immediate circumstances suggests that the magnitude of what is in question today is *not* whether some people are capable only of being "hewers of wood and drawers of water." Professor Jensen's conclusions on a practical level are therefore very different from the conclusions of Margaret Sanger, Madison Grant or Sir Francis Galton in earlier years:

Whenever we select a person for some special educational purpose, whether for special instruction in a grade-school class for children with learning problems, or for a "gifted" class with an advanced curriculum, or for college attendance, or for admission to graduate training or a professional school, we are selecting an *individual*, and we are selecting him and dealing with him as an individual for reasons of his individuality. Similarly, when we employ someone, or promote someone in his occupation, or give some special award or honor to someone for his accomplishments, we are doing this to an individual. The variables of social class, race, and national origin are correlated so imperfectly with any of the valid criteria on which the above decisions should depend, or, for that matter, with any behavioral characteristic, that these background factors are irrelevant as a basis for dealing with individuals— as students, as employees, as neighbors. Furthermore, since, as far as we know, the full range of human talents is represented in all the major races of man and in all socioeconomic levels, it is unjust to allow the mere fact of an individual's racial or social background to affect the treatment accorded to him.[5]

Nor was Arthur R. Jensen as confident as the writers of the Progressive era had been about the meaning of a mental test score. Professor Jensen said he had "very little confidence in a single test score, especially if it is the child's first test and more especially if the child is from a poor background and of a different race from the examiner."[6] He also acknowledged the possible effect of home environment. Professor Jensen pointed out that "3 out of 4 Negroes failing the Armed Forces Qualification Test come from families of four or more children."[7]

Jensen's article, which renewed a controversy that has since lasted for decades, was titled "How Much Can We Boost IQ and Scholastic Achievement?" His answer— long since lost in the storms of controversies that followed— was that scholastic achievement could be much improved by different teaching methods, but that these different teaching methods were not likely to change I.Q. scores much.[8]

Far from concluding that lower I.Q. groups were not educable, Jensen said: "One of the great and relatively untapped reservoirs of mental ability in the disadvantaged, it appears from our research, is the basic ability to learn. We can do more to marshal this strength for educational purposes."[9] He argued for educational reforms, saying that "scholastic performance— the acquisition of the basic skills— can be boosted much more, at least in the early years, than can the IQ" and that, among "the disadvantaged," there are "high school students who have failed to learn basic skills which they could easily have learned many years earlier" if taught in different ways.[10]

As someone writing against a later orthodoxy— one in which only such non-genetic factors as test bias and social environment were acceptable as factors behind racial differences in IQ scores— Jensen confronted not only opposing beliefs, but also a dogmatism about those beliefs reminiscent of the opposite dogmatism of genetic determinists of an earlier time. Professor Jensen wrote in 1969: "A preordained, doctrinaire stance with regard to this issue hinders the achievement of a scientific understanding of the problem. To rule out of court, so to speak, any reasonable hypotheses on purely ideological grounds is to argue that static ignorance is preferable to increasing our knowledge of reality."[11]

Jensen was also concerned with social consequences, as well as with questions of scientific findings. He pointed out that "Negro middle- and upper-class families have fewer children than their white counterparts, while Negro lower-class families have more," and that these facts "have some relationship to intellectual ability," as shown by the disproportionate representation of blacks from large families among those who failed the Armed Forces Qualification Test. He said that "current welfare policies"— presumably because they subsidized the birth of more children by black lower-class families— could lead to negative effects on black educational achievement. Jensen concluded that these welfare policies and "the possible consequences of our failure seriously to study these questions may well be viewed by future generations as our society's greatest injustice to Negro Americans."[12]

While controversies about race and I.Q. focus on explanations for the differences in median I.Q.s among groups, the magnitude of those differences is also crucial. Research by Professor James R. Flynn, an American expatriate in New Zealand, concluded that the average I.Q. of Chinese Americans in 1945 to 1949 was 98.5, compared to a norm of 100 for whites.[13] Even if we were to arbitrarily assume, for the sake of argument— as Professor Flynn did *not*— that this difference at that time was due solely to genetics, the magnitude of the difference would hardly justify the kinds of drastic policies advocated by eugenicists. In reality, the occupational achievements of both Chinese

Americans and Japanese Americans exceed those of white Americans with the same I.Q.s. Japanese Americans were found to have occupational achievements equal to that of those whites who had 10 points higher I.Q.s than themselves, and Chinese Americans to have occupational achievements equal to those of those whites who had 20 points higher I.Q.s than themselves.[14]

In short, even though much research has shown that I.Q. differences matter for educational, occupational and other achievements,[15] the magnitude of those differences also matters, and in particular cases other factors may outweigh I.Q. differences in determining outcomes. Incidentally, other IQ studies at different times and places show people of Chinese and Japanese ancestry with *higher* IQs than whites[16] though the differences are similarly small in these studies as well.

The importance of other factors besides IQ is not a blank check for downplaying or disregarding mental test scores when making employment, college admissions or other decisions. Although empirical evidence shows that Chinese Americans and Japanese Americans tend to perform better in educational institutions than whites with the same mental test scores as themselves, other empirical evidence shows that blacks tend to perform *below* the level of those whites with the *same* test scores as themselves.[17] Clearly, then, with blacks as with Chinese and Japanese Americans, *other* factors besides IQs have a significant influence on actual educational outcomes, even though these other factors operate in a different direction for different groups.

None of this means that mental tests— whether I.Q. tests, college aptitude tests, or others— can be disregarded when it comes to making practical decisions about individuals, even if they do not justify sweeping inferences about genes or discrimination. When deciding whom to hire, admit to college or select for other kinds of endeavors, the relevant question about tests is: What has been the track record of a particular test in predicting subsequent performances— both absolutely and in comparison with alternative criteria? It is essentially an empirical statistical question, rather than a matter of speculation or ideology.

The issue is not even whether the particular questions in the test seem plausibly relevant to the endeavor at hand, as even courts of law have sometimes misconceived the issue.[18] If knowing fact *A* enables you to make predictions about outcome *B* with a better track record than alternative criteria, then plausibility is no more relevant than it was when wine experts dismissed Professor Orley Ashenfelter's use of weather statistics to predict wine prices— which predictions turned out to have a better track record than the methods used by wine experts.[19]

PREDICTIVE VALIDITY

Even if I.Q. tests or college admissions tests do not accurately measure the "real" intelligence of prospective students or employees— however "real" intelligence might be defined— the practical question is whether whatever they do measure is correlated with future success in the particular endeavor. Despite numerous claims that mental tests under-estimate the "real" intelligence of blacks, a huge body of research has demonstrated repeatedly that the future scholastic performances of blacks are *not* under-estimated by these tests which tend, if anything, to predict a slightly higher performance level than that which actually follows, contrary to the situation with Chinese Americans or Japanese Americans. While blacks tend to score lower than whites on a variety of aptitude, academic achievement and job tests, empirical evidence indicates that those whites with the *same* test scores as blacks have, on average, a track record of higher subsequent performances than blacks, whether academically or on the job. This includes academic performance in colleges, law schools, and medical schools, and job performance in the civil service and in the Air Force.[20]

Nor is this pattern unique to American blacks. In the Philippines, for example, students from low-income and rural backgrounds have not only had lower than average test scores, but have also done worse academically at the University of the Philippines than other students with the *same* low test scores as themselves.[21] In Indonesia, where men have averaged lower test scores than women, men with the same test scores as women have done poorer academic work than women at the University of Indonesia.[22]

A long-range study by Lewis Terman, beginning in 1921, followed children with I.Q.s of 140 and above in their later lives and found that those children who came from homes where the parents were less educated, and were from a lower socioeconomic level, did not achieve prominence in their own lives as often as other children in the same I.Q. range who had the further advantage of coming from homes with a higher cultural level.[23] In short, other factors besides those captured by IQ tests affect performances in various endeavors— and affect them differently for different groups. But one cannot just arbitrarily wave test results aside in order to get more demographic "representation" of racial or other groups with lower test scores as employees, students or in other contexts.

ABSTRACT QUESTIONS

A common finding among groups with low mental test scores, in various countries around the world, has been a lack of interest and proficiency in answering abstract questions. A study in England, for example, showed that rural working class boys trailed their urban peers more on abstract questions than on other kinds of questions.[24] In the Hebrides Islands off Scotland, where the average I.Q. of the Gaelic-speaking children was 85— the same as that among blacks in the United States— the Gaelic-speaking youngsters did well on informational items but trailed their English-speaking peers most on items involving such abstractions as time, logic, and other non-verbal factors.[25] In Jamaica, where I.Q.s averaged below normal, the lowest performance was on the least verbal test.[26] A 1932 study of white children living in isolated mountain communities in the United States showed that they not only had low I.Q. scores over all, but were especially deficient on questions involving abstract comprehension.[27]

Indian children being tested in South Africa were likewise reported as showing a "lack of interest in non-verbal materials."[28] Lower class youngsters in Venezuela were described as "non-starters" on one of the well-known abstract tests used there.[29] Inhabitants of the Hebrides likewise gave evidence of not being fully oriented toward such questions.[30] Black American soldiers tested during the First World War tended to "lapse into inattention and almost into sleep" during abstract tests, according to observers.[31]

That black-white mental test score differences in America are likewise greatest on abstract questions[32] is hardly surprising in view of this common pattern among groups that score low in various countries around the world, regardless of the race of the particular group. But the fact that low-scoring groups tend to do their worst on abstract questions is also contrary to the claim made by some critics of mental tests that group differences in scores on these tests are due primarily to the words used in these tests or to the culturally loaded subjects in the questions. However, an interest in abstractions is itself something characteristic of particular cultures and not of others. When H.H. Goddard said of the immigrants he tested at Ellis Island that they "cannot deal with abstractions," he overlooked the possibility that they had no real interest in abstractions.

Even if those who take tests try to do their best on abstract questions, as on other questions, a lifetime of disinterest in such things can mean that their best is not very good, even if that is not due to a lack of innate potential. If Asian American youngsters were to do their best playing basketball against black American youngsters on a given day, their best might not be nearly as good as the best of youngsters who had spent far more time on this activity before. Similarly if black youngsters try their best on a test measuring mental skills that they have not spent as much time developing as Asian youngsters have.

Neither genes nor a biased test is necessary to explain such results. If there were some group which assiduously pursued intellectual development and yet ended up with low IQs, the case for genetic determinism might be overwhelming. But there seems to be no such group anywhere.

If one chooses to call tests that require the mastery of abstractions culturally biased, because some cultures put more emphasis on abstractions than others do, that raises fundamental questions about what the tests are for. In a world where the ability to master abstractions is fundamental to mathematics, science and other endeavors, the measurement of that ability is not an arbitrary bias. A culture-free test might be appropriate in a culture-free society— but there are no such societies.

Nor is the importance of particular kinds of abilities constant over time, even in the same endeavors. Criteria that might have been suited to selecting individuals to be shepherds or farmers in centuries past may not be adequate for selecting individuals for a different range of occupations today— or even to be shepherds or farmers today, in an age of scientific agriculture and scientific animal husbandry.

TEST SCORE DIFFERENCES

Whether or not whatever factors make for high or low mental test scores make these tests a good measure of innate mental potential, what matters from a practical standpoint is whether those factors are important in education, in the economy and in life. Disregarding test scores, in order to get a higher demographic "representation" of black students in colleges and universities, for example, has systematically mismatched these students with the particular institutions in which they have been enrolled.

When the top tier colleges and universities accept black students whose test scores are like those of students in the second tier of academic institutions, then those colleges and universities in the second tier, which now find themselves with a smaller pool of black applicants whose qualifications are suited to their institutions, are thus left to accept black students whose test scores are more like those of students in the third tier— and so on down the line. In short, mismatching at the top tier institutions has a domino effect across the field of academic institutions, leading to far higher rates of academic failure among black students than among other students.

A widely-praised book on the effects of affirmative action— *The Shape of the River* by former college presidents William Bowen and Derek Bok— claimed to have refuted this mismatching hypothesis with data showing that black students "graduated at *higher* rates, the more selective the school that they attended" (emphasis in the original).[33] But what would be relevant to testing the mismatching hypothesis is the *difference* in test scores between black and white students at the same institutions— and this difference has been less at Harvard (95 points on the combined SAT test scores) than at Duke (184 points) or Rice (271 points).[34] Other data likewise indicate that black students graduate at a higher rate in colleges where their test scores are more similar to those of white students at the same institutions.[35] As Bowen and Bok themselves say: "There has been a much more pronounced narrowing of the black-white gap in SAT scores among applicants to the most selective colleges."[36]

That the high rate of college dropouts found among black students in general is not as great at institutions where the racial mental test score gap is not as great is a *confirmation* of the mismatching hypothesis that Bowen and Bok claim to have *refuted*. The fact that access to their raw data has been refused to others[37] suggests that the great praise showered on their book in the media may reflect agreement with its message and its vision, rather than a critical examination of its evidence and reasoning.

Although most controversies about racial differences in intelligence focus on *averages*, such as those of I.Q. scores, what is also relevant is the *range* of these scores. Much of what was said in the early twentieth century seemed to indicate a belief that there was some ceiling to intelligence that was lower for some races than for others. This was another way in which Professor Jensen differed from early twentieth century believers in genetic determinism, since he acknowledged that "as far as we know, the full range of human talents is represented in all the major races of man."[38]

Among the "beaten men from beaten races" disdained during the Progressive era were Jews— who were later in the forefront of those whose scientific work made the United States the first nuclear power, and Jews have been wholly disproportionately represented among Nobel laureates worldwide.[39] World chess championships have been won by any number of members of another group of "beaten men from beaten races," the Slavs— and the first human being to go into space was a Slav. The idea of an intellectual ceiling for particular races seems unsustainable, whatever might be said of intellectual averages.

There have been studies of blacks with I.Q.s significantly above the national average, these studies having lower cutoff I.Q. scores of 120, 130, and 140.[40] One of these studies turned up a nine-year-old girl "of apparently pure Negro stock" with an I.Q. of 143 on the Porteus mazes test, 180 on the Otis test and "approximately 200" on the Binet I.Q. test.[41] If there is an intelligence *ceiling* for blacks, and it is up near an I.Q. of 200, then its practical significance would be wholly different from what was proclaimed by genetic determinists of the Progressive era, who depicted some races as being unfit for survival in any role above that of the proverbial "hewers of wood and drawers of water." No one of course knows whether there is a racial ceiling on anyone's I.Q., much less what that ceiling might be.

Although the most common and most heated controversies about racial differences in I.Q. have centered on black and white Americans, the singling out of any given racial or ethnic group for comparison with the national average in any country creates an implication of uniqueness that is belied by empirical facts, since the national average itself is simply an amalgam of very different I.Q. levels among a variety of racial, social, regional and other groups.*

There is nothing unique about the average black American I.Q. of 85, compared to a national average of 100. At various times and places, other racial or social groups have had very similar I.Q.s. Studies during the era of mass immigration to the United States in the early twentieth century often found immigrant children from various countries with average I.Q.s in the 80s. A 1923 survey of studies of Italian American I.Q.s, for example, found their average I.Q. to be 85 in one study, 84 in three studies, 83 in another study and 77.5 in still another study. A 1926 survey of I.Q. studies found median I.Q.s of 85.6 for Slovaks, 83 for Greeks, 85 for Poles, 78 for Spaniards, and 84 for Portuguese.[42]

Similar I.Q.s in the 80s have been found among people living in the Hebrides Islands off Scotland and in white mountaineer communities in the United States in the 1930s[43]— both groups being of Nordic extraction, people who were supposed to be intellectually superior, according to

---

* These differences are by no means limited to racial or ethnic groups. In Indonesia, residents of Java score higher than Indonesians living in the outer islands, and women score higher than men. (Robert Klitgaard, *Elitism and Meritocracy in Developing Countries* [Baltimore: Johns Hopkins University Press, 1986], pp. 119, 124). In China, low-income and rural youngsters score lower on examinations (Ibid., p. 19). First-born children in general tend to score higher on mental tests and to do better in school than later children in the same families. (Lillian Belmont and Francis A. Marolla, "Birth Order, Family Size, and Intelligence," *Science*, December 14, 1973, p. 1096. But see also Phillip R. Kunz and Evan T. Peterson, "Family Size and Academic Achievement of Persons Enrolled in High School and the University," *Social Biology*, December 1973, pp. 454–459; Phillip R. Kunz and Evan T. Peterson, "Family Size, Birth Order, and Academic Achievement," *Social Biology*, Summer 1977, pp. 144–148).

Madison Grant and others. A 1962 study of the children of people from India tested in South Africa found them to have a mean I.Q. of 86.8, the same as that of African children there.[44]

Although mental test pioneer Carl Brigham wrote in 1923 that the Army tests provided an "inventory" of "mental capacity" with "a scientific basis,"[45] in 1930 he recanted his earlier view that low mental test scores among various immigrant groups in the United States reflected low innate intelligence. He belatedly pointed out in 1930 that many of the immigrant men tested by the Army during the First World War were raised in homes where the language spoken was not English. Although Brigham said in his 1923 book that he and other testers had "demonstrated the accuracy of the combined scale as a measure of the intelligence of the groups under consideration,"[46] he said candidly in his 1930 article that his previous conclusions were— in his own words— "without foundation."[47]

For blacks who took those same tests, their very low level of literacy at the time was likewise a factor to be considered, though few commentators took that into account. One sign of that low level of literacy among black soldiers taking the Army mental tests, and how that affected the results, was that more black soldiers were able to answer some of the more difficult test questions that did not require understanding the meaning of written words than were able to answer much simpler questions that did.[*]

One section of one of the Army tests required information such as the color of sapphires, the location of Cornell University, the profession of Alfred Noyes and the city in which the Pierce Arrow automobile was manufactured.[48] Why

---

[*] In many parts of the Army Alpha test used during the First World War, the modal score of black soldiers was *zero*— derived by subtracting incorrect answers from correct answers, in order to neutralize the effect of guessing— even though the actual intellectual substance of some of these questions involved only knowing that "yes" and "no" were opposites, as were "night" and "day," "bitter" and "sweet" and other similarly extremely easy questions— questions too simple to be missed by anyone who knew what the word "opposite" meant. However, in the Army Beta test, given to soldiers who could not read, some of the questions involved looking at pictures of a pile of blocks and determining how many blocks there were, including blocks that were not visible, but whose presence had to be inferred (and counted) from the shape of the piles. Yet fewer than half of the black soldiers received a score of zero on such questions, which were more intellectually demanding, but did not require the ability to read and understand words. Given the very small quantity and low quality of

blacks would have any reason to know any of these things at that time is a mystery— and why such questions could be considered measures of either black or white innate intelligence is an even bigger mystery.

DURATION OF MENTAL TEST RESULTS

During the Progressive era, one of the strongest arguments advanced for eugenics was that the tendency of people with lower I.Q.s to have larger families would, over time, lead to a decline in the national I.Q. But the later research of Professor James R. Flynn showed that, in more than a dozen countries around the world, the average performance on I.Q. tests *rose* substantially— by one standard deviation or more— in a generation or two.[49] Only the fact that I.Q. tests are repeatedly renormed, in order to keep the average I.Q. at its definitional level of 100, as the average number of questions answered correctly increased, had concealed this rise— and only the fact that Professor Flynn went back to the original raw scores revealed the facts which the renorming had concealed.

Much has been made of the fact that the average I.Q. among blacks has remained at about 85 over the generations, suggesting that the tests are measuring an unchanging genetic potential. But the apparent permanence of the performance of black Americans on I.Q. tests is an artifact of the renorming of those tests. The average number of questions answered correctly on I.Q. tests by blacks in 2002 would have given them an average I.Q. of 104 by the norms used in 1947–1948, which is to say, slightly higher than the average performance of Americans in general during the earlier

---

education received by that generation of blacks, even those who were technically literate were unlikely to have a large vocabulary of written words, so it is hardly surprising that the completely illiterate black soldiers did better on more challenging questions than did blacks with some ability to read. For details, see Carl Brigham, *A Study of American Intelligence* (Princeton: Princeton University Press, 1923), pp. 16–19, 36–38; [Robert M. Yerkes,] National Academy of Sciences, *Psychological Examining in the United States Army* (Washington: Government Printing Office, 1921), Vol. XV, Part III, pp. 874, 875; Thomas Sowell, "Race and IQ Reconsidered," *Essays and Data on American Ethnic Groups*, edited by Thomas Sowell and Lynn D. Collins (Washington: The Urban Institute, 1978), pp. 226–227.

period.[50] In short, the performances of blacks on I.Q. tests have risen significantly over time, just as the performances of other people in the United States and in other countries have, even though the renorming of those tests concealed these changes. While the persistence of a gap between blacks and whites in America on I.Q. tests leads some to conclude that genetic differences are the reason, the large changes in I.Q. test performance by both black and white Americans, as well as by the populations of other whole nations around the world, undermines the notion that I.Q. tests measure an unchanging genetic potential.

The fervor and persistence of the racial I.Q. debate cannot be assumed to be a measure of its practical implications,[*] as distinguished from its ideological importance for competing social visions. As already noted, even the leading advocate of genetic theories of I.Q. differences, Professor Arthur R. Jensen, has seen scholastic achievement as amenable to different teaching methods and has treated I.Q. differences as an over-estimate of differences in intelligence between children from lower socioeconomic classes and others. Since concrete capabilities matter much more in the real world than do abstract potentialities, educational outcomes are the practical issue, however much this practical issue has been overshadowed by ideological issues.

The leading scholar in the opposing, environmentalist school of thought, Professor James R. Flynn, expressed the narrowness of the practical issues in 2008:

> The race and IQ debate has raged for almost forty years. I have been entangled in it for thirty years. It has been a constant and unwelcome companion, rather like living with an uncongenial spouse from an arranged marriage. It has occupied the time of legions of scholars and laid waste acres of trees. Will we ever see the end of it? At least the debate is entering a new and more sophisticated stage. Given the relatively high values for black IQ in infancy and age 4, the focus should now be on whatever causes the decline of black IQ (compared to white) with age. If that can be settled, the main event will be over.[51]

---

[*] Anyone with experience teaching in American schools or colleges may well question whether either the average black or white student is working so close to his or her ultimate mental capacity as to make that ultimate capacity a matter of practical concern.

Professor Flynn has argued that the culture in which most black Americans grow up has had a negative effect on their intellectual development. He pointed out that the offspring of black and white American soldiers, who fathered children with German women during the American occupation of Germany after the Second World War, had no such I.Q. differences as that among black and white children in the United States. Professor Flynn concluded that the reason for results being different in Germany was that the offspring of black soldiers in Germany "grew up in a nation with no black subculture."[52]

There is other evidence that the black subculture has a negative effect on intellectual achievement. An empirical study published by the National Bureau of Economic Research found that "a higher percentage of Black schoolmates has a strong adverse effect on achievement of Blacks and, moreover, that the effects are highly concentrated in the upper half of the ability distribution."[53] In other words, brighter black students do not perform as well in settings where there are many other black students around them, contrary to the theory that what is needed in educational institutions is some larger "critical mass" of black students, in order to make them feel socially comfortable and thus able to do their best academically. Yet the unsubstantiated "critical mass" theory has flourished from academic journals to Supreme Court briefs.[54]

Another study, focussing on the effect of ability-grouping on the performances of students in general, mentioned among its conclusions: "Schooling in a homogeneous group of students appears to have a positive effect on high-ability students' achievements, and even stronger effects on the achievements of high-ability minority youth."[55] In other words, high-ability minority youngsters do better in classes that are *intellectually* homogeneous, rather than racially homogeneous.

The negative effects of the black subculture on intellectual development are manifested in other ways as well. A study of high-IQ black adults found that they described their childhoods as "extremely unhappy" more often than other blacks.[56] This study was done long before the current reports of academically striving black students being accused by their peers of "acting white." Empirical studies during this later era show a negative correlation between black students' academic achievement and their popularity among other black students. An opposite pattern was found among white Americans and Asian Americans.[57] In England, lower-class whites show a pattern strikingly similar to that among American blacks who resent academically achieving classmates. British physician Theodore Dalrymple reports lower class school children being beaten up so badly by their lower class classmates as to require hospital treatment, simply because they are doing well in school.[58]

There is other evidence against the "critical mass" theory. In earlier times, from 1892 to 1954, all-black Dunbar High School in Washington sent 34 graduates to Amherst College, usually very few at any given time, and certainly nothing that could be called a "critical mass." Seventy-four percent of those black students graduated from Amherst, 28 percent of these graduating as Phi Beta Kappas.[59] Dunbar did not promote a black subculture. As Senator Edward Brooke, one of its alumni, put it:

> Negro History Week was observed, and in American history they taught about the emancipation of the slaves and the struggle for equality and civil rights. But there was no demand by students for more, no real interest in Africa and its heritage. We knew about Africa as we knew about Finland.[60]

Yet the "critical mass" theory continues to flourish, with no evidence behind it, but with a peer consensus among the intelligentsia, which is apparently sufficient for many.

The cultural explanation of black-white IQ differences is also consistent with the fact that very young black American children do not lag behind very young white American children on mental tests, but that the gap begins and widens as they grow up. Research as far back as the 1920s found this pattern, as Otto Klineberg reported in a 1941 summary:

> A study by Lacy, for example, showed that the average I.Q. of colored children dropped steadily from 99 to 87 in the first four school grades, whereas the White I.Q. remained almost stationary. Wells also noted that Negro children were equal to Whites at ages six, seven and eight; only slightly inferior at ages nine, ten and eleven; and showed a progressively more marked inferiority from the ages of twelve to sixteen.[61]

Professor Jensen offers an alternative, genetic explanation for this pattern,[62] but a similar pattern was also found among low-IQ European immigrant groups in studies in 1916 to 1920, and among white American children in isolated mountain communities studied in 1930 and 1940,[63] so it is not a racial peculiarity in a genetic sense. Professor Flynn's explanation of this same pattern is consistent with the data cited by Klineberg. But these data are completely inconsistent with the prevailing multiculturalists' doctrine that all cultures are equal. Flynn's cultural explanation of black-white differences in I.Q. is also consistent with the otherwise puzzling anomaly that the mental test scores of white soldiers from various Southern states during the First World War were lower than the mental test scores of black soldiers from various Northern states at that time.[64]

Striking differences between the regional cultures of the South and the North in times past were noted by many, including Alexis de Tocqueville, Frederick Law Olmsted and Hinton Helper in the nineteenth century and Gunnar Myrdal in the twentieth century.[65] Moreover, those differences went back for centuries, when similar differences existed in different regions of Britain, among people who would later settle in the American South and others who would later settle in New England.[66]

Some of these cultural differences have been detailed in *Cracker Culture* by Grady McWhiney and in *Albion's Seed* by David Hackett Fischer, as well as in my book *Black Rednecks and White Liberals*. The fact that whites who came out of that Southern culture scored lower on mental tests than Northern whites— as well as whites from some Southern states scoring lower than blacks from some Northern states— is much more difficult to reconcile with genetic theories than with cultural explanations. In fact, neither of the two main explanations of mental test score differences by the twentieth century intelligentsia— genetic differences or racial discrimination— can account for white Southerners scoring low on the Army mental tests in the First World War. But the cultural explanation is consistent with both blacks and Southern whites scoring low on these tests at that time.

Much has changed in the South in later generations, and especially in the latter decades of the twentieth century, in part as a result of interregional migrations which have changed the demographic and cultural makeup of the South, perhaps more so than other regions of the country. However, as late as the middle of the twentieth century, most blacks in America had been born in the old South, even when they lived in the North, so the culture of the South, which Gunnar Myrdal saw as common to both blacks and whites born in that region, lived on in black ghettos across the country.[67] Many features of that culture have continued to live on today, often insulated from change by being regarded as a sacrosanct part of black culture and identity.

There is another striking phenomenon which cannot be explained by either the hereditary or the environmental theory of I.Q. differences— as heredity and environment are usually conceived. That is the fact that females are several times as numerous as males among blacks with high I.Q.s,[68] despite the fact that black males and black females inherit the same genes and are raised in the same homes and neighborhoods. Yet a cultural explanation seems more consistent with these findings as well, since the particular culture in which most blacks have lived for centuries, like the culture of white Southerners in the past, has emphasized especially macho roles for males.[*] It is hardly surprising if such a culture inhibited the intellectual development of both blacks and whites— especially males— in the South.

Further evidence that the male-female difference in IQs among blacks is cultural is that black orphans raised by white families show no such female superiority in IQs, in addition to both sexes having higher average IQs than other black children.[69] It should also be noted that the male-female

---

[*] There may be another, but different, environmental reason for the male-female differences in IQs among blacks. There is evidence that females in general are less affected by environmental disadvantages of various sorts than are males. (Arthur R. Jensen, "How Much Can We Boost IQ and Scholastic Achievement?" *Harvard Educational Review,* Winter 1969, pp. 32, 67). This possibility is independent of the peculiarities of the culture of the South and would apply to other groups with a very different culture, but who have low IQs for other reasons. Which factor carries more weight is hard to determine. Since there was no mass mental testing of white Southern females during the era when there was mass mental testing of white Southern males in the U.S. Army, we have no way to know whether there was a similar I.Q. difference between the sexes in the white Southern population at that time. However, there are data on sex differences between males and females among Jews, back during the early twentieth century, when Jews scored below average on mental tests. In that era, Jewish girls scored higher than Jewish boys on mental tests. Clifford Kirkpatrick, *Intelligence and Immigration* (Baltimore: The Williams & Wilkins Co., 1926), pp. 26–27.

difference in *average* IQs among blacks is only a few points but, due to the characteristics of a bell curve, a small difference in average IQs translates into a large difference in male-female representation at high IQ levels. Since these high IQ levels are common among students at elite colleges and among people in elite occupations, their impact on demographic representation in such conspicuous places can be considerable.

There is other evidence that "environment" cannot be usefully defined solely in terms of current gross external circumstances, such as income levels or even levels of education. More important, environment cannot be defined solely in terms of surrounding circumstances *at a given time*.

During the era of mass immigration to the United States, for example, it was common for Italian and Jewish children to be raised in similar low-income neighborhoods and to sit side-by-side in the same classrooms. Yet the Jewish children began to improve educationally before the Italian children, who were mostly the offspring of southern Italian parents. Nor was this at all surprising, in light of different cultural attitudes that prevailed among Jews and among southern Italians, long before these children were born. Even uneducated Jews respected education, while the imposition of compulsory education in southern Italy was not only resisted but evaded, and in places even led to riots and the burning of school houses.[70] However similar the immediate circumstances of Italian and Jewish school children were on the Lower East Side of New York, each trailed the long shadow of the cultural history and tradition in which they were raised, and those histories and traditions were very different.

Just as the preferences of Progressive-era intellectuals for genetic explanations of group differences led them to give little attention to cultural explanations of intergroup differences in educational achievement, so the preferences of intellectuals in the second half of the twentieth century for external social explanations— racial segregation and/or discrimination in schools being prominent— led them to also overlook cultural explanations. But research on a school in a large metropolitan area in the North from 1932 to 1953 found I.Q. differences between Jewish and Italian children attending that school to be as persistent over the years as black-white I.Q. differences in racially segregated schools in the South, and I.Q. differences between Jewish and Puerto Rican youngsters in that same school to be not only as persistent, but as large, as I.Q. differences between black and white youngsters attending different, racially segregated schools in the Jim Crow-era South.[71]

There were similar I.Q. differences among Mexican American and Japanese American youngsters living in the same school district out west, at a place and time where there was little occupational difference among their parents.[72] Cultural differences with educational consequences are not peculiar to the United States. When Maori students, admitted under preferential policies at New Zealand's University of Auckland, fail to show up for tutorials as often as other students,[73] their academic failures cannot be attributed automatically to institutional racism or to not having enough "role models"— not if the purpose is to advance Maoris rather than to protect a vision.

It should be noted that an *internal* explanation of racial differences— even if it is cultural, rather than genetic— deprives intellectuals of a moral melodrama and the opportunity that presents to be on the side of the angels against the forces of evil. There are, of course, times to take moral stands on particular issues, but that is very different from saying that issues in general, or racial issues in particular, are to be automatically conceived in ways that create a moral melodrama. Yet internal explanations of economic outcome differences among Americans have become so taboo that it was literally front-page news in the *New York Times* when a conference was held on the possibility that "a culture of poverty" existed, and that this culture helped explain disparate economic and other outcomes among the poor in general or blacks in particular.[74]

Near the end of the twentieth century, another firestorm among the intelligentsia was ignited by the publication of a major study of intelligence testing in general, and the social implications of its results, by Richard J. Herrnstein and Charles Murray, in their book *The Bell Curve*. Although most of the data and analysis in this book dealt with samples of white Americans, its two chapters on ethnic differences in mental test scores dominated discussions of the book, and especially attacks on the book. Yet one of the most important— and most ignored— statements in *The Bell Curve* appears there completely italicized:

*That a trait is genetically transmitted in individuals does not
mean that group differences in that trait are also genetic in origin.*[75]

As an example of that principle, it is known that differences in height among individuals are due mostly to genetics, but the difference in height between the people of North Korea and South Korea cannot be explained that way, because North Koreans were not shorter than South Koreans before drastic differences in living standards between the two halves of Korea began with that country's partitioning after the Second World War,[76] with North Korea being run by a draconian dictatorship that left its people in dire poverty. So, although genetics may explain *most* differences in height among most individuals and groups, it cannot explain *all* differences in height among all individuals and groups.

Whether there are, or have been, environmental differences of comparable magnitudes between other groups at various times and places, in ways that would affect mental capabilities, is a question that is open to empirical investigation. But what *The Bell Curve* says about the relative effects of heredity and environment on intergroup differences is that there is simply no foregone conclusion either way— which is the opposite of what was said by most of the intelligentsia in either the Progressive era or the later liberal and multicultural eras. While *The Bell Curve* says that "the instability of test scores across generations should caution against taking the current ethnic differences as etched in stone,"[77] it also refuses to accept the arguments of those who "deny that genes have *anything* to do with group differences, a much more ambitious proposition."[78] Authors Richard J. Herrnstein and Charles Murray declared themselves "resolutely agnostic" on the relative weight of heredity and environment in ethnic differences in cognitive abilities, because "the evidence does not yet justify an estimate."[79]

Saying that existing evidence is inadequate to make sweeping conclusions on a complex question like the existence or non-existence of differences in innate mental potential among races might not seem to be something to stir heated controversies, unless someone can point to definitive evidence, one way or the other, which no one has.[*] Nevertheless, *The Bell Curve* has been widely treated in the media, and even among many academics, as if it were just a restatement of the arguments of people like Madison Grant, despite the fact that (1) only two of its 22 chapters deal with ethnic differences and (2) their conclusions as to both facts and policies are as different from those of the Progressive era as from those of the later liberal and multicultural eras.

Like James R. Flynn, Herrnstein and Murray mention the fact that the children of black and white soldiers on occupation duty in Germany after the Second World War do not show the same I.Q. differences found between black and white children in the United States,[80] though Herrnstein and Murray do not discuss it at length or offer any explanation. It is simply part of a general presentation of evidence on both sides of the issue, in a book that refuses to pretend that current knowledge permits a definitive answer that would validate the racial views prevailing among intellectuals in either the Progressive era or the later eras.

Whatever the merits or demerits of *The Bell Curve* in general (which I have discussed elsewhere[**]), neither seems to explain the heated reactions it has provoked. Perhaps the fact that Herrnstein and Murray publicly discussed the taboo subject of race and I.Q. at all— and did so without repeating the prevailing social pieties— was what offended many, including many who never read the book. The authors of *The Bell Curve* also did not share the prevailing optimism among people who see an environmental explanation of intergroup differences in cognitive ability as showing such differences to be readily amenable to enlightened social policies. Herrnstein and Murray pointed out that environmental differences among groups are passed on from parents to children, just like genetic differences,[81] so their

---

[*] Even if such definitive evidence were possible, its practical effect would be questionable, given the limited magnitude of the differences in scientific dispute today. If science were to prove, for example, that the innate mental potential of blacks is 5 percent more than that of whites, of what practical value would that be, except to alert us to an even greater waste of potential than we might have thought? But that would tell us nothing about how to stop this waste. Moreover, the practical relevance of concerns about the limits of mental potential seems questionable when it is by no means clear that either black or white American students are operating anywhere close to those limits.

[**] My comments on both can be found in the essay "Ethnicity and IQ" in *The Bell Curve Wars*, edited by Steven Fraser (New York: Basic Books, 1995), pp. 70–79.

conception of environment is clearly not limited to current surrounding socioeconomic conditions, but includes the cultural heritage as well. Moreover, they did not see the mental tests which *convey* unwelcome news about intergroup differences in current mental capabilities as being the *cause* of those differences or due to "culture bias" in the tests themselves.

Just as Franz Boas had to argue against the *dogmatism* of the prevailing vision of race among the Progressives in the 1920s, in order to get his empirical evidence to the contrary even considered, so the authors of *The Bell Curve* have had to do the same in a later and supposedly more enlightened time. Even being agnostic about ultimate answers to the very complex questions that they explored was not enough to save them from the wrath of those whose social vision and agenda they undermined.

In an all too familiar pattern, the analysis and evidence in *The Bell Curve* were often side-stepped by critics, who instead attacked its authors as people with unworthy motives. John B. Judis of *The New Republic* dismissed *The Bell Curve* as "a combination of bigotry and of metaphysics," using "linguistic legerdemain."[82] Michael Lind of *Harper's* magazine called it part of an "astonishing legitimation" of "a body of racialist pseudoscience" representing "a right-wing backlash," and "covert appeals to racial resentments on the part of white Americans."[83] *Time* magazine called the book a work of "dubious premises and toxic conclusions."[84] Such arguments without arguments were not confined to the media, but were also used by academics, including a number of well-known Harvard professors.

Professor Randall Kennedy, for example, declared that Herrnstein and Murray were "bankrolled by wealthy supporters of right wing reaction,"[85] as if large-scale research projects of all sorts— including those at Harvard— are not bankrolled by somebody and, more fundamentally, as if an arbitrary characterization of those who financed the research says anything about the validity or lack of validity of the work itself. Professor Stephen Jay Gould depicted Herrnstein and Murray as promoting "anachronistic social Darwinism" and "a manifesto of conservative ideology."[86] Professor Henry Louis Gates said that the "most pernicious aspect of Murray and Herrnstein's dismissal of the role of environment" is the implication that social programs to advance blacks are futile,[87] though Professor Gates did not quote anything from *The Bell Curve* to substantiate this claim.

Professor Nathan Glazer likewise questioned "the motivations of the authors"[88] and concluded that, even if Herrnstein and Murray were correct in saying that currently prevailing beliefs are based on an untruth, "I ask myself whether the untruth is not better for American society than the truth."[89]

By falsely portraying the authors of *The Bell Curve* as genetic determinists, and then offering little besides vituperation against them, intellectuals may inadvertently promote the false conclusion that there is no serious argument or evidence against genetic determinism. With certainty remote and the magnitudes now in dispute of questionable social consequence, the ferocity of the attacks on those who deviate from the prevailing orthodoxy may signal little more than the sanctity of a vision or fear of the truth.

Chapter 18

Liberalism and Multiculturalism

*No issue in American society in recent times has generated
more pious rhetoric, unctuousness, and sheer hypocrisy than
race relations and racial problems.*

Paul Hollander[1]

B etween the earliest years of the twentieth century and the last half of
that century, the prevailing ideologies about race among intellectuals
did a complete reversal. But, just as there was not simply one view among
intellectuals in either period, so there were transitions within both the first
half of the century and the second half. The biggest transition during the
second half of the twentieth century was the transition to what can be called
the liberal era on race in the United States, which in turn metamorphosed
into the multicultural era. Moreover, such transitions were not confined to
the United States, but were common in Western civilization, whether in
Europe, the Western Hemisphere or Australia and New Zealand. In both
the liberal and the multicultural eras, the issue of "racial justice" loomed
large, though the meaning of that term changed over time, as well as
differing among different intellectuals at the same time.

THE LIBERAL ERA

Just as the horrors of the First World War led to an about-face among
Progressives who had before supported overseas expansions that conquered

other races during the Spanish-American war and later American interventions in Latin America, as well as the historic intervention in the war raging in Europe, so the horrors of the Second World War— and, more specifically, the Holocaust— led to painful reconsiderations of racial beliefs and policies in the Western world.

This is not to say that there had been no change in attitudes toward race since the Progressive era until the Second World War. A coherent school of thought, opposed to the prevailing Progressive era view of race, emerged in the 1920s under the leadership of anthropologist Franz Boas, a professor at Columbia University, to challenge the Progressive era orthodoxy. Boas and his followers emphasized environmental explanations of racial and ethnic differences, and apparently this approach made some inroads into the way some intellectuals saw race. Some changes were apparent by the 1930s. As already noted, in 1930 Carl Brigham recanted his earlier views on what the Army mental tests implied about the intelligence of men of various ethnicities.

As the Jewish population in America, whom Brigham had especially singled out for their low scores on Army mental tests during the First World War, became more assimilated and more educated, later mental test studies usually showed them doing far better than on the Army tests— and better than the American population as a whole.[2]

By the 1930s, the climate of opinion had changed sufficiently that Madison Grant's last book, *The Conquest of a Continent*, was panned by reviewers and *Clashing Tides of Color* by his prize pupil, Lothrop Stoddard, was ridiculed.[3] *The Christian Century* magazine, for example, said of Grant's book: "It gave to prejudice and hatred the false rationalization of an argument having the form, if not the substance, of science."[4] A 1934 survey of opinions among psychologists found 25 percent still believing that blacks had innately inferior intelligence, while 11 percent believed that blacks had equal intelligence and 64 percent believed the data to be inconclusive.[5]

What had eroded were not only the particular beliefs of the Progressive era but also the dogmatic tone of certainty of the Progressives. Otto Klineberg, one of Boas' disciples who promoted the alternative, environmental explanation of mental test differences, did so without the claims of scientific certainty made by Progressives, when he said: "We have no right to conclude that there are no racial differences in mental ability, since it is conceivable that new techniques may some day be developed which will indicate that such differences do exist."[6]

The Liberal Vision

Despite these developments in both beliefs and methods, however, it was the Second World War that marked a decisive turning point in American intellectuals' views of race relations. If there is a single book that might be said to mark that turning point in thinking about race among the intelligentsia, it would be *An American Dilemma* by Swedish economist Gunnar Myrdal, published in 1944. It was a massive study— more than a thousand pages long— of the many aspects of black-white relations in the United States, and its thesis was that American racial policies, especially in the South, marked a glaring contradiction between the nation's fundamental founding principles of freedom and equality and its actual practices as regards blacks. How to resolve that contradiction was the dilemma posed by Myrdal.

By this time, Progressives had begun calling themselves liberals, so this now became the prevailing liberal vision, as it evolved in the second half of the twentieth century.

Broadly speaking, while in the Progressive era socioeconomic differences between races were attributed to race— genetics— in the liberal era such differences between races were often attributed to racism. In neither era were alternative explanations taken seriously by much of the intelligentsia. In the liberal era, attributing any part of the differences between blacks and whites in incomes, crime, education, etc., to internal causes— even if social or cultural, rather than genetic— was often dismissed as "blaming the victim," a phrase preempting the issue rather than debating it.

If heredity was the reigning orthodoxy of the Progressive era, environment became the reigning orthodoxy of the liberal era. Moreover, "environment" usually meant the *external* contemporary environment, rather than including the internal cultural environment of minorities themselves. If minorities were seen as the problem before, the majority was seen as the problem now.

These premises were stated quite clearly in the introduction to *An American Dilemma*, where that dilemma was described as "a white man's problem" and Myrdal added, "little, if anything, could be scientifically explained in terms of the peculiarities of the Negroes themselves."[7] Despite the invocation of science, so reminiscent of the earlier Progressive era intellectuals, this was an arbitrary premise which, if followed consistently, would treat black Americans as simply abstract people with darker complexions, who were victims of what Myrdal called "confused and contradictory attitudes" in the minds of white Americans.[8] Yet Myrdal's own massive study brought out many behavioral and attitudinal differences between blacks and whites, though in the end none of this changed the basic premise of *An American Dilemma*, which remained the central premise of liberal intellectuals for decades thereafter.

This premise— that the racial problem was essentially one inside the minds of white people— greatly simplified the task of those among the intelligentsia who did not have to research the many behavioral differences between blacks and whites in America— or the many comparable or larger differences between other groups in other countries around the world— that have led to other intergroup complications, frictions and polarizations, which were in many cases at least as great as those between black and white Americans. Nor did intellectuals have to confront the constraints, costs and dangers inherent in group differences in behavior and values. To the intelligentsia of this later period, racial problems could be reduced to problems inside people's minds, and especially to racism, not only simplifying problems but enabling intellectuals to assume their familiar stance of being on the side of the angels against the forces of evil— and morally superior to the society in which they lived.

Life magazine, for example, greeted publication of *An American Dilemma* as showing that America was a "psychotic case among nations."[9] As with many other such sweeping pronouncements, it was not based on any empirical comparisons. For example, the number of blacks lynched in the entire history of the United States would be a fraction of the Armenians slaughtered by Turkish mobs in *one year* in the Ottoman Empire, the Ibos slaughtered by Hausa-Fulani mobs in one year in Nigeria, not to mention the number of Jews slaughtered by mobs in one year in a number of countries at various times scattered throughout history. While specifically black-white relations in the United States— especially in the South— were more polarized than black-white relations in some other countries, there were even more polarized relations between other groups that were not different in skin color in many other places and times, the Balkans and Rwanda being just two examples in our own times.

Gunnar Myrdal's basic premise— that racial problems in America were fundamentally problems inside the heads of white people, and that the resulting discrimination or neglect explained black-white differences in economic and other outcomes— was to remain the fundamental assumption of liberal thinking and policies for decades thereafter. As Professor Alfred Blumrosen of Rutgers University, an important figure in the evolution of federal racial policies, put it, discrimination should be "broadly defined," for example, by "including all conduct which adversely affects minority group employment opportunities."[10] This particular formulation preempts the very possibility that any behavior or performance by minorities themselves plays a role in the economic, educational and other "disparities" and "gaps" which are common among racial or other groups in countries around the world.

Such feats of verbal virtuosity were not peculiar to Professor Blumrosen, but were common among the intelligentsia of the liberal era. Even where there were demonstrable differences in behavior among racial or ethnic groups— whether in crime rates or rates of unwed motherhood, for example— these were more or less automatically attributed to adverse treatment, past or present, by the white majority.

Celebrated black writer James Baldwin, for example, claimed that blacks took the building of a subsidized housing project in Harlem as "additional proof of how thoroughly the white world despised them" because "people in Harlem know they are living there because white people do not think they are good enough to live anywhere else." Therefore "they had scarcely moved in" to the new housing project, before "naturally" they "began smashing windows, defacing walls, urinating in the elevators, and fornicating in the playgrounds."[11]

From this perspective, anything negative that blacks do is the fault of whites. But however much Baldwin's picture might fit the prevailing vision of the 1960s, anyone who is serious about whether it also fits the facts would have to ask such questions as: (1) Was there a time before the 1960s when it was common for blacks to urinate in public areas of buildings where they lived? and (2) If not, was that because they felt that whites had higher regard for them in earlier times?

To ask such questions is to answer them, and the answer in both cases is clearly *No!** But few asked such questions, which remained outside the sealed bubble of the prevailing vision. What was different about the 1960s was the proliferation of people like James Baldwin, promoting resentments and polarization, and making excuses for counterproductive and even barbaric behavior. Nor is this a phenomenon peculiar to blacks or even to the United States. Writing about lower-class whites in British public housing projects, Dr. Theodore Dalrymple observed: "The public spaces and elevators of all public housing blocks I know are so deeply impregnated with urine that the odor is ineradicable. And anything smashable has been smashed."[12]

The people behaving this way in Britain have none of the history that is supposed to explain black behavior in the United States. What is the same in both situations has been a steady drumbeat of grievance and victimhood ideologies from the media, from educational institutions and from other institutions permeated by the vision of the intelligentsia. In the United States, the racial version of such notions has not been confined to a fringe of

---

* As a personal note, I lived in Harlem in the 1940s and 1950s, when no one expected the smell of urine to be the norm in places where blacks lived. Others familiar with that period likewise paint a radically different picture of the projects of that era. For example: "These were not the projects of idle, stinky elevators, of gang-controlled stairwells where drug deals go down. In the 1940s, '50s and '60s, when most of the city's public housing was built, a sense of pride and community permeated well-kept corridors, apartments and grounds." Lizette Alvarez, "Out, and Up," *New York Times*, May 31, 2009, Metropolitan section p. 1. The projects in which economist Walter Williams grew up in Philadelphia in that era were likewise radically different from the projects of later years. Walter E. Williams, *Up From the Projects: An Autobiography* (Stanford: Hoover Institution Press, 2010), pp. 4–8. There was certainly not less discrimination or racism in this earlier period, so the difference was not due to white people. Among the differences between the two eras was that the intelligentsia, both black and white, became more prone in the later period to make excuses such as James Baldwin made for moral squalor and barbaric behavior. After such notions permeated the society, barbaric behavior and moral squalor became accepted norms within some segments of society— and among many intellectuals observing those segments of society.

extremists. Urban League director Whitney M. Young, regarded as a racial moderate, echoed the same 1960s vision when he said, in an article in *Ebony* magazine, "most white Americans do not link the rapid spread of blight and decay of our central cities to racism. But it is the main cause." He added, "The white man creates the ghettos and brutalizes and exploits the people who inhabit them— and then he fears them and then he flees from them." The white man, according to Young, "creates a climate of despair and then acts surprised when the protest marches fill the streets and riots erupt."[13]

Jean-Paul Sartre has been credited, if that is the word, with originating the practice of excusing violence by depicting the violence of some as reactions to other things that have been analogized to violence or redefined as violence.[14] That verbal tactic has since crossed the Atlantic. After the ghetto riots of the 1960s, whose violence shocked many Americans, Professor Kenneth B. Clark, best known for his work being cited in the case of *Brown v. Board of Education*, responded by saying:

> The real danger of Harlem is not in the infrequent explosions of random lawlessness. The frightening horror of Harlem is the chronic day-to-day quiet violence to the human spirit which exists and is accepted as normal.[15]

A writer in *The Nation* magazine likewise referred to "the quiet violence in the very operation of the system." The "institutional form of quiet violence operates when people are deprived of choices in a systematic way by the very manner in which transactions normally take place."[16] A committee of black clergymen took out an ad in the *New York Times*, deploring "the silent and covert violence which white middle-class America inflicts upon the victims of the inner city."[17]

Although many of those who said such things spoke in the name of the black community, or claimed to be conveying what most blacks believed, a 1967 poll found that 68 percent of blacks said that they had more to lose than to gain from rioting.[18] After the Rodney King riots in 1992, 58 percent of blacks condemned those riots, while only 32 percent found the violence even partially justified.[19]

This, however, was not the impression created in the media, after either the earlier or the later ghetto riots. In 1967, under the headline, "The Hard-Core Ghetto Mood," *Newsweek* quoted those individuals, inside and outside the ghetto, who expressed the militant vision accepted by the intelligentsia. "Rage is common to all of them," black academician Alvin Poussaint said of ghetto blacks. A white academic in California likewise said that the Watts riots represented "the metamorphosis of the Negroes" from victims to master. "The people of Watts felt that for those four days they represented all Negroes; the historic plight of the Negroes; all the rebellions against all injustice. . . . What must be understood by the rest of America is that, for the lower-class Negro, riots are not criminal, but a legitimate weapon in a morally justified civil war."[20] None of those who made such sweeping pronouncements had to offer hard evidence to have their pronouncements echoed throughout the media.

Nothing is easier than to find some individuals— in any group— who share a given writer's opinion, and to quote such individuals as if their views were typical. This approach became common in media coverage of ghetto riots. *Newsweek* magazine, for example, quoted various black youths, including one described as *"a child of Detroit's ravaged ghetto,"*[21] even though (1) the poverty rate among Detroit's black population before the riots was only half of that of blacks nationwide, (2) the homeownership rate among blacks in Detroit was the highest in the nation, and (3) the unemployment rate of blacks in Detroit was 3.4 percent— lower than that among whites nationwide.[22]

It was *after* the riots that Detroit became a ravaged community, and remained so for decades thereafter, as businesses withdrew, taking jobs and taxes with them. But here, as elsewhere, an idea that fit the vision did not have to meet the additional requirement of fitting the facts.

Racism and Causation

At the heart of the prevailing liberal vision of race today is the notion of "racism"— a concept with multiple, elusive and sometimes mutually contradictory meanings. Sometimes the term refers simply to any adverse opinion about any racially different group, whether a minority in a given society or a group that may be a majority in some other society. This immediately transforms any adverse judgment of any aspect of a different racial group into an indictment of whoever expressed that adverse judgment, without any need to assess the evidence or analysis behind it. In short, this approach joins the long list of arguments without arguments.

At other times, the term "racism" refers more specifically to an adverse conclusion based on a belief that the genetic endowment of a particular racial group limits their potential. Other meanings include a preference for advancing the interests of one race over another, with or without any genetic theories or even any adverse assessment of the behavior, performance or potential of the group to be disfavored. For example, an argument has been made in various countries around the world for policies preferring one group over another on the ground that the group to be discriminated against is *too* formidable for others to compete against on even terms. This argument has been made in Sri Lanka, Nigeria, Malaysia, in India's states of Assam and Andhra Pradesh, and even in early twentieth century America, where Japanese immigrants were feared on grounds that their high capability and lower standard of living would permit them to undercut the prices charged by white American farmers, workers, or commercial business owners.[23]

In other words, racism defined as a preference for one race over another need not depend upon any belief that the group to be discriminated against is inferior in performance or potential, and at various times and places has been based on the opposite belief that the group that is to be discriminated against was too proficient for others to compete with on equal terms, for whatever reason. As a book advocating group preferences for Malays in Malaysia put it, "Whatever the Malays could do, the Chinese could do better and more cheaply."[24] A leader in a campaign for preferential policies in India's state of Andhra Pradesh said: "Are we not entitled to jobs just because we are not as qualified?"[25] In Nigeria, an advocate of group representation policies deplored what he called "the tyranny of skills."[26]

Racism not only has varying definitions, its role in arguments by intellectuals can vary greatly from its use simply as a descriptive term to its role as a causal explanation. How one chooses to characterize adverse decisions against a particular racial group may be a matter of personal semantic preferences. But to assert a causal role is to enter the realm of evidence and verification, even if the assertion contains neither. For example, a *New York Times* editorial presented a classic example of the liberal vision of racism:

> Every index of misery continues to show that the devastating effects of racism linger on in America. Blacks make up a disproportionate number of the citizens dependent on public assistance. The unemployment rates among black males and teen-agers remain at least twice as high as among whites. The proportion of blacks dropping out of the labor force altogether has doubled over the last two decades.[27]

The bare facts cited are undoubtedly true. But two of the three facts— higher unemployment and lower labor force participation among blacks than among whites— are worse today than in earlier times. By the logic of this editorial, that would imply that there was less racism in the past, *which no one believes*.

Black labor force participation rates were higher than that of whites generations ago.[28] Black unemployment rates were lower than that of whites in 1890 and, for the last time, in 1930.[29] Black 16-year-olds and 17-year-olds had a slightly lower unemployment rate than white youngsters of the same age in 1948 and only slightly higher unemployment rates than their white peers in 1949.[30] Moreover, these unemployment rates for black teenagers were a *fraction* of what they would become in later times. These low unemployment rates existed just before the minimum wage law was amended in 1950 to catch up with the inflation of the 1940s which had, for all practical purposes, repealed the minimum wage law, since inflated wages for even unskilled labor were usually well above the minimum wage level specified when the Fair Labor Standards Act was passed in 1938.

The key role of federal minimum wage laws can be seen in the fact that black teenage unemployment, even in the recession year of 1949, was a fraction of what it would become in even prosperous later years, after the series of minimum wage escalations that began in 1950.[31]

The last year in which black unemployment was lower than white unemployment— 1930— was also the last year in which there was no federal minimum wage law. The Davis-Bacon Act of 1931 was openly advocated by some members of Congress on grounds that it would stop black construction workers from taking jobs from white construction workers by working for less than the union wages of white workers.[32] Nor was the use of minimum wage laws to deliberately price competing workers out of the labor market unique to the Davis-Bacon Act or to the United States. Similar arguments were made in Canada in the 1920s, where the object was to price Japanese immigrants out of the labor market, and in South Africa in the era of apartheid, to price non-whites out of the labor market.[33]

Any group whose labor is less in demand, whether for lack of skills or for other reasons, is disproportionately priced out of labor markets when there are minimum wage laws, which are usually established in disregard of differences in skills or experience. It has not been uncommon in Western Europe, for example, for young people to have unemployment rates above 20 percent.[34]

The point here is not to claim that pricing competitors out of the market was the motivation of all or most of the supporters of the Fair Labor Standards Act. The point is that this was its effect, regardless of the intentions. In short, the empirical evidence is far more consistent with the changing patterns of black labor force participation rates and unemployment rates over time being results of minimum wage laws than with changes in the degree of racism in American society. Indeed, these patterns over time are completely inconsistent with the fact that racism was worse in the earlier period. Only the fact that the intelligentsia tend to make racism the default setting for explaining adverse conditions among blacks enables such statements as those in the *New York Times* editorial to pass muster without the slightest demand for either evidence or analysis.

It is much the same story when racism is used as an explanation for the existence of black ghettoes. If racism is simply a characterization, there may be others who prefer different characterizations, but these are matters of subjective preferences. However, if a *causal* proposition is being advanced, then it is subject to empirical verification like other causal propositions.

When racism is offered as a *causal* explanation, as distinguished from a characterization, that makes the predispositions of whites the reason for the residential segregation of blacks, among other forms of racially disparate treatment. But seeing that as a hypothesis to be tested brings us face to face with inconvenient but inescapable facts of history. For example, most blacks were not residentially segregated in such cities as New York, Chicago, Detroit, Philadelphia, and Washington by the end of the nineteenth century[35]— even though they had been before and would be again in the twentieth century. Do the racial predispositions of white people just come and go unpredictably? That would be an especially strange thing for predispositions to do, even if reasoned opinions change with changing circumstances.

It is a matter of historical record that there were in fact changing circumstances preceding changing racial policies in the United States, both when these were changes for the better and when they were changes for the worse. Moreover, where the circumstances changed at different times from one place to another, racial attitudes and policies also changed correspondingly at different times.

As of the early nineteenth century, residential segregation was just one of a number of restrictions placed on free blacks in both the North and the South. However, by the last decade of the nineteenth century, such residential restrictions had eroded in Northern cities to the point where W.E.B. Du Bois could write in the 1890s of "a growing liberal spirit toward the Negro in Philadelphia," in which "the community was disposed to throw off the trammels, brush away petty hindrances and to soften the harshness of race prejudice"— leading, among other things, to blacks being able to live in white neighborhoods.[36] Nor was Philadelphia unique. There were similar developments in New York, Detroit, Washington and other Northern cities.[37] Census data show a lower rate of urban residential segregation of blacks nationwide in 1890–1910 than in later decades of the twentieth century and even as late as the 2010 census.[38]

Other restrictions had eroded as well. In Detroit, blacks who had been denied the vote in 1850 were voting in the 1880s, and in the 1890s blacks were being elected to public office by a predominantly white electorate in Michigan. The black upper class in Detroit at that time had regular social interactions with whites, and their children attended high schools and colleges with whites. In Illinois during this same era, legal restrictions on access to public accommodations for blacks were removed from the law, even though there were not enough black voters at the time to influence public policy, so that this represented changes in white public opinion.[39]

In New York City, by the 1890s most blacks did not work as unskilled laborers but held modest but respectable jobs as barbers, waiters, caterers, and skilled craftsmen. Distinguished historian Oscar Handlin characterized blacks in New York at that time as being "better off than the mass of recent white immigrants."[40] The visible improvement in the living standards of blacks was noted in Jacob Riis' 1890 classic, *How the Other Half Lives.*[41]

In Philadelphia, blacks were among the leading caterers in the city, serving a predominantly white clientele.[42] In Chicago, there were also successful black businesses serving a predominantly white clientele[43] and, as late as 1910, more than two-thirds of the city's black residents lived in neighborhoods that were predominantly white.[44]

To maintain that residential and other racial restrictions on blacks were simply a matter of the predispositions of the white population— racism— immediately raises the question of why such predispositions should have changed so much during the course of the nineteenth century— and then changed back again, drastically, and within a very few years— during the early twentieth century. But this pattern of progress in race relations in Northern urban communities during the nineteenth century, followed by retrogression in the early twentieth century, followed again by progress in the latter part of the twentieth century, is more readily understood in terms of causes other than pure subjective mood swings in the white population. In short, whether or not attitudes within the white population deserve the *characterization* of racism, a *causal* analysis of the major changes that occurred in residential and other restrictions on blacks cannot explain such *changes* by simply saying "racism."

Turning from the white population to the black population, we find developments that make the changing residential patterns explicable without resorting to inexplicable changes inside the heads of white people. Beginning at the beginning, African slaves were brought into American society at the bottom, and concentrated in the South— a region with its own cultural handicaps that produced marked differences between the *white* populations of the North and South that many observers noted during the antebellum era.[45] This meant that those blacks who came out of the South to live in Northern cities would be very different in many ways from the white populations of those cities. The visible racial differences made blacks easy to identify and restrict.

During the course of the nineteenth century, however, over a period of generations Northern blacks tended to acquire more of the culture of the surrounding white urban population of the North, just as other groups often have when living surrounded by a vastly larger population with a different culture and a higher socioeconomic level. By the end of the nineteenth century, this cultural assimilation had reached the point where racial barriers eased considerably in the Northern cities, where the black populations of these cities were now predominantly native-born residents, rather than migrants from the South.[46]

This situation changed drastically, however, and within a relatively few years, with the mass migrations of millions of blacks out of the South, beginning in the early twentieth century. This not only greatly multiplied the black populations living in many Northern cities, the newcomers were seen by both the pre-existing black populations and the white populations of these cities as creating greatly increased social problems such as crime, violence and offensive behavior in general.[47]

If these were mere "prejudices," "perceptions" or "stereotypes" in the minds of white people, as so many adverse judgments have been automatically characterized, why did the very same views appear among Northern-born blacks at the same time?

Where hard data are available, these data substantiate the pattern of behavioral differences between the pre-existing Northern black populations and the newcomers from the South. In early twentieth-century Pennsylvania, for example, the rate of violent crimes among blacks from the South was nearly five times that among blacks born in Pennsylvania.[48] In Washington, D.C., where the influx from the South occurred decades earlier, the effect of the Southerners' arrival could be seen decades earlier. For example, out of wedlock births were just under 10 percent of all births among blacks in Washington in 1878, but this more than doubled by 1881, following a large influx of Southern blacks, and remained high for years thereafter.[49]

The new majorities of Southern blacks in the Northern black urban communities were sufficiently large, and their culture sufficiently reinforced by continuing new arrivals from the South, that their rate of assimilation to the cultural norms of the surrounding white society was neither as rapid nor as complete as that of the much smaller numbers of blacks who had preceded them in these cities in the nineteenth century. Moreover, as late as 1944, Gunnar Myrdal's *An American Dilemma* pointed out that a majority of blacks living in the North at that time had been born in the South.[50]

During the early years of mass migration of blacks out of the South, many Northern-born blacks condemned the Southern newcomers, and saw in them a danger that the white population would put up new barriers against all blacks[51]— which is in fact what happened. After the massive inflow of Southern blacks into Northern cities in which small black populations had once lived scattered in predominantly white neighborhoods, these now became cities in which blacks were prevented from living in white neighborhoods by methods ranging from legal prohibitions and restrictive covenants to outright violence. All this happened within a very few years of the mass migrations of Southern blacks to Northern cities.

The massive black ghettoes which became common in the twentieth century were just one aspect of a more general retrogression in race relations, in which various public accommodations once open to blacks were now closed to them, and black children who had once gone to schools with white children in Northern cities were now segregated into different schools.[52]

The conclusion that this change was a reaction to a mass in-migration of less acculturated blacks from the South is reinforced by the history of cities on the west coast, where this mass in-migration from the South took place decades later, largely during the Second World War, and was likewise followed by retrogressions in race relations there at this later time.[53] A similar pattern had already unfolded among Jews in the United States in the late nineteenth century, when the highly acculturated German Jews lost much of the social acceptance which they had already achieved, after larger masses of much less acculturated Jews from Eastern Europe arrived, followed by new barriers against Jews in general. To say that this retrogression was caused by anti-Semitism would likewise be to transform a characterization into a causal explanation, implicitly treating those adversely affected as abstract people whose problems originated solely in other people's minds.

Whether among blacks, Jews or others, leaders within these groups themselves saw behavioral problems among some of their own people as creating backlashes in the larger society around them, from which the entire group suffered. As a result, organized social uplift groups, both secular and religious, arose within the black community, the Jewish community, as well as within other communities, aimed at changing the behavior of members of their own respective groups, in order to facilitate the advancement of these groups as a whole.[54]

Among Jews, during the era of mass immigration from Eastern Europe, the already acculturated German Jews living in America took the lead in seeking to acculturate the Jewish newcomers from Eastern Europe. A German Jewish publication of that era described the Eastern European Jews as "slovenly in dress, loud in manners, and vulgar in discourse."[55] As a leading study of American Jews noted: "The Germans found it hard to understand what could better serve their ill-mannered cousins than rapid lessons in civics, English, and the uses of soap." Such problems were not peculiar to Jews but were common among the Irish immigrants before them and to blacks after them.

During the mass migrations of blacks out of the South during the early twentieth century, both the *Chicago Defender* (a black newspaper) and the Urban League offered such published advice as:

DON'T USE VILE LANGUAGE IN PUBLIC PLACES.
DON'T THROW GARBAGE IN THE BACKYARD OR ALLEY
OR KEEP DIRTY FRONT YARDS.
DO NOT CARRY ON LOUD CONVERSATIONS IN STREET
CARS AND PUBLIC PLACES.[56]

Although these efforts produced positive results over the years, whether among blacks, Jews or others, that whole approach was antithetical to a new social philosophy that emerged in the late twentieth century— multiculturalism.

THE MULTICULTURALISM ERA

The era of multiculturalism might be considered an extension of the liberal era, but it has evolved characteristics that go not only beyond, but in some cases counter to, the characteristics of the liberal era, as that era had developed in the wake of Myrdal's *An American Dilemma* and the immediate post-World War II years. The earlier liberalism was universalistic, in that it emphasized equal treatment for all individuals, "regardless of race, color or creed," in a common phrase of that era. In some places, race was not even allowed to be recorded on job applications or various other records. The initial thrust of the civil rights movement, and of laws like the Civil Rights Act of 1964, was the extension of the same rights to all citizens, irrespective of race.

It was understood that such an extension would be especially valuable to those citizens— such as blacks and other minority group members— who had previously been denied some of those rights in one way or another. But while such policies would especially benefit particular groups, the larger implication of the civil rights movement was seen as being in effect a completion of the American Revolution, by bringing its ideals to fruition for all, the goal being aimed at being to make race irrelevant to laws and policies. Whatever the merits or demerits of this particular conception, it was one attracting a broad consensus across racial lines, among both intellectuals and the general public, and bipartisan support in Congress, where a higher percentage of Republicans than Democrats voted for the Civil Rights Act of 1964, since Congressional Democrats from the South were the main opposition.

Despite the breadth of this consensus, it was short-lived. Various segments of the population began to go in different directions for different reasons. The ghetto riots that swept across many American cities in the 1960s— the first in Los Angeles, just days after passage of the Voting Rights Act of 1965, and culminated in a wave of such riots in cities across the country after the assassination of Martin Luther King, Jr., in 1968— forfeited much sympathy for blacks among the general public. Among blacks, disappointment that the economic and social advances did not match the high expectations of the social revolution that the civil rights laws and policies were to produce, provided fertile ground for more radical elements urging more extreme actions.

The consensus on racial issues that had existed just a few years earlier was giving way to polarization over those issues, within as well as between the black population and the white population, and among intellectuals. While there was little or no support among the intelligentsia for undoing the recent civil rights advances, there were bitter disputes over the direction that racial policies were taking, as those policies moved in the direction of what can broadly be called multiculturalism.

The Multicultural Vision

Multiculturalism involves more than a simple recognition of differences in cultures among different groups. It is an insistence, *a priori*, that the effects of these differences are on net balance positive and that the particular cultures found among less fortunate groups are not to be blamed for disparities in income, education, crime rates, or family disintegration, lest observers be guilty of "blaming the victim" instead of indicting society. Given that premise, it was consistent for multiculturalists to decry educators who sought to get black youngsters to speak standard English or to force Hispanic students to speak English rather than Spanish in school. An all too typical example was an author who referred to "the white Harlem schoolmarm who carps over her students' speaking differently from herself."[57]

More generally, trying to get minority groups to acculturate to the social, linguistic and other norms of the larger society around them has been viewed negatively by multiculturalists as a form of cultural imperialism.

The key word among advocates of multiculturalism became "diversity." Sweeping claims for the benefits of demographic and cultural diversity in innumerable institutions and circumstances have prevailed without a speck of evidence being asked for or given. It is one of the purest examples of arguments without arguments, and of the force of sheer repetition, insistence and intimidation.

Among many multiculturalists, saying the word "diversity" trumps mundane concerns about empirical consequences and converts preferential treatment by race— the principle fought against so long by liberals— into "social justice" when the preferences are for those minorities currently in favor among the intelligentsia. That preferential college admissions of blacks and Hispanics may have a negative effect on the admissions of Asian Americans, not to mention whites, is something usually ignored or brushed aside. Treating races as intertemporal abstractions enables those with this vision to treat discrimination against contemporary whites as somehow offsetting discrimination against blacks in the past. For example, Professor James M. McPherson, a distinguished historian at Princeton University, made the case for affirmative action this way:

> Having benefitted in so many ways from these older forms of affirmative action that favored white males, I cannot feel censorious about the newer version that may seem to disadvantage this same category— either in faculty recruitment or student admissions. And in the area of faculty promotions, if not recruitment, white males still dominate the senior ranks in many departments of history.[58]

By reducing contemporary individuals to a verbally collectivized "category," in addition to portraying whites as an intertemporal abstraction, Professor McPherson makes discrimination against flesh-and-blood individuals palatable— or at least something that can be done with only a passing expression of "empathy" for them.[59] But affirmative action costs nothing to those individuals of his generation who presumably received the unfair advantages which are to be repaid by discrimination against younger individuals who had nothing to do with past advantages or disadvantages.

Sometimes there is an implicit assumption that any lack of skills or other qualifications among blacks today is solely a result of previous discrimination— rather than any of the innumerable other factors producing equal or greater differences among other racial or ethnic groups in other countries around the world. Sometimes this belief even became explicit, as when Justice Harry Blackmun declared in the *Weber* case in 1979 that there could be "little doubt that any lack of skill has its roots in purposeful discrimination of the past."[60] Justice William J. Brennan advanced similar reasoning in the **Bakke** case, saying that Allan Bakke, a white applicant for medical school who was passed over while blacks with lesser qualifications were admitted, "would have failed to qualify" for admission in a non-discriminatory world, being outperformed in such a hypothetical world by sufficient numbers of minority applicants, whose current failure to qualify in the existing world "was due principally to the effects of past discrimination."[61]

Given these premises, four justices in the *Bakke* case saw the Supreme Court's task as "putting minority applicants in the position they would have been in if not for the evil of racial discrimination."[62] In short, those with this vision see whites who outperform blacks— economically, educationally or otherwise— as simply unjust beneficiaries of past discrimination. Only the implicit and unsubstantiated assumption that blacks would have the same skills as others in the absence of racial discrimination gives this line of reasoning any semblance of plausibility. It is as if blacks arrived in the United States from Africa with the same skills as those of whites who arrived here from Europe. The fact that whites from different parts of Europe arrived here with very different skills from one another, as well as different cultures in general, has not been allowed to disturb this vision that proceeds as if discussing abstract people in an abstract world.

Not only have the large and numerous differences in a wide range of skills among various white ethnic groups in the United States today been utterly ignored in such arguments, so have similarly wide (or wider) differences among innumerable other groups in other countries around the world, as reflected in minorities dominating whole industries in many of these countries.

While the intelligentsia may wax surprised or indignant at the low representation of blacks among the top executive officers of major American corporations, and regard that as proof of discrimination, blacks are nevertheless better represented in such elite places than Turks were among bankers or stockbrokers in the Ottoman Empire, *which the Turks controlled*, and better represented than the Malays were in the 1960s among recipients of engineering degrees from Malaysia's universities, *which the Malays controlled*, and in which therefore no one was in any position to discriminate against them.

At various places and times, similar things could be said of the Fijians in Fiji, the Poles in Poland, the Argentines in Argentina, the Ugandans in Uganda and many other majorities grossly outperformed by their respective minorities.

While facts would undermine the hypothesis of current intergroup differentials being automatically a result of current or past discrimination, such facts have no effect on beliefs that are treated as axioms essential to a desired conclusion, rather than as hypotheses subject to verification. Those who question the prevailing vision have been accused of denying a history of racial discrimination. But, although such discrimination exists, just as cancer exists, nevertheless intergroup differences cannot be assumed *a priori* to be due to discrimination, any more than deaths can be assumed *a priori* to be due to cancer.

The premises of multiculturalism are more than an intellectual issue that might be debated around a seminar table or in academic publications. They have real world consequences affecting millions of human beings, both minorities and non-minorities, as well as the cohesion or polarization of whole societies. These consequences have been both practical and psychic, affecting economic and educational outcomes, as well as people's sense of group identity. Those who promote the preservation of racial or ethnic identities have seldom investigated what happens when lagging groups do that, compared to what happens when they follow the opposite approach. The benefits of separate cultures and identities are instead treated as axioms rather than hypotheses— in short, as arguments without arguments.

Cultural Changes

If, instead of judging beliefs about cultures and identities by how well they fit the prevailing multicultural vision, we treat these issues in terms of how well they fit the facts, we reach very different conclusions. David Hume's urging of his fellow eighteenth century Scots to learn the English language, and the remarkable rise of the Scots as a result of moving into a wider world of cultural possibilities by acquiring the knowledge and skills available in the English language, have been noted in Chapter 16. Something very similar happened in nineteenth century Japan, a technologically and economically backward country at that time, and one very painfully aware of its backwardness and publicly lamenting its lag behind countries like the United States.[63]

Not only did Japan import Western technology on a massive scale, it imported European and American technological experts and sent its promising young people to Western nations to study Western technology and organizational methods.[64] During this era, nineteenth-century Japan engaged in one of the most remarkable public denigrations of its own culture ever seen in a major nation, extolling the United States as an "earthly paradise"[65] as part of a general depiction of Western peoples and nations as enviable, beautiful, and great.[66] Government-issued textbooks in Japan held up Abraham Lincoln and Benjamin Franklin as models to be imitated, even more so than Japanese heroes.[67] Not only was the English language introduced into Japanese secondary schools, it was for a time even suggested that English become the national language of Japan.[68]

If this kind of behavior, which has often been dismissed as a "cultural cringe" is compared in its consequences to what has been extolled as the pride of "identity," it is by no means clear that what intellectuals extol has a better track record than what they deplore. But of course no such empirical comparison is likely to be made. Nor are Scotland and Japan the only examples where the deliberate seeking of a different culture has produced striking advances. On a much smaller scale, something similar has happened, at isolated times and places, in the history of black Americans.

In the wake of the Civil War and the emancipation of millions of Southern blacks from slavery, thousands of New Englanders and other Northern whites went into the South to educate black children there. Whether this education stressed traditional academic subjects or emphasized vocational training of the sort taught at Hampton Institute in Virginia and Tuskegee Institute in Alabama, both schools of thought emphasized the importance of *replacing* the existing Southern culture in which blacks were steeped with a very different culture. Both the head of the American Missionary Association and the head of the Hampton Institute, where Booker T. Washington was trained, very plainly and emphatically stressed the importance of supplanting the existing culture among Southern blacks with an imported culture from the North in general and often from New England specifically.

In a speech in 1882, the head of the American Missionary Association declared that what the younger generation of blacks needed was "a total change of environment" by removing young people to residential institutions "where morals are pure; where manners are refined; where language is grammatical."[69] Hampton Institute's founder, General Samuel Chapman Armstrong, likewise declared that the "average Negro student" needed a residential boarding school that could "control the entire twenty-four hours of each day— only thus can old ideas and ways be pushed out and new ones take their place."[70] Addressing the American Missionary Association in 1877, General Armstrong said: "There is no lack of those who have mental capacity. The question with him is not one of brains, but of right instincts, of morals, and of hard work."[71] Contrary to later caricatures, neither Hampton Institute nor Tuskegee Institute was based on an assumption that blacks had the capacity to be only hewers of wood and drawers of water.

These isolated educational efforts began to pay off in a remarkably short time after the abolition of slavery, for those black young people who developed within these small and highly atypical enclaves. An official board of white visitors to Atlanta University in 1871 expressed amazement at the demonstrated abilities of black students in Latin, Greek and geometry, as reported in the *Atlanta Constitution*, which said that they could hardly "believe what we witnessed."[72] Another of these atypical educational institutions for blacks, founded by people likewise steeped in a very different cultural tradition from that of the South, was an academic high school in Washington which, in 1899, outscored two of the three white academic high schools in the same city on tests that they all took.[73] Nor was this an isolated fluke. This school had impressive academic records throughout an 85-year period.[74] Ironically, it was located within walking distance of the Supreme Court, which virtually declared its existence impossible when it ruled in 1954 that racially separate schools were "inherently unequal."[75]

However radically different the academic achievements of this particular high school were from that of most other black schools, these achievements were not unique. Other black schools with similar achievements today differ just as radically from the common run of black schools today. As of 2010, the *Wall Street Journal* reported:

> Nationwide, the average black 12th grader reads at the level of a white eighth grader. Yet Harlem charter students at schools like KIPP and Democracy Prep are outperforming their white peers in wealthy suburbs.[76]

Many of the schools that have been successful with black students have gone against the cultural values that permeate ghetto communities and ghetto schools. In doing so, their practices have also gone against the theories of multiculturalism.

The Cultural Universe

On the world stage, the multicultural dogma of the equality of cultures flies in the face of massive borrowings of cultural, technological and other advances from one civilization to another that has gone on for millennia.[77] There would be no real point in abandoning features of one's own culture and substituting features of an alien culture, unless the substitutes were found to be better.

So-called Arabic numerals, for example, were in fact created in India and then spread to the West after Europeans encountered these numbers in use among the Arabs. Moreover, Arabic numerals are not simply *different* from Roman numerals— as the verbal fetishes of multiculturalism would require us to say— they are *superior* to Roman numerals, as demonstrated by their displacement of Roman numerals even in nations whose civilizations derived from Rome, as well as their displacement of other numbering systems in countries around the world.

It is hard even to imagine the complex operations of higher mathematics being carried out today using cumbersome Roman numerals, when merely expressing the year of American independence— MDCCLXXVI— requires more than twice as many Roman numerals as Arabic numerals. Moreover, Roman numerals offer more opportunities for errors, since the same digit may be either added or subtracted, depending on its place in the sequence. More fundamentally, Roman numerals have no zero or negative numbers to indicate either debits or declining mathematical functions. Like other cultural features, numbers do not exist simply as badges of cultural identity, but to get a particular job done— and some cultural features get the job done better than others, which is why virtually every culture discards some of its own features and replaces them with features borrowed from other cultures.

Perpetuating cultural features as if they were butterflies preserved in amber, or other museum pieces, and using verbal virtuosity to make this seem like cosmic justice, may exalt the anointed but it condemns lagging groups— the ostensible beneficiaries of multiculturalism— to needless handicaps in the real world, where concrete capabilities matter more than purely symbolic equality. For similar reasons, the promotion of separate group identities not only fragments a society into warring factions, it keeps those groups that are lagging— whether lagging economically or educationally or both— from fully utilizing the existing culture of the larger society around them for their own advancement.

Massive borrowings of one culture from other cultures not only belie the arbitrary multicultural pronouncement that all cultures are equal— in some undefinable and hence empirically untestable sense— these borrowings raise deeper questions about the extent to which such borrowings are facilitated or inhibited by the particular settings in which particular racial groups have evolved. In short, the question is not simply what kinds of cultures have been internally generated by particular races but how large is the cultural universe from which the cultural achievements of others can be borrowed.

When the British first crossed the Atlantic to settle in North America, they were enabled to navigate at sea by using knowledge of the stars derived from the Middle East, one of a number of kinds of knowledge stored in letters from an alphabet created by the Romans and disseminated by mass-production printing, invented by the Chinese. The Britons' navigational calculations were made with a numbering system created in India and they used compasses invented in China. Societies isolated from such far flung sources of knowledge— whether isolated by deserts, mountains or other impediments, such as an absence of draft animals— have whole ways of life denied to them by geography alone. Cultures evolving over the centuries in radically different settings are unlikely to have the same values or imperatives, especially when they are untempered by exposure to other cultures.

When the British confronted the Iroquois on the eastern coast of North America, their cultural differences were due not solely to those features generated internally by the British themselves and by the Iroquois themselves. These differences reflected the vastly larger cultural universe available to the British, including the decisive advantage of gunpowder, invented in China. Lacking the long-range transportation advantages of

Europeans, based ultimately on draft animals,* the Iroquois had no way of knowing of the very existence of the Incas and the Maya, much less incorporating cultural features from Incan and Mayan societies into their own. We need not resort to genes, racism, perceptions or injustices to explain why the British ultimately prevailed against the Iroquois.

In various other parts of the world as well, the cultural universe could shrink to the dimensions of an isolated village, whether in the mountain valleys of the Balkans or in geographically fragmented regions of sub-Saharan Africa. Literacy could expand the dimensions of the mind beyond the immediate physical setting and illiteracy could shrink the cultural universe, even among peoples not as severely limited by geography as others. But access to literacy has also been radically different for different peoples in different parts of the world.

The cultural universe can also be affected by what has been aptly called "the radius of trust," which can profoundly affect economic development. Without the ability to draw economic resources from vastly more people than can possibly know each other, huge economic projects, creating great economies of scale, would not be possible, except in the rare cases where a very few very rich people are both able and willing to commit a major portion of their own personal fortunes to a particular enterprise. While millions of strangers will seldom blindly trust their money to other strangers, in any kind of society, in those societies whose legal and political institutions can be relied upon to maintain some level of integrity in the protection of returns on investments, modest sums invested by millions of individuals can be aggregated into the vast amounts of money required for such major economic undertakings as building railroads or financing multinational corporations.

Conversely, in societies where the radius of trust seldom extends beyond the family, and where people in the next village are an unknown quantity,

---

* While many cultural features of distant societies arrived by ship, what made ships economically viable, during the millennia before modern transportation technology created self-propelled vehicles, was the availability of draft animals to transport the large cargoes which these ships carried. In the absence of heavy-duty draft animals in the Western Hemisphere, an absence of large-scale ships is hardly surprising.

while the national legal and political institutions may be a distant and unreliable mystery, economic activities may be severely limited, regardless of the natural endowments of the land or the people. Moreover, limited economic interactions can also mean limited cultural interactions. There are reasons why port cities, especially those engaged in international trade, have often been centers of cultural advancement more so than the interior hinterlands. Even the most advanced peoples borrow from others, including borrowing particular features from other peoples who lag behind in general technological, cultural or economic development, but who develop particular advances that others have not developed.

In short, the size of the cultural universe has been enormously important in the cultural and economic development of peoples, races and nations, however much the factor of cultural universes may be overlooked or downplayed by those pursuing the more heady visions of genetic determinism or social injustice.

Geography does not lend itself to moral melodramas. As the distinguished economic historian David S. Landes put it in his book *The Wealth and Poverty of Nations*: "No one can be praised or blamed for the temperature of the air, or the volume and timing of rainfall, or the lay of the land."[78]

Chapter 19

Race and Cosmic Justice

The kind of collective justice demanded for racial or ethnic groups is often espoused as "social justice," but could more aptly be called *cosmic* justice, since it seeks to undo disparities created by circumstances, as well as those created by the injustices of human beings. Moreover, cosmic justice not only extends from individuals to groups, it extends beyond contemporary groups to intertemporal abstractions, of which today's groups are conceived as being the current embodiments.

DISPARITIES VERSUS INJUSTICES

Against the background of world history, the idea that an absence of an even distribution of groups in particular endeavors is something strange, or is weighty evidence of discrimination, is a dogma for which evidence is seldom asked or given— and a dogma that defies vast amounts of evidence to the contrary. Yet that dogma survives on the basis of contemporary peer consensus, even among those who take pride in considering themselves to be "thinking people." Yet this unsubstantiated presupposition of the prevailing vision is so powerful that its reverberations are felt, not only among people in the media who are ready to burst into indignation or outrage at statistical differences in outcomes among groups, but even in courts of law where employers, mortgage lenders and others whose decisions *convey* some of the differences among groups are presumed to be the *cause* of those differences— and are charged with proving their innocence, completely contrary to the practice in most other aspects of American law.

468

Among intellectuals who confuse blame with causation, the question-begging phrase "blaming the victim" has become a staple in discussions of intergroup differences. No individual or group can be blamed for being born into circumstances (including cultures) that lack the advantages that other people's circumstances have. But neither can "society" be automatically assumed to be either the cause or the cure for such disparities. Still less can a particular institution whose employment, pricing or lending decisions *convey* intergroup differences be automatically presumed to be *causing* those differences.

Even if one believes that environment is the key to intergroup differences, that environment includes a cultural legacy from the past— and the past is as much beyond our control as the geographic settings and historic happenstances that have left not only different individuals or races, but whole nations and civilizations, with very different heritages. Too often "environment" is conceived as the immediate surroundings today, when the cultural legacy of the past may be an equal or greater environmental influence, depending on the circumstances.

If the dogmas of multiculturalism declare different cultures equally valid, and hence sacrosanct against efforts to change them, then these dogmas simply complete the sealing off of a vision from facts— and sealing off many people in lagging groups from the advances available from other cultures around them, leaving nothing but an agenda of resentment-building and crusades on the side of the angels against the forces of evil— however futile or even counterproductive these may turn out to be for those who are the ostensible beneficiaries of such moral melodramas.

Nor can whole cultures always be left unchanged while simply tacking on new skills, since the very desire, efforts and perseverance required to acquire and master those skills are not independent of the existing culture. Moreover, the corollary of the presumed equality of cultures— that existing disparities are due to injustices inflicted by others— reduces a felt need to subject oneself to the demanding process of changing one's own capabilities, habits and outlook.

The perspective of cosmic justice is implicit in much of what is said and done by many intellectuals on many issues— for example, best-selling author Andrew Hacker's depiction of people like himself who tend "to murmur, when seeing what so many blacks endure, that there but for an accident of birth, go I."[1] However valid this may be as a general statement of the vision of cosmic justice and cosmic injustice, the word "endure" implies something more than that. It implies that the misfortunes of those on the short end of cosmic injustices are due to what they must endure at the hands of other people, rather than being due to either external circumstances that presented fewer opportunities for them to acquire valuable human capital or internal cultural values which worked against their taking advantage of the opportunities already available to them.

In this, Professor Hacker has been in the long tradition of intellectuals who more or less automatically transform differences into inequities and inequities into the evils or shortcomings of society. Among the many feats of verbal virtuosity by Andrew Hacker and others is transforming negative facts about the group that is considered to be the victim of society into mere *perceptions* by that society. Thus Professor Hacker refers to "what we call crime," to "so-called riots," and to "what we choose to call intelligence."[2] Such exercises in verbal cleansing extend to racism, from which blacks are definitionally exempt, according to Hacker, by the newly minted proviso of possessing power[3]— a proviso which serves no other purpose than providing an escape hatch from the obvious. All this clearly puts Hacker on the side of the angels, rather explicitly when he says "On the whole, conservatives don't really care whether black Americans are happy or unhappy,"[4] as presumably liberals like himself do.

Professor Hacker expresses empathy with those blacks who work in predominantly white organizations and "are expected to think and act in white ways"[5]— the same kind of objection made by Latvians and Czechs in times past, when acquiring another culture was the price of their rising in a world where their own culture did not equip them with the same prerequisites for achievement as Germans already had. Apparently people are to think and behave as they have in the past and yet somehow get better results in the future— and, if they don't get better results, that is considered to be society's fault. Achieving the same results as others, without having to change, in order to acquire the same cultural prerequisites that others acquired without changing, would be cosmic justice, *if it happened*, but hardly a promising agenda in the real world.

Multiculturalism, like the caste system, tends to freeze people where the accident of birth has placed them. Unlike the caste system, multiculturalism holds out the prospect that, all cultures being equal, one's life chances should be the same— and that it is society's fault if these chances are not the same. Although both caste and multiculturalism suppress individual opportunities, they differ primarily in that the caste system preaches resignation to one's fate and multiculturalism preaches resentment of one's fate. Another major difference between caste and multiculturalism is that no one was likely to claim that the caste system was a boon to the lower castes.

As for more general questions about racial or ethnic identity, the costs of an identity ideology include not only the advancement that is forfeited, but also the needless disadvantages of letting people who represent the lowest common denominator of a group have a disproportionate influence on the fate of the group as a whole.

If criminals, rioters and vandals from within the group are to be automatically defended or excused for the sake of group solidarity, then the costs of that solidarity include not only a lower standard of living, since such people raise the costs of doing business in their neighborhoods and thereby raise the prices of goods and services above what they are in other neighborhoods, such people also cause fewer businesses to locate in their neighborhoods and fewer taxis to be willing to take people to such neighborhoods. Worst of all, the damage committed by those representing the lowest common denominator— encompassing crimes up to and including murder— is overwhelmingly against other members of their own group.

The high costs of putting race-based solidarity ahead of behavior and its consequences include letting the lowest common denominator become a disproportionate influence in defining the whole community itself, not only in the eyes of the larger society but also within the community. When middle-class black youngsters feel a need or pressure to adopt some of the counterproductive attitudes, values or lifestyles of the lowest common denominator, including negative attitudes toward education, lest they be accused of "acting white," then the life chances of whole generations can be sacrificed on the altar to racial solidarity. Yet a sense of the overriding importance of solidarity based on race extends far beyond children in school and goes far back in history. Gunnar Myrdal's 1944 classic, *An American Dilemma*, pointed out that it had long been the practice of black Americans to "protect any Negro from the whites, even when they happen not to like that individual Negro."[6]

When outsiders' criticisms of any segment of a community cannot be either accepted or refuted, the response is often to claim that these critics are "blaming the victim." But this whole concept confuses blame with causation. The masses of less educated and less acculturated blacks, whose migrations out of the South in the twentieth century and whose arrival in Northern cities led to retrogressions in race relations in the early part of the century— and whose later arrival in west coast cities during the Second World War led to similar retrogressions on the west coast, could hardly be blamed for having been born where they were and having absorbed the culture which existed around them in the South. But that does not deny these migrants' causal role in the changes for the worse which occurred in cities outside the South after the Southern blacks' arrivals there.

No one in John Rawls' "original position" as a disembodied being contemplating alternative circumstances into which to be born would have chosen to be born black in the South of that era. From a cosmic perspective, it was an injustice to those who were. But that is very different from saying that their mass migrations in search of a better life did not impose large costs on both the black and white populations already residing in the Northern cities to which they moved, or that the latter had no right to resent these costs or to try to protect themselves from them. The inherent conflict of these different legitimate desires and interests in each of these groups is part of the tragedy of the human condition— as contrasted with a simple moral melodrama starring the intelligentsia on the side of the angels against the forces of evil.

RACE AND CRIME

The intelligentsia's feats of verbal virtuosity reach their heights— or depths— when discussing the crime rate among blacks in America. For example, *New York Times* columnist Tom Wicker responded to an incident in which a white woman jogging in Central Park was gang raped by black youths, by denying that this was a racially motivated crime. Wicker said, "the fact that the victim was white and the attackers black does not seem to have caused the crime." He added:

> But if race does not explain this crime, race was relevant to it. The attackers lived surrounded and surely influenced by the social pathologies of the inner city. They hardly could have reached teen age without realizing and resenting the wide economic and social gap that still separates blacks and whites in this country; and they could not fail to see, and probably return, the hostility that glares at them undisguised across that gap. These influences are bound to have had some consequences—perhaps long repressed, probably not realized or understood— in their attitudes and behavior.[7]

The "wide economic and social gap" between blacks and whites that Wicker referred to was even wider in earlier years, when it was common for whites to go up to Harlem at night for public entertainment or private parties, and common for both blacks and whites to sleep out in the city's parks on hot summer nights during an era when most people could not afford air-conditioning. But sleeping in parks— or in some cases, even walking through some of those same parks in broad daylight— became dangerous in later and more prosperous times. Yet here, as elsewhere, the prevailing vision often seems impervious to even the plainest facts.

The role played by many people who, like Tom Wicker himself, have incessantly emphasized "gaps" and "disparities" as injustices to be resented, rather than lags to be overcome, is seldom considered to be among the candidates for inclusion among the "root causes" of crime, even though the rise of crime is far more consistent with the increasing prevalence of such grievance and resentment ideologies than with other things that are considered to be "root causes," such as poverty levels, which have been declining as crime rates rose. Resentments, based on ideologies of cosmic justice, are not confined to the intelligentsia but "trickle down" to others. For example, right after charges of gang rape of a black woman were filed against white students on Duke University's lacrosse team in 2006, angry reactions from a black college in the same town reflected that same vision, as reported in *Newsweek*:

Across town, at NCCU, the mostly black college where the alleged
victim is enrolled, students seemed bitterly resigned to the players'
beating the rap. "This is a race issue," said Candice Shaw, 20. "People at
Duke have a lot of money on their side." Chan Hall, 22, said, "It's the
same old story. Duke up, Central down." Hall said he wanted to see the
Duke students prosecuted "whether it happened or not. It would be
justice for things that happened in the past."[8]

Implicit in these statements are the key elements of the cosmic justice
vision of the intelligentsia— seeing other people's good fortune as a
grievance, rather than an incentive for self-improvement, and seeing flesh-
and-blood contemporaries as simply part of an intertemporal abstraction, so
that a current injustice against them would merely offset other injustices of
the past. There could hardly be a more deadly inspiration for a never-ending
cycle of revenge and counter-revenge— the Hatfields and the McCoys writ
large, with a whole society caught in the crossfire.

The built-in excuse has become as standard in discussions of black crime
as it is unsubstantiated, except by peer consensus among the intelligentsia.
The phrase "troubled youth" is a common example of the unsubstantiated
but built-in excuse, since those who use that phrase usually feel no need to
offer any specific evidence about the specific individuals they are talking
about, who may be creating big trouble for others, while enjoying themselves
in doing so. An all too common pattern across the country was that in an
episode in Milwaukee:

Shaina Perry remembers the punch to her face, blood streaming from a
cut over her eye, her backpack with her asthma inhaler, debit card and
cellphone stolen, and then the laughter. . . "They just said, 'Oh, white girl
bleeds a lot,'" said Perry, 22, who was attacked at Kilbourn Reservoir Park
over the Fourth of July weekend. . . Milwaukee Police Chief Edward
Flynn noted Tuesday that crime is colorblind... "I saw some of my friends
on the ground getting beat pretty severely.". . . Perry needed three stitches
to close a cut above her eye. She said she saw a friend getting kicked and
when she walked up to ask what was happening, a man punched her in
the face. "I heard laughing as they were beating everybody up. They were
eating chips like it was a picnic," said Perry, a restaurant cashier. . . Most
of the 11 people who told the Journal Sentinel they were attacked or
witnessed the attacks on their friends said that police did not take their
complaints seriously. . . "About 20 of us stayed to give statements and
make sure everyone was accounted for. The police wouldn't listen to us,

they wouldn't take our names or statements. They told us to leave. It was completely infuriating."[9]

Variations on such episodes of unprovoked violence by young black gangs against white people on beaches, in shopping malls or in other public places have occurred in Philadelphia, New York, Denver, Chicago, Cleveland, Washington, Los Angeles and other places across the country, often with the attackers voicing anti-white invective and mocking those they left injured or bleeding.[10] But such episodes are often either ignored or downplayed in most of the media, and by officials— and the *Chicago Tribune* even offered an excuse for not reporting the race of the attackers in a series of such episodes that alarmed the Chicago public.[11] Yet race is widely reported when it comes to imprisonment rates or other racial disparities. For example:

> In March of 2010, Secretary of Education Arne Duncan delivered a speech that highlighted racial disparities in school suspension and expulsion and that called for more rigorous civil rights enforcement in education. He suggested that students with disabilities and Black students, especially males, were suspended far more often than their White counterparts. These students, he also noted, were often punished more severely for similar misdeeds. Just months later, in September of 2010, a report analyzing 2006 data collected by the U.S. Department of Education's Office for Civil Rights found that more than 28% of Black male middle school students had been suspended at least once. This is nearly three times the 10% rate for white males. Further, 18% of Black females in middle school were suspended, more than four times as often as white females (4%). Later that same month, U.S. Attorney General Eric Holder and Secretary Duncan each addressed a conference of civil rights lawyers in Washington, D.C., and affirmed their departments' commitment to ending such disparities.[12]

The very possibility that there might be behavioral differences behind the punishment differences does not surface in such discussions. To believe that there are no behavioral differences between black and white school-age males is to assume that the large and undeniable differences in crime rates— including murder rates— between black and white young adults suddenly and inexplicably materialize after they finish school.

Professor David D. Cole of the Georgetown University Law School expressed views similar to those of Tom Wicker and many others among the intelligentsia of the multicultural era, when he lamented the increasing imprisonment of black men:

> In the 1950s, when segregation was still legal, African-Americans comprised 30 percent of the prison population. Sixty years later, African-Americans and Latinos make up 70 percent of the incarcerated population, and that population has skyrocketed. The disparities are greatest where race and class intersect— nearly 60 percent of all young black men born between 1965 and 1969 who dropped out of high school went to prison at least once on a felony conviction before they turned thirty-five.[13]

Professor Cole posed the issue explicitly in the cosmic justice terms of John Rawls:

> Were we in John Rawls' "original position," with no idea whether we would be born a black male in an impoverished urban home... would we accept a system in which one out of every three black males born today can expect to spend time in jail during his life?[14]

The preemptive assertion in passing that it is the *system*— something external, created by others in the larger society— that is the cause of the problem arbitrarily puts off limits at the outset the very possibility that the problem may be elsewhere. By sheer verbal virtuosity, rather than by any facts or evidence, collective responsibility is put on those in the larger society. There is clearly *something* in the circumstances into which many black males are born that makes it far more likely that they will commit crimes than is true of the population in general, including the majority of the black population that does *not* end up behind bars. But that tells us absolutely nothing about what that something is. If it is being "impoverished," then clearly there is a lot less poverty today than in 1950, when the imprisonment rate among black males was lower, even though invoking poverty remains at least as much a part of the rituals— as distinguished from arguments— of intellectuals today as then.

Professor Cole adds some other statistics, that "only 5 percent of college-educated African-Americans" have spent time in prison, while the imprisonment rate for black male high-school dropouts "is nearly fifty times the national average."[15] He also notes, "Children with parents in prison are in turn seven times more likely to be imprisoned at some point in their lives than other children."[16] None of this supports the claim that the cause is an external "system," as asserted by Professor Cole, rather than an internal counterproductive culture, perhaps aided and abetted by outsiders who excuse or even celebrate that counterproductive underclass culture— an underclass culture which has produced very similar results among lower class whites in Britain,[17] where similar ideologies of envy and resentment have long been promoted by the British intelligentsia.

Both in Britain and in the United States, as well as in other countries, there has been a steady ideological drumbeat of rhetoric from intellectuals depicting "gaps" and "disparities" as grievances against those who are better off. In both Britain and America, this resentment and hostility generated by the intelligentsia has been directed by those who accept it, not only against members of the larger society, but also against those members of their own group who are working to do well in school, in order to have a better life later on.

What is truly remarkable in its implications is the contrast between the higher rate of imprisonment among young men in the black ghettos of America today compared to the 1950s, and how that undermines the very argument in which these imprisonment rates are cited. Surely the supposed "root causes" of crime—poverty, discrimination and the like— were not *less* in the 1950s, before the civil rights laws and policies of the 1960s. And what of those blacks who do not drop out of high school but who go on to college instead— and seldom end up in prison? It should also be noted that, from 1994 on into the twenty-first century, the poverty rate among black husband-wife families was below 10 percent.[18] Are these blacks living in a different external "system" or do they have a different internal culture, representing different values in their families or among others who have influenced them?

Yet such questions are seldom asked, much less answered. Instead, today's higher rate of incarceration is blamed on drug laws, tighter sentencing rules, and a general failure of society. In short, society is to blame, except apparently for those members of society who actually commit the crimes. But, whatever the reasons for the higher crime rate now than then, or between blacks and whites, it is indeed a tragic injustice— *from a cosmic perspective*— to be born into circumstances that make it more likely that one will commit crimes and be imprisoned, with negative consequences for the rest of one's life. If some personified Fate had decreed this, then that would be the perpetrator of the injustice. But, if this is just part of the way the world has evolved, then it is a cosmic injustice— if something as impersonal as the cosmos can be considered capable of being unjust.

As noted in Chapter 8, a *cosmic* injustice is not a *social* injustice, and proceeding as if society has both the omniscience and the omnipotence to "solve" the "problem" risks *anti-social* justice, in which others are jeopardized or sacrificed, in hopes of putting some particular segment of the population where they would be "but for" being born into adverse circumstances that they did not choose. It is certainly no benefit to blacks in general to take a sympathetic view of those blacks who commit crimes, since most of the crimes committed by blacks— especially murder— are committed against other blacks.

Whatever the injustices of society that might be blamed as "root causes" of crime, the black victims of crime are not responsible for those injustices. Here, especially, "social justice" in theory becomes *anti-social* justice in practice, sacrificing innocent people's well-being— or even their lives— because some other individuals are considered not to have been born into circumstances that would have given them as good a chance as others have had to achieve their own well-being without becoming criminals. Moreover, it is wholly arbitrary to imagine oneself in Rawls' "original position" as a potential black criminal, rather than as one of the far more numerous blacks who are victims of criminals.

Those who say that we should "do something" seldom face the fact that everything depends on just what specifically that something is. Being lenient with criminals has not worked. Relieving poverty has not reduced crime. And certainly being "non-judgmental" has not done so either. Crime rates skyrocketed when all these things were tried, whether among blacks or whites, and whether in America or in England.

The automatic "celebration" of cultural differences, or the non-judgmental view of socially counterproductive behavior, for example, cannot be continued if the goal is to improve the well-being of actual flesh-and-blood people, rather than seeking cosmic justice for an intertemporal abstraction. One can be humane or inhumane only to living people, not to abstractions.

SLAVERY

Nowhere have intellectuals seen racial issues as issues about intertemporal abstractions more so than in discussions of slavery. Moreover, few facts of history have been so distorted by highly selective filtering as has the history of slavery. To many people today, slavery means white people holding black people in bondage. The vast millions of people around the world who were neither white nor black, but who were either slaves or enslavers for centuries, fade out of this vision of slavery, as if they had never existed, even though they may well have outnumbered both blacks and whites. It has been estimated that there were more slaves in India than in the entire Western Hemisphere.[19] China during the era of slavery has been described as "one of the largest and most comprehensive markets for the exchange of human beings in the world."[20] Slaves were a majority of the population in some of the cities in Southeast Asia.[21] At some period or other in history, as John Stuart Mill pointed out, "almost every people, now civilized, have consisted, in majority, of slaves."[22]

When Abraham Lincoln said, "If slavery is not wrong, nothing is wrong,"[23] he was expressing an idea peculiar to Western civilization at that time, and by no means universally accepted throughout Western civilization. What seems almost incomprehensible today is that there was no serious challenge to the moral legitimacy of slavery prior to the eighteenth century. Christian monasteries in Europe and Buddhist monasteries in Asia both had slaves. Even Thomas More's fictional ideal society, Utopia, had slaves.

Although intellectuals today may condemn slavery as a historic evil of "our society," what was peculiar about Western society was not that it had slaves, like other societies around the world, but that it was the first civilization to turn *against* slavery— and that it spent more than a century destroying slavery, not only within Western civilization itself, but also in other countries around the world, over the often bitter and sometimes armed resistance of people in other societies. Only the overwhelming military power of Western nations during the age of imperialism made this possible. Slavery did not quietly die out of its own accord. It went down fighting to the bitter end, in countries around the world, and it has still not totally died out to this day, in parts of the Middle East and Africa.[24]

It is the image of *racial* slavery— white people enslaving black people— that has been indelibly burned into the consciousness of both black and white Americans today by the intelligentsia— and not simply as a fact about the past but as a *causal* factor used to explain much of the present, and an enduring *moral* condemnation of the enslaving race. Yet two crucial facts have been filtered out of this picture: (1) the institution of slavery was not based on race and (2) whites as well as blacks were enslaved. The very word "slave" is derived from the name of a European people— Slavs— who were enslaved for centuries before the first African was brought in bondage to the Western Hemisphere. It was not only in English that the word for slave derived from the word for Slav; the same was true in various other European languages and in Arabic.[25]

For most of the history of slavery, which covers most of the history of the human race, most slaves were not racially different from those who enslaved them. Not only did Europeans enslave other Europeans, Asians enslaved other Asians, Africans enslaved other Africans, Polynesians enslaved other Polynesians and the indigenous peoples of the Western Hemisphere enslaved other indigenous peoples of the Western Hemisphere.

Moreover, after it became both technologically and economically feasible to transport masses of slaves from one continent to another— that is, to have a whole population of slaves of a different race— Europeans as well as Africans were enslaved and transported from their native lands to bondage on another continent. Pirates alone transported a million or more Europeans as slaves to the Barbary Coast of North Africa— at least twice as many European slaves as there were African slaves transported to the United States and to the thirteen colonies from which it was formed.[26] Moreover, white slaves were still being bought and sold in the Islamic world, decades after blacks had been freed in the United States.

What marked the modern era of slavery in the West was the fact that, as distinguished historian Daniel Boorstin pointed out, "Now for the first time in Western history, the status of slave coincided with a difference of race."[27] But to claim that race or racism was the basis of slavery is to cite as a cause something that happened thousands of years after its supposed effect. As for the legacy of slavery in the world of today, that is something well worth investigating— as distinguished from simply making sweeping assumptions. Too many assumptions that have been made about the effects of slavery on both blacks and whites will not stand up under scrutiny.

Back during the era of slavery in the United States, such prominent writers as the French visitor and observer Alexis de Tocqueville, Northern traveler in the antebellum South Frederick Law Olmsted and prominent Southern writer Hinton Helper all pointed to striking differences between the North and the South, and attributed the deficiencies of the Southern region to the effects of slavery on the *white* population of the South.[28] These differences between Northern and Southern whites were not mere "perceptions" or "stereotypes." They were factually demonstrable in areas ranging from literacy rates to rates of unwed motherhood, as well as in attitudes toward work and violence.[29] But attributing these differences to slavery ignored the fact that the ancestors of white Southerners differed in these same ways from the ancestors of white Northerners, when they both lived in different parts of Britain, and when neither had ever seen a black slave.

Does the moral enormity of slavery give it any more decisive *causal* weight in explaining the situation of blacks today than it did in explaining that of whites in the antebellum South? There is no *a priori* answer to that question, which must be examined empirically, like many other questions.

The fact that so many black families today consist of women with fatherless children has been said by many to be a legacy of slavery. Yet most black children grew up in two-parent families, even under slavery itself, and for generations thereafter.[30] As recently as 1960, two-thirds of black children were still living in two-parent families.[31] A century ago, a slightly higher percentage of blacks were married than were whites.[32] In some years, a slightly higher percentage of blacks were in the labor force than were whites.[33] In 1890 and in 1930, the unemployment rate for blacks was lower than it was for whites.[34] The reasons for changes for the worse in these and other patterns must be sought in our own times. Whatever the reasons for the disintegration of the black family, it escalated to the current disastrous level well over a century after the end of slavery, though less than a generation after a large expansion of the welfare state and its accompanying non-judgmental ideology.

To say that slavery will not bear the full weight of responsibility for all subsequent social problems among black Americans is not to say that it had negligible consequences among either blacks or whites or that its consequences ended when slavery itself ended. But this is only to say that answers to questions about either slavery or race must be sought in facts, not in assumptions or visions, and certainly not in attempts to reduce questions of causation to only those which provide moral melodramas and an opportunity for the intelligentsia to be on the side of the angels.

Just as Western Europeans in post-Roman times benefitted from the fact that their ancestors had been conquered by the Romans, with all the brutality and oppression that entailed, blacks in America today have a far higher standard of living than most Africans in Africa as a result of the injustices and abuses that their ancestors suffered by being enslaved. There is no question that both conquest and enslavement were traumatic experiences for those on whom they were inflicted. Nor is either morally justified by whatever benefits might come of this to subsequent generations of their offspring. But history cannot be undone. Nor does conceiving of races as intertemporal abstractions have any such track record as to make it look like a promising approach to the present or the future.

PART VIII

AN OVERVIEW

The study of history is a powerful antidote to contemporary arrogance. It is humbling to discover how many of our glib assumptions, which seem to us novel and plausible, have been tested before, not once but many times and in innumerable guises; and discovered to be, at great human cost, wholly false.

Paul Johnson[1]

Chapter 20

Patterns and Visions

M any specific issues have been discussed in the preceding chapters, not simply for the sake of critiquing those particular issues (many of which are now moot) or for the sake of critiquing particular intellectuals (many of whom are now dead and largely forgotten), but for understanding enduring patterns among intellectuals in general— and how those patterns have impacted society in the past and can be expected to impact society in the future. These patterns include the underlying assumptions which give a coherence to conclusions reached by intellectuals on a wide range of otherwise unrelated issues, whether on law, economics, war, race or other concerns. These underlying assumptions might be internal value premises of intellectuals or they might be assumptions about the facts of the external world. We need to examine both possibilities, in order to understand the thrust of intellectuals' ideas and the imperatives that give direction to that thrust.

To understand the role of intellectuals in society, we must understand what they do— not what they say they do, or even what they may think they are doing, but what in fact are their actions and the social consequences of those actions. For that, we need to understand not only their internal assumptions but also the external incentives and constraints inherent in the role of intellectuals, as compared to people who are in other occupations. Individual intellectuals may say and do all sorts of things for all sorts of reasons but, when we try to understand general patterns among the intelligentsia as a whole, we need to examine the circumstances in which they operate, their track records and their impact on the larger society around them.

Since this is an attempt to discover patterns among intellectuals and to seek reasons for those patterns, history obviously provides a far larger sample than the present. It is also a sample from many very different eras, covering far greater variations in circumstances than the current slice of history before our eyes. Patterns that have endured for generations, or for centuries, suggest more fundamental and enduring reasons for the ways that intellectuals have thought and acted. Moreover, our ability to dispassionately examine those ideas of the past in which we have no such emotional investment as we may have in the ideas of our own time, can give us a clearer view of patterns and their implications.

Nothing is easier to detect than the absurdities of ideas in the past. Nor are such absurdities simply those of the village idiot. All too often, they have been the absurdities of the village genius, who may not realize that the depth of his genius says nothing about the limits of its scope. Moreover, the village idiot seems unlikely to have acquired the same influence as the village genius or to have the same capacity for generating major disasters. Intellect— even intellect that reaches the level of genius— is not the same as wisdom.

In surveying the past, we have focussed especially on the ideas of eminent thinkers in the past, people who were not only "in the mainstream" but who were the elite of the mainstream, people recognized by the many honors heaped upon them by their contemporaries, even if their luster may later have grown dimmer with the passage of time and the unfolding of the consequences of their ideas when put into practice. If nothing else, their obvious— in retrospect— missteps in logic, and vast gaps in empirical evidence, can make painfully clear what a weak reed to lean on is peer consensus, even when it is the peer consensus of those who consider themselves to be "thinking people." But, however superior the capacity to think, an unused capacity is as fruitless in the brain as it is in an economy with unemployed labor and idle factories. The question in both cases is why valuable resources are not used.

VALUE PREMISES

There is no question that different people see the world in fundamentally different ways. Among the explanations offered are differences in their value premises and differences in their assumptions about the facts of the real world.

Many among the intelligentsia say that how one conceives of issues, or reaches policy conclusions, depends on the "value premises" from which one begins. Plausible as this may sound, and however much this belief may have peer approval among intellectuals, ultimately it is an assertion subject to verification. An alternative explanation of how people reach opposing views on particular policy conclusions, or differences in their more general ideological positions, is that they begin with different beliefs about the facts of the world (including the nature of human beings) and/or a different analysis of causation.[1] The distinction between these two explanations of differences in social visions is plain: John Rawls' categorical priority of justice is a value premise, but Alfred Marshall's theories of supply and demand are testable hypotheses about observable facts.

Conceivably, either internal value premises or assumptions about the facts of the external world can form the basis of conclusions about why things are what they are, or about what is desirable in individual life or social policy. Yet the value premises explanation of differences in social visions seems to be much more widely accepted, and is more consistent with the ferocity of attacks on those who dissent from the prevailing vision of the anointed. But is it a foregone conclusion that ideological differences are ultimately based on different value premises?

It would be hard to think of two economists whose ideological positions on capitalism were more different from one another than those of Adam Smith and Karl Marx. Yet Marx's extensive discussions of Adam Smith in his *Theories of Surplus Value* make no criticisms of Smith's value premises. Nor is it obvious what fundamental differences there are between Marx and Smith as regards their value premises. J.A. Schumpeter, perhaps the leading scholar on the history of economic thought, pointed out an "inconveniently large expanse of common ground" between Marx and classical liberals in general[2]— that is, inconvenient for a revolutionary.[3] Smith and Marx in fact had very similar opinions about businessmen, for example, and a case could be made that Smith's views of businessmen were even more negative than Marx's.[4]

Where Smith and Marx differed was in their economic analyses and in their assumptions about empirical facts, on which their economic analyses were based. Even here, however, in Marx's criticisms of Smith's economic conceptions and analysis, he called Smith historically "justified" as a pioneer feeling his way toward the development of new concepts for the emerging field of economics.[5] Marx went even further in defense of Adam Smith, and dismissed some criticisms of particular aspects of Smith's economic analysis by later economists as "the hobby-horse of the second-rate."[6]

In Marx's extensive critique of the next great classical economist, David Ricardo, there is likewise no criticism of Ricardo's value premises,[7] much less the kinds of smears advanced by later critics on the left against free market economists, that they are apologists for the status quo or defenders of the powers that be. Marx did not hesitate to make such charges against particular individuals but it was not a blanket charge that included economists of the caliber of Smith and Ricardo.

In general, it is by no means clear that differences in conclusions about social issues among other intellectuals are due to differences in value premises, rather than differences in assumptions about the nature of the facts of the real world or differences in analytical approaches. That is a question whose answer can vary according to the particular intellectuals involved, rather than being a foregone conclusion. But the "value premises" argument is seldom questioned by most of the intelligentsia today, perhaps because it affords them a safe harbor when their stands on issues are challenged on either logical or empirical grounds.

When no other reply to their critics is possible, the intelligentsia can at least say that they are basing themselves on their own "value premises" which, like tastes, cannot be disputed. The long-standing— and long untested— assumption among the anointed that those who have a different vision of the world are not as humane as themselves is an assumption consonant with the view that differing value premises explain ideological differences. But whether it is consonant with the facts is another question entirely. What is telling is that the value premise assumption has usually not even been treated as a question, but as an axiom.

Sudden changes of mind on ideological issues by large numbers of people at the same time, whether in response to the First World War, which turned many hawks into pacifists, or in response to the Nazi-Soviet Pact that led to many defections from the Communist Party in Western democracies, are hard to explain by changes in value premises. Both happened too fast for large numbers of people to have coincidentally changed their fundamental values all at the same time. What such events presented were new *facts* that undermined old assumptions about the realities of the world. So too did the French Revolution, the Great Depression and other traumatic events which led many people to sudden "road to Damascus" conversions in their thinking about the *facts* of life, leading to the abandonment of previous assumptions and policy positions based on those assumptions.

ASSUMPTIONS ABOUT FACTS

What is remarkable is how few are the differences in underlying assumptions that are necessary to produce a sweeping array of opposing views on a wide spectrum of very disparate issues. The centuries-long conflicts between those with the tragic vision and those with the vision of the anointed have had many ramifications, but these conflicts seemed to require only a few differences in how knowledge is conceived and in how effective reason is assumed to be in the real world.

When knowledge is conceived as all the information that has consequences in the real world, then the distribution of that knowledge is radically different from what it is when knowledge is conceived as the much narrower range of information in which intellectuals specialize. Much of the latter kinds of knowledge may be little known or understood by the population at large, whose articulated reasoning may also not be nearly as highly developed as that among intellectuals. But the practical implications of such disparities between the intelligentsia and the masses depend on how consequential both knowledge and reason— as narrowly conceived— are in the real world.

Just as one side and two angles are enough to determine all the dimensions and relationships of a triangle (the principle on which rangefinders are based), so these few assumptions about knowledge and reason seem to determine the broad outlines of differences in a wide spectrum of conclusions about disparate issues in society that have marked a conflict of visions that goes back for centuries.

In the twentieth century, for example, Swedish economist Gunnar Myrdal and Peter Bauer of the London School of Economics offered diametrically opposite prescriptions for increasing the economic development of Third World nations, based on different assessments of the amount and relevance of the knowledge of Westernized intellectuals in those countries.[8] Although the importance of value premises was insisted upon by Myrdal,[9] it is by no means clear what differences in value premises there were between Myrdal and Bauer. Although Myrdal put more emphasis on equalization in the distribution of income, Bauer's different emphasis was based *not* on a value preference for inequality but on a different analysis of consequences: "The promotion of economic equality and the alleviation of poverty are distinct and often conflicting."[10] Whatever the merits or demerits of Professor Bauer's conclusion, it was based on his different assessment of facts, not a difference in values.

Similarly, as noted in Chapter 11, H.G. Wells saw social problems as fundamentally *intellectual* problems, conferring on intellectuals a leading role in solving those problems, while George J. Stigler in a later era would dismiss the idea that even a monumental human tragedy implied a need for new intellectual input. To Wells, "escape from economic frustration to universal abundance and social justice" requires "a mighty intellectual effort"[11] and creating a lasting peace "is a huge, heavy, complex, distressful piece of mental engineering."[12] But to Stigler, "A war may ravage a continent or destroy a generation without posing new theoretical questions."[13] These contrasting views are *not* based on different beliefs about the desirability of wars— that is, different value premises— but are based on differences in the assumed roles of intellectual activity in preventing wars.

The vast disparity in knowledge and understanding between intellectuals and the population at large assumed by the intelligentsia is crucial to the vision of the anointed, whether in discussions of law, economics, race, war or innumerable other issues. But, if the knowledge that is consequential includes a range of mundane information too vast to be known to any given individual— whether among the intellectuals or the masses— then top-down decision-making processes like economic central planning, directed by an intellectual elite, are less promising than market competition, where millions of individual decisions and mutual accommodations bring into play a vastly larger range of consequential knowledge, even if this knowledge is available to each individual in unimpressively small fragments of the total knowledge in society. As Robert L. Bartley of the *Wall Street Journal* expressed this point of view: "In general, 'the market' is smarter than the smartest of its individual participants."[14]

The sharp rise and sharper fall of central planning in the twentieth century, even in countries run by communists or socialists, suggests a flaw in the assumptions of those with the vision of the anointed, a flaw not necessarily confined to economic policies. The failure of central planning, despite its having all the advantages that the intelligentsia consider crucial— advantages of intellect, education, vast amounts of statistical and other information, and a coherent plan, backed by government power— suggests that something must have been left out of the equation. The enormous fragmentation of consequential knowledge is one of those things, and the heterogeneity of people, not only among groups but even among individuals, including members of the same family, is another. Thinking in terms of abstract people in an abstract world makes it possible to glide over such things. But reality does not go away when it is ignored.

The same assumptions about knowledge and reason— their definition, distribution and efficacy— underlie conflicts of vision in the law. If the knowledge that is most consequential is mundane knowledge— as implied in Oliver Wendell Holmes' famous statement, "The life of the law has not been logic: it has been experience"[15]— then systemic processes tapping the experiences of millions of contemporaries, as well as the experiences of generations before them, count for more than brilliant innovations by a contemporary intellectual elite.[*] The Constitution of the United States governs one of those systemic processes by which laws are created, modified

---

[*] According to Holmes, some "great intellects" had made contributions to the development of the law, "the greatest of which," he added, "is trifling when compared with the mighty whole." Oliver Wendell Holmes, Jr., *Collected Legal Papers* (New York: Peter Smith, 1952), p. 194.

or repealed in response to a broad electorate, which can with a sufficiently sustained effort— as distinguished from a transient majority— amend the Constitution itself.

To those with the vision of the anointed, however, this whole process— which undercuts any claim for special decision-making influence by intellectual elites— is too confining for the role of "enlightened" government policies, which they envision as necessary to overcome the inertia and deficiencies of the masses. Nor is amending the Constitution considered to be a sufficient remedy, since it too depends on the decisions of the many, rather than the insights of an intellectual elite. Just as logically as those with the tragic vision— but with opposite assumptions— those with the vision of the anointed seek to have the power of legal innovation vested in judges, who are in Woodrow Wilson's words to determine "the adequacy of the Constitution in respect of the needs and interests of the nation" and to be the nation's "conscience" in matters of law, exercising "statesmanlike judicial control."[16]

This lofty rhetoric boils down to surrogate decision-making, preempting the decisions of individuals in their own lives and the Constitutional rights of voters to live under laws passed by their elected representatives, instead of under arbitrary rules imposed by judges responding to elite opinion, and with the added insult of pretending to be merely "interpreting" the Constitution— by which is meant ruling according to the underlying "values" or "spirit" of the Constitution, rather than its explicit instructions, and using the insights of "modern social science" or of foreign laws to reach decisions that meet "the needs of the time." What "values," "modern social science," the "needs of the time" and foreign laws all have in common is that they expand the arbitrary power of judges beyond the written laws passed by elected representatives of the people and beyond the Constitution of the United States.

The vision of the law pioneered in the early twentieth century by Progressive-era intellectuals had, by the second half of the twentieth century, become the prevailing vision in elite law schools and to a considerable extent in the courts themselves, as well as pervasive among the intelligentsia in the media and in educational institutions.

With other issues and in other fields, the public's decision-making power in a Constitutional democracy likewise became something to either circumvent or redirect in accordance with the agenda of the anointed. The filtering and slanting of information, whether in the media or in educational institutions from the public schools to the universities, are perfectly consistent with this vision. So too is seeing opposing views as not being things to engage but to discredit and, if possible, penalize, whether by informal sanctions, campus speech codes or by laws against "hate speech." Not all intellectuals have supported all these tactics, for the continuing influence of principles and ideas from earlier times did not evaporate immediately. But the trend has nevertheless been apparent— and perfectly consistent with the underlying assumptions of superior knowledge and reasoning concentrated in an intellectual elite.

In short, the tactics used by many of these elites— especially the evasion of serious engagement with opposing views— show that intellectuals' agendas can conflict with intellectual *standards*, and the outcome cannot be predicted in any particular case, so that the best we can do is examine how that conflict has generally turned out.

INTELLECTUAL STANDARDS

While the word "intellectual" as a noun refers to a set of people in a given range of occupations, as an adjective it connotes a set of standards and achievements which may or may not characterize the actual behavior of most people in those occupations.

Certainly as public intellectuals, commenting on issues and events outside the realm of their respective specialties, intellectuals have not always adhered to intellectual standards, to put it mildly. Yet the many violations of those standards by intellectuals themselves have demonstrated repeatedly the distinction which they often seek to blur between the noun and the adjective. These violations of intellectual standards include such blatant examples of illogic as the one-observation "trend" (capitalism having made workers poor, as if they were more prosperous before) and the one-country international comparison, in which Professor Lester Thurow pronounced the United States the "worst" of the industrial nations when it comes to unemployment, by citing unemployment problems solely within the United States, while ignoring chronically worse unemployment problems in Western Europe and elsewhere.

One of the most common violations of intellectual standards by intellectuals has been the practice of attributing an emotion (racism, sexism, homophobia, xenophobia, etc.) to those whose views differ from theirs, rather than answering their arguments.* In addition to examples from history already noted in earlier chapters, today Professor Robert H. Nelson of the University of Maryland is among those using this tactic, depicting "the common antagonism of most leading members of the Chicago school to the scientific management of society through government planning and implementation."[17] The invocation of "science" to buttress a political preference also goes back for centuries.

Another common tactic and flaw in the arguments of the intelligentsia is *eternalizing the transient*. Thus statistical trends in the share of the nation's income going to "the rich" (however defined) and "the poor" (however defined), treat the people in these different income brackets as if they are enduring residents in those brackets, despite all evidence that the turnover includes most of the people in these brackets, due to the mundane fact that most people begin their careers at the bottom and progress upward. The same principle of eternalizing the transient was also at the heart of the genetic determinism of the Progressive era intelligentsia, who took the demonstrable contemporary differences in achievements between different races, nations and civilizations as signs of innate superiority and inferiority— again, ignoring the changes over time (centuries in this case) in the relative achievements of races, nations and civilizations.

What the Progressives of the early twentieth century and those of the late twentieth century had in common, in addition to their faith in surrogate decision-making by elites, was a belief that uneven distributions of achievements among racial or ethnic groups was weighty evidence of some given and overriding factor— whether genetics in the early twentieth century or discrimination in the late twentieth century.

---

* Ironically, a classic example of evading confrontation with substantive arguments by imputing negative attitudes appeared in a review of the first edition of this book. See, Alan Wolfe, "The Joyless Mind," *New Republic*, February 9, 2010, on-line edition.

There is sufficient confusion between the meaning of the noun "intellectual" and the connotations of the same word as an adjective that critics of the behavior of intellectuals are often dismissed as people who are either hostile to intellectual endeavors or people who fail to appreciate intellectual processes or intellectual achievements. Richard Hofstadter's Pulitzer Prize-winning book *Anti-Intellectualism in American Life* perpetuated this confusion, both in its title and in its contents, where people who criticized intellectuals were depicted as people who exhibit "the national disrespect for mind" and a "dislike of specialists and experts."[18] H.L. Mencken likewise wrote of America as a country with "not only a great dearth of ideas in the land, but also an active and relentless hostility to ideas."[19] Even the loss of an election by Adlai Stevenson— a man with only the image of an intellectual— was declared by Russell Jacoby in *The Last Intellectuals* to be an example of "the endemic anti-intellectualism of American society."[20]

Yet the American public honors intellectual achievements in science, engineering or the medical profession, among others— which is to say, fields whose practitioners exhibit high intellectual ability but who are not intellectuals in the occupational sense defined here. As in many other contexts, imputing unworthy influences such as "anti-intellectualism" to others serves as a substitute for answering their arguments.

Despite the high levels of brainpower available to intellectuals for analyzing problems and confronting issues, what is remarkable is the wide range of ways that intellectuals have devised for *not* analyzing problems and *not* confronting issues. Verbal preemption has substituted for hypothesis-testing on issues ranging from poverty and race to war and peace.

Whether military deterrence or disarmament is more likely to preserve peace are hypotheses that might be tested. But the intelligentsia have often simply preempted that question by labeling military deterrence as an "arms race" and disarmament advocates as a "peace movement"— in utter disregard of any historical evidence that might be examined as to which approach has more often produced which result. Issues involved in alternative ways of organizing an economy or society are likewise often preempted by depicting advocates of some policies or institutions as being for "change" while those with different views are depicted as "defenders of the status quo," even if the specifics advocated by the latter are further from the status quo than the specifics advocated by the former, as noted in Chapter 9. The ability to wave aside realities with the turn of a phrase is one of the most dangerous talents of the intelligentsia.

The arsenal of evasion ranges from "simplistic" to "blaming the victim" to "no panacea" to "mean-spirited," "racist," "sexist," "homophobic," and differential caring, as in Andrew Hacker's statement, "conservatives don't really care whether black Americans are happy or unhappy."[21] More sophisticated evasions include the argument that there is no argument— that "science" has already proved something, whether what science is supposed to have proved is the genetic inequality of races or catastrophic consequences from man-made global warming. Related to this is the notion that some statements are simply "hate speech," rather than alternative views, and are therefore to be banned and sanctioned, as is common on academic campuses, the institutions most under the direct control of intellectuals.

The same mindset was demonstrated by the adverse and alarmed reactions among the intelligentsia to a Supreme Court decision in 2010— *Citizens United v. FEC*— which said that a law restricting the spending of corporations and labor unions on political advertisements was unconstitutional, as an infringement of the free speech guaranteed by the First Amendment.

Under a *New York Review of Books* headline proclaiming this decision to be one that "threatens democracy," Professor Ronald Dworkin declared that "allowing rich corporations to swamp elections" will produce a "worse-informed" public because corporate advertising "will mislead the public."[22] Given the political makeup of the existing media, not to mention academia, the idea that allowing corporations to run ads giving their side of the story will "swamp" everyone else seems either laughable, if seriously believed, or a cynical scare tactic otherwise. More fundamentally, it betrays a belief that others should not have the same rights as the intelligentsia, and harkens back to the ages of religious intolerance under the doctrine that "error has no rights." At the very least, it is yet another attempt at restriction or evasion of the substance of opposing arguments.

Also reflecting the view that there is no argument are such expressions as "raising the consciousness" of others, as distinguished from debating their views with evidence and logic on a plane of equality. But to do the latter would be to surrender the anointed's vision of themselves at the outset.

Filtering out discordant facts in the media and refusing to release raw data on which some favored conclusion has been reached— whether about the supposed success of affirmative action in college admissions or the conclusiveness of the case for catastrophic global warming— are all part of the pattern of preempting issues rather than confronting them.

Filtering can distort reality, not only in what it presents to the general public, but also in what it presents to the filterers themselves. While each filterer knows what part of reality he has suppressed, what each filterer cannot know is what part of reality innumerable like-minded peers around the world have suppressed, and therefore how valid or invalid are the empirical bases for his own general conclusions, which in turn prompted his decision to engage in filtering out particular parts of reality.

If there really was a coordinated conspiracy to deceive the public, then at least the conspirators themselves would know what was true and what was false. But, when there is instead devotion to a vision, and uncoordinated individual efforts to defend and sustain that vision, none of the individuals involved in that effort may be aware of how much of their own beliefs are based on the falsehoods or filtering of facts by similarly disposed peers. For example, someone who is filtering facts about race or crime may be doing so as a result of believing filtered distortions about income disparities or the effects of government interventions in the economy. In short, filterers can deceive each other as well as they deceive the public, adding painful contemporary relevance to the adage, "Oh, what a tangled web we weave, when first we practice to deceive."

Changing the meaning of words has been another of the many other ways of *not* confronting the substance of issues, as with the redefinition of "judicial activism" discussed in Chapter 12, the redefinition of "power" discussed in Chapter 5 or the redefinition of "racism" mentioned in Chapter 19.

"Democracy" has long been redefined to lend a positive glow to things that would be more difficult to advocate or defend in a straightforward way with logic or facts. As far back as the Progressive era at the beginning of the twentieth century, Herbert Croly's *The Promise of American Life* changed the meaning of "democracy" from that of a particular political process to that of a particular social purpose— in his words, "the democratic purpose,"[23] a "collective purpose" which included among other things regulating "the distribution of wealth in the national interest."[24] Later variations on this theme by others have included "economic democracy" and some even called various Communist dictatorships "people's democracies," presumably pursuing "democratic purposes" unhindered by political democracy.

Freedom has likewise been redefined to mean things remote from what most people have long meant by freedom— namely, exemption from other people's restrictions. Through verbal virtuosity, that is now called "freedom *from*" but not "freedom *to*." In Woodrow Wilson's book *The New Freedom*, this "new freedom" was described as "a Liberty widened and deepened to match the broadened life of man in modern America"— a freedom whose meaning was expanded from that of "the old-fashioned days when life was very simple." According to Wilson, "Life has become complex," so that "Freedom to-day is something more than being let alone."[25]

The redefinition of freedom continues to the present day. A well-known book by two Yale professors defined freedom as "the absence of obstacles to the realisation of desires."[26] Thus freedom "depends upon attaining important prime goals such as dignity, respect, love, affection, solidarity, friendship. To the extent that individuals lack these, they cannot be free."[27] Someone who "cannot achieve his goals" is not free, they say.[28] They added, "security and freedom are much the same thing."

Through such verbal virtuosity, those who promote a *dirigiste* agenda can claim not to be reducing people's freedom, but enhancing it, by having government provide things that they could not afford otherwise. Thus such intellectuals need not debate critics who say that a *dirigiste* world reduces people's freedom, but can evade such debates with verbal sleight of hand, by redefining freedom.

Another of the ways of evading opposing views has been simply putting the burden of proof on others. What does the phrase "*glass* ceiling" mean, except that no visible evidence is necessary to support the conclusion that a dearth of women above some occupational level is due to discrimination, rather than to innumerable other factors that are involved?[29]

What does "disparate impact" mean, except that it is presumptively the particular criteria used to judge and select people which creates a false appearance of differences in capabilities among people, when there is no real or relevant difference between the people themselves? Similarly, the benefits of "diversity" need only be asserted, reiterated and insisted upon— but never demonstrated or even illustrated empirically, much less proved.

The simplicity, not to say crudeness, of some of these many ways of evading the responsibility of substantive engagement with opposing arguments is not only striking in itself but is even more striking in its success, especially among those who consider themselves to be "thinking people." Merely saying words like "diversity," "glass ceiling" or "disparate impact" banishes any need for evidence to supplement the peer consensus which produces automatic responses not unlike those of Pavlov's dog.

Because some beliefs may be lacking in logic and/or evidence does not mean that such beliefs are just random irrationalities. There can be a consistency and logic in the patterns of beliefs which are themselves inconsistent and illogical. One such consistency that has already been seen at various points in previous chapters is that beliefs can survive discordant evidence when those beliefs enable the intelligentsia to see issues as moral melodramas, starring themselves on the side of the angels against the forces of evil. Focus on "disparities" between groups and a related zero-sum conception of the economy facilitate such moral melodramas, however much damage these misconceptions do to both policy-making and social cohesion. Beliefs that offer opportunities for influence, renown, power, popularity or career advancement may also be embraced without insisting on strict logic or compelling evidence.

Sometimes beliefs need only be emotionally satisfying in order to pass muster. For example, depicting people who are envied or resented as being the cause of the lags or misfortunes of others obviously meets that modest standard, whether at the level of "exploitation" theories about individuals, classes or races domestically or at the level of "imperialism" theories as explanations of differences in economic levels among nations.* Such charges need not be defined, much less proved, to pass muster politically.

Simplicity is another reason for some theories to be preferred over others. However, more complex theories may be preferred to simpler theories when those complex theories meet emotional or other criteria. Conspiracy theories, for example, are often more complex than a straightforward theory that fails to provide as emotionally or ideologically satisfying an explanation.

While the various reasons for preferring beliefs or theories that do not meet intellectual criteria can apply to anyone in any walk of life, where such non-intellectual criteria prevail among intellectuals— as has been painfully obvious they often do— that presents a puzzle, in view of intellectuals' obvious mental capacity to do better. However, it is less of a puzzle when the distinction is kept in mind between the word "intellectual" as a noun denoting particular occupations and the word "intellectual" as an adjective describing certain mental processes or standards. Once that distinction is clear, it becomes an open question whether intellectuals maintain intellectual standards any better than— or even as well as— people in other occupations, whether elite or mundane occupations.

However counterproductive the ideas of intellectuals may be for society at large, there are few, if any, adverse consequences for intellectuals themselves. That is why explaining the patterns of their behavior requires consideration of the particular incentives and constraints that they face, which affect both the supply and the demand for intellectuals.

---

* Lenin's theory of imperialism is almost laughably easy to refute. See, for example, my *Economic Facts and Fallacies*, second edition (New York: Basic Books, 2011), pp. 225–227.

Chapter 21

Incentives and Constraints

A mong people whose occupations require high levels of mental ability—including mathematicians, scientists, chess grandmasters and others—we have defined as intellectuals those whose end products are ideas, as distinguished from tangible creations such as those of engineers, or services such as those of physicians and pilots.* This dichotomy is not arbitrary. It conforms more or less to general usage and, more important, there are behavioral differences between intellectuals so defined and others whose work is likewise mentally demanding, and who may in many cases be academic colleagues on the same campuses.

These differences have much to do with both the supply and the demand for intellectuals in their roles as public intellectuals, people whose words contribute to the general atmosphere in which consequential decisions are made for society as a whole. Sometimes public intellectuals affect social outcomes by their direct advocacy of particular policies, but sometimes their effect is indirect, when they simply explain their particular specialty—whether economics, criminology or some other subject with policy implications— in a way that laymen can understand and which therefore influences public understanding and public opinion, whether or not these particular public intellectuals directly advocate one policy or another.

Perhaps more consequential than either of these roles of intellectuals is their creating a general set of presumptions, beliefs and imperatives— a

---

* What has also been part of our definition is that these are ideas whose validation is peer consensus. Mathematicians' end products are ideas, but they are ideas subject to empirical validation. The Pythagorean theorem would not have survived for thousands of years unless actual measurements validated its reasoning.

vision— that serves as a framework for the way particular issues and events that come along are perceived by the population at large. For this, it is not necessary to be a "public intellectual" who addresses the population at large. Such disparate figures as Sigmund Freud and Friedrich Hayek have had enormous influence over people who never read a word of theirs, but who absorbed their vision from others who had read them and received their direct impact. What John Maynard Keynes called "the gradual encroachment of ideas" can change the way we see the world as it exists and change how we think the world ought to be.[1]

THE SUPPLY OF PUBLIC INTELLECTUALS

Ideologically, poll after poll has shown sociologists and scholars in the humanities, for example, to be more often liberal or left politically than are engineers or scientists. In addition to such ideological differences, there are more fundamental differences in incentives and constraints between intellectuals in the sense defined here and other academic or non-academic specialists in mentally demanding fields. For one thing, an engineer can become famous for his work *as an engineer* but the world's leading authority on French literature or the history of Mayan civilization is unlikely to be known, much less celebrated, beyond the narrow confines of the particular specialty.

The incentives to become a "public intellectual"— that is, someone known for comments on issues of the day, whether within or outside that person's specialty— are obviously stronger for intellectuals, as defined here, than for others who can gain fame and/or fortune without ever bothering to either go beyond their own special expertise or even to explain their specialty in layman's language to the general public. A pioneer in heart surgery can gain national or even worldwide acclaim, without ever having to explain either the heart or surgery to a lay audience, much less volunteer opinions on politics or social philosophy. But a pioneer in linguistics like Noam Chomsky would never become as widely known beyond the confines of his specialty as he has become by commenting on issues and events well beyond the realm of linguistics.

The intellectuals we have been studying have usually been public intellectuals, people whose comments help create a climate of opinion in which issues of the day are discussed and ultimately acted upon by those with political power. People in more utilitarian fields, whether in the academic world or not, may also choose as individuals to step outside the boundaries of their competence to comment on a range of issues at large, but there are fewer built-in incentives for them to do so.

Professor Richard A. Posner's landmark study *Public Intellectuals* points out that many individuals may become far better known, and more highly regarded, by the general public than they are by peers within their own respective professions. "Many public intellectuals are academics of modest distinction fortuitously thrust into the limelight" by their activities as public intellectuals, he asserts, noting a "tendency of a public intellectual's media celebrity to be inverse to his scholarly renown."[2]

While it would not be difficult to think of individuals who fit that description,[3] and who would therefore have incentives to seek recognition beyond their respective specialties that they have not achieved within those specialties, it would also not be difficult to think of other individuals of the highest levels of achievements within their own specialties who also chose either to write introductory textbooks for students or popular articles and books for the general public on subjects ranging from astronomy to zoology. Intellectuals who popularize the field of their own expertise would include Nobel Prizewinning economists like Paul Samuelson, Milton Friedman, and Gary Becker. However, among the 100 public intellectuals mentioned most often in the media, Posner found only 18 who were also among the 100 intellectuals mentioned most often in the scholarly literature.[4]

Whatever the validity of Professor Posner's observation as an explanation of intellectuals' motivations, what we are ultimately concerned about is the empirical validity of their beliefs, especially when these are beliefs relied upon as a basis for decisions of governments. In this context, what may be far more relevant than Posner's conclusion is Schumpeter's observation, "the degree of truth of a doctrine is by no means always positively correlated with the ability of its exponents."[5]

Many of the leading intellectuals in America, for example, called for a vote for the Communist Party of the United States in 1932, and many internationally renowned intellectuals in Western democracies in general were throughout the 1930s holding up the Soviet Union as a favorable contrast to American capitalism, and a model for the world— the "moral top of the world" in renowned literary critic Edmund Wilson's words[6]— at a time when people were literally starving to death by the millions in the Soviet Union and many others were being shipped off to slave labor camps. A learned scholar like professor Harold Laski spent years denouncing military equipment producers in Britain, who were all that stood between him and dehumanization and extermination in a Nazi concentration camp.

More fundamentally, there is no reason to adopt the criteria of the intellectuals for rankings among themselves as criteria for evaluating the validity or value of what they say for society at large. Academic intellectuals, especially, are evaluated according to whether their ideas are original, rather than— the ultimate putdown— "derivative." But Edmund Burke said, "I do not aim at singularity." He added: "I give you opinions which have been accepted amongst us, from very early times to this moment, with a continued and general approbation, and which indeed are so worked into my mind, that I am unable to distinguish what I have learned from others from the results of my own meditation."[7] He was openly proclaiming his ideas to be derivative but was putting those ideas forth as valid for the real world, rather than as enhancements of his own reputation.

By contrast many, if not most, intellectuals *do* aim at singularity, and academic intellectuals especially must, from the time of their doctoral dissertations onward. But that is no reason for the rest of society to adopt similar criteria when deciding which of the ideas of intellectuals to take seriously as guides to practices in the real world. To do so would be to disregard the history of the tragic consequences of being influenced by the ideas of even leading intellectuals of unquestioned ability, which have supported or promoted trends which have led to such things as totalitarian dictatorship and the Holocaust.

When we are talking about the intellectuals of the 1930s being mistaken about the Soviet Union or about foreign policy toward Nazi Germany, we are not talking about simply making mistakes like those that everyone makes at some time or other. We are talking about being monumentally and grotesquely wrong, while also being smugly and arrogantly wrong. Much the same could be said about the earlier intellectuals of the Progressive era, writing off the Jews, among others, as "beaten men from beaten races." The connection of the writings of Madison Grant and the Nazi persecutions is not a matter of speculation but is as tangible as a letter that Hitler sent to Grant— and that Grant proudly showed to others— calling *The Passing of the Great Race* his "Bible." Even those intellectuals of today who readily acknowledge and condemn such errors of the past seldom draw any implications about relying on the consensus of distinguished peers today and dismissing views to the contrary as simply beyond the pale.

Media celebrity and scholarly renown are indeed often areas that attract different people. Whatever the relative attractions of the two roles, to be a top scholar and a top popular public intellectual at the same time would require a rare ability to write at very different intellectual levels and in very different styles for a scholarly audience and for the general public. John Maynard Keynes, for example, was one of those with this rare ability. He was internationally known as a public intellectual, writing on issues inside and outside of economics, years before he became both the most famous and the most professionally influential economist of the twentieth century. Milton Friedman, so different from Keynes in other respects, likewise had that same rare ability to write at the highest intellectual level of his profession and at the same time write and speak in a way that made economics understandable to people with no background whatever in the subject. But people with the intellectual and literary versatility of Keynes and Friedman have been extremely rare.

While particular intellectually stellar individuals may choose to become public intellectuals for any of a variety of reasons, there are few *generally* compelling incentives for them to go outside the bounds of their specialty, except for those whom we have defined as intellectuals in the sense of people whose end products are ideas. For intellectuals in this sense, the choice may often be either accepting severe limits on the range of public recognition and public influence available to them, even when they are the best in the world at what they do, or to venture out beyond the bounds of their professional expertise— or even competence— to appeal to a vastly larger and much less discriminating audience.*

For intellectuals in general, where the primary constraint is peer response, rather than empirical criteria, currently prevailing attitudes among peers may carry more weight than enduring principles or the weight of evidence. This can produce patterns much like those found among another group heavily influenced by their peers— namely adolescents, among whom particular fashions or fads can become virtually obligatory for a given time, and later become completely rejected as *passé*, without in either period having been subjected to serious examination, either empirically or analytically. Racial issues are just one example. As Oliver Wendell Holmes pointed out in the 1920s, the widespread outrage among the intelligentsia over the trial of Sacco and Vanzetti was in stark contrast with their lack of interest in the legal travesties and personal tragedies in the contemporary trials of black defendants convicted by all-white juries in the Jim Crow South.

Today, when blacks are often treated by the intelligentsia as mascots du jour, black students beating up Asian students in schools in New York and Philadelphia *for years*[8] is simply not an issue that either the media or academia want to discuss, much less an issue to arouse moral outrage. Had these been Hispanic students, for example, being beaten up by white students, cries of outrage would no doubt have rung out across the land from those in the media, in academia and in politics. There is no principle involved in these inconsistencies, but simply the fact that some groups happen to be in vogue among intellectuals at a particular time and other groups are not— and that peer consensus carries great weight, even among individuals with high intellects who consider themselves to be "thinking people." This peer

---

* By contrast with the pattern we are considering, distinguished economist Frank Knight was described by one of his Nobel Prizewinning students this way: "He was not a consultant to great bodies or small, whether public or private; he did not ride the lecture circuit; he did not seek a place in the popular press. He conducted himself as if the pursuit of academic knowledge was a worthy full-time career for a first-class mind." George J. Stigler, *Memoirs of an Unregulated Economist* (New York: Basic Books, 1988), p. 18.

consensus might be jeopardized by criticizing a group which is currently in vogue for violence against a group not currently in vogue.

Like adolescent fads, many other beliefs can flourish unchallenged among the intelligentsia, when those beliefs are shared by their peers. For example, the notion that there were "earlier and simpler times" has been endlessly repeated without a speck of evidence being cited, much less anything resembling a thorough examination of history that would be required to establish the validity of this sweeping assumption. The popularity of the notion of "earlier and simpler times" has nothing to do with either evidence or logic, and much to do with its facilitating the disregard of historical experience, traditional values and Constitutional limits on the scope of government.

THE DEMAND FOR PUBLIC INTELLECTUALS

Turning from the incentives that lead to a supply of public intellectuals to the demand for such people, we again find an important distinction between those people with high-level mental skills who are intellectuals in our sense and others who are in mentally demanding fields whose end products are more tangible or more empirically testable. There is a spontaneous demand from the larger society for the end products of engineering, medical, and scientific professions, while whatever demand there is for the end products of sociologists, linguists, or historians comes largely from educational institutions or is created by intellectuals themselves, mostly by stepping outside of whatever academic specialty they are in, to operate as "public intellectuals" offering "solutions" to social "problems" or by raising alarms over some dire dangers which they claim to have discovered.

In short, the demand for public intellectuals is to a considerable extent manufactured by themselves. Otherwise, whatever the views of such intellectuals about the current state of the world, or about how it might be made better, such views are unlikely to make much difference to the public or to have much effect on government policy in a democracy, so long as those intellectuals stay within the bounds of their expertise.

The general public contributes to the income of intellectuals in a variety of ways, often involuntarily as taxpayers who support schools, colleges, and various other institutions and programs subsidizing intellectual and artistic endeavors.

The humanities are a classic example of a field where the only relevant criterion of success is what is accepted or rewarded by peers. Under academic pressures to "publish or perish," and with growing tangible rewards for publishing available from organizations such as the taxpayer-financed National Endowment for the Humanities, the number of publications on such long-standing literary figures as Shakespeare and Milton skyrocketed, while the number of readers of these publications declined. Moreover, the thrust of literary criticism was no longer an attempt to explain or unearth the meaning of what these historic literary figures had written but to find some new meaning that the literary critic could read into classic works.[9] In short, the rewards were for going beyond one's competence as someone familiar with literature and venturing into unchecked subjective speculations, however elegantly phrased those speculations might be.

By contrast, other occupations requiring great mental ability— engineers, for example— have a vast spontaneous market for their end products, whether computers, planes or buildings. But that is true far less often of people whose end products are ideas. There is neither a large nor a prominent role for them to play in society, unless they create such a role for themselves, outside their own special expertise.

Among academic intellectuals especially, the spontaneous demand, and even acclaim, for the work of their colleagues in the sciences, engineering, medicine and other fields provides yet another incentive for them to seek their own "place in the sun." So too does the prominence of many people outside of academia— people in politics, sports or entertainment, for example. But most of these non-intellectuals first achieve public recognition or acclaim by their achievements within their respective areas of specialization, while many intellectuals could achieve comparable public recognition only by going beyond their expertise or competence. They need not be outright charlatans, just people whose vast knowledge and understanding of one subject may conceal from themselves, as well as from others, their fundamental ignorance of the things that bring them to public attention.

There could hardly be a set of incentives and constraints more conducive to getting people of great intellect to say sweeping, reckless, or even foolish things. Some of those foolish and dangerous things have already been noticed in earlier chapters but, even so, these samples barely scratch the surface of a vast vein of reckless pronouncements by the intelligentsia, stretching back over the generations and no doubt also stretching well into the future.

We have noted an ideological fault line between intellectuals defined as people whose end products are ideas whose validation process is the approval of peers and others with high-level mental skills, but whose end products are technological, medical, scientific or other goods and services. While the existence of that ideological fault line has been demonstrated by numerous studies,[10] the reasons for that ideological fault line are not as readily demonstrable. It is certainly true that, once having accepted a particular set of assumptions— a particular vision— a whole range of positions on particular issues then follows, differing in each case from the positions taken by those who began with a different vision. But, since both visions were available, why did so many intellectuals choose one, rather than the other?

There may be no definitive answer to that question, but there are some suggestive patterns. Intellectuals, defined as people whose work begins and ends with ideas whose validation is peer consensus, work in what are often called "soft" fields— that is, fields with less rigorous standards of validation and fields that are, on the whole, easier to master. Given that these are also fields for which there is no great spontaneous market demand from the population at large, there has long been a concern that there was a chronic over-supply of people trained to work in such fields, relative to the demand, leading to many disappointed individuals, frustrated in finding occupations, incomes or recognition commensurate with their investments of time, talent and effort, and with the expectations that such investments generate.

These concerns are not peculiar to our time nor even to Western civilization. Studies in Third World countries often find large numbers of educated people without marketable skills, many of them unemployed or under-employed, who are often resentful or hostile to others without as much education as themselves but with technical or economic skills that are much more in demand and more highly rewarded. As noted in Chapter 16, the "well-educated but underemployed" Czech young men promoted ethnic identity movements in the nineteenth century Habsburg Empire,[11] as the newly educated class of Latvians did likewise in the Russian Empire.[12] So did a newly-educated intelligentsia in the Ottoman Empire[13]— and as likewise the soft-subject intelligentsia have promoted polarization, discrimination and violence in a long list of other countries.

Studies have highlighted the role of an over-supply of those with higher education in insurgencies in Europe, Asia, Africa and the Western Hemisphere.[14] In some countries, bureaucracies have been expanded to absorb such people, highly educated but economically superfluous, in order to neutralize the political dangers they can pose.

It is not hard to see how an intelligentsia of this sort would be more likely to gravitate toward the vision of the anointed, in which society is perceived as unfair, rather than toward the tragic vision, in which it is the inherent flaws of human nature that underlie much of the unhappiness and frustrations of life, while social institutions seek to mitigate these problems, but necessarily do so imperfectly, since these institutions are themselves products of imperfect human beings. Even intellectuals who end up espousing the tragic vision often begin in their earlier adulthood as believers in the vision of the anointed, whether because of their personal situations or because of the pervasiveness of the vision of the anointed in the institutions in which they have been educated.[15]

The most obvious examples in the American context have been leaders of the neo-conservative movement, such as Norman Podhoretz and Irving Kristol, who began on the left. But many others who ended up as leading "conservatives" in the American sense, including Milton Friedman and Friedrich Hayek, began as either "liberals" in the American sense (Friedman) or as outright socialists (Hayek). In short, the attraction of the vision of the anointed to intellectuals has extended even to those who later repudiated it and became its strongest opponents.

While bureaucracies, ideological movements and post-doctoral fellowships can absorb much of the surplus of highly educated people whom the market does not absorb, there are few constraints against the continued over-production of such people. Complaints about the over-production of Ph.D.s in the humanities, for example, with vastly more applicants for faculty positions in these fields than there are appointments available, have continued for generations. But universities have few incentives to reduce the supply, which is often subsidized by government, foundations and individual or corporate donors. Moreover, the availability of graduate students in these fields not only provides professors with research assistants and teaching assistants, the need to teach such students provides a rationale for the employment of as many professors as there are in these fields.

In short, institutional incentives seem unlikely to fit the supply of the intelligentsia to the demand, certainly not the spontaneous demand of the society at large, for whom an over-supply of such people can represent not only a cost but a danger.

A Sense of Mission

More than career incentives are involved in the behavior of intellectuals. There is also often a sense of a social mission— perhaps including a sense of personal grievance, growing out of the frustrations inherent in their chronic over-supply— that can long outlast even eventual individual success and renown.

The zeal of many intellectuals with the vision of the anointed to lead others to conclusions that will facilitate the kinds of economic and social changes they prefer, especially as regards the distribution of wealth, is in sharp contrast with their very limited, or even non-existent, interest in economics in general, and in particular their lack of interest in the question of how wealth has been produced in the first place, and what will facilitate or impede its future production. It is not only tangible wealth whose origins and production the intelligentsia show little interest in. The same is true of human capital— the skills, experience and cultural orientations that enable human beings to produce not only tangible wealth but also large and viable societies, in which they can co-exist with innumerable and disparate strangers without ruinous frictions, and with a degree of mutual accommodation and cooperation.

When both tangible wealth and human capital are treated as things that just exist *somehow*, not only is an arduous task of explanation avoided, so is the possibility that the many prerequisites for tangible wealth and human capital can come together very differently, and to very different degrees, in different geographic, historic and social circumstances, producing people who are grossly unequal in the ability to create wealth or to maintain large-scale societies of mutually accommodating strangers. Both history and the contemporary world show such differences to be the rule, not the exception. Yet many, if not most, intellectuals proceed as if statistical differences in outcomes— often christened "disparities," "inequities" or "injustices"— are deviations from the norm that require explanations as well as condemnations.

Instead of the equality of abstract people in an abstract world, differences in the radius of trust and in the size of the cultural universe available to different social, racial or other groups make equal outcomes virtually impossible in the real world, even in the complete absence of genetic differences or social injustices. These cultural differences are not faults for which the less fortunate are personally responsible but neither are the less fortunate automatically "victims" of others. However grossly unjust the statistical distribution of wealth-producing capacity, and the consequent differences in income and wealth, they are unjust from a cosmic perspective— undeserved fates— but not necessarily as a result of social decisions. The confusion between *cosmic* injustices and *social* injustices is a crucial confusion, which enables many intellectuals to see issue after issue as opportunities to be on the side of the angels against the forces of evil.

Things look very different in a vision built on a foundation of inherent constraints— that is, the tragic vision. Progress, including remarkable progress when favorable conditions are maintained over long spans of time, is possible within the tragic vision. But such progress does not necessarily entail either the extermination or subordination of those currently less capable, as many intellectuals assumed in the Progressive era. Nor does progress necessarily take the form of "liberation" of the less fortunate from evils created by the more fortunate, as many of the intelligentsia have assumed in later times. Once that is recognized, it means a much reduced role for intellectuals in either case, which may be why this conclusion is not more readily considered. Moreover, what is called "liberation" is often the abandonment of the restraints socially evolved from experience over generations or centuries, and replacing them with the newly minted and very different restraints and taboos of contemporary intellectuals.

The path to progress is very different in the tragic vision from what it is in the vision of the anointed. One of those differences is in whether the circle of trust and the cultural universe are to be expanded or contracted. Where the less fortunate are conceived to be so because they are victims of the more fortunate, promoting a struggle between the two, as many with the vision of the anointed do, is the antithesis of expanding the circle of trust or even the circle of mutual accommodation. Where victimhood is seen by those with the vision of the anointed as the main explanation of intergroup differences in outcomes, there is less reason to emphasize changing the group cultures that have been less successful. "Multiculturalism" is a virtual denial of any such need and instead paints the less successful into the corner of the cultural happenstances into which they were born.

In this, as in other things, a relatively few differences in fundamental assumptions between the two visions lead to a wide spectrum of opposite conclusions on a sweeping range of very different issues.

Among those with a sense of mission are those who teach the young, whether teachers in the schools or professors in colleges and universities. Those among the academics or school teachers who lack either the inclination or the talent to become public intellectuals can instead vent their opinions in the classroom to a captive audience of students, operating in a smaller arena but in a setting with little chance of serious challenge. In such settings, their aggregate influence on the mindset of a generation may be out of all proportion to their competence— not simply in what they directly impart, but more fundamentally in habituating their students to reaching sweeping conclusions after hearing only one side of an issue and then either venting their emotions or springing into action, whether by writing letters to public officials as part of classroom assignments or taking part in other, more direct, activism. In these cases as well, there are few, if any, constraints beforehand and no accountability for the consequences afterwards.

School teachers are one of the elements of the intelligentsia in the penumbra surrounding the inner core of intellectuals. Like many others, the school teachers' role is quite modest and little noticed, and their influence on the course of national policy or historical events virtually nil, so long as they remain within the confines of their competence in their assigned role as transmitters of the cultural achievements of the past to the younger generation. Only by stepping outside that role to take on responsibilities for which they have neither qualifications nor accountability do they greatly expand their influence— whether by ideological indoctrination of students or by psychological manipulation of students in order to change the values which those students received from their parents.[16]

In either case, the teachers are unaccountable for the consequences, either to the students or to the society. For example, when the long downward trend in teenage pregnancy and venereal disease suddenly reversed after the attitude-changing exercises known as "sex education" were introduced into American schools in the 1960s,[17] it was the parents who were left to pick up the pieces when a teenage daughter became pregnant or an adolescent son caught some venereal disease. No teacher had to pay anything toward the financial costs or to lose a moment's sleep over what had happened in these young people's personal lives, and verbal virtuosity enabled the changed values which "sex education" promoted to not only escape censure but even to continue to foster the impression that what was called "sex education" was the solution, even when it turned out empirically to be an aggravation of the problem.

Like so much else, "sex education" fit the vision, which exempted it from the requirement of fitting the facts. Moreover, because these indoctrination exercises in promoting different values were called "education," their legitimacy in the schools escaped serious scrutiny, as did their role in the results that followed.

As early as elementary school, students have been encouraged or recruited to take stands on complex policy issues ranging up to and including policies concerning nuclear weapons, on which whole classes have been assigned to write to members of Congress or to the President of the United States. College admissions committees can give weight to various forms of environmentalism or other activism in considering which applicants to admit, and it is common for colleges to require "community service" as a prerequisite for applicants to be considered at all— with the admissions committee arbitrarily defining what is to be considered a "community service," as if, for example, it is unambiguously clear that aiding and abetting vagrancy ("the homeless") is a service rather than a disservice to a community.

In these and other ways, intellectual prerequisites for reaching serious policy conclusions are, ironically, undermined by the intelligentsia themselves. In short, at all levels of the intelligentsia, and in a wide range of specialties, the incentives tend to reward going beyond whatever expertise the particular members of the intelligentsia may have, and the constraints against falsity are few or non-existent. It is not that most of the intelligentsia deliberately lie in a cynical attempt to gain notoriety or to advance themselves or their cause in other ways. However, the general ability of people to rationalize to themselves, as well as to others, is certainly not lacking among the intelligentsia.

Are whole societies to be put at risk for such vanities and conceits among a relatively small segment of the population? As we have already seen, especially in discussions of the role of Western intellectuals between the two World Wars, whole nations have already been put at risk and indeed led into disaster, by a climate of opinion to which the intelligentsia have made major contributions. Nor is this all simply a matter of history, as shown by the revival among the intelligentsia and the media in our own times of the attitudes, arguments and the very phrases of the period between the two World Wars.

Constraints

Unlike engineers, physicians, or scientists, the intelligentsia face no serious constraint or sanction based on empirical verification. None could be sued for malpractice, for example, for having contributed to the hysteria over the insecticide DDT, which led to its banning in many countries around the world, costing the lives of literally millions of people through a resurgence of malaria. By contrast, doctors whose actions have had a far more tenuous connection with the medical complications suffered by their patients have had to pay millions of dollars in damages— illustrating once again a fundamental difference between the circumstances of the intelligentsia and the circumstances of people in other mentally demanding professions.

Even the liability of journalists under the laws against slander and libel has been reduced almost to the vanishing point in the case of slandered or libeled individuals who are considered to be "public figures." Yet, in terms of social consequences, slander or libel against individuals holding or aspiring to high government offices harms the general public as well as the particular individuals who are targeted. If voters are persuaded to abandon someone whom they were otherwise prepared to vote for, as a result of false charges spread by the media, that is as harmful as any other voter fraud. If nominees to be federal judges, including Supreme Court justices, can find their nominations derailed by false charges of racism or sexual harassment spread by the media, that can deprive the public not only of the services of those particular individuals but also the services of many others later, who refuse to jeopardize their reputations, built up over a lifetime, by entering a confirmation process where reckless and inflammatory accusations, spread nationwide through the media, have become the norm and proving oneself innocent is virtually impossible.

Not only the external world, but even their professional peers, impose few constraints on intellectuals— so long as those intellectuals are propounding the prevailing vision of the anointed, especially to a lay audience. Nor is the ultimate constraint— one's own personal standards— a constraint that is at all difficult to escape. As Jean-François Revel has observed:

> Each of us should realize that one possesses within oneself the formidable capacity to construct an explanatory system of the world and along with it a machine for rejecting all facts contrary to this system.[18]

Intellectuals are certainly not lacking in the ability to rationalize and, if anything, are likely to be more gifted with that talent than are most other people.

Given their incentives— and the weak or non-existent constraints— it is possible to understand why so many intellectuals fail to see that stepping out beyond their competence can be like stepping off a cliff. For example, many— if not most— intellectuals have no knowledge of economics, but nevertheless insist on making sweeping pronouncements on economic issues. Some may have much miscellaneous information about economic matters but no conception of economic *analysis*. Knowing all the Roman numerals and all the Arabic numerals would not be enough to make someone competent in arithmetic, much less calculus, without the systematic analysis that constitutes mathematics.

Similarly, no amount of sheer information about the economy can substitute for the systematic analysis that constitutes economics. In various other specialized fields as well, having a vast amount of superficial information in no way precludes someone from being fundamentally ignorant— or, worse yet, misinformed— without the specialized analysis necessary to reach valid and verifiable conclusions.

While the human tendency to over-estimate the range of one's own competence is not confined to intellectuals, the ability to persist in that error is limited by the contexts in which most other people operate. General Motors, for example, makes millions of automobiles but no tires— not because of an innate modesty of General Motors executives in realizing that their abilities in automobile production do not translate into comparable abilities in producing tires, but because the inescapable economic realities of the marketplace could cost them millions of dollars if they tried to make their own tires, instead of buying them from companies whose years of specialized expertise and experience in producing tires enable them to produce better tires at lower costs than an automobile company can.

Similarly, the head coach of a football team has specialists on his staff who coach defensive linemen, or who plan offensive plays or who coach special units that go on the field for punts or kickoffs. Again, it is not innate modesty that leads to head coaches' implicit recognition of their own inherent limitations, but the inescapable fact that losing football games can quickly lead to losing one's own job. But there are few incentives for intellectuals to even consider whether they may be ignorant or misinformed outside the narrow range of their own particular specialty when their ultimate validation rests on their peers, who tend to share both their talents and their limitations, as well as their social vision.

Against this background of incentives and constraints, many of the things that are said and done by the intelligentsia are understandable, however detrimental or even disastrous those things have been for the societies around them.

Chapter 22

The Influence of Intellectuals

Before assessing the influence of intellectuals, we must define in what sense we consider influence. Professor Richard A. Posner, for example, considers public intellectuals to be not very influential and regards their predictions in particular as "generally not heeded."[1] He may well be correct in the terms in which he discusses the issue. That is, the public did not panic over Paul Ehrlich's predictions of impending economic and environmental disasters or George Orwell's fictional depictions of what to expect in 1984. However, we must distinguish the influence of particular intellectuals, with their own special agendas and predictions, from the influence of the intelligentsia as a whole on matters in which, as a group, they generally advance the same prevailing vision and, in many cases, filter out facts which go counter to that vision.

While the British public did not follow the specific prescriptions of Bertrand Russell to disband British military forces on the eve of the Second World War, that is very different from saying that the steady drumbeat of anti-military-preparedness rhetoric among the intelligentsia in general did not impede the buildup of a military deterrence or defense to offset Hitler's rearming of Germany. It was not that Britain's leaders necessarily believed what the intelligentsia were saying, but that these leaders had to take into account what the voting public believed, as a result of the climate of opinion created by the intelligentsia.

The impact of those whom we have defined as intellectuals— that is, people whose work begins and ends with ideas— has been growing over the centuries, with the increasing numbers of intellectuals that more affluent societies are able to support, the increasing audience for their ideas provided by an ever wider spread of literacy and higher education, and with the vast increase in the reach of the mass media. Their influence has been felt not only in the law and in matters of national defense, but also in the erosion of the social cohesion without which a society cannot continue to remain a society. That influence has been most pronounced in modern, democratic nations, where intellectuals have their greatest scope.

A distinguished historian referred to "the thin sliver of the upper crust" of czarist Russian society "that constituted significant public opinion."[2] An even thinner sliver of those with consequential opinions has characterized modern totalitarian dictatorships, whether in Russia or in other countries around the world. It is democracies that are most vulnerable to whatever unsubstantiated notions are prevalent among the intelligentsia and promoted to the public via the media and to the next generation through educational institutions.

THE NATURE OF INTELLECTUALS' INFLUENCE

Equally important as the question of the magnitude of the influence of intellectuals is the question of the directions in which that influence is exercised. In addition to the specific ways in which intellectuals have influenced particular issues, there have been certain general patterns of their influence. These include their tendency to verbally localize in "our society" the worldwide evils and shortcomings of the human race, their confusion of conveyances with causes, their exaltation of intellect over experience and their confining the very meaning of knowledge to the narrow band of learning in which they excel. In all these things, intellectuals have shown a remarkable ability to ignore or defy evidence to the contrary.

Intellectuals have every incentive to believe in the effectiveness of their own specialty— articulated ideas— and to correspondingly undervalue competing factors, such as the experience of the masses or especially the use of force by the police or the military. The unarticulated cultural distillations of mass experience over the generations are often summarily dismissed as mere prejudices. Force or the threat of force is likewise deemed far inferior to articulated reason, whether in dealing with criminals, children or hostile nations. "Military service is the remedy of despair— despair of the power of intelligence,"[3] according to John Dewey.

Reason tends to be considered preferable *categorically*, with little consideration of differing circumstances in which one of these approaches— that is, reason or force— may be incrementally better than the other in some cases but not in other cases. The intelligentsia seem especially to reject the idea of private individuals using force in defense of themselves and their property or private individuals having guns with which to do so.*

In international issues of war and peace, the intelligentsia often say that war should be "a last resort." But much depends on the context and the specific meaning of that phrase. War should of course be "a last resort" in terms of our *preferences*. But so too should heart surgery, divorce and many other negative experiences in other contexts. Yet in other contexts we readily recognize that our own preferences are by no means all that matter, nor are necessarily even relevant when confronted with sufficiently dire circumstances and catastrophic alternatives. To say that war should be "a last resort" is very different from simply hoping against hope while dangers and provocations accumulate unanswered, and while wishful thinking or illusory agreements substitute for serious military preparedness— or, if necessary, military action. The repeated irresolution of France during the 1930s, and on into the period of the "phony war" that ended in its sudden collapse in 1940, gave the world a painful example of how caution can be carried to the point where it becomes dangerous.

While the kinds of ideas prevalent among today's intellectuals have a long pedigree that reaches back at least as far as the eighteenth century, the *predominance* of those ideas in both intellectual circles and in the society at large, through their influence in the educational system, the media, the courts and in politics, is a much more recent phenomenon. As just one factor, a number of occupations that did not require years of academic training now do. In times past lawyers, for example, did not have to have

---

* Using a gun in self-defense need not require pulling the trigger, since would-be robbers or assailants usually have enough common sense to back off when a gun is pointed at them.

studied in law schools but could study law on their own, as Abraham Lincoln and many others did. What that means, not only for lawyers but for people in many other occupations, is that the price of their professional training is spending years as a captive audience for academic intellectuals promoting the vision of the anointed.

This is not to say that intellectuals had no influence at all in earlier eras, but in previous centuries there were fewer intellectuals and far fewer of their penumbra among the intelligentsia to carry their ideas into the schools, the media, the courts and the political arena. In earlier times, they had not yet acquired the ability to filter out what information and ideas reach the public through the media and through the educational system, or what ideas would become the touchstone of advanced thinking in the courts. For one thing, inherited traditional beliefs— both religious and secular— were more of a limitation on the influence of newly minted notions among the intellectuals.

The influence of intellectuals on the course of events in society at large through their influence on the general public was, in the past, less than today because, in most countries, the general public itself had far less influence on the direction of national policy in earlier eras. The American government was, after all, a major and historic departure in the kinds of governments that existed in the world when the United States was founded in 1776. Before that— and in other countries long after that— even if the intelligentsia had had the kind of influence on the public that they have today, that would not have made nearly as much of a difference in government policies controlled by autocratic rulers. Moreover, neither the masses nor the elite expected intellectuals to have a major influence on governmental decisions. That influence grew in recent centuries with the spread of literacy and the spread of political power down the socioeconomic pyramid.

In autocratic nations, the understanding that matters— for decision-making and for the course of events that follows— is the understanding of those who wield power. Whatever misconceptions may arise among the people at large, whether spontaneously or by being induced by the intelligentsia, has far less influence on decisions made in autocratic societies than in democratic nations. In short, along with the benefits of free and democratic societies comes a special danger from the vulnerability of a trusting public to the fashions and presumptions embodied in the visions of an intelligentsia seeking their place in the sun.

The period from the 1960s to the 1980s was perhaps the high tide of the influence of the intelligentsia in the United States. Though the ideas of the intelligentsia still remain the prevailing ideas, their overwhelming dominance ideologically has been reduced somewhat by counter-attacks from various quarters— for example, by an alternative vision presented by Milton Friedman and the Chicago school of economists, by the rise of small but significant numbers of conservative and neo-conservative intellectuals in general, and by the rise of conservatives to a minority, but no longer negligible, role in the media, especially talk radio, cable television and the Internet, which have reduced the ability of the intelligentsia with the vision of the anointed to block from the public information that might undermine that vision.

Nevertheless, any announcement of the demise of the vision of the anointed would be very premature, if not sheer wishful thinking, in view of the continuing prevalence of that vision in the educational system, as well as in television and in motion pictures that deal with social or political issues. In short, the intellectuals' vision of the world— as it is and as it should be— remains the prevailing vision.

Not since the days of the divine right of kings has there been such a presumption of a right to direct others and constrain their decisions, largely through expanded powers of government. Everything from economic central planning to environmentalism epitomizes the belief that third party elites know best and should be empowered to over-ride the decisions of others. This includes preventing children from growing up with the values taught them by their parents if different— and presumptively more "advanced"— values are preferred by those who teach in the schools and colleges.

We have already seen how Ronald Dworkin declared, "a more equal society is a better society even if its citizens prefer inequality."[4] In a similar vein, Simone de Beauvoir said, "No woman should be authorized to stay at home to raise her children. Society should be totally different. Women should not have that choice, precisely because if there is such a choice, too many women will make that one."[5] Even earlier, as noted in Chapter 6, Woodrow Wilson as an academic saw his job to be "to make the young gentlemen of the rising generation as unlike their fathers as possible."[6] There was no suggestion that anyone had given him any such mandate, or that parents would even tolerate and pay for such a mission, if they knew that this was his intention. Over-riding or circumventing other people's values and choices is at the heart of the vision of the anointed.

Such frank expressions of a desire to pre-empt other people's decisions may be rare, but the ideas behind such statements have long been expressed in more circumspect language. Herbert Croly's Progressive era classic, *The Promise of American Life* advocated going beyond democracy "defined as popular government"[7] to a government pursuing a "democratic purpose,"[8] which would include regulating "the distribution of economic power" and a "democratic economic system."[9] Given the redefinition of "democracy" in terms of social goals, rather than political processes, even those who seek to circumvent the voting public and micro-manage their lives through government can call themselves democrats, as Herbert Croly did a century ago, and as other intellectuals continue to do today.

Against this background, it is remarkable to read the description of liberals by Professor Tony Judt of New York University:

> A liberal is someone who opposes interference in the affairs of others: who is tolerant of dissenting attitudes and unconventional behavior. Liberals have historically favored keeping other people out of our lives, leaving individuals the maximum space in which to live and flourish as they choose.[10]

This picture is as clear as it is common among those with the vision of the anointed. But, however consistent it is with that vision, it is painfully inconsistent with facts, whether the facts of eugenics policies and anti-miscegenation laws urged by Progressive-era intellectuals or the restrictive speech codes of academia today that have made campuses among the least free forums in free nations for ideas that differ from the prevailing vision among academics. Communities long dominated politically by the left, such as San Francisco and New York, abound with nanny-state restrictions that micro-manage what people can and cannot do in their own daily lives. Tolerance for violations of the norms of the larger society in no way translates into tolerance for violating the norms of the vision prevailing among the intelligentsia.

Such disdain or contempt for the views of ordinary people has further implications. Given the fallibility of human beings, which intellectuals have amply demonstrated applies to themselves as to others, feedback as to the actual consequences of the ideas of the intelligentsia can be important or even crucial. But when feedback from people with different experiences or perspectives is taken only as signs of an intellectual or moral gap between those people and the intelligentsia with superior understanding, then feedback is not only negated but regarded as confirmation of the rightness of what is being said or done by the anointed. Thus it can be a point of honor to dismiss "public clamor" against the words or deeds of "progressive" judges, politicians or members of the intelligentsia.

We have seen in Chapter 2 how the warnings of a retired police commissioner were not only dismissed but ridiculed at a conference of judges and law professors. Very similar attitudes can prevail among the anointed in different contexts. For example, the publisher of the *New York Times* "told a crowd of people that alienating older white male readers meant 'we're doing something right,' and if they were *not* complaining, 'it would be an indication that we were not succeeding.'"[11]

One of the many arrogant assumptions of the intelligentsia is that outsiders have to bring meaning into the lives of ordinary people, mobilize them behind some common cause and give them a sense of importance. But anyone who thinks that a mother is not important to a child or a child to a mother has no understanding of human beings. There are few things as important to lovers as each other. Most people already have someone to whom they are enormously important and whose lives would never be the same without them. That such people may seem unimportant to intellectuals says more about intellectuals than about them. And to project that sense of their unimportance onto the people themselves is one of the many violations of fundamental intellectual standards by intellectuals.

The importance that matters to the intelligentsia is *invidious* importance, publicly displayed importance to strangers. But a mother's sense of her importance to her child, and the child to her, is in no way diminished by the fact that this is an importance within the confines of the family, or that there are millions of other mothers elsewhere with millions of other children who feel the same way. If anything, that sense of purpose and importance may be enhanced by the knowledge that motherhood is a role whose importance has been recognized around the world and over the centuries. Mothers do not need intellectuals to bring meaning into their lives or to give them some public benediction. Lovers are even less likely to want the attention of third parties.

Emphasis on the invidious is not simply a happenstance or an individual idiosyncrasy. It is an essential factor in the evolution of the careers of intellectuals in general, and often a major component in their sense of themselves. Having been treated as special and apart, from early school through college and university, intellectually gifted individuals would have to be more than human not to think of themselves, and others like themselves, as superior to the common herd. Moreover, the terms of competition among themselves likewise reinforce invidious comparisons.

A COGNITIVE ELITE

Just as the intellectuals proper are surrounded by a penumbra of others among the intelligentsia, so the intelligentsia as a whole are part of a larger cognitive elite that includes people whose work requires high levels of mental ability, but whose output is not confined to ideas. These would include technologists of various sorts, medical practitioners, lawyers and administrative officials in both private and governmental organizations, for example. While these occupations need not involve the active production or promotion of ideological visions, neither are they immune to those visions. Moreover, these other members of the cognitive elite have usually been trained at the same academic institutions as the intelligentsia, and their undergraduate education has involved being taught by many of the same professors with the same ideological slant.

Perhaps equally or more important, these other members of the cognitive elite are more likely to continue to move in many of the same social circles as the intelligentsia, rather than living at random among members of the larger society. There have always been elites of one sort or another, but the nature of those elites has changed in different eras, often with important consequences for the society at large. The evolution of the cognitive elite of our own time is highly relevant to the influence of the intellectuals.

Over time— and especially during the twentieth century— the growing access of individuals with high levels of mental ability to institutions of higher education, even when such individuals originate in families unable to afford to pay the full costs of higher education, has had both economic and social consequences. Among the obvious economic consequences have been not only the social mobility enjoyed by the particular individuals whose education has been subsidized by either private philanthropy or the government but, more fundamentally, a growing ability of society at large to benefit from a growing opportunity to tap and develop outstanding abilities and talents wherever they may occur, across a broader social spectrum. But these economic benefits have a social cost that is relevant to the influence of the intelligentsia.

At the beginning of the twentieth century, most people with high IQs were unlikely to go to college, and most people who did go to college were not as much selected for their mental abilities or academic performances as would be the case later in the century. For many years, what mattered most was the ability to pay. As late as 1952, two-thirds of the applicants to Harvard were admitted,[12] as contrasted with fewer than one-tenth today. But, during the decade of the 1950s, some striking changes occurred. By the end of that decade, most applicants to Harvard were now rejected as academic standards rose, so that the average SAT scores of Harvard's entering freshmen rose nearly a hundred points on both the verbal and mathematics portions of the SAT. Changes in social origins accompanied these changes in intellectual standards. The proportion of freshmen entering Harvard from private schools declined and they were outnumbered by freshmen from public schools.[13]

What was happening at Harvard was part of a more general trend toward opening higher education in general, and especially education at the more elite colleges and universities, to students selected more for their mental abilities than for their socioeconomic origins. The benefits of this to these individuals, and ultimately to society, are obvious. But there are also other consequences. When a society divided into socioeconomic compartments is replaced by a society divided into cognitive compartments, there is still a social isolation of the people in the elite compartments from those of the great majority of the people, whose lives they live apart from and cannot help having difficulties understanding— even though the elites in either case have disproportionate influence over the lives of the people who are not part of their intimate circles. In short, a more egalitarian access to higher education can create other social divisions:

> When people live in encapsulated worlds, it becomes difficult for them, even with the best of intentions, to grasp the realities of worlds with which they have little experience but over which they also have great influence, both public and private. Many of those promising undergraduates are never going to live in a community where they will be disabused of their misperceptions, for after education comes another sorting mechanism, occupations, and many of the holes that are still left in the cognitive partitions begin to get sealed.[14]

This social sealing off of a cognitive elite from the lives of the great majority of the society in which they live— and which the elites influence— is one of the main themes of *The Bell Curve*, from which this observation was quoted. While casual encounters may continue among the members of society at large, their intimate lives move in different orbits as regards their marriages, their careers and their lifestyles. Even if the cognitive elite take an interest in others and support efforts to better their lives, their isolation from direct personal experience of those lives can leave their understanding lacking in the mundane knowledge that only direct personal experience can supply— and for which abstract notions about abstract people are no substitute.

In short, even the benevolent interest of a cognitive elite in people unlike themselves, whose real lives they have few ways of understanding, can give these elites an influence whose actual consequences can range from unpromising to catastrophic. It is all too easy for cognitive elites to generalize from their repeatedly demonstrated superiority, within the realms in which they have moved for years, to imagine that the consensus of their similarly insulated peers is superior to the mundane direct experience of the people at large. This is confusing intellect with wisdom, despite history's painful record of how often and how far the two can diverge.

INTELLECTUALS AND POLITICIANS

Although politicians and intellectuals are separate occupations, and only two Presidents of the United States— Theodore Roosevelt and Woodrow Wilson— have been intellectuals in the sense used here, there can be a symbiotic relationship between intellectuals and politicians in general or between particular intellectuals and particular politicians. Intellectuals may acquire greater visibility from their association with famous politicians, and politicians may find intellectuals a useful source of ideas or of at least a source of enhancement of a politician's image as someone carrying out big ideas.

Symbiotic relationships between intellectuals and politicians can take many forms. One of the more common forms is intellectuals' general promotion of expanding government preemption of decision-making from private individuals and organizations. The verbal virtuosity of the intelligentsia can aid this process in many ways, including by making it seem as if that process is not taking place. For example, use of the word "society" instead of the word "government"— as in John Rawls' statements about how "society" should "arrange" certain results,[15] or John Dewey's advocacy of "socially organized intelligence in the conduct of public affairs,"[16] and "organized social reconstruction"[17] or about how "we" should "set hopefully at work upon a course of social intervention and experimental engineering."[18]

Such verbal camouflage for the transfer of decisions from private individuals and organizations to politicians, bureaucrats and judges makes such a transfer easier to carry out when the awareness of it is reduced. Use of the word "public" as a euphemism for government, as in "public schools" or "public service" serves the same purpose.

When government is spoken of explicitly by the intelligentsia, it is often depicted as if it is simply an expression of a Rousseauian "general will," rather than a collection of politicians, bureaucrats and judges, responding to the incentives and constraints confronting politicians, bureaucrats and judges. That there should be such a separate specialty as "public choice" economics, in which government officials' actions are analyzed in terms of the incentives and constraints of their circumstances, is a sign of how atypical such an approach is among intellectuals.

The relationship between politicians and intellectuals of course also depends on what kind of politician is involved. Old-fashioned machine politicians, such as the two Mayor Daleys in Chicago, were essentially non-ideological and had no special need for intellectuals. But politicians with more sweeping ambitions not only may find intellectuals useful, but also themselves face incentives similar to those of intellectuals— and can therefore constitute similar dangers. Judges are another set of government officials who can have a symbiotic relationship with intellectuals, when court decisions are made with an eye to how these decisions will be received by "the thoughtful part" of the population, as expressed by the Supreme Court of the United States in its *Planned Parenthood v. Casey* decision.[19]

In addition to politicians who are successful in the more or less routine sense of getting elected and re-elected, or perhaps being appointed to prestigious Cabinet or judicial posts, there are politicians whose ambitions soar higher, in terms of visibility on the national or world stage and in the pages of history. The incentives facing such politicians are especially similar to those facing intellectuals. When looking at their own society and nation, neither has a viable option of leaving well enough alone, which would leave them far less visible to their contemporaries and in all likelihood utterly invisible to history.

Abraham Lincoln understood such incentives and the dangers they posed. A quarter of a century before the Gettysburg address, Lincoln spelled out the inherent, internal dangers to a free society in another speech, this one in Springfield, Illinois. Moreover, Lincoln spelled out these dangers within the framework of a constrained vision— a tragic vision— of human nature, when he spoke of "the jealousy, envy, and avarice, incident to our nature," as well as "the deep-rooted principles of *hate*, and the powerful motive of *revenge*." During the war for American independence, such passions were turned against the British, he said, "instead of being turned against each other."[20] But that was an exceptional time.

According to Lincoln, many had "won their deathless names" creating the United States of America. Once that was accomplished, however, that particular "field of glory" had been "harvested." How were the highly talented and highly ambitious individuals of later generations to achieve similar glory? Lincoln said:

> It is to deny, what the history of the world tells us is true, to suppose that men of ambition and talents will not continue to spring up amongst us. And, when they do, they will as naturally seek the gratification of their ruling passion, as others have so done before them. The question then, is, can that gratification be found in supporting and maintaining an edifice that has been erected by others? Most certainly it cannot.[21]

While many highly talented people "would aspire to nothing beyond a seat in Congress, a gubernatorial or a presidential chair," he said, there are others whose ambitions soar higher:

> Towering genius disdains a beaten path. It seeks regions hitherto unexplored.— It sees *no distinction* in adding story to story, upon the monuments of fame, erected to the memory of others. It *denies* that it is glory enough to serve under any chief. It *scorns* to tread in the footsteps of *any* predecessor, however illustrious. It thirsts and burns for distinction; and, if possible, it will have it, whether at the expense of emancipating slaves, or enslaving freemen.[22]

The preservation of a free society, Lincoln argued, required vigilance against such driven leaders, for in a time of turmoil and confusion "men of sufficient talent and ambition will not be wanting to seize the opportunity, strike the blow, and overturn that fair fabric, which for the last half century, has been the fondest hope, of the lovers of freedom, throughout the world."[23] Lincoln clearly understood that the ostensible goal was not what was crucial, for driving ambitions could be satisfied by doing the opposite of whatever the ostensible goal might be— that is, whether by "emancipating slaves, or enslaving freemen."

If the internal dangers to a free society arose only from individuals "of towering genius," those dangers might not be as great as they are today. But towering *presumptions* of genius can drive both politicians and intellectuals to undermine or destroy the institutions and norms of the existing society, precisely because these are the *existing* norms of the *existing* society, and ambitious politicians— like intellectuals— want to create different norms and a different society, even if that means sacrificing other people's freedom. In this, some politicians are not only like intellectuals in the incentives they respond to, but may also share the same vision of the anointed as the intellectuals and likewise treat its principles and beliefs as axioms rather than hypotheses. A coalescing of a political leader bent on remaking a free society to fit a vision widely shared among the intelligentsia can bring together the ingredients of a "perfect storm" that a free society may or may not be able to survive.

THE TRACK RECORD OF INTELLECTUALS

What have the intellectuals actually done for society— and at what cost?

The areas in which we have seen great advances— science, industry, and medicine, for example— are largely areas outside the scope and influence of intellectuals, as the term has been used here. In areas more within the scope and influence of the intelligentsia, such as education, politics and the law, we have seen significant, and even dangerous, retrogressions.

Beginning in the 1960s, in the wake of "innovative" and "exciting" new educational theories by the intelligentsia, test scores went down in American schools, despite greatly increased spending per student. Also beginning in the 1960s, the previous decades-long decline in the murder rate reversed dramatically and tripled in the wake of the intelligentsia's new theories about crime being applied in the courts. Similarly, downward trends in sexually transmitted diseases and teenage pregnancy reversed dramatically in the 1960s, as indoctrination programs that the intelligentsia called "sex education" spread through the schools. The black family, which had survived centuries of slavery and generations of discrimination, began disintegrating disastrously in the wake of welfare state policies and corresponding non-judgmental social doctrines promoted by the intelligentsia.

Many great advances in medicine, science, and technology have come out of the universities, research institutes, and industrial development departments of businesses, benefitting society at large and ultimately people around the world. Many of these benefits have been produced by individuals of extraordinary mental abilities, as well as other valuable qualities— but seldom have these individuals been intellectuals in our sense of people whose end products are ideas whose only validation process is the approval of peers. What is striking about intellectuals in this sense is how difficult it is to think of benefits they have conferred on anyone outside their own circles— and how painfully apparent it is how much they have in fact cost the rest of society at large, not only economically but in many other ways, including vulnerability to external enemies bent on these societies' destruction.

While virtually anyone can name a list of medical, scientific, or technological things that have made the lives of today's generation better in some way than that of people in the past, including people just one generation ago, it would be a challenge for even a highly informed person to name three ways in which our lives today are better as a result of the ideas of sociologists or deconstructionists. One could, of course, define "better" as being aware of sociology, deconstruction, etc., or carrying out their policy agendas, but this circular reasoning would amount to just another of the many arguments without arguments.

There have been landmark writings, even works of genius, in what are called the social sciences. But so many of these have been implicitly or explicitly attacks on things said by other writers in the social sciences that it is not at all clear how much net loss the society would have suffered if none of them in the whole profession had said anything. For example, the writings of James Q. Wilson on crime have been enormously valuable, but primarily by rebutting the prevailing ideas of other writers on crime, ideas which have produced social disasters on both sides of the Atlantic. It was other intellectuals— not the general public— who were the source of the fashionable notions behind counterproductive policies on crime, as well as on other social issues. Prior to the ascendancy of the intelligentsia's notions in the criminal justice system of the United States, murder rates had been going down for decades, under the traditional ideas and practices so much disdained by the intelligentsia.

Something similar could be said of other outstanding writings which rebutted other intellectual fashions, but which would have been unnecessary had not those fashions arisen and prevailed among the intelligentsia— and then found their way into public policy.

Obviously the net balance can differ among fields of specialization. Empirically-based fields, such as history and economics, can enrich people's understanding to the extent that practitioners in these fields act like historians or economists, rather than philosopher-kings. However, even assuming that there has been a net benefit from the work of contemporary intellectuals, it is hard to believe that it has approached the benefits from such fields as engineering, medicine or agriculture.

There is an old saying that even a clock that is stopped is nevertheless right twice a day. Intellectuals can claim credit for largely supporting the American civil rights revolution of the 1960s but much of the credit must go to others who put themselves in danger in the South or who put their political careers on the line for the sake of civil rights, beginning with President Harry Truman in the 1940s, in order to make the legal changes which began the breaking down of state-sponsored racial discrimination. Moreover, whatever contributions the intelligentsia made as regards racial progress in the latter half of the twentieth century must be balanced off against the role of Progressive era intellectuals in promoting racial discrimination and even, in the case of Madison Grant, providing a rationale for Hitler's racial beliefs that ended in genocide.

Even as regards the intelligentsia of the late twentieth century, whatever contributions they made as regards racial progress must be balanced off against their role in justifying or rationalizing the undermining of law and order, whether in racial or non-racial contexts, with blacks being the primary victims of the increased violence, including in some years more blacks than whites being murdered, in absolute numbers, despite the large differences in the sizes of the two populations.

In an earlier era, intellectuals in France, led by Émile Zola, exposed the fraudulence of the charges that had sent Captain Alfred Dreyfus to a Devil's Island prison. In fact, the very term "intellectual" has been said to have originated in that episode.[24] Though others in France— some in the military and Georges Clemenceau in politics— had taken up the cause of Captain Dreyfus, even before Zola's famous article "J'accuse,"[25] nevertheless the Dreyfus episode was something to be put on the credit side of the ledger for the intelligentsia. But we have already seen how much was on the other side of that ledger, especially in France.

While it is difficult to put together a case that intellectuals as producers of ideas have created major and lasting benefits for the vast majority of people at all comparable to what people in other professions, or even in many mundane occupations, have created, what would be far less of a challenge would be to name things made *worse* by intellectuals, both in our own times and in other times. Many of these things can be listed here in summary fashion, because they have either been discussed at some length in earlier chapters or because they are matters of common knowledge.

SOCIAL COHESION

One of the things intellectuals have been doing for a very long time is loosening the bonds that hold a society together. They have sought to replace the groups into which people have sorted themselves with groupings created and imposed by the intelligentsia. Ties of family, religion, and patriotism, for example, have long been treated as suspect or detrimental by the intelligentsia, while new ties that intellectuals have promoted, such as class— and more recently "gender"— have been projected as either more real or more important. More generally, the tendency of the intelligentsia to turn statistical disparities into moral melodramas virtually guarantees unending sources of polarization among flesh-and-blood human beings who differ from each other in innumerable ways, unlike abstract people in an abstract world.

The tendency of intellectuals toward extreme and dramatic explanations of social phenomena— genetic determinism or social injustice, for example— can create alternatives which are each intolerable to believers in the other alternative. Large economic differences, whether among individuals or groups in a given country or among nations, have at various times and places been attributed to innate inferiority among those who are poorer, and at other times and places have been attributed to injustice and exploitation by those who are more prosperous. Given the alternatives proposed, those who are less prosperous have been confronted with either believing themselves inferior or hating those who are more prosperous, and hence guilty of making them poor. Those who are more prosperous are confronted with either accepting that guilt or denouncing the poor— if they accept the visions that prevailed among intellectuals during the early or the later twentieth century.

There could hardly be a more polarizing set of alternatives. There could hardly be more of an incentive to embrace an unsubstantiated theory than having the only apparent alternative be another unsubstantiated theory, which has the additional quality of being deeply wounding. This is the high price of dramatic visions, and why they represent a danger to the social cohesion at the heart of a viable society.

Either belief can have devastating consequences. Relegating whole races to the role of hewers of wood and drawers of water is an obvious tragedy for them, and no small loss to a society that throws away the talents and potentialities of millions. Descendants of the supposed "beaten men from beaten races" have made medical, technological and other breakthroughs that have benefitted human beings around the world. These would include the inventor of alternating current, which made the electrification of the world economically viable (Nikola Tesla), the scientist who created the first controlled nuclear reaction (Enrico Fermi), and the man who revolutionized the whole scientific conception of the universe (Albert Einstein)— a Serb, an Italian and a Jew, respectively. We can only guess how many others might have made similar contributions had they not perished in the Holocaust, the end result of intellectuals' speculations translated into political ideology.

The opposite view, that the poverty of the poor is caused by the injustices of the rich, has led to whole generations remaining needlessly poor in Third World countries, until some of these countries— most notably China and India— belatedly opened their markets to both domestic and international private investment, leading to sharp increases in economic growth and millions rising out of poverty. Earlier, the Marxist "exploitation" theory led to Communist societies in the Soviet Union and in China under Mao, each of which had deaths by starvation alone that were more numerous than the deaths in the Holocaust. Here too, speculations for which intellectuals paid no price ended up imposing ghastly costs on millions of others.

We have seen in Chapter 14 some of the ways in which leading intellectuals in Western democracies undermined their own countries' national defense between the two World Wars. But before there can be national defense in a military sense, there has to be some feeling that the nation is worth defending, whether in a social, cultural or other sense. Most modern intellectuals seldom contribute toward that feeling. Some have even made statements such as this by George Kennan:

Show me first an America which has successfully coped with the problems of crime, drugs, deteriorating educational standards, urban decay, pornography and decadence of one sort or another— show me an America that. . . is what it ought to be, then I will tell you how we are going to defend ourselves from the Russians.[26]

Not all intellectuals are as blunt as this but it is by no means uncommon for some among the intelligentsia to depict the United States as being on trial and needing to prove its innocence— a standard seldom applied to other countries— before it can claim the public's allegiance in its defense against other nations, or perhaps even before its laws and social norms can expect voluntary compliance at home. Nor is the United States unique in this respect. The intelligentsia in some European nations have gone further— being apologetic to Muslims at home and abroad, and having acquiesced in the setting up of de facto Muslim enclaves with their own rules and standards within Europe, as well as overlooking their violations of the national laws in the European countries in which Muslim immigrants have settled.[27]

What does the intelligentsia's vogue of being "non-judgmental" mean, except a refusal to uphold the society's standards and values, despite how much those standards and values may be responsible for the benefits which the members of that society have inherited? How can standards and values be upheld, if those who violate them pay no price for doing so, either from the law or from the disapproval of others around them?

Fictitious complimentary images of foreign countries are among the many ways in which intellectuals undermine their own. In other ways as well, many intellectuals erode or destroy a sense of the shared values and shared achievements that make a nation possible, or a sense of national cohesion with which to resist those who would attack it from within or without. To condemn their country's enemies would be to be like the masses, but to condemn their own society itself sets the anointed apart as moral exemplars and incisive minds— at least to like-minded peers.

If we take the word "critical" to mean "involving or requiring skillful judgment as to truth, merit, etc.,"[28] then what is called "critical thinking," especially in academic institutions, is too often *uncritical* negativism towards their own society and uncritical admiration or apologetics for other societies. Intellectuals who decry a "Eurocentric" view of the world are often themselves very Eurocentric, when it comes to criticizing the sins and shortcomings common to the human race around the world.

Given the incentives and constraints, it is hard to see how intellectuals would do otherwise, when whatever significance they might have in the larger society so often depends on their criticisms of that society and their claims to have created "solutions" to whatever they define as its "problems." This is not to say that intellectuals cynically play on the gullibility of the public in order to parlay their professional expertise into social acclaim or political influence. They may sincerely believe what they say, but those beliefs often have no substance behind them nor— more important— any test in front of them.

Under the influence of the intelligentsia, we have become a society that rewards people with admiration for violating the society's own norms and for fragmenting that society into jarring segments. In addition to explicit denigrations of their own society for its history or current shortcomings, intellectuals often set up standards for their society which no society of human beings has ever met or is ever likely to meet. Neither American society nor any other society has ever been simply the embodiment of its ideals, "the word made flesh."

Comparing any society to ideals virtually guarantees that that society will be condemned as a failure, if only because it costs nothing to imagine something better than what exists— that is, to create ideals— while everything created in the real world has a cost. Moreover, our only choice in the real world is between different societies compared to each other— not compared to ideals such as "social justice." The enormous influence of geographic, climatic and other forces, utterly beyond the control of any given society, makes the resulting gross inequalities among peoples— not only in their immediate economic circumstances, but in their own internal "human capital," developing in cultural universes of widely varying sizes — something far more than an injustice that can be attributed to any given society or that can blithely be assumed to be remediable by every society.

Calling unrealistic standards "social justice" enables intellectuals to engage in endless complaints about the particular ways in which a particular society fails to meet their criteria, along with a parade of groups entitled to a sense of grievance, exemplified in the "race, class and gender" formula today, though the same kind of thinking behind that particular formula has also been used to depict children as victims of their parents and illegal immigrants as victims of a calloused or xenophobic society in the country they enter, in violation of its laws.

"The creation of nations out of tribes, in early modern times in Europe and in contemporary Asia and Africa, is the work of intellectuals," according to distinguished scholar Edward Shils.[29] But intellectuals in Western nations today are largely engaged in creating tribes out of nations. What Peter Hitchens in Britain has aptly called the "atomization of society," which has "sundered many of the invisible bonds which once held our society together"[30] is a pattern which has not been confined to Britain or even to Western nations.

The positive achievements of the society in which intellectuals live seldom receive attention even remotely comparable to the amount of attention paid to grievances or supposed grievances. This asymmetry, together with factual and logical deficiencies of many laments made in the name of "social justice," can create the image of a society not worth preserving, much less defending. The benefits of existing social arrangements are taken for granted as things that happen more or less automatically— even when they seldom happen in many other countries— and not as things for which sacrifice (or at least forbearance) is required, much less things that can be jeopardized by some of the zeal for generic "change," often promoted with little regard to the many possible repercussions of those changes.

Western civilization, with all its faults, may nevertheless provide a more decent life for more people than any competing civilization that is likely to replace it. But the filtering and distortions of the intelligentsia can prevent enough people from fully understanding that, without actually experiencing the change, so that the knowledge may come too late, after all is irretrievably lost.

The intelligentsia have changed the high achievements and rewards of some members of society from an inspiration to others into a source of resentment and grievance for others. The intelligentsia encourage people who are contributing nothing to the world to complain, and even organize protests, because others are not doing enough for them. They have rationalized the breaking of laws by those who choose to picture themselves as underdogs fighting an oppressive "system," even when these are college students from affluent homes, being subsidized by their parents and/or the taxpayers. Intellectuals have, both in America and in France, verbally turned military heroes who put their lives on the line for their country into victims of war, people whom one might pity but never want to emulate.

They have put the people whose work creates the goods and services that sustain a rising standard of living on the same plane as people who refuse to work, but who are depicted as nevertheless entitled to their "fair share" of what others have created— this entitlement being regardless of whether the recipients observe even common decency, much less the laws.

Intellectuals have largely ignored or downplayed the things in which Americans lead the world— including philanthropy, technology, and the creation of life-saving medical advances— and treated the errors, flaws and shortcomings that Americans share with human beings around the world as special defects of "our society."

ANTI-INTELLECTUAL INTELLECTUALS

After one of their ideas or policies is adopted, the intelligentsia almost never ask the follow-up question: What has gotten better as a result? Often things have gotten demonstrably worse[31]— and then the verbal virtuosity of the intelligentsia is deployed, to claim that the evidence doesn't prove anything because it was not necessarily what they did that caused things to go wrong. While it is fine to warn against the *post hoc* fallacy, what intellectuals seldom do is put the burden of proof on themselves to show what has gotten better when their ideas were put into practice.

Despite intellectuals' *capacity* to analyze and clarify beliefs and issues, among the recurring confusions exhibited and spread by the intelligentsia is a confusion between *causes* and *conveyances*. Perhaps the greatest damage done by intellectuals who confuse conveyances with causes is turning the innumerable differences among races, classes and other subdivisions of the human species into sources of unending strife that can tear whole nations apart. In a world where levels of capabilities in various endeavors can vary greatly among both individuals and groups— and rewards vary correspondingly— for innumerable reasons, some going far back into the past, intellectuals have made those differences either reasons to label those who lag as incorrigibly inferior (as during the early twentieth century) or to blame their lags on those who do not lag (as in the later twentieth century).

Whether discussing races, classes, nations or other segments of the human species, many among the intelligentsia have often depicted the more fortunate groups as the *cause* of others being less fortunate. In many cases, evidence for this conclusion is non-existent, and in other cases the available evidence points in the opposite direction— namely, that the presence of the more fortunate groups, whether Germans living in Eastern Europe in centuries past or multinational corporations in Third World countries today, has expanded the opportunities of others, rather than contracted them.

In the schools and colleges, the intelligentsia have changed the role of education from equipping students with the knowledge and intellectual skills to weigh issues and make up their own minds into a process of indoctrination with the conclusions already reached by the anointed.

The intelligentsia have treated the conclusions of their vision as axioms to be promoted, rather than hypotheses to be tested— and those who teach have often passed the same dogmatism on to their students, along with habits of using arguments without arguments.

Some among the intelligentsia have treated reality itself as subjective or illusory, thereby putting current intellectual fashions and fads on the same plane as verified knowledge and the cultural wisdom distilled from generations, or even millennia, of human experience.

Intellectuals have romanticized cultures that have left people mired in poverty, ignorance, violence, disease and chaos, while trashing cultures that have led the world in prosperity, education, medical advances and law and order. In doing so, the intelligentsia have often disregarded, or even filtered out, the fact that masses of people were fleeing the societies intellectuals romanticized to go to the societies they condemned.

The intelligentsia have been quick to find excuses for crime and equally quick to attribute wrong-doing to police, even when discussing things for which intellectuals have neither expertise nor experience, such as shooting.

Intellectuals give people who have the handicap of poverty the further handicap of a sense of victimhood. They have encouraged the poor to believe that their poverty is caused by the rich— a message which may be a passing annoyance to the rich but a lasting handicap to the poor, who may see less need to make fundamental changes in their own lives that could lift themselves up, instead of focusing their efforts on dragging others down. The intelligentsia have acted as if their ignorance of why some people earn unusually high incomes is a reason why those incomes are either suspect or ought not to be permitted.

Intellectuals have— on issues ranging across the spectrum from housing policies to laws governing organ transplants— sought to have decision-making discretion taken from those directly involved, who have personal knowledge and a personal stake, and transferred to third parties who have neither, and who pay no price for being wrong. The presumption of the superior wisdom and virtue of intellectuals has made the actual track record of intellectuals of the past, whether on foreign or domestic policies, a matter of minimal interest to their successors, if any interest at all.

IMPLICATIONS

The characteristics of intellectuals and the roles that they seek to play mesh well together. That applies both to intellectuals proper— people whose occupation is producing ideas as end products— and to the intelligentsia as a whole, including the large surrounding penumbra of those whose views reflect and disseminate the views of the intellectuals.

The revealed preference of the intelligentsia— whether the specific subject is crime, economics or other things— is not only to be conspicuously different from society at large but also, and almost axiomatically, superior to society, either intellectually or morally, or both. Their vision of the world is not only a vision of causation in the world as it exists and a vision of what the world ought to be like, it is also a vision of *themselves* as a self-anointed vanguard, leading toward that better world.

This vision of the anointed represents a huge investment of ego in a particular set of beliefs, and this investment is a major obstacle to reconsideration of those beliefs in the light of evidence and experience. No one likes to admit being wrong but few have such a large personal investment in a set of beliefs as those with the vision of the anointed— or so few countervailing incentives to reconsider. The ruthlessness with which the anointed assail others[32] and the doggedness with which they cling to their beliefs, in defiance of ever mounting evidence against the "root causes" of crime and other social theories, for example, is evidence of that large ego investment in a set of beliefs about social or political issues that also involve beliefs about themselves.

Intellectuals have no monopoly on dogmatism or ego, or on the power to rationalize. But the institutional constraints facing people in many other fields, from science to athletics, confront others with high and often ruinous costs for persisting in ideas that turn out not to work in practice. The history of prevailing beliefs among scientists that they were forced to abandon in the face of contrary evidence is a major part of the entire history of science. In athletics, whether professional or collegiate, no theory or belief can survive incessant losses and seldom can any manager or coach.

No such inescapable constraints confront people whose end products are ideas, and whose ideas face only the validation of like-minded peers. That is especially the case with academic intellectuals, who control their own institutions and select their own colleagues and successors. No tenured professor can be fired because he or she voted for campus policies that turned out to be either economically or educationally disastrous for the college or university, or advocated policies that turned out to be catastrophic for society as a whole.

This unaccountability to the external world is not a happenstance but a deeply rooted principle enshrined under the title of "academic freedom." From unaccountability to irresponsibility can be a very short step. Other members of the intelligentsia, including both broadcast media and entertainment media, likewise have very wide latitude as far as checks on the validity of what they say is concerned. Their main constraint is whether they can draw an audience, whether with truth or falsehoods, and whether with constructive or destructive effects on the society at large.

However few are the constraints on what the intelligentsia choose to do in their work, the role that they aspire to play in society at large can be achieved by them only to the extent that the rest of society accepts what they say uncritically and fails to examine their track record. Despite formidable weapons wielded by the intelligentsia in their crusades for cultural, moral, and ideological hegemony, they are not always able to neutralize the countervailing force of facts, experience and common sense. That is especially so in the United States, where intellectuals have never gotten the kind of deference they have long received in Europe and in some other parts of the world. Yet, even among Americans, the steady encroachment of policies, practices, and laws based on the notions and ideologies prevalent among the intelligentsia has steadily narrowed the scope of the freedoms traditionally enjoyed by ordinary people to run their own lives, much less to shape the laws that govern them.

Some intellectuals' downplaying of objective reality and enduring criteria extends beyond social, scientific, or economic phenomena into art, music, and philosophy. The one over-riding consistency across all these disparate venues is the self-exaltation of the intellectuals. Unlike great cultural achievements of the past, such as magnificent cathedrals, which were intended to inspire kings and peasants alike, the hallmark of self-consciously "modern" art and music is its inaccessibility to the masses and often even its deliberate offensiveness to, or mockery of, the masses.

Just as a physical body can continue to live, despite containing a certain amount of microorganisms whose prevalence would destroy it, so a society can survive a certain amount of forces of disintegration within it. But that is very different from saying that there is no limit to the amount, audacity and ferocity of those disintegrative forces which a society can survive, without at least the will to resist.

NOTES

PREFACE

1. J.A. Schumpeter, *History of Economic Analysis* (New York: Oxford University Press, 1954), p. 475.

2. Mark Lilla, *The Reckless Mind: Intellectuals in Politics* (New York: New York Review Books, 2001), p. 198.

PART I: INTRODUCTION

CHAPTER 1: INTELLECT AND INTELLECTUALS

1. Alfred North Whitehead, "December 15, 1939," *Dialogues of Alfred North Whitehead as Recorded by Lucien Price* (Boston: Little, Brown and Company, 1954), p. 135.

2. Michael St. John Packe, *The Life of John Stuart Mill* (New York: The Macmillan Company, 1954), p. 315.

3. For example, according to the *Chronicle of Higher Education*: "Conservatives are rarest in the humanities (3.6 percent) and social sciences (4.9 percent), and most common in business (24.5 percent) and the health sciences (20.5 percent)." Among faculty in the social sciences and humanities at elite, Ph.D.-granting universities, "not a single instructor reported voting for President Bush in 2004," when the President received a majority of the popular vote in the country at large. See David Glenn, "Few Conservatives but Many Centrists Teach in Academe," *Chronicle of Higher Education*, October 19, 2007, p. A10. In the health sciences, a study showed that the proportion of the faculty who called themselves conservative was the same as the proportion who called themselves liberal (20.5 percent), with the remainder calling themselves moderate. In business there were slightly more self-styled conservatives than self-styled liberals (24.5 percent versus 21.3 percent). Neil Gross and Solon Simmons, "The Social and Political Views of American Professors," Working Paper, September 24, 2007, p. 28. But in the social sciences and humanities, people who identified themselves as liberals were an absolute majority, with moderates outnumbering conservatives several times over among the remainder. See also Howard Kurtz, "College Faculties A Most Liberal Lot, Study Finds," *Washington Post*, March 29, 2005, p. C1; Stanley Rothman, S. Robert Lichter, and Neil Nevitte, "Politics and

Professional Advancement Among College Faculty," *The Forum*, Vol. 3, Issue 1 (2005), p. 6; Christopher F. Cardiff and Daniel B. Klein, "Faculty Partisan Affiliations in All Disciplines: A Voter-Registration Study," *Critical Review*, Vol. 17, Nos. 3–4, pp. 237–255.

4. Oliver Wendell Holmes, "The Profession of the Law," *Collected Legal Papers* (New York: Peter Smith, 1952), p. 32.

5. Gunnar Myrdal, for example, said, "The major recastings of economic thought that we connect with the names of Adam Smith, Malthus, Ricardo, List, Marx, John Stuart Mill, Jevons and Walras, Wicksell and Keynes were all responses to changing political conditions and opportunities." Gunnar Myrdal, *Asian Drama: An Inquiry Into the Poverty of Nations* (New York: Pantheon, 1968), Vol. I, p. 9.

6. George J. Stigler, *Essays in the History of Economics* (Chicago: University of Chicago Press, 1965), p. 21.

7. See Thomas Sowell, *On Classical Economics* (New Haven: Yale University Press, 2006), pp. 143–146.

8. Eric Hoffer, *Before the Sabbath* (New York: Harper & Row, 1979), p. 3. Richard Posner also said that public intellectuals "who do not expect to undergo the close scrutiny of a biographer pay little cost in reputation even for being repeatedly proved wrong by events." Richard A. Posner, *Public Intellectuals: A Study of Decline* (Cambridge, Massachusetts: Harvard University Press, 2001), p. 63.

9. Paul R. Ehrlich, *The Population Bomb* (New York: Ballantine Books, 1968), p. xi.

10. The results of the government study of the safety of the Corvair were reported in the *Congressional Record: Senate*, March 27, 1973, pp. 9748–9774.

CHAPTER 2: KNOWLEDGE AND NOTIONS

1. Daniel J. Flynn, *Intellectual Morons: How Ideology Makes Smart People Fall for Stupid Ideas* (New York: Crown Forum, 2004), p. 4.

2. Bertrand Russell, *Which Way to Peace?* (London: Michael Joseph, Ltd., 1937), p. 146.

3. League of Professional Groups for Foster and Ford, *Culture and the Crisis: An Open Letter to the Writers, Artists, Teachers, Physicians, Engineers, Scientists and Other Professional Workers of America* (New York: Workers Library Publishers, 1932), p. 32.

4. "Shaw Bests Army of Interviewers," *New York Times*, March 25, 1933, p. 17.

5. "G.B. Shaw 'Praises' Hitler," *New York Times*, March 22, 1935, p. 21.

6. Letter to *The Times* of London, August 28, 1939, p. 11.

7. George J. Stigler, *Memoirs of an Unregulated Economist* (New York: Basic Books, 1988), p. 178. "A full collection of public statements signed by laureates whose work gave them not even professional acquaintance with the problem addressed by the statement would be a very large and somewhat depressing collection." Ibid., p. 89.

8. Roy Harrod, *The Life of John Maynard Keynes* (New York: Augustus M. Kelley, 1969), p. 468.

9. Richard Overy, *The Twilight Years: The Paradox of Britain Between the Wars* (New York: Viking, 2009), p. 374.

10. Brad Stone, "The Empire of Excess," *New York Times*, July 4, 2008, p. C1. Wal-Mart has likewise put much emphasis on choosing the locations of its stores. Richard Vedder and Wendell Cox, *The Wal-Mart Revolution: How Big-Box Stores Benefit Consumers, Workers, and the Economy* (Washington: AEI Press, 2006), pp. 53–54.

11. F.A. Hayek, *The Constitution of Liberty* (Chicago: University of Chicago Press, 1960), p. 26.

12. Robert L. Bartley, *The Seven Fat Years: And How To Do It Again* (New York: The Free Press, 1992), p. 241.

13. John Dewey, *Human Nature and Conduct: An Introduction to Social Psychology* (New York: The Modern Library, 1957), p. 148.

14. Edmund Morris, *The Rise of Theodore Roosevelt* (New York: Modern Library, 2001), p. 466.

15. Eligio R. Padilla and Gail E. Wyatt, "The Effects of Intelligence and Achievement Testing on Minority Group Children," *The Psychosocial Development of Minority Group Children*, edited by Gloria Johnson Powell, et al (New York: Brunner/Mazel, Publishers, 1983), p. 418.

16. Stuart Taylor, Jr. and K.C. Johnson, *Until Proven Innocent: Political Correctness and the Shameful Injustices of the Duke Lacrosse Rape Case* (New York: St. Martin's Press, 2007), pp. 12–13, 186, 212, 233–234.

17. Jeff Schultz, "Wrong Message for Duke Women," *Atlanta Journal-Constitution*, May 27, 2006, p. C1; Harvey Araton, "At Duke, Freedom of Speech Seems Selective," *New York Times*, May 26, 2006, pp. D1 ff; John Smallwood, "School Should Ban 'Innocent' Sweatbands," *Philadelphia Daily News*, May 26, 2006, Sports, p. 107; Stephen A. Smith, "Duke Free-Falling from Grace," *Philadelphia Inquirer*, May 28, 2006, p. D1.

18. See Thomas Sowell, *Basic Economics: A Common Sense Guide to the Economy*, fourth edition (New York: Basic Books, 2011), pp. 319–326 for a discussion of resource

allocation over time and pp. 21–24 and 29–30 for a discussion of resource allocation as of a given time.

19. See, for example, Ibid., p. 275.

20. Randal O'Toole, *The Best-Laid Plans: How Government Planning Harms Your Quality of Life, Your Pocketbook, and Your Future* (Washington: Cato Institute, 2007), p. 190.

21. Ibid., p. 194.

22. Nikolai Shmelev and Vladimir Popov, *The Turning Point: Revitalizing the Soviet Economy* (New York: Doubleday, 1989), p. 170.

23. See, for example, Thomas Sowell, *The Vision of the Anointed: Self-Congratulation as a Basis for Social Policy* (New York: Basic Books, 1995), Chapter 2.

24. Sidney E. Zion, "Attack on Court Heard by Warren," *New York Times*, September 10, 1965, pp. 1 ff.

25. U. S. Bureau of the Census, *Historical Statistics of the United States: Colonial Times to 1970* (Washington: Government Printing Office, 1975), Part 1, p. 414.

26. James Q. Wilson and Richard J. Herrnstein, *Crime and Human Nature* (New York: Simon and Schuster, 1985), p. 409.

27. William Godwin, *Enquiry Concerning Political Justice and Its Influence on Morals and Happiness* (Toronto: University of Toronto Press, 1946), Vol. I, p. 85.

28. Michael J. Hurley, *Firearms Discharge Report*, Police Academy Firearms and Tactics Section, New York, 2006, p. 10. See also Al Baker, "A Hail of Bullets, a Heap of Uncertainty," *New York Times*, December 9, 2007, Week in Review section, p. 4.

29. Oliver Wendell Holmes, *Collected Legal Papers* (New York: Peter Smith, 1952), p. 197.

30. Richard A. Epstein, *How Progressives Rewrote the Constitution* (Washington: The Cato Institute, 2006), p. viii.

31. N. J. G. Pounds, *The Culture of the English People: Iron Age to the Industrial Revolution* (Cambridge: Cambridge University Press, 1994), p. 303.

32. "The life of the law has not been logic: it has been experience. The felt necessities of the time, the prevalent moral and political theories, intuitions of public policy, avowed or unconscious, even the prejudices which judges share with their fellow-men, have had a good deal more to do than the syllogism in determining the rules by which men should be governed." Oliver Wendell Holmes, Jr., *The Common Law* (Boston: Little, Brown and Company, 1923), p. 1.

33. Eugene Davidson, *The Unmaking of Adolf Hitler* (Columbia, Missouri: University of Missouri Press, 1996), p. 198.

34. Winston Churchill, *Churchill Speaks 1897–1963: Collected Speeches in Peace & War*, edited by Robert Rhodes James (New York: Chelsea House, 1980), p. 552.

35. Ibid., pp. 642–643.

PART II: INTELLECTUALS AND ECONOMICS

George J. Stigler, *The Economist as Preacher and Other Essays* (Chicago: University of Chicago Press, 1982), p. 61.

CHAPTER 3: "INCOME DISTRIBUTION"

1. Quoted in Arthur C. Brooks, "Philanthropy and the Non-Profit Sector," *Understanding America: The Anatomy of An Exceptional Nation*, edited by Peter H. Schuck and James Q. Wilson (New York: Public Affairs, 2008), pp. 548–549.

2. "Class and the American Dream," *New York Times*, May 30, 2005, p. A14.

3. Evan Thomas and Daniel Gross, "Taxing the Super Rich," *Newsweek*, July 23, 2007, p. 38.

4. Eugene Robinson, "Tattered Dream; Who'll Tackle the Issue of Upward Mobility?" *Washington Post*, November 23, 2007, p. A39.

5. Janet Hook, "Democrats Pursue Risky Raising-Taxes Strategy," *Los Angeles Times*, November 1, 2007.

6. E.J. Dionne, "Overtaxed Rich Is A Fairy Tale of Supply Side," *Investor's Business Daily*, July 29, 2010, p. A11.

7. Peter Corning, *The Fair Society: The Science of Human Nature and the Pursuit of Social Justice* (Chicago: University of Chicago Press, 2011), p. ix.

8. Andrew Hacker, *Money: Who Has How Much and Why* (New York: Scribner, 1997), p. 10.

9. See, for example, David Wessel, "As Rich-Poor Gap Widens in the U.S., Class Mobility Stalls," *Wall Street Journal*, May 13, 2005, pp. A1 ff.

10. "Movin' On Up," *Wall Street Journal*, November 13, 2007, p. A24.

11. David Cay Johnston, "Richest Are Leaving Even the Rich Far Behind," *New York Times*, June 5, 2005, section 1, pp. 1 ff.

12. U.S. Department of the Treasury, "Income Mobility in the U.S. from 1996 to 2005," November 13, 2007, p. 12.

13. Tom Herman, "There's Rich, and There's the 'Fortunate 400,'" *Wall Street Journal*, March 5, 2008, p. D1.

14. "The 400 Individual Income Tax Returns Reporting the Highest Adjusted Gross Incomes Each Year, 1992–2000," Statistics of Income Bulletin, U.S. Department of the Treasury, Spring 2003, Publication 1136 (Revised 6–03).

15. W. Michael Cox and Richard Alm, "By Our Own Bootstraps: Economic Opportunity & the Dynamics of Income Distribution," *Annual Report, 1995*, Federal Reserve Bank of Dallas, p. 8.

16. Peter Saunders, "Poor Statistics: Getting the Facts Right About Poverty in Australia," *Issue Analysis*, No. 23, Centre for Independent Studies (Australia), April 3, 2002, p. 5; David Green, *Poverty and Benefit Dependency* (Wellington: New Zealand Business Roundtable, 2001), pp. 32, 33; Jason Clemens & Joel Emes, "Time Reveals the Truth about Low Income," *Fraser Forum*, September 2001, pp. 24–26.

17. U.S. Department of Labor, Bureau of Labor Statistics, *Characteristics of Minimum Wage Workers: 2005* (Washington: Department of Labor, Bureau of Labor Statistics, 2006), p. 1 and Table 1.

18. U.S. Department of the Treasury, "Income Mobility in the U.S. from 1996 to 2005," November 13, 2007, p. 2.

19. Computed from Carmen DeNavas-Walt, et al., "Income, Poverty, and Health Insurance Coverage in the United States: 2005," *Current Population Reports*, P60–231 (Washington: U.S. Bureau of the Census, 2006), p. 4.

20. See, for example, "The Rich Get Richer, and So Do the Old," *Washington Post*, National Weekly Edition, September 7, 1998, p. 34; John Schmitt, "No Economic Boom for the Middle Class," *San Diego Union-Tribune*, September 5, 1999, p. G3.

21. Computed from *Economic Report of the President* (Washington: U.S. Government Printing Office, 2009), p. 321.

22. Herman P. Miller, *Income Distribution in the United States* (Washington: U.S. Government Printing Office, 1966), p. 7.

23. Rose M. Kreider and Diana B. Elliott, "America's Family and Living Arrangements: 2007," *Current Population Reports*, P20–561 (Washington: U.S. Bureau of the Census, 2009), p. 5.

24. Robert Rector and Rea S. Hederman, *Income Inequality: How Census Data Misrepresent Income Distribution* (Washington: The Heritage Foundation, 1999), p. 11.

25. Data on numbers of heads of household working in high-income and low-income households in 2000 are from Table HINC–06 from the *Current Population Survey*, downloaded from the Bureau of the Census web site.

26. Alan Reynolds, *Income and Wealth* (Westport, CT: Greenwood Press, 2006), p. 28.

27. Michael Harrington, *The Other America: Poverty in the United States* (New York: Penguin Books, 1981), pp. xiii, 1, 12, 16, 17.

28. Alan Reynolds, *Income and Wealth*, p. 67.

29. Peter Corning, *The Fair Society*, p. ix.

30. Andrew Hacker, *Money*, p. 14.

31. Ibid., p. 31.

32. Steve DiMeglio, "With Golf Needing a Boost, Its Leading Man Returns," *USA Today*, February 25, 2009, pp. 1A ff.

33. Jeffrey S. Gurock, *When Harlem Was Jewish: 1870–1930* (New York: Columbia University Press, 1979).

34. Conor Dougherty, "States Imposing Interest-Rate Caps to Rein in Payday Lenders," *Wall Street Journal*, August 9–10, 2008, p. A3.

35. "Pay Pals," *New York Times*, June 10, 2009, p. A26.

CHAPTER 4: ECONOMIC SYSTEMS

1. John Dewey, *Liberalism and Social Action* (Amherst, N.Y.: Prometheus Books, 2000), p. 43.

2. Bernard Shaw, *The Intelligent Woman's Guide to Socialism and Capitalism* (New York: Brentano's Publishers, 1928), p. 208.

3. Bertrand Russell, *Sceptical Essays* (New York: W.W. Norton & Co., Inc., 1928), p. 230.

4. John Dewey, *Liberalism and Social Action*, p. 65.

5. Aida D. Donald, *Lion in the White House: A Life of Theodore Roosevelt* (New York: Basic Books, 2007), p. 10.

6. Robert B. Reich, *Supercapitalism: The Transformation of Business, Democracy, and Everyday Life* (New York: Vintage Books, 2008), p. 21.

7. Harold A. Black, et al., "Do Black-Owned Banks Discriminate against Black Borrowers?" *Journal of Financial Services Research*, February 1997, pp. 185–200.

8. Board of Governors of the Federal Reserve System, *Report to the Congress on Credit Scoring and Its Effects on the Availability and Affordability of Credit*, submitted to the Congress pursuant to Section 215 of the Fair and Accurate Credit Transactions Act of 2003, August 2007, p. 80.

9. United States Commission on Civil Rights, *Civil Rights and the Mortgage Crisis* (Washington: U.S. Commission on Civil Rights, 2009), p. 53.

10. Karl Marx, *Capital: A Critique of Political Economy* (Chicago: Charles H. Kerr & Co., 1909), Vol. III, pp. 310–311.

11. Karl Marx, "Wage Labour and Capital," section V, Karl Marx and Frederick Engels, *Selected Works* (Moscow: Foreign Languages Publishing House, 1955), Vol. I, p. 99. See also Karl Marx, *Capital*, Vol. III, pp. 310–311.

12. Karl Marx, *Theories of Surplus Value: Selections* (New York: International Publishers, 1952), p. 380.

13. Karl Marx and Frederick Engels, *Selected Correspondence 1846–1895*, translated by Dona Torr (New York: International Publishers, 1942), p. 476.

14. Ibid., p. 159.

15. John Dewey, *Liberalism and Social Action*, p. 73. "Unless freedom of individual action has intelligence and informed conviction back of it, its manifestation is almost sure to result in confusion and disorder." John Dewey, *Intelligence in the Modern World: John Dewey's Philosophy*, edited by Joseph Ratner (New York: Modern Library, 1939), p. 404.

16. John Dewey, *Human Nature and Conduct: An Introduction to Social Psychology* (New York: Modern Library, 1957), p. 277.

17. John Dewey, *Liberalism and Social Action*, p. 56.

18. Ibid., p. 50.

19. Ibid., p. 65.

20. Ronald Dworkin, *Taking Rights Seriously* (Cambridge, Mass.: Harvard University Press, 1980), p. 147.

21. Adam Smith denounced "the mean rapacity, the monopolizing spirit of merchants and manufacturers" and "the clamour and sophistry of merchants and manufacturers," whom he characterized as people who "seldom meet together, even for merriment and diversion, but the conversation ends in a conspiracy against the public." As for policies recommended by such people, Smith said: "The proposal of any new law or regulation of commerce which comes from this order, ought always to be listened to with great

precaution, and ought never to be adopted till after having been long and carefully examined, not only with the most scrupulous, but with the most suspicious attention. It comes from an order of men, whose interest is never exactly the same with that of the public, who have generally an interest to deceive and even to oppress the public, and who accordingly have, upon many occasions, both deceived and oppressed it." Adam Smith, *The Wealth of Nations* (New York: Modern Library, 1937), pp. 128, 250, 460. Karl Marx wrote, in the preface to the first volume of *Capital*: "I paint the capitalist and the landlord in no sense *couleur de rose*. But here individuals are dealt with only in so far as they are the personifications of economic categories, embodiments of particular class-relations and class-interests. My stand-point, from which the evolution of the economic formation of society is viewed as a process of natural history, can less than any other make the individual responsible for relations whose creature he socially remains, however much he may subjectively raise himself above them." In Chapter X, Marx made dire predictions about the fate of workers, but not as a result of subjective moral deficiencies of the capitalist, for Marx said: "As capitalist, he is only capital personified" and "all this does not, indeed, depend on the good or ill will of the individual capitalist." Karl Marx, *Capital: A Critique of Political Economy* (Chicago: Charles H. Kerr & Company, 1919), Vol. I, pp. 15, 257, 297.

22. Adam Smith, *The Wealth of Nations*, p. 423.

23. My own sketch of these arguments can be found in Chapters 2 and 4 of my *Basic Economics: A Common Sense Guide to the Economy*, fourth edition (New York: Basic Books, 2011). More elaborate and more technical accounts can be found in more advanced texts.

24. Herbert Croly, *The Promise of American Life* (Boston: Northeastern University Press, 1989), pp. 44, 45.

25. See, for example, Nikolai Shmelev and Vladimir Popov, *The Turning Point: Revitalizing the Soviet Economy* (New York: Doubleday, 1989), pp. 141, 170; Midge Decter, *An Old Wife's Tale: My Seven Decades in Love and War* (New York: Regan Books, 2001), p. 169.

26. Frederick Engels, "Introduction to the First German Edition," Karl Marx, *The Poverty of Philosophy* (New York: International Publishers, 1963), p. 19.

27. John Dewey, *Characters and Events: Popular Essays in Social and Political Philosophy*, edited by Joseph Ratner (New York: Henry Holt and Company, 1929), Vol. II, p. 555.

28. Karl Marx, *Capital*, Vol. I, p. 15.

29. Peter Corning, *The Fair Society: The Science of Human Nature and the Pursuit of Social Justice* (Chicago: University of Chicago Press, 2011), p. 125.

30. Harold J. Laski, Letter to Oliver Wendell Holmes, September 13, 1916, *Holmes-Laski Letters: The Correspondence of Mr. Justice Holmes and Harold J. Laski 1916–1935*, edited by Mark DeWolfe Howe (Cambridge, Massachusetts: Harvard University Press, 1953), Vol. I, p. 20.

31. Holman W. Jenkins, Jr., "Business World: Shall We Eat Our Young?" *Wall Street Journal*, January 19, 2005, p. A13.

32. Lester C. Thurow, *The Zero-Sum Society: Distribution and the Possibilities for Economic Change* (New York: Basic Books, 2001), p. 203.

33. Beniamino Moro, "The Economists' 'Manifesto' On Unemployment in the EU Seven Years Later: Which Suggestions Still Hold?" *Banca Nazionale del Lavoro Quarterly Review*, June-September 2005, pp. 49–66; *Economic Report of the President* (Washington: U.S. Government Printing Office, 2009), pp. 326–327.

34. Theodore Caplow, Louis Hicks and Ben J. Wattenberg, *The First Measured Century: An Illustrated Guide to Trends in America, 1900–2000* (Washington: AEI Press, 2001), p. 47.

35. Lester C. Thurow, *The Zero-Sum Society*, p. 203.

36. "The Turning Point," *The Economist*, September 22, 2007, p. 35.

37. John Dewey, *Liberalism and Social Action*, p. 53. See also p. 88.

38. Ibid., p. 89.

39. Ibid., p. 44.

CHAPTER 5: GOVERNMENT AND THE ECONOMY

1. John Dewey, *Liberalism and Social Action* (Amherst, N.Y.: Prometheus Books, 2000), p. 78.

2. Edward Bellamy, *Looking Backward: 2000–1887* (New York: Modern Library, 1917), p. 43.

3. V.I. Lenin, *The State and Revolution* (Moscow: Progress Publishers, 1969), p. 92.

4. V.I. Lenin, "The Role and Functions of the Trade Unions Under the New Economic Policy," *Selected Works* (Moscow: Foreign Languages Publishing House, 1952), Vol. II, Part 2, p. 618.

5. V.I. Lenin, "Ninth Congress of the Russian Communist Party (Bolsheviks)," ibid., p. 333.

6. Edmund Morris, *Theodore Rex* (New York: Modern Library, 2002), p. 360.

7. Ibid., pp. 10–11.

8. Loc. cit.

9. John Maynard Keynes, *The General Theory of Employment Interest and Money* (New York: Harcourt, Brace and Company, 1936), p. 19.

10. Woodrow Wilson, *Woodrow Wilson: Essential Writings and Speeches of the Scholar-President*, edited by Mario R. DiNunzio (New York: New York University Press, 2006), p. 342.

11. Charles F. Howlett, *Troubled Philosopher: John Dewey and the Struggle for World Peace* (Port Washington, N.Y.: Kennikat Press, 1977), p. 31.

12. Daniel J. Flynn, *A Conservative History of the American Left* (New York: Crown Forum, 2008), p. 137.

13. John Kenneth Galbraith, *American Capitalism: The Concept of Countervailing Power*, Sentry edition (Boston: Houghton Mifflin Co., 1956), p. 113.

14. Ibid., pp. 114–115.

15. Ibid., p. 136.

16. Ibid., p. 137.

17. Ibid., p. 44.

18. Ibid., p. 26.

19. Jim Powell, *Bully Boy: The Truth About Theodore Roosevelt's Legacy* (New York: Crown Forum, 2006), pp. 82, 89–90.

20. Theodore Roosevelt, *The Rough Riders: An Autobiography* (New York: The Library of America, 2004), p. 692.

21. Ibid., p. 685.

22. Ibid., p. 691.

23. Jim Powell, *Bully Boy*, p. 112.

24. Ibid., p. 111.

25. Ibid., pp. 109–110.

26. Edmund Morris, *Theodore Rex*, p. 427.

27. Jim Powell, *Bully Boy*, p. 135.

28. "Spare a Dime? A Special Report on the Rich," *The Economist*, April 4, 2009, p. 4 of special report.

29. Richard Vedder and Lowell Gallaway, *Out of Work: Unemployment and Government in Twentieth-Century America* (New York: Holmes & Meier, 1993), p. 77.

30. Ibid.

31. Milton Friedman and Anna Jacobson Schwartz, *A Monetary History of the United States: 1867–1960* (Princeton: Princeton University Press, 1963), p. 407; John Kenneth Galbraith, *The Great Crash, 1929* (Boston: Houghton Mifflin, 1961), p. 32.

32. Jim Powell, *FDR's Folly: How Roosevelt and His New Deal Prolonged the Great Depression* (New York: Crown Forum, 2003), p. 92.

33. Harold L. Cole and Lee E. Ohanian, "New Deal Policies and the Persistence of the Great Depression: A General Equilibrium Analysis," *Journal of Political Economy*, Vol. 112, No. 4 (August 2004), pp. 779–816.

34. "Reagan Fantasies, Budget Realities," *New York Times*, November 5, 1987, p. A34.

35. Mary McGrory, "Fiddling While Wall St. Burns," *Washington Post*, October 29, 1987, p. A2.

36. "What the US Can Do," *Financial Times* (London), October 28, 1987, p. 24.

37. Roger C. Altman, "If Reagan Were F.D.R.," *New York Times*, November 20, 1987, p. A39.

38. "The Turning Point," *The Economist*, September 22, 2007, p. 35.

39. Jim Powell, *FDR's Folly*, pp. xv–xvi.

PART III: INTELLECTUALS AND SOCIAL VISIONS

Walter Lippmann, *Public Opinion* (New York: The Free Press, 1965), p. 80.

CHAPTER 6: A CONFLICT OF VISIONS

1. Paul Johnson, *Enemies of Society* (New York: Atheneum, 1977), p. 145.

2. Joseph A. Schumpeter, *History of Economic Analysis* (New York: Oxford University Press, 1954), p. 41.

3. John Stuart Mill, "Utilitarianism," *Collected Works of John Stuart Mill* (Toronto: University of Toronto Press, 1969), Vol. X, p. 215. Yet, in his autobiography, Mill said that he realized as a young man that, if all the goals he was pursuing were realized, that would not make him happy. John Stuart Mill, "Autobiography," *Collected Works of John Stuart Mill* (Toronto: University of Toronto Press, 1963), Vol. I, p. 139.

4.   John Stuart Mill, "De Tocqueville on Democracy in America [I]," *Collected Works of John Stuart Mill* (Toronto: University of Toronto Press, 1977), Vol. XVIII, p. 86; John Stuart Mill, "Civilization," ibid., pp. 121, 139; John Stuart Mill, "On Liberty," ibid., p. 222.

5.   Jean-Jacques Rousseau, *The Social Contract*, translated by Maurice Cranston (New York: Penguin Books, 1968), p. 49.

6.   Donald Kagan, *On the Origins of War and the Preservation of Peace* (New York: Doubleday, 1995), p. 414.

7.   Mark DeWolfe Howe, editor, *Holmes-Laski Letters: The Correspondence of Mr. Justice Holmes and Harold J. Laski 1916–1935* (Cambridge, Massachusetts: Harvard University Press, 1953), Volume I, p. 12.

8.   Richard A. Epstein, *Overdose: How Excessive Government Regulation Stifles Pharmaceutical Innovation* (New Haven: Yale University Press, 2006), p. 15.

9.   Adam Smith, *The Wealth of Nations* (New York: Modern Library, 1937), Book I, Chapter I.

10.   John Rawls, for example, said: "I should note that a well-ordered society does not do away with the division of labor in the most general sense. To be sure, the worst aspects of this division can be surmounted: no one need be servilely dependent on others and made to choose between monotonous and routine occupations which are deadening to human thought and sensibility. Each can be offered a variety of tasks so that the different elements of his nature find a suitable expression." John Rawls, *A Theory of Justice* (Cambridge, Massachusetts: Harvard University Press, 1971), p. 529.

11.   See my *A Conflict of Visions*, second edition (New York: Basic Books, 2007).

12.   Ibid., pp. 9–17, 166–167, 198–199.

13.   Ibid., pp. 147–153.

14.   See, for example, William Godwin, *Enquiry Concerning Political Justice and Its Influence on Morals and Happiness* (Toronto: University of Toronto Press, 1946), Vol. II, Chapter XVI; John Dewey, *Human Nature and Conduct: An Introduction to Social Psychology* (New York: Modern Library, 1957), pp. 114–115; Bernard Shaw, *The Intelligent Woman's Guide to Socialism and Capitalism* (New York: Brentano's Publishers, 1928), pp. 158–160.

15.   Donald Kagan, *On the Origins of War and the Preservation of Peace*, p. 212.

16. Will and Ariel Durant, *The Lessons of History* (New York: Simon and Schuster, 1968), p. 81.

17. Alexander Hamilton et al., *The Federalist Papers* (New York: New American Library, 1961), p. 87.

18. Ibid., p. 46.

19. Jonah Goldberg, *Liberal Fascism: The Secret History of the American Left from Mussolini to the Politics of Meaning* (New York: Doubleday, 2008), pp. 17, 25–26.

20. See, for example, G. Kinne, "Nazi Stratagems and their Effects on Germans in Australia up to 1945," *Royal Australian Historical Society*, Vol. 66, Pt. 1 (June 1980), pp. 1–19; Jean Roche, *La Colonisation Allemande et Le Rio Grande Do Sul* (Paris: Institut des Hautes Études de L'Amérique Latine, 1959), pp. 541–543.

21. Valdis O. Lumans, *Himmler's Auxiliaries* (Chapel Hill: University of North Carolina Press, 1993), pp. 77–87.

22. Hélène Carrère d'Encausse, *Decline of an Empire: The Soviet Socialist Republics in Revolt* (New York: Newsweek Books, 1980), pp. 146, 150–151.

23. Jonah Goldberg, *Liberal Fascism*, pp. 45–46, 410–413.

24. Ibid., pp. 324–325, 344–357; William Godwin, *Enquiry Concerning Political Justice*, Vol. I, p. 47.

25. See, for example, Chapter 3 of my *Inside American Education: The Decline, the Deception, the Dogmas* (New York: The Free Press, 1993).

26. Lewis A. Coser, *Men of Ideas: A Sociologist's View* (New York: The Free Press, 1970), p. 141.

27. "The statesman, who should attempt to direct private people in what manner they ought to employ their capitals, would not only load himself with a most unnecessary attention, but assume an authority which could safely be trusted, not only to no single person, but to no council or senate whatever, and which would nowhere be so dangerous as in the hands of a man who had folly and presumption enough to fancy himself fit to exercise it." Adam Smith, *The Wealth of Nations*, p. 423.

28. Oliver Wendell Holmes, Jr., *The Common Law* (Boston: Little, Brown and Company, 1923), p. 1.

29. Jonah Goldberg, *Liberal Fascism*, p. 52.

30. Jean-Jacques Rousseau, *The Social Contract*, translated by Maurice Cranston, p. 89.

31. William Godwin, *Enquiry Concerning Political Justice,* Vol. I, p. 446; Antoine-Nicolas de Condorcet, *Sketch for a Historical Picture of the Progress of the Human Mind,* translated by June Barraclough (London: Weidenfeld and Nicolson, 1955), p. 114.

32. Karl Marx and Frederick Engels, *Selected Correspondence 1846–1895,* translated by Dona Torr (New York: International Publishers, 1942), p. 190.

33. Bernard Shaw, *The Intelligent Woman's Guide to Socialism and Capitalism,* p. 456.

34. Edmund Wilson, *Letters on Literature and Politics 1912–1972,* edited by Elena Wilson (New York: Farrar, Straus and Giroux, 1977), p. 36. Nor was this due to the racism of Southern whites, for Wilson himself referred to how distasteful Chattanooga was to him because of "the niggers and the mills." Ibid., pp. 217, 220. Years later, upon seeing the poverty of Italy at the end of World War II, Wilson said, "that isn't the way that white people ought to live." Ibid., p. 423.

35. Quoted in Jonah Goldberg, *Liberal Fascism,* p. 38.

36. Lincoln Steffens, "Stop, Look, Listen!" *The Survey,* March 1, 1927, pp. 735–737, 754–755. Nor was he the only prominent American radical or progressive to do so. See Jonah Goldberg, *Liberal Fascism,* pp. 28–29.

37. Jonah Goldberg, *Liberal Fascism,* p. 21. A year later, after Hitler had come to power, Wells characterized him as "a clumsy lout" with "his idiotic symbols" and "his imbecile cruelties." "H.G. Wells Scores Nazis as 'Louts,'" *New York Times,* September 22, 1933, p. 13. By 1939 he was attacking both Mussolini and Hitler, though he exempted the Soviet Union from his condemnation. See "Wells Sees in U.S. Hope for Mankind," *New York Times,* August 4, 1939, p. 3.

38. Jonah Goldberg, *Liberal Fascism,* pp. 100–101, 103–104.

39. Ibid., pp. 26–27.

40. Ibid., p. 103.

41. Ibid., p. 10.

42. Daniel J. Flynn, *Intellectual Morons: How Ideology Makes Smart People Fall for Stupid Ideas* (New York: Crown Forum, 2004), p. 173.

43. Jonah Goldberg, *Liberal Fascism,* p. 140.

44. Ibid., pp. 122–123, 146–148.

45. Keith Michael Baker, editor, *Condorcet: Selected Writings* (Indianapolis: The Bobbs-Merrill Company, 1976), pp. 5–6.

46. William Godwin, *Enquiry Concerning Political Justice,* Vol. I, p. 107.

47. Ibid., p. 47.

48. William Godwin, *The Enquirer: Reflections on Education, Manners, and Literature* (London: G. G. and J. Robinson, 1797), p. 70.

49. Ibid., p. 67.

50. Adam Smith, *The Theory of Moral Sentiments* (Indianapolis: Liberty Classics, 1976), p. 529.

51. Edmund Burke, *Speeches and Letters on American Affairs* (New York: E.P. Dutton & Co., Inc., 1961), p. 203.

52. Woodrow Wilson, "What is Progress?" *American Progressivism: A Reader*, edited by Ronald J. Pestritto and William J. Atto (Lanham, MD: Lexington Books, 2008), p. 48.

53. John Stuart Mill, "On Liberty," *Collected Works of John Stuart Mill*, Vol. XVIII, p. 245.

54. Richard Hofstadter, *Anti-Intellectualism in American Life* (New York: Vintage Books, 1963), p. 361.

55. Ibid.

56. John Dewey, *Democracy and Education: An Introduction to the Philosophy of Education* (New York: The Free Press, 1966), p. 79.

57. John Dewey, *The Child and the Curriculum and The School and Society* (Chicago: University of Chicago Press, 1956), p. 18. Despite the much later vogue of regarding various things as a microcosm of a larger world, schools are a specialized institution to do a specialized job— just as the eye is not a microcosm of the body but a specialized part of the body that does something that no other part of the body does.

CHAPTER 7: ABSTRACT PEOPLE IN AN ABSTRACT WORLD

1. Oscar Handlin, *Boston's Immigrants* (New York: Atheneum, 1970), p. 114.

2. Carl Wittke, *The Irish in America* (New York: Russell & Russell, 1970), p. 101; Oscar Handlin, *Boston's Immigrants*, pp. 169–170; Jay P. Dolan, *The Irish Americans: A History* (New York: Bloomsbury Press, 2008), pp. 118–119.

3. Arthur R. Jensen, "How Much Can We Boost IQ and Scholastic Achievement?" *Harvard Educational Review*, Vol. 39, No. 1 (Winter 1969), p. 35; Richard J. Herrnstein and Charles Murray, *The Bell Curve: Intelligence and Class Structure in American Life* (New York: The Free Press, 1994), p. 110.

4. Lawrence E. Harrison, *Underdevelopment Is a State of Mind: The Latin American Case* (Cambridge, Massachusetts: Center for International Affairs, Harvard University, 1985), p. 164.

5.   Arthur Herman, *How the Scots Invented the Modern World* (New York: Crown Publishers, 2001), Chapter 5; Maldwyn A. Jones, "Ulster Emigration, 1783–1815," *Essays in Scotch-Irish History*, edited by E. R. R. Green (London: Routledge & Kegan Paul, 1969), p. 49; Eric Richards, "Australia and the Scottish Connection 1788–1914," *The Scots Abroad: Labour, Capital, Enterprise, 1750–1914*, edited by R. A. Cage (London: Croom Helm, 1984), p. 122; E. Richards, "Highland and Gaelic Immigrants," *The Australian People*, edited by James Jupp (North Ryde, Australia: Angus & Robertson, 1988), pp. 765–769.

6.   Philip E. Vernon, *Intelligence and Cultural Environment* (London: Methuen & Co., Ltd., 1970), pp. 157–158.

7.   Nathan Glazer and Daniel Patrick Moynihan, *Beyond the Melting Pot: The Negroes, Puerto Ricans, Jews, Italians, and Irish of New York City*, second edition (Cambridge, Massachusetts: MIT Press, 1963), pp. 257–258; Andrew M. Greeley, *That Most Distressful Nation: The Taming of the American Irish* (Chicago: Quadrangle Books, 1972), p. 132.

8.   Vladimir G. Treml, *Alcohol in the USSR: A Statistical Study* (Durham, NC: Duke University Press, 1982), p. 73.

9.   Mohamed Suffian bin Hashim, "Problems and Issues of Higher Education Development in Malaysia," *Development of Higher Education in Southeast Asia: Problems and Issues*, edited by Yip Yat Hoong (Singapore: Regional Institute of Higher Education and Development, 1973), Table 8, pp. 70–71.

10. See, for example, Yuan-li Wu and Chun-hsi Wu, *Economic Development in Southeast Asia: The Chinese Dimension* (Stanford: Hoover Institution Press, 1980), p. 70; Haraprasad Chattopadhyaya, *Indians in Africa: A Socio-Economic Study* (Calcutta: Bookland Private Limited, 1970), p. 69; Neil O. Leighton, "Lebanese Emigration: Its Effect on the Political Economy of Sierra Leone," *The Lebanese in the World: A Century of Emigration*, edited by Albert Hourani and Nadim Shehadi (London: The Center for Lebanese Studies, 1992), p. 582; Jean Roche, *La Colonisation Allemande et le Rio Grande do Sul* (Paris: Institut Des Hautes Études de L'Amérique Latine, 1959), pp. 385–386; Hans Juergen Hoyer, "Germans in Paraguay, 1881–1945: A Study of Cultural and Social Isolation," Ph.D. dissertation, American University, 1973, pp. 46, 49, 51–56.

11. Charles Issawi, "The Transformation of the Economic Position of the *Millets* in the Nineteenth Century," *Christians and Jews in the Ottoman Empire: The*

Functioning of a Plural Society, edited by Benjamin Braude and Bernard Lewis (New York: Holmes and Meier, 1982), Vol. I: *The Central Lands*, pp. 262–263.

12. Bernard Lewis, *The Jews of Islam* (Princeton: Princeton University Press, 1984), p. 214.

13. Yuan-li Wu and Chu-hsi Wu, *Economic Development in Southeast Asia*, p. 51.

14. R. Bayly Winder, "The Lebanese in West Africa," *Comparative Studies in Society and History*, Vol. IV (1961–62), p. 309.

15. Charles Issawi, "The Transformation of the Economic Position of the *Millets* in the Nineteenth Century," *Christians and Jews in the Ottoman Empire*, edited by Benjamin Braude and Bernard Lewis, Vol. I: *The Central Lands*, pp. 262–263, 266.

16. Winthrop R. Wright, *British-Owned Railways in Argentina: Their Effect on Economic Nationalism, 1854–1948* (Austin: University of Texas Press, 1974).

17. John P. McKay, *Pioneers for Profit: Foreign Entrepreneurship and Russian Industrialization 1885–1913* (Chicago: University of Chicago Press, 1970), p. 35.

18. Jonathan I. Israel, *European Jewry in the Age of Mercantilism 1550–1750* (Oxford: Clarendon Press, 1985), p. 139.

19. Carl Solberg, *Immigration and Nationalism: Argentina and Chile, 1890–1914* (Austin: University of Texas Press, 1970), p. 68.

20. S. J. Thambiah, "Ethnic Representation in Ceylon's Higher Administrative Services, 1870–1946," *University of Ceylon Review*, Vol. 13 (April–July 1955), p. 130.

21. Jean Roche, *La Colonisation Allemande et le Rio Grande do Sul*, pp. 388–389.

22. James L. Tigner, "Japanese Immigration into Latin America: A Survey," *Journal of Interamerican Studies and World Affairs*, November 1981, p. 476.

23. H.L van der Laan, *The Lebanese Traders in Sierra Leone* (The Hague: Mouton & Co., 1975), p. 65.

24. Ibid., p. 137.

25. Ezra Mendelsohn, *The Jews of East Central Europe between the World Wars* (Bloomington: Indiana University Press, 1983), pp. 23, 26.

26. Haraprasad Chattopadhyaya, *Indians in Africa*, p. 394.

27. Haraprasad Chattopadhyaya, *Indians in Sri Lanka: A Historical Study* (Calcutta: O.P.S. Publishers Private Ltd., 1979), pp. 143, 144, 146.

28. Carl Solberg, *Immigration and Nationalism*, p. 50.

29. Felice A. Bonadio, *A.P. Giannini: Banker of America* (Berkeley: University of California Press, 1994), p. 28.

30. Carl Solberg, *Immigration and Nationalism*, p. 63.

31. Pablo Macera and Shane J. Hunt, "Peru," *Latin America: A Guide to Economic History 1830–1930*, edited by Roberto Cortés Conde and Stanley J. Stein (Berkeley: University of California Press, 1977), p. 565.

32. Carlo M. Cipolla, *Clocks and Culture: 1300–1700* (New York: W. W. Norton & Co., 1978), p. 68.

33. Nena Vreeland, et al., *Area Handbook for Malaysia*, third edition (Washington: U. S. Government Printing Office, 1977), p. 303.

34. Winthrop R. Wright, *British-Owned Railways in Argentina*; Gino Germani, "Mass Immigration and Modernization in Argentina," *Studies in Comparative International Development*, Vol. 2 (1966), p. 170.

35. John P. McKay, *Pioneers for Profit*, pp. 33, 34, 35.

36. Jean W. Sedlar, *East Central Europe in the Middle Ages, 1000–1500* (Seattle: University of Washington Press, 1994), p. 131.

37. Charles Issawi, "The Transformation of the Economic Position of the *Millets* in the Nineteenth Century," *Christians and Jews in the Ottoman Empire*, edited by Benjamin Braude and Bernard Lewis, Vol. I: *The Central Lands*, pp. 262, 263, 265, 266, 267.

38. Victor Purcell, *The Chinese in Southeast Asia*, second edition (Kuala Lumpur: Oxford University Press, 1980), pp. 7, 68, 83, 180, 245, 248, 540, 559.

39. Robert J. Sharer, *The Ancient Maya*, fifth edition (Stanford: Stanford University Press, 1994), p. 455.

40. See, for example, Roy E.H. Mellor and E. Alistair Smith, *Europe: A Geographical Survey of the Continent* (New York: Columbia University Press, 1979), pp. 1–17; Norman J.G. Pounds, *An Historical Geography of Europe: 1800–1914* (Cambridge: Cambridge University Press, 1985), pp. 37–65; Jocelyn Murray, editor, *Cultural Atlas of Africa* (New York: Facts on File Publications, 1981), pp. 10–22; Thomas Sowell, *Conquests and Cultures: An International History* (New York: Basic Books, 1998), pp. 99–109.

41. J. F. Ade Ajayi and Michael Crowder, editors, *Historical Atlas of Africa* (Cambridge: Cambridge University Press, 1985), Section 2; Kathleen Baker, "The Changing Geography of West Africa," *The Changing Geography of Africa and the Middle East*, edited by Graham P. Chapman and Kathleen M. Baker (London: Routledge, 1992), p. 105.

42. Fernand Braudel, *The Mediterranean and the Mediterranean World in the Age of Philip II*, translated by Siân Reynolds (Berkeley: University of California Press, 1995), Vol. I, p. 35.

43. William S. Maltby, *The Rise and Fall of the Spanish Empire* (New York: Palgrave Macmillan, 2009), p. 18; Peter Pierson, *The History of Spain* (Westport, CT: Greenwood Press, 1999), pp. 7–8.

44. John H. Chambers, *A Traveller's History of Australia* (New York: Interlink Books, 1999), pp. 22–24.

45. H. J. de Blij and Peter O. Muller, *Geography: Regions and Concepts*, sixth edition (New York: John Wiley & Sons, Inc., 1992), p. 394.

46. Oscar Handlin, "Introduction," *The Positive Contribution by Immigrants* (Paris: United Nations Educational, Scientific and Cultural Organization, 1955), p. 13.

47. Ulrich Bonnell Phillips, *The Slave Economy of the Old South: Selected Essays in Economic and Social History*, edited by Eugene D. Genovese (Baton Rouge: Louisiana State University Press, 1968), p. 269.

48. See, for example, Thomas Sowell, *Conquests and Cultures*, pp. 175–176.

49. See, for example, "We're Doing All Right, But What About You?" *The Economist*, August 16, 2003, p. 43. Russia has a Gross Domestic Product per capita that is less than half that of Britain, France or Germany and less than one-third that of Norway or Luxembourg. The Economist, *Pocket World in Figures*, 2011 edition (London: Profile Books, Ltd., 2010), p. 27. Meanwhile, the per capita income of black Americans is 64 percent of that of white Americans. Carmen DeNavas-Walt, et al., "Income, Poverty, and Health Insurance Coverage in the United States: 2009," *Current Population Reports*, P60–238 (Washington: US Census Bureau, 2010), p. 6.

50. Angelo M. Codevilla, *The Character of Nations: How Politics Makes and Breaks Prosperity, Family, and Civility* (New York: Basic Books, 1997), p. 50.

51. See Thomas Sowell, *Conquests and Cultures*, pp. 177–184.

52. Robert Bartlett, *The Making of Europe: Conquest, Colonization and Cultural Change, 950–1350* (Princeton: Princeton University Press, 1993), p. 235.

53. Jean W. Sedlar, *East Central Europe in the Middle Ages, 1000–1500*, pp. 126–127.

54. Such disparities, found just in my own research include the following: *Conquests and Cultures*, pp. 125, 210, 211, 217; *Migrations and Cultures: A World View* (New York: Basic Books, 1996), pp. 4, 17, 31, 57, 123, 130, 135, 152, 154, 157, 176, 179, 193, 196, 211, 258, 265, 275, 277, 278, 289, 297, 298, 300, 320, 345–346, 353–354, 355, 358, 366, 372–373.

55. *Wal-Mart Stores, Inc. v. Dukes et al.* (slip opinion), June 20, 2011, opinion of Justice Ginsburg, pp. 3, 11.

56. Elizabeth Wiskemann, *Czechs & Germans: A Study of the Struggle in the Historic Provinces of Bohemia and Moravia* (London: Oxford University Press, 1938), pp. 142, 148.

57. Stephen Steinberg, *The Ethnic Myth: Race, Ethnicity, and Class in America* (New York: Atheneum, 1981), pp. 99–103.

58. See, for example, U.S. Bureau of the Census, *We the People: Asians in the United States*, Census 2000 Special Reports, December 2004, p. 6; U.S. Bureau of the Census, *We the People: Hispanics in the United States*, Census 2000 Special Reports, December 2004, p. 5; U.S. Bureau of the Census, *We the People: Blacks in the United States*, Census 2000 Special Reports, August 2005, p. 4.

59. U.S. Bureau of the Census, *We the People: Asians in the United States*, Census 2000 Special Reports, December 2004, p. 6.

60. The Economist, *Pocket World in Figures*, 2011 edition, p. 18.

61. "Discrimination and Loans," *USA Today*, October 23, 1991, p. 12A; "Racial Gap Persists in Mortgage Lending," *St. Louis Post-Dispatch*, October 25, 1991, p. 2C; Michael Quint, "Racial Gap Detailed on Mortgages," *New York Times*, October 22, 1991, p. D1.

62. United States Commission on Civil Rights, *Civil Rights and the Mortgage Crisis* (Washington: U.S. Commission on Civil Rights, 2009), p. 53.

63. Harold A. Black, et al., "Do Black-Owned Banks Discriminate against Black Borrowers?" *Journal of Financial Services Research*, February 1997, pp. 185–200.

64. Malcolm Gladwell, *Outliers: The Story of Success* (Boston: Little, Brown and Co., 2008), p. 112.

65. Padma Ramkrishna Velaskar, "Inequality in Higher Education: A Study of Scheduled Caste Students in Medical Colleges of Bombay," Ph.D. dissertation, Tata Institute of Social Sciences (Bombay), 1986.

66. See, for example, Robert Klitgaard, *Choosing Elites* (New York: Basic Books, 1985), p. 162; Sammy Smooha and Yochanan Peres, "The Dynamics of Ethnic Inequalities: The Case of Israel," *Studies of Israeli Society*, edited by Ernest Krausz (New Brunswick, New Jersey: Transaction Books, 1981), Vol. I, p. 173.

67. Antoine-Nicolas de Condorcet, *Sketch for a Historical Picture of the Progress of the Human Mind*, translated by June Barraclough (London: Weidenfeld and Nicolson, 1955), p. 174.

68. "...undeserved inequalities call for redress; and since inequalities of birth and natural endowment are undeserved, these inequalities are to be somehow compensated for. Thus the principle holds that in order to treat all persons equally, to provide genuine equality of opportunity, society must give more attention to those with fewer native assets and to those born into the less favorable social positions." John Rawls, *A Theory of Justice* (Cambridge, Massachusetts: Harvard University Press, 1971), p. 100.

69. Diana Furchtgott-Roth, "Testimony on the Gender Pay Gap," *Hearing Before the Joint Economic Committee*, Congress of the United States, September 28, 2010, p. 9.

70. Diana Furchtgott-Roth and Christine Stolba, *Women's Figures: An Illustrated Guide to the Economic Progress of Women in America* (Washington: American Enterprise Institute, 1999), p. 33.

71. Warren Farrell, *Why Men Earn More: The Startling Truth Behind the Pay Gap and What Women Can Do About It* (New York: Amacom, 2005), p. xxiii.

72. Diana Furchtgott-Roth, "Testimony on the Gender Pay Gap," *Hearing Before the Joint Economic Committee*, Congress of the United States, September 28, 2010, p. 5.

73. Ibid., pp. 1–17.

74. Ibid., p. 10.

75. Ibid., p. 11.

76. Martin Loney, *The Pursuit of Division: Race, Gender, and Preferential Hiring in Canada* (Montreal: McGill-Queen's University Press, 1998), p. 28.

77. Diana Furchtgott-Roth, "Testimony on the Gender Pay Gap," *Hearing Before the Joint Economic Committee*, Congress of the United States, September 28, 2010, p. 12.

78. See, for example, studies cited in Chapter 3 of my *Economic Facts and Fallacies*, second edition (New York: Basic Books, 2011).

CHAPTER 8: ARGUMENTS WITHOUT ARGUMENTS

1. J.A. Schumpeter, *History of Economic Analysis* (New York: Oxford University Press, 1954), p. 90.

2. Ian Ayres, *Super Crunchers: Why Thinking-by-Numbers Is the New Way to Be Smart* (New York: Bantam Books, 2007), p. 3.

3. Ibid., pp. 1–9. See also Mark Strauss, "The Grapes of Math," *Discover*, January 1991, pp. 50–51; Jay Palmer, "Grape Expectations," *Barron's*, December 30, 1996, pp. 17–19.

4. Ian Ayres, *Super Crunchers*, pp. 82–83.

5. Tom Wicker, "Freedom for What?" *New York Times*, January 5, 1990, p. A31.

6. Joseph Epstein, "True Virtue," *New York Times Magazine*, November 24, 1985, p. 95.

7. Thomas Robert Malthus, *Population: The First Essay* (Ann Arbor: University of Michigan Press, 1959), p. 3.

8. William Godwin, *Of Population* (London: Longman, Hurst, Rees, Orme, and Brown, 1820), pp. 520, 550, 554.

9. Edmund Burke, *The Correspondence of Edmund Burke*, edited by R. B. McDowell (Chicago: University of Chicago Press, 1969), Vol. VIII, p. 138.

10. Alexander Hamilton, "Federalist No. 1: General Introduction for the Independent Journal, Saturday, October 27, 1787," Alexander Hamilton et al., *The Federalist Papers* (New York: New American Library, 1961), p. 34.

11. F.A. Hayek, *The Road to Serfdom* (Chicago: University of Chicago Press, 1944), pp. 55, 185.

12. Charles Murray, "Introduction to the Tenth-Anniversary Edition," *Losing Ground: American Social Policy, 1950–1980* (New York: Basic Books, 1994), p. xv.

13. Winston S. Churchill, *The Second World War*, Vol. I: *The Gathering Storm* (Boston: Houghton Mifflin Co., 1983), p. 346.

14. Winston Churchill, *Churchill Speaks 1897–1963: Collected Speeches in Peace & War*, edited by Robert Rhodes James (New York: Chelsea House, 1980), pp. 734–735.

15. Ibid., p. 866.

16. See my *A Conflict of Visions*, second edition (New York: Basic Books, 2007), pp. 58–60, 256–260.

17. Lewis Feuer, *Imperialism and the Anti-Imperialist Mind* (Buffalo, NY: Prometheus Books, 1986), p. 154.

18. Andrew Hacker, *Two Nations: Black and White, Separate, Hostile, Unequal* (New York: Charles Scribner's Sons, 1992), p. 52.

19. Arthur C. Brooks, *Who Really Cares: The Surprising Truth About Compassionate Conservatism* (New York: Basic Books, 2006), pp. 21–22, 24.

20. Peter Schweizer, *Markers and Takers* (New York: Doubleday, 2008), p. 63.

21. Bertrand Russell, *Which Way to Peace?* (London: Michael Joseph, Ltd., 1937), p. 179.

22. John Dewey, "If War Were Outlawed," *New Republic*, April 25, 1923, p. 235.

23. J.B. Priestley, "The Public and the Idea of Peace," *Challenge to Death*, edited by Storm Jameson (New York: E.P. Dutton & Co., Inc., 1935), p. 313.

24. Ibid., p. 309.

25. See, for example, William Godwin, *Enquiry Concerning Political Justice and Its Influence on Morals and Happiness* (Toronto: University of Toronto Press, 1946), Vol. I, pp. 456–457.

26. Corey Robin, "Why Conservatives Love War," *Chronicle of Higher Education*, October 29, 2010, p. B10; Michael Nelson, "Warrior Nation," Ibid., p. B7.

27. See, for example, "Fuzzy Economic Thinking; Job Czar for the Jobless," *New York Times*, September 3, 2003, p. A18; "Yo-Yo Economics," *Washington Post*, May 23, 2003, p. A24; Robert H. Frank, "In the Real World of Work and Wages, Trickle-Down Theories Don't Hold Up," *New York Times*, April 12, 2007, p. C3; Paul Krugman, "The Hostage Economy," *New York Times*, March 28, 2001, p. A21; Peter Corning, *The Fair Society: The Science of Human Nature and the Pursuit of Social Justice* (Chicago: University of Chicago Press, 2011), p. 117; Amity Shlaes, *The Forgotten Man: A New History of the Great Depression* (New York: HarperCollins, 2007), p. 128; S.M. Michael, editor, *Dalits in Modern India* (New Delhi: Vistaar Publications, 1999), p. 288.

28. John Maynard Keynes, "The Means to Prosperity," *The Means to Prosperity* (Buffalo: Economica Books, 1959), p. 11.

29. "In short, it is a paradoxical truth that tax rates are too high today and tax revenues are too low and the soundest way to raise the revenues in the long run is to cut the rates now." *Public Papers of the Presidents of the United States: John F. Kennedy, 1962* (Washington: U.S. Government Printing Office, 1963), p. 879.

30. Amity Shlaes, *The Forgotten Man*, p. 128. Much the same argument was made even earlier, in William Jennings Bryan's famous "cross of gold" speech in 1896.

31. M. Jay Wells, "Why the Mortgage Crisis Happened," *Investor's Business Daily*, October 30, 2008, p. A1.

32. Andrew W. Mellon, *Taxation: The People's Business* (New York: The Macmillan Company, 1924), pp. 127–138, 199–204.

33. Some years ago, in my syndicated column, I defied anyone to cite any economist, of any school of thought, who had ever advocated a trickle-down theory. No example has yet been offered, though many examples of critics who said that others had a trickle-down theory were suggested.

34. James Gwartney and Richard Stroup, "Tax Cuts: Who Shoulders the Burden?" *Federal Reserve Bank of Atlanta Economic Review*, March 1982, pp. 19–27; Benjamin G. Rader, "Federal Taxation in the 1920s: A Re-examination," *Historian*,

Vol. 33, No. 3, p. 433; Robert L. Bartley, *The Seven Fat Years: And How to Do It Again* (New York: The Free Press, 1992), pp. 71–74; Burton W. Folsom, Jr., *The Myth of the Robber Barons: A New Look at the Rise of Big Business in America*, sixth edition (Herndon, VA: Young America's Foundation, 2010), pp. 108, 116; Adrian Dungan and Kyle Mudry, "Individual Income Tax Rates and Shares, 2007," *Statistics of Income Bulletin*, Winter 2010, p. 63.

35. Benjamin G. Rader, "Federal Taxation in the 1920s: A Re-examination," *Historian*, Vol. 33, No. 3, pp. 432–433.

36. Andrew W. Mellon, *Taxation*, pp. 72, 74.

37. Ibid., p. 76.

38. Ibid., p. 201.

39. Burton W. Folsom, Jr., *The Myth of the Robber Barons*, sixth edition, p. 109.

40. Andrew W. Mellon, *Taxation*, p. 72.

41. Ibid., pp. 152, 158.

42. Ibid., p. 160.

43. Ibid., pp. 79–80, 141–142, 171–172.

44. Ibid., pp. 13, 15–16, 81–82, 141–142, 170.

45. Ibid., p. 79.

46. Ibid., pp. 106–107.

47. Ibid., p. 167.

48. Ibid., p. 79.

49. Treasury Department, U.S. Internal Revenue, *Statistics of Income from Returns of Net Income for 1925* (Washington: U.S. Government Printing Office, 1927), p. 21.

50. U. S. Bureau of the Census, *Historical Statistics of the United States: Colonial Times to 1970* (Washington: Government Printing Office, 1975), Part 1, p. 126.

51. *The Facts: La Follette-Wheeler Campaign Text-Book* (Chicago: La Follette-Wheeler Campaign Headquarters, 1924), pp. 77, 80, 81.

52. Jacob S. Hacker and Paul Pierson, *Winner-Take-All Politics: How Washington Made the Rich Richer— and Turned Its Back on the Middle Class* (New York: Simon and Schuster, 2010), p. 20.

53. Arthur M. Schlesinger, Jr., *The Age of Roosevelt: The Crisis of the Old Order, 1919–1933* (Boston: Houghton Mifflin Company, 1957), p. 62.

54. U.S. Bureau of the Census, *Historical Statistics of the United States: Colonial Times to 1970*, Part 2, p. 1117.

55. Irwin Unger, *These United States: The Questions of Our Past*, concise edition (Upper Saddle River, NJ: Prentice-Hall, 1999), p. 591.

56. Burton W. Folsom, Jr., *The Myth of the Robber Barons*, sixth edition, p.116.

57. John M. Blum, et al., *The National Experience: A History of the United States*, eighth edition (New York: Harcourt, Brace and Jovanovich, 1991), p. 640.

58. Andrew W. Mellon, *Taxation*, p. 9.

59. Ibid., pp. 54–57.

60. Ibid., pp. 61–62.

61. John A. Garraty, *The American Nation: A History of the United States* (New York: Harper & Row, 1966), p. 713.

62. Thomas A. Bailey, David M. Kennedy and Lizabeth Cohen, *The American Pageant: A History of the Republic*, eleventh edition (Boston: Houghton-Mifflin, 1998), p. 768.

63. Tom Wicker, "A Trojan Horse Indeed," *New York Times*, November 13, 1981, p. A35.

64. David S. Broder, "The Reagan Year: Conviction and Callousness," *Washington Post*, January 20, 1982, p. A23.

65. Haynes Johnson, "Resurrection of Coolidge— the Stamping of Nostalgia's Clay Feet," *Washington Post*, June 7, 1981, p. A3.

66. John Kenneth Galbraith, "The Heartless Society," *New York Times Magazine*, September 2, 1984, p. 44.

67. Leonard Silk, "A Tax Policy for the Rich," *New York Times*, June 12, 1981, p. D2; Alan Brinkley, "Calvin Reagan," *New York Times*, July 4, 1981, p. 19; Mark Green, "Economic Democracy," *New York Times*, March 7, 1982, p. E19; Ira C. Magaziner, "'Trickle Down' And Away," *New York Times*, May 25, 1982, p. A23; "After the Tax Spree," *New York Times*, July 29, 1981, p. A22; "There Is a Better Bet," *New York Times*, January 31, 1982, p. E20.

68. *Public Papers of the Presidents of the United States: George W. Bush, 2001* (Washington: U.S. Government Printing Office, 2003), pp. 144–145.

69. Arthur Schlesinger, Jr., "A Poor Tax Reduction Strategy," Letters to the Editor, *Washington Post*, March 25, 2001, p. B6; Paul Krugman, "The Hostage Economy," *New York Times*, March 28, 2001, p. A21; Jonathan Chait, "Going for Gold," *New Republic*, May 21, 2001, p. 25; David S. Broder, "Return to Reaganomics," *Washington Post*, February 6, 2001, p. A17.

70. *Public Papers of the Presidents of the United States: John F. Kennedy, 1962*, pp. 878, 880. In a similar vein, decades earlier Andrew Mellon deplored the "flight of capital into safe but unproductive forms of investment." Andrew W. Mellon, *Taxation*, p. 93.

71. "Special Message to the Congress on Tax Reduction and Reform," January 24, 1963, *Public Papers of the Presidents of the United States: John F. Kennedy, 1963* (Washington: U.S. Government Printing Office, 1964), p. 75.

72. "Address Before a Joint Session of the Congress on the Program for Economic Recovery," *Public Papers of the Presidents of the United States: Ronald Reagan, 1981* (Washington: U.S. Government Printing Office, 1982), pp. 112, 113.

73. Edmund L. Andrews, "Surprising Jump in Tax Revenues Curbs U.S. Deficit," *New York Times*, July 9, 2006, p. A1.

74. See, for example, Ronald Dworkin, "The Court's Embarrassingly Bad Decisions," *New York Review of Books*, May 26, 2011, p. 50; George Packer, "The Broken Contract: Inequality and American Decline," *Foreign Affairs*, November/December 2011, pp. 23–25.

75. Alfred Lief, editor, *Representative Opinions of Mr. Justice Holmes* (Westport, CT: Greenwood Press, 1971), pp. 160, 282.

76. Mark DeWolfe Howe, editor, *Holmes-Laski Letters: The Correspondence of Mr. Justice Holmes and Harold J. Laski 1916–1935* (Cambridge, Massachusetts: Harvard University Press, 1953), Volume II, p. 888.

77. Ibid., pp. 822–823. He also used the phrase in a letter to British jurist Sir Frederick Pollock. Mark DeWolfe Howe, editor, *Holmes-Pollock Letters: The Correspondence of Mr. Justice Holmes and Sir Frederick Pollock 1874–1932* (Cambridge, Massachusetts: Harvard University Press, 1942), Vol. 2, p. 215.

78. Alfred Lief, editor, *The Dissenting Opinions of Mr. Justice Holmes* (New York: The Vanguard Press, 1929), p. 33.

79. John Bartlett, *Bartlett's Familiar Quotations* (Boston: Little, Brown and Company, 1968), p. 802.

80. Edmund Burke, *Reflections on the Revolution in France* (New York: Everyman's Library, 1967), p. 56.

81. Alexander Hamilton, *The Papers of Alexander Hamilton*, edited by Harold C. Syrett (New York: Columbia University Press, 1961), Volume I, p. 104.

82. Alexander Hamilton, *The Works of Alexander Hamilton*, edited by Henry Cabot Lodge (New York: G.P. Putnam's Sons, 1904), Volume I, p. 410.

83.   Peter Sacks, "How Colleges Perpetuate Inequality," *Chronicle of Higher Education*, January 12, 2007, p. B9.

84.   John Rawls, *A Theory of Justice* (Cambridge, Mass.: Harvard University Press, 1971), pp. 3–4.

85.   Peter Corning, *The Fair Society*, p. 124.

86.   Ronald Dworkin, *Taking Rights Seriously* (Cambridge, Mass.: Harvard University Press, 1980), p. xi; Laurence H. Tribe, *Constitutional Choices* (Cambridge, Massachusetts: Harvard University Press, 1985), p. 5.

87.   William Godwin, *Enquiry Concerning Political Justice*, Vol. I, p. 166.

88.   Adam Smith, *The Theory of Moral Sentiments* (Indianapolis: Liberty Classics, 1976), p. 167.

89.   Ibid., p. 169.

90.   Edmund Burke, *Reflections on the Revolution in France*, p. 253.

91.   Edmund Burke, *The Correspondence of Edmund Burke*, edited by Alfred Cobban and Robert A. Smith (Chicago: University of Chicago Press, 1967), Vol. VI, p. 47.

92.   F.A. Hayek, *Law, Legislation and Liberty*, Vol. 2: *The Mirage of Social Justice* (Chicago: University of Chicago Press, 1976), p. 78.

93.   Richard A. Posner, *The Economics of Justice* (Cambridge, Mass.: Harvard University Press, 1981).

94.   See, for example, John Rawls, *A Theory of Justice*, pp. 43, 60, 61, 265, 302.

95.   Ibid., p. 15.

96.   Ibid., p. 104.

97.   Ibid., p. 73.

98.   Ibid., p. 278.

99.   Ibid., p. 276.

100.   Ibid., p. 301.

101.   Ibid., pp. 3–4.

102.   Alfred Lief, editor, *Representative Opinions of Mr. Justice Holmes*, p. 69.

103.   Oliver Wendell Holmes, *Collected Legal Papers* (New York: Peter Smith, 1952), p. 304.

104.   Loc. cit.

105.   Oliver Wendell Holmes, Jr. *The Common Law* (Boston: Little, Brown and Company, 1923), p. 43.

106.   Ibid., p. 48.

107.   Mark DeWolfe Howe, editor, *Holmes-Laski Letters*, Volume I, p. 264.

108. Edmund Burke, *Reflections on the Revolution in France*, p. 28.

109. *Terminiello v. Chicago*, 337 U.S. 1 (1949), at 37.

110. Margaret Bush Wilson, "Commentary: Reflections on Discrimination in the Private Sector," *Washington University Law Quarterly*, Vol. 1979, p. 785.

111. *Public Papers of the Presidents of the United States: Lyndon B. Johnson, 1965*, Book II (Washington: U.S. Government Printing Office, 1966), p. 636.

112. Adam Smith, *The Theory of Moral Sentiments*, pp. 380–381.

CHAPTER 9: PATTERNS OF THE ANOINTED

1. John Dewey, *Liberalism and Social Action* (Amherst, N.Y.: Prometheus Books, 2000), p. 13.

2. Edmund Burke, "A Letter to the Right Hon. Henry Dundas, One of His Majesty's Principal Secretaries of State with the Sketch of a Negro Code," Edmund Burke, *The Works of the Right Honorable Edmund Burke*, third edition (Boston: Little, Brown, and Company, 1869), Vol. VI, pp. 256–289.

3. Adam Smith, *The Theory of Moral Sentiments* (Indianapolis: Liberty Classics, 1976), p. 337.

4. John Dewey, *Liberalism and Social Action*, p. 66.

5. Joe Williams, "New Attack at Horror HS: Top Senior Jumped at Brooklyn's Troubled Lafayette," *New York Daily News*, December 7, 2002, p. 7; Maki Becker, "Asian Students Hit in Rash of HS Attacks," *New York Daily News*, December 8, 2002, p. 7; Erin Texeira, "Asian Americans Bullied at School; Laws and Conferences Address Problem," *Washington Post*, December 25, 2005, p. A10; Samuel G. Freedman, "Students and Teachers Expect a Battle in Their Visits to the Principal's Office," *New York Times*, November 22, 2006, p. B7; Kristen A. Graham, "Asian Students Describe Violence at South Philadelphia High," *Philadelphia Inquirer*, December 10, 2009, p. A1; G.W. Miller, III, "Aggregated Assault: Asian Students Seek Refuge from School Violence," *Philadelphia Weekly*, September 2–8, 2009, pp. 15, 17, 19–20; Kristen A. Graham, "Attacking Immigrant Students Not New, Say Those Involved," *Philadelphia Inquirer*, December 18, 2009, p. B1; Kristen A. Graham, "Other Phila. Schools Handle Racial, Ethnic Tensions," *Philadelphia Inquirer*, February 4, 2010, p. A1; Jeff Gammage and Kristen A. Graham, "Feds Find Merit in Asian Students' Claims Against Philly School," *Philadelphia Inquirer*,

August 28, 2010, p. A1; Kristen A. Graham and Jeff Gammage, "Two Immigrant Students Attacked at Bok," *Philadelphia Inquirer,* September 21, 2010, p. B1.

6. Mark DeWolfe Howe, editor, *Holmes-Laski Letters: The Correspondence of Mr. Justice Holmes and Harold J. Laski 1916–1935* (Cambridge, Massachusetts: Harvard University Press, 1953), Volume II, p. 974.

7. David S. Landes, *The Wealth and Poverty of Nations: Why Some Are So Rich and Some So Poor* (New York: W.W. Norton, 1998), p. 94.

8. Ibid., p. 95.

9. Ibid., p. 96.

10. Ibid., p. 135.

11. John Larkin, "Newspaper Nirvana?" *Wall Street Journal,* May 5, 2006, p. B1; Tim Harford, *The Undercover Economist* (New York: Oxford University Press, 2005), p. 3.

12. Raymond Aron, *The Opium of the Intellectuals,* translated by Terence Kilmartin (London: Secker & Warburg, 1957), p. 227.

13. See, for example, Abigail and Stephan Thernstrom, *No Excuses: Closing the Racial Gap in Learning* (New York: Simon & Schuster, 2003), pp. 43–50; Thomas Sowell, "Patterns of Black Excellence," *The Public Interest,* Spring 1976, pp. 26–58.

14. T.S. Eliot, "The Cocktail Party," *The Complete Poems and Plays* (New York: Harcourt, Brace and Company, 1952), p. 348.

15. Gunnar Myrdal, *Asian Drama: An Inquiry Into the Poverty of Nations* (New York: Pantheon, 1968), Vol. III, pp. 1569–1570.

16. Walter Olson, "Law School and Leftist Orthodoxy," *Commentary,* March 2011, p. 45.

PART IV: OPTIONAL REALITY

Jean-François Revel, *The Flight from Truth: The Reign of Deceit in the Age of Information,* translated by Curtis Cate (New York: Random House, 1991), p. 34.

CHAPTER 10: FILTERING REALITY

1. J.A. Schumpeter, *History of Economic Analysis* (New York: Oxford University Press, 1954), p. 43n.

2. Daniel J. Flynn, *A Conservative History of the American Left* (New York: Crown Forum, 2008), p. 214.

3. Jean-François Revel, *The Flight from Truth: The Reign of Deceit in the Age of Information*, translated by Curtis Cate (New York: Random House, 1991), p. 259.

4. Carmen DeNavas-Walt, et al., "Income, Poverty, and Health Insurance Coverage in the United States: 2006," *Current Population Reports*, P60–233 (Washington: U.S. Bureau of the Census, 2007), p. 5; Glenn B. Canner, et al., "Home Mortgage Disclosure Act: Expanded Data on Residential Lending," *Federal Reserve Bulletin*, November 1991, p. 870; Glenn B. Canner and Dolores S. Smith, "Expanded HMDA Data on Residential Lending: One Year Later," *Federal Reserve Bulletin*, November 1992, p. 808; Rochelle Sharpe, "Unequal Opportunity: Losing Ground on the Employment Front," *Wall Street Journal*, September 14, 1993, pp. A1 ff.

5. Bernard Goldberg, *Bias: A CBS Insider Exposes How the Media Distort the News* (Washington: Regnery Publishing Inc., 2002), p. 63.

6. Brian C. Anderson, *South Park Conservatives: The Revolt Against Liberal Media Bias* (Washington: Regnery Publishing Inc., 2005), p. 14. An earlier study found that more than half of all corporate heads in television dramas "do something illegal, ranging from fraud to murder." Paul Hollander, *Anti-Americanism: Critiques at Home and Abroad 1965–1990* (New York: Oxford University Press, 1992), p. 231.

7. Bernard Goldberg, *Bias*, p. 81.

8. Daniel Golden, "Aiming for Diversity, Textbooks Overshoot," *Wall Street Journal*, August 19, 2006, pp. A1 ff.

9. Walter Duranty, "All Russia Suffers Shortage of Food; Supplies Dwindling," *New York Times*, November 25, 1932, p. 1.

10. S. J. Taylor, *Stalin's Apologist: Walter Duranty, The New York Times's Man in Moscow* (New York: Oxford University Press, 1990), p. 182.

11. Ibid., p. 205.

12. Gregory Wolfe, *Malcolm Muggeridge: A Biography* (Grand Rapids: William B. Eerdmans Publishing Co., 1997), p. 119.

13. Robert Conquest, *The Harvest of Sorrow: Soviet Collectivization and the Terror-Famine* (New York: Oxford University Press, 1986), p. 303.

14. See, for example, Michael Ellman, "A Note on the Number of 1933 Famine Victims," *Soviet Studies*, Vol. 43, No. 2 (1991), p. 379; R.W. Davies and Stephen G. Wheatcroft, *The Years of Hunger: Soviet Agriculture, 1931–1933* (New York: Palgrave Macmillan, 2004), p. 415; Steve Smith, "Comment on Kershaw," *Contemporary European History*, February 2005, p. 130; James E. Mace, "The

Politics of Famine: American Government and Press Response to the Ukrainian Famine, 1932–1933," *Holocaust and Genocide Studies*, Vol. 3, No. 1 (1988), p. 77; Hiroaki Kuromiya, *Stalin* (Harlow, England: Pearson Education Limited, 2005), pp. 103–104. Even Soviet publications carried reports for the country as a whole "that the number of victims of hunger and terror during the 1930s and during the war, according to the no longer tongue-tied Soviet demographers, far exceeded the harshest evaluations of anti-communist historiography." Jean-François Revel, *The Flight from Truth*, translated by Curtis Cate, p. 208.

15. S. J. Taylor, *Stalin's Apologist*, p. 206.

16. James E. Mace, "The Politics of Famine: American Government and Press Response to the Ukrainian Famine, 1932–1933," *Holocaust and Genocide Studies*, Vol. 3, No. 1 (1988), p. 82.

17. Ronald Dworkin, "Affirming Affirmative Action," *New York Review of Books*, October 22, 1998, pp. 91 ff; Alan Wolfe, "Affirmative Action: The Fact Gap," *New York Times*, October 25, 1998, Book Review section, p. 15; Richard Flacks, "Getting to Yes; *The Shape of the River*," *Los Angeles Times*, July 4, 1999, Book Review section, p. 7; Ellis Cose, "Cutting Through Race Rhetoric," *Newsweek*, September 28, 1998, p. 75; David Karen, "Go to the Head of the Class," *The Nation*, November 16, 1998, pp. 46 ff.

18. Stephan Thernstrom and Abigail Thernstrom, "Reflections on *The Shape of the River*," *UCLA Law Review*, Vol. 46, No. 5 (June 1999), p. 1589.

19. Gail Heriot, "Affirmative Action Backfires," *Wall Street Journal*, August 24, 2007, p. A15; "Race Data for Bar Admissions Research Stays Under Wraps," *California Bar Journal*, December 2007, pp. 1 ff.

20. Peter Hitchens, *A Brief History of Crime: The Decline of Order, Justice and Liberty in England* (London: Atlantic Books, 2003), p. 168.

21. Gary Mauser, "Some International Evidence on Gun Bans and Murder Rates," *Fraser Forum*, October 2007, p. 24. An international statistical study found that Switzerland, Israel and New Zealand "have relatively lax gun control laws and/or high firearms availability, yet have homicide rates that differ little from those in England or Japan"— which is to say, homicide rates a fraction of those in the United States. Jeffrey A. Miron, "Violence, Guns, and Drugs: A Cross-Country Analysis," *Journal of Law and Economics*, Vol. 44, No. 2, Part 2 (October 2001), p. 616. New York City has had a murder rate some multiple of the murder rate in London for more than two centuries— and for most of those two centuries neither place had

serious gun control laws. Joyce Lee Malcolm, *Guns and Violence: The English Experience* (Cambridge, Massachusetts: Harvard University Press, 2002), p. 225.

22. Joyce Lee Malcolm, *Guns and Violence*, p. 225.

23. David B. Kopel, "Children and Guns," *Guns: Who Should Have Them?*, edited by David B. Kopel (Amherst, N.Y.: Prometheus Books, 1995), p. 346.

24. James Q. Wilson, "Criminal Justice," *Understanding America: The Anatomy of an Exceptional Nation*, edited by Peter H. Schuck and James Q. Wilson (New York: Public Affairs, 2008), p. 479.

25. Joyce Lee Malcolm, *Guns and Violence*, p. 61.

26. Ibid., p. 82.

27. Ibid., p. 92.

28. Ibid., p. 128.

29. Ibid., p. 167.

30. James B. Jacobs, *Can Gun Control Work?* (New York: Oxford University Press, 2002), p. 13.

31. William McGowan, *Coloring the News: How Crusading for Diversity Has Corrupted American Journalism* (San Francisco: Encounter Books, 2001), pp. 99–100.

32. For example, in a report from the Family Research Institute in June 2005 titled "Homosexual Child Molestation: Part 2" and another report from the same organization titled "Domestic Violence Higher Among Homosexuals?" in August 2008.

33. William McGowan, *Coloring the News*, p. 105.

34. Ibid., pp. 235, 236.

35. Jennifer Harper, "To Be 'Illegal' or Not to Be: Newsroom Question," *Washington Times*, March 6, 2009, p. A1.

36. William McGowan, *Coloring the News*, p. 89.

37. Ibid., p. 90.

38. Loc. cit.

39. Ibid., pp. 90–94.

40. David Murray, Joel Schwartz, and S. Robert Lichter, *It Ain't Necessarily So: How Media Make and Unmake the Scientific Picture of Reality* (Lanham, Maryland: Rowman & Littlefield, 2001), p. 71.

41. "Media Eat Up Hunger Study," *Media Watch*, April 1991, p. 1.

42. Loc. cit.

43. Robert E. Rector, "Hunger and Malnutrition Among American Children," *Backgrounder* No. 843 (August 2, 1991), The Heritage Foundation, p. 2.

44. Jonah Goldberg, *Liberal Fascism: The Secret History of the American Left from Mussolini to the Politics of Meaning* (New York: Doubleday, 2008), pp. 127–128.

45. See, for example, John Kenneth Galbraith, *The Great Crash, 1929* (Boston: Houghton Mifflin, 1961), pp. 143–146; Arthur M. Schlesinger, *Paths to the Present* (Boston: Houghton Mifflin, 1964), p. 237.

46. Amity Shlaes, *The Forgotten Man: A New History of the Great Depression* (New York: HarperCollins, 2007), pp. 148–149.

47. Paul Johnson, *A History of the American People* (New York: HarperCollins, 1997), p. 757.

48. Herbert Hoover, *The Memoirs of Herbert Hoover: The Great Depression 1929–1941* (New York: The Macmillan Company, 1952), p. 29.

49. Herbert Hoover, *The Memoirs of Herbert Hoover: The Cabinet and the Presidency 1920–1933* (New York: The Macmillan Company, 1952), pp. 99, 103–104.

50. Amity Shlaes, *The Forgotten Man*, p. 131.

51. Herbert Hoover, *The Memoirs of Herbert Hoover: The Great Depression 1929–1941*, pp. 43–46.

52. Oswald Garrison Villard, "Pity Herbert Hoover," *The Nation*, June 15, 1932, p. 669.

53. "Wanted— A Government," *New Republic*, March 4, 1931, p. 58.

54. Edmund Wilson, *The Shores of Light: A Literary Chronicle of the Twenties and Thirties* (New York: Farrar, Straus and Young, Inc., 1952), p. 498.

55. Edmund Wilson, *The American Jitters: A Year of the Slump* (New York: Charles Scribner's Sons, 1932), p. 296.

56. Robert S. Allen and Drew Pearson, *Washington Merry-Go-Round* (New York: Horace Liveright, 1931), p. 55.

57. Harold Laski, "Persons and Personages: President Hoover," *Living Age*, June 1931, p. 367.

58. "Ickes Says Hoover Let Needy 'Starve,'" *New York Times*, April 7, 1936, p. 5.

59. Robert S. McElvaine, *The Great Depression: America, 1929–1941* (New York: Times Books, 1993), p. 52.

60. Paul Krugman, "Fifty Herbert Hoovers," *New York Times*, December 29, 2008, p. A25.

61. David McCullough, *Truman* (New York: Simon & Schuster, 1992), pp. 389–390.

62. Merle Miller, *Plain Speaking: An Oral Biography of Harry S. Truman* (New York: Berkley Publishing Corp., 1974), p. 220.

63. "Adlai E. Stevenson," *New York Times*, July 15, 1965, p. 28.

64. Russell Jacoby, *The Last Intellectuals: American Culture in the Age of Academe* (New York: Basic Books, 2000), p. 81.

65. Michael Beschloss, "How Well-Read Should a President Be?" *New York Times*, June 11, 2000, section 4, p. 17.

66. David McCullough, "Harry S. Truman: 1945–1953," *Character Above All: Ten Presidents from FDR to George Bush*, edited by Robert A. Wilson (New York: Simon & Schuster, 1995), p. 58.

67. Robert H. Ferrell, *Harry S. Truman: A Life* (Columbia, Missouri: University of Missouri Press, 1994), p. 19.

68. Michael Straight, "Truman Should Quit," *New Republic*, April 5, 1948, p. 5.

69. "Truman as Leader," *New Republic*, May 17, 1948, p. 13.

70. Drew Pearson, "Washington Merry-Go-Round: Truman Explains 'Rights' Passion," *Washington Post*, November 7, 1948, p. B5.

71. Merle Miller, *Plain Speaking*, p. 243.

72. Glen Jeansonne, *A Time of Paradox: America from the Cold War to the Third Millennium, 1945–Present* (Lanham, Maryland: Rowman & Littlefield, 2007), p. 225.

73. Ron Suskind, *A Hope in the Unseen: An American Odyssey from the Inner City to the Ivy League* (New York: Broadway Books, 1998), p. 116.

74. Jeffrey Toobin, "The Burden of Clarence Thomas," *The New Yorker*, September 27, 1993, p. 43.

75. Carl T. Rowan, "Thomas is Far From 'Home,'" *Chicago Sun-Times*, July 4, 1993, p. 41.

76. Mary McGrory, "Thomas Walks in Scalia's Shoes," *Washington Post*, February 27, 1992, p. A2.

77. Kevin Merida, et al., "Enigmatic on the Bench, Influential in the Halls," *Washington Post*, October 10, 2004, pp. A1 ff.

78. Loc. cit.

79. Ken Foskett, *Judging Thomas: The Life and Times of Clarence Thomas* (New York: William Morrow, 2004), pp. 274–276.

80. Kevin Merida and Michael A. Fletcher, *Supreme Discomfort: The Divided Soul of Clarence Thomas* (New York: Doubleday, 2007), p. 340.

81. David C. Lipscomb, "Thomas Inspires Boys School Grads," *Washington Times*, May 30, 2008, p. A1.

82. Jan Crawford Greenburg, *Supreme Conflict: The Inside Story of the Struggle for Control of the United States Supreme Court* (New York: Penguin Press, 2007), p. 117.

83. Arch Ward, "Talking It Over," *Chicago Daily Tribune*, February 10, 1937, p. 27.

84. Jack Cuddy, "'Condemned Man' Arrives for Louis Bout," *Los Angeles Times*, April 22, 1936, p. A9.

85. "$500,000 Bid for Contest Claimed," *Washington Post*, December 17, 1936, p. X22.

86. Westbrook Pegler, "Adolph Hitler's Boy," *Washington Post*, December 15, 1936, p. X9.

87. Albion Ross, "Nazi Regime Backs Berlin Fight Plan," *New York Times*, March 12, 1937, p. 27.

88. Joseph D'O'Brian, "The Business of Boxing," *American Heritage*, October 1991, p. 78.

89. "Schmeling's Departure for U.S. Practically Ignored in Germany," *New York Times*, April 16, 1936, p. 31; "Hitler Still Frowns on Max Fighting Joe Louis in U.S.," *Chicago Defender*, May 2, 1936, p. 14.

90. Albion Ross, "Schmeling, Home, Hailed by Reich," *New York Times*, June 27, 1936, p. 12.

91. Ibid.

92. Shirley Povich, "This Morning. . ." *Washington Post*, June 16, 1936, p. 19.

93. Jack Cuddy, "'Condemned Man' Arrives for Louis Bout," *Los Angeles Times*, April 22, 1936, p. A9.

94. Robert Weisbord and Norbert Hedderich, "Max Schmeling: Righteous Ring Warrior?" *History Today*, January 1993, p. 40.

95. Frank Deford, "Almost a Hero," *Sports Illustrated*, December 3, 2001, p. 74.

96. Edmund Wilson, *Travels in Two Democracies* (New York: Harcourt, Brace and Company, 1936), p. 321.

97. "After the Slaughter, What Hope?" *The Economist*, March 9, 2002, p. 45.

98. "Caste and The Durban Conference," *The Hindu* (India), August 31, 2001 (online).

99. "Reservation Policy Not Implemented in Full," *The Hindu* (India), November 18, 2001 (online).

100. Tom O'Neill, "Untouchable," *National Geographic*, June 2003, pp. 2–31.

101. Jim Yardley, "In India, Castes, Honor and Killings Intertwine," *New York Times*, July 10, 2010, pp. A1 ff.

102. Martin A. Klein, "Introduction," *Breaking the Chains: Slavery, Bondage, and Emancipation in Modern Africa and Asia*, edited by Martin A. Klein (Madison: University of Wisconsin Press, 1993), pp. 19, 20. As of 1840, there were still more slaves in India than those emancipated by the British in the Caribbean. David Brion Davis, *The Problem of Slavery in the Age of Revolution, 1770–1823* (Ithaca: Cornell University Press, 1975), p. 63.

103. Nicholas D. Kristof, "She's 10 and May Be Sold To a Brothel," *New York Times*, June 2, 2011, p. A23.

104. Winston Churchill was one of those who was not taken in by benign depictions of India by Western or Indian intellectuals. "These Brahmins who mouth and patter the principles of Western Liberalism, and pose as philosophic and democratic politicians, are the same Brahmins who deny the primary rights of existence to nearly sixty millions of their own fellow countrymen whom they call 'untouchable,' and whom they have by thousands of years of oppression actually taught to accept this sad position." Winston Churchill, *Churchill Speaks 1897–1963: Collected Speeches in Peace & War*, edited by Robert Rhodes James (New York: Chelsea House, 1980), p. 536.

105. Paul Hollander, *Political Pilgrims: Travels of Western Intellectuals to the Soviet Union, China, and Cuba 1928–1978* (New York: Oxford University Press, 1981), p. 13.

106. Anthony Daniels, "Preface," Jean-François Revel, *Last Exit to Utopia: The Survival of Socialism in a Post-Soviet Era*, translated by Diarmid V.C. Cammell (New York: Encounter Books, 2000), p. xvii.

107. "A Reaffirmation of Principle," *New York Times*, October 26, 1988, p. A21.

108. Richard Hofstadter, *Anti-Intellectualism in American Life* (New York: Vintage Books, 1963), pp. 3, 24.

109. Nicholas D. Kristof, "Obama and the War on Brains," *New York Times*, November 9, 2008, Week in Review section, p. 10.

110. Jacques Barzun, *The House of Intellect* (New York: Perennial Classics, 2002), p. 2.

111. Clark Hoyt, "Keeping Their Opinions to Themselves," *New York Times*, October 19, 2008, Week in Review section, p. 12.

112. J.A. Schumpeter, *History of Economic Analysis*, p. 43.

113. "Hardcover Advice & Misc." *New York Times*, March 20, 2011, Book Review section. See also Ibid., March 27, 2011.

CHAPTER 11: SUBJECTIVE TRUTH

1. Jonah Goldberg, *Liberal Fascism: The Secret History of the American Left from Mussolini to the Politics of Meaning* (New York: Doubleday, 2008), p. 343.

2. "Historical Poverty Tables: Table 4," U.S. Bureau of the Census, Current Population Survey, Annual Social and Economic Supplements. Downloaded June 29, 2007 from: http://www.census.govhhes/www/poverty/histpov/hstpov4.html.

3. Arnold P. Hinchliffe, *Harold Pinter* (New York: Twayne Publishers, Inc., 1967), p. 101.

4. Paul Johnson, *Enemies of Society* (New York: Atheneum, 1977), p. 230.

5. Will Rogers, *A Will Rogers Treasury: Reflections and Observations*, edited by Bryan B. Sterling and Frances N. Sterling (New York: Crown Publishers, 1982), p. 88.

6. Jacques Barzun, *The House of Intellect* (New York: Perennial Classics, 2002), p. 15.

7. Jean-François Revel, *The Flight from Truth: The Reign of Deceit in the Age of Information*, translated by Curtis Cate (New York: Random House, 1991), p. 16.

8. Peter F. Sugar, *Southeastern Europe under Ottoman Rule, 1354–1804* (Seattle: University of Washington Press, 1977), pp. 55–56.

9. Nikolai Shmelev and Vladimir Popov, *The Turning Point: Revitalizing the Soviet Economy* (New York: Doubleday, 1989), p. 170.

10. Eric Hoffer, *First Things, Last Things* (New York: Harper & Row, 1971), p. 117.

11. H.G. Wells, *The Anatomy of Frustration: A Modern Synthesis* (New York: The Macmillan Company, 1936), p. 115.

12. Ibid., p. 100.

13. George J. Stigler, *Essays in the History of Economics* (Chicago: University of Chicago Press, 1965), pp. 20–22, *passim.*

14. Tim Harford, *The Undercover Economist* (New York: Oxford University Press, 2005), p. 3.

15. Paul Johnson, *Intellectuals* (New York: Harper & Row, 1988), p. 319.

16. Ibid., p. 246.

17. Eric Hoffer, *First Things, Last Things*, p. 117.

PART V: INTELLECTUALS AND THE LAW

Richard A. Epstein, *How Progressives Rewrote the Constitution* (Washington: The Cato Institute, 2006), p. viii.

CHAPTER 12: CHANGING THE LAW

1. *Constitution of the United States*, Article I, Section 9 (3).

2. Oliver Wendell Holmes, Jr., *The Common Law* (Boston: Little, Brown and Company, 1923), p. 1.

3. *Lauren Hill Cemetery v. City and County of San Francisco*, 216 U.S. 358 (1910), at 366.

4. Oliver Wendell Holmes, *Collected Legal Papers* (New York: Peter Smith, 1952), p. 194.

5. Antoine-Nicolas de Condorcet, *Sketch for a Historical Picture of the Progress of the Human Mind*, translated by June Barraclough (London: Weidenfeld and Nicolson, 1955), p. 112.

6. Ronald Dworkin, *Taking Rights Seriously* (Cambridge, Massachusetts: Harvard University Press, 1980), p. 147.

7. Ibid., p. 145.

8. Ibid., p. 239.

9. Theodore Roosevelt, *The Rough Riders: An Autobiography* (New York: The Library of America, 2004), p. 614. See also p. 721.

10. Edmund Morris, *Theodore Rex* (New York: The Modern Library, 2002), p. 165.

11. Sidney M. Milkis, *Theodore Roosevelt, the Progressive Party, and the Transformation of American Democracy* (Lawrence, Kansas: University of Kansas Press, 2009), p. 186.

12. Loc. cit.

13. Woodrow Wilson, *Constitutional Government in the United States* (New Brunswick, N.J.: Transaction Publishers, 2006), p. 158.

14. Ibid., p. 167.

15. Ibid., p. 169.

16. *Roe v. Wade*, 410 U.S. 113 (1973).

17. *Engel v. Vitale*, 370 U.S. 421 (1962).

18. *Miranda v. Arizona*, 384 U.S. 436 (1966).

19. *Brown v. Board of Education of Topeka, Kansas*, 347 U.S. 483 (1954).

20. *Furman v. Georgia*, 408 U.S. 238 (1972).

21. *Lynch v. Donnelly*, 465 U.S. 668 (1984); *Allegheny County v. American Civil Liberties Union*, 492 U.S. 573 (1989); *Rosenberger v. Rector and Visitors of University of Virginia*, 515 U.S. 819 (1995); *McCreary County, Kentucky v. American Civil Liberties Union*, 545 U.S. 844 (2005); *Van Orden v. Perry*, 545 U.S. 677 (2005).

22. *Baker v. Carr*, 369 U.S. 186 (1962).

23. Herbert Croly, *The Promise of American Life* (Boston: Northeastern University Press, 1989), pp. 35–36.

24. Ibid., p. 200.

25. Stephen Breyer, *Making Our Democracy Work: A Judge's View* (New York: Alfred A. Knopf, 2010), p. 230.

26. Roscoe Pound, "Mechanical Jurisprudence," *Columbia Law Review*, Vol. 8 (December 1908), p. 615.

27. Ibid., pp. 605, 609, 612.

28. Ibid., pp. 612, 614.

29. Roscoe Pound, "The Need of a Sociological Jurisprudence," *The Green Bag*, October 1907, pp. 611, 612.

30. Roscoe Pound, "Mechanical Jurisprudence," *Columbia Law Review*, Vol. 8 (December 1908), p. 614.

31. Roscoe Pound, "The Need of a Sociological Jurisprudence," *The Green Bag*, October 1907, pp. 614, 615.

32. Ibid., pp. 612, 613.

33. Roscoe Pound, "Mechanical Jurisprudence," *Columbia Law Review*, Vol. 8 (December 1908), pp. 605, 606, 610, 612, 613, 618, 620, 622.

34. Richard A. Epstein, *How Progressives Rewrote the Constitution* (Washington: The Cato Institute, 2006), pp. 4–5, 39.

35. Louis D. Brandeis, "The Living Law," *Illinois Law Review*, February 1916, p. 461.

36. Ibid., p. 462.

37. Ibid., p. 464.

38. Loc cit.

39. Loc cit.

40. Ibid., p. 471.

41. Archibald Cox, "The Effect of the Search for Equality Upon Judicial Institutions," *Washington University Law Quarterly*, Volume 1979, p. 795.

42. Ibid., pp. 804–805.

43. Ruth Bader Ginsburg, "Sexual Equality Under the Fourteenth and Equal Rights Amendments," Ibid., p. 161.

44. John Dewey, *Liberalism and Social Action* (Amherst, New York: Prometheus Books, 2000), p. 68.

45. Herbert Croly, *The Promise of American Life*, p. 150.

46. *Dred Scott v. Sandford*, 60 U.S. 393 (1857), at 407.

47. Ibid., at 562, 572–576.

48. *Wickard v. Filburn*, 317 U.S. 111 (1942), at 114.

49. Ibid., at 118.

50. Ibid., at 128.

51. Stephen Breyer, *Making Our Democracy Work*, p. 128.

52. Ibid., p. 127.

53. *United Steelworkers v. Weber*, 443 U.S. 193 (1979), at 201, 202.

54. Ibid., at 222.

55. United States Equal Employment Opportunity Commission, *Legislative History of Titles VII and XI of the Civil Rights Act of 1964* (Washington: U.S. Government Printing Office, no date), p. 3005.

56. Oliver Wendell Holmes, *Collected Legal Papers*, p. 307.

57. *Adkins v. Children's Hospital*, 261 U.S. 525 (1923), at 570.

58. *Constitution of the United States*, Article VI (2).

59. See, for example, *Day-Brite Lighting, Inc. v. Missouri*, 342 U.S. 421 (1952), at 423.

60. *Griswold v. Connecticut*, 381 U.S. 479 (1965), at 484.

61. Michael Kinsley, "Viewpoint: Rightist Judicial Activism Rescinds a Popular Mandate," *Wall Street Journal*, February 20, 1986, p. 25.

62. Linda Greenhouse, "Justices Step In as Federalism's Referee," *New York Times*, April 28, 1995, pp. A1 ff.

63. Ruth Colker and James J. Brudney, "Dissing Congress," *Michigan Law Review*, October 2001, p. 100.

64. "Federalism and Guns in School," *Washington Post*, April 28, 1995, p. A26.

65. Joan Biskupic, "Top Court Ruling on Guns Slams Brakes on Congress," *Chicago Sun-Times*, April 28, 1995, p. 28.

66. Linda Greenhouse, "Farewell to the Old Order in the Court," *New York Times*, July 2, 1995, section 4, pp. 1 ff.

67. Cass R. Sunstein, "Tilting the Scales Rightward," *New York Times*, April 26, 2001, p. A23.

68. Cass R. Sunstein, "A Hand in the Matter," *Legal Affairs*, March-April 2003, pp. 26–30.

69. Jeffrey Rosen, "Hyperactive: How the Right Learned to Love Judicial Activism," *New Republic*, January 31, 2000, p. 20.

70. Adam Cohen, "What Chief Justice Roberts Forgot in His First Term: Judicial Modesty," *New York Times*, July 9, 2006, section 4, p. 11.

71. "The Vote on Judge Sotomayor," *New York Times*, August 3, 2009, p. A18.

72. Ronald Dworkin "The 'Devastating' Decision," *New York Review of Books*, February 25, 2010, p. 39.

73. Alan S. Blinder, "It's Time for Financial Reform Plan C," *Wall Street Journal*, February 16, 2010, p. A19.

74. Ronald Dworkin, "The 'Devastating' Decision," *New York Review of Books*, February 25, 2010, p. 39.

75. Ronald Dworkin, "The Court's Embarrassingly Bad Decisions," *New York Review of Books*, May 26, 2011, p. 40.

76. *Constitution of the United States*, Amendment I.

77. Ronald Dworkin, "The 'Devastating' Decision," *New York Review of Books*, February 25, 2010, p. 39.

78. Cass R. Sunstein, "Tilting the Scales Rightward," *New York Times*, April 26, 2001, p. A23.

79. "Inside Politics," CNN Transcripts, July 11, 2005.

80. See, for example, Anthony Lewis, "A Man Born to Act, Not to Muse," *New York Times Magazine*, June 30, 1968, pp. 9 ff.

81. Jack N. Rakove, "Mr. Meese, Meet Mr. Madison," *Atlantic Monthly*, December 1986, p. 78.

82. Antonin Scalia, *A Matter of Interpretation: Federal Courts and the Law* (Princeton: Princeton University Press, 1997), pp. 17, 45.

83. William Blackstone, *Commentaries on the Laws of England* (New York: Oceana Publications, 1966), Vol. 1, p. 59.

84. Oliver Wendell Holmes, *Collected Legal Papers*, p. 204.

85. Ibid., p. 207.

86. Mark DeWolfe Howe, editor, *Holmes-Pollock Letters: The Correspondence of Mr. Justice Holmes and Sir Frederick Pollock 1874–1932* (Cambridge, Massachusetts: Harvard University Press, 1942), Vol. 1, p. 90.

87. *Northern Securities Company v. United States*, 193 U.S. 197 (1904), at 401.

88. Robert H. Bork, *Tradition and Morality in Constitutional Law* (Washington: American Enterprise Institute, 1984), p. 7.

89. *Constitution of the United States*, Article I, Section 9 (3).

90. *McDonald et al. v. City of Chicago, Illinois* (slip opinion), June 28, 2010, dissenting opinion of Justice Breyer, p. 5.

91. Oliver Wendell Holmes, *Collected Legal Papers*, p. 289.

92. Jack N. Rakove, "Mr. Meese, Meet Mr. Madison," *Atlantic Monthly*, December 1986, p. 81.

93. Ibid., pp. 81, 82.

94. Ibid., p. 84.

95. Ronald Dworkin, *A Matter of Principle* (Cambridge, Massachusetts: Harvard University Press, 1985), pp. 40, 43, 44.

96. Ibid., p. 42.

97. Jack N. Rakove, "Mr. Meese, Meet Mr. Madison," *Atlantic Monthly*, December 1986, p. 78.

98. Anthony Lewis, "A Supreme Difference," *New York Review of Books*, June 10, 2010, pp. 49–50.

99. Ronald Dworkin, *A Matter of Principle*, p. 318.

100. Ibid., p. 331.

101. "The High Court Loses Restraint," *New York Times*, April 29, 1995, section 1, p. 22.

102. Mark DeWolfe Howe, editor, *Holmes-Laski Letters: The Correspondence of Mr. Justice Holmes and Harold J. Laski 1916–1935* (Cambridge, Massachusetts: Harvard University Press, 1953), Volume I, p. 752.

103. *Abrams v. United States*, 250 U.S. 616 (1919), at 629.

104. Mark DeWolfe Howe, editor, *Holmes-Laski Letters*, Volume I, p. 389.

105. Mark DeWolfe Howe, editor, *Holmes-Laski Letters*, Volume II, p. 913.

CHAPTER 13: LAW AND "RESULTS"

1.   R.R. Palmer, *Twelve Who Ruled: The Year of the Terror in the French Revolution* (Princeton: Princeton University Press, 1989), pp. 132–133.

2.   See, for example, Michael Rothfeld, "Officials Urge End to Prison Oversight," *Los Angeles Times*, January 28, 2009, p. B1; Solomon Moore, "The Prison Overcrowding Fix," *New York Times*, February 11, 2009, p. A17; William Robbins, "Tax for School Desegregation Upheld," *New York Times*, August 20, 1988, section 1, p. 7; Frank J. Murray, "Schools Plan Will End; Feud Will Not; Desegregation Case Leaves Judge Bitter," *Washington Times*, March 27, 1997, p. A1; Mary Jordan, "Kansas City's

Costly Integration Strategy; Results Mixed in $1.2 Billion School Plan," *Washington Post*, April 11, 1992, p. A1.

3.   See, for example, Charles Murray, *Human Accomplishment: The Pursuit of Excellence in the Arts and Sciences, 800 B.C. to 1950* (New York: HarperCollins, 2003), pp. 92, 99, 100, 101, 258, 279, 282, 301–304, 356; Malcolm Gladwell, *Outliers: The Story of Success* (New York: Little, Brown and Co., 2008), Chapter 1; Thomas Sowell, *The Vision of the Anointed: Self-Congratulation as a Basis for Social Policy* (New York: Basic Books, 1995), pp. 35–37.

4.   Linda Greenhouse, "The Year the Court Turned Right," *New York Times*, July 7, 1989, pp. A1 ff.

5.   Linda Greenhouse, "Shift to Right Seen," *New York Times*, June 13, 1989, pp. A1 ff.

6.   Tom Wicker, "Bush and the Blacks," *New York Times*, April 16, 1990, p. A19.

7.   "A Red Herring in Black and White," *New York Times*, July 23, 1990, p. A14.

8.   William T. Coleman, Jr., "A False 'Quota' Call," *Washington Post*, February 23, 1990, p. A23.

9.   "A Gentler Civil Rights Approach," *Boston Globe*, August 3, 1991, p. 18.

10. "A Civil Rights Setback," *Boston Globe*, June 9, 1989, p. 16.

11. Ronald Dworkin, *Freedom's Law: The Moral Reading of the American Constitution* (Cambridge, Massachusetts: Harvard University Press, 1996), p. 157.

12. Tamar Jacoby, "A Question of Statistics," *Newsweek*, June 19, 1989, p. 58.

13. Reginald Alleyne, "Smoking Guns Are Hard to Find," *Los Angeles Times*, June 12, 1989, p. 5.

14. Howard Eglit, "The Age Discrimination in Employment Act, Title VII, and the Civil Rights Act of 1991: Three Acts and a Dog That Didn't Bark," *Wayne Law Review*, Spring 1993, p. 1190.

15. Alan Freeman, "Antidiscrimination Law: The View From 1989," *The Politics of Law: A Progressive Critique*, revised edition, edited by David Kairys (New York: Pantheon Books, 1990), p. 147.

16. Candace S. Kovacic-Fleischer, "Proving Discrimination After *Price Waterhouse* and *Wards Cove*: Semantics as Substance," *American University Law Review*, Vol. 39 (1989–1990), p. 662.

17. U.S. Equal Employment Opportunity Commission, *Legislative History of Titles VII and XI of Civil Rights Act of 1964* (Washington, D.C.: U.S. Government Printing Office, no date), pp. 3005, 3006–3007, 3160, and *passim*.

18. Ibid., p. 3015.

19. Ibid., p. 1014.

20. Edwin S. Mills, "The Attrition of Urban Real-Property Rights," *The Independent Review*, Fall 2007, p. 209.

21. Laurence H. Tribe, *Constitutional Choices* (Cambridge, Massachusetts: Harvard University Press, 1985), p. 187.

22. Loc. cit.

23. See, for example, Martin Anderson, *The Federal Bulldozer: A Critical Analysis of Urban Renewal, 1949–1962* (Cambridge, Mass.: MIT Press, 1964), pp. 56–59, 64–65; Dick M. Carpenter and John K. Ross, *Victimizing the Vulnerable: The Demographics of Eminent Domain Abuse* (Arlington, Virginia: Institute for Justice, 2007), pp. 1–7; Steven Greenhut, *Abuse of Power: How the Government Misuses Eminent Domain* (Santa Ana, California: Seven Locks Press, 2004), p. 109; Leslie Fulbright, "Neighborhood Closes a Checkered Chapter," *San Francisco Chronicle*, July 21, 2008, p. B1.

24. For examples, see my *The Housing Boom and Bust*, second edition (New York: Basic Books, 2010), pp. 8–17.

25. Will Oremus, "Bay Meadows Vote to Have Broad Repercussions," *Inside Bay Area*, April 21, 2008.

26. *Home Builders Association of Northern California v. City of Napa*, 90 Cal. App. 4th 188 (June 6, 2001).

27. Leslie Fulbright, "S.F. Moves to Stem African American Exodus," *San Francisco Chronicle*, April 9, 2007, pp. A1 ff; Bureau of the Census, *1990 Census of Population: General Population Characteristics California, 1990* CP–1–6, Section 1 of 3, pp. 27, 28, 30, 31; U.S. Census Bureau, *Profiles of General Demographic Characteristics 2000: 2000 Census of Population and Housing, California*, Table DP–1, pp. 2, 20, 39, 42.

28. See, for example, William Godwin, *Enquiry Concerning Political Justice and Its Influence on Morals and Happiness* (Toronto: University of Toronto Press, 1946), Vol. II, p. 462; John Dewey, *Human Nature and Conduct: An Introduction to Social Psychology* (New York: Modern Library, 1957), p. 18; Edward Bellamy, *Looking Backward: 2000–1887* (Boston: Houghton Mifflin, 1926), pp. 200–201.

29. James Q. Wilson and Richard J. Herrnstein, *Crime and Human Nature* (New York: Simon and Schuster, 1985), p. 409.

30. Joyce Lee Malcolm, *Guns and Violence: The English Experience* (Cambridge, Massachusetts: Harvard University Press, 2002), pp. 164–165.

31. James Q. Wilson and Richard J. Herrnstein, *Crime and Human Nature*, pp. 423–425; Joyce Lee Malcolm, *Guns and Violence*, pp. 166–168, 171–189; David Fraser, *A Land Fit for Criminals: An Insider's View of Crime, Punishment and Justice in England and Wales* (Sussex: Book Guild Publishing, 2006), pp. 352–356; Theodore Dalrymple, "Protect the Burglars of Bromsgrove!" *City Journal*, October 20, 2008.

32. Joyce Lee Malcolm, *Guns and Violence*, p. 184.

33. C. H. Rolph, "Guns and Violence," *New Statesman*, January 15, 1965, pp. 71, 72.

34. C. H. Rolph, "Who Needs a Gun?" *New Statesman*, January 16, 1970, p. 70.

35. Peter Hitchens, *A Brief History of Crime: The Decline of Order, Justice and Liberty in England* (London: Atlantic Books, 2003), p. 151.

36. Ibid., p. 166.

37. Joyce Lee Malcolm, *Guns and Violence*, p. 168.

38. Franklin E. Zimring, *The Great American Crime Decline* (New York: Oxford University Press, 2008), pp. 6, 15.

39. Department of the Treasury, Bureau of Alcohol, Tobacco & Firearms, "Commerce in Firearms in the United States," February 2000, p. 6.

40. Joyce Lee Malcolm, *Guns and Violence*, pp. 5, 204.

41. Ibid., p. 184.

42. Chris Henwood, "Council Tells Gardener: Take Down Barbed Wire In Case It Hurts Thieves Who Keep Burgling You," *Birmingham Evening Mail*, October 11, 2008, p. 9.

43. Stephan Thernstrom and Abigail Thernstrom, *America in Black and White: One Nation, Indivisible* (New York: Simon and Schuster, 1997), p. 162.

44. Joyce Lee Malcolm, *Guns and Violence*, pp. 90–91.

45. See, for example, Franklin E. Zimring, *The Great American Crime Decline*, p. 55.

46. Sidney E. Zion, "Attack on Court Heard by Warren," *New York Times*, September 10, 1965, pp. 1 ff.

47. Tom Wicker, "In the Nation: Which Law and Whose Order?" *New York Times*, October 3, 1967, p. 46.

48. "The Unkindest Cut," *The Economist*, January 3, 2009, p. 42.

49. See, for example, David Fraser, *A Land Fit for Criminals*, especially Chapters 3, 6, 7.

50. Ibid., p. xviii.

51. Fox Butterfield, "Crime Keeps on Falling, but Prisons Keep on Filling," *New York Times*, September 28, 1997, p. WK1. Earlier, Fox Butterfield said: "Oddly, during the 1960's, as crime rose, the number of Americans in prison actually declined." Fox Butterfield, "U.S. Expands Its Lead in the Rate of Imprisonment," *New York Times*, February 11, 1992, p. A16. In other words, the inverse relationship between crime and punishment seemed puzzling in both eras.

52. "Prison Nation," *New York Times*, March 10, 2008, p. A16.

53. Tom Wicker, "The Punitive Society," *New York Times*, January 12, 1991, p. 25.

54. Dirk Johnson, "More Prisons Using Iron Hand to Control Inmates," *New York Times*, November 1, 1990, p. A18.

55. David Fraser, *A Land Fit for Criminals*, p. 97; Peter Saunders and Nicole Billante, "Does Prison Work?" *Policy* (Australia), Vol. 18, No. 4 (Summer 2002–03), pp. 3–8.

56. David Fraser, *A Land Fit for Criminals*, pp. 71–73.

57. "A Nation of Jailbirds," *The Economist*, April 4, 2009, p. 40.

58. David Fraser, *A Land Fit for Criminals*, p. 72.

59. "A Nation of Jailbirds," *The Economist*, April 4, 2009, p. 40.

60. David Fraser, *A Land Fit for Criminals*, p. 109.

61. Daniel Seligman and Joyce E. Davis, "Investing in Prison," *Fortune*, April 29, 1996, p. 211.

62. "Prison Nation," *New York Times*, March 10, 2008, p. A16.

63. David Fraser, *A Land Fit for Criminals*, p. 38; "Criminal Statistics 2004," *Home Office Statistical Bulletin*, November 2005, Table 1.2.

64. David Barrett, "Thousands of Criminals Spared Prison Go on to Offend Again," *Daily Telegraph* online (London), 20 December 2008.

65. David Fraser, *A Land Fit for Criminals*, pp. 7–8, 277–278.

66. Ibid., pp. 13–14.

67. Ibid., Chapters 6, 7.

68. James Q. Wilson and Richard J. Herrnstein, *Crime and Human Nature*, pp. 428–434.

69. Jaxon Van Derbeken, "Homicides Plummet as Police Flood Tough Areas," *San Francisco Chronicle*, July 6, 2009, pp. C1 ff.

PART VI: INTELLECTUALS AND WAR

CHAPTER 14: THE WORLD WARS

1. Eugen Weber, *The Hollow Years: France in the 1930s* (New York: W.W. Norton, 1994), p. 5.

2. Donald Kagan, *On the Origins of War and the Preservation of Peace* (New York: Doubleday, 1995), pp. 132–133.

3. Martin Gilbert, *The First World War: A Complete History* (New York: Henry Holt, 1994), pp. 29, 34; Barbara W. Tuchman, *The Guns of August* (New York: Bonanza Books, 1982), pp. 125, 127.

4. Jonah Goldberg, *Liberal Fascism: The Secret History of the American Left from Mussolini to the Politics of Meaning* (New York: Doubleday, 2008), p. 83.

5. William E. Leuchtenburg, "Progressivism and Imperialism: The Progressive Movement and American Foreign Policy, 1898–1916," *Mississippi Valley Historical Review*, Vol. 39, No. 3 (December 1952), pp. 483–504; Jonah Goldberg, *Liberal Fascism*, pp. 106–111.

6. Herbert Croly, *The Promise of American Life* (Boston: Northeastern University Press, 1989), p. 259.

7. Ibid., p. 256.

8. William E. Leuchtenburg, "Progressivism and Imperialism: The Progressive Movement and American Foreign Policy, 1898–1916," *Mississippi Valley Historical Review*, Vol. 39, No. 3 (December 1952), pp. 486, 487, 497.

9. Herbert Croly, *The Promise of American Life*, pp. 302, 303.

10. Ibid., p. 169.

11. Jonah Goldberg, *Liberal Fascism*, p. 107.

12. Jim Powell, *Wilson's War: How Woodrow Wilson's Great Blunder Led to Hitler, Lenin, Stalin, and World War II* (New York: Crown Forum, 2005), pp. 80–81. See also Arthur S. Link, *Woodrow Wilson and the Progressive Era: 1910–1917* (New York: Harper & Brothers, 1954), Chapters 4, 5.

13. The great economist Alfred Marshall saw in Britain's attempt to starve the German population a lasting source of bitterness and a future war. Writing in 1915 to his most famous student, John Maynard Keynes, Marshall said: "I shall not live to see our next war with Germany; but you will, I expect." *Memorials of Alfred Marshall*, edited by A.C. Pigou (New York: Kelley & Millman, Inc., 1956), p. 482.

14. Woodrow Wilson, "Address to a Joint Session of Congress Calling for a Declaration of War," *Woodrow Wilson: Essential Writings and Speeches of the Scholar-President*, edited by Mario R. DiNunzio (New York: New York University Press, 2006), p. 401.

15. Ibid., p. 402.

16. Jim Powell, *Wilson's War*, p. 136.

17. Jonah Goldberg, *Liberal Fascism*, p. 105.

18. Ibid., p. 63.

19. Charles F. Howlett, *Troubled Philosopher: John Dewey and the Struggle for World Peace* (Port Washington, N.Y.: Kennikat Press, 1977), p. 20.

20. Thomas J. Knock, *To End All Wars: Woodrow Wilson and the Quest for a New World Order* (New York: Oxford University Press, 1992), pp. 77–78. Intellectuals were not alone in idolizing Woodrow Wilson. "Across Europe there were squares, streets, railway stations and parks bearing Wilson's name." Margaret MacMillan, *Paris 1919: Six Months That Changed the World* (New York: Random House, 2002), p. 15.

21. Quoted in Daniel Patrick Moynihan, *Pandaemonium: Ethnicity in International Politics* (Oxford: Oxford University Press, 1993), pp. 81, 82.

22. Ibid., p. 83.

23. David C. Smith, *H.G. Wells: Desperately Mortal* (New Haven: Yale University Press, 1986), p. 221.

24. H.G. Wells, *The War That Will End War* (New York: Duffield & Company, 1914), p. 54.

25. Daniel Patrick Moynihan, *Pandaemonium*, p. 100.

26. Woodrow Wilson, "Address to a Joint Session of Congress Calling for a Declaration of War," *Woodrow Wilson*, edited by Mario R. DiNunzio, p. 402.

27. Daniel J. Flynn, *A Conservative History of the American Left* (New York: Crown Forum, 2008), p. 178.

28. Jonah Goldberg, *Liberal Fascism*, pp. 108–111, *passim*.

29. Ibid., pp. 112–113.

30. John Dewey, *Characters and Events: Popular Essays in Social and Political Philosophy*, edited by Joseph Ratner (New York: Henry Holt and Company, 1929), Vol. II, p. 517.

31. Eugen Weber, *The Hollow Years*, p. 11.

32. Alistair Horne, *To Lose A Battle: France 1940* (New York: Penguin Books, 1990), p. 49.

33. Eugen Weber, *The Hollow Years*, pp. 13, 14.

34. Ibid., pp. 18, 24.

35. Derek W. Lawrence, "The Ideological Writings of Jean Giono (1937–1946)," *The French Review*, Vol. 45, No. 3 (February 1972), p. 589.

36. Richard Overy, *The Twilight Years: The Paradox of Britain Between the Wars* (New York: Viking, 2009), p. 370.

37. Robert Shepherd, *A Class Divided: Appeasement and the Road to Munich, 1938* (London: Macmillan, 1988), p. 17.

38. Martin Ceadel, *Semi-Detached Idealists: The British Peace Movement and International Relations, 1854–1945* (Oxford: Oxford University Press, 2000), p. 242.

39. Harold J. Laski, *A Grammar of Politics* (London: George Allen & Unwin, Ltd., 1925), p. 587.

40. John Dewey, "Outlawing Peace by Discussing War," *New Republic*, May 16, 1928, p. 370; John Dewey, "If War Were Outlawed," *New Republic*, April 25, 1923, p. 235.

41. Robert Shepherd, *A Class Divided*, p. 50.

42. Martin Ceadel, *Semi-Detached Idealists*, p. 359.

43. Martin Ceadel, *Pacifism in Britain 1914–1945: The Defining of a Faith* (Oxford: Clarendon Press, 1980), p. 253.

44. Robert Skidelsky, *John Maynard Keynes*, Vol. 3: *Fighting for Britain 1937–1946* (New York: Viking Penguin, 2001), p. 34.

45. Bertrand Russell, *Which Way to Peace?* (London: Michael Joseph, Ltd., 1937), p. 179.

46. H.G. Wells, *The Anatomy of Frustration: A Modern Synthesis* (New York: The Macmillan Co., 1936), p. 102.

47. Kingsley Martin, "Russia and Mr. Churchill," *New Statesmanship: An Anthology*, edited by Edward Hyams (London: Longmans, 1963), p. 70.

48. Kingsley Martin, "The Educational Role of the Press," *The Educational Role of the Press*, edited by Henry de Jouvenel, et al (Paris: International Institute of Intellectual Co–Operation, 1934), pp. 29–30.

49. When Churchill in 1937— two years before the beginning of the Second World War— advocated doubling the size of the Royal Air Force, the leader of the Liberal Party declared this to be the language of Malays "running amok." A year later, when Churchill again rose in Parliament to chastise the government for not

rearming, this was the response: "An embarrassed silence greeted Churchill as he ended. Then members anxious to turn to more pleasant thoughts rattled their papers, stood, and shuffled out to the lobby, many heading for tea. One member told his Visitor's Gallery guest, Virginia Cowles, 'It was the usual Churchill filibuster— he likes to rattle the saber and he does it jolly well but you have to take it with a grain of salt.'" This was one year before the Second World War began. James C. Humes, *Churchill: Speaker of the Century* (New York: Stein and Day, 1982), p. 175.

50. David James Fisher, *Romain Rolland and the Politics of Intellectual Engagement* (Berkeley: University of California Press, 1988), pp. 61–65.

51. "Ask League to Act to End Army Draft," *New York Times*, August 29, 1926, p. E1.

52. The book was written by H.C. Engelbrecht and F.C. Hanighen. See Robert Skidelsky, *John Maynard Keynes*, Vol. 3: *Fighting For Britain 1937–1946*, p. 34.

53. Charles F. Howlett, *Troubled Philosopher*, p. 134.

54. "Romain Rolland Calls for a Congress against War," *New Republic*, July 6, 1932, p. 210.

55. H.G. Wells, *The Work, Wealth and Happiness of Mankind* (Garden City, N.Y.: Doubleday, Doran & Co., Inc., 1931), Vol. II, p. 669.

56. Harold J. Laski, "If I Were Dictator," *The Nation*, January 6, 1932, p. 15.

57. Aldous Huxley, *Aldous Huxley's Hearst Essays*, edited by James Sexton (New York: Garland Publishing, Inc., 1994), pp. 9–10.

58. J.B. Priestley, "The Public and the Idea of Peace," *Challenge to Death*, edited by Storm Jameson (New York: E.P. Dutton & Co., Inc., 1935), p. 319.

59. E.M. Forster, "Notes on the Way," *Time and Tide*, June 2, 1934, p. 696; E.M. Forster, "Notes on the Way," *Time and Tide*, November 23, 1935, p. 1703.

60. Charles F. Howlett, *Troubled Philosopher*, pp. 55–56.

61. Donald Kagan, *On the Origins of War and the Preservation of Peace*, p. 314.

62. "Romain Rolland Calls for a Congress against War," *New Republic*, July 6, 1932, p. 210.

63. Georges Duhamel, *The French Position*, translated by Basil Collier (London: Dent, 1940), p. 107.

64. "A Speech by Anatole France," *The Nation*, September 6, 1919, p. 349.

65. Mona L. Siegel, *The Moral Disarmament of France: Education, Pacifism, and Patriotism, 1914–1940* (Cambridge: Cambridge University Press, 2004), pp. 127, 132.

66. Ibid., p. 146.

67. Daniel J. Sherman, *The Construction of Memory in Interwar France* (Chicago: University of Chicago Press, 1999), p. 300.

68. Mona L. Siegel, *The Moral Disarmament of France*, p. 160.

69. Ernest R. May, *Strange Victory: Hitler's Conquest of France* (New York: Hill and Wang, 2000), p. 283.

70. Mona L. Siegel, *The Moral Disarmament of France*, p. 217.

71. Malcolm Scott, *Mauriac: The Politics of a Novelist* (Edinburgh: Scottish Academic Press, 1980), p. 79.

72. Winston Churchill, *Churchill Speaks 1897–1963: Collected Speeches in Peace & War*, edited by Robert Rhodes James (New York: Chelsea House, 1980), p. 554.

73. Alistair Horne, *To Lose A Battle*, p. 189.

74. Ernest R. May, *Strange Victory*, pp. 18–23.

75. See, for example, B.H. Liddell Hart, *History of the Second World War* (New York: Paragon Books, 1979), pp. 35–36; Ernest R. May, *Strange Victory*, pp. 5–6, 278.

76. Ernest R. May, *Strange Victory*, pp. 103–106.

77. Ibid., pp. 215, 220, 245, 252, 276–277, 278, 287, 289, 439, 454, 455, 456.

78. Ibid., p. 17.

79. Ibid., pp. 17, 280.

80. William L. Shirer, *Berlin Diary: The Journal of a Foreign Correspondent 1934–1941* (Tess Press, 2004), pp. 167, 189, 201, 219, 242, 260, 332–333, 345, 347, 348, 349, 372. Hitler shrewdly anticipated and encouraged French quiescence. Shirer in Berlin wrote in his diary on September 3: "The High Command lets it be known that on the western front the Germans won't fire *first* against the French." Ibid., p. 163.

81. Kingsley Martin, "War and the Next Generation," *New Statesman and Nation*, April 11, 1931, p. 240.

82. Bertrand Russell, *Sceptical Essays* (New York: W.W. Norton & Co., Inc., 1928), p. 184.

83. Martin Ceadel, *Pacifism in Britain 1914–1945*, p. 105.

84. Ibid., pp. 106, 131; André Gide, *The André Gide Reader*, edited by David Littlejohn (New York: Alfred A. Knopf, 1971), pp. 804–805.

85. Martin Ceadel, *Pacifism in Britain 1914–1945*, p. 137.

86. Winston Churchill, *Churchill Speaks 1897–1963*, edited by Robert Rhodes James, p. 645. Earlier Churchill said: "Many people think that the best way to escape war is to dwell upon its horrors, and to imprint them vividly upon the minds of the younger generation. They flaunt the grisly photographs before their eyes. They fill their ears with tales of carnage. They dilate upon the ineptitude of generals and admirals. They denounce the crime and insensate folly of human strife." Ibid., p. 586.

87. David C. Smith, *H.G. Wells*, pp. 317, 321.

88. H.G. Wells, *The Anatomy of Frustration*, p. 98.

89. J.B. Priestley, "The Public and the Idea of Peace," *Challenge to Death*, edited by Storm Jameson, p. 316.

90. "Spreading the Spirit of Peace," *The Times* (London), August 28, 1936, p. 8.

91. Ernest R. May, *Strange Victory*, pp. 103–106.

92. William Godwin, *Enquiry Concerning Political Justice and Its Influence on Morals and Happiness* (Toronto: University of Toronto Press, 1946), Vol. II, pp. 144–145.

93. Bertrand Russell, *Which Way to Peace?*, p. 139.

94. Ibid., pp. 140, 144.

95. Ibid., pp. 144–145.

96. Raymond Leslie Buell, "Even in France They Differ on Armaments," *New York Times*, February 21, 1932, Book Review section, pp. 10 ff.

97. Bertrand Russell, *Which Way to Peace?*, pp. 99, 122.

98. Kingsley Martin, "Dictators and Democrats," *New Statesman and Nation*, May 7, 1938, p. 756.

99. Kingsley Martin, "The Inescapable Facts," *New Statesman and Nation*, March 19, 1938, p. 468.

100. Richard J. Golsan, *French Writers and the Politics of Complicity: Crises of Democracy in the 1940s and 1990s* (Baltimore: Johns Hopkins University Press, 2006), p. 83.

101. Simone Weil, *Formative Writings 1929–1941*, edited and translated by Dorothy Tuck McFarland and Wilhelmina Van Ness (Amherst: University of Massachusetts Press, 1987), p. 266.

102. Martin Ceadel, *Pacifism in Britain 1914–1945*, pp. 216, 218.

103. Mona L. Siegel, *The Moral Disarmament of France*, pp. 218–219. The teachers' union encouraged other teachers to join the resistance. Among other things, this indicated that these teachers were not lacking in personal patriotism, even though

they had for years attempted to blend internationalism and patriotism when teaching the young, producing the effect of the proverbial trumpet that makes an uncertain sound.

104. Paul Johnson, *Modern Times: The World from the Twenties to the Nineties*, revised edition (New York: Perennial Classics, 2001), p. 348.

105. Robert Shepherd, *A Class Divided*, p. 41.

106. Harold Laski, "The People Wait for a Lead," *Daily Herald*, January 4, 1937, p. 10.

107. Talbot C. Imlay, *Facing the Second World War: Strategy, Politics, and Economics in Britain and France 1938–1940* (New York: Oxford University Press, 2003), pp. 199, 303–304; Robert Shepherd, *A Class Divided*, pp. 102–103; Robert Paul Shay, Jr., *British Rearmament in the Thirties: Politics and Profits* (Princeton: Princeton University Press, 1977), pp. 217–218; Tom Buchanan, *Britain and the Spanish Civil War* (New York: Cambridge University Press, 1997), pp. 78–79.

108. "Trade Unionism and Democracy," *New Statesman and Nation*, September 10, 1938, p. 369.

109. Charles F. Howlett, *Troubled Philosopher*, p. 77.

110. Oswald Garrison Villard, "Issues and Men: The President's Disarmament Opportunity," *The Nation*, January 31, 1934, p. 119.

111. William Manchester, *American Caesar: Douglas MacArthur 1880–1964* (Boston: Little, Brown and Company, 1978), pp. 154, 156; Matthew F. Holland, *Eisenhower Between the Wars: The Making of a General and Statesman* (Westport, CT: Praeger, 2001), pp. 171–172.

112. Charles F. Howlett, *Troubled Philosopher*, pp. 55–56.

113. "The Way of Appeasement," *The Times* (London), November 25, 1937, p. 15.

114. Winston Churchill, *Churchill Speaks 1897–1963*, edited by Robert Rhodes James, pp. 624, 627.

115. Winston S. Churchill, *The Second World War*, Vol. I: *The Gathering Storm* (Boston: Houghton Mifflin Co., 1983), p. 216.

116. Ibid., pp. 216–217.

117. Eugen Weber, *The Hollow Years*, p. 126.

118. Ernest R. May, *Strange Victory*, p. 138.

119. Eugen Weber, *The Hollow Years*, p. 127.

120. Ibid., p. 126.

121. Ibid., p. 128.

122. Ibid., pp. 102, 107–108.

123. Ian Kershaw, *Making Friends with Hitler: Lord Londonderry, the Nazis and the Road to World War II* (New York: Penguin Press, 2004), pp. 28, 30, 31.

124. H.J. Laski, "Hitler— Just a Figurehead," *Daily Herald*, November 19, 1932, p. 8.

125. Ian Kershaw, *Making Friends with Hitler*, pp. 29–30.

126. John Evelyn Wrench, *Geoffrey Dawson and Our Times* (London: Hutchinson, 1955), p. 361. In 1935, American foreign correspondent William L. Shirer recorded in his diary that a *Times* of London correspondent "has complained to me in private that the *Times* does not print all he sends, that it does not want to hear too much of the bad side of Nazi Germany and apparently has been captured by the pro-Nazis in London." William L. Shirer, *Berlin Diary*, p. 33. Dawson's filtering of the news extended to his coverage of German troops marching into Czechoslovakia's Sudetenland in 1938, where the predominantly German population warmly greeted them, while the Czechs fled from Nazi rule. "Every day there were photographs of the triumphant German troops marching into the Sudetenland. . . In the photographs the joyful welcome accorded to the German soldiers bore witness to the apparent justice of the Munich settlement. Photographs of refugees *had* reached *The Times*. Dawson refused to print them." Martin Gilbert and Richard Gott, *The Appeasers* (Boston: Houghton Mifflin Co., 1963), p. 191.

127. Winston S. Churchill, *The Second World War*, Volume I: *The Gathering Storm*, p. 73.

128. William L. Shirer, *The Rise and Fall of the Third Reich: A History of Nazi Germany* (New York: Simon and Schuster, 1960), pp. 292–294. See also William L. Shirer, *Berlin Diary*, pp. 44–45.

129. William L. Shirer, *The Rise and Fall of the Third Reich*, p. 293.

130. Loc. cit. The conclusion that a German retreat could have spelled the end of the Nazi regime was also shared by Winston Churchill. See Winston S. Churchill, *The Second World War*, Vol. I: *The Gathering Storm*, p. 194. Although a later historian questioned this conclusion (Ernest R. May, *Strange Victory*, pp. 36–38),William L. Shirer pointed out, contrary to Professor May, that the German troops in the Rhineland were to be ordered to beat a hasty retreat back over the Rhine in the event that French troops intervened. The mere concentration of French troops near the German border, to reinforce the Maginot Line, caused the top German generals to urge Hitler to pull their troops back out of the Rhineland, which Hitler refused to do. (William L. Shirer, *The Rise and Fall of the Third Reich*, pp. 290–291, 293).

131. Winston S. Churchill, *The Second World War*, Vol. I: *The Gathering Storm*, pp. 196–197.

132. Eugen Weber, *The Hollow Years*, p. 23; Ernest R. May, *Strange Victory*, pp. 142–143.

133. Ernest R. May, *Strange Victory*, pp. 142–143.

134. Winston S. Churchill, *The Second World War*, Vol. I: *The Gathering Storm*, p. 197.

135. "Harold Macmillan later observed of the period immediately following Munich, 'The whole world seemed united in gratitude to the man who had prevented war. No wonder the Prime Minister lived in an exalted, almost intoxicated mood. To question his authority was treason; to deny his inspiration almost blasphemy.'" Robert Shepherd, *A Class Divided*, p. 225. See also pp. 1–5.

136. Eugen Weber, *The Hollow Years*, pp. 175, 260.

137. Ibid., p. 261.

138. Ernest R. May, *Strange Victory*, p. 7.

139. Patrick J. Buchanan, *Churchill, Hitler, and the Unnecessary War: How Britain Lost Its Empire and the West Lost the World* (Westminster, MD: Crown Publishing, 2008), pp. 329–334.

140. Winston Churchill, *Churchill Speaks 1897–1963*, edited by Robert Rhodes James, p. 809.

141. "Washington in August, I'm told, had almost given Britain up as lost and was in a state of jitters for fear the British navy would fall into Hitler's hands and thus place the American eastern seaboard in great danger." William L. Shirer, *Berlin Diary*, pp. 444–445. Winston Churchill himself had warned President Franklin D. Roosevelt in May 1940 that if he— Churchill— and his government were replaced by others who would "parley amid the ruins" with a victorious Germany, the British fleet would be "the sole remaining bargaining counter" they could use to try to win "the best terms they could for the surviving inhabitants." Winston S. Churchill, *The Second World War*, Vol. II: *Their Finest Hour* (Boston: Houghton Mifflin, 1949), pp. 56–57.

142. "At the climax of what he called the Battle of Britain, Churchill, on a September Sunday afternoon, drove with his wife from the prime minister's country residence at Chequers to Uxbridge, the underground nerve center of the Royal Air Force. On the wall were electronic maps revealing the disposition of the twenty-five squadrons of the RAF. As discs began to dot the electrified chart indicating each

successive wave of German aircraft swooping in from France, the Fighter Command released its squadrons one by one to meet each onslaught. Soon the red lights signaled that all 25 squadrons were in the air. By then the British fighters were winging on their last ounce of fuel and firing their last round of ammunition.

"'What other reserves have we?' asked Churchill.

"'There are none,' the air marshal answered.

"Silence descended on the room."

James C. Humes, *Churchill*, p. 191.

143. Victor Davis Hanson, *Carnage and Culture: Landmark Battles in the Rise of Western Power* (New York: Doubleday, 2001), Chapter 9.

144. "Policy for a National Opposition," *New Statesman and Nation*, October 22, 1938, p. 596.

145. "Passing the Buck," *New Statesman and Nation*, February 25, 1939, p. 272.

CHAPTER 15: THE COLD WAR AND BEYOND

1. A. Solzhenitsyn, "Nobel Lecture in Literature, 1970," *Literature 1968–1980: Nobel Lectures Including Presentation Speeches and Laureates' Biographies*, edited by Tore Frangsmyr and Sture Allen (Singapore: World Scientific, 1993), p. 42.

2. "Victory in Europe," *Time*, May 14, 1945, p. 17.

3. David Halberstam, *The Fifties* (New York: Random House, 1993), p. 46.

4. Victor Davis Hanson, "If the Dead Could Talk," *Hoover Digest*, 2004, No. 4, pp. 17–18.

5. Bertrand Russell, "The International Bearings of Atomic Warfare," *United Empire*, Vol. XXXIX, No. 1 (January–February 1948), p. 21. See also Bertrand Russell, "International Government," *The New Commonwealth*, January 1948, p. 80.

6. "Fight Before Russia Finds Atom Bomb," *The Observer* (London), November 21, 1948, p. 1. After his comments were reported on both sides of the Atlantic, Bertrand Russell in a letter to *The Times* of London said: "I did not, as has been reported, urge immediate war with Russia. I did urge that the democracies should be *prepared* to use force if necessary, and that their readiness to do so should be made perfectly clear to Russia, for it has become obvious that the Communists, like the Nazis, can only be halted in their attempts to dominate Europe and Asia by determined and combined resistance by every means in our power, not

excluding military means if Russia continues to refuse all compromise." "Lord Russell's Address," *The Times* (London), November 30, 1948, p. 5.

7.　Joseph Alsop, "Matter of Fact," *Washington Post and Times Herald*, February 19, 1958, p. A15.

8.　Paul Johnson, *Intellectuals* (New York: Harper & Row, 1988), pp. 208, 209, 210.

9.　Steven F. Hayward, *Greatness: Reagan, Churchill, and the Making of Extraordinary Leaders* (New York: Crown Forum, 2005), p. 147.

10.　Peter Braestrup, *Big Story: How the American Press and Television Reported and Interpreted the Crisis of Tet 1968 in Vietnam and Washington* (Garden City, NY: Anchor Books, 1978), pp. 49–54.

11.　Ibid., pp. ix–xi.

12.　Jim and Sybil Stockdale, *In Love and War: The Story of a Family's Ordeal and Sacrifice During the Vietnam Years* (New York: Harper & Row, 1984), p. 181.

13.　Stanley Karnow, "Giap Remembers," *New York Times Magazine*, June 24, 1990, p. 36.

14.　Ibid., p. 62.

15.　"How North Vietnam Won the War," *Wall Street Journal*, August 3, 1995, p. A8.

16.　Ibid.

17.　Arthur Schlesinger, Jr., "A Middle Way Out of Vietnam," *New York Times*, September 18, 1966, p. 112.

18.　"Needed: A Vietnam Strategy," *New York Times*, March 24, 1968, section 4, p. 16.

19.　Drew Pearson, "Gen. Westmoreland Ouster Is Urged," *Washington Post, Times Herald*, February 10, 1968, p. B11.

20.　"The Logic of the Battlefield," *Wall Street Journal*, February 23, 1968, p. 14.

21.　Peter Braestrup, *Big Story*, pp. 465–468; Victor Davis Hanson, *Carnage and Culture: Landmark Battles in the Rise of Western Power* (New York: Doubleday, 2001), pp. 404–405.

22.　Walter Lippmann, "Negotiated Settlement in Vietnam— It Makes Sense," *Los Angeles Times*, February 12, 1967, p. F7; Arthur Schlesinger, Jr., "A Middle Way Out of Vietnam," *New York Times*, September 18, 1966, pp. 111–112.

23.　Peter Braestrup, *Big Story*, pp. ix–xi.

24.　Walter Lippmann, "The Vietnam Debate," *Washington Post, Times Herald*, February 18, 1965, p. A21.

25.　Walter Lippmann, "'Defeat,'" *Newsweek*, March 11, 1968, p. 25.

26. Joseph Kraft, "Khesanh Situation Now Shows Viet Foe Makes Strategy Work," *Washington Post, Times Herald*, February 1, 1968, p. A21.

27. Richard Parker, *John Kenneth Galbraith: His Life, His Politics, His Economics* (Chicago: University of Chicago Press, 2005), pp. 432–433.

28. Victor Davis Hanson, *Carnage and Culture*, p. 425.

29. See, for example, Peter Braestrup, *Big Story*, Chapter 6; Victor Davis Hanson, *Carnage and Culture*, pp. 393, 395.

30. "The My Lai Massacre," *Time*, November 28, 1969, pp. 17–19; "Cite Pilot for Valor at My Lai," *Chicago Tribune*, November 29, 1969, p. 8; Nell Boyce, "Hugh Thompson: Reviled, then honored, for his actions at My Lai," *U.S. News & World Report*, August 27, 2001, pp. 33–34; Victor Davis Hanson, *Carnage and Culture*, p. 394.

31. Peter Braestrup, *Big Story*, p. 24.

32. B.G. Burkett and Glenna Whitley, *Stolen Valor: How the Vietnam Generation Was Robbed of Its Heroes and Its History* (Dallas: Verity Press, 1998), p. 44.

33. Victor Davis Hanson, *Carnage and Culture*, pp. 422–423.

34. B.G. Burkett and Glenna Whitley, *Stolen Valor*, Chapters 4–5, 19.

35. Victor Davis Hanson, *Carnage and Culture*, p. 393.

36. Loc. cit.

37. Ibid., pp. 394–398.

38. Lewis Feuer, *Imperialism and the Anti-Imperialist Mind* (Buffalo, N.Y.: Prometheus Books, 1986), p. 183.

39. Leslie Cauley and Milo Geyelin, "Ex-Green Beret Sues CNN, Time Over Retracted Nerve-Gas Report," *Wall Street Journal*, August 7, 1998, p. 1.

40. Albert L. Kraus, "Two Kinds of Warfare," *New York Times*, February 14, 1968, p. 61.

41. Victor Davis Hanson, *Carnage and Culture*, p. 418.

42. Winston Churchill, *Churchill Speaks 1897–1963: Collected Speeches in Peace & War*, edited by Robert Rhodes James (New York: Chelsea House, 1980), p. 881.

43. "Churchill Visit Scored," *New York Times*, March 7, 1946, p. 5.

44. "Mr. Churchill's Plea," *Chicago Daily Tribune*, March 7, 1946, p. 18.

45. Marquis Childs, "Churchill's Speech," *Washington Post*, March 6, 1946, p. 8.

46. "Press Reaction to Churchill Plan For Closer U.S. Ties With Britain," *United States News*, March 15, 1946, p. 39; Walter Lippmann, "Mr. Churchill's Speech,"

Washington Post, March 7, 1946, p. 11; "Let's Hang Together— Churchill," *Los Angeles Times*, March 7, 1946, p. A4.

47. "Europe's Capitals Stirred by Speech," *New York Times*, March 7, 1946, p. 5; "Mr. Churchill's Speech," *The Times* (London), March 6, 1946, p. 5.

48. Kenneth Tynan, "The Price of Berlin," *Time and Tide*, August 3, 1961, p. 1263.

49. Neville Chamberlain, *In Search of Peace* (New York: G.P. Putnam's Sons, 1939), p. 288.

50. *Public Papers of the Presidents of the United States: John F. Kennedy, 1961* (Washington: United States Government Printing Office, 1962), p. 2.

51. Neville Chamberlain, *In Search of Peace*, pp. 34, 40, 120, 209, 216, 230, 240, 242, 250, 271. The same idea, in different words, recurs repeatedly elsewhere in the same book.

52. Writing in his diary on August 31, 1939— the day before the German invasion of Poland that set off the Second World War— American foreign correspondent in Berlin, William L. Shirer, said: "Everybody against the war. People talking openly. How can a country go into a major war with a population so dead against it?" William L. Shirer, *Berlin Diary: The Journal of a Foreign Correspondent 1934–1941* (Tess Press, 2004), p. 153.

53. Charles F. Howlett, *Troubled Philosopher: John Dewey and the Struggle for World Peace* (Port Washington, NY: Kennikat Press, 1977), p. 53. John Dewey, *Characters and Events: Popular Essays in Social and Political Philosophy*, edited by Joseph Ratner (New York: Henry Holt and Company, 1929), Vol. I, pp. 199, 201. (This was a reprint of an essay by Dewey that was first published in 1922).

54. John Dewey, *Characters and Events*, edited by Joseph Ratner, Vol. I, p. 201.

55. Neville Chamberlain, *In Search of Peace*, pp. 119, 132, 198.

56. Ibid., pp. 53, 174, 208, 251–252.

57. Loc. cit.

58. See, for example, Tom Wicker, "2 Dangerous Doctrines," *New York Times*, March 15, 1983, p. A25; Strobe Talbott, "Behind the Bear's Angry Growl," *Time*, May 21, 1984, pp. 24, 27; Anthony Lewis, "Onward, Christian Soldiers," *New York Times*, March 10, 1983, p. A27; Colman McCarthy, "The Real Reagan: Can He See the Forest for the Trees?" *Washington Post*, March 27, 1983, p. G7; TRB, "Constitutional Questions," *New Republic*, March 28, 1983, p. 4; "The Lord and the Freeze," *New York Times*, March 11, 1983, p. A30.

59. Dinesh D'Souza, *Ronald Reagan: How an Ordinary Man Became an Extraordinary Leader* (New York: The Free Press, 1997), p. 189.

60. Ronald Reagan, *An American Life* (New York: Simon and Schuster, 1990), pp. 680–681.

61. Ibid., p. 683.

62. Ibid., pp. 677, 679.

63. William Raspberry, "Why the Freeze Is on the Ballot," *Washington Post*, October 29, 1982, p. A29.

64. Anthony Lewis, "The Diabolical Russians," *New York Times*, November 18, 1985, p. A21.

65. Tom Wicker, "30 Years of Futility," *New York Times*, November 22, 1985, p. A35.

66. George F. Kennan, "First Things First at the Summit," *New York Times*, November 3, 1985, section 4, p. 21.

67. Colman McCarthy, "The Disarming, Modest Manner of Alva Myrdal," *Washington Post*, October 24, 1982, p. H8.

68. Paul W. Valentine, "Economist Hits Reagan Policies: Galbraith, as AU Speaker, Assails 'Reverse Logic,'" *Washington Post*, May 14, 1984, p. B1.

69. "Voters' Real Opportunity to Help Stop the Nuclear Arms Race," *New York Times*, November 1, 1982, p. A18.

70. Adam Clymer, "Strong 1984 Role Vowed by Kennedy," *New York Times*, February 6, 1983, p. 28.

71. Margot Hornblower, "Votes Arms Freeze; 27 For, 9 Against Resolution," *Washington Post*, March 9, 1983, pp. A1 ff.

72. "'The Best Way to End the Nuclear Arms Race,'" *New York Times*, March 16, 1983, p. A26.

73. Helen Dewar, "Senate Rejects Arms Freeze; Debt Ceiling Rise Voted Down," *Washington Post*, November 1, 1983, pp. A1 ff.

74. Jonathan Fuerbringer, "Senators Reject Spending Freeze," *New York Times*, May 3, 1984, p. B15. See also *Congressional Record*, Vol. 130, Part 8, pp. 10671–10679.

75. See, for example, Mona Charen, *Useful Idiots: How Liberals Got It Wrong in the Cold War and Still Blame America First* (New York: Perennial, 2004), pp. 110–115.

76. "SDI, Chernobyl Helped End Cold War, Conference Told," *Washington Post*, February 27, 1993, p. A17.

77. Peter Huessy, "Whining About Winners: Cold Warriors Received the Cold Shoulder," *Washington Times*, June 16, 2004, p. A19.

78. Herbert I. London, *Armageddon in the Classroom: An Examination of Nuclear Education* (Lanham, MD: University Press of America, 1987), p. vii.

79. Mona L. Siegel, *The Moral Disarmament of France: Education, Pacifism, and Patriotism, 1914–1940* (Cambridge: Cambridge University Press, 2004), p. 80.

80. National Education Association, *NEA Handbook 1999–2000* (Washington: National Education Association, 1999), p. 343.

81. National Education Association, *NEA Handbook 1980–81* (Washington: National Education Association, 1980), p. 244.

82. National Educational Association, *NEA Handbook 1982–83* (Washington: National Education Association, 1982), p. 237.

83. National Education Association, *NEA Handbook 1985–86* (Washington: National Education Association, 1985), p. 247.

84. Loc. cit.

85. National Education Association, *Proceedings of the Sixty–First Representative Assembly, 1982* (Washington: National Education Association, 1983), p. 62.

86. National Education Association, *Proceedings of the Sixty–Fourth Representative Assembly, 1985* (Washington: National Education Association, 1986), pp. 107–108; Carl Luty, "Thinking the Unthinkable. . . Thoughtfully," *NEA Today*, March 1983, pp. 10–11.

87. Mona L. Siegel, *The Moral Disarmament of France*, p. 136.

88. National Education Association, *Proceedings of the Sixty–First Representative Assembly, 1982*, p. 67.

89. National Education Association, *NEA Handbook 1982–83*, p. 237.

90. "Statement of Mr. Willard McGuire," *Twelfth Special Session, United Nations General Assembly*, June 25, 1982, A/S–12/AC.1/PV.7, p. 12.

91. National Education Association, *Proceedings of the Sixty-Third Representative Assembly, 1984* (Washington: National Education Association, 1985), p. 10.

92. Keith Geiger, "The Peace Dividend: Meeting America's Needs," *NEA Today*, March 1990, p. 2.

93. Keith Geiger, "A Time for Hope," *Washington Post*, December 23, 1990, p. C4.

94. Robert D. Novak, *The Prince of Darkness: 50 Years Reporting in Washington* (New York: Crown Forum, 2007), p. 432.

95. Tom Wicker, "The War Option," *New York Times*, October 31, 1990, p. A25.

96. Anthony Lewis, "The Argument for War," *New York Times*, December 14, 1990, p. A39.

97. Barton Gellman, "How Many Americas Would Die in War with Iraq?" *Washington Post*, January 6, 1991, p. A21.

98. Donald Kagan, "Colin Powell's War," *Commentary*, June 1995, p. 45.

99. Maureen Dowd, "Monkey on a Tiger," *New York Times*, January 6, 2007, p. A15.

100. Paul Krugman, "Quagmire of the Vanities," *New York Times*, January 8, 2007, p. A19.

101. "A Detached Debate; Have the Senators Arguing over Iraq War Resolutions Read the National Intelligence Estimate?" *Washington Post*, February 6, 2007, p. A16.

102. "The One that Brung Him," *St. Louis Post-Dispatch*, July 5, 2007, p. B8.

103. Ron Walters, "Bush Won't Face Truth about the War in Iraq," *Philadelphia Tribune*, January 21, 2007, p. 6A.

104. "Funeral Surge," *New Republic*, February 12, 2007, p. 7.

105. Jon Ward, "Democrats Ready to Fight New War Plan," *Washington Times*, January 11, 2007, p. A1; *Congressional Record: Senate*, January 30, 2007, p. S1322; Shailagh Murray, "Obama Bill Sets Date for Troop Withdrawal," *Washington Post*, January 31, 2007, p. A4.

106. Jon Ward, "Democrats Ready to Fight New War Plan," *Washington Times*, January 11, 2007, p. A1.

107. *Congressional Record: Senate*, January 18, 2007, p. S722.

108. Jon Ward, "Kennedy Proposal Uncovers Party Rift; Leave Iraq Now vs. Slow Retreat," *Washington Times*, January 10, 2007, p. A1.

109. Eric Pfeiffer, "Pelosi Threatens to Reject Funds for Troop Surge," *Washington Times*, January 8, 2007, p. A1.

110. Jon Ward, "Democrats Ready to Fight New War Plan," *Washington Times*, January 11, 2007, p. A1.

111. Michael E. O'Hanlon and Jason H. Campbell, *Iraq Index: Tracking Variables of Reconstruction & Security in Post-Saddam Iraq:* (http://www.brookings.edu/iraqindex), May 28, 2009, pp. 5, 14.

112. "Peace Talks Now," *Los Angeles Times*, June 12, 2007, p. A20.

113. Paul Krugman, "Snow Job in the Desert," *New York Times*, September 3, 2007, p. A13.

114. Frank Rich, "As the Iraqis Stand Down, We'll Stand Up," *New York Times*, September 9, 2007, section 4, p. 14.

115. Jason Campbell, et al., "The States of Iraq and Afghanistan," *New York Times*, March 20, 2009, p. A27.

116. Michael E. O'Hanlon and Kenneth M. Pollack, "A War We Just Might Win," *New York Times*, July 30, 2007, p. A17.

117. Paul Krugman, "A Surge, and Then a Stab," *New York Times*, September 14, 2007, p. A21.

118. Alan Nathan, "Slamming the Messenger," *Washington Times*, September 18, 2007, p. A17.

119. Farah Stockman, "Intelligence Calls Iraq's Government Precarious," *Boston Globe*, August 24, 2007, p. A1.

120. Advertisement, "General Petraeus or General Betray Us?" *New York Times*, September 10, 2007, p. A25.

121. Howard Kurtz, "New York Times Says It Violated Policies Over MoveOn Ad," *Washington Post*, September 24, 2007, p. A8.

122. Kathy Kiely, "Senators Have Their Say During Marathon Hearings; 'Take Off Your Rosy Glasses,' General Told in 10 Hours of Inquiries," *USA Today*, September 12, 2007, p. 6A.

123. Ibid.

124. Elisabeth Bumiller, "A General Faces Questions from Five Potential Bosses," *New York Times*, September 12, 2007, p. A10.

125. S. A. Miller, "Petraeus' Integrity under Fire on Hill," *Washington Times*, September 10, 2007, p. A1.

126. Susan Page, "A Mixed Reception, with No Sign of Consensus on War," *USA Today*, September 11, 2007, p. 1A.

127. Frank Rich, "Will the Democrats Betray Us?" *New York Times*, September 16, 2007, section 4, p. 11.

128. Susan Page, "A Mixed Reception, with No Sign of Consensus on War," *USA Today*, September 11, 2007, p. 1A.

129. Dan Frosch and James Dao, "A Military Deception, Made Easier by a Reluctance to Ask Questions," *New York Times*, June 8, 2009, p. A10.

130. Diana B. Henriques, "Creditors Press Troops Despite Relief Act," *New York Times*, March 28, 2005, pp. A1 ff; Dan Barry, "A Teenage Soldier's Goodbyes on the Road to Over There," *New York Times*, March 4, 2007, section 1, pp. 1 ff.

131. Eric Schmitt, "Medal of Honor to Be Awarded to Soldier Killed in Iraq, a First," *New York Times*, March 30, 2005, p. A13; Sarah Abruzzese, "Bush Gives Medal of Honor to Slain Navy Seals Member," *New York Times*, April 9, 2008, p. A14; Raymond Hernandez, "A Protector As a Child, Honored As a Hero," *New York Times*, October 22, 2007, p. B1.

132. See, for example, John F. Burns, "Pillagers Strip Iraqi Museum of Its Treasure," *New York Times*, April 13, 2003, pp. A1 ff; "Lawlessness in Iraq Puts U.S. Military Gains at Risk," *USA Today*, April 14, 2003, p. 12A; Maria Puente, "The Looting of Iraq's Past," *USA Today*, April 15, 2003, p. 7D; Douglas Jehl and Elizabeth Becker, "Experts' Pleas to Pentagon Didn't Save Museum," *New York Times*, April 16, 2003, p. B5; Constance Lowenthal and Stephen Urice, "An Army for Art," *New York Times*, April 17, 2003, p. A25; Frank Rich, "And Now: 'Operation Iraqi Looting,'" *New York Times*, April 27, 2003, section 2, pp. 1 ff; Andrew Gumbel and David Keys, "The Iraq Conflict: U.S. Blamed for Failure to Stop Sacking of Museum," *The Independent* (London), April 14, 2003, p. 6.

133. William Booth and Guy Gugliotta, "All Along, Most Iraqi Relics Were 'Safe and Sound,'" *Washington Post*, June 9, 2003, p. A12; Charles Krauthammer, "Hoaxes, Hype and Humiliation," *Washington Post*, June 13, 2003, p. A29; Matthew Bogdanos, "The Casualties of War: The Truth About the Iraq Museum," *American Journal of Archaeology*, Vol. 109, No. 3 (July 2005), pp. 477–526.

134. *WWII: Time-Life Books History of the Second World War* (New York: Prentice Hall Press, 1989), p. 401; *The Columbia Encyclopedia*, fifth edition (New York: Columbia University Press, 1993), p. 116.

135. Clark Hoyt, "The Painful Images of War," *New York Times*, August 3, 2008, Week in Review section, p. 10.

136. See, for example, Christian Davenport, "From Serving in Iraq to Living on the Streets; Homeless Vet Numbers Expected to Grow," *Washington Post*, March 5, 2007, pp. B1 ff. The problems of returning Iraq war veterans going to college were headlined in the *New York Times*' education section: "Crowded classrooms can send them into a panic. They have trouble focusing. They can't remember facts. And no one around them understands what they've seen. . . These new students will need

help. Are campuses ready?" *New York Times*, November 2, 2008, Education Life section, p. 1. Despite how radically this differs from the experience of veterans going to college after World War II, where troops had longer individual tours in combat and higher fatality rates, isolated anecdotes were all that were offered to substantiate these sweeping claims in the story itself. See Lizette Alvarez, "Combat to College," Ibid., pp. 24 ff.

137. Deborah Sontag and Lizette Alvarez, "Across America, Deadly Echoes of Foreign Battles," *New York Times*, January 13, 2008, section 1, pp. 1, 14.

138. Ralph Peters, "Smearing Soldiers," *New York Post*, January 15, 2008.

139. Lizette Alvarez and Dan Frosch, "A Focus on Violence by G.I.'s Back from War," *New York Times*, January 2, 2009, pp. A1 ff.

140. "Suicide Rate for Soldiers Rose in '07," *New York Times*, May 30, 2008, p. A18.

141. Pauline Jelinek, "Soldier Suicides Hit Highest Rate–115 Last Year," Associated Press Online, May 30, 2008.

142. Mona L. Siegel, *The Moral Disarmament of France*, pp. 218–219.

143. Edmund Burke, *The Correspondence of Edmund Burke*, edited by R. B. McDowell (Chicago: University of Chicago Press, 1969), Vol. VIII, p. 138.

144. Mona L. Siegel, *The Moral Disarmament of France*, p. 167.

145. William Godwin, *Enquiry Concerning Political Justice and Its Influence on Morals and Happiness* (Toronto: University of Toronto Press, 1946), Vol. II, p. 180.

146. Ibid., p. 146.

147. John Dewey, *Characters and Events*, edited by Joseph Ratner, Vol. II, pp. 800, 801.

148. Alistair Horne, *To Lose A Battle: France 1940* (New York: Penguin Books, 1990), p. 189.

149. Neville Chamberlain, *In Search of Peace*, pp. 307–308.

150. William L. Shirer, *The Rise and Fall of the Third Reich: A History of Nazi Germany* (New York: Simon and Schuster, 1960), pp. 595–596.

151. Neville Chamberlain, *In Search of Peace*, p. 33. It should be noted that Hitler presented his position in terms of "the national honour of a great people" in a letter to Chamberlain. Ibid., p. 170.

152. Ibid., p. 107.

153. Ibid., p. 305.

154. Ibid., p. 170.

155. Ibid., p. 174.

156. Richard Overy, *The Twilight Years: The Paradox of Britain Between the Wars* (New York: Viking, 2009), p. 357.

157. Patrick J. Buchanan, *Churchill, Hitler, and the Unnecessary War: How Britain Lost Its Empire and the West Lost the World* (Westminster, MD: Crown Publishing, 2008), Chapter 9.

158. J.M. Keynes, "A Positive Peace Programme," *New Statesman and Nation*, March 26, 1938, p. 510.

159. Ibid., p. 509.

160. Alistair Horne, *To Lose A Battle*, p. 129.

PART VII: INTELLECTUALS AND RACE

G. M. Trevelyan, *English Social History: A Survey of Six Centuries, Chaucer to Queen Victoria* (London: Longmans, Green and Co., 1942), p. 339.

CHAPTER 16: DISPARITIES AND THEIR CAUSES

1. See, for example, various chapter titles in Madison Grant, *The Passing of the Great Race or the Racial Basis of European History*, revised edition (New York: Charles Scribner's Sons, 1918).

2. Ibid., p. 16.

3. Mark H. Haller, *Eugenics: Hereditarian Attitudes in American Thought* (New Brunswick: Rutgers University Press, 1963), p. 11.

4. Madison Grant, *The Passing of the Great Race*, revised edition, p. 100. The book was a best-seller according to Paul Johnson, *Modern Times: The World from the Twenties to the Nineties*, revised edition (New York: Perennial Classics, 2001), p. 203.

5. Reports of the Immigration Commission, *The Children of Immigrants in Schools* (Washington: Government Printing Office, 1911), Vol. I, p. 110.

6. Carl C. Brigham, *A Study of American Intelligence* (Princeton: Princeton University Press, 1923), p. xx.

7. Ibid., p. 119.

8. Robert M. Yerkes, *Psychological Examining in the United States Army*, Memoirs of the National Academy of Sciences (Washington: Government Printing Office, 1921), Vol. 15, pp. 123–292; Carl C. Brigham, *A Study of American Intelligence*, pp. 80, 121.

9. Rudolph Pintner and Ruth Keller, "Intelligence Tests of Foreign Children," *Journal of Educational Psychology*, Vol. 13, Issue 4 (April 1922), p. 215.

10. Nathaniel D. Mttron Hirsch, "A Study of Natio-Racial Mental Differences," *Genetic Psychology Monographs*, Vol. 1, Nos. 3 and 4 (May and July, 1926), p. 302.

11. Otto Klineberg, *Race Differences* (New York: Harper & Brothers, 1935), pp. 183–184.

12. Ibid., p. 182. For critiques of the World War I data, from differing points of view, see Audrey M. Shuey, *The Testing of Negro Intelligence*, second edition (New York: Social Science Press, 1966), pp. 310–311; Carl C. Brigham, "Intelligence Tests of Immigrant Groups," *Psychological Review*, Vol. 37, Issue 2 (March 1930); Thomas Sowell, "Race and IQ Reconsidered," *Essays and Data on American Ethnic Groups*, edited by Thomas Sowell and Lynn D. Collins (Washington: The Urban Institute, 1978), pp. 226–227.

13. Carl C. Brigham, *A Study of American Intelligence*, p. 190.

14. H.H. Goddard, "The Binet Tests in Relation to Immigration," *Journal of Psycho-Asthenics*, Vol. 18, No. 2 (December 1913), p. 110.

15. Quoted in Leon J. Kamin, *The Science and Politics of I.Q.* (New York: John Wiley and Sons, 1974), p. 6.

16. Carl Brigham, for example, said, "The decline of American intelligence will be more rapid than the decline of the intelligence of European national groups, owing to the presence here of the negro." Carl C. Brigham, *A Study of American Intelligence*, p. 210.

17. "The Control of Births," *New Republic*, March 6, 1915, p. 114.

18. Sidney Webb, "Eugenics and the Poor Law: The Minority Report," *Eugenics Review*, Vol. II (April 1910-January 1911), p. 240; Thomas C. Leonard, "Eugenics and Economics in the Progressive Era," *Journal of Economic Perspectives*, Vol. 19, No. 4 (Fall 2005), p. 216.

19. Richard Overy, *The Twilight Years: The Paradox of Britain Between the Wars* (New York: Viking, 2009), pp. 93, 105, 106, 107, 124–127.

20. Matthew Pratt Guterl, *The Color of Race in America: 1900–1940* (Cambridge, Massachusetts: Harvard University Press, 2001), p. 67.

21. Madison Grant, *The Passing of the Great Race*, revised edition, p. 17.

22. Ibid., p. 48.

23. Ibid., p. 60.

24. Ibid., p. 77.

25. Ibid., p. 32.

26. Ibid., p. 19.

27. Ibid., p. 20.

28. Ibid., p. 104.

29. Ibid., p. 257.

30. Ibid., p. 258.

31. Ibid., p. 260.

32. Ibid., p. 101.

33. Ibid., p. 105.

34. Ibid., p. xxi.

35. Ibid., p. 49.

36. Ibid., p. 58.

37. Ibid., p. 59.

38. Ibid., p. 89.

39. Ibid., p. 16.

40. Ibid., p. 91.

41. Ibid., p. 263.

42. Jonathan Peter Spiro, *Defending the Master Race: Conservation, Eugenics, and the Legacy of Madison Grant* (Burlington: University of Vermont Press, 2009), pp. 6, 10, 17, 22–34.

43. "Scientific Books," *Science*, Vol. 48, No. 1243 (October 25, 1918), p. 419.

44. Madison Grant, *The Conquest of a Continent or the Expansion of Races in America* (York, SC: Liberty Bell Publications, 2004), p. xii.

45. Jonathan Peter Spiro, *Defending the Master Race*, pp. 98, 99.

46. Edward Alsworth Ross, *The Principles of Sociology* (New York: The Century Co., 1920), p. 63.

47. Edward Alsworth Ross, "Who Outbreeds Whom?" *Proceedings of the Third Race Betterment Conference* (Battle Creek, Michigan: Race Betterment Foundation, 1928), p. 77.

48. Edward Alsworth Ross, *The Old World in the New: The Significance of Past and Present Immigration to the American People* (New York: The Century Company, 1914), pp. 285–286.

49. Ibid., p. 288.

50. Ibid., pp. 288–289.

51. Ibid., p. 293.

52. Ibid., p. 295.

53. "Social Darwinism," *American Journal of Sociology*, Vol. 12, No. 5 (March 1907), p. 715.

54. Edward A. Ross, "The Causes of Race Superiority," *Annals of the American Academy of Political and Social Science*, Vol. 18 (July 1901), p. 89.

55. Ibid., p. 85.

56. Francis A. Walker, "Methods of Restricting Immigration," *Discussions in Economics and Statistics*, Volume II: *Statistics, National Growth, Social Economics*, edited by Davis R. Dewey (New York: Henry Holt and Company, 1899), p. 430.

57. Ibid., p. 432.

58. Francis A. Walker, "Restriction of Immigration," Ibid., p. 438.

59. Ibid., p. 447.

60. Thomas C. Leonard, "Eugenics and Economics in the Progressive Era," *Journal of Economic Perspectives*, Vol. 19, No. 4 (Fall 2005), p. 211.

61. *Annual Report of the Commissioner of Indian Affairs to the Secretary of the Interior for the Year 1872* (Washington: Government Printing Office, 1872), p. 11.

62. Richard T. Ely, "Fraternalism vs. Paternalism in Government," *The Century Magazine*, Vol. 55, No. 5 (March 1898), p. 781.

63. Richard T. Ely, "The Price of Progress," *Administration*, Vol. III, No. 6 (June 1922), p. 662.

64. Sidney Fine, "Richard T. Ely, Forerunner of Progressivism, 1880–1901," *Mississippi Valley Historical Review*, Vol. 37, No. 4 (March 1951), pp. 604, 609.

65. Ibid., p. 610.

66. Ibid., p. 603.

67. "Dr. R.T. Ely Dies; Noted Economist," *New York Times*, October 5, 1943, p. 25; Richard T. Ely, "Fraternalism vs. Paternalism in Government," *The Century Magazine*, Vol. 55, No. 5 (March 1898), p. 784.

68. "Dr. R.T. Ely Dies; Noted Economist," *New York Times*, October 5, 1943, p. 25.

69. Thomas C. Leonard, "Eugenics and Economics in the Progressive Era," *Journal of Economic Perspectives*, Vol. 19, No. 4 (Fall 2005), p. 215.

70. Ibid., p. 214.

71. Ibid., p. 221.

72. Ibid., p. 212.

73. Ibid., p. 213.

74. Ibid., p. 216.

75. Ibid.

76. William E. Spellman, "The Economics of Edward Alsworth Ross," *American Journal of Economics and Sociology*, Vol. 38, No. 2 (April 1979), pp. 129–140; Howard W. Odum, "Edward Alsworth Ross: 1866–1951, *Social Forces*, Vol. 30, No. 1 (October 1951), pp. 126–127; John L. Gillin, "In Memoriam: Edward Alsworth Ross," *The Midwest Sociologist*, Vol. 14, No. 1 (Fall 1951), p. 18.

77. Edward Alsworth Ross, *Seventy Years of It: An Autobiography* (New York: D. Appleton-Century Company, 1936), pp. 97–98.

78. Julius Weinberg, *Edward Alsworth Ross and the Sociology of Progressivism* (Madison: The State Historical Society of Wisconsin, 1972), p. 136.

79. William E. Spellman, "The Economics of Edward Alsworth Ross," *American Journal of Economics and Sociology*, Vol. 38, No. 2 (April 1979), p. 130.

80. Edward Alsworth Ross, *Sin and Society: An Analysis of Latter-Day Iniquity* (Boston: Houghton-Mifflin Company, 1907), pp. ix–xi.

81. Edward Alsworth Ross, *Seventy Years of It*, p. 98.

82. Henry C. Taylor, "Richard Theodore Ely: April 13, 1854-October 4, 1943," *The Economic Journal*, Vol. 54, No. 213 (April 1944), p. 133; "Dr. R.T. Ely Dies; Noted Economist," *New York Times*, October 5, 1943, p. 25.

83. Henry C. Taylor, "Richard Theodore Ely: April 13, 1854-October 4, 1943," *The Economic Journal*, Vol. 54, No. 213 (April 1944), p. 133.

84. Ibid., p. 134.

85. Ibid., p. 137.

86. Loc. cit.

87. George McDaniel, "Madison Grant and the Racialist Movement," in Madison Grant, *The Conquest of a Continent*, p. iv.

88. Jonathan Peter Spiro, *Defending the Master Race*, pp. xv–xvi.

89. Ibid., p. 17.

90. Ibid., p. 250.

91. Jan Cohn, *Creating America: George Horace Lorimer and the Saturday Evening Post* (Pittsburgh: University of Pittsburgh Press, 1989), p. 5.

92. Ibid., pp. 49, 92, 95–96.

93. Ibid., p. 155.

94. "The Great American Myth," Saturday Evening Post, May 7, 1921, p. 20.

95. Kenneth L. Roberts, "Lest We Forget," Saturday Evening Post, April 28, 1923, pp. 158, 162.

96. Kenneth L. Roberts, *Why Europe Leaves Home* (Bobbs-Merrill Company, 1922), p. 15.

97. Ibid., p. 21.

98. Ibid., p. 22.

99. Ibid., p. 119.

100. Kenneth L. Roberts, "Slow Poison," *Saturday Evening Post*, February 2, 1924, p. 9.

101. George Creel, "Melting Pot or Dumping Ground?" *Colliers*, September 3, 1921, p. 10.

102. Ibid., p. 26.

103. George Creel, "Close the Gates!" *Collier's*, May 6, 1922, p. 10.

104. Henry L. Mencken, *The Philosophy of Friedrich Nietzsche* (Boston: Luce and Company, 1908), pp. 167–168.

105. "Mencken's Reply to La Monte's Fourth Letter," *Men versus The Man: A Correspondence Between Robert Rives La Monte, Socialist and H.L. Mencken, Individualist* (New York: Henry Holt and Company, 1910), p. 162.

106. H.L. Mencken, "The Aframerican: New Style," *The American Mercury*, February 1926, pp. 254, 255.

107. Ibid., p. 255.

108. H.L. Mencken, "Utopia by Sterilization," *The American Mercury*, August 1937, pp. 399, 408.

109. H.G. Wells, *The Work, Wealth and Happiness of Mankind* (Garden City, NY: Doubleday, Doran & Company, 1931), pp. 733, 734, 746.

110. H.G. Wells, *What Is Coming?: A European Forecast* (New York: The Macmillan Company, 1916), p. 254.

111. Jack London, *The Unpublished and Uncollected Articles and Essays*, edited by Daniel J. Wichlan (Bloomington, IN: AuthorHouse, 2007), pp. 60, 66.

112. George McDaniel, "Madison Grant and the Racialist Movement," in Madison Grant, *The Conquest of a Continent*, p. ii.

113. Arthur S. Link, *Woodrow Wilson and the Progressive Era: 1910–1917* (New York: Harper & Brothers Publishers, 1954), pp. 64–66. The number of black postmasters declined from 153 in 1910 to 78 in 1930. Gunnar Myrdal, *An American Dilemma:*

The Negro Problem and Modern Democracy (New York: Harper & Brothers Publishers, 1944), p. 327. See also Henry Blumenthal, "Woodrow Wilson and the Race Question," *Journal of Negro History*, Vol. 48, No. 1 (January 1963), pp. 1–21.

114. S. Georgia Nugent, "Changing Faces: The Princeton Student of the Twentieth Century," *Princeton University Library Chronicle*, Vol. LXII, Number 2 (Winter 2001), pp. 215–216.

115. Edmund Morris, *The Rise of Theodore Roosevelt* (New York: The Modern Library, 2001), p. 483.

116. In his memoirs, looking back on his days as a police commissioner in New York, Theodore Roosevelt said: "The appointments to the police force were made as I have described in the last chapter. We paid not the slightest attention to a man's politics or creed, or where he was born, so long as he was an American citizen; and on an average we obtained far and away the best men that had ever come into the Police Department." Theodore Roosevelt, *The Rough Riders: An Autobiography* (New York: The Library of America, 2004), p. 428.

117. Edmund Morris, *Theodore Rex* (New York: Modern Library, 2002), pp. 52–53.

118. Quoted in Bernard Lewis, *The Muslim Discovery of Europe* (New York: W. W. Norton, 1982), p. 139.

119. Edward Byron Reuter, *The Mulatto in the United States* (Boston: Richard G. Badger, The Gorham Press, 1918).

120. Theodore Hershberg and Henry Williams, "Mulattoes and Blacks: Intra-group Color Differences and Social Stratification in Nineteenth-Century Philadelphia," *Philadelphia*, edited by Theodore Hershberg (New York: Oxford University Press, 1981), p. 402.

121. For examples of the latter assumption, see, for example, Michael Tonry, *Punishing Race: A Continuing American Dilemma* (New York: Oxford University Press, 2011), pp. 65–66.

122. See, for example, E. Franklin Frazier, *The Negro in the United States*, revised edition (New York: The Macmillan Co, 1957), p. 67; David W. Cohen and Jack P. Greene, "Introduction," *Neither Slave Nor Free: The Freedmen of African Descent in the Slave Societies of the New World*, edited by David W. Cohen and Jack P. Greene (Baltimore: The Johns Hopkins University Press, 1972), p. 7; A.J.R. Russell-Wood, "Colonial Brazil," Ibid., p. 91.

123. Calculated from data in *The Seventh Census of the United States: 1850* (Washington: Robert Armstrong, 1853), pp. xliii, lxi; U.S. Bureau of the Census, *Historical Statistics of the United States: Colonial Times to 1970* (Washington: Government Printing Office, 1975), Part I, p. 382.

124. Thomas Sowell, "Three Black Histories," *Essays and Data on American Ethnic Groups*, edited by Thomas Sowell and Lynn D. Collins, p. 12.

125. Ibid.

126. Madison Grant, *The Conquest of a Continent*, pp. 283–284.

127. As noted in Chapter 7 a study of military forces in countries around the world found that "militaries fall far short of mirroring, even roughly, the multi-ethnic societies" from which they come. Cynthia H. Enloe, *Police, Military and Ethnicity: Foundations of State Power* (New Brunswick: Transaction Books, 1980), p. 143. Another massive scholarly study of ethnic groups in countries around the world concluded that, when discussing "proportional representation" of ethnic groups, "few, if any, societies have ever approximated this description." Donald L. Horowitz, *Ethnic Groups in Conflict* (Berkeley: University of California Press, 1985), p. 677. Yet another such international study of ethnic groups referred to "the universality of ethnic inequality" and pointed out that these inequalities are multi-dimensional: "All multi-ethnic societies exhibit a tendency for ethnic groups to engage in different occupations, have different levels (and, often, types) of education, receive different incomes, and occupy a different place in the social hierarchy." Myron Weiner, "The Pursuit of Ethnic Equality Through Preferential Policies: A Comparative Public Policy Perspective," *From Independence to Statehood: Managing Ethnic Conflict in Five African and Asian States*, edited by Robert B. Goldmann and A. Jeyaratnam Wilson (London: Frances Pinter, 1984), p. 64.

128. James Buchan, *Crowded with Genius: The Scottish Enlightenment, Edinburgh's Moment of the Mind* (New York: HarperCollins, 2003), p. 129.

129. See, for example, Olive and Sydney Checkland, *Industry and Ethos: Scotland 1832–1914* (Edinburgh: Edinburgh University Press, 1989), pp. 147–150; William R. Brock, *Scotus Americanus: A Survey of the Sources for Links between Scotland and America in the Eighteenth Century* (Edinburgh: Edinburgh University Press, 1982), pp. 114–115; Esmond Wright, "Education in the American Colonies: The Impact of Scotland," *Essays in Scotch-Irish History*, edited by E. R. R. Green (London: Routledge & Kegan Paul, 1969), pp. 40–41; Bruce Lenman, *Integration,*

Enlightenment, and Industrialization: Scotland 1746–1832 (Toronto: University of Toronto Press, 1981), p. 91.

130. Anders Henriksson, *The Tsar's Loyal Germans: The Riga German Community: Social Change and the Nationality Question, 1855–1905* (Boulder: East European Monographs, 1983), pp. 1, 4.

131. Ingeborg Fleischhauer, "The Germans' Role in Tsarist Russia: A Reappraisal," *The Soviet Germans*, edited by Edith Rogovin Frankel (London: C. Hurst & Company, 1986), p. 16.

132. Anders Henriksson, *The Tsar's Loyal Germans*, p. 2.

133. Ibid., pp. 15, 35, 54.

134. Ibid., p. 15.

135. Robert A. Kann and Zdeněk V. David, *The Peoples of the Eastern Habsburg Lands, 1526–1918* (Seattle: University of Washington Press, 1984), p. 201.

136. Gary B. Cohen, *The Politics of Ethnic Survival: Germans in Prague, 1861–1914* (Princeton: Princeton University Press, 1981), p. 3.

137. Ibid., Chapters 1, 2; Anders Henriksson, *The Tsar's Loyal Germans*, pp. x, 12, 34, 35, 54, 57–59, 61; Donald L. Horowitz, *Ethnic Groups in Conflict*, p. 286.

138. Gary B. Cohen, *The Politics of Ethnic Survival*, p. 28.

139. Gunnar Myrdal, *Asian Drama: An Inquiry Into the Poverty of Nations* (New York: Pantheon, 1968), Vol. III, p. 1642.

140. Mary Fainsod Katzenstein, *Ethnicity and Equality: The Shiv Sena Party and Preferential Policies in Bombay* (Ithaca: Cornell University Press, 1979), pp. 48–49.

141. Ezra Mendelsohn, *The Jews of East Central Europe Between the World Wars* (Bloomington: Indiana University Press, 1983), pp. 98–99, 106.

142. Larry Diamond, "Class, Ethnicity, and the Democratic State: Nigeria, 1950–1966," *Comparative Studies in Society and History*, Vol. 25, No. 3 (July 1983), pp. 462, 473; Donald L. Horowitz, *Ethnic Groups in Conflict*, p. 225.

143. Anatoly M. Khazanov, "The Ethnic Problems of Contemporary Kazakhstan," *Central Asian Survey*, Vol. 14, No. 2 (1995), pp. 244, 257.

144. Joseph Rothschild, *East Central Europe between the Two World Wars* (Seattle: University of Washington Press, 1992), p. 293; Irina Livezeanu, *Cultural Politics in Greater Romania: Regionalism, Nation Building, & Ethnic Struggle, 1918–1930* (Ithaca: Cornell University Press, 1995), *passim.*

145. Gunnar Myrdal, *Asian Drama*, Vol. I, p. 348; Donald L. Horowitz, *Ethnic Groups in Conflict*, p. 133.

146. Conrad Black, "Canada's Continuing Identity Crisis," *Foreign Affairs*, Vol. 74, No. 2 (March-April 1995), p. 100.

147. See, for example, Gary B. Cohen, *The Politics of Ethnic Survival*, pp. 26–28, 32, 133, 236–237; Ezra Mendelsohn, *The Jews of East Central Europe Between the World Wars*, p. 167; Hugh LeCaine Agnew, *Origins of the Czech National Renascence* (Pittsburgh: University of Pittsburgh Press, 1993), *passim*.

148. William Pfaff, *The Wrath of Nations: Civilization and the Furies of Nationalism* (New York: Simon & Schuster, 1993), p. 156.

149. Maurice Pinard and Richard Hamilton, "The Class Bases of the Quebec Independence Movement: Conjectures and Evidence," *Ethnic and Racial Studies*, Volume 7, Issue 1 (January 1984), pp. 19–54.

150. Joseph Rothschild, *East Central Europe between the Two World Wars*, p. 20; Irina Livezeanu, *Cultural Politics in Greater Romania*, pp. 56, 218, 242, 298–299.

151. Irina Livezeanu, *Cultural Politics in Greater Romania*, p. 385.

152. Chandra Richard de Silva, "Sinhala-Tamil Relations and Education in Sri Lanka: The University Admissions Issue— The First Phase, 1971–7," *From Independence to Statehood*, edited by Robert B. Goldmann and A. Jeyaratnam Wilson, p. 126.

153. Warren Zimmerman, "The Last Ambassador: A Memoir of the Collapse of Yugoslavia," *Foreign Affairs*, March-April 1995, pp. 9, 17; William Pfaff, *The Wrath of Nations*, p. 55.

154. Paul Johnson, *Modern Times*, revised edition, pp. 654–655.

155. Quoted in William Pfaff, *The Wrath of Nations*, p. 96.

156. Myron Weiner, *Sons of the Soil: Migration and Ethnic Conflict in India* (Princeton: Princeton University Press, 1978), p. 107; Donald L. Horowitz, *Ethnic Groups in Conflict*, pp. 219–224.

157. S. J. Tambiah, *Sri Lanka: Ethnic Fratricide and the Dismantling of Democracy* (Chicago: University of Chicago Press, 1986), pp. 20–21, 26; William McGowan, *Only Man is Vile: The Tragedy of Sri Lanka* (New York: Farrar, Straus and Giroux, 1992), pp. 97, 98.

158. Joseph Rothschild, *East Central Europe between the Two World Wars*, p. 92.

159. Radomír Luža, *The Transfer of the Sudeten Germans: A Study of Czech-German Relations, 1933–1962* (New York: New York University Press, 1964), pp. 9, 11, 42.

160. Ibid., p. 34.

161. Ibid., p. 290.

162. Cacilie Rohwedder, "Germans, Czechs are Hobbled by History as Europe Moves toward United Future," *Wall Street Journal*, November 25, 1996, p. A15.

163. P.T. Bauer, *Equality, the Third World and Economic Delusion* (Cambridge, Massachusetts: Harvard University Press, 1981), pp. 70–71.

164. Michael Ornstein, *Ethno-Racial Inequality in the City of Toronto: An Analysis of the 1996 Census*, May 2000, p. ii.

165. Charles H. Young and Helen R.Y. Reid, *The Japanese Canadians* (Toronto: University of Toronto Press, 1938), pp. 9–10, 49, 53, 58, 76, 120, 129, 130, 145, 172.

166. Thomas Sowell, *Black Rednecks and White Liberals* (San Francisco: Encounter Books, 2005), p. 251.

167. Elissa Gootman, "City to Help Curb Harassment of Asian Students at High School," *New York Times*, June 2, 2004, p. B9; Joe Williams, "New Attack at Horror HS; Top Senior Jumped at Brooklyn's Troubled Lafayette," *New York Daily News*, December 7, 2002, p. 7; Maki Becker, "Asian Students Hit in Rash of HS Attacks," *New York Daily News*, December 8, 2002, p. 7; Kristen A. Graham and Jeff Gammage, "Two Immigrant Students Attacked at Bok," *Philadelphia Inquirer*, September 21, 2010, p. B1; Jeff Gammage and Kristen A. Graham, "Feds Find Merit in Asian Students' Claims Against Philly School," *Philadelphia Inquirer*, August 28, 2010, p. A1; Kristen A. Graham and Jeff Gammage, "Report Released on Racial Violence at S. Phila. High," *Philadelphia Inquirer*, February 24, 2010, p. A1; Kristen A. Graham, "Other Phila. Schools Handle Racial, Ethnic Tensions," *Philadelphia Inquirer*, February 4, 2010, p. A1; Kristen A. Graham and Jeff Gammage, "Attacking Immigrant Students Not New, Say Those Involved," *Philadelphia Inquirer*, December 18, 2009, p. B1; Kristen A. Graham, "Asian Students Describe Violence at South Philadelphia High," *Philadelphia Inquirer*, December 10, 2009, p. A1.

168. See, for example, Ian Urbina, "Mobs Are Born as Word Grows By Text Message," *New York Times*, March 25, 2010, p. A1; Kirk Mitchell, "Attacks Change Lives on All Sides," *Denver Post*, December 6, 2009, pp. A1 ff; Alan Gathright, 7News Content Producer, "Black Gangs Vented Hatred for Whites in Downtown Attacks," *The DenverChannel.com*, December 5, 2009; Meg Jones, "Flynn Calls Looting, Beatings in Riverwest Barbaric," *Milwaukee Journal Sentinel*, July 6, 2011, pp. A1 ff; Mareesa Nicosia, "Four Skidmore College Students Charged in Assault; One

Charged with Felony Hate Crime," *The Saratogian* (online), December 22, 2010; "Concealing Black Hate Crimes," *Investor's Business Daily*, August 15, 2011, p. A16; Joseph A. Slobodzian, "West Philly Man Pleads Guilty to 'Flash Mob' Assault," *Philadelphia Inquirer*, June 21, 2011, pp. B1 ff; Alfred Lubrano, "What's Behind 'Flash Mobs'?" *Philadelphia Inquirer*, March 28, 2010, pp. A1 ff; Stephanie Farr, "'Geezer' Won't Let Thugs Ruin His Walks," *Philadelphia Daily News*, October 20, 2011, Local section, p. 26; Barry Paddock and John Lauinger, "Subway Gang Attack," *New York Daily News*, July 18, 2011, News, p. 3.

CHAPTER 17: RACE AND INTELLIGENCE

1. Arthur R. Jensen, *Straight Talk About Mental Tests* (New York: The Free Press, 1981), p. 171. See also, Robert C. Nichols, "Heredity, Environment, and School Achievement," *Measurement and Evaluation in Guidance*, Vol. 1, No. 2 (Summer 1968), p. 126.

2. Mark H. Haller, *Eugenics: Hereditarian Attitudes in American Thought* (New Brunswick: Rutgers University Press, 1963), p. 11.

3. The article was Arthur R. Jensen, "How Much Can We Boost IQ and Scholastic Achievement?" *Harvard Educational Review*, Vol. 39, No. 1 (Winter 1969). For examples of the reactions, see for example, Lawrence E. Davies, "Harassment Charged by Author of Article About Negroes' I.Q.'s," *New York Times*, May 19, 1969, p. 33; "Campus Totalitarians," *New York Times*, May 20, 1969, p. 46; "Panelists Assail View on Black I.Q.," *New York Times*, November 23, 1969, p. 88; Robert Reinhold, "Psychologist Arouses Storm by Linking I.Q. to Heredity," *New York Times*, March 30, 1969, p. 52; "Born Dumb?" *Newsweek*, March 31, 1969, p. 84; Maurice R. Berube, "Jensen's Complaint," *Commonweal*, October 10, 1969, pp. 42–44; "Intelligence and Race," *New Republic*, April 5, 1969, pp. 10–11; "The New Rage at Berkeley," *Newsweek*, June 2, 1969, p. 69; "Let There Be Darkness," *National Review*, October 7, 1969, pp. 996–997. For early intellectual responses by professionals, see *Environment, Heredity, and Intelligence*, Reprint Series No. 2, a 246-page reprint of articles compiled from the *Harvard Educational Review*, Vol. 39, Nos. 1 and 2 (Winter and Spring 1969).

4. Arthur R. Jensen, "How Much Can We Boost IQ and Scholastic Achievement?" *Harvard Educational Review*, Winter 1969, p. 100.

5. Ibid., p. 78.

6. Ibid., p. 100.

7. Ibid., p. 95.

8. Ibid., pp. 106, 115–117.

9. Ibid., p. 117.

10. Ibid., pp. 106, 116.

11. Ibid., p. 79.

12. Ibid., p. 95.

13. James R. Flynn, *Asian Americans: Achievement Beyond IQ* (Hillsdale, NJ: Lawrence Erlbaum Associates, Publishers, 1991), p. 1.

14. Ibid., pp. 116–117.

15. Richard J. Herrnstein and Charles Murray, *The Bell Curve: Intelligence and Class Structure in American Life* (New York: The Free Press, 1994), pp. 70–74; Robert Klitgaard, *Choosing Elites* (New York: Basic Books, 1985), pp. 104–115; Stanley Sue and Jennifer Abe, *Predictors of Academic Achievement Among Asian American and White Students* (New York: College Entrance Examination Board, 1988), p. 1; Robert A. Gordon and Eileen E. Rudert, "Bad News Concerning IQ Tests," *Sociology of Education*, July 1979, p. 176; Frank L. Schmidt and John E. Hunter, "Employment Testing: Old Theories and New Research Findings," *American Psychologist*, October 1981, p. 1131; Arthur R. Jensen, "Selection of Minority Students in Higher Education," *University of Toledo Law Review*, Spring-Summer 1970, pp. 440, 443; Donald A. Rock, "Motivation, Moderators, and Test Bias," Ibid., pp. 536, 537; Ronald L. Flaugher, *Testing Practices, Minority Groups, and Higher Education: A Review and Discussion of the Research* (Princeton: Educational Testing Service, 1970), p. 11; Arthur R. Jensen, *Bias in Mental Testing* (New York: The Free Press, 1980), pp. 479–490.

16. Richard Lynn, *Race Differences in Intelligence: An Evolutionary Analysis* (Augusta, GA: Washington Summit Publishers, 2006), pp. 124–125.

17. Robert Klitgaard, *Choosing Elites*, pp. 161–165.

18. The Supreme Court said, in *Griggs v. Duke Power Company*, that any job criteria "must have a manifest relationship to the employment in question." *Griggs v. Duke Power Company*, 401 U.S. 424 (1971), at 432. But what is "manifest" to third parties with neither expertise in psychometrics nor practical experience in the particular business, much less a stake in the outcome, is something that can be

known only after the fact, and is thus essentially *ex post facto* law that is expressly forbidden by the Constitution in Article I, Section 9.

19. Ian Ayres, *Super Crunchers: Why Thinking-by-Numbers Is the New Way to Be Smart* (New York: Bantam Books, 2007), pp. 2–3, 6; Mark Strauss, "The Grapes of Math," *Discover*, January 1991, pp. 50–51; Jay Palmer, "Grape Expectations," *Barron's*, December 30, 1996, pp. 17–19.

20. Robert Klitgaard, *Choosing Elites*, pp. 161–165.

21. Robert Klitgaard, *Elitism and Meritocracy in Developing Countries: Selection Policies for Higher Education* (Baltimore: The Johns Hopkins University Press, 1986), pp. 77–84.

22. Ibid., pp. 124, 147.

23. Malcolm Gladwell, *Outliers: The Story of Success* (New York: Little, Brown and Company, 2008), pp. 74, 112.

24. Philip E. Vernon, *Intelligence and Cultural Environment* (London: Methuen & Co., Ltd., 1969), p. 145.

25. Ibid., pp. 157–158.

26. Ibid., p. 168.

27. Mandel Sherman and Cora B. Key, "The Intelligence of Isolated Mountain Children," *Child Development*, Vol. 3, No. 4 (December 1932), p. 284.

28. Philip E. Vernon, *Intelligence and Cultural Environment*, p. 104.

29. Ibid., p. 101.

30. Ibid., p. 155.

31. Robert M. Yerkes, *Psychological Examining in the United States Army*, Memoirs of the National Academy of Sciences (Washington: Government Printing Office, 1921), Vol. 15, p. 705.

32. Arthur R. Jensen, "How Much Can We Boost IQ and Scholastic Achievement?" *Harvard Educational Review*, Winter 1969, p. 81.

33. William G. Bowen and Derek Bok, *The Shape of the River: Long-Term Consequences of Considering Race in College and University Admissions* (Princeton: Princeton University Press, 1998), p. 61. See also p. 259.

34. Bob Zelnick, *Backfire: A Reporter's Look at Affirmative Action* (Washington: Regnery Publishing, 1996), p. 132.

35. Robert Lerner and Althea K. Nagai, "Racial Preferences in Colorado Higher Education," Center for Equal Opportunity, pp. 6, 11.

36. William G. Bowen and Derek Bok, *The Shape of the River*, p. 21.

37. Stephan Thernstrom and Abigail Thernstrom, "Reflections on *The Shape of the River*," *UCLA Law Review*, Vol. 46, No. 5 (June 1999), p. 1589.

38. Arthur R. Jensen, "How Much Can We Boost IQ and Scholastic Achievement?" *Harvard Educational Review*, Winter 1969, p. 78.

39. Charles Murray, *Human Accomplishment: The Pursuit of Excellence in the Arts and Sciences, 800 B.C. to 1950* (New York: HarperCollins, 2003), p. 282.

40. Paul A. Witty and Martin D. Jenkins, "The Educational Achievement of a Group of Gifted Negro Children," *Journal of Educational Psychology*, Vol. 25, Issue 8 (November 1934), p. 593; Paul Witty and Viola Theman, "A Follow-up Study of Educational Attainment of Gifted Negroes," *Journal of Educational Psychology*, Vol. 34, Issue 1 (January 1943), pp. 35–47; Edelbert G. Rodgers, *The Relationship of Certain Measurable Factors in the Personal and Educational Backgrounds of Two Groups of Baltimore Negroes, Identified as Superior and Average in Intelligence as Fourth Grade Children, to their Educational, Social and Economic Achievement in Adulthood* (Unpublished Doctoral Dissertation, New York University, 1956), University Microfilms, unpaged introduction and pp. 75–94.

41. Otto Klineberg, "Mental Testing of Racial and National Groups," *Scientific Aspects of the Race Problem*, edited by H.S. Jennings, et al (Washington: Catholic University Press, 1941), p. 282.

42. Rudolf Pintner, *Intelligence Testing: Methods and Results* (New York: Henry Holt and Company, 1923), p. 352; Clifford Kirkpatrick, *Intelligence and Immigration* (Baltimore: The Williams & Wilkins Company, 1926), pp. 24, 31, 34.

43. Philip E. Vernon, *Intelligence and Cultural Environment*, p. 155; Lester R. Wheeler, "A Comparative Study of the Intelligence of East Tennessee Mountain Children," *The Journal of Educational Psychology*, Vol. XXXIII, No. 5 (May 1942), pp. 322, 324.

44. Philip E. Vernon, *Intelligence and Cultural Environment*, p. 104.

45. Carl C. Brigham, *A Study of American Intelligence* (Princeton: Princeton University Press, 1923), p. xx.

46. Ibid., p. 110.

47. Carl C. Brigham, "Intelligence Tests of Immigrant Groups," *Psychological Review*, Vol. 37, Issue 2 (March 1930), p. 165.

48. Carl C. Brigham, *A Study of American Intelligence*, p. 29.

49. James R. Flynn, "The Mean IQ of Americans: Massive Gains 1932 to 1978," *Psychological Bulletin*, Vol. 95, No. 1, pp. 29–51; James R. Flynn, "Massive IQ Gains in 14 Nations: What IQ Tests Really Measure," *Psychological Bulletin*, Vol. 101, No. 2, pp. 171–191.

50. James R. Flynn, *Where Have All the Liberals Gone?: Race, Class, and Ideals in America* (Cambridge: Cambridge University Press, 2008), pp. 72–73, 87.

51. Ibid., pp. 110–111.

52. Ibid., pp. 89, 90.

53. Eric A. Hanushek, et al., "New Evidence About *Brown v. Board of Education*: The Complex Effects of School Racial Composition on Achievement," National Bureau of Economic Research, Working Paper 8741 (Cambridge, Massachusetts: National Bureau of Economic Research, 2002), Abstract.

54. See, for example, Paul Brest, "Some Comments on *Grutter v. Bollinger*," *Drake Law Review*, Vol. 51, p. 691; Gabriel J. Chin, "*Bakke* to the Wall: The Crisis of *Bakkean* Diversity," *William & Mary Bill of Rights Journal*, Vol. 4, No. 3 (1995–1996), pp. 888, 921–923; *Hopwood v. Texas Litigation Documents*, Part I, Volume 3, compiled by Kumar Percy (Buffalo, N.Y.: William S. Hein & Co., Inc., 2002), Document No. 57, "Deposition of Dean Paul Brest," pp. 32, 33–34, 35, 36, 38–39; *Hopwood v. Texas Litigation Documents*, Part I, Volume 3, compiled by Kumar Percy, Document No. 58, "Deposition of Lee Carroll Bollinger," pp. 35–36, 38–39; *Hopwood v. Texas Litigation Documents*, Part I, Volume 3, compiled by Kumar Percy, Document No. 60, "Oral Deposition of Judith Wegner," pp. 14–15.

55. Ellis B. Page and Timothy Z. Keith, "The Elephant in the Classroom: Ability Grouping and the Gifted," *Intellectual Talent: Psychometric and Social Issues*, edited by Camilla Persson Benbow and David Lubinski (Baltimore: The Johns Hopkins University Press, 1996), p. 208.

56. Edelbert G. Rodgers, *The Relationship of Certain Measurable Factors in the Personal and Educational Backgrounds of Two Groups of Baltimore Negroes, Identified as Superior and Average in Intelligence as Fourth Grade Children, to their Educational, Social and Economic Achievement in Adulthood* (Unpublished Doctoral Dissertation, New York University, 1956), University Microfilms, p. 50.

57. Stuart Buck, *Acting White: The Ironic Legacy of Desegregation* (New Haven: Yale University Press, 2010), pp. 11–17.

58. Theodore Dalrymple, *Life at the Bottom: The Worldview that Makes the Underclass* (Chicago: Ivan R. Dee, 2001), p. 69.

59. See Mary Gibson Hundley, *The Dunbar Story (1870–1955)* (New York: Vantage Press, 1965), p. 75.

60. Jervis Anderson, "A Very Special Monument," *The New Yorker,* March 20, 1978, p. 105.

61. Otto Klineberg, "Mental Testing of Racial and National Groups," *Scientific Aspects of the Race Problem,* edited by H.S. Jennings, et al., p. 280.

62. Arthur R. Jensen, "How Much Can We Boost IQ and Scholastic Achievement?" *Harvard Educational Review,* Winter 1969, pp. 86–87.

63. Clifford Kirkpatrick, *Intelligence and Immigration,* p. 31; Lester R. Wheeler, "A Comparative Study of the Intelligence of East Tennessee Mountain Children," *The Journal of Educational Psychology,* Vol. XXXIII, No. 5 (May 1942), pp. 326–327.

64. H.J. Butcher, *Human Intelligence: Its Nature and Assessment* (New York: Harper & Row, 1968), p. 252.

65. Alexis de Tocqueville, *Democracy in America* (New York: Alfred A. Knopf, 1966), Vol. I, p. 365; Frederick Law Olmsted, *The Cotton Kingdom: A Traveller's Observations on Cotton and Slavery in the American Slave States,* edited by Arthur M. Schlesinger (New York: Modern Library, 1969), pp. 476n, 614–622; Hinton Rowan Helper, *The Impending Crisis of the South: How to Meet It,* enlarged edition (New York: A. B. Burdick, 1860), p. 34; Gunnar Myrdal, *An American Dilemma: The Negro Problem and Modern Democracy* (New York: Harper & Brothers, 1944), p. 70n.

66. David Hackett Fischer, *Albion's Seed: Four British Folkways in America* (Oxford: Oxford University Press, 1989), pp. 31–36, 72–77, 89–90, 120–121, 130–134, 233, 236–240, 252, 256–261, 284–285, 298, 303, 344–349, 368, 618–639, 674–675, 680–681, 703–708, 721–723. See also Grady McWhiney, *Cracker Culture: Celtic Ways in the Old South* (Tuscaloosa: University of Alabama Press, 1988), pp. 16–18.

67. Gunnar Myrdal, *An American Dilemma,* p. 70n.

68. Paul A. Witty and Martin D. Jenkins, "The Educational Achievement of a Group of Gifted Negro Children," *Journal of Educational Psychology,* Vol. 25, Issue 8 (November 1934), p. 593; Paul Witty and Viola Theman, "A Follow-up Study of Educational Attainment of Gifted Negroes," *Journal of Educational Psychology,* Vol. 34, Issue 1 (January 1943), p. 43; Edelbert G. Rodgers, *The Relationship of Certain Measurable Factors in the Personal and Educational Backgrounds of Two*

Groups of Baltimore Negroes, Identified as Superior and Average in Intelligence as Fourth Grade Children, to their Educational, Social and Economic Achievement in Adulthood (Unpublished Doctoral Dissertation, New York University, 1956), University Microfilms, unpaged introduction and pp. 75–94.

69.   Sandra Scarr and Richard A. Weinberg, "IQ Test Performance of Black Children Adopted by White Families," *American Psychologist*, October 1976, p. 731.

70.   See, for example, Leonard Covello, *The Social Background of the Italo-American School Child* (Totowa, N.J.: Rowman and Littlefield, 1972), pp. 241–261; Charles Murray, *Human Accomplishment*, p. 291; Richard Gambino, *Blood of My Blood: The Dilemma of the Italian-Americans* (Garden City, N.Y.: Doubleday & Co., 1974), p. 225.

71.   Thomas Sowell, "Assumptions versus History in Ethnic Education," *Teachers College Record*, Volume 83, Number 1 (Fall 1981), pp. 43–45.

72.   Ibid., p. 45.

73.   Kathryn G. Caird, "A Note on the Progress of Preference Students in First Year Accounting Courses," internal memorandum, University of Auckland (undated but probably 1989).

74.   Patricia Cohen, "'Culture of Poverty' Makes a Comeback," *New York Times*, October 18, 2010, pp. A1 ff.

75.   Richard J. Herrnstein and Charles Murray, *The Bell Curve*, p. 298.

76.   Daniel Schwekendiek, "Height and Weight Differences Between North and South Korea," *Journal of Biosocial Science*, Vol. 41, No. 1 (January 2009), p. 51–55.

77.   Richard J. Herrnstein and Charles Murray, *The Bell Curve*, p. 309.

78.   Ibid., p. 304.

79.   Ibid., p. 311.

80.   Ibid., p. 310.

81.   Ibid., p. 314.

82.   John B. Judis, "Hearts of Darkness," *The Bell Curve Wars: Race, Intelligence, and the Future of America*, edited by Steven Fraser (New York: Basic Books, 1995), pp. 126–127, 128.

83.   Michael Lind, "Brave New Right," Ibid., pp. 172, 174.

84.   Steven Fraser, "Introduction," Ibid., p. 1.

85.   Randall Kennedy, "The Phony War," Ibid., p. 182.

86.   Stephen Jay Gould, "Curveball," Ibid., pp. 11, 20.

87. Henry Louis Gates, Jr., "Why Now?" Ibid., pp. 95–96. As a matter of fact, *The Bell Curve* does not say that environment plays no role. Moreover, the word "dismissal" implies not simply a rejection but a rejection without consideration. Nevertheless, even when a proposition is rejected after extensive examination and consideration, the word "dismissal" is often used by those more interested in its propaganda effect than with its accuracy.

88. Nathan Glazer, "Scientific Truth and the American Dilemma," Ibid., p. 141.

89. Ibid., p. 147.

CHAPTER 18: LIBERALISM AND MULTICULTURALISM

1. Paul Hollander, *Anti-Americanism: Critiques at Home and Abroad 1965–1990* (New York: Oxford University Press, 1992), p. 455.

2. See, for example, Richard Lynn, "The Intelligence of American Jews," *Personality and Individual Differences*, Vol. 36, No. 1 (January 2004), p. 204; Richard Lynn and David Longley, "On the High Intelligence and Cognitive Achievements of Jews in Britain," *Intelligence*, Vol. 34, No. 6 (November-December 2006), p. 542.

3. Matthew Pratt Guterl, *The Color of Race in America 1900–1940* (Cambridge, Mass.: Harvard University Press, 2001), p. 67.

4. "The Passing of the Nordic Myth," *The Christian Century*, June 16, 1937, p. 765.

5. Franz Samelson, "From 'Race Psychology' to 'Studies in Prejudice': Some Observations on the Thematic Reversal in Social Psychology," *Journal of the History of the Behavioral Sciences*, Vol. 14 (1978), p. 268.

6. Otto Klineberg, "Mental Testing of Racial and National Groups," *Scientific Aspects of the Race Problem*, edited by H.S. Jennings, et al (Washington: Catholic University Press, 1941), p. 284.

7. Gunnar Myrdal, *An American Dilemma: The Negro Problem and Modern Democracy* (New York: Harper & Brothers, 1944), p. li. Within the main body of the book itself, this premise was explicitly repeated— "The Negro problem is primarily a white man's problem" (p. 669)— as well as being implicit in the whole approach taken.

8. Ibid., p. xlvii.

9. David W. Southern, *Gunnar Myrdal and Black-White Relations* (Baton Rouge: Louisiana State University Press, 1987), p. 74.

10. Alfred W. Blumrosen, *Black Employment and the Law* (New Brunswick: Rutgers University Press, 1971), p. vii.

11. James Baldwin, "Fifth Avenue, Uptown," *Esquire*, July 1960, pp. 73, 76.

12. Theodore Dalrymple, *Life at the Bottom: The Worldview That Makes the Underclass* (Chicago: Ivan R. Dee, 2001), p. 150.

13. Whitney M. Young, "The High Cost of Discrimination," *Ebony*, August 1965, p. 51.

14. Paul Johnson, *Enemies of Society* (New York: Atheneum, 1977), p. 237.

15. Kenneth Clark, "Behind the Harlem Riots— Two Views," *New York Herald Tribune*, July 20, 1964, pp. 1, 7.

16. Newton Garver, "What Violence Is," *The Nation*, June 24, 1968, pp. 821, 822.

17. National Committee of Negro Churchmen, "'Black Power,'" *New York Times*, July 31, 1966, p. E5.

18. Louis Harris, "U.S. Riots: Negroes, Whites Offer Views," *Los Angeles Times*, August 14, 1967, p. A5.

19. Frank Clifford and David Farrell, "L.A. Strongly Condemns King Verdicts, Riots," *Los Angeles Times*, May 6, 1992, pp. A1, A4.

20. "The Hard-Core Ghetto Mood," *Newsweek*, August 21, 1967, pp. 20, 21.

21. Ibid., p. 20.

22. Stephan Thernstrom and Abigail Thernstrom, *America in Black and White: One Nation, Indivisible* (New York: Simon & Schuster, 1997), p. 162.

23. Donald L. Horowitz, *Ethnic Groups in Conflict* (Berkeley: University of California Press, 1985), pp. 170–181; Robert A. Wilson and Bill Hosokawa, *East to America: A History of the Japanese in the United States* (New York: William Morrow, 1980), p. 123.

24. Mahathir bin Mohamad, *The Malay Dilemma* (Singapore: Asia Pacific Press, 1970), p. 25.

25. Myron Weiner, *Sons of the Soil: Migration and Ethnic Conflict in India* (Princeton: Princeton University Press, 1978), p. 250.

26. John A. A. Ayoade, "Ethnic Management of the 1979 Nigerian Constitution," *Canadian Review of Studies in Nationalism*, Spring 1987, p. 127.

27. "America Can't Be Colorblind Yet," *New York Times*, June 10, 1981, p. A30.

28. U.S. Bureau of the Census, *Historical Statistics of the United States: Colonial Times to 1957* (Washington, D.C.: U.S. Government Printing Office, 1960), p. 72.

29. Richard Vedder and Lowell Galloway, "Declining Black Employment," *Society*, July-August 1993, p. 57.

30. Walter Williams, *Race & Economics: How Much Can Be Blamed on Discrimination?* (Stanford: Hoover Institution Press, 2011), p. 42.

31. Ibid.

32. Ibid., pp. 33–34.

33. Charles H. Young and Helen R.Y. Reid, *The Japanese Canadians* (Toronto: University of Toronto Press, 1938), p. 49; Merle Lipton, *Capitalism and Apartheid: South Africa, 1910–84* (Totowa, New Jersey: Rowman & Allanheld, 1985), pp. 19–20; George M. Fredrickson, *White Supremacy: A Comparative Study in American and South African History* (New York: Oxford University Press, 1981), p. 233.

34. "A Divided Self: A Survey of France," *The Economist*, November 16, 2002, p. 11; Holman W. Jenkins, Jr., "Shall We Eat Our Young?" *Wall Street Journal*, January 19, 2005, p. A13; Nelson D. Schwartz, "Young, Down and Out in Europe," *New York Times*, January 1, 2010, pp. B1, B4.

35. See, for example, Gilbert Osofsky, *Harlem: The Making of a Ghetto* (New York: Harper and Row, 1966), p. 12; David Katzman, *Before the Ghetto: Black Detroit in the Nineteenth Century* (Urbana, IL: University of Illinois Press, 1973), pp. 35, 37, 102, 138, 139, 160; W.E.B. Du Bois, *The Philadelphia Negro: A Social Study* (New York: Schocken Books, 1967), p. 7; Constance McLaughlin Green, *The Secret City: A History of Race Relations in the Nation's Capital* (Princeton: Princeton University Press, 1967), p. 127; St. Clair Drake and Horace R. Cayton, *Black Metropolis: A Study of Negro Life in a Northern City* (New York: Harper & Row, 1962), Vol. I, pp. 44–45, 176n; Allan H. Spear, *Black Chicago: The Making of a Negro Ghetto, 1890–1920* (Chicago: University of Chicago Press, 1970), Chapter 1; Reynolds Farley, et al., *Detroit Divided* (New York: Russell Sage Foundation, 2000), pp. 145–146; Oliver Zunz, *The Changing Face of Inequality: Urbanization, Industrial Development, and Immigrants in Detroit, 1880–1920* (Chicago: University of Chicago Press, 1982), p. 353; Willard B. Gatewood, *Aristocrats of Color: The Black Elite, 1880–1920* (Bloomington: Indiana University Press, 1990), pp. 119, 125.

36. W.E.B. Du Bois, *The Philadelphia Negro*, pp. 41–42, 305–306.

37. Jacob Riis, *How the Other Half Lives: Studies among the Tenements of New York* (Cambridge, Mass.: Harvard University Press, 1970), p. 99; David Katzman, *Before the Ghetto*, pp. 35, 37, 102, 138, 139, 160; St. Clair Drake and Horace R.

Cayton, *Black Metropolis*, Vol. I, pp. 44–45; Willard B. Gatewood, *Aristocrats of Color*, pp. 119, 125.

38. Edward Glaeser and Jacob Vigdor, "The End of The Segregated Century: Racial Separation in America's Neighborhoods, 1890–2010," *Civic Report*, No. 66 (January 2012), pp. 3–4.

39. David Katzman, *Before the Ghetto*, pp. 35, 37, 102, 138, 139, 160; St. Clair Drake and Horace R. Cayton, *Black Metropolis*, Vol. I, pp. 44–45.

40. Oscar Handlin, *The Newcomers: Negroes and Puerto Ricans in a Changing Metropolis* (New York: Anchor Books, 1962), p. 46.

41. Jacob Riis, *How the Other Half Lives*, p. 99.

42. W.E.B. Du Bois, *The Philadelphia Negro*, pp. 33–36, 119–121.

43. E. Franklin Frazier, *The Negro in the United States*, revised edition (New York: The Macmillan Company, 1957), p. 405.

44. St. Clair Drake and Horace R. Cayton, *Black Metropolis*, Vol. I, p. 176n. See also Allan H. Spear, *Black Chicago*, Chapter 1.

45. See the title article in my *Black Rednecks and White Liberals* (San Francisco: Encounter Books, 2005).

46. W.E.B. Du Bois, *The Black North in 1901: A Social Study* (New York: Arno Press, 1969), p. 39.

47. Gilbert Osofsky, *Harlem*, pp. 43–44.

48. E. Franklin Frazier, *The Negro in the United States*, revised edition, p. 643.

49. Ibid., p. 630.

50. Gunnar Myrdal, *An American Dilemma*, p. 965.

51. See, for example, Willard B. Gatewood, *Aristocrats of Color*, pp. 186–187, 332; Allan H. Spear, *Black Chicago*, p. 168; E. Franklin Frazier, *The Negro in the United States*, revised edition, pp. 284–285; Florette Henri, *Black Migration: Movement North, 1900–1920* (Garden City, New York: Anchor Press, 1975), pp. 96–97; Gilbert Osofsky, *Harlem*, pp. 43–44; Ivan H. Light, *Ethnic Enterprise in America* (Berkeley: University of California Press, 1972), Figure 1 (after p. 100); W.E.B. Du Bois, *The Black North in 1901*, p. 25.

52. Willard B. Gatewood, *Aristocrats of Color*, pp. 65, 250; E. Franklin Frazier, *The Negro in the United States*, revised edition, pp. 250–251, 441; Davison M. Douglas, *Jim Crow Moves North: The Battle over Northern School Segregation, 1865–1954* (Cambridge: Cambridge University Press, 2005), pp. 137–153.

53. Douglas Henry Daniels, *Pioneer Urbanites: A Social and Cultural History of Black San Francisco* (Philadelphia: Temple University Press, 1980), pp. 171–173; E. Franklin Frazier, *The Negro in the United States*, revised edition, pp. 270–271.

54. See, for example, Isabel Wilkerson, *The Warmth of Other Suns: The Epic Story of America's Great Migration* (New York: Random House, 2010), p. 291; Irving Howe, *World of Our Fathers* (New York: Harcourt Brace Jovanovich, 1976), pp. 229–230.

55. Irving Howe, *World of Our Fathers*, pp. 229–230.

56. Isabel Wilkerson, *The Warmth of Other Suns*, p. 291.

57. Michael Tobias, "Dialectical Dreaming: The Western Perception of Mountain People," *Mountain People*, edited by Michael Tobias (Norman: University of Oklahoma Press, 1986), p. 191.

58. James M. McPherson, "Deconstructing Affirmative Action," *Perspectives* (American Historical Association), April 2003, online edition.

59. Ibid.

60. *United Steelworkers of America, AFL-CIO-CLC v. Weber*, 443 U.S. (1979), at 212.

61. *Regents of the University of California v. Bakke*, 438 U.S. (1978), at 265, 365–366.

62. Ibid., at 374 n.58.

63. Yasuo Wakatsuki, "Japanese Emigration to the United States, 1866–1924: A Monograph," *Perspectives in American History*, edited by Donald Fleming (Cambridge, Mass.: Crimson Printing Company, 1979), Vol. XII, pp. 441–442.

64. See, for example, Tetsuro Nakaoka, "The Transfer of Cotton Manufacturing Technology from Britain to Japan," *International Technology Transfer: Europe, Japan and the USA, 1700–1914*, edited by David J. Jeremy (Brookfield, VT: Edward Elgar, 1991), pp. 181–198; Takeshi Yuzawa, "The Transfer of Railway Technologies from Britain to Japan, with Special Reference to Locomotive Manufacture," Ibid., pp. 199–218; Hoshimi Uchida, "The Transfer of Electrical Technologies from the United States to Japan, 1869–1914," Ibid., pp. 219–241.

65. Yasuo Wakatsuki, "Japanese Emigration to the United States, 1866–1924: A Monograph," *Perspectives in American History*, edited by Donald Fleming, Vol. XII, p. 431. See also p. 434.

66. Ibid., pp. 430–434.

67. Ibid., p. 440.

68. Ibid., pp. 430, 438.

69.   President Wm. W. Patton, "Change of Environment," *The American Missionary*, Vol. XXXVI, No. 8 (August 1882), p. 229.

70.   James D. Anderson, *The Education of Blacks in the South, 1860–1935* (Chapel Hill: University of North Carolina Press, 1988), p. 46.

71.   "Principal of the Hampton Institute at the Anniversary Meeting of the American Missionary Association at Syracuse, N.Y., October 24, 1877," *Southern Workman*, Vol. VI, No. 12 (December 1877), pp. 94–95.

72.   James M. McPherson, *The Abolitionist Legacy: From Reconstruction to the NAACP* (Princeton: Princeton University Press, 1975), p. 178.

73.   Henry S. Robinson, "The M Street High School, 1891–1916," *Records of the Columbia Historical Society*, Washington, D.C., Vol. LI (1984), p. 122; *Report of the Board of Trustees of Public Schools of the District of Columbia to the Commissioners of the District of Columbia: 1898–99* (Washington: Government Printing Office, 1900), pp. 7, 11.

74.   See my *Black Rednecks and White Liberals*, pp. 39–40, 204–211, 213–214.

75.   "Separate educational facilities are inherently unequal." *Brown v. Board of Education*, 347 U.S. 483 (1954), at 495. Among other unsubstantiated assertions in the *Brown* decision was that a racially segregated school system "generates a feeling of inferiority as to their status in the community that may affect their hearts and minds in a way unlikely ever to be undone" and that this "sense of inferiority affects the motivation of a child to learn." Ibid., at 494. As one of those black children who went to a segregated school in the South in the 1930s, I cannot recall anyone who even commented on the absence of white children in our school, much less anyone so preoccupied with their absence as to interfere with our learning. There were no white children in our neighborhood, on our playgrounds or in our churches. If we had found them in our schools, we would have wondered what was going on. Whether the Constitution of the United States permits government to racially segregate school children or other people is a serious legal question. But sociological and psychological speculations hardly seem like a serious legal basis for such a landmark Supreme Court decision.

76.   Jason L. Riley, "Charter Schools Flourish in Harlem," *Wall Street Journal*, March 8, 2010, p. A21.

77.   See, for example, William H. McNeill, *The Rise of the West: A History of the Human Community* (Chicago: University of Chicago Press, 1991), pp. xxvi, 48, 63, 68, 98,

102–103, 108, 148, 168, 229, 233, 250, 251, 252, 272–287, 298, 299, 330, 357, 361, 373–374, 379, 384, 390–391, 392, 398, 412, 419, 420, 437–438, 448n, 464, 465n, 469, 476, 477, 478, 479, 483, 485, 501, 506, 512, 530–531, 535, 536, 548, 550, 555, 558, 566, 578, 599, 600–601, 606, 633, 643, 646n, 651, 656, 660, 665, 666, 671, 674, 730, 776–777, 782, 787–788; John K. Fairbank, Edwin O. Reischauer, and Albert M. Craig, *East Asia: Tradition & Transformation*, revised edition (Boston: Houghton Mifflin Co., 1989), pp. 38, 77, 107, 112, 174, 243, 260, 300–302, 310, 324, 335, 354, 355, 429, 515, 530, 562–563; E. L. Jones, *The European Miracle: Environments, Economies, and Geopolitics in the History of Europe and Asia*, second edition (Cambridge: Cambridge University Press, 1987), pp. xxi, 45, 54, 57–58, 60, 73, 83, 115–116, 179–180.

78.   David S. Landes, *The Wealth and Poverty of Nations: Why Some Are So Rich and Some So Poor* (New York: W.W. Norton, 1998), p. 4.

CHAPTER 19: RACE AND COSMIC JUSTICE

1.   Andrew Hacker, *Two Nations: Black and White, Separate, Hostile, Unequal* (New York: Charles Scribner's Sons, 1992), p. 53.

2.   Ibid., pp. xi, 19, 27.

3.   Ibid., p. 29.

4.   Ibid., p. 51.

5.   Ibid., p. 23.

6.   Gunnar Myrdal, *An American Dilemma: The Negro Problem and Modern Democracy* (New York: Harper & Brothers 1944), p. 964.

7.   Tom Wicker, "The Worst Fear," *New York Times*, April 28, 1989, p. A39.

8.   Susannah Meadows and Evan Thomas, "What Happened At Duke?" *Newsweek*, May 1, 2006, p. 51.

9.   Meg Jones, "Flynn Calls Looting, Beatings in Riverwest Barbaric," *Milwaukee Journal Sentinel*, July 6, 2011, pp. A1 ff.

10.   See, for example, Ian Urbina, "Mobs Are Born as Word Grows By Text Message," *New York Times*, March 25, 2010, p. A1; Kirk Mitchell, "Attacks Change Lives on All Sides," *Denver Post*, December 6, 2009, pp. A1 ff; Alan Gathright, 7News Content Producer, "Black Gangs Vented Hatred for Whites in Downtown Attacks," *The DenverChannel.com*, December 5, 2009; Meg Jones, "Flynn Calls Looting, Beatings in Riverwest Barbaric," *Milwaukee Journal Sentinel*, July 6, 2011, pp. A1 ff; Mareesa

Nicosia, "Four Skidmore College Students Charged in Assault; One Charged with Felony Hate Crime," *The Saratogian* (online), December 22, 2010; "Concealing Black Hate Crimes," *Investor's Business Daily*, August 15, 2011, p. A16; Joseph A. Slobodzian, "West Philly Man Pleads Guilty to 'Flash Mob' Assault," *Philadelphia Inquirer*, June 21, 2011, pp. B1 ff; Alfred Lubrano, "What's Behind 'Flash Mobs'?" *Philadelphia Inquirer*, March 28, 2010, pp. A1 ff; Stephanie Farr, "'Geezer' Won't Let Thugs Ruin His Walks," *Philadelphia Daily News*, October 20, 2011, Local section, p. 26; Barry Paddock and John Lauinger, "Subway Gang Attack," *New York Daily News*, July 18, 2011, News, p. 3.

11. Steve Chapman, "Race and the 'Flash Mob' Attacks," *Chicago Tribune*, June 8, 2011 (online).

12. Daniel J. Losen, Executive Summary, "Discipline Policies, Successful Schools, and Racial Justice," National Education Policy Center, School of Education, University of Colorado Boulder, October 2011.

13. David D. Cole, "Can Our Shameful Prisons Be Reformed?" *New York Review of Books*, November 19, 2009, p. 41.

14. Ibid.

15. Ibid.

16. Ibid.

17. See, for example, Theodore Dalrymple, *Life at the Bottom: The Worldview That Makes the Underclass* (Chicago: Ivan R. Dee, 2001), p. 69.

18. "Historical Poverty Tables: Table 4," U.S. Bureau of the Census, Current Population Survey, Annual Social and Economic Supplements. Downloaded June 29, 2007 from: http://www.census.govhhes/www/poverty/histpov/hstpov4.html.

19. Martin A. Klein, "Introduction," *Breaking the Chains: Slavery, Bondage, and Emancipation in Modern Africa and Asia*, edited by Martin A. Klein (Madison: University of Wisconsin Press, 1993), pp. 19, 20. As of 1840, there were still more slaves in India than those emancipated by the British in the Caribbean. David Brion Davis, *The Problem of Slavery in the Age of Revolution 1770–1823* (Ithaca: Cornell University Press, 1975), p. 63.

20. Martin A. Klein, "Introduction," *Breaking the Chains*, edited by Martin A. Klein, p. 8.

21. Ibid., p. 11.

22. John Stuart Mill, "Considerations on Representative Government," *Collected Works of John Stuart Mill*, Vol. XIX: *Essays on Politics and Society*, edited by J.M. Robson (Toronto: University of Toronto Press, 1977), p. 395.

23. Abraham Lincoln to Albert G. Hodges, April 4, 1864, reprinted in *The Collected Works of Abraham Lincoln*, edited by Roy P. Basler (New Brunswick: Rutgers University Press, 1953), Vol. VII, p. 281.

24. Kevin Bales, "The Social Psychology of Modern Slavery," *Scientific American*, April 2002, pp. 80–88.

25. Orlando Patterson, *Slavery and Social Death: A Comparative Study* (Cambridge, Mass.: Harvard University Press, 1982), pp. 406–407; W. Montgomery Watt, *The Influence of Islam on Medieval Europe* (Edinburgh: Edinburgh University Press, 1972), p. 19; Bernard Lewis, *Race and Slavery in the Middle East: An Historical Enquiry* (New York: Oxford University Press, 1990), p. 11; Daniel Evans, "Slave Coast of Europe," *Slavery & Abolition*, Vol. 6, Number 1 (May 1985), p. 53, note 3; William D. Phillips, Jr., *Slavery from Roman Times to the Early Transatlantic Trade* (Minneapolis: University of Minnesota Press, 1985), p. 57.

26. Robert C. Davis, *Christian Slaves, Muslim Masters: White Slavery in the Mediterranean, the Barbary Coast, and Italy, 1500–1800* (New York: Palgrave Macmillan, 2003), p. 23; Philip D. Curtin, *The Atlantic Slave Trade: A Census* (Madison: University of Wisconsin Press, 1969), pp. 72, 75, 87.

27. Daniel J. Boorstin, *The Americans*, Vol. II: *The National Experience* (New York: Random House, 1965), p. 203.

28. Alexis de Tocqueville, *Democracy in America* (New York: Alfred A. Knopf, 1966), Vol. I, p. 365; Frederick Law Olmsted, *The Cotton Kingdom: A Traveller's Observations on Cotton and Slavery in the American Slave States*, edited by Arthur M. Schlesinger (New York: Modern Library, 1969), pp. 476n, 614–622; Hinton Rowan Helper, *The Impending Crisis of the South: How to Meet It*, enlarged edition (New York: A. B. Burdick, 1860), p. 34.

29. David Hackett Fischer, *Albion's Seed: Four British Folkways in America* (Oxford: Oxford University Press, 1989), pp. 31–33, 89–91, 130–134, 252, 284–285, 298, 303, 345–346, 365–368, 621–630, 674–675, 680–682, 703–708, 721–723.

30. Herbert G. Gutman, *The Black Family in Slavery and Freedom, 1750–1925* (New York: Vintage Press, 1977), pp. 32, 45; Leon F. Litwack, *Been in the Storm So Long* (New York: Alfred A. Knopf, 1979), p. 238.

31. Stephan Thernstrom and Abigail Thernstrom, *America in Black and White: One Nation, Indivisible* (New York: Simon and Schuster, 1997), p. 238.

32. Henry A. Walker, "Black-White Differences in Marriage and Family Patterns," *Feminism, Children and the New Families*, edited by Sanford M. Dornbusch and Myra H. Strober (New York: The Guilford Press, 1988), p. 92.

33. U.S. Bureau of the Census, *Historical Statistics of the United States: Colonial Times to 1957* (Washington, D.C.: U.S. Government Printing Office, 1960), p. 72.

34. Richard Vedder and Lowell Galloway, "Declining Black Employment," *Society*, July-August 1993, p. 57.

PART VIII: AN OVERVIEW

Paul Johnson, *The Quotable Paul Johnson: A Topical Compilation of His Wit, Wisdom and Satire*, edited by George J. Marlin, et al (New York: Farrar, Straus and Giroux, 1994), p. 138.

CHAPTER 20: PATTERNS AND VISIONS

1. The question of the effect of value premises is explored at greater length in my *A Conflict of Visions*, second edition (New York: Basic Books, 2007).

2. Joseph A. Schumpeter, *Capitalism, Socialism, and Democracy* (New York: Harper & Brothers, 1950), p. 313.

3. Some of those similarities are explored in my "Karl Marx and the Freedom of the Individual," *Ethics*, Vol. 73, No. 2 (January 1963).

4. See, for example, Adam Smith, *The Wealth of Nations* (New York: Modern Library, 1937), pp. 128, 250, 460; Karl Marx, *Capital: A Critique of Political Economy* (Chicago: Charles H. Kerr & Company, 1919), Vol. I, pp. 15, 257, 297.

5. Karl Marx, *Theories of Surplus Value: Selections* (New York: International Publishers, 1952), pp. 202–203.

6. Ibid., p. 175.

7. Marx, in fact, praised Ricardo for his conception of wages as the share of output received by workers, rather than the absolute amount of goods and services that the worker could purchase. To Marx, "It is one of Ricardo's greatest merits that he made an examination of relative wages and established them as a definite category. Previously wages had always been looked upon as a simple element, and

consequently the worker had been regarded as an animal. In Ricardo, however, he is considered in his social relationship. The position of the classes in relation to each other depends to a greater extent on the proportion which the wage forms than on the absolute amount of the wage." (Karl Marx, *Theories of Surplus Value: Selections*, p. 320.) In other words, Marx depicted Ricardo's definition of real wages as indicating that Ricardo shared a value premise with Marx. In reality, Ricardo's special definition of real wages in relative terms carried no such implication, as far as Ricardo himself was concerned. In a work unpublished at the time Marx wrote, Ricardo said, "I should first enquire what the labourers money wages were, and should estimate his condition by the abundance of necessaries which those money wages would procure him." David Ricardo, *The Works and Correspondence of David Ricardo*, edited by Piero Sraffa, Vol. II: *Notes on Malthus's Principles of Political Economy* (Cambridge: Cambridge University Press, 1957), p. 250.

8. See my *A Conflict of Visions*, second edition, pp. 174–179.

9. Gunnar Myrdal, *Asian Drama: An Inquiry Into the Poverty of Nations* (New York: Pantheon, 1968), Vol. I, pp. 7n, 49–125.

10. Peter Bauer, *Equality, The Third World and Economic Delusion* (Cambridge, Mass.: Harvard University Press, 1981), p. 23.

11. H.G. Wells, *The Anatomy of Frustration: A Modern Synthesis* (New York: The Macmillan Company, 1936), p. 115.

12. Ibid., p. 100.

13. George J. Stigler, *Essays in the History of Economics* (Chicago: University of Chicago Press, 1965), pp. 20–22, *passim*.

14. Robert L. Bartley, *The Seven Fat Years: And How to Do It Again* (New York: The Free Press, 1992), p. 241.

15. Oliver Wendell Holmes, Jr., *The Common Law* (Boston: Little, Brown and Company, 1923), p. 1.

16. Woodrow Wilson, *Constitutional Government in the United States* (New Brunswick, N.J.: Transaction Publishers, 2006), pp. 158, 167.

17. Robert H. Nelson, *The New Holy Wars: Economic Religion vs. Environmental Religion in Contemporary America* (University Park, PA: Pennsylvania State University Press, 2010), p. 283.

18. Richard Hofstadter, *Anti-Intellectualism in American Life* (New York: Vintage Books, 1963), pp. 3, 14. Hofstadter's caveat jeopardizes the main thrust of his

argument: "It seems clear that those who have some quarrel with intellect are almost always ambivalent about it: they mix respect and awe with suspicion and resentment; and this has been true in many societies and phases of human history. In any case, anti-intellectualism is not the creation of people who are categorically hostile to ideas. Quite the contrary: just as the most effective enemy of the educated man may be the half-educated man, so the leading anti-intellectuals are usually men deeply engaged with ideas, often obsessively engaged with this or that outworn or rejected idea." Ibid., p. 21. Because this caveat still does not distinguish intellectual processes and achievements, on the one hand, from the behavior of people in one subset of those whose work involves such processes and achievements, on the other, it perpetuates the confusion that hostility to one is hostility to the other. Admitting that many of the critics of intellectuals are themselves men of ideas, Hofstadter can dispose of their ideas by characterizing these ideas as "outworn or rejected"— which is to say, ideas with which he disagrees. In short, an ideological disagreement has been verbally transformed by Hofstadter into an issue of hostility to intellectual processes, even though he admits evidence to the contrary, including the fact that Edison "was all but canonized by the American public." (Ibid., p. 25.)

19.   H.L. Mencken, *Prejudices: Second Series* (New York: Alfred A. Knopf, 1920), p. 47.

20.   Russell Jacoby, *The Last Intellectuals: American Culture in the Age of Academe* (New York: Basic Books, 2000), p. 81.

21.   Andrew Hacker, *Two Nations: Black and White, Separate, Hostile, Unequal* (New York: Charles Scribner's Sons, 1992), p. 51.

22.   Ronald Dworkin, "The Decision That Threatens Democracy," *New York Review of Books*, May 13, 2010, p. 63.

23.   Herbert Croly, *The Promise of American Life* (Boston: Northeastern University Press, 1989), p. 212.

24.   Ibid., p. 409.

25.   Woodrow Wilson, *The New Freedom: A Call for the Emancipation of the Generous Energies of a People* (New York: Doubleday, Page & Company, 1913), pp. 19, 283, 284, 294; Ibid (New York: BiblioBazaar, 2007), pp. 20, 140, 145.

26.   Robert A. Dahl and Charles E. Lindblom, *Politics Economics and Welfare: Planning and Politico-Economic Systems Resolved into Basic Social Processes* (Chicago: University of Chicago Press, 1976), pp. 29, 36. They did not originate this redefinition but adopted it as theirs, giving credit— if that is the word— to Bertrand Russell.

27. Ibid., p. 518.

28. Ibid., p. 49.

29. See, for example, Chapter 3 of my *Economic Facts and Fallacies,* second edition (New York: Basic Books, 2011).

CHAPTER 21: INCENTIVES AND CONSTRAINTS

1. John Maynard Keynes, *The General Theory of Employment Interest and Money* (New York: Harcourt, Brace and Company, 1936), p. 383.

2. Richard A. Posner, *Public Intellectuals: A Study of Decline* (Cambridge, Massachusetts: Harvard University Press, 2001), pp. 5, 7.

3. Among economists, for example, data in Posner's study showed Lester Thurow to have been mentioned more than twice as often as Nobel Prizewinner Gary Becker in the media, while Becker was cited more than eight times as often as Thurow in scholarly publications. Ibid., pp. 194, 205.

4. Ibid., pp. 174, 194–206, 209–214.

5. J.A. Schumpeter, *History of Economic Analysis* (New York: Oxford University Press, 1954), p. 573.

6. Edmund Wilson, *Travels in Two Democracies* (New York: Harcourt, Brace and Company, 1936), p. 321.

7. Edmund Burke, *Reflections on the Revolution in France* (London: J.M Dent & Sons, Ltd., 1967), pp. 95–96.

8. Elissa Gootman, "City to Help Curb Harassment of Asian Students at High School," *New York Times,* June 2, 2004, p. B9; Joe Williams, "New Attack at Horror HS; Top Senior Jumped at Brooklyn's Troubled Lafayette," *New York Daily News,* December 7, 2002, p. 7; Maki Becker, "Asian Students Hit in Rash of HS Attacks," *New York Daily News,* December 8, 2002, p. 7; Kristen A. Graham and Jeff Gammage, "Two Immigrant Students Attacked at Bok," *Philadelphia Inquirer,* September 21, 2010, p. B1; Jeff Gammage and Kristen A. Graham, "Feds Find Merit in Asian Students' Claims Against Philly School," *Philadelphia Inquirer,* August 28, 2010, p. A1; Kristen A. Graham and Jeff Gammage, "Report Released on Racial Violence at S. Phila. High," *Philadelphia Inquirer,* February 24, 2010, p. A1; Kristen A. Graham, "Other Phila. Schools Handle Racial, Ethnic Tensions," *Philadelphia Inquirer,* February 4, 2010, p. A1; Kristen A. Graham and Jeff Gammage, "Attacking Immigrant Students Not New, Say Those Involved," *Philadelphia Inquirer,* December 18, 2009, p. B1;

Kristen A. Graham, "Asian Students Describe Violence at South Philadelphia High," *Philadelphia Inquirer*, December 10, 2009, p. A1.

9.   Mark Bauerlein, "Diminishing Returns in Humanities Research," *Chronicle of Higher Education*, July 24, 2009, pp. B4–B5.

10.   According to the *Chronicle of Higher Education*: "Conservatives are rarest in the humanities (3.6 percent) and social sciences (4.9 percent), and most common in business (24.5 percent) and the health sciences (20.5 percent)." Among faculty in the social sciences and humanities at elite, Ph.D.-granting universities, "not a single instructor reported voting for President Bush in 2004," when the President received a majority of the popular vote in the country at large. See David Glenn, "Few Conservatives but Many Centrists Teach in Academe," *Chronicle of Higher Education*, October 19, 2007, p. A10. In the health sciences, a study showed that the proportion of the faculty who called themselves conservative was the same as the proportion who called themselves liberal (20.5 percent), with the remainder calling themselves moderate. In business there were slightly more self-styled conservatives than self-styled liberals (24.5 percent versus 21.3 percent). Neil Gross and Solon Simmons, "The Social and Political Views of American Professors," Working Paper, September 24, 2007, p. 28. But in the social sciences and humanities, people who identified themselves as liberals were an absolute majority, with moderates outnumbering conservatives several times over among the remainder. See also Howard Kurtz, "College Faculties A Most Liberal Lot, Study Finds," *Washington Post*, March 29, 2005, p. C1; Stanley Rothman, S. Robert Lichter, and Neil Nevitte, "Politics and Professional Advancement Among College Faculty," *The Forum*, Vol. 3, Issue 1 (2005), p. 6; Christopher F. Cardiff and Daniel B. Klein, "Faculty Partisan Affiliations in All Disciplines: A Voter-Registration Study," *Critical Review*, Vol. 17, Nos. 3–4, pp. 237–255.

11.   Gary B. Cohen, *The Politics of Ethnic Survival: Germans in Prague, 1861–1914* (Princeton: Princeton University Press, 1981), p. 28.

12.   Anders Henriksson, *The Tsar's Loyal Germans: The Riga German Community: Social Change and the Nationality Question, 1855–1905* (Boulder: East European Monographs, 1983), p. 15.

13.   Kemal H. Karpat, "*Millets* and Nationality: The Roots of the Incongruity of Nation and State in the Post-Ottoman Era," *Christians and Jews in the Ottoman Empire: The Functioning of a Plural Society*, edited by Benjamin Braude and

Bernard Lewis (New York: Holmes and Meier, 1982), Vol. I: *The Central Lands,* pp. 159–161.

14. Gunnar Myrdal, *Asian Drama: An Inquiry Into the Poverty of Nations* (New York: Pantheon, 1968), Vol. III, pp. 348, 1642; Ezra Mendelsohn, *The Jews of East Central Europe Between the World Wars* (Bloomington: Indiana University Press, 1983), pp. 99, 167; Mary Fainsod Katzenstein, *Ethnicity and Equality: The Shiv Sena Party and Preferential Policies in Bombay* (Ithaca: Cornell University Press, 1979), pp. 48–49; Larry Diamond, "Class, Ethnicity, and the Democratic State: Nigeria, 1950–1966," *Comparative Studies in Society and History,* Vol. 25, No. 3 (July 1983), pp. 462, 473; Anatoly M. Khazanov, "The Ethnic Problems of Contemporary Kazakhstan," *Central Asian Survey,* Vol. 14, No. 2 (1995), pp. 244, 257; Joseph Rothschild, *East Central Europe between the Two World Wars* (Seattle: University of Washington Press, 1992), p. 293; Irina Livezeanu, *Cultural Politics in Greater Romania: Regionalism, Nation Building, & Ethnic Struggle, 1918–1930* (Ithaca: Cornell University Press, 1995), *passim*; Conrad Black, "Canada's Continuing Identity Crisis," *Foreign Affairs,* Vol. 74, No. 2 (March-April 1995), p. 100; Gary B. Cohen, *The Politics of Ethnic Survival,* pp. 26–28, 32, 133, 236–237; Hugh LeCaine Agnew, *Origins of the Czech National Renascence* (Pittsburgh: University of Pittsburgh Press, 1993), *passim.*

15. While academics in the harder fields are not as overwhelmingly on the political left as those in the softer fields, they may nevertheless be on the left more often than the general population. The number of leading "conservative" intellectuals who began on the left may provide a clue as to why this is so. The pervasiveness of the vision of the left in schools and colleges means that those who spend years being trained in fields such as engineering or accounting are subjected for years to that vision in courses outside their specialties. In short, the vision of the anointed is a more or less natural consequence of spending many years being trained in academic institutions, even if one is being trained in specialties other than those in which most intellectuals specialize, leading even many of those who later turn against that vision to require additional years. Engineers, accountants, and others whose professional work does not force them to confront the ideas of intellectuals have less reason to invest the time and effort required to reassess the vision they were taught than do specialists in fields where that vision is constantly before them, whether as something to follow or something to oppose.

16.   See, for example, Chapter 3 of my *Inside American Education: The Decline, the Deception, the Dogmas* (New York: The Free Press, 1993).

17.   See Thomas Sowell, *The Vision of the Anointed: Self-Congratulation as a Basis for Social Policy* (New York: Basic Books, 1995), pp. 15–21.

18.   Jean-François Revel, *The Flight from Truth: The Reign of Deceit in the Age of Information*, translated by Curtis Cate (New York: Random House, 1991), p. 361.

CHAPTER 22: THE INFLUENCE OF INTELLECTUALS

1.   Richard A. Posner, *Public Intellectuals: A Study of Decline* (Cambridge, Massachusetts: Harvard University Press, 2001), p. 135.

2.   Donald Kagan, *On the Origins of War and the Preservation of Peace* (New York: Doubleday, 1995), p. 104.

3.   Charles F. Howlett, *Troubled Philosopher: John Dewey and the Struggle for World Peace* (Port Washington, N.Y.: Kennikat Press, 1977), p. 73.

4.   Ronald Dworkin, *Taking Rights Seriously* (Cambridge, Mass.: Harvard University Press, 1980), p. 239.

5.   Mona Charen, *Do-Gooders: How Liberals Hurt Those They Claim to Help— and the Rest of Us* (New York: Sentinel, 2004), p. 124.

6.   Woodrow Wilson, "What is Progress?" *American Progressivism: A Reader*, edited by Ronald J. Pestritto and William J. Atto (Lanham, MD: Lexington Books, 2008), p. 48.

7.   Herbert Croly, *The Promise of American Life* (Boston: Northeastern University Press, 1989), p. 177.

8.   Ibid., pp. 179, 206

9.   Ibid., pp. 202, 203.

10.   Tony Judt, "Ill Fares the Land," *New York Review of Books*, April 29, 2010, p. 17.

11.   William McGowan, *Gray Lady Down: What the Decline and Fall of the New York Times Means for America* (New York: Encounter Books, 2010), p. 27.

12.   Richard J. Herrnstein and Charles Murray, *The Bell Curve: Intelligence and Class Structure in American Life* (New York: The Free Press, 1994), pp. 30, 31.

13.   Ibid., p. 30.

14.   Ibid., p. 50.

15.   See, for example, John Rawls, *A Theory of Justice* (Cambridge, Massachusetts: Harvard University Press, 1971), pp. 43, 60, 61, 265, 302.

16. John Dewey, *Liberalism and Social Action* (Amherst, N.Y.: Prometheus Books, 2000), p. 53. See also p. 88.

17. Ibid., p. 89.

18. John Dewey, *Human Nature and Conduct: An Introduction to Social Psychology* (New York: The Modern Library, 1957), p. 148.

19. *Planned Parenthood of Southeastern Pennsylvania v. Casey,* 505 U.S. 833 (1992), at 864.

20. Abraham Lincoln, "The Perpetuation of Our Political Institutions: Address Before the Young Men's Lyceum of Springfield, Illinois, January 27, 1838," *Abraham Lincoln: His Speeches and Writings*, edited by Roy P. Basler (Millwood, N.Y.: Kraus Reprint, 1981), p. 83.

21. Ibid., p. 82.

22. Ibid., p. 83.

23. Ibid., p. 80.

24. Lewis A. Coser, *Men of Ideas: A Sociologist's View* (New York: The Free Press, 1970), p. 215.

25. Ibid., p. 216.

26. Paul Hollander, *Anti-Americanism: Critiques at Home and Abroad 1965–1990* (New York: Oxford University Press, 1992), p. 242.

27. See, for example, Theodore Dalrymple, *Our Culture, What's Left of It: The Mandarins and the Masses* (Chicago: Ivan R. Dee, 2005), pp. 296–310; Bruce Thornton, *Decline and Fall: Europe's Slow-Motion Suicide* (New York: Encounter Books, 2007), Chapter 3; Christopher Caldwell, *Reflections on the Revolution in Europe: Immigration, Islam, and the West* (New York: Doubleday, 2009).

28. *Random House Webster's College Dictionary* (New York: Random House, 1991), p. 322.

29. Edward Shils, *The Constitution of Society* (Chicago: University of Chicago Press, 1982), p. 182.

30. Peter Hitchens, *The Abolition of Britain: From Winston Churchill to Princess Diana* (San Francisco: Encounter Books, 2002), pp. 4, 7.

31. See, for example, Chapter 2 of my *The Vision of the Anointed: Self-Congratulation as a Basis for Social Policy* (New York: Basic Books, 1995).

32. In addition to examples in earlier chapters of this book, see *Slander: Liberal Lies About the American Right* (New York: Crown, 2002) by Ann Coulter.

INDEX